# WORLD ERAS

## VOLUME 1

## EUROPEAN RENAISSANCE AND REFORMATION
### 1350 – 1600

# WORLD ERAS

## VOLUME 1

## EUROPEAN RENAISSANCE AND REFORMATION

### 1350 – 1600

# NORMAN J. WILSON

A MANLY, INC. BOOK

**GALE GROUP**

™

**THOMSON LEARNING**

*Detroit • New York • San Diego • San Francisco*
*Boston • New Haven, Conn. • Waterville, Maine*
*London • Munich*

# WORLD ERAS VOL. 1
# EUROPEAN RENAISSANCE
# AND REFORMATION
## 1350-1600

Matthew J. Bruccoli and Richard Layman, *Editorial Directors*

Anthony J. Scotti Jr., *Series Editor*

Library Of Congress Cataloging-in-Publication Data

World Eras vol. 1: European Renaissance and Reformation, 1350-1600 /
edited by Norman J. Wilson.
p. cm.— (World Eras)
"A Manly, Inc. book."
Includes bibliographical references and index.
ISBN 0-7876-1706-7 (alk. paper)
1. Renaissance. 2. Reformation. 3. Religion and culture—Europe—
History. 4. Europe—History—1492-1648. I. Wilson, Norman J.
II. Series.
CB359.W67 2001
940.2'1—dc21                                    00-052802

Printed in the United States of America
10 9 8 7 6 5 4 3 2 1

# ADVISORY BOARD

*to Tarja Tuulikki Wilson*

# CONTENTS

## CHAPTER 8: FAMILY AND SOCIAL TRENDS

### Topics in Family and Social Trends

### Significant People

## Chapter 9: RELIGION AND PHILOSOPHY

### Topics in Religion and Philosophy

## Significant People

## Chapter 10: SCIENCE, TECHNOLOGY, AND HEALTH

### Topics in Science, Technology, and Health

### Significant People

# ABOUT THE SERIES

## PROJECT DESCRIPTION

Patterned after the well-received *American Decades* and *American Eras* series, *World Eras* is a cross-disciplinary reference series. It comprises volumes examining major civilizations that have flourished from antiquity to modern times, with a global perspective and a strong emphasis on daily life and social history. Each volume provides in-depth coverage of one era, focusing on a specific cultural group and its interaction with other peoples of the world. The *World Eras* series is geared toward the needs of high-school students studying subjects in the humanities. Its purpose is to provide students—and general reference users as well—a reliable, engaging reference resource that stimulates their interest, encourages research, and prompts comparison of the lives people led in different parts of the world, in different cultures, and at different times.

The goal of *World Eras* volumes is to enrich the traditional historical study of "kings and battles" with a resource that promotes understanding of daily life and the cultural institutions that affect people's beliefs and behavior.

What kind of work did people in a certain culture perform?

What did they eat?

How did they fight their battles?

What laws did they have and how did they punish criminals?

What were their religious practices?

What did they know of science and medicine?

What kind of art, music, and literature did they enjoy?

These are the types of questions *World Eras* volumes seek to answer.

## VOLUME DESIGN

*World Eras* is designed to facilitate comparative study. Thus volumes employ a consistent ten-chapter structure so that teachers and students can readily access standard topics in various volumes. The chapters in each *World Eras* volume are

1. World Events
2. Geography
3. The Arts
4. Communication, Transportation, and Exploration
5. Social Class System and the Economy
6. Politics, Law, and the Military
7. Leisure, Recreation, and Daily Life
8. The Family and Social Trends
9. Religion and Philosophy
10. Science, Technology, and Health

*World Eras* volumes begin with two chapters designed to provide a broad view of the world against which a specific culture can be measured. Chapter 1 provides students today with a means to understand where a certain people stood within our concept of world history. Chapter 2 describes the world from the perspective of the people being studied—what did they know of geography and how did geography and climate affect their lives? The following eight chapters address major aspects of people's lives to provide a sense of what defined their culture. The ten chapters in *World Eras* will remain constant in each volume. Teachers and students seeking to compare religious beliefs in Roman and Greek cultures, for example, can easily locate the information they require by consulting chapter 9 in the appropriate volumes, tapping a rich source for class assignments and research topics. Volume-specific glossaries and a checklist of general references provide students assistance in studying unfamiliar cultures.

## CHAPTER CONTENTS

Each chapter in *World Eras* volumes also follows a uniform structure designed to provide users quick access to the information they need. Chapters are arranged into five types of material:

- **Chronology** provides an historical outline of significant events in the subject of the chapter in timeline form.

- **Overview** provides a narrative overview of the chapter topic during the period and discusses the material of the chapter in a global context.

- **Topical Entries** provide focused information in easy-to-read articles about people, places, events, institutions, and matters of general concern to the people of the time. A references rubric includes sources for further study.

- **Biographical Entries** profiles people of enduring significance regarding the subject of the chapter.
- **Documentary Sources** is an annotated checklist of documentary sources from the historical period that are the basis for the information presented in the chapter.

Chapters are supplemented throughout with primary-text sidebars that include interesting short documentary excerpts or anecdotes chosen to illuminate the subject of the chapter: recipes, letters, daily-life accounts, excerpts from important documents. Each *World Eras* volume includes about 150 illustrations, maps, diagrams, and line drawings linked directly to material discussed in the text. Illustrations are chosen with particular emphasis on daily life.

## INDEXING

A general two-level subject index for each volume includes significant terms, subjects, theories, practices, people, organizations, publications, and so forth, mentioned in the text. Index citations with many page references are broken down by subtopic. Illustrations are indicated both in the general index, by use of italicized page numbers, and in

a separate illustrations index, which provides a description of each item.

## EDITORS AND CONTRIBUTORS

An advisory board of history teachers and librarians has provided valuable advice about the rationale for this series. They have reviewed both series plans and individual volume plans. Each *World Eras* volume is edited by a distinguished specialist in the subject of his or her volume. The editor is responsible for enlisting other scholar-specialists to write each of the chapters in the volume and of assuring the quality of their work. The editorial staff at Manly, Inc., rigorously checks factual information, line edits the manuscript, works with the editor to select illustrations, and produces the books in the series, in cooperation with Gale Group editors.

The *World Eras* series is for students of all ages who seek to enrich their study of world history by examining the many aspects of people's lives in different places during different eras. This series continues Gale's tradition of publishing comprehensive, accurate, and stimulating historical reference works that promote the study of history and culture.

The following timeline, included in every volume of *World Eras,* is provided as a convenience to users seeking a ready chronological context.

# TIMELINE

This timeline, compiled by editors at Manly, Inc., is provided as a convenience for students seeking a broad global and historical context for the materials in this volume of World Eras. *It is not intended as a self-contained resource. Students who require a comprehensive chronology of world history should consult sources such as William L. Langer, comp. and ed.,* The New Illustrated Encyclopedia of World History, *2 volumes (New York: Harry N. Abrams, 1975).*

## CIRCA 4 MILLION TO 1 MILLION B.C.E.
Era of *Australopithecus*, the first hominid

## CIRCA 1.5 MILLION TO 200,000 B.C.E.
Era of *Homo erectus*, "upright-walking human"

## CIRCA 1,000,000-10,000 B.C.E.
Paleothic Age: hunters and gatherers make use of stone tools in Eurasia

## CIRCA 250,000 B.C.E.
Early evolution of *Homo sapiens*, "consciously thinking humans"

## CIRCA 40,000 B.C.E.
Migrations from Siberia to Alaska lead to the first human inhabitation of North and South America

## CIRCA 8000 B.C.E.
Neolithic Age: settled agrarian culture begins to develop in Eurasia

## 5000 B.C.E.
The world population is between 5 million and 20 million

## CIRCA 4000-3500 B.C.E.
Earliest Sumerian cities: artificial irrigation leads to increased food supplies and populations in Mesopotamia

## CIRCA 3000 B.C.E.
Bronze Age begins in Mesopotamia and Egypt, where bronze is primarily used for making weapons; invention of writing

## CIRCA 2900-1150 B.C.E.
Minoan society on Crete: lavish palaces and commercial activity

## CIRCA 2700-2200 B.C.E.
Egypt: Old Kingdom and the building of the pyramids

## CIRCA 2080-1640 B.C.E.
Egypt: Middle Kingdom plagued by internal strife and invasion by the Hyksos

## CIRCA 2000-1200 B.C.E.
Hittites build a powerful empire based in Anatolia (present-day Turkey) by using horse-drawn war chariots

## CIRCA 1792-1760 B.C.E.
Old Babylonian Kingdom; one of the oldest extant legal codes is compiled

## CIRCA 1766-1122 B.C.E.
Shang Dynasty in China: military expansion, large cities, written language, and introduction of bronze metallurgy

## CIRCA 1570-1075 B.C.E.
Egypt: New Kingdom and territorial expansion into Palestine, Lebanon, and Syria

## CIRCA 1500 B.C.E.
The Aryans, an Indo-European people from the steppes of present-day Ukraine and southern Russia, expand into northern India

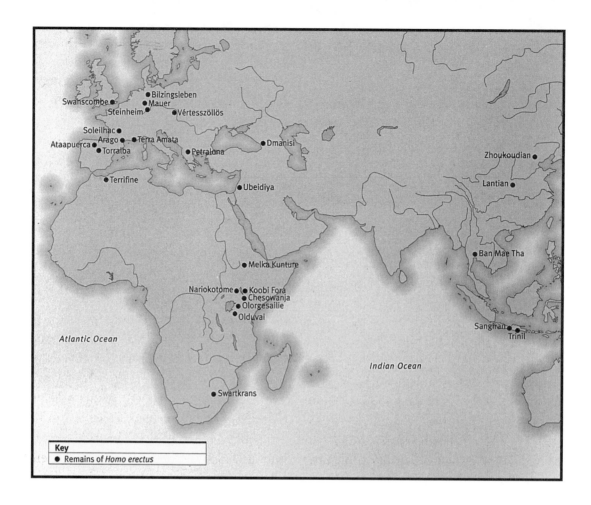

Key
● Remains of *Homo erectus*

**CIRCA 1500 B.C.E.**
Phoenicians create the first alphabet

**CIRCA 1400-1200 B.C.E.**
Hittites develop the technology of iron-smelting, improving weaponry and agricultural implements, as well as stimulating trade

**CIRCA 1200-800 B.C.E.**
Phoenicians establish colonies throughout the Mediterranean

**CIRCA 1122- 221 B.C.E.**
Zhou Dynasty in China: military conquests, nomadic invasions, and introduction of iron metallurgy

**CIRCA 1100-750 B.C.E.**
Greek Dark Ages: foreign invasions, civil disturbances, decrease in agricultural production, and population decline

**1020-587 B.C.E.**
Israelite monarchies consolidate their power in Palestine

**CIRCA 1000-612 B.C.E.**
Assyrians create an empire encompassing Mesopotamia, Syria, Palestine, and most of Anatolia and Egypt; they deport populations to various regions of the realm

**1000 B.C.E.**
The world population is approximately 50 million

**CIRCA 814-146 B.C.E.**
The city-state of Carthage is a powerful commercial and military power in the western Mediterranean

**753 B.C.E.**
Traditional date of the founding of Rome

**CIRCA 750-700 B.C.E.**
Rise of the polis, or city-state, in Greece

**558-330 B.C.E.**
Achaemenid Dynasty establishes the Persian Empire (present-day Iran, Turkey, Afghanistan, and Iraq); satraps rule the various provinces

**509 B.C.E.**
Roman Republic is established

**500 B.C.E.**
The world population is approximately 100 million

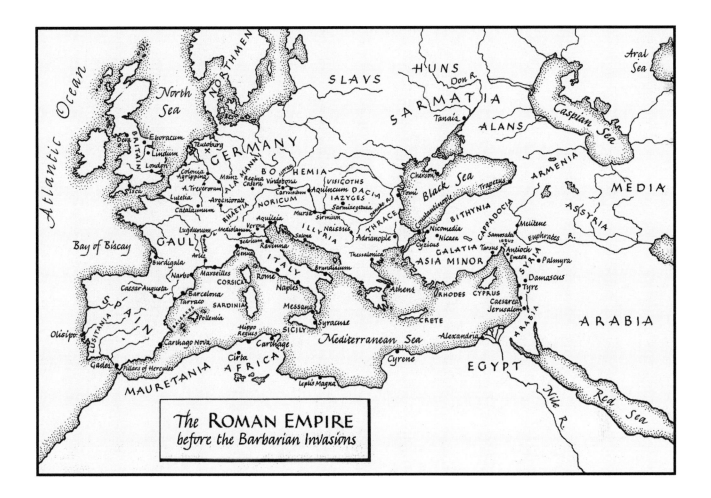

The ROMAN EMPIRE
before the Barbarian Invasions

**CIRCA 400 B.C.E.**
Spread of Buddhism in India

**338-323 B.C.E.**
Macedon, a kingdom in the central Balkan peninsula, conquers the Persian Empire

**323-301 B.C.E.**
Ptolemaic Kingdom (Egypt), Seleucid Kingdom (Syria), and Antigonid Dynasty (Macedon) are founded

**247 B.C.E.-224 C.E.**
Parthian Empire (Parthia, Persia, and Babylonia): clan leaders build independent power bases in their satrapies, or provinces

**215-168 B.C.E.**
Rome establishes hegemony over the Hellenistic world

**206 B.C.E. TO 220 C.E.**
Han Dynasty in China: imperial expansion into central Asia, centralized government, economic prosperity, and population growth

**CIRCA 100 B.C.E.**
Tribesmen on the Asian steppes develop the stirrup, which eventually revolutionizes warfare

**1 C.E.**
The world population is approximately 200 million

**CIRCA 100 C.E.**
Invention of paper in China

**224-651 C.E.**
Sasanid Empire (Parthia, Persia, and Babylonia): improved government system, founding of new cities, increased trade, and the introduction of rice and cotton cultivation

**340 C.E.**
Constantinople becomes the capital of the Eastern Roman, or Byzantine, Empire

**CIRCA 320-550 C.E.**
Gupta Dynasty in India: Golden Age of Hindu civilization marked by stability and prosperity throughout the subcontinent

**395 C.E.**
Christianity becomes the official religion of the Roman Empire

**CIRCA 400 C.E.**
The first unified Japanese state arises and is centered at Yamato on the island of Honshu; Buddhism arrives in Japan by way of Korea

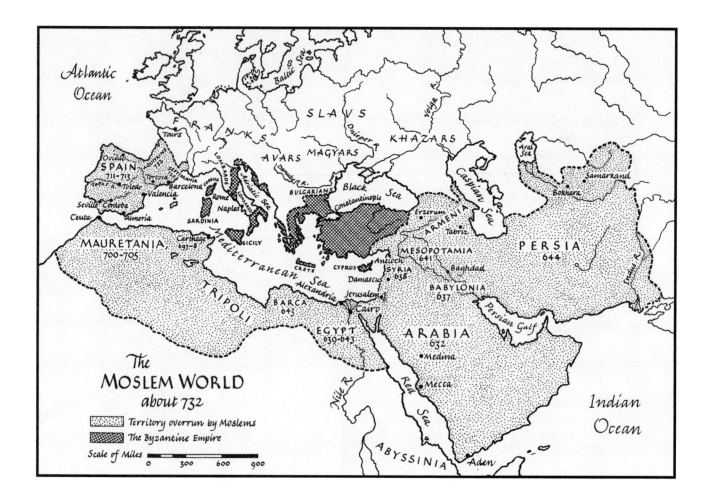

The MOSLEM WORLD about 732

Territory overrun by Moslems

The Byzantine Empire

Scale of Miles
0   300   600   900

## CIRCA 400 C.E.
The nomadic Huns begin a westward migration from central Asia, causing disruption in the Roman Empire

## CIRCA 400 C.E.
The Mayan Empire in Mesoamerica evolves into city-states

## 476 C.E.
Rome falls to barbarian hordes and the Western Roman Empire collapses

## CIRCA 500-1500 C.E.
Middle Ages, or medieval period, in Europe: gradual recovery from political disruption and increase in agricultural productivity and population

## 618-907 C.E.
Tang Dynasty in China: territorial expansion, government bureaucracy, agricultural improvements, and transportation and communication networks

## 632-733 C.E.
Muslim expansion and conquests in Arabia, Syria, Palestine, Mesopotamia, Egypt, North Africa, Persia, northwestern India, and Iberia

## CIRCA 700 C.E.
Origins of feudalism, a political and social organization that dominates Europe until the fifteenth century; based on the relationship between lords and vassals

## CIRCA 900 C.E.
Introduction of the horseshoe in Europe and black powder in China

## 960-1279 C.E.
Song Dynasty in China: civil administration, industry, education, and the arts

## 962-1806 C.E.
Holy Roman Empire of western and central Europe, created in an attempt to revive the old Roman Empire

## 1000 C.E.
The world population is approximately 300 million

## 1096-1291 C.E.
Western Christians undertake the Crusades, a series of religiously inspired military campaigns, to recapture the Holy Land from the Muslims

## 1200 to 1400 C.E.
The Mali empire in Africa dominates the trans-Saharan trade network of camel caravans

## 1220-1335 C.E.
The Mongols, nomadic horsemen from the high steppes of eastern central Asia, build an empire that includes China, Persia, and Russia

## Circa 1250 C.E.
Inca Empire develops in Peru: Civil administration, road networks, and sun worshipping

## 1299-1919 C.E.
Ottoman Empire, created by nomadic Turks and Christian converts to Islam, encompasses Asia Minor, the Balkans, Greece, Egypt, North Africa, and the Middle East

## 1300 C.E.
The world population is approximately 396 million

## 1337-1453 C.E.
Hundred Years' War, a series of intermittent military campaigns between England and France over control of continental lands claimed by both countries

## 1347-1350 C.E.
Black Death, or the bubonic plague, kills one-quarter of the European population

## 1368-1644 C.E.
Ming Dynasty in China: political, economic, and cultural revival; the Great Wall is built

## 1375-1527 C.E.
The Renaissance in Western Europe, a revival in the arts and learning

## 1428-1519 C.E.
The Aztecs expand in central Mexico, developing trade routes and a system of tribute payments

## 1450 C.E.
Invention of the printing press

## 1453 C.E.
Constantinople falls to the Ottoman Turks, ending the Byzantine Empire

## 1464-1591 C.E.
Songhay Empire in Africa: military expansion, prosperous cities, control of the trans-Saharan trade

## 1492 C.E.
Discovery of America; European exploration and colonization of the Western Hemisphere begins

## Circa 1500-1867 C.E.
Transatlantic slave trade results in the forced migration of between 12 million and 16 million Africans to the Western Hemisphere

## 1500 C.E.
The world population is approximately 480 million

## 1517 C.E.
Beginning of the Protestant Reformation, a religious movement that ends the spiritual unity of western Christendom

## 1523-1763 C.E.
Mughal Empire in India: military conquests, productive agricultural economy, and population growth

## 1600-1867 C.E.
Tokugawa Shogunate in Japan: shoguns (military governors) turn Edo, or Tokyo, into the political, economic, and cultural center of the nation

## 1618-1648 C.E.
Thirty Years' War in Europe between Catholic and Protestant states

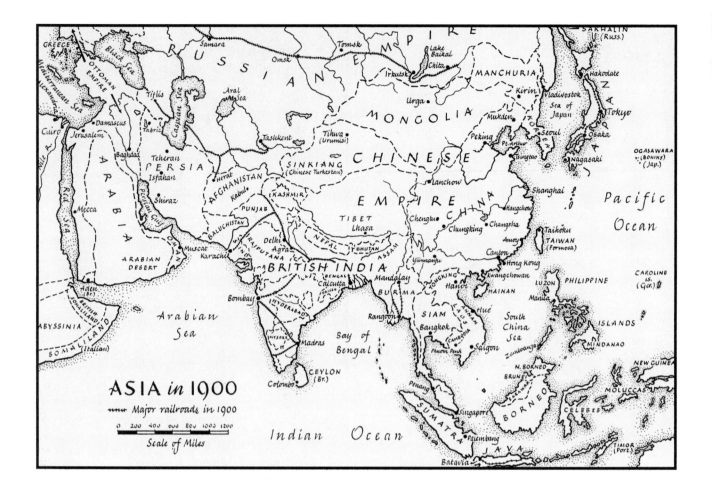

ASIA in 1900

~~~~ Major railroads in 1900

0 200 400 600 800 1000 1200
Scale of Miles

**1644-1911 c.e.**
Qing Dynasty in China: military expansion and
scholar-bureaucrats

**1700 c.e.**
The world population is approximately 640 million

**Circa 1750 c.e.**
Beginning of the Enlightenment, a philosophical
movement marked by an emphasis on rationalism and
scientific inquiry

**1756-1763 c.e.**
Seven Years' War: England and Prussia versus Austria, France, Russia, Saxony, Spain, and Sweden

**Circa 1760-1850 c.e.**
Industrial Revolution in Britain is marked by mass
production through the division of labor, mechanization, a great increase in the supply of iron, and the use
of the steam engine

**1775-1783 c.e.**
American War of Independence; the United States
becomes an independent republic

**1789 c.e.**
French Revolution topples the monarchy and leads
to a period of political unrest followed by a dicta-
torship

**1793-1815 c.e.**
Napoleonic Wars: Austria, England, Prussia, and
Russia versus France and its satellite states

**1794-1824 c.e.**
Latin American states conduct wars of independence against Spain

**1900 c.e.**
The world population is approximately 1.65 billion

**1914-1918 c.e.**
World War I, or the Great War: the Allies
(England, France, Russia, and the United States)
versus Central Powers (Austria-Hungary, Germany, and the Ottoman Empire)

**1917-1921 c.e.**
Russian Revolution: a group of Communists
known as the Bolsheviks seize control of the country following a civil war

**1939-1945** C.E.
World War II: the Allies (China, England, France, the Soviet Union, and the United States) versus the Axis (Germany, Italy, and Japan)

**1945** C.E.
Successful test of the first atomic weapon; beginning of the Cold War, a period of rivalry, mistrust, and, occasionally, open hostility between the capitalist West and communist East

**1947-1975** C.E.
Decolonization occurs in Africa and Asia as European powers relinquish control of colonies in those regions

**1948**
Israel becomes the first independent Jewish state in nearly two thousand years

**1949**
Communists seize control of China

**1950-1951**
Korean War: the United States attempts to stop Communist expansion in the Korean peninsula

**1957** C.E.
The Soviet Union launches *Sputnik* ("fellow traveler of earth"), the first man-made satellite; the Space Age begins

**1965-1973**
Vietnam War: the United States attempts to thwart the spread of Communism in Vietnam

**1989** C.E.
East European Communist regimes begin to falter and multiparty elections are held

**1991** C.E.
Soviet Union is dissolved and replaced by the Commonwealth of Independent States

**2000** C.E.
The world population is 6 billion

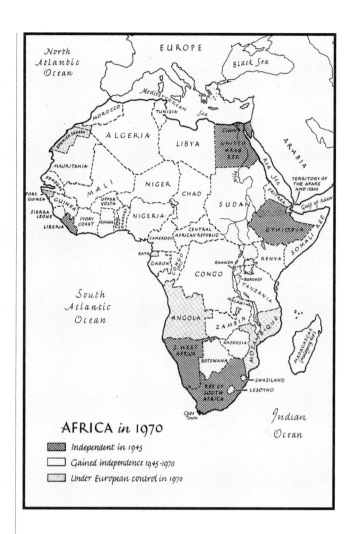

# INTRODUCTION

**Symbols of the Era.** During the period 1350 to 1600, two monumental events occurred in European history: the Renaissance, a rebirth or revival in classical learning, and the Reformation, a religious revolution that led to the founding of Protestantism. Three figures have come to epitomize this era in one form or another: Niccolò Machiavelli, Martin Luther, and Elizabeth I. Machiavelli, a Florentine humanist and diplomat, was unemployed when he wrote a short treatise on political theory titled *Il principe* (The Prince, 1513). The book was dedicated to the local prince because Machiavelli wanted a position in the Florentine government. *Il principe* won Machiavelli historical fame but did not gain him employment. Luther, the grandson of a peasant and son of a successful copper miner, was an obscure professor at the newly founded (1502)—and thus academically remote—University of Wittenberg in Saxony. In 1517 Luther drafted his Ninety-five Theses objecting to the church's sale of indulgences. His persistence over the topic resulted in a 1519 debate against Dr. Johann Eck, a prominent professor of theology at the better-known University of Ingolstadt. In 1520 Luther wrote three treatises that formalized his break with the Roman Church, and Eck assisted the Pope in drafting a papal bull excommunicating Luther. King Henry VIII of England ordered a ghostwriter to compose a response to Luther that won Henry the title *Defender of the Faith* from Pope Leo X in 1521. A dozen years later Henry himself broke with Rome because his mistress was pregnant and the Pope refused to annul Henry's marriage to Catherine of Aragon. In 1533 Princess Elizabeth was born, but within three years her parents' marriage was declared invalid and her mother, Ann Boleyn, was beheaded. Elizabeth was third in line for the crown of England when Henry died. She ruled England from 1558 until 1603. Known as the Virgin Queen or Good Queen Bess, Elizabeth maintained an image of female authority and regal magnificence. Elizabeth stands out as a representative of postmedieval monarchy. Although from diverse backgrounds and different regions of Europe, these three individuals profoundly influenced ideology, religion, and politics.

**Legacy.** Machiavelli, Luther, and Elizabeth not only define the period under consideration—their names have evolved into modern terms. *Machiavellian* means "expedi-

ent, deceitful, and cunning" while *Machiavellianism* (also *Machiavellism*) is the rejection of morality as a guide for political action. Whereas *Machiavellian* is derogatory, *Lutheran* is a label proudly employed by adherents to Luther's teachings. Lutherans are part of a Protestant tradition, the name of which is derived from Luther's "protest" against the Roman Catholic Church. While Lutherans and Machiavellians are still in present-day society, Elizabethans exist only in the literary, artistic, and cultural legacy that they have left behind. The term *Elizabethan* describes an entire era of history: the Elizabethan Age at the end of the sixteenth century.

**Historical Categories.** Machiavelli lived beyond Luther's break with the Roman Catholic Church, yet he is decidedly a Renaissance, not a Reformation, figure. Luther is the best-known person from the Reformation despite the fact that his scholastic education was more consistent with the late medieval period than with the Renaissance. Of the three, only Elizabeth is readily identified as a Reformation and Renaissance figure. Her personal success is evidence of the rise of dynastic, national kingdoms with strong centralized governments. The Elizabethan Age is also famous for literature and arts that are decidedly Renaissance. The Reformation followed the Renaissance, but the two also overlapped. Despite this overlap, historians tend to place individuals into one category or the other. Relatively few people are, like Elizabeth, considered both Renaissance and Reformation figures.

**Ideals of Ancient Rome.** Fifteenth-century Italians developed the term *Middle Ages* to describe everything between the world of ancient Rome and that of fourteenth-century, urban Italy. Italian urbanites of the period found that they had more in common with the ideals of ancient Rome than with the ideals of feudal Europe. Their efforts to revive ancient texts and ideals have become a key determinant in the title *Renaissance*. Jakob Burckhardt, a nineteenth-century Swiss historian, first used the term *Renaissance* to define the emergence of modern individualism. For Burckhardt, individuality arose first in Italy because the Italian political scene lacked a strong national sovereign. Social mobility was a valid possibility in Italy, and thus the ideal of the many-sided man, the individual who sought outward distinction and glory, became a Renaissance ideal.

**Humanism.** The Renaissance was a cultural movement that had profound implications for education and for the arts. During the fourteenth century, a new type of learning appeared in Italy that became known as humanism. Its focus on rhetoric, poetry, history, and most importantly, Latin classical works, distinguished humanism from the mathematical logic of medieval scholasticism. Humanism was a type of education that emphasized words and the precise analysis of the original texts. When Renaissance ideas spread beyond Italy, the Italian artistic and intellectual models were adapted and revised to fit local situations. The civic humanism of Italian republics, with its focus on civic liberties, was inappropriate for humanists living under strong northern monarchs. Northern humanists adopted the techniques and vocabulary of the civic humanists, but they focused their study on different texts: namely, the sources of Christianity and the Bible. Known as Christian humanists, they were frequently critical of the Roman Catholic Church on the eve of the Reformation. Many historians of northern Europe refer to the period under study as early modern Europe instead of Renaissance Europe, in part because the Renaissance was also a period of brutal warfare and harsh living conditions. Most northern Europeans did not experience a sense of rebirth during the Renaissance.

**Church Reform.** The term *Reformation* is less contentious because most residents of Europe had some notion of Luther's changes in religion, even if they were not aware of all of the theological implications. Luther's insistence that people turn to translations of the Bible as the ultimate source of truth became a cornerstone of church reformers known as Protestants. The Protestants placed the Bible over the traditions of the Church and redefined the sacraments, such as the Eucharist. The various factions among the Protestants tend to be derived from differences between individual reformers, such as followers of Luther, Huldrych Zwingli, John Calvin, and Menno Simons. In England, the Elizabethan Settlement was named after Elizabeth's reinterpretation of Henry VIII's newly founded Church of England. The Roman Catholic Church responded to Protestantism and to internal currents of reform by establishing higher standards for the clergy and by defining doctrine more precisely at the Council of Trent (1545–1563). While most modern followers of the various sixteenth-century churches coexist peacefully, the doctrinal disputes of the Reformation led to a century of religious warfare in Europe.

**Cultural Diversity.** The Reformation overlaps the Renaissance and both concepts are somewhat ambiguous, but the two eras also distinguish something that occurred in Europe without occurring elsewhere. Other intellectual and religious movements were taking place around the world, but they lacked the Renaissance's revival of classical Greek and Roman thought and the Reformation's revisions to the beliefs of the Roman Catholic Church. Similarly, the Renaissance and Reformation did not touch all corners of Europe because some areas were neither Roman Catholic nor under political systems that looked to Rome and Greece for models. The eastern border of Europe, consisting of the Ural Mountains, the Caspian Sea, and the Caucasus Mountains, experienced little of what is traditionally called the Renaissance and Reformation. For purposes of this book, it is best to think of Europe not as a simple geographical expression but rather as a range of cultural identities, religious beliefs, and diverse languages. The authors of the individual chapters have gone to great lengths to include this diversity in their analysis, yet the broad focus of this work tends to be areas of Europe where a definable Renaissance and Reformation are evident.

**Black Death.** The title of this book also bears a chronological framework. The concluding date of 1600 is based on a base ten calendar, but it is easily rationalized as an approximation of a French proclamation of religious tolerance (the Edict of Nantes, 1598) and the end of religious warfare in France. The 1350 opening date was chosen in recognition of the profound historical consequences of the Black Death (1347–1351). The Black Death killed so many people in Europe that it altered the ways humans interacted with each other and with the environment. The ensuing preoccupation with death gave rise to mechanical forms of religiosity, such as the pursuit of pious acts to lessen God's wrath. The papacy, or the system of the Roman Church's government under the pope, was in Avignon, France, instead of in Rome in the decades before and after the Black Death. After seven decades in Avignon, the papacy returned to Rome in 1377 only to see the election of two popes in 1378. The rival popes established themselves at Avignon and Rome. This Great, or Western, Schism was finally resolved at the Council of Constance (1414–1417), which also dealt with heresy, reform of the clergy and conciliarism, the idea that a general assembly of the church was superior to the pope.

**Economic Opportunities.** Those who were fortunate enough to survive the Black Death experienced opportunities favorable to the accumulation of wealth. Land was abundant, wages remained high, and population began to increase. Economic development was regional and sporadic until discoveries of sea passages to India and the Americas provided the European economy with different products and new sources of precious metals. Voyages of exploration and colonization created a new world and necessitated a new way of mapping and describing the world. This new world changed the focal point of European economies and trade from Rome and the Mediterranean Sea to the Atlantic Ocean at the same time that religious reformers were shifting the focal point of church authority from Rome to individual theologians in Wittenberg, Geneva, and London.

**Political Consolidation.** The focal point of politics also shifted from local rulers to powerful dynastic families who ruled vast territories. Strong monarchies and centralized governments became possible in part because of changes in military technology. Knights had been able to withstand sieges and thus defy their kings until mid-fifteenth-century developments in gunpowder artillery gave the kings a decisive advantage. Monarchs began to wrestle local power from the petty nobility and to expand royal kingdoms. The costs of warfare escalated as huge armies armed with crossbows, longbows, pikes, and gunpowder weapons supplemented the cavalry. Kings imposed new laws and taxes in order to consolidate power and to fund the military. Spain, France, and England are examples of the rising national kingdoms where the borders of the kingdom corresponded with the dominant ethnic group. In such kingdoms, the ruler was expected to be part of the dominant ethnic group, and the religion of the realm was determined by the ruler.

**Technological Innovations.** Technology played a central role in all of these political and military changes. Technological innovations also transformed ship construction and rigging, thus allowing navigators to attempt new voyages. The use of movable type for printing books created a communications revolution that influenced the humanists, reformers, cartographers, artists, and scientists. Readers of printed books knew with certainty that scholars in other parts of Europe were reading the exact same text. For the first time, historical writings in the sciences were placed aside as the anti-Galenic and anti-Aristotelian views of Paracelsian medicine called for fresh observations. It was not chemistry and medicine, but rather astronomy and the physics of motion, that created the most profound revisions in science. Nicholas Copernicus argued that the earth was not the center of the universe and astronomers began to contemplate new laws of motion. The Renaissance established the basis for the seventeenth-century scientific revolution.

**Question of Perspective.** Historians of science and medicine generally use the term *Renaissance* to define the entire sixteenth century, whereas Reformation historians apply the term *Reformation* to the sixteenth century after Luther posted his Ninety-five Theses in 1517. Historians of the period have long debated the accuracy of the titles *Renaissance* and *Reformation*. Joan Kelly called into question the traditional "periods" of history in her groundbreaking article "Did Women Have a Renaissance?" (1977). Kelly asked: "Suppose we look again at this age, the Renaissance, reputed for its liberation from old confining forms, renowned for its revival of classical and republican ideas? Suppose we look at the Renaissance from the vantage point of women?" Kelly examined women's economic and political roles, the prevailing ideology about women, their cultural role in shaping society, and the regulation of sexuality. She concluded "that events which change the course of history for men, liberating them from the natural, social, or ideological restraints upon power, may have quite different effects upon women." The titles *Renaissance* and *Reformation* are in large part a question of perspective.

**Interdependence.** Traditionally, historians of the Renaissance and Reformation have placed all of history within the framework of political, religious, and intellectual factors. Thus far, this introduction has also focused on those factors because they are important. Traditional topics of political development, religious conflict, and the history of ideas are included as subthemes in certain chapters, but economics, technology, daily life, and social history are equally prevalent. This book is emphatically oriented toward social and cultural history. This decision was based on the assumption that social-cultural history and political-religious history are continuous, each offering insights into the other.

**Art and Communications.** Art and communications offer a vivid example of the interplay between various types of historical analysis. The tumultuous politics of the Italian city-states favored the emergence of new ideas. Innovative political leaders seized power and Italian intellectuals believed that they were part of a rebirth of civilization based on ideals of ancient Greece and Rome. Prosperous urbanites in Italy had sufficient wealth to allow their children to pursue education, literature, and art. Individuals and corporate groups commissioned art at a previously unprecedented rate. Art became a more prominent avenue for the church to reveal the mysteries of the Christian faith to a wide audience, especially those who could not read and write. Merchant elites in Italian city-states used their discretionary income to support the arts. The fifteenth-century patrons of art began to take new interest in the standards of artistic production. They were especially impressed with the graceful figures of the international style of artists from northern Europe. The highly symbolic nature of northern painting merged with an Italian style that, as a consequence of humanism, drew heavily on classical traits. Meanwhile, reform-minded churchmen of the Protestant Reformation attacked the medieval doctrine of salvation and opposed forms of piety that encouraged works, such as indulgences and pilgrimages. Their emphasis on faith had profound implications for the arts because the reformers were suspicious of the notion that art objects could possess sacred power. Yet, the reformers were quick to employ new printing technologies to convey their ideas. Printmaking became popular because a broad audience of Europeans could view the pictures and grasp the message, even if they were unable to read the captions. The Roman Church's response to the Reformation included an emphasis on simple art that told stories and stressed the intercessory role of saints. Thus, in various ways, religious art became an important tool for teaching religion. However, art is not produced in a vacuum, and thus it is not discussed here without reference to political, economic, social, and cultural factors. Yet, the arts were also important determinants in political, economic, social, and religious developments.

**Family and Daily Life.** The political, religious, and intellectual changes of the Renaissance and Reformation clearly shaped culture, large institutions, and structures of society, but they also influenced daily life by redefining the family, health, emotions, and daily habits. Conversely, small and seemingly private things such as the family and practices of daily life also influenced larger developments. Politicians, religious reformers, artists, writers, and explorers all grew up in families and experienced the practices of daily life. This point may seem obvious, yet historians for centuries studied the politics and ideas of the Renaissance and Reformation without paying adequate attention to the private lives, family surroundings, and living habits of individuals. Great individuals were also often discussed as if they never had been children, never married, never lived in households with other people, and never grew old. To redress these various inadequacies, chapters 7 and 8 examine leisure activities, recreation, daily life, and family trends during the period. Chapter 8 outlines notions of life cycle from the period and shows the extent to which families were units of production. This role for families had significant implications for women, people who remained unmarried, widows, and society as a whole. Chapters 7 and 8 combine to offer an important comparison with modern notions of the family, manners, and social differentiation.

**Why This Volume?** There are many books available on the European Renaissance and Reformation, including some outstanding recent studies. This book is meant to be a reference work, not a textbook. The *World Eras* series offers cross-disciplinary overviews of world history from a global perspective with a strong emphasis on daily life, social history, and cultural history. This particular volume is a perfect fit for students in traditional Western Civilization courses, in World Civilization courses, and in a range of more focused history courses. The series provides students with the factual information necessary for comparative study of cultures and cultural interactions. The structure was in part dictated by the *World Eras* series, but chapter lengths have been adjusted to accommodate the amount of information pertinent to the European Renaissance and Reformation. Each chapter contains alphabetically arranged topical entries that focus on events, ideas, developments, material conditions, and personalities. The authors have woven global perspectives into the text when possible in order to facilitate comparisons with other geographical regions and diverse chronological periods.

**Acknowledgments.** Anyone who has participated in a multi-author project is aware of potential pitfalls. I was blessed with a disciplined group of authors. Their participation has resulted in outstanding chapters written by specialists in their respected fields. The authors maintained an eye on global issues and took into consideration the neces-

sity of comparative analysis. The focus required presentation of canonized orthodoxy, and thus the authors have shied away from some of the daring new hypotheses that are evident in their other works. I want to thank the chapter authors for their efforts: Fred Baumgartner, Melanie Casey, Amanda Eurich, Jay Goodale, Carol Janson, Jole Shackelford, John Theibault, and Merry Wiesner-Hanks. Thanks also to the many colleagues, friends, students, and family members that have assisted the various authors. Special recognition goes to Fred Baumgartner for assistance on a number of topics, Pamela Long for guidance on the history of technology, and Frankie Shackelford for assistance on chapter 10. In addition, a work of this scope would not be possible without the generous support of the Methodist College administration. I am especially fortunate to have wonderful colleagues who have encouraged me throughout the writing process. Special thanks go to Grayson Carter, Carl Dyke, Helen Graham, Sal Mercagliano, Trevor Morris, and Peter Murray. Melanie Casey, a graduate of Methodist College, assisted immeasurably at every stage of this project. She did an exceptional job editing the various drafts of each chapter for content and style. I also wish to acknowledge and thank the Bruccoli Clark Layman/Manly staff for their professional assistance. They did an excellent job of editing, formatting, and providing graphics. In particular, Anthony Scotti was a patient and industrious editor. He offered a balanced mixture of encouragement, prodding, and direction. Finally, my wife, Tarja Wilson, has become all too familiar with the planning, writing, revising, and rewriting of this book. Her patience throughout and her willingness to adjust her own teaching schedule are greatly appreciated. I hope that my three young sons, James, Christopher, and David, will one day read this book with the intense curiosity that they currently possess.

**Goal.** Lastly, it is worth mentioning the reason the chapter authors and I initially set out to write such a volume: the students. Having devoted the better part of our lives to this topic, our goal was to share aspects of the Renaissance and Reformation Europe with students in a book that is both valuable and enjoyable. I hope that some of our enthusiasm for the period, and for history in general, will be contagious.

Norman J. Wilson
Methodist College
Fayetteville, N.C.

# ACKNOWLEDGMENTS

This book was produced by Manly, Inc. Karen L. Rood is senior editor and Anthony J. Scotti Jr. is series editor. James F. Tidd Jr. was the assistant in-house editor.

Production manager is Philip B. Dematteis.

Administrative support was provided by Ann M. Cheschi, Amber L. Coker, and Angi Pleasant.

Accounting supervisor is Ann-Marie Holland.

Copyediting supervisor is Phyllis A. Avant. The copyediting staff includes Brenda Carol Blanton, Allen E. Friend Jr., Melissa D. Hinton, William Tobias Mathes, Rebecca Mayo, Nancy E. Smith, and Elizabeth Jo Ann Sumner.

Editorial associates are Andrew Choate and Michael S. Martin.

Database manager is José A. Juarez.

Layout and graphics supervisor is Janet E. Hill. The graphics staff includes Karla Corley Brown and Zoe R. Cook.

Office manager is Kathy Lawler Merlette.

Photography supervisor is Paul Talbot. Photography editors are Charles Mims and Scott Nemzek.

Permissions editor is Jeff Miller.

Digital photographic copy work was performed by Joseph M. Bruccoli.

The SGML staff includes Frank Graham, Linda Dalton Mullinax, Jason Paddock, and Alex Snead.

Systems manager is Marie L. Parker.

Typesetting supervisor is Kathleen M. Flanagan. The typesetting staff includes Patricia Marie Flanagan, Mark J. McEwan, Pamela D. Norton, and Alison Smith. Freelance typesetters are Wanda Adams and Vicki Grivetti.

Walter W. Ross supervised library research. He was assisted by Steven Gross and the following librarians at the Thomas Cooper Library of the University of South Carolina: circulation department head Tucker Taylor; reference department head Virginia W. Weathers; Brette Barclay, Marilee Birchfield, Paul Cammarata, Gary Geer, Michael Macan, Tom Marcil, Rose Marshall, and Sharon Verba; interlibrary loan department head John Brunswick; and interlibrary loan staff Robert Arndt, Hayden Battle, Barry Bull, Jo Cottingham, Marna Hostetler, Marieum McClary, Erika Peake, and Nelson Rivera.

Anthony J. Scotti Jr. wrote the entries on Abraham Ortelius and the Sargasso Sea in the Geography chapter and Elizabeth I in Politics, Law, and the Military. James F. Tidd Jr. helped compile the data for the World Events chapter and wrote the chronology for Politics, Law, and the Military. Amanda Eurich and Carol Janson wrote the biography of Aldus Manutius for the Communication, Transportation, and Exploration chapter.

# WORLD EVENTS:
## SELECTED OCCURRENCES OUTSIDE EUROPE

by MELANIE CASEY

## 1350

- Sixteen-year-old Javan ruler Hayam Wuruk takes the throne of the Hindu state of Majapahit when his mother, Tribhuvana, abdicates. Along with his powerful minister Gajah Mada, he extends Javan control throughout Indonesia.

- Ramathibodi I, a Utong (Thai) general, becomes king and moves the capital to Ayutthaya, a settlement on an island north of Bangkok. He engages in warfare against the Cambodians—who are defeated, but they introduce Khmer culture into that of their conquerors—and establishes coded laws. He becomes a Buddhist priest and rules until his death in 1369.

## 1351

- Abū al-Hasan ʿAli, sultan of Morocco—who defeated Tunis (1347), controlled Algeria, and attempted to capture Spain—abdicates his throne in favor of his son.

- Fīrūz Shāh Tughluq becomes sultan of Delhi and attacks Bengal (1353). He rules until 1388.

## 1352

- The Ottoman Turks establish a settlement on Gallipoli, near Tzympe.
- Arab traveler Ibn Battūtah crosses the Sahara and visits the Mandingo Empire.

## 1353

- Fa Ngum unites the Laotian people and introduces Khmer civilization. He leads his country until he is exiled in 1371.

- Chinese general Hsü Ta and rebel Hung-wu join their forces and fight against the Mongols, eventually leading to the downfall of Mongol control and the start of a new Chinese dynasty.

*Denotes circa date

1

- After a series of short-lived reigns, Idris I Nigalemi becomes emperor of Kanem-Bornu. He rules until 1377.

## 1354

- The Ottoman Turks invade Thrace on the Balkan Peninsula.

## 1355

- Chu Yüan-chang becomes leader of rebel forces in China, after the death of Kuo-Tzu-hsing.

## 1356

- Yüan-chang's forces take the city of Nanking.
- Mobarez od-Din Mohammad, son of southern Iranian ruler Sharaf od-Din Mozaffar, captures Tabriz in northwest Iran.

## 1358

- Od-Din Mohammad is deposed by his sons Qotb od-Din Shah Mahmud and Jalal od-Din Shah Shoja', who divide the kingdom between themselves.

## 1359

- Angora (later Ankara) is captured by the Ottomans. It will become the capital of modern Turkey.

## 1360

- Murad I becomes sultan of the Ottoman Empire. He establishes an elite corps of soldiers known as the Janissaries, comprised of prisoners of war and Christian youths. They achieve great power until they are eliminated in 1826—massacred in their barracks.
- Mari Jata II becomes the mansa of the Mali Empire in West Africa. He rules until 1374.

## 1362

- Adrianpole (now Edirne, Turkey) is captured by the Ottomans under Murad I.

**1364**
- Javan minister Gajah Mada dies, possibly after being poisoned by Hayam Wuruk, who may have feared the influence of his powerful subordinate.

**1365**
- Indonesian poet Prapanca writes *Nāgarakertāgama,* an epic poem featuring the rule of Wuruk.

**1367**
- Four hundred thousand Hindus are massacred after a Bahmani victory in Vijayanagar.

**1368**
- The Yüan dynasty in China, a period of Mongol control initiated by Kublai Khan in 1260, ends. It is replaced by the Ming Dynasty, founded by the monk Chu Yüan-chang, whose forces capture Khahbalik (later Beijing).
- Ashikaga Yoshimitsu becomes a shogun in Japan. He serves in many government posts, reorganizes civil service, and suppresses piratical activities.

**1369**
- Ewostatewos, founder of many Ethiopian monasteries, dies.
- Japanese soldier and author Kitabatake Chikafusa's *Jinnō shōtōki,* written in 1339, is published. Kitabatake declares Japanese superiority over other nations in this work.
- Thai ruler Ramathibodi I, who unified the Thai kingdom and set the foundation of its legal system, dies. His son Prince Ramesuan takes the throne, but abdicates one year later in favor of his uncle Boromaraja.
- Korea submits to Chinese authority.

**1370**
- Indian theologian Vedāntadeśika, founder of the Vadakalai sect of Srivaisnava Hindus, dies.
- Timur (Tamerlane) becomes king of Samarghand, beginning a reign that will include the control of much of Central Asia and the Middle East.

**1371\***
- Arab jurist ad-Damīrī writes the *Hayāt al-hayawān,* an encyclopedia of animals that appear in the Koran.

**1371**    26 Sept.    The army of the allied Serb princes of Macedonia, led by King Vukasin, is defeated by the Ottoman Turks at Chernomen on the Maritsa River. Bulgaria and Serbia are forced to accept Turkish control.

**1373**    •    Sam Sene Thai becomes the ruler of the Lan Xang kingdom of Laos and rules for forty-four years of peace and prosperity.

**1375**    •    Suleiman-Mar wins independence for the Songhai, who controlled the western Sahara, from the Mali Kingdom.

**1377**    •    Islamic traditionalist theologian al-Jurjānī arrives to teach in Shīrāz, where he stays for ten years. He is best known for his dictionary *Kitāb at-taʿrifāt*.

**1381**    •    Ottoman theologian Bedreddin converts to Sūfism; he later becomes tutor to the royal house in Egypt.

**1382**    •    The Mongols are driven out of China and the country is unified.

         •    T'aigo Wangsa, founder of the T'aigo sect of Korean Buddhism, dies.

**1385**    •    Japanese poet Kanami, who is credited with transforming primitive dance into Nō drama, dies.

**1386**    •    Serbian prince Lazar Hrebeljanović defeats the Turks at the battle of Pločnik.

**1388**    •    Fīruz Shāh Tughluq dies, opening the door for palace intrigues, a reduction in the power of the Delhi sultanate, and a bitter civil war.

## 1389

- Hrebeljanović is killed, and his forces are crushed by the Turks at the battle of Kosovo. Also killed, however, is the Ottoman sultan Murad I, who is replaced by Bayazid I.

- Hayam Wuruk dies and his kingdom is divided between a nephew and a son from one of his lesser queens, which leads to a breakup of his empire and reduction of Hindu strength in Indonesia.

## 1390

- Bayazid I captures Anatolia.

## 1392

- Korean general Yi Sŏnggye overthrows the Koryŏ dynasty, names his kingdom Chosŏn, and establishes his capital at Hanyang (Seoul). The Yi dynasty rules Korea until 1910, when Japan annexes the country.

## 1393

- The Thais invade Cambodia, capturing Angkor and ninety thousand people. The policy of seizing and subjugating whole populations, often removing them to the home state, leads to much intermixing of peoples in the region.

- Bayazid I continues his conquests of northern Anatolia and captures the capital of Bulgaria.

## 1394

- Turkish ruler Timur captures Baghdad and controls Mesopotamia.

## 1395

- Thai king Ramesuan dies and is replaced by his son Ramraja. Fourteen years of peace follow.

## 1397

- The Ming law code is introduced in China, reinforcing traditional authority and the responsibility of the paterfamilias along hereditary groupings. A system of social organization (ten-family groups organized into one-hundred-family communities) is developed to regulate and indoctrinate the populace.

## 1398

- Timur's Turkish troops invade India, destroying the province of Delhi and massacring more than one hundred thousand Hindus before capturing the city of the same name.

**1399** • Faraj becomes ruler of Egypt. He allows a defensive alliance with the Turks to lapse and is later captured by the Turks while trying to regain Syria.

**1400\*** • Five Iroquois nations (Mohawk, Oneida, Onondaga, Cayuga, and Seneca) emerge as distinct tribal entities in North America.

**1400** • Damascus and Aleppo in Syria fall to Timur's armies.

**1402** • Chu Ti overthrows his father Chu Yüan-chang. During his reign, which lasts until 1424, China dominates Japan, expands its territory, establishes the capital in Beijing, defeats the Mongols, and sends sailing vessels on voyages to lands as far away as Africa.

• The first of several ambassadors from Ethiopia arrive in Europe.

• Mehmed I becomes the Ottoman sultan.

28 July Bayazid is defeated, and later dies in captivity, by Timur at the Battle of Angora.

**1403** • Prince Paramesvara founds Malacca (Melaka) on the west coast of the Malay Peninsula. The area will become a major supplier of spices.

**1404** • Narameikhla begins a thirty-year reign as king of Arakan (now Rakhine, Myanmar), but is driven from the land.

**1405** • Chinese explorer Cheng Ho (Zheng He) begins the first of seven expeditions, which will last until 1433, to Asia, India, East Africa, Egypt, Ceylon, and the Persian Gulf.

• Timur dies during an expedition to conquer China. Shah Rokh, his son, begins his reign of Persia (Iran) and Central Asia, which lasts until 1447.

**1407** • The Chinese defeat the kingdom of Palembang (Sumatra) and remove its ruler to China. They also invade Vietnam, setting up direct Chinese administration.

**1408**
- The king of Ceylon is taken to China as a prisoner.

**1409**
- Thai prince Nakonin overthrows Ramraja and takes the title Intharaja.

**1410**
- Sultan Ahmad Jalayir of Iraq is killed in a dispute with the chief of the Black Sheep Turkmen tribal confederation from eastern Anatolia.

**1412**
- Faraj is killed by the Turks in Damascus while trying to recapture Syria.

**1413**
- Mehmed defeats Mûsa at Camurlu, in Serbia, and declares himself the sultan of Rumelia and Anatolia.

**1414**
- Khizr Khan, former governor of the Punjab, becomes ruler of the Delhi sultanate, beginning a reign known as the Sayyid dynasty, because the leaders claimed to be descendants of the Prophet Muhammad. North India is divided among military chiefs for half a century.

**1416**
- A revolt begins in Iznik, Turkey, initiated by the communalistic social theories pushed by Moslem theologian Bedreddin, who had been exiled to the city. He is captured and hanged after the rebellion is crushed by Mehmed I.

**1418**
- Le Loi begins a Vietnamese independence movement in the Red River basin against the Chinese.

**1419**
- Sejong becomes the king of Korea. His reign, which lasts until 1450, is known for cultural achievement, development of a phonetic alphabet, and reduction of the power of the Buddhists.
- Tibetan Buddhist lama Tsongkhapa, founder of the Yellow Hat sect, dies.

**1420**

- Islamic calligrapher Mīr ʿAlī of Tabriz, a leading developer of cursive Persian script, dies.

**1421**

- Murad II becomes the Ottoman sultan.
- China establishes its capital at Beijing.

**1422**

- Indian Bahami Shihāb-ud-Dīn Ahmad I becomes sultan of the Deccan and expands the territorial holdings of his country during his reign, which lasts until 1436.

**1423**

- Mongol leader Aruqtai, chief of the As, declares himself khan of the Mongols and attacks North China.

**1424**

- Chu Chan-chi becomes emperor of China, following a one-year rule by his father, Chu Kao-chih, the son of Chu Ti. Chan-chi enjoys a peaceful reign that lasts until 1435.
- Intharaja dies, setting off a war between his three sons for control of Siam. His youngest son, Boromaraja II, defeats his siblings and assumes the throne.

**1425**

- The lands and rule of the Mentese Dynasty of the Mugla-Milas region of south-western Anatolia are annexed by the Ottomans.

**1428**

- Aztec ruler Itzcóatl begins his reign, which lasts until 1440.
- Vietnamese resistance leader Le Loi pushes the Chinese from his land and earns Vietnam its independence. He becomes emperor and begins instituting reforms. He will remain emperor until his death in 1443.

**1430**

- Narameikhla regains Arakan and begins the Mrohaung dynasty.

**1432**
- The Kara Koyunlu destroy remnants of the Jalayirid dynasty of Iraq, which had fled to areas around Basra.

**1434**
- The Cambodians establish a new capital at Phnom Penh, after having tried a new site on the Mekong River two years earlier. The new site was necessary because the former capital, Angkor, was vulnerable to raids by the Thais.

**1435**
- Chu Ch'i-chen, son of Chu Chan-chi, begins his rule of China.

**1436***
- Muslim theologian Muhammad ibn Falāh begins converting Arab tribesmen to what will become the Musha'sha' sect. He later settles in Iran.

**1438***
- Jahān Shān unites the Turkeman tribes in Azerbaijan and begins his quest to control Iraq and Fars (Persia), which he achieves by 1453.

**1438**
- Pachacuti begins his thirty-three-year reign, expanding and reorganizing the social and political system of the Inca Empire. His domain stretches from present-day Ecuador to southern Peru.

**1439**
- Esen Taiji becomes chief of the Oyat Mongols, extending Mongolian holdings into Korea and China.

**1440**
- Kabīr, whose teachings attempt to unite Hindi and Muslim thought, is born. After his death in 1518, Kabir's followers establish Sikhism.
- Aztec ruler Montezuma I begins his reign, which lasts until 1469. He extends the control of his people over what will become known as Mexico.

**1442**
- The Portuguese enslave captured Berbers from North Africa.

| | | |
|---|---|---|
| **1444** | 10 Nov. | The Ottomans, led by Murad II, who had been coaxed out of retirement from public life, defeat Christian Hungarians, led by János Hunyadi, at Varna. |
| **1446** | • | A revolt of the Janissaries, who opposed a planned attack on Constantinople, calls Murad II back to Edirne from a second retirement because of the weakness of his fourteen-year-old son Mehmet's rule. |
| **1447** | • | Tartar prince Ulūgh Beg becomes ruler of Turkestan. His short reign, which lasts until 1449, marks the transition of Central Asia, as after his death the Timurid Empire breaks up. |
| | • | The Bolewa people move from Lake Chad to the Daniski Hills, displacing the native Ngamo tribe from the region. |
| **1448** | • | Boromaraja II dies and is replaced on the Thai throne by King Trailok, who rules for forty years. He installs a system of nonhereditary nobility, reforms government administration, and distributes land to his favorites. |
| **1449** | • | Chu Ch'i-chen, emperor of China, is captured by the Mongols and imprisoned for one year. His place is taken by Chu Ch'i-yü, who leads until his death in 1457. |
| **1451** | • | Ottoman sultan Mehmed II (Mehmed the Conqueror) succeeds his father, Murad II. He is considered the true founder of the Ottoman Empire. |
| | • | Afghan king Bahlūl Lodī begins his reign, initiating the Lodī dynasty. |
| **1453** | • | Following an eighteen-year period of civil war, Uzun Hasan emerges as the ruler of the Turkmen Ak Koyunlu dynasty, which controls lands including Iran, Iraq, and Armenia. |
| | 29 May | Sultan Mehmed II captures Constantinople, thereby ending the Byzantine Empire. He renames the city Istanbul, promotes learning, and institutes Islam in the city. |

**1454**

- The Greek Orthodox Patriarchate is restored to Istanbul by Mehmed, who also allows a Jewish rabbi and Armenian patriarch into the city.

**1456**

- Tun Perak, the chief minister of Malacca, leads his forces to a victory over the invading Siamese.

**1457**

- Chu Ch'i-chen returns as emperor of China, remaining on the throne until his death in 1464.

**1458**

- Herāt, an ancient town on the trade route through Afghanistan, is captured by Jahān Shān of Azerbaijan.

**1460**

- Le Thanh Tong becomes ruler of Vietnam. He institutes Chinese-style government, develops an efficient provincial system, employs centrally appointed officials, institutes new taxes, and promotes education.

**1464**

- Chu Chien-shen, son of Chu Ch'i-chen, starts his twenty-three-year rule of China. He is dominated by his wife and advisers.
- Sonni ʿAlī (Alī the Great) becomes king of Gao and Songhai, beginning an expansion of territory that leads to the development of the Songhai Empire.

**1466**

- The Kara Koyunlu fail to conquer the Diyarbikar, a province of Turkey, and within two years they will be destroyed by Ak Koyunlu.

**1467**

- The devastating Ōnin War, which lasts for ten years, begins in Japan. The conflict started over who would succeed Ashikaga Yoshimasa, who became shogun at the age of thirteen in 1449.

**1468**
- Mengli Giray begins nearly half a century of rule as Khan of the Crimean Tartars.
- Sonni ʿAlī drives the Tuaregs out of Timbuktu.

**1469**
- Zen priest and artist Sesshū, who adapted Chinese techniques to Japanese ideals in painted scrolls and screens, returns to Japan from China.

**1471**
- The conquest of Champa by Le Thanh Tong, who establishes military colonies in the southern parts of Vietnam, is completed. This victory allows the Vietnamese the freedom to take border areas from the Cambodians.
- Topa Inca Yupanqui, son of Pachacuti, assumes the Incan throne.

**1472**
- Chinese Ming philosopher Wang Yang-ming is born. Trained as a Taoist, he brings new interpretations to Confucianism, advocating the philosophy of subjectivism. He serves as a governor and war minister in the Chinese government.

**1474**
- Maharaja Tilok, ruler of Chiang Mai, which has constantly been at war with the Thais, massacres all the members of the Thai embassy. This action sparks an inconclusive war.

**1476**
- Japanese painter and art critic Nōami compiles a catalogue of Chinese artists, titled the *Kundaikan sayū*.

**1478**
- The last Sayyid ruler in India, ʿAla'-ud-Din ʿAlam Shah, dies.

**1481**

3 May — Sultan Mehmed II dies, possibly from poisoning, and is replaced by his eldest son Bayezid II, despite the dead leader's wish that his favorite son, Cem, get the throne. Cem attempts a revolt, but is defeated and exiled to Rhodes. Bayezid rules until 1512.

**1482**

- The mouth of the Congo River is located by Portuguese navigator Diogo Cão, who soon finds the Kongo people. Trade between Kongo and Portugal commences, and the Kongo people become Christianized and Europeanized.

- Indian Bahmani Shihāb-ud-Dīn becomes sultan of the Deccan.

**1483**

- Bābur (Zahīrud-Din Muhammad), founder of the Mughal dynasty in India and its first emperor, is born. He rules until 1530.

**1485**

- Saluva Narasimha begins a new dynasty in India, opening ports on the west coast to trade, revitalizing the army, and establishing centralized rule.

**1486**

- Japanese poet Ike Sōgi, a Buddhist monk and master of linked verse, writes *Minase Sangin Hyakuin*.

**1487**

- Chu Chien-shen's son Chu Yu-t'ang begins his rule, a mostly peaceful reign, of China. He controls the throne until his death in 1505.

**1488**

- King Trailok dies and is replaced by his son and deputy Boromaraja III, who leads the Thais for only three years.

- The True Pure Land Sect in northern Japan rebels against a local lord and kills him, leading to a series of uprisings by this group.

**1489**

- The reign of Bahlul Lodi comes to a end. The most powerful Punjab chief and first Lodi ruler who replaced (1451) the Sayyid dynasty in India, Bahlul had successfully held together a confederacy of Afghan and Turkish chiefs, extending his empire to the borders of Bengal.

**1491**

- Saluva Narasimha is imprisoned, and then dies, after the siege of Udayagiri by Hindu soldiers from Orissa, a kingdom in eastern India.

**1492**
- Sonni ʿAlī of Songhai dies.
- Rustam Shah of Persia succeeds to the throne for a short five-year reign.

**1493**
- Muhammad I Askia (Askia the Great) gains the throne of Songhai after defeating the son of Sonni ʿAlī at the battle of Anfao. He reforms Songhai politics and establishes Islam as the state religion, making Songhai the strongest power and intellectual center of West Africa.
- Husayn Shāh ʿAlāʾ ad-Dīn declares himself king of Bengal, founding a new dynasty.
- Hosokawa Masamoto drives the shogun Yoshitane out of Kyoto.

**1495**
- Muhammad I Askia begins a two-year pilgrimage to Mecca.
- Sumayla Ndewura Dyakpa becomes king of the newly founded Gonja, a state on the Ghana-Ivory Coast. Gonja lasts until it is conquered in 1713 by Dagomba.

**1498**
- Husayn Shāh ʿAlāʾ ad-Dīn leads Bengal in conquering Kamrup and Assam.

**1500\***
- For approximately forty years, two queens, Rafohy and Rangita, successively rule the island nation of Imerinanjaka, located on Madagascar.

**1501**
- Esmāʿīl I, Shah of Iran, begins his reign. He establishes Jafari Shia Islam as the state religion and begins to convert the mostly Sunni population to the Shīʿah sect. With his rule also begins the Safavid Empire, which lasts until 1722, the first time since the seventh century that Iran is unified as an independent state.
- The enslavement of Africans is introduced into the West Indies to replace the rapidly dying off Native American population, which had been pressed into service. Nicolás de Ovando of Hispaniola imports some Spanish-born blacks for the purpose of using them as slaves.

**1502**
- Ahuitzotl dies and is succeeded by his nephew Montezuma II, who is destined to lose the Aztec Empire to the Spanish.

**1504**

- Amara Dunkas founds the Funj Sultanate around Sennar, in central Sudan.

**1505**

- Emperor Chu Yu-t'ang dies, leaving the throne in the hands of his son, Chu Hou-chao, whose reign is marked with rampant corruption, dominance by the eunuchs, and internal strife.

- Ozolua (the Conquerer) dies after a twenty-three-year reign as king of Benin (Nigeria). He expanded the size of his kingdom and traded with the Portuguese.

**1506**

- Afonso I, sixth Manikongo (ruler) of Kongo, converts to Roman Catholicism and encourages Portuguese colonization.

- Behzād, one of the greatest Persian miniaturist painters, becomes the head of an art academy in Herat. He will later become the court painter to Esmāʿīl I and director of the royal library.

**1509**

- An Arab-Egyptian fleet is destroyed off Diu (northwest of Bombay, India) by a Portuguese navy led by Francisco de Almeida, who had established forts along the Indian coast.

**1512**

- Selim I (the Grim) becomes Sultan upon the abdication of his father, Bayezid II. He doubles Ottoman territory, moves the capital to Istanbul, brings the Arab world into the Ottoman Empire, and becomes an Islamic Caliph (or protector) of the Sunni Muslims. He rules until 1520.

- Afonso I of Kongo signs a treaty with Manuel I of Portugal.

**1513**

- Selim I defeats and executes his brother in Anatolia.

**1514**

23 Aug. The Ottomans, led by Selim I, temporarily occupy the Safavid capital at Tabrīz (in Iran) after the Battle of Chāldirān.

**1515**

- The Turks capture Anatolia and Kurdistan.

## 1516

- Ang Chan becomes the king of Cambodia, resists Thai dominance, and rules until 1566.

- Syria is annexed by the Ottoman Empire.

- Aleppo and Damascus fall to the Turks after the Battle of Marjdabik (24 August).

## 1517

- The Spanish crown, under Charles I, authorizes slave trade to its South American colonies; a rapid increase in the importation of slaves to the New World follows.

22 Jan.  Egypt is annexed by the Ottoman Empire after Cairo is sacked.

## 1520

- Cuauhtémoc becomes the last emperor of the Aztecs, but is hanged in 1522 by Cortés.

- Sultan Süyeiman the Magnificent, son of Selim I, begins his reign. Under his rule the Ottoman Empire will reach its height of power, becoming a dominant power in the region. He promotes learning, sponsors reforms, and builds many public works.

- Babur invades northern India.

- Photisarath becomes ruler of Lan Chang (Laos), builds monasteries and temples, and promotes Buddhism. He rules until 1547.

## 1521

- The cruel Chu Hou-tsung, cousin of the previous emperor, assumes control of China. His reign is marked by lawlessness and disorder while court favorites control policy.

- Magellan is the first European to sight one of the Polynesian Islands, that of Pukapuka.

## 1524

- Tahmasp I, son of Esmā'īl I, takes the Persian throne after the death of his father. He is a weak leader, losing land and influence to Turkey.

## 1525

- Huáscar, son of Huayna Capac, shares the Incan throne with his half brother Atahualpa after their father steps down. Capac dies in 1535.

**1526**

- Babur routs the forces of the Delhi sultan Ibrahim Lodi at the First Battle of Panipat. By 1530 he controls all of northern India, establishing Mughal control.

- The Hungarians are defeated by the Ottoman Turks at the Battle of Mohács.

**1527**

- The Incan civil war breaks out between sides led by brothers Atahualpa and Huáscar.

- Somali chieftan Ahmed Gran, a Moslem, invades Ethiopia.

- Mac Dang Dung, governor of Hanoi, becomes ruler of Vietnam, deposing the Le rulers and their generals.

**1528**

- Muhammad I Askia is deposed by his son Musa and is exiled. He returns, but not to power, in 1537, and dies in 1538.

**1529**

- Mexico City (formerly Tenochtitlán) becomes capital of the Viceroyalty of New Spain.

- Barbary pirate Khayr ad-Dīn (Barbarossa, Redbeard) captures Algiers.

**1530**

- Babur dies and is replaced on the Indian throne by his son Humāyūn, who rules until 1540.

- Atahualpa becomes the Incan king of Peru, after deposing his half brother Huáscar.

**1531**

- Tabinshweti becomes the king of Burma.

**1533**

- Four-year-old Prince Ratsadatiratkumar becomes ruler of Siam, but is killed by his half brother Prince Prajai.

**1534**

- Khayr ad-Dīn conquers Tunisia as a base for pirate activities.

**1535**

- The first printing press arrives in the Western Hemisphere, brought to Mexico by the viceroy of New Spain, Antonio de Mendoza.
- Aztec leader Manco Inca Yupanqui attacks the Spanish in Peru, but is defeated by the following year.

**1537**

- A period of peace and stability in China begins with the ascension to the throne of Chu Tsai-kou, son of Chu Hou-tsung.

**1539**

- The Afghan ruler of North India, Shēr Shah, conquers Bengal and defeats Humāyūn at Chausa.
- Tabinshweti conquers the kingdom of Pegu (Myanmar).

**1540**

- Humāyūn is defeated again by Shēr Shah, this time at Kanauj, and is driven from India, but he returns in 1555.

**1541**

- Ahmed Gran's Somali army is pushed out of Ethiopia with the help of Portuguese arms. The Portuguese then send missionaries to Ethiopia, where they succeed in converting the next two rulers.

**1543**

- Altan Kahn becomes chief of the eastern Mongols. His army breaches the Great Wall of China in 1550.

**1544**

- Lima becomes capital of the Viceroyalty of Peru.
- Hindu religious reformer Dādū, founder of the Dādūpanthīs sect, is born.

**1545**

- The Spanish discover silver at Potosí, Bolivia, and begin mining operations using Indian labor.
- The Le dynasty in Vietnam regains control of the Red River region of Vietnam.

**1546**

- Thai ruler King Prajai dies, reportedly after being poisoned by his wife, Tao Sri Sudachan, who assumes powers of state as regent.

**1548**

- Sinan, considered the greatest Ottoman architect, builds the Sehzade Mosque in Istanbul. He is credited with designing more than three hundred buildings.

- Tao Sri Sudachan and her lover take the Thai throne outright but are murdered in a palace revolt led by Khun Pirentoratep, who rules as regent for King Chakrapat. Their rule is almost immediately interrupted by a Burmese invasion.

**1549**

- Spanish missionary Francis Xavier, who helped found the Jesuit order and preached in Gao and India, arrives in Kagoshima, Japan, where he works for two years. He returns to India in 1551 and dies on Sancian Island.

**1550**

- Jón Arason, a prelate of Iceland who resists the expansion of Lutheranism into his country, is beheaded.

- Arab traveler Leo Africanus's *Descittione dell' Africa*, the only source of information on the Sudan, is published.

**1551**

- Bayinnaung proclaims himself king of Burma after the assassination of his brother-in-law Tabinshweti, and suppresses a rebellion against his rule.

**1555**

- Humāyūn returns to India, seizing Delhi from its Afghan rulers, but he dies six months later.

- Turkish poet Bâkî gains the favor of Sultan Süleyman I, helping to revitalize lyric poetry in Turkey.

**1556**

- Abū-ul-Fath Jalāl-ud-Din Muhammad Akbar (Akbar the Great) becomes the Mughal emperor of India. He reigns until 1605, conquers most of India, and promotes reforms, learning, and art.

**1557**
- Shaybanid ruler 'Abd Allāh ibn Iskandar conquers Bukhara in Central Asia, as well as several regional kingdoms, and attacks Persia (1593–1594, 1595–1596).

**1558**
- The Nguyen family begins ruling southern Vietnam from the capital of Hue.

**1561\***
- The warrior Kongolo invades southern Zaire and unites the local chiefdoms into the Luba Empire. He is overthrown around 1620 by his son, Ilunga Kalala.

**1562**
- A cargo of African slaves is deposited in Hispaniola by Englishman John Hawkins, the first of three such slaving voyages, initiating English participation in the trade.

**1563**
- Burmese king Bayinnaung invades Siam, assaulting the capital of Ayutthaya.

**1566**
- Selim II becomes sultan of the Ottoman Empire.

**1568**
- The Azuchi-Momoyama period begins in Japan, an era of unification under military rule that lasts until the turn of the century.

**1569**
- Ayutthaya falls to the Burmese after a seven-month siege, as King Chakrapat dies (possibly by murder). A large portion of the population is removed to Burma, but the Burmese do not completely destroy the kingdom.

**1570\***
- The Mohawk, Oneida, Onondaga, Cayuga, and Seneca tribes unite into the Iroquois League. This accomplishment is credited to chiefs Hiawatha and Dekanawidah.
- The Ashanti people (Ghana) found a state of loosely bound tribes that becomes the Ashanti Empire around 1680.

## 1571

- The Ottomans capture Cyprus.

- A fleet of more than two hundred ships, under the command of Don John of Austria, defeats a Turkish fleet, commanded by Ali Pasha at Lepanto.

- Safavid philosopher-author Mullah Sadra is born; he will lead the Iranian cultural renaissance into the early seventeenth century.

- Idris Alooma, progenitor of what becomes the Sefawa Dynasty of Kanem Borno in northern Nigeria, around Lake Chad, begins his reign, which lasts until his death in 1603. It will become the most fully Islamic state in West Africa.

## 1572

- Chu Tsai-kou's son Chu I-chun begins his forty-eight-year reign in China.

- Palestinian Hebrew mystic Isaac ben Solomon Luria dies.

- Rana Pratāp Singh becomes the maharaja of Mewar (now part of Rajasthan, India) and defends his people against Akbar the Great.

- Tupac Amarú, the last male in the Incan chief line, is beheaded by Spanish conquistadors.

## 1574

- Murad III, the son of Selim II, becomes the sultan of the Ottomans.

- Rām Dās becomes the fourth Sikh Gurū and founds Amritsar (in Punjab, India).

- Hindu poet Tulsīdās writes *Rāmcaritmānas* (Lake of the Acts of Rama), one of the greatest Hindi literary works.

- The Spanish are pushed out of Tunis by the Turks. While the Spanish are losing in Tunis, they are establishing a settlement in Angola.

## 1576

- Esmā'īl II succeeds his father Tahmāsp I to the Persian throne, but he rules for just one year.

## 1578

- Italian Jesuit Matteo Ricci becomes a missionary to China and works to promote Christianity. In 1601 he founds a mission in Beijing.

- Sultan Ahmad al-Mansūr of Morocco begins his twenty-five-year reign, expanding Moroccan control of North Africa, after defeating a Portuguese force under Sebastian.

- Fez is captured from the Portuguese by Murad III.

**1580**

- Altan Kahn imposes the Dge-lugs-pa (Yellow Hat) sect of Lamaism upon the Mongol people and bestows the title of Dalai Lama on his grandson.

- Chinese dramatist Liang Ch'en-yü, whose K'un-shan style of singing dominates Chinese theater for nearly three centuries, dies.

**1581**

- King Bhueng Noreng of Burma, who had conquered the Thais, is succeeded by his son Nanda Bhueng.

**1584**

- Prince Naresuan (The Black Prince) of Siam defends his country against a Burmese invasion by employing a scorched-earth policy.

**1586**

- Japanese dancer Izumo Okuni, considered the founder of Kabuki, begins performing works inspired by Buddhist prayers.

**1587**

- Both Burma and Cambodia attack Siam, but again the leadership of Naresuan is pivotal in beating back the incursions. He becomes king in 1590.

**1588**

- Abbās I (Abbas the Great), the son of Shāh Soltān Mohammad, begins his reign in Persia. He rules the empire, defeating the Uzbeks and Ottoman Turks and regaining Persian lands, until 1629.

**1590**

- Japan, including the islands of Shikoku and Kyushu, is united under the leadership of Hideyoshi Toyotomi. He brings peace and infrastructural improvements, and will lead his nation (though he relinquishes his official title), until his death in 1598.

- Naresuan becomes the king of Siam and liberates Siam from Burmese control.

**1591**

- A Moroccan army made up largely of Spanish and Portuguese mercenaries, under the command of Ahmad al-Mansūr, defeats a Songhai army and the Songhai Empire collapses. The Moroccans capture Gao and Timbuktu.

**1592**

- Ming troops defending Korea battle Hideyoshi's Japanese army in its unsuccessful attempt to capture the country.

**1593**

- After another attack by Burma, with more than 250,000 troops, is defeated by Siam, Naresuan takes lands in southern Burma, as well as attacks Cambodia, forcing its leaders to flee. The conquered territory is placed under a military governor. Naresuan rules until his death in 1605.

**1595**

- Mehmed III succeeds Murad III to the Ottoman sultanate. He continues the wars with Europe and Iran.

**1596**

- Mexican historian Agustín Dávila Padilla publishes *Historia de la fundación de la provincia de Santiago de México de la Orden de predicadores.*

**1598**

- Abbās I defeats the Uzbeks near Herāt.
- Trade between Ayutthaya and Spain begins.

**1599**

- Manchurian chief Nurhachi begins conquering the Juchen tribes in his quest to unite the Manchu, which will become the Ch'ing dynasty starting in 1644.

**1600**

- Tokugawa Ieyasu, who was involved in a power struggle with Japanese warlords (*daimyos*) after the death of Toyotomi Hideyoshi, wins the battle of Sekigahara, defeating Konishi Yukinaga. Three years later he is appointed shogun by the emperor, thereby beginning the Tokugawa shogunate, centered in Edo (Tokyo).

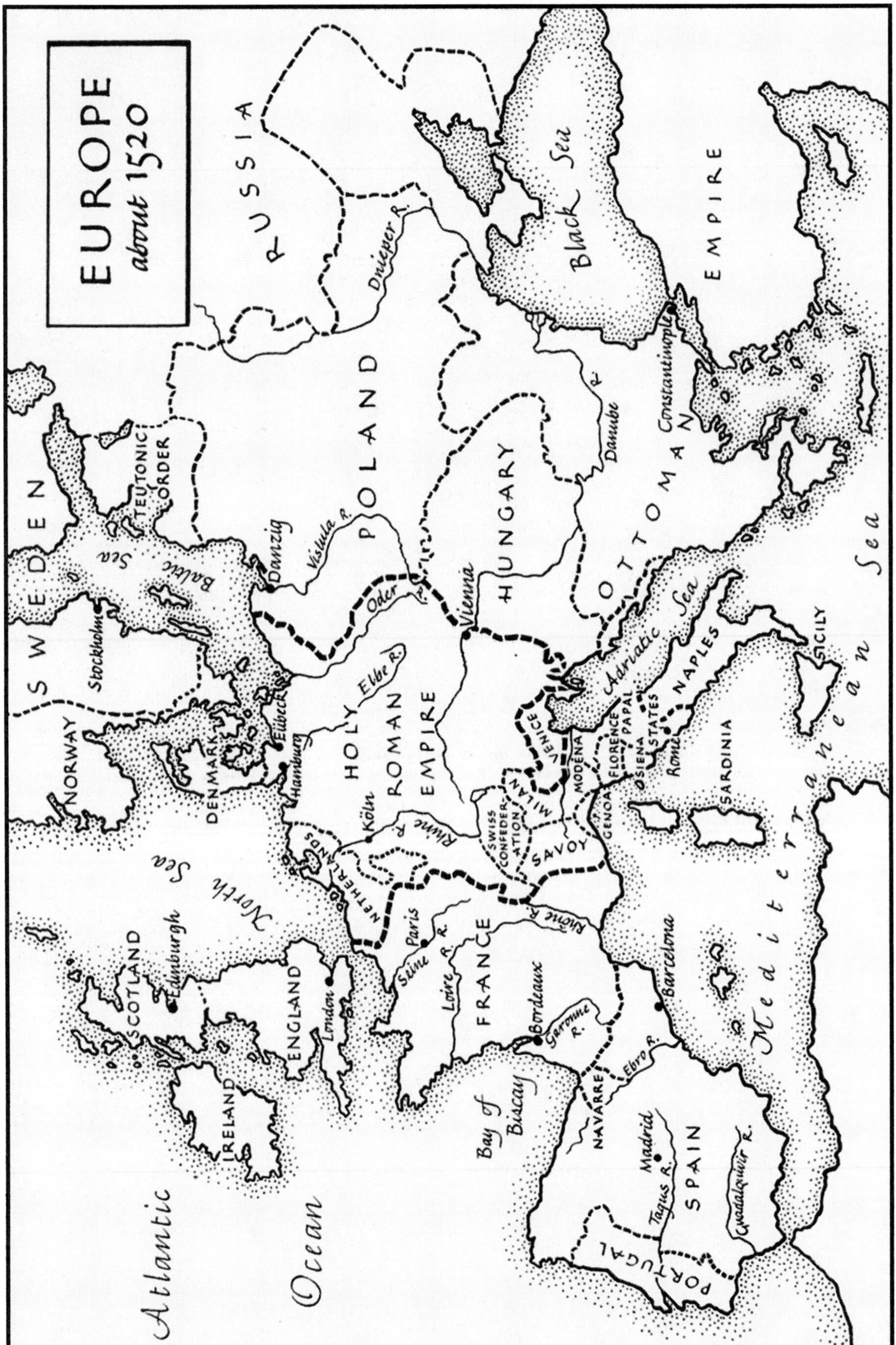

EUROPE
*about 1520*

RUSSIA

POLAND

SWEDEN

NORWAY

DENMARK

TEUTONIC ORDER

Danzig

*Vistula R.*

*Oder R.*

*Elbe R.*

Hamburg

Lübeck

*Baltic Sea*

Stockholm

HOLY ROMAN EMPIRE

Köln

*Rhine R.*

NETHERLANDS

SWISS CONFEDERATION

SAVOY

MILAN

MODENA

GENOA

FLORENCE

SIENA

PAPAL STATES

Rome

VENICE

*Adriatic Sea*

NAPLES

SARDINIA

SICILY

HUNGARY

Vienna

*Danube R.*

OTTOMAN EMPIRE

Constantinople

*Black Sea*

*Dnieper R.*

*Mediterranean Sea*

*North Sea*

*Atlantic Ocean*

SCOTLAND

Edinburgh

IRELAND

ENGLAND

London

FRANCE

Paris

*Seine R.*

*Loire R.*

Bordeaux

*Garonne R.*

*Rhône R.*

*Bay of Biscay*

NAVARRE

*Ebro R.*

Barcelona

SPAIN

Madrid

*Tagus R.*

*Guadalquivir R.*

PORTUGAL

Europe during the Renaissance and the Reformation

CHAPTER TWO

# GEOGRAPHY

by NORMAN J. WILSON

## CONTENTS

*Sidebars and tables are listed in italics.*

**1350**

- Portuguese sailors begin to chart the coastlines of the Canary Islands 823 miles off the northwest coast of Africa. In ancient times the Canaries were called the "Fortunate Islands" and were believed to be the western limit of the world. Arab, Portuguese, and French mariners had visited the islands in the Middle Ages.

**1402**

- Jean de Béthencourt and Gadifer de La Salle claim the Canary Islands for the kingdom of Castile.

**1410**

- Claudius Ptolemy's *Geography*, a second-century C.E. book, is translated into Latin. Scholars discover that Ptolemy had used a system of latitude and longitude in his maps.

**1418**

- The Madeira Islands, off the coast of Morocco, are officially discovered by the Portuguese explorer Joao Goncalves Zarco. This island group was possibly known in ancient times and probably had been visited by Genoese sailors in the mid 1300s.

**1419**

- Prince Henry of Portugal, more commonly known as Prince Henry the Navigator, becomes governor of the Algarve, the southernmost province of Portugal. There he attracts a following of astronomers, cartographers, instrument makers, seamen, and shipwrights. The next year he begins to sponsor expeditions down the coast of western Africa, searching for the southerly route to India.

**1427**

- The Portuguese sailor Diego de Sevilha lands in the Azores, a group of islands in the North Atlantic about eight hundred miles off the coast of Portugal. Although the exact date of discovery is uncertain, the Azores were known to European sailors in the fourteenth century.

**1456**

- The Cape Verde Islands in the North Atlantic are discovered by Ca'da Mosto, a Venetian navigator in the service of Prince Henry of Portugal.

**1460**

- Prince Henry the Navigator dies. During his lifetime the expeditions he sent along the African coast reached as far south as present-day Sierra Leone, although some evidence suggests his ships reached the Ivory Coast, approximately four hundred miles beyond.

**1462**

• The Portuguese begin to settle the Cape Verde Islands.

**1475**

• The first European edition of Ptolemy's *Geography* is printed.

**1479**

• The Canary Islands become a Spanish possession.

**1480**

• Under provisions of the Treaty of Alcatçovas, the Azores are assigned to Portugal.

**1482**

• Trade develops between the African kingdom of the Congo and Portugal.

**1485**

• Martin Behaim voyages down the west coast of Africa with Diogo Cao.

**1488**

• Bartholomeu Dias sails around the Cape of Good Hope and into the Indian Ocean, thereby dispelling the Ptolemaic belief that the Indian Ocean is a land-locked sea.

**1492**

• Behaim constructs a terrestrial globe for the city of Nuremberg, Germany. It is the oldest surviving terrestrial globe, and its creator shares the same geographical ideas as Christopher Columbus about the distance to the Indies. However, Behaim's depiction of the world is inaccurate, especially in relation to the African coast.

• Columbus sails to San Salvador on his first voyage to the Americas.

**1493**

• In an attempt to avoid conflicts over newly discovered lands, Spanish-born Pope Alexander VI declares a line of demarcation 100 leagues (about 320 miles) west of the Cape Verde Islands. All territory west of the line belongs to Spain, while the lands to the east are given to Portugal.

**1494**

- After protests from John II of Portugal, Spanish, and Portuguese delegates revise the papal division of the previous year. The Treaty of Tordesillas moves the boundary between the two countries' territorial claims 370 leagues (1,185 miles) west of the Cape Verde Islands. Pope Julius II does not approve the change until 1506.

**1497**

- John Cabot, an Italian in the service of King Henry VII of England, sails from Bristol in the *Matthew*. Searching for a route to India, he lands after fifty-two days at a spot variously identified as Labrador, Newfoundland, or Cape Breton Island. He makes a second voyage the next year but is lost at sea.

- The Portuguese explorer Vasco da Gama begins a two-year voyage during which he sails around the Cape of Good Hope and trades on the Malabar Coast of India.

**1499**

- The Italian merchant Amerigo Vespucci acts as the navigator for four Spanish ships under the command of Alonso de Ojeda. The yearlong expedition sails along the coast of South America and discovers the mouth of the Amazon River.

**1500**

- The navigator Pedro Alvares Cabral, under the provisions of the Treaty of Tordesillas, claims Brazil for Portugal.

**1501**

- Under Portuguese auspices Vespucci embarks on a second expedition and sails along the coast of Brazil, concluding that Columbus had discovered a new continent. He returns to Lisbon in 1502.

**1506**

- Congo king Afonso I converts to Roman Catholicism.

**1507**

- German cartographer Martin Waldseemüller issues the *Cosmographie Introductio*. He uses Vespucci's name to designate the New World.

**1508**

- Vespucci becomes *piloto mayor* (master navigator) in Seville, a position he holds until his death in 1512. As master navigator, he examines pilots' and shipmasters' licenses for all voyages and prepares a royal map of newly discovered lands.

**1513**

- The Spaniard Vasco Núñez de Balboa crosses the Isthmus of Panama and sights the *El Mar del Sur* (the South Sea), or what becomes known as the Pacific Ocean.

**1515**

- The first printed edition of Ptolemy's *Almagest* appears in Europe. It describes a universe in which the Sun and planets all revolve around Earth.

**1517**

- The Spanish Crown authorizes the importation of African slaves to its New World colonies.

**1519**

- The Spanish conquistador Hernán Cortés arrives in Mexico and conquers the Aztecs, killing their king, Montezuma, and destroying Tenochtitlán (present-day Mexico City). Over the next thirty years Spanish authority expands throughout Central and South America. Meanwhile, smallpox begins to decimate the natives of the region.

- The Portuguese navigator Ferdinand Magellan leaves Spain with five ships in an attempt to reach the Spice Islands (Moluccas) by sailing westward. Although Magellan is killed in the Philippines, one of his ships returns to Spain in 1522 after circumnavigating the globe.

**1524**

- A ship under the command of Giovanni da Verrazano, a Florentine in the pay of Francis I of France, ranges along the coast of North America from present-day North Carolina to Maine.

**1529**

- Mexico City becomes the capital of the viceroyalty of New Spain.

**1533**

- The Spanish conquistador Francisco Pizarro conquers the Incan capital of Cuzco and secures a large quantity of gold. Two years later he establishes the city of Lima, Peru.

- Peter Apian's *Cosmographia* explains how triangulation (a trigonometric method for finding a location between two fixed points a known distance apart) could be used to accurately create land maps.

**1534** • The Frenchman Jacques Cartier explores the Gulf of St. Lawrence. The next year he sails up the river as far as present-day Montreal. He names the nearby rapids *La Chine* because he believes that he has reached China.

**1538** • Gerardus Mercator, a Flemish cartographer, draws a world map with a heart-shaped design. He uses this pattern in order to take into account that he is projecting a globe onto a flat surface. In 1569 he perfects this type of map, which becomes known as the Mercator Projection Map.

**1543** • Portuguese ships arrive in Japan, marking the first time that Europeans had visited the islands. A Spanish expedition arrives in 1587.

**1544** • Lima becomes the capital of the viceroyalty of Peru.

**1545** • The Spanish discover a lode of silver at Potosí in present-day Bolivia.

**1564** • The Flemish engraver and cartographer Abraham Ortelius, an associate of Mercator, compiles maps of the world on a heart-shaped projection. He draws one of Egypt in 1565 and Asia in 1567.

**1570** • Ortelius's *Theatrum orbis terrarum* (Epitome of the Theater of the Worlde) is published and quickly becomes the most popular atlas of its time.

**1571** • The Spanish conquer the Philippine Islands.

**1575** • Ortelius is appointed royal cosmographer to King Philip II of Spain.

**1580**
- Michel Eyquem de Montaigne's *Travel Journey* describes inns and dining habits in Italy, Germany, and Switzerland.

**1584**
- Sir Walter Raleigh receives permission from Queen Elizabeth I of England to send an expedition to the present-day Outer Banks of North Carolina. Attempts to colonize Roanoke Island in both 1585 and 1587 fail.

**1600**
- The British establish the East India Company to regulate trading factories in the Indian subcontinent.

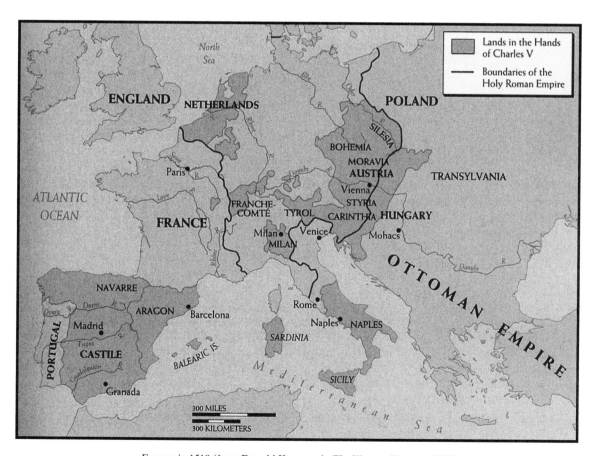

Europe in 1519 (from Donald Kagan, ed., *The Western Heritage*, 1998)

# OVERVIEW

**Interdependence.** Physical geography is the study of the earth's surface and natural features. Geographers consider climate, but they focus primarily on topography, which consists of the physical characteristics, land formations, and bodies of water in a given region. The earth's topography rarely changes, but any change can have severe repercussions for humans. Natural disasters, such as tidal waves or volcanoes, and major alterations in weather patterns, such as the end of the Ice Age, are the main causes of changes in topography. Climate and topography provide a static and inescapable setting to history. The interdependence of people and the physical earth means that physical geography influences human life, but it need not be seen in a purely deterministic sense because ingenuity and innovation allow humans to overcome geographical factors. For instance, the Netherlands rose to international prominence in the period 1350–1600 after the combination of wind-driven water pumps and huge dykes allowed the Dutch to reclaim fertile land and to irrigate fields. The resulting agricultural productivity was sufficient to feed an urban population of merchants, workers in small industry, and soldiers. Moreover, advancements in shipping allowed the Dutch to extend their political position and influence around the globe. Water, more so than ever before in human history, shaped the destiny of the Dutch and all Europeans during the period of the Renaissance and Reformation.

**Europe.** Geographers tend to study clearly distinguishable units, or regions, such as the seven continents. The Euro-Asian landmass is traditionally divided into the continents of Europe and Asia. Europe is a huge landmass with small peninsulas, or pieces of land that project into bodies of water, such as Italy extending into the Mediterranean Sea or Denmark into the North Sea. Europe itself is a peninsula. Like the Indian and Arabian peninsulas, the European peninsula protrudes from the Asian landmass, but the European peninsula differs from other Asian peninsulas due to the Mediterranean Sea, a vast but protected body of water. Europe is bounded by the Mediterranean Sea to the south, the Atlantic Ocean to the west, and the Arctic Ocean to the north. The eastern border is less clearly defined. The Ural Mountains in Russia offer a potential natural border; yet, early modern inhabitants of the region recognized no official distinctions between the eastern and western sides of the wide, but relatively low, Ural Mountains. The fluid eastern frontier complicates any attempt to define Europe in purely topographical terms.

**Cultural Identities.** The borders of Europe become more complicated in the era of the Renaissance and Reformation when one considers that Europeans on the shores of the Mediterranean frequently shared more in common with their neighbors in North Africa than with Europeans in northern Europe. A topographical definition of Europe is thus limited both by the lack of clear borders and by cultural factors. Therefore, cultural geographers and ethnographers bypass the topographical definitions of Europe and focus instead on social institutions, cultural values, religion, language, and a range of other factors. Examinations of the social and cultural factors that make something European frequently reveal the profound diversity of Europe. In this book the term *European* is best defined as a range of cultural identities and not a simple geographical expression.

**Black Death.** Geographers also seek to define the changing interrelationships between the physical environment and human activities. Europe's fertile soil and mild temperate climate make it one of the most favored places on earth for human habitation and population growth. Population in Europe does not follow a linear pattern of growth because as populations grow they influence the physical environment and become susceptible to disasters. Nineteenth-century social critic Thomas Malthus argued that population growth is checked by human actions, such as war, or by natural phenomena, such as plague and famine. Malthus's theory correctly describes most preindustrial societies and is especially pertinent to Europe at the beginning of the Renaissance and Reformation. The Black Death (1347–1351) killed so many Europeans that it altered the way humans interacted both with each other and with their geographical environment. Centuries of population growth and the requisite expansion into previously unsettled or sparsely settled land suddenly came to an end in the mid fourteenth century. The massive depopulation decimated small towns by removing the market for cash crops, such as grapes used in the production of wine. In the century after the Black Death the amount of plowed land decreased substantially as Europeans ceased to produce grains and cereals on previously cultivated land.

Plowed lands in areas with weaker soil and on the frontiers of society were simply abandoned. Forests and wastelands filled these areas and fostered a revival of wild game. The depopulation and the changes in cultivated land altered the ways that families controlled land and thereby influenced the makeup of the average family as well as the role of communities.

**Dawn of a New Era.** The geography of Europe influenced historical development between 1350 and 1600, but geography's influence on human activity need not be reduced to a strict geographical determinism. Human ingenuity and knowledge allowed people to overcome geographical limitations. During the Renaissance and Reformation, Europeans made significant accomplishments in science, medicine, and technology. One example of human ingenuity overcoming geographical limitations during the period is the way that advancements in shipping and transportation turned previous geographic hindrances into new opportunities for travel and trade. Europeans had long sought overland routes to the Far East. These pursuits eventually took them around the southern edge of the African continent and up into the Indian Sea. Shortly thereafter, Europeans in pursuit of new trade routes to Asia went west across the Atlantic Ocean. Suddenly, the Atlantic Ocean ceased to be a seemingly insurmountable border. It was transformed into a vast highway connecting humans from diverse lands. European culture began to change as the focus shifted from the world of the Mediterranean Sea to that of the Atlantic Ocean. The shape of the known world changed at an unprecedented pace, and within two generations all of the great urban civilizations of the earth became aware of one another for the first time in human history. A true world history and world geography emerged as these cultures interacted for the first time.

# TOPICS IN GEOGRAPHY

## CARTOGRAPHERS AND GEOGRAPHERS

**Stagnant Field of Study.** Geography had no independent status as a field of study in the early Renaissance. Geographical analysis did occur in travel literature, in works of nonfiction that purported to be universal histories, and in maps. The travel literature, such as accounts of Marco Polo or Sir John Mandeville, lacked precise distances and frequently incorporated purely fictional material. The universal histories were largely based on the accounts of the travel literature and thus further distorted reality. Moreover, the travel literature of the late fifteenth century was basically the same, especially in terms of accuracy, as that of the thirteenth century. During the fifteenth century Europeans sailed to the Americas and India, but little new appeared in the way of geographical studies. Printers well into the early sixteenth century preferred to republish these older and geographically incorrect accounts rather than take the financial risk of assimilating the current information into a new genre.

**Revival.** Mapmakers, also known as cartographers, were more interested in appeasing the political ambitions of their noble patrons than in achieving objectivity and accuracy. European maps in the Renaissance were usually meant for public display in churches and civic buildings. These "world maps" were essentially useless, and thus travelers found their way by asking directions at each settlement they encountered. However, late in the sixteenth century European geographers and cartographers created accurate maps that displayed a clear understanding of modern geography. The origins of this change can be traced to the early humanists, whose interest in ancient geographers and Greek learning contributed to a revival of works written by classical geographers such as Claudius Ptolemy and Strabo. As late as 1550, world maps were of no value to mariners and navigational maps grossly distorted the world. By the end of the century the mathematical methods of both Ptolemy and the Italian military engineers allowed mapmakers to merge the previously distinct world and navigational maps. Gerardus Mercator and Abraham Ortelius combined these traditions into maps that the modern reader would readily recognize. World geography was thus born a century after Christopher Columbus and Bartholomeu Dias made their historic voyages.

**T-O World Maps.** World maps prior to the sixteenth century were schematic representations of the world. Most were based on Isidore of Seville's "T-O" map, although some were zone maps known as Macrobian maps. Despite being called *mappae mundi* (world maps), the T-O maps followed the classical division of the habitable world into the three continents of Asia, Africa, and Europe. The name *T-O* derives from the location of the continents on a flat circular map. The "O" is the ocean that encircles the three continents, and the "T" is a water line that divides the continents. The stem of the "T" is the Mediterranean Sea that separates Europe on the left from Africa on the right. The cross of the "T" represents the Nile

A T-O map showing the five climata (zones) of the earth, in which the tropical region is divided by the "ocean river," 1485 (Huntington Library, San Marino, California, HEH 91528)

and Don rivers that separate Africa and Europe respectively from Asia. T-O maps grotesquely distorted reality, but they served an ecclesiastical function by supporting Christian ideas such as the biblical account that lands had been distributed to the sons of Noah. Jerusalem appears at the center of the ecclesiastically based T-O world maps.

**Portolan Charts.** By 1350 the magnetic compass was a common tool of European navigators. The compass transformed sailors' *portolani* (notebooks) into charts with traverse tables that explained distances of daily travel. Portolan charts allowed sailors to use their knowledge of the Mediterranean coasts and islands for a method of sailing known as "plain sailing," whereby navigators followed straight, or rhumb lines. These straight rhumb lines intersected each other and ran to key ports. The system worked well in the Mediterranean, where coastal markings were easily recognizable, but portolan charts did not allow for the fact that the earth is not flat. A curved surface cannot be mapped on a flat plane without a system of projection. Only slight latitudinal variations exist in the Mediterranean and shorelines were nearby, but Portuguese sailors who were sailing south along the coast of Africa crossed a wide latitudinal range. Moreover, the African coast has

fewer islands and more dangerous winds than the Mediterranean. A navigational error on the Mediterranean Sea might send a boat to the wrong shore, whereas the same error for the Portuguese in the Atlantic could send the boat clear across the ocean. Portuguese sailors were thus forced to forsake straight-line sailing and to seek other ways to determine latitude.

**Forgotten Solution.** Ptolemy had actually solved the problem of representing a spherical section of the earth's surface on a flat map more than one thousand years before the Renaissance. A Greek manuscript of Ptolemy's *Geography* was brought to Florence in 1406 and translated into Latin in 1410. Ptolemy introduced a difference in scale and a clear difference between unmeasured works, such as the *mappae mundi,* and maps based on coordinates. Ptolemy's use of coordinates was slowly assimilated into European mapmaking, and in the 1460s many maps of northern Europe were added to Ptolemy's book. The first printed edition of *Geography* appeared in 1475, complete with new maps. The coordinates of latitude and longitude were frequently incorrect in early editions of the book, but the work stimulated the pursuit of better ways to represent the earth's curvature.

The earliest known terrestrial globe, made by Martin Behaim on the basis of Ptolemaic ideas, 1492
(Germanisches Nationalmuseum, Nuremberg)

The author of *The Travels of Sir John Mandeville* remains unknown but many scholars believe it was written by an exiled Irish physician living in France. It circulated around Europe in the late fourteenth century and includes several adventurous and outlandish stories. The stories are now known to be hoaxes, but they nonetheless serve as a mirror to the medieval mind. The legendary story of Prester John, about an all-powerful ruler who receives the rite of baptism and ordination, appears first in the chronicle of Otto of Freising in 1145, but probably originated during the expansion of Christianity many years earlier. The validity of the story was still being seriously debated as late as 1646 and the Nuremberg globe of Renaissance geographer Martin Behaim includes Mandeville's magnetic rocks between Java Major and the mainland of India.

This emperor, Prester John, holds full great land, and hath many full noble cities and good towns in his realm, and many great diverse isles and large. For all the country of Ind is devised in isles for the great floods that come from Paradise, that depart all the land in many parts. And also in the sea he hath full many isles. And the best city in the Isle of Pentexoire is Nyse. . . .

This Prester John hath under him many kinds and many isles and many diverse folk of diverse conditions. And this land is full good and rich, but not so rich as is the land of the great Chan. For the merchants come not thither so commonly for to buy merchandises, as they do in the land of the great Chan, for it is too far to travel to. And on that other part, in the Isle of Cathay, men find all manner of thing that is need to man—cloths of gold, of silk, of spicery and all manner avoirdupois. And therefore, albeit that men have greater cheap in the Isle of Prester John . . . men dread the long way and the great perils in the sea in those parts. . . .

In the land of Prester John be many diverse things and many precious stones, so great and so large, that men make of them vessels, as platters, dishes and cups. And many other marvels be there, that it were too cumbrous and too long to put it in scripture of books; but of the principal isles and of his estate and of his law, I shall tell you some part.

This Emperor Prester John is Christian, and a great part of his country also. But yet, they have not all the articles of our faith as we have. They believe well in the Father, in the Son, and in the Holy Ghost. And they be full devout and right true one to another.

**Source:** *The Travels of Sir John Mandeville* (New York: Dover, 1964) pp. 178–179.

**Cosmography.** Ptolemy's mapping of the entire world on a framework of celestially derived circles became the standard model until Dias circumnavigated the Cape of Good Hope (1488), Columbus voyaged to the Americas (1492), and Ferdinand Magellan circumnavigated the globe (1519–1522). The Ptolemaic map evolved into an oval map that depicted the whole spherical globe on a flat surface. World maps in the sixteenth century became known as *cosmographia*. The oval world projection replaced the ecclesiastically determined *mappae mundi*. The basic textbook for cartogrpahers in the sixteenth century was Peter Apian's *Cosmographia* (1533). Apian's work relied heavily on Ptolemy's *Geographia* but with a new addition drawn from the mathematics of military engineers. Military and civil engineers of the Renaissance became interested in scaled representations that were mathematically precise. They developed mathematical methodology using scales and projections. Their techniques influenced Apian, who explained in his volume how triangulation could be used to accurately create land maps.

**Gerardus Mercator.** Maps of navigation and the world *cosmographia* were two distinct types of maps until Mercator merged them in his famous 1569 projection map. A former land surveyor, Mercator employed a projection that incorporated the cosmographical grid that allowed the globe's surface to be projected onto a flat surface while simultaneously allowing compass courses to be plotted with a straight edge. The Mercator projector was further refined by Edward Wright in 1599, and the Wright-Mercator projection became the basis for navigation until the twentieth century.

**Politics of Mapmaking.** Despite the technological advances of Mercator's world map, the map itself has a distinctive pro-Spanish bent. Mercator was employed by the king of Spain when the Spanish and Portuguese crowns essentially divided the two hemispheres. The Spanish Western Hemisphere, the Americas, is in the top left of the map in a manner that overstates the significance and size of the Spanish area. Cartography in the sixteenth century was a way to advertise, be it the Church advertising the centrality of Jerusalem and Christianity in the T-O maps or the cartographers in the pay of the Spanish throne, who advertised the promise of Spanish domains. Noble patronage of maps decreased dramatically after Mercator's map because shipping fell into the hands of commercial companies. These shipping companies wanted maps that were accurate and reliable to ensure that vessels and investments were not lost. By 1600, cartographers owed their allegiance to Dutch and English joint-stock companies and not to the royal families of Europe.

Sources:

Jerry Brotton, *Trading Territories: Mapping the Early Modern World* (Ithaca, N.Y.: Cornell University Press, 1998).

J. H. Parry, *The Age of Reconnaissance: Discovery, Exploration and Settlement, 1456-1650* (Berkeley: University of California Press, 1981).

J. R. S. Phillips, *The Medieval Expansion of Europe* (Oxford & New York: Clarendon Press, 1988).

David Woodward, *Maps as Prints in the Italian Renaissance: Makers, Distributors & Consumers* (London: British Library, 1996).

## CLIMATE

**Latitude.** The climate of any region is largely determined by the region's relation to the sun, which is called latitude, as well as its relation to water, winds, and elevation. Latitude is the most obvious and sometimes most deceptive determinant of climate. The southern extremes of Europe, such as Barcelona and Rome, are at a latitude equal to northern portions of the United States, such as New York. But the European climate of Madrid and Rome is much warmer than that of New York due to ocean currents and high-altitude winds known as the jetstreams. Most of Europe has a mild, temperate, and humid climate. Temperate-zone climates have a pronounced difference between winter and summer conditions. The most notable exception is the snow forest climate in some portions of Scandinavia.

**Ocean and Wind Currents.** Europe, the only continent with no desert region, is a peninsula jutting off the Eurasian landmass, and thus its climate is greatly influenced by the huge bodies of water to the west, north, and south. Water currents and winds coming off of the water have a great influence on European climate. The influence is especially evident in the northern plains where there are neither mountains nor highlands to interfere with wind patterns. The North Atlantic Drift is a broad ocean current, essentially an eastward extension of the North American Gulf Stream, of relatively warm water that hits the western shores of Europe. Prevailing westerly winds coming off of the Atlantic Ocean combine with the currents to create a temperate, humid, marine climate. Europe's mild, moist winters and cool, wet summers diminish as one travels east across the continent. The Atlantic Ocean heats up and cools off more slowly than the lands, and thus mild, moist climates along the coast differ from the cooler, drier winters and warmer, drier summers of the eastern portions of the Great European Plain. No north-south mountain barriers prevent warm Atlantic maritime air masses from moving east across Europe. As a result, climatic changes from the Atlantic to the Ural Mountains tend to be slow and gradual. Conversely, the absence of mountains also allows cold continental air to move westward in the winter, thereby creating long periods of winter weather across the Great European Plain.

**Mediterranean Basin.** The most dramatic variations in temperature are based not on the Atlantic but rather on proximity to the Mediterranean Sea, which borders Europe to the south. The climate of the Mediterranean Basin consists of dry, hot summers and moist, mild winters. A large high-pressure belt covers the Mediterranean Basin in the summer and creates droughtlike conditions. This subtropical high-pressure belt shifts slightly south in the winter, and the prevailing westerly winds bring enough humid air from the Atlantic Ocean to create wet, rainy winters. The northern edge of the Mediterranean Basin is clearly delineated by the various mountain ranges: Pyrenees, Appenines, Alps, Balkans, and the Caucasus. The mountains separate the northern humid climate from the dry subtropical climate of the Mediterranean Basin.

**Six Climatic Zones.** Europe can be divided into six broad climatic zones: the Mediterranean Basin (subtropical with fall and winter precipitation), Alpine Europe (climatic variation due to different elevations), Western-Northwestern Europe (mild winters and moderate to heavy precipitation), Central Europe (cold winters and summer rainfall), Eastern Europe (very cold, dry winters), and the Scandinavian Mountains (snowforests with heavy precipitation on the west). The Mediterranean Basin has a warm climate with dry summers. Climate is not uniform in the basin because of the various peninsulas and the diversity of the many smaller seas that make up the Mediterranean Sea. The Mediterranean Basin has less cloudiness than the rest of Europe in summer because the westerly winds move to its north. In the fall and winter the Mediterranean Sea is warmer than in the spring; hence, precipitation is higher in the fall and winter. The high elevation and diversity of altitudes create climatic variations in Alpine Europe. North of the Alps the rainiest season is the winter, whereas south of the mountains the rainiest season is fall. The mountains themselves have a fairly narrow high altitude area, and thus only a small region experiences the typical snow forest climate found in the Scandinavian Mountains. The maritime influence is most strongly noticeable in Western-Northwestern Europe, where southwesterly winds create a humid, temperate climate. Winters are mild and precipitation is moderate to heavy. The northern edges of this region are some of the cloudiest areas on earth. The maritime influence is less obvious as one travels east to Central Europe, but the absence of mountains makes it a transitional zone between the mild, wet northwest winters and the cold, dry Russian winters. Winter is the cloudiest season, but summer has the highest precipitation. Eastern Europe continues the gradual variation in climate. Late-summer rains lead to heavier precipitation in the fall than in the spring. The Scandinavian Mountains form a barrier that keeps much of the cloud cover and precipitation on the western side of Norway.

Sources:

Bernhard Haurwitz and James M. Austin, *Climatology* (New York & London: McGraw-Hill, 1944).

Emmanuel Le Roy Ladurie, *Times of Feast, Times of Famine: A History of Climate since the Year 1000,* translated by Barbara Bray (Garden City, N.Y.: Doubleday, 1971).

## CULTURAL GEOGRAPHY

**Villages.** Christian Europe was full of villages and walled cities. Villages typically had a population of three hundred to five hundred people who lived in windowless houses with thatched roofs. Villages were relatively isolated but were usually not far from a market town or city. Peasants in villages were self-sufficient, which means that virtually all of their needs were supplied locally. Most villages were dependent on the local production of grain, the staple product of villagers' diets, but villagers also needed to produce other essential crops. Frequently the local land or climate was not optimal for the production of staple items, but villagers would continue to produce poor exemplars of staples rather than live without them. Agriculture in the

Mediterranean Basin was based on the same three crops that had dominated in ancient times: wheat, olive oil, and grapes for wine. A plow that simply scratched the surface was used for the light soils, and grains were planted in alternating years. The heavier soils north of the Alps were well suited to a wide range of cereal crops such as wheat, rye, oats, and barley. Fields were farmed in a three-field rotation whereby one field was planted with a summer crop, one with a winter crop, and one was left fallow. This system was well suited to maintaining livestock who could pull a heavier plow and also provide manure to fertilize the fields. Local towns and cities relied on village-based grain production. At the end of the sixteenth century, grain from the Baltics was sufficient to free the Dutch farmers from grain production, and thus the Low Countries became the first to develop extensive specialization in nongrain crops.

**Towns and Cities.** A villager traveling to a city would be shocked to see the high stone ramparts, built out of quarry stone, that surrounded towns and cities. Urbanites lived, ate, and dressed in a manner that was drastically different from that of villagers. The contrast between urban and rural was great, and cities went to great lengths to monitor and restrict visitors from outside the city walls. Entry gates were closed at night and night watchers walked the streets looking for noncitizen vagrants as well as keeping a watch for potential fires. Beyond the walls of a city lay a river, fields, various buildings of religious orders, and the city hospital. Ill people went to the hospital not to be cured but rather to be isolated from the other residents until the illness passed or the person died. Within the city walls streets frequently rambled without any logical pattern because urban planners were generally not employed until late in the Renaissance and Reformation.

**Types of Cities.** Towns varied considerably, but all towns were distinguishable from villages based on legal, economic, and strategic factors: towns had courts and a hierarchy of church officials; towns housed markets, artisans, handworkers, and a school or university; and towns were always fortified. Free city-states and ordinary cities were similar in shape and size, but they differed consider-

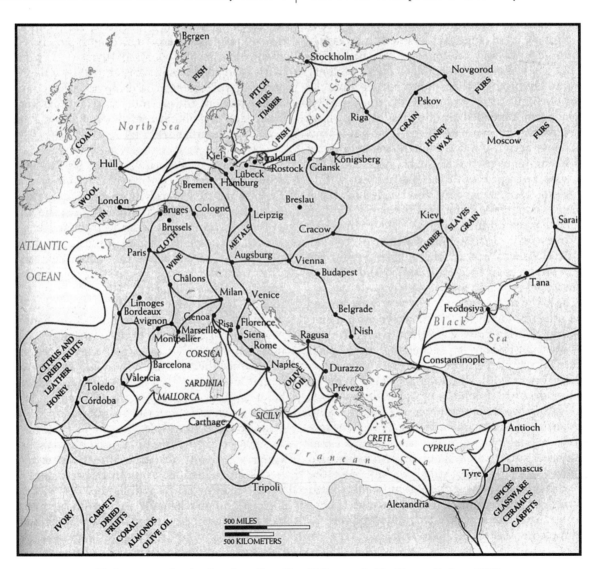

Trade routes and regional products (from Donald Kagan, ed., *The Western Heritage,* 1998)

ably in terms of governance within the city and control over the surrounding countryside. Free city-states were autonomous self-governing political entities that controlled the agricultural lands around their walls. Ordinary cities were controlled by aristocrats who also controlled the surrounding agricultural lands. One ruler could control many cities, but usually the city where the ruler resided, known as the court city, was the most prosperous in a territory.

**Trade.** Large urban areas tend to fall along one of two "urban belts." One flows north-south, from the Netherlands to Italy, and the other moves east-west along the Mediterranean Sea. Trade routes in Europe followed the urban patterns and formed a north-south axis that connected the world of the northern Hansa traders to that of the Mediterranean south, and an east-west corridor that connected the Mediterranean Basin to traders in Asia. Italians monopolized the east-west corridor and dominated the north-south corridor. The Hansa, the northern arm of the north-south corridor, also controlled trade in the Baltic that went east-west. This trade corridor prospered in the sixteenth century as grains from Russia and Poland made their way into urban areas to their west.

**Iberian Peninsula.** Inhabitants of the Iberian Peninsula were isolated from both trade corridors and therefore turned to northern Africa for trade. On the far western edge of the Iberian Peninsula, Portugal was initially one of the areas most isolated from European trade. The Portuguese sought trade routes around the southern African Cape and into the Indian Ocean. Their success was a strong impetus for the Spaniards to explore a western route to the Indies. The resulting exploration led to the ability to sail the Atlantic Ocean. As the center of European trade shifted from the Mediterranean to the Atlantic, the role of Portugal shifted from remote outpost to the center of shipping.

Sources:

Fernand Braudel, *Civilization and Capitalism 15th–18th Century*, 3 volumes, translated by Siân Reynolds (New York: Harper & Row, 1982–1984).

George Huppert, *After the Black Death: A Social History of Early Modern Europe* (Bloomington & Indianapolis: Indiana University Press, 1986).

## LANGUAGE

**Localism.** The limit of daily travel and thus the limits of sending information in preindustrial society was roughly thirty miles per day. Someone from more than thirty miles away was therefore foreign to an area. As a result it is better to think of Europe not as one entity but rather as a complex patchwork of small local units. Localism is evident in the variations in customs, coinage, and dialects. The oral culture of late-medieval Europe consisted of a wide range of diverse dialects. The rise of printing in the fifteenth century eventually created a standard written form of most languages. The standard form was usually the result of a small group of popular writers who chanced to be from the same region, such as Dante, Petrarch, and Boccacio from Tuscany. By 1600 most languages had a "high," or written, version that the educated elite began to use and a "low," or local, dialect that was spoken in geographically defined areas.

**Indo-European Languages.** Most European languages are of Indo-European origins. The Indo-European family of languages is the world's largest and most frequently spoken family of languages in the modern world. Indo-European languages from the Renaissance and Reformation may be further divided into seven main language groups: Romance, Germanic, Baltic, Slavic, Celtic, Hellenic, and other. The Romance languages are derived from Latin, which was the language of the ancient Romans. Thus, the Romance languages are spoken in the western Mediterranean portion of Europe that had been part of the ancient Roman Empire. Italian, French, Spanish, Portuguese, and Rumanian are the main Romance languages. Modern forms of these languages emerged from a wide range of dialects that existed throughout the Renaissance and Reformation. Printing codified languages and eliminated many of the dialects, but several regional Romance languages remained vibrant throughout the period, such as Catalan, Provençal, Rhaeto-Romanic, Sardinian, and Moldavian. Areas north of the Romance-speaking regions spoke Germanic languages such as English, German, Yiddish, Dutch, Flemish, Frisian, and Luxembourgian. In far northern Scandinavia a northern grouping of Germanic languages consists of Swedish, Danish, Icelandic, and Faroese. Nestled between the Germanic and the Scandinavian-Germanic languages were Lithuanian and Latvian (also called Lettish), two Baltic languages that are distantly related to the Slavic languages but distinct from the Germanic. The Slavic languages of northeastern and central Europe are spoken in areas east of the Germanic-speaking and Romance-speaking sections of Europe. They include an eastern grouping of Russian, Ukrainian, and Belorussian; a western grouping of Polish, Czech, Slovak, and Sorbian (Lusatian); and a southern grouping of Bulgarian, Serbo-Croatian, and Macedonian. Further south is Greek, a Hellenic language that influenced the other European languages during the late Renaissance because intellectuals across Europe revived Greek studies. Two languages from the edge of the Greek-speaking world that fail to fall into specific divisions are Albanian and Armenian. Celtic, the final group or subfamily within the Indo-European languages that are spoken in Europe, is limited to two branches of language spoken on the British Isles. The Brythonic branch consists of Welsh and Breton, and the Goidelic branch consists of Gaelic (Irish and Scottish).

**Non-Indo-European Languages.** Non-Indo-European languages are limited to Basque in Western Europe and two main families, Finno-Ugric and Altaic, in eastern Europe. Basque is the only non-Indo-European language spoken in the western sections of Europe. It is spoken in the mountainous area around the modern border of Spain and France. In eastern Europe the Uralic and Finno-Ugric languages consists of two distinct branches. The Finnic languages (Finnish, Lappish, Estonian, and Komi) are spoken to the northeast of the Germanic languages, and the Ugric languages (Hungarian) are spoken to the southeast of the Germanic languages in modern-day Hungary. Turkish, a member of the Altaic language family, came to be of central importance to European history during the Renaissance and Reformation because the Ottoman Turks came from the south and moved north across eastern Europe as far as Austria. Turkish, the official language of modern Turkey, is also spoken by groups of people in modern Bulgaria, Greece, and Cyprus.

**Source:**
Kenneth Katzner, *The Languages of the World* (London & New York: Routledge, 1995).

Christopher Moseley and R. E Asher, eds., *Atlas of the World's Languages* (London & New York: Routledge, 1994).

## PHYSICAL GEOGRAPHY

**Borders.** Europe is bordered by water on three sides. The western boundary is the Atlantic Ocean, the northern boundary is the Arctic Ocean, and the southern boundary includes the Mediterranean Sea and the Black Sea. These bodies of water provide clear boundaries but are themselves so distinct that Europeans living on the shores of one body of water have a radically different experience with the water than inhabitants living on a different body of water. The sheltered coasts and many natural harbors fostered sea-oriented, or maritime, economies that prospered during the late Renaissance and Reformation periods as naval developments turned the vast stretches of water into highways for trade and travel. The Ural Mountains, the Caspian Sea, and the Caucasus Mountains form an eastern frontier that is more ambiguous than the other borders.

**Great European Plain.** Between the low Ural Mountains and the relatively high Caucasus Mountains lies the eastern edge of the Great European Plain. This vast flatland stretches from the Pyrenees Mountains that divide modern France and Spain and across Germany, Poland, and Russia before ending at the Ural Mountains. The Caspian Gate, a mountain pass south of the Urals and north of the landlocked Caspian Sea, allows one to pass from Amsterdam in the west straight through to the borders of Western China, with elevations that barely exceed sea level. Glaciers on the northwestern edge of the plain, in what is now the eastern border of modern Finland, have receded and left more varied geography with tens of thousands of small lakes, but other regions of the plain have relatively few lakes.

**Rivers.** The Great European Plain is drained by various rivers, such as the Volga, Dneiper, Vistula, Oder, Elbe, Seine, and Loire. These and other rivers of Europe provided access to the seas and better transportation opportunities for early-modern Europeans than overland routes. As a result, most major cities in Europe are located along waterways: London on the Thames; Paris on the Seine; Vienna and Budapest on the Danube; Warsaw on the Vistula; Copenhagen, Stockholm, and St. Petersburg on the Baltic Sea; Amsterdam on the North Sea; Lisbon on the Atlantic; and a shoreline full of cities on the Mediterranean. Furthermore, river valleys tend to be suitable for intensive agriculture, which is a prerequisite for urban development. Cities even dot the shores of rivers that were not navigable in the Renaissance and Reformation periods because river valleys also provided an opportunity to travel long distances with only slight variation in altitude. In fact, one can travel at water level from the Mediterranean Sea to the Atlantic Ocean over the French isthmus, a land bridge that connects two bodies of land. In the early Renaissance these travel opportunities made France the only area of Europe that clearly belonged to both the Atlantic world of Northern Europe and the Mediterranean world of Southern Europe.

**Peninsulas and Isthmuses.** France is part of a long isthmus that connects the Iberian Peninsula (Spain and Portugal) to the Asian continent. France also includes smaller peninsulas, such as Brittany and Normandy, which jut into the English Channel toward the British Isles. The European continent itself is a peninsula of smaller peninsulas, or landmasses that jut into water. These peninsulas are connected to the great Eurasian landmass by a wide isthmus known as the Great European Plain. The Iberian, Italian, Balkan, Scandinavian, and Danish peninsulas are the five most prominent peninsulas. Inhabitants of four of these peninsulas were forced to turn to the seas for trade because mountains hindered land travel: the Pyrenees isolated Spain and Portugal on the Iberian Peninsula, the Alps isolated the Italian peninsula, the Balkans isolated the Balkan peninsula, and the mountains of the Scandinavian peninsula limited travel across it. Island and peninsular inhabitants therefore turned to the seas at an unprecedented pace in the Renaissance and Reformation. The ability to cross the oceans dramatically changed Europe because remote outposts such as Portugal suddenly became the center of European shipping.

**Islands.** Advances in shipping were also significant for the many large inhabitable islands that are located in the Atlantic Ocean to the west of the continent. The largest of these islands, Iceland and the British Isles, are virtually small-scale continents. Access to these islands was greatly enhanced by Renaissance shipping technology, yet many Atlantic islands remained largely isolated. Danish islands in the Baltic Sea formed a bridge from the Danish to the Swedish peninsula and were important for Hanseatic trade in the Baltic. Mediterranean islands prospered in the late Middle Ages from Venetian and Genoese trade routes. Sardinia, Corsica, Sicily, Cyprus, Crete, and Rhodes, the largest of the Mediterranean islands, provided stopping points for sea routes and visual points for navigation. When these islands were integrated into shipping routes, their main port cities flourished, but the economic prosperity rarely spread to the interior of the islands. The interior of wealthy Sicily lacked the roads, bridges, and agricultural production found on the continent. Changes in shipping routes, due to technology or political factors, could quickly demolish the economic prosperity of port cities. Smaller islands also had a pattern of boom and bust as nonnative crops such as sugar cane were introduced. The shift from Mediterranean to Atlantic trade negatively influenced Mediterranean islands but proved to be a tremendous boon to Atlantic islands.

**Three Geographical Regions.** European geography can be broken into three general regions: the fold mountains, the highlands or uplands, and the lowlands. Each region can be further divided, such as dividing the highlands into the Central Uplands and the Northwestern Highlands, but the three general regions have distinct features that influence inhabitants. Higher elevations, be they uplands or fold mountains, border Europe on the northwest, the east, and the south. Nestled between these higher elevation areas are fertile plains, coastal lowlands, and river-valley basins.

**Fold Mountains.** The Alpine mountain system in Europe consists of high mountains and rugged plateaus that extend on a west-east axis from the Sierra Nevada and Pyrenees to the Caucasus Mountains. The Pyrenean Mountains, or Pyrenees, form a boundary between France and Spain on the western Mediterranean basin. The Baetic cordillera, or Sierra Nevada, is the westernmost alpine range situated in the southeast of Spain. The Balearic Islands are part of a submerged ridge of mountains that rises above the sea to form Cabrera, Formentera, Ibiza, Majorca, Minorca, and eleven other smaller islands. The Alpes Maritimes form an east-west line of mountains in southern France. To their north the Alps run from the French Riviera to Austria. Rugged peaks, such as the Matterhorn, and deep valleys are evidence of earlier glacial erosion that created this majestic band of mountains. Rugged peaks are also evident to the west of the Alps, in the Jura, which stretch from the cities of Basel and Geneva in Switzerland westward into eastern France. East of the Alps the Carpathians are a long range of rounded, forested mountains that consist of three distinct sections: the northern Carpathians in Czechoslovakia and Poland; the eastern Carpathians, which arc from the Ukraine to Romania; and the Transylvanian Alps, or southern Carpathians, which run from east to west across Romania. The Appennines run south of the Alps through the Italian peninsula. To their south the triangular island of Sicily is itself a mountain range famous for the volcanic Mount Etna, although the highest peak is Mount Madonie. Parallel to the Italian Appennines and to the east, across the Adriatic Sea, run the Dinaric Alps. A southern continuation of the Dinaric mountains is called the Hellenic mountains, or Greek mountains. The Cretan arc on the Island of Crete is the southern extent of the Alps. The Balkan highlands run west-east parallel to and just south of the Danube River through Bulgaria to the Black Sea. The Crimean peninsula on the northern side of the Black Sea has mountains on the south that fall to the Crimean steppes, or highlands, to the north and then fall further north into the Great European Plain. The easternmost Alpine region of Europe is the Caucasus Mountains that form the southeastern border of Europe. This rugged range can be divided into the greater Caucasus to the north and the lesser Caucasus to the south. The highest peaks are in the western edges of the greater Caucasus. The eastern border of Europe is formed by the Ural mountain range that consists of the heavily glaciated northern Urals and the wide central and southern Urals.

## THE SARGASSO SEA

During the initial voyage of Christopher Columbus to the New World in 1492, his ships encountered a strange expanse of water in the central North Atlantic west of the Azores. This large tract of comparatively still but clear water was oval in shape and filled with seaweed. Columbus took the presence of the weed as a sign that land was near, although his sailors had misplaced fears that their ships would become ensnared in the tangle of floating vegetation.

What Columbus did not know at the time was that he was still hundreds of miles from land. The area of water he encountered has been dubbed the Sargasso Sea by mariners and scientists. (Free-floating brown seaweed is from the genus *Sargassum*.) The Sargasso Sea covers approximately 2 million square miles (two-thirds the size of the contiguous United States) and because of clockwise-flowing currents it can be found in the area bordered by the parallels 20°N and 35°N and the meridians 30°W and 70°W. A shallow warm pool covers deeper, colder waters with depths ranging from 5,000 feet to 23,000 feet. Light winds, weak currents, low precipitation, and high evaporation all combine to create an aquatic desert almost totally devoid of plankton, the basic food source for most marine life, although the sea is home to certain species of crabs, shrimp, eels, and flying fish.

Source: John and Mildred Teal, *The Sargasso Sea* (Boston: Little, Brown, 1975).

**Interior Trade.** The southern Alpine belt would appear to hamper European trade, but in fact the topography allows for trade within Europe. Wide river valleys are suitable for land transportation in the French Languedoc, between the Alps and the Pyrenees, the long Danube valley between the Alps and the Carpathians, and the valleys of the Morava and Vardar rivers that flow through the Balkan ranges. Glaciers carved deep valleys into the Alps and the Carpathians, the longest mountain ranges, which are connected by mountain passes for transportation. However, the Pyrenees to the southwest and the Caucasus to the southeast pose severe hindrances to trade except along the narrow seashores. Mountains thus pose serious boundaries for trade into and out of Europe on the southeast and southwest but only limited hindrances to trade within Europe.

**Highlands.** Running alongside the diverse mountains of Europe are the half-mountain plateaus, hills, and foothills that are quite distinct from the mountains. The Massifs, or Central Uplands, are highlands that border or lay between the southern Alpine mountain ranges and thus also follow a west-east axis: Spanish Meseta (Iberian Peninsula), Massif Central (France), Ardennes Plateau, Bavarian Plateau,

Volga Heights, and Podolian Plateau (north of the Carpathians). These scattered uplands are grassy and suitable for fodder crops. As a result, they are areas which developed intensive animal husbandry. The Northwestern or Atlantic Highlands follow a southwest-northeast axis running from the Breton Peninsula in northwestern France northeast to Lapland: France, Ireland, Scotland, Iceland, Norway, Sweden, and Lapland. These highlands have thin soil and rugged topography that is suitable for sheep and cattle grazing. The craggy, hilly uplands in many areas are known for their isolation and ruggedness.

**Lowlands and Plains.** The coastal lowlands and river-valley plains consist of rolling plains that are suitable for intensive agricultural development: the Great European Plain, Po Basin, Paris Basin, Southern England and Eastern Ireland, Hungarian Plain, Wallachian Plain, and the Bohemian Plain. The Great European Plain is a vast flatland that stretches from western France to the Ural Mountains. The name *plains* suggests abundance, fertility, and good living, but in fact the Great European Plain was easily traversed and thus susceptible to outside invasions. This situation allowed Russia to move eastward and create an empire, but it also left Poland vulnerable to attacks from the east and the west. The cleared forests of the northern European plains are quite different from the much smaller Mediterranean plains. The Mediterranean plains frequently faced severe water and drainage problems. Communal efforts to alleviate these problems resulted in fertile farmland that was conducive to intensive agricultural production. All European plains shared the responsibility of providing agricultural resources for an urban world that existed quite distinctly from the rural plains.

Sources:

Fernand Braudel, *The Mediterranean and the Mediterranean World in the Age of Philip II,* 2 volumes (New York: Harper & Row, 1972–1973).

Edwin Michael Bridges, *World Geomorphology* (Cambridge & New York: Cambridge University Press, 1990).

David L. Clawson and James S. Fisher, *World Regional Geography,* sixth edition (Upper Saddle River, N.J.: Prentice Hall, 1998).

# SIGNIFICANT PEOPLE

## MARTIN BEHAIM

### 1459-1507
### NAVIGATOR AND GEOGRAPHER

**Nuremberg Globe.** Although the fourteenth-century French prelate Nicholas of Oresme outlined a technique for making a globe in *De Sphaera,* Martin Behaim is responsible for making the oldest surviving terrestrial globe. Behaim's 1492 globe is consistent with Christopher Columbus's perspective of the earth. The globe was being created at the exact time when Columbus was under sail, so it is unclear if one influenced the other or if the two men simply shared the same idea at the same time. The globe is based in part on a *mappa mundi* (world map), a decorative draft that Behaim constructed. Both projects were meant for public display in Behaim's hometown, the Free Imperial City of Nuremberg in southern Germany.

**Background.** A Nuremberg cloth merchant, Behaim traveled to Lisbon in hopes of benefiting from Portuguese trade along the African coast. Behaim claimed to have sailed on Portuguese ships as far south as the Tropic of Capricorn, but he was not a true businessman-turned-explorer like Amerigo Vespucci. He established a successful business in Portugal and maintained ties to Nuremberg citizens who were interested in Portuguese exploration and trade. Upon returning to Nuremberg in 1490, he was persuaded to utilize his knowledge of Portuguese exploration in the construction of a world map. City financiers who had profited nicely in the German silver boom were especially interested in the growing Portuguese gold trade along the west coast of Africa. Other city leaders were simply interested in the commercial potential of Portuguese trade with Asia.

**Narrow Atlantic Theory.** Behaim's spherical representation of the earth was not new to navigators who did not really believe Columbus would fall off the surface of a flat earth. The globe does represent a new use of maps to illustrate geographical theories. Behaim was clearly indebted to both the ancient scholar Ptolemy and to a group of geographers from Nuremberg that included Hieronymus Münzer. In 1493, Münzer wrote to the king of Portugal to encourage a westward pursuit of a route to Asia. Apparently unaware that such an attempt had been tried, Münzer made his case for a western route based on a theory about the Atlantic Ocean that was circulating among cosmographers. This theory was not entirely new. Early in the fifteenth century Pierre d'Ailly, the Frenchman responsible for the revival of Ptolemy's theories in Europe, combined Ptolemy's estimate of the earth's size with Roger Bacon's thirteenth-century belief that a narrow body of water separated western Spain from eastern India. The narrow Atlantic theory was communicated to the king of Portugal as early as 1474 by the Florentine cosmographer, Paolo Toscanelli dal Pozzo. This view came to be accepted by the Nuremberg circle of cosmographers that included Münzer and Behaim.

**Earth Apple.** Behaim called his globe an *Erdapfel* (earth apple). The actual mapping shares remarkable similarities to Henricus Martellus's 1490 world maps, which suggests that both Martellus and Behaim shared the same prototype. The globe was constructed by three workers, but Behaim was responsible for the geographical details. The artistic work, done by George Glockenthon the Elder, included color illustration, forty-eight flags (ten of which were Portuguese), fifteen coats of arms, forty-eight miniatures of kings and local rulers, and 1,100 place names. The Christian theme of the map is obvious from illustrations of missionaries meeting with natives and four full-length portraits of saints. The final globe was completed before July 1493 and was housed in the Nuremberg City Hall. The Christian message and the pro-Portuguese slant suggest that the globe was meant for public display to encourage Nuremberg's trade ties with Portugal.

**Legacy.** Behaim offered little new in terms of geographical ideas, but his globe is evidence that Columbus's ideas were not unique. Columbus's notion that San Salvador was an outlying Japanese island is consistent with Behaim's placement of islands across the Atlantic. Both could have reached these conclusions by combining the land distances of the late-thirteenth-century-traveler Marco Polo with Ptolemy's estimate of the earth's size. The only new information on the globe involves information about the western coast of Africa, such as place names and an awareness that Bartholomeu Dias had voyaged around the Cape of Good Hope. Yet, Behaim placed this known information on a scaled globe that included latitude and, to the extent it was known, longitude. This fact allowed landmasses to be drawn in their true shapes and placed Africa at the center of the map, whereas most political and commercial maps of the period placed Africa on the periphery. The globe's true legacy is evident in the extent to which later cartographers struggled to make new discoveries fit Behaim's framework rather than revise Behaim's world.

Sources:

Jerry Brotton, *Trading Territories: Mapping the Early Modern World* (Ithaca, N.Y.: Cornell University Press, 1998).

G. R. Crone, *Maps and Their Makers: An Introduction to the History of Cartography* (London: Hutchinson's University Library, 1962).

# ABRAHAM ORTELIUS

## 1527-1598
### BOOK DEALER AND CARTOGRAPHER

**Beginnings.** Abraham Ortelius, or Oertel, was born in Antwerp on 14 April 1527 to an affluent Flemish merchant family. Little is known about his early life; apparently he had no university training. In 1547 Ortelius entered the guild of St. Luke as an illuminator of maps, and seven years later he and his sister established a prosperous book and antiquary business. Ortelius corresponded with many learned men, including the French printer Christophe Plantin and the Flemish humanist Justus Lipsius.

**Mapping the World.** Some historians consider Ortelius to be second only to Gerhardus Mercator as the leading cartographer of the period, although he was actually more of a map collector who edited other people's work. Ortelius and Mercator developed a close friendship between 1559 and 1560 when the two traveled through Lorraine and Poitou in France. After receiving encouragement from Mercator, Ortelius in 1564 produced his first world map. (It showed the St. Lawrence River in North America as a gateway to the Pacific Ocean.) Over the next six years he published maps of Egypt, Asia, and Spain.

**Famous Atlas.** In 1570 Ortelius produced his most famous work, *Theatrum orbis terrarum* (Epitome of the Theater of the Worlde). A compilation of all the geographical research undertaken up to that point, the *Theatrum orbis terrarum* is considered by many scholars to be the first modern world atlas. Ortelius scrupulously credited eighty-seven other mapmakers for their work (an unusual attribute for a cartographer in the sixteenth century) and dedicated the atlas to Philip II of Spain. By 1612 it had been published in forty-two editions and translated into seven languages.

**Royal Favorite.** The exploration and colonization efforts of maritime powers during the 1500s dictated the need for the type of atlas produced by Ortelius, and he quickly became renowned throughout European scientific and government circles. In 1575 he received an appointment as the royal cosmographer to the court of King Philip II. The substantial income from this position in turn allowed him to travel extensively and make collections. In 1577 he journeyed to England and conferred with John Dee, Richard Hakluyt, and other British geographers. He spent his later life collecting insects, plants, and ancient coins. Ortelius died in Antwerp on 4 July 1598.

Sources:
Marcel P. R. van den Broecke, *Ortelius Atlas Maps: An Illustrated Guide* (Houten, Netherlands: HES, 1996).

Cornelius Koeman, *The History of Abraham Ortelius and His* Theatrum orbis terrarum (New York: American Elsevier, 1964).

# AMERIGO VESPUCCI

## 1454-1512

### MERCHANT, EXPLORER, AND NAVIGATOR

**Early Wealth.** A native of Florence, Amerigo Vespucci was a wealthy businessman who traveled extensively. He was in Spain as a representative of the Medici family when Columbus sailed in 1492. While in Seville, Vespucci turned his hobby of geography and navigation into a new midlife career as an explorer. He made the first of at least two voyages to the Americas in 1499–1500. The first voyage was to Venezuela aboard a Spanish ship. Vespucci calculated longitude on the voyage by mapping the planets and the moon, a method so complicated that it was rarely used, despite remaining in navigation manuals for hundreds of years. After his second voyage he returned to Spain and was promoted to Chief Pilot of Spain, the first person to hold the office.

**Brazil.** Vespucci's second voyage was a direct result of Portuguese navigator Pedro Alvares Cabral's sighting of Brazil. Cabral had sailed in a south-southwesterly direction and sighted the coast of Brazil in 1500. However, he did not explore the land because he was actually attempting to repeat Vasco da Gama's voyage around the southern tip of Africa. Vespucci set sail in 1501 under the Portuguese flag in order to find and chart the Brazilian coast. He continued south along the coast of South America for more than two thousand miles until he crossed the "Line of Demarcation" (an imaginary boundary that divided the Portuguese and Spanish areas of exploration). Vespucci's two known voyages thus covered most of the Atlantic coast of South America. It was obvious to him and others that South America was a vast continent.

**Propaganda.** Unlike Columbus, who thought he was in the Indies, Vespucci claimed that he had sailed to a new land: "It is proper to call [it] a new world." Vespucci was the first to popularize the wonders of the Americas despite the fact that he may not have actually written material attributed to him. In 1507, Fracanzano da Montalboddo published a collection of accounts titled *Paesi novamente retrovati* that included two essays purportedly written by Vespucci. The author's sexual imagination and eye for the outlandish filled the work with accounts of Amazon women, cannibals, and giants. For instance, a 1504 letter to Piero Sodarini vividly describes Vespucci's voyage of 1501–1502 to Brazil. He offers a stark contrast between the inhabitants of the new land and the Europeans, whom he refers to as Christians. One incident in the letter details how a woman killed a Christian on the beach. Within open eyesight of his ship, other women dragged the body to higher land, where it was butchered and cooked over a fire. Men and women from the new lands then flaunted their victory by waving portions of the body in the air. To make matters worse, they then reenacted how they had earlier killed and eaten two missing Christians. Vespucci expressed his disgust, yet his exotic descriptions were clearly meant to stir emotions in Europe.

**Legacy.** Vespucci's propaganda allowed him to win much of the fame that should have gone to Columbus. His claim of "a new world" so influenced German cartographer Martin Waldseemüller that his *Cosmographiae introductio* (1507) proposed the name *America*, after Amerigo Vespucci, for the newly found western lands. Waldseemüller's great world map states across the top that it is "according to the tradition of Ptolemy and the voyages of Amerigo Vespucci and others." (Ptolemy's view of the world was not consistent with Vespucci's claim of new lands, and Waldseemüller later abandoned his support of Ptolemaic theory.) Vespucci's real legacy is in Waldseemüller's use of Amerigo's name for the new lands. Decades later Gerardus Mercator used the name for North America and South America. The term remains today despite the fact that Vespucci never saw the North American shore.

Sources:

G. R. Crone, ed., *The Explorers: Great Adventurers Tell Their Own Stories of Discovery* (New York: Crowell, 1962).

J. H. Parry, *The Age of Reconnaissance: Discovery, Exploration and Settlement, 1450-1650* (Cleveland: World, 1963).

Frederick J. Pohl, *Amerigo Vespucci, Pilot Major* (New York: Octagon, 1966).

# Documentary Sources

Pietro Martire d'Anghiera (Peter Martyr), *De Orbe Novo* (1530)—Written in Latin for a specialized audience, this text is the best early account of the New World.

Peter Apian, *Cosmographia* (1533)—A discussion of how to draw accurate land maps by using trigonometric formulas.

Nicholas Copernicus, *De revolutionibus orbium coelestium* (On the Revolutions of the Celestial Spheres) (1543)—An astronomical and mathematical explanation of the heliocentric theory, the belief that the sun is the center of the universe.

Leonardo Fibonacci (Pisano), *Liber Abaci* (Book of the Abacus) (1400)—Originally published in 1202, *Book of the Abacus* popularized the use of Hindu-Arabic numerals, which proved to be useful to mariners during the period of the Renaissance and Reformation.

Michel Eyquem de Montaigne, *Travel Journey* (1580)—A traveler's account of Europe.

Muhammad Ibn Abdullah Ibn Batuta, *Rhilah* (Travels) (circa 1353)—An important source for the history and geography of the medieval Muslim world.

Abraham Ortelius, *Theatrum orbis terrarum* (Epitome of the Theater of the Worlde) (1570)—Considered to be the first modern atlas. It contains seventy maps drawn by eighty-seven cartographers and is engraved in a uniform style. It was revised and updated in successive editions until 1612. Mapmaking in early modern Europe was one of the means that political authorities had of staking and maintaining territorial claims and was therefore an important part of the European expansion and hegemony process.

Enea Silvio Piccolomini, *De ritu, situ, morbus et conditione Germaniae* (Germania) (1457)—Silvio became Pope Pius II one year after the publication of *Germania*. Contemporaries used Book II as a model for geographical and historical descriptions of the region and people. Silvio's defense of the papacy and scathing comments about Germans also made the work a target of German hostility to Rome on the eve of the Reformation.

Claudius Ptolemy, *Geography* (1410)—Originally written in the second century C.E. by an astronomer, mathematician, and geographer from Alexandria, it contains an estimate of the size of the earth, geographic and topographic descriptions, and a list of places located by a crude form of latitude and longitude.

Ptolemy, *Megale Syntaxis tes Astronomias* (Almagest) (1515)—It describes a system of astronomy and geography based on the theory that the sun, planets, and stars all revolve around the earth.

Martin Waldseemüller, *Carta marina* (1516)—A chart version of the author's famous *Cosmographiae introductio*.

Waldseemüller, *Cosmographiae introductio* (1507)—The tome in which the German humanist suggests that the newly discovered world should be named *"ab Americo Inventore . . . quasi Americi terram sive Americam"* ("from Amerigo the discoverer . . . as if it were the land of Americus or America").

Waldseemüller, *Quattuor Americi navigationes* (Four Voyages of Amerigo) (1507)—A compilation of Amerigo Vespucci's private letters to the Medici, his employers. Although this volume indicates Vespucci made four expeditions to the New World, only two of those can be dated with any certainty (1499–1500 and 1501–1502).

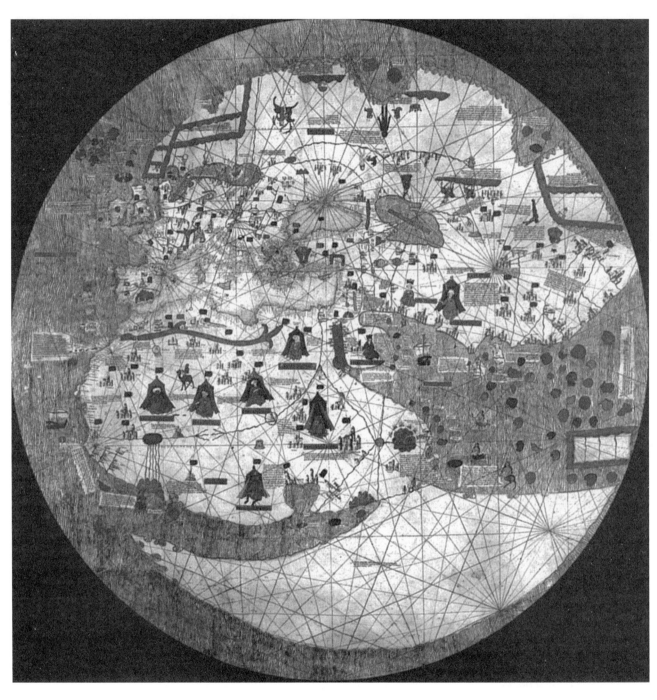

A fifteenth-century Catalan map of the world, which includes the Mediterranean Sea, West Africa,
and the Gulf of Guinea (from Franco Cardini, *Europe 1492,* 1989)

CHAPTER THREE

# THE ARTS

by AMANDA EURICH and CAROL JANSON

## CONTENTS

*Sidebars and tables are listed in italics.*

**1373-1410***

- Italian narrative painter Spinello Aretino is active in Tuscany, painting fresco cycles at St. Benedict and St. Catherine of Alexandria, both in Florence, as well as one at the Siena Town Hall.

**1374**

- Italian scholar Francesco Petrarch, one of the founders of humanism, dies in Arqua Petrarca in northeastern Italy. His poems and essays were widely read among the Renaissance aristocracy.

**1375-1400***

- English poet Geoffrey Chaucer writes *The Canterbury Tales,* comprised of twenty-three stories told by a group of pilgrims.

**1378-1444***

- The unknown Master of Flémalle, who might have been Robert Campin, helps found the Netherlandish School of painting, with such works as *The Werle Altarpiece* (1438) and *The Marriage of the Virgin* (undated).

**1395***

- Italian artist Pisanello (Antonio Pisano) is born in Verona. He will become the leading Italian representative of the International Gothic style of painting.

**1400***

- Civic humanism flourishes in Florence under the leadership of Leon Battista Alberti, Leonardo Bruni, and Lino Coluccio di Piero Salutati.

**1401**

- Tommaso Giovanni di Mone Masaccio is born near Florence. In his short life he helps revolutionize Renaissance painting, particularly in the use of light to highlight form.

**1411-1412**

- Italian sculptor Donato di Niccolò di Bettu Bardi, known as Donatello, produces a series of standing figures for two churches in Florence, marking the start of a brilliant career. Between 1415 and 1420 he sculpts *St. George and the Dragon.*

*\* Denotes circa date*

**1416**
- *Très Riches Heures* is illuminated by the Limbourg brothers for Burgundian duke Jean de Berry.

**1420-1436**
- A cathedral dome is constructed for the Santa Maria del Fiore in Florence, marking the early Renaissance style. Architect Filippo Brunelleschi designs the dome as well as the Foundling Hospital and other buildings in Florence.

**1422**
- Sigismondo Pandolfo Malatesta begins his reign as lord of Rimini, in northeastern Italy, which lasts until 1468. During this period he commissions the *Tempio*, the former church of San Francesco, into which were introduced many classical architectural elements.

**1423**
- Italian painter Gentile da Fabriano (Niccolò di Giovanni Massio) completes his masterpiece, *Adoration of the Magi*, in the International Gothic style, for Santa Trinita Church in Florence.

**1434**
- Flemish painter Jan van Eyck completes the *Arnolfini Wedding Portrait*. His greatest work may have been completing *The Adoration of the Lamb*, which was started by his brother Hubert.

**1435**
- Alberti, an architect, mathematician, and artist, writes *De pictura* (*On Painting*), in which he describes the rules for painting three-dimensional scenes. His book greatly influences Italian painting and relief sculpture.
- German goldsmith and printer Johannes Gutenberg, who invented movable type, prints the first book in Europe. His invention and techniques opened the way for the mass production of books, including his famous forty-two line Bible (circa 1454–1455).
- *The Adoration of the Magi* is painted by Veronese School painter Stefano da Zevio.

**1435-1436***
- Alberti writes *De re aedificatoria* (*Ten Books on Architecture*), based on his study of the Vitruvius manuscript. Alberti incorporated classical styles into contemporary theory, which he will himself use in designing several churches and palaces, including the Palazzo Rucellai.

**1439**
- A manuscript of first century B.C.E. Roman architect Vitruvius (Marcus Vitruvius Pollio) is discovered.

**1440-1491\***
- Italian sculptor Bertoldo di Giovanni, who was a student of Donatello and an instructor of Michelangelo, develops a new style of sculpture, small bronze figures designed for private collections.

**1447\***
- Florentine sculptor Lorenzo Ghiberti, known particularly for his bronze doors, statues, and reliefs, produces his *I Commentarii* (*Commentaries*), which includes three books on the history of ancient art and art theory, as well as an autobiography.

**1450\***
- A German engraver, known as the Master of the Playing Cards, initiates a simple, unornamented style of printmaking, using diagonal parallel cuts for shading. German engravers dominate printmaking for nearly a century.

**1452**
- Ghiberti finishes *The Gates of Paradise,* begun in 1425, his second set of bronze doors for the Florence Cathedral baptistry. He had received a commission for the first set of doors, after winning an open competition, in 1403.

**1453**
- Constantinople falls to the forces of Sultan Mehmed II, thereby ending the Byzantine Empire. He renames the city Istanbul and promotes Islam, which prompts an exodus of Greek scholars to the West, especially to Italy.

**1460**
- Italian painter Andrea Mantegna is appointed court painter for Mantua.

**1462**
- Italian philosopher Marsilio Ficino becomes the head of the Platonic Academy in Florence. He soon begins to translate Plato into Latin, which he finishes about 1470 (published in 1484), with the financial backing of Cosimo de' Medici. He also translates the Greek text *Corpus Hermeticum* (printed in 1471), which is attributed to the Greek mystic Hermes Trismegistus.

**1465**
- Florentine artist and engraver Antonio Pollaiuolo produces *The Battle of the Nudes.*

**1470**
- Italian painter Sandro Botticelli (Alessandro di Mariano Filipepi), influenced by Alberti and classical art, begins painting mythologies, the most famous of which are *The Primavera* (1477–1478) and *The Birth of Venus* (circa 1485). He also assists in decorating the Sistine Chapel (1480–1481).
- Alberti designs the Saint Andrea Church in Mantua, Italy. The building, which incorporates many classical elements in the design, will not be built until after his death.

**1473-1474**
- Flemish artist Justus of Ghent (Joos van Wassenhove) paints the *Communion of the Apostles.*

**1475-1476***
- Flemish painter Hugo van der Goes paints the *Portinari Altarpiece* for the church of the Hospital of Saint Maria Nuova in Florence.

**1480***
- The Master of Mary of Burgundy, an unknown artist, completes *The Hours of Mary of Burgundy,* an example of the Ghent-Bvuges style of illumination he established.

**1481**
- Botticelli, Perugino, Cosimo Rosselli, and Ghirlandaio all work on frescoes for the Sistine Chapel. Perugino's *Christ Delivering the Keys to St. Peter* helps establish him as a leading painter.

**1483**
- Raphael (Raffaello Sanzio), one of the most important painters in the Renaissance period, is born in Urbino. His works include *Coronation of the Virgin* (1502–1503), *Sistine Madonna* (1512), and *Galatea* (1511–1512), as well as many frescoes in Rome.

**1485**
- Florentine artist Domenico Ghirlandaio paints the *Adoration of the Shepherds.*

- Netherlandish painter Hieronymus Bosch paints *Tabletop of The Seven Deadly Sins and the Four Last Things.*

**1486**

- Italian humanist Giovanni Pico della Mirandola composes *De hominus digitate oratio* (*Oration on the Dignity of Man*) to defend publicly the nine hundred theses he had developed out of his study of ancient texts.

**1487-1491**

- The *Granovitaya Palata* (Faceted Palace) in Moscow is designed and built in the Italian Renaissance style by Pietro Antonio Solario, an Italian sculptor and architect.

**1488***

- Italian architect Donato Bramante, who also was a noted painter, begins designing the Sta. Maria delle Grazie in Milan, which he will complete around 1499. He designs the Tempietto of Saint Pietro in Montorio (1502), as well as an amphitheater and St. Peters Basilica in the Vatican, the foundation of which was laid in 1506.

**1490**

- The Aldine Press is established in Venice by Italian editor and printer Aldo Mannucci (Aldus Manutius the Elder). His first dated book is Greek grammarian Constantine Lascarius's *Erotemata* (1495), the first book printed entirely in Greek. The press printed many first editions of Greek and Latin classics, and printed smaller books that were more convenient to use.

**1491**

- Martin Schongauer, the most famous German painter and engraver of his day, dies in Colmar.

**1494**

- Ludovico Sforza (*Il Moro*) becomes the ruler of Milan. He becomes a great patron of the arts and artisans, including such notables as Amadeo, Bramante, and Leonardo da Vinci.

**1495-1497**

- Leonardo da Vinci paints *The Last Supper* in Milan for the refectory of Sta. Maria delle Grazie.

**1501-1504**

- Italian painter and sculptor Michelangelo sculpts *David*.

**1504**

- German painter and engraver Albrecht Dürer paints *Adam and Eve*.

**1504-1507**

- Florentine school painter Fra Baccio Della Porta Bartolommeo paints the *Vision of St. Bernard*. A contemporary of Raphael, he helped contribute to the transition of painting to the High Renaissance style.

**1506**

- Italian painter Lorenzo Costa takes Mantegna's place as court painter in Mantua, and receives several commissions from Isabella d'Este.
- *Votive Picture of Jacopo Pesaro*, the earliest known painting of the Venetian master Titian (Tiziano Vecellio), is completed. Some of his masterpieces include *St. Mark with Four Saints* (circa 1511), *Three Ages of Man* (circa 1515), *Sacred and Profane Love* (circa 1516), *Worship of Venus* (circa 1518), *Presentation of the Virgin* (1534–1538), *Ecce Homo* (1543), *Martyrdom of St. Lawrence* (1550–1555), and *Shepherd and Nymph* (circa 1570). He painted portraits of kings and patrons, as well as erotic pieces for private collectors.

**1507-1511**

- Flemish artist Quentin Massys paints the *Altarpiece of St. Anne* and the *Lamentation*.

**1508**

- *The Emperor Maximilian on Horseback* is designed by German engraver Hans Burgkmair. This woodcut is the earliest dated example of chiaroscuro, which through the use of several blocks produced light and dark images that gave the print a three-dimensional look.

**1509***

- Raphael paints *The School of Athens*.

**1512**

- Dutch artist Jacob Cornelisz van Oostsanen paints *Adoration of the Shepherds*. He is, however, more important as a designer of woodcuts.

**1513**
- Italian political philosopher Niccolò Machiavelli finishes writing *Il principe* (*The Prince*).

**1514**
- Italian painter Andrea del Sarto, who promotes a Florentine classical vocabulary, completes the fresco *The Nativity of the Virgin* for a cloister in Florence.
- Dutch painter, engraver, and graphic artist Lucas van Leyden joins the Painter's Guild in Leyden, where he established himself as a formidable artist by the age of fifteen. Until his death in 1533 he will dominate Dutch engraving and painting, along with Dürer.

**1516**
- German printer Johann Froben, who began a press in Basel in 1491, publishes Desiderius Erasmus's *New Testament*. He also publishes leading English humanist and statesman Sir Thomas More's *Utopia*, with a title-page cut by Augsburg engraver and painter Hans Holbein, who will also design the title page for Martin Luther's Bible and a portrait of Erasmus.

**1519**
- Netherlandish painter Jan van Scorel sets out to tour Germany, Italy, and other Mediterranean states. He will bring Italian painting techniques to Holland.

**1521**
- Italian artist Francesco Mazzola Parmigianino paints *The Marriage of St. Catherine* in the mannerist style.

**1525**
- German brothers and noted engravers Hans Sebald Beham and Bartel Beham, members of a group known as the Little Masters, are expelled from Nuremberg for blasphemy and sedition.

**1526**
- Giovanni Antonio Bazzi, a painter in Siena, completes the fresco *The Life of St. Catherine*.

**1528**
- Italian diplomat Baldassare Castiglione's *Il cortegiano* (*The Courtier*), which celebrates ideal courtly life, is published.

**1531**

- Italian architect Sammichele goes to Venice to serve as a military engineer. His major contribution, though, is as a designer of palaces, including the Pompeii (circa 1530s), Canossa (circa 1530s), Palazzo Bevilacqua (circa 1538), Corner-Mocenigo (circa 1543), and Grimani (circa 1556).

- Spanish architect Machuca, who evidently studied painting in Italy and was an accomplished painter of altarpieces, begins designing the palace of Charles V in Granada.

**1534**

- French monk, doctor, and writer François Rabelais publishes *Gargantua*.

- Italian painter Francesco de' Rossi completes the fresco *Visitation*. He travels throughout Europe, painting frescoes and designing tapestry.

- Jacopo Tatti Sansovino becomes city architect of Venice, beginning many new buildings, including the Library of St. Mark and Palazzo Corner.

**1541**

- Italian architect Sebastiano Serlio is appointed court painter and architect to Francis I of France. He publishes a seven-part treatise on architecture.

**1545-1554**

- Florentine sculptor Benvenuto Cellini, who also worked in marble, casts the bronze *Perseus*.

**1550**

- Italian painter and art historian Giorgio Vasari publishes *Vite de' più eccelenti architetti, pittori ed scultori italiani* (*Lives of the Most Eminent Painters, Sculptors, and Artists*, commonly known as *Lives of the Artists*).

**1560**

- Vasari begins building the Uffizi for Cosimo I of Tuscany and finishes in 1574. The palace will become an art museum housing many important Renaissance works, including many pieces from the Medici family treasures.

**1562**

- Cosimo de' Medici founds the *Accadèmia del Disegno* in Florence to reduce the power of guilds over artists and to increase their social prestige.

* *The Finding of the Body of St. Mark* is completed by Venetian painter Jacopo Robusti Tintoretto. He produces many works, mastering chiaroscuro, including the *Presentation of the Virgin in the Temple* (1552), *St. Peter's Vision of the Cross* (circa 1556), *The Decapitation of St. Paul* (circa 1556), and *The Last Supper* (1594).

**1563**

* Flemish painter and engraver Pieter Bruegel draws *Flight into Egypt*.

  John Shute publishes the first English book on architecture, *The First and Chief Groundes of Architecture*.

**1571-1575**

* Italian sculptor Bartolommeo Ammannati produces a marble *Neptune* with bronze *Nymphs* for the fountain of the Piazza della Signoria in Florence.

**1584**

* Italian painter Giovanni Paola Lomazzo, who went blind at age thirty-three, publishes the *Trattato dell' Arte de la Pittura*, promoting the style known as Mannerism.

**1591**

* Swiss engraver Jost Amman, who worked primarily in Nuremberg, dies. He had been one of the most prolific illustrators of his day.

# OVERVIEW

**Introduction.** Surviving images, texts, and artifacts from the fourteenth, fifteenth, and sixteenth centuries provide scholars with a partial, somewhat opaque, picture of early modern society. Europeans of this period had ways of seeing and habits of thought that were profoundly different from modern ways. Scholars can only reconstruct the emotional tenor, belief systems, behavioral codes, and symbolic systems of this distant past. Analyzing the context, function, location, commission, and intended audience of visual culture is crucial to uncovering the various dimensions of meaning that contemporaries attributed to these works. Most artwork in early modern Europe was commissioned by either individuals or corporate institutions, such as church bodies, city governments, or guilds. Artists were at the center of a system of exchange, negotiating the contours of visual and spiritual reality, human knowledge, and understanding with their patrons and audiences.

**Uses of Art.** Art, even a specific work of art, had multiple functions. The patron who commissioned a work of art realized that the location of the piece would create a larger political, social, and religious context for its viewers. Princes and other ruling elite recognized that both secular and sacred commissions enhanced their power and legitimacy. Guilds and other corporate institutions commissioned artwork as an expression of their fundamental place in the social and civic fabric. Pious patrons donated sacred works of art with expectations of rewards in this life and the next. Art was produced for both private and public consumption. For instance, illuminated prayer books, or Books of Hours, were used only by their owners. Family chapels privatized public devotional space and restricted important works of art to a narrow audience. In the ritual life of the Church, however, art became a crucial vehicle through which the mysteries of the Christian faith were rendered visible to the entire community.

**Artistic Invention.** Artists had to work within established traditions and visual conventions that constrained and shaped artistic invention. The contractual nature of artistic production created a complex matrix of interrelationships among artist, patron, and the institutional setting. The cultural and religious codes of early modern society established a certain framework and visual language within which the artist had to operate. Between 1350 and 1550 momentous changes in religion, politics, intellectual culture, technology, and the market challenged the fundamental convictions and conventions of European society and provoked vital changes in the role of the arts and artists in society.

**Black Death.** In 1348 the bubonic plague spread to Sicily from Italian galleys trading in Byzantium and the Crimea, and from there it spread along trade routes throughout Italy and Western Europe. Over the next several years, aggregate figures suggest that the population fell by 25 to 30 percent across Europe. The demographic, political, and economic crises triggered by the Black Death affected artistic production and patronage in several ways. Modern scholars dispute older studies that argued that the plague inspired a complete shift toward pessimistic religious art and an increasingly sober style of presentation, because they placed too much weight on the events of a single year and on the Italian context. In other cases, such as the Netherlands, the limited number of surviving works from this period renders such judgments highly problematic. What is certain is that the loss of a generation of artists from the plague had a strong impact on artistic training and traditions. Moreover, greater prosperity with higher wages across the social spectrum encouraged an expanding market for art, especially for traditional devotional works. In the city-states of central Italy the plague further concentrated wealth in the hands of the merchant elite, who had accumulated vast capital resources thanks to the revival of Mediterranean trade and commerce. Individuals, families, and institutions, such as guilds as well as the Church, increasingly used their discretionary wealth to support the arts. As artists and their workshops struggled to meet the demands of buyers less familiar with the dynamics of artistic invention, composition, and production, they sacrificed quality and innovation. Artists continued to work within established conventions, replicating standard images of the Virgin and Child, as well as other popular religious themes. Only in the fifteenth century did patrons and artists begin to focus again on more-demanding standards of artistic production.

**Court Commissions.** The wealth available at courts found in late-medieval France and Flanders enabled their rulers to commission tapestries, small devotional statues, and illuminated manuscripts for their libraries, family chapels, and castles. Such works were usually products of the late Gothic or International Style, characterized by its focus on gentle swaying figures whose graceful gestures emphasized their noble demeanor. Much of the art created was portable and lavish in its execution. It emphasized the activities of the nobility depicted through rich materials and fabrics. Elements of naturalism were introduced into landscape scenes or details of human interaction. Artists throughout Western Europe shared the visual vocabulary of the International Style into the fourteenth century. The patronage of rulers such as Charles V of France, and his two brothers, Philip the Bold (1342–1404) and Jean, the Duke de Berry (1340–1416), led to the cross-fertilization of the arts.

**Flemish Art.** The visual vocabulary of the first generation of Northern Renaissance artists developed from the illuminated manuscript traditions and monumental tomb sculptures commissioned by the nobility. Flemish painters such as Jan van Eyck applied their training in illuminated manuscripts to the new commissions of altarpieces for family chapels and portraiture. His *Arnolfini Wedding Portrait* (1434) represented an Italian merchant and his wife, with the gender distinctions of their social roles highlighted in full-length portraits. Patronage expanded to include the urban middle class. Artists including Robert Campin painted small portable altarpieces for these families. New themes such as the Virgin as the Madonna of Humility placed her in the domestic setting of a Flemish household. Northern painting often conveyed religious meanings through symbolic language that used ordinary material goods. The Virgin's purity was shown through an image of a lily or a spotless towel as part of a larger symbolic program. Guild commissions, such as Flemish painter Rogier van der Weyden's *Descent from the Cross* (circa 1435–1440), solidified civic pride and devotion to the church. The commissioners of this work, the Crossbowmen's Guild of Louvain, met regularly to celebrate mass in their chapel, reinforcing their communal solidarity. The next generation of artists expanded on the visual vocabulary already in place. Altarpieces placed greater emphasis on their donors. Independent occupational portraits developed as well. The cross-fertilization of art between Italy and the north increased with the importation of work in each other's countries.

**The Italian Context.** By the early fourteenth century the revival of trade throughout the Mediterranean and northern Europe encouraged the rise of powerful city-states in central Italy. The tumultuous politics of these city-states favored the emergence of new ideas and new men. Endemic warfare among the states opened the door for ambitious and innovative leaders to seize political power. Largely independent of papal and imperial authority, the merchant oligarchies who governed the Italian city-states legitimized their political hegemony by surrounding themselves with talented writers and artists who heralded the dawn of a new age. The intellectual and political elite in Italy believed that they were witnesses to the rebirth of true civilization, based on the ideals and achievements of classical Greece and Rome. Classical ruins provided a continuing stimulus for such reflections and encouraged the growth of a kind of nationalist sentiment among Italians, for whom the recovery of antiquity became a patriotic duty. The wealthy elite spent enormous sums in their desire to accumulate manuscripts, coins, small objets d'art, and other relics of antiquity. They also invested heavily in public and private building projects, inspired by Ciceronian ideals of civic virtue championed by Renaissance humanists, who argued that true greatness of the soul manifested itself in the desire to use talent and fortune for the public good. In their appreciation of antiquity, Renaissance humanists were not antagonistic to the essential beliefs and rituals of Christianity. They were committed instead to a philosophical enterprise that they believed would only enhance the authority of the Christian faith by revealing the common truths shared by classical and Christian belief systems. Within the population at large the critical importance of religious values and imagery meant that everyone needed art.

**Classical Revival.** By the fifteenth century the flowering of humanist scholarship and the arts across Italy testified to a general cultural revival. Italian Renaissance artists and architects employed a new visual vocabulary inspired by Greco-Roman antiquity. Artists such as Donatello, Tommaso Giovanni di Mone Masaccio, and Filippo Brunelleschi demonstrated their understanding and mastery of a whole new range of skills and techniques that made it possible to emulate the classical style. The ability to imitate nature by creating convincing conventions of space and light became the most admired artistic skill. This technical achievement further encouraged the reevaluation of the standards of artistic production in which the artist's skill, not the expense and beauty of materials used, was recognized by both artists and patrons. In vernacular treatises on painting and architecture, Leon Battista Alberti articulated the new aesthetic and underscored the vital exchange between artists and humanists, whose studies of antiquity had revitalized the arts by reintroducing the classical canon. By the late fifteenth century the circle of Neoplatonic scholars around Marsilio Ficino in Florence ascribed a kind of divine genius to artists whose creative talents allowed them to render visible the mind of God.

**Noble Expressions.** The princely courts of northern Italy readily embraced humanist culture and adapted it to suit their own diplomatic and dynastic interests. Ruling families such as the Montefeltro of Urbino, the Estes of Ferrara, and Gonzaga of Mantua laid claim to the princely magnificence of their more-powerful counterparts in Milan and northern Europe through ambitious programs of artistic patronage. As in northern Europe, the center of artistic production was the court itself, where a constantly changing stable of artists gave visual expression to the cultural and political ambitions of these minor warlords anxious to refashion themselves as men of letters as well as men of war. Whole palace complexes—in Mantua, the entire city itself—were redesigned. Within the palace, private apartments called *studioli,* where princely rulers displayed their manuscript and art collections, showcased their wealth, aesthetic taste, and sensibilities. By the late fifteenth century, princely courts were considered to be loci of refinement and civility, reflecting the increasing aristocratization of late Renaissance society.

**Religious Culture and the Arts.** In late-medieval devotional culture, sight was considered the primary medium of spiritual experience. In the late thirteenth century John of Genoa argued that feelings of devotion "were more effectively aroused by things seen rather than things heard." The liturgy or devotional rituals employed images, prayers, relics, music, and sermons to emotionally stimulate and teach the congregation. Artists made manifest a common repertoire of images mediated by local clergymen and theologians. At various points during the liturgical year priests in their sermons explained the mysteries represented in the sacred arts, rehearsing the proper boundaries of internal devotional experience.

**Devotional Piety.** Late-medieval piety placed its devotional focus on the Blessed Sacrament, the mystic body of Christ present in the Catholic Mass, which represented individual and corporate renewal of unity in heart and mind. The theme of the Seven Sacraments, illustrated in stained-glass windows, baptismal fonts, and painted altarpieces, gave central place to the ceremony of the Eucharist when the priest raised the host aloft. Weyden's *Seven Sacraments Altarpiece* (circa 1451–1455) clearly illustrated this sentiment by placing a living image of the crucified Christ in the foreground. The viewer looked past this vision to the celebration of the Mass taking place at the high altar. The side panels traced the whole sacramental cycle from the baptism of a baby to the death of an elderly man blessed by the priest.

**Religious Celebrations.** Affective piety developed in the context of regular attendance at Mass on Sundays and feast days, and annual confession and communion at Easter. During the Golden Mass, the *Missa aurea,* celebrated during Advent in Flemish churches, two costumed choirboys sang the responses of Mary and the Angel Gabriel from the Annunciation story. The congregant heard the Gospel account read by the deacon, saw it enacted by the choirboys, and encountered it in the Annunciation scenes of Flemish artists who employed their symbolic gestures. During the fourteenth, fifteenth, and sixteenth centuries, the Church sanctioned the cycle of life through sacramental celebrations of birth, baptism, marriage, and death. The changing seasons of winter and spring marked the celebration of Christmas and Easter, joining the sacred and secular calendar. Secular traditions of games and dances explored the tensions between body and spirit, feast and famine, rule and misrule. These elements were accommodated within religious celebrations, drawing together sacred and secular life. At the public bonfires held on Midsummer's eve in England, the poor were fed and entertained on the day dedicated to St. John the Baptist. These overlapping domains of sacred and secular time were visualized in the prayer books of the laity, where calendar illustrations recorded the major feast days of the Church and illustrated the labors associated with each month.

**Controversies and Reform.** Fourteenth-century religious controversies threatened the authority of the Latin Church in the West. The Avignon Papacy (1304–1377) and Great Schism (1378–1417) divided the religious allegiances of Europeans and undermined the moral and political authority of the papacy. Eager to reestablish papal supremacy, popes in the late fifteenth and sixteenth centuries engaged in a program of artistic patronage that transformed Rome into one of the most important art centers in Europe. To finance their ambitions they revived the practice of selling indulgences, certificates stamped with papal insignia promising to acquit the purchaser of temporal punishments for sin to be carried out in Purgatory. Indulgences sold throughout the Holy Roman Empire by Dominican agents helped finance the construction of St. Peter's Basilica, the emblem of the revival of papal authority. By the early sixteenth century, reform-minded churchmen, such as Martin Luther, challenged the sale of indulgences as one of the most-egregious examples of corruption of the medieval Church. In the 1520s Luther broadened his call for the reform of the Church and targeted several religious practices, such as the veneration of saints, pilgrimages, and eucharistic devotion, which had stimulated a tremendous traffic in religious art and artifacts. Luther's vehement attack on monasticism promoted the dissolution of monasteries and convents throughout Protestant Europe, and in so doing, destroyed an important locus of art production.

**Reformation Challenges.** At the heart of the Protestant Reformation, however, was an even more fundamental attack on the medieval doctrine of salvation that had profound implications for the arts. According to the medieval Church, a person could assist in his or her salvation by performing any number of good works, including commissioning works of art to instruct and to stimulate the religious devotion of the faithful. In 1507, for example, the wealthy cloth merchant, Jacob Heller, renowned for his piety and patronage of the arts, employed Albrecht Dürer to paint a large altarpiece depicting the Assumption and Coronation of the Virgin for the Dominican church in his native city of Frankfurt. When he died several years later, Heller was buried in the church beneath Dürer's dramatic painting, an action that clearly underscored the connections Heller and his contemporaries drew between patronage, piety, and their hopes for salvation. In striking contrast, Protestant reformers emphasized that salvation was achieved solely through faith, nourished by the disciplines of Bible reading and prayer. The idea that paintings and sculptures, even those invested with especial sanctity, possessed a kind miraculous or even visionary power that could convey benefits of salvation to the beholder or donor, was considered idolatrous. The relationship between the

Reformation and the arts, however, was complex. Vehement in their repudiation of superstitious medieval doctrines that invested material objects with sacred power, mainstream Protestant reformers such as Luther and John Calvin also harshly denounced popular religious riots, where enthusiasts of the Reformed faith smashed statues, stained-glass windows, and religious artifacts to purify the church of the "idols" of the faith.

**Reform By Print.** Protestant reformers also proved particularly adept at using the new print technologies to disseminate and popularize their ideas. Cheap portraits of Luther and his fellow reformers legitimized their challenge to papal authority by depicting them as nationalist and humanist heroes of the faith. Some prints even mimicked medieval devotional images, showing Luther with his monastic tonsure (shaven hairstyle) and a halo of sainthood around his head. On both sides of the religious divide, inexpensive woodcuts, broadsheets, and tracts also demonized the opposition and its beliefs and practices. Printmakers frequently relied on pictorial conventions and codes to assure the intended message was readily accessible to the semiliterate. Especially popular were woodcuts that connected to popular anticlericalism by portraying the Pope as the Antichrist. Printmakers attempted to create a new devotional vocabulary acceptable to Protestant sensibilities. Pious images printed for domestic consumption usually drew from a much-narrower pictorial tradition. Old Testament patriarchs such as Abraham, New Testament heroes such as Paul, and biblical stories and parables like the Prodigal Son, replaced the images of the Virgin Mary, the Christ child, and the saints that were emblematic of medieval religious practices and beliefs. The popularity of moralistic ballads and religious ABCs all reflect the didactic function of print in sixteenth-century Protestant Europe.

**Catholic Reformation.** The Sack of Rome in 1527 accentuated the movement toward religious reform within the Catholic Church. In Rome itself, the local population interpreted the event as God's punishment for their sins and for the abuses of the Church, and they responded by founding lay confraternities and new religious orders. Alessandro Farnese, elected to the papal see as Paul III in 1534, spearheaded spiritual renewal throughout the Catholic world. His two great legacies were the support of new religious orders, such as the Society of Jesus (Jesuits) founded by Ignatius Loyola, and his 1545 opening of the Council of Trent, the first pan-European council called to respond to the Protestant challenge. Artists such as Michelangelo experienced and expressed this renewed interest in religious reform and piety in works such as *The Last Judgment* (1534–1541), commissioned by Paul III for the Sistine Chapel. The Council of Trent, which met three times between 1545 and 1563, envisioned education, preaching, and missionary work as pivotal tools in the continuing campaign of the Church to check the spread of Protestantism throughout Europe. Regulation for the arts resulting from the decrees of the Council, like earlier Protestant treatises, promulgated through the print medium, prompted a unity of style and common concern for propagating the faith through Catholic Europe and the New World. The Council emphasized that art should be simple and direct and tell a story. The reaffirmation of the crucial intercessory role of saints and eucharistic devotion also stimulated and revised artistic activity to focus on religious art for teaching.

**Sixteenth-Century Implications.** People living in the sixteenth century witnessed increasing traffic in luxury goods, furnishings, and art between northern and southern Europe. Northern artists also traveled much more widely, journeying to Italy, and Rome in particular, to witness Roman antiquities and contemporary Italian art firsthand. As a consequence, northern artists absorbed Italian styles into their work, and Italian artists in turn were influenced by the northern Renaissance. Prints became the primary mechanism by which artistic innovations were assimilated with greater rapidity. The French invasions of Italy in 1495 and 1499 became another mechanism of cultural exchange. The forced exchange of goods as war trophies stimulated fears among Italians that their country was being dispossessed of its cultural and artistic heritage. As a consequence of war, diplomacy, and the growing market economy, the traffic in luxury art and objects diversified, and the aesthetic taste of noble connoisseurs and collectors became more eclectic. Beyond the aesthetic pleasure and enhanced reputations that collectors sought through this traffic in rarities, silverplate, jewelry, and art, these items also functioned as collateral that funded the military, political, and cultural initiatives of princes and aristocrats.

**Commerce and Innovation.** The increasingly fluid commerce in artifacts and artistic styles prompted growing concerns about the potential pollution and conflation of indigenous art, with recognizable "national" characteristics. From the late fifteenth century onward, anti-Italian sentiment in northern Europe, fueled by humanist sensitivities to Italian claims of superiority and nascent national identities, fostered a growing discourse about indigenous visual languages, artistic styles, and aesthetic taste. Northern Europeans sought to define the distinctive qualities and expressive vocabulary of dance, music, and art as part of a continued search for an autonomous northern aesthetic. The increasing interest in and exposure to other traditions prompted concerns about the loss of distinctive cultural norms and identities in Italy as well. At the same time, the creation of new print technologies, growth of market economies, and emergence of communities of like-minded artists, patrons, and scholars in sixteenth-century Europe expanded artists' ways of knowing, appropriating, and transforming artistic innovation.

# TOPICS IN THE ARTS

## ARCHITECTURE AND URBAN LANDSCAPE

**Palaces.** During the fifteenth century, extensive domestic building projects were undertaken in many Renaissance Italian cities. In Florence, for example, the banking and commercial elite employed architects to design palazzi (palaces) as markers of their political, social, and cultural power. In the mid fifteenth century, Cosimo de' Medici commissioned Filippo Brunelleschi to build a family palace near the center of town, not far from a cluster of older family houses. The design turned out to be too grand for de' Medici's taste, and Michelozzo di Bartolomeo, a collaborator of Lorenzo Ghiberti and Donatello, was called upon to design the palace, which still exists. Architects wanted to express the humanist value of magnificence, conflating architectural design with the dignity and social standing of the owners. In the early fourteenth century, they continued to employ designs that fortified the palace against public attacks and rebellions, but they gradually drafted plans that expressed an increasing refinement of form based upon classical motifs. Renaissance palazzi usually featured an interior courtyard with open loggias (galleries) for the reception and entertainment of guests and foreign dignitaries. These loggias were also the site of family festivities such as wedding feasts. Often several generations and branches of the family lived in the palazzo, a domestic arrangement that reinforced patriarchal power and authority in Italian city-states. Members of the immediate family usually lived in rooms on the *piano nobile* (the floor with the largest rooms on the second story). The third story was reserved for or used by servants. In the sixteenth century a new domestic building type was the *villa suburbana*, where the secular and sacred elite retired for a day of leisure. The design of most villas was inspired by classical texts, by such authors as first-century B.C.E. Roman architect Vitruvius, who described ancient villas and the arrangement of rooms. Architects exploited the natural topography, especially outside Rome, building hidden grottoes, fountains, and theaters that intensified the pleasures of rural life.

**Northern Palaces.** Whereas Italian palazzi were essentially urban structures, in northern Europe palaces were built in the countryside. French palaces constructed in the Loire Valley during the reign of Francis I incorporated new architectural elements inspired by the classical vocabulary of galleries or loggia. The galleries at Fontainebleau were intended for the display of tapestries and paintings, many of which mythologized Francis's achievements. In Spain the palace of Charles V in Granada was situated within the Alhambra. The square plan and circular court, designed by Spanish architect Machuca, recalled the Renaissance ideals of perfected form and magnificence.

**Town Halls.** Toward the end of the thirteenth century the establishment of communal governments led to a building boom in new town halls, which symbolized the emergence of popular sovereignty. In Siena, Florence, and other Tuscan cities these town halls signaled a new definition of power and authority in Italian society. The Palazzo Vecchio in Florence set the pattern for Italian civic architecture during the fourteenth century. Like its counterpart in Siena, it featured battlements decorated with the coats of arms of the commune, which were typical of the fortification of the secular buildings after the emergence of free communes. The instability and factionalism of communal life often made it necessary for members of the government to seek refuge beyond the fortified facade of the palazzi. Town council chambers were often located above the level of surrounding streets and squares. Bell towers were also an important architectural element in these palaces and a powerful symbol of the new governments. They tolled warnings during times of unrest and danger and summoned citizens for public meetings. Decorative schemes inside these buildings celebrated communal history and politics. In the Palazzo Pubblico in Siena, Ambrogio Lorenzetti created a series of frescoes that illustrated the consequences of good and bad government.

**Churches.** Renaissance cities vied with each other to build and recast their cathedrals as markers of civic pride. Humanist scholars and historians such as Leonardo Bruni praised their native city and their architectural structures. Cathedrals such as the Duomo in Florence (Santa Maria del Fiore) were focal points of the urban skyline. Brunelleschi's successful design for the Duomo was an engineering feat based upon his trial-and-error efforts, which he worked out in his 1418 model supplied for the competition. The architect subsequently developed a new aesthetic for Renaissance churches based upon a Latin-cross plan (a long nave and short cross arm or transept) that used a

The Palazzo Vecchio in Florence, attributed to thirteenth-century architect Arnolfo Di Cambrio and redesigned in the sixteenth century by Giorgio Vasari

square module. The simple use of stucco and stone, as evidenced by his designs for Santo Spirito (completed after his death) and San Lorenzo, changed the dynamics of interior decor, eliminating expansive fresco cycles and replacing them with small panel altarpieces.

**Patronage.** The architectural patronage and financial responsibilities for most church-building campaigns was often assumed by civic and private parties. The intimate connection between religious piety and political power inspired many members of the ruling elite to commission and fund substantial architectural projects and renovations. Cosimo de' Medici's extensive funding of San Lorenzo demonstrates such activities. In the 1450s, Giovanni Ruccellai, a rival of the Medici, commissioned the renovation of the church of Santa Maria Novella, one of the most important Dominican churches in Italy. Underneath the triangular pediment of the exterior facade, a Latin dedica-

tory inscription documented his role in funding the church. On the frieze above the main entrance a line of ships with billowing sails, a well-known symbol of the winds of fortune, also recalled Ruccellai's patronage. This symbol had been adopted and displayed by the Ruccellai family as their personal insignia. Toward the end of his life Ruccellai wrote that spending money, especially on buildings that immortalized his achievements, had given him more pleasure than earning it.

**Urban Planning.** Renaissance civic and classical values inspired secular and religious leaders to reinvent the urban landscape. The most-complete transformation of urban space was the city of Pienza, named by Pius II to honor his birthplace. Leon Battista Alberti's ideas were used in the reconstruction of the city. The center of the city was completely redesigned between 1459 and 1464, around a trapezoid-shaped piazza flanked by the bishop's palace, the cathedral, and Pius's private residence. Some forty buildings were constructed or refurbished. Pius was directly involved in the decision-making process, which transformed the city into a model of Renaissance urban planning. The strategic siting of public and private buildings expressed the close connection between church and state. In his commentaries Pius penned an extremely detailed description of the church and its decorations, which is one of the few surviving accounts by a Renaissance patron of his or her architectural achievements.

**Renovation.** The centerpiece of urban revitalization in Rome was St. Peter's Basilica, begun in 1506. Italian architect Donato Bramante, commissioned by Julius II, totally renovated the basilica. He had to accommodate two programmatic needs: a central space for the tomb of Julius and greater space around the main altar, beneath which the relics of St. Peter were located. Bramante undertook several designs and ultimately settled on a Greek cross within a square. The cross symbolized the sacrificial Christ, while the encompassing square reflected the perfection of the church militant. Bramante's earlier project to erect a church on the site of St. Peter's martydom and next to the cloister in San Pietro in Montorio (1502) enabled him to explore the dynamic tensions of a centrally planned building. He derived his architectural concept from the surviving ruins of the Temple of Hercules Victor, excavated in Rome during the reign of Sixtus IV (1471–1484). After Bramante's death in 1514 and the Sack of Rome in 1527, work on St. Peter's was completely suspended for many years. In 1546 Michelangelo reconceptualized the project, revitalizing the Greek-cross plan to convey the majesty of earth and heaven symbolized by the square and circle. The architectural unity also recalled the oneness of the body of Christ and the Church at the point when the return of Protestants to the Catholic Church was clearly improbable.

**Impact of the Reformation.** The earliest Protestant assemblies took place in private homes. Where Protestants achieved a measure of political power, they appropriated public buildings and churches. On the continent, Calvinists called their meeting places "temples," a term that recalled the ancient temple of Jerusalem and allowed the Calvinists to distinguish their place of worship from their Catholic rivals. Inside Protestant churches the internal organization of furnishings reflected their objections to images and other visual elements of medieval religious culture and doctrine. The placement of pews, pulpits, and communion table in Protestant churches stressed two key reform principles: the priesthood of all believers and the centrality of the Word. Churches provided benches or pews for the congregation, which expressed the priesthood of all believers and the equality of the clergy and laity. Protestants also considered the pulpit, not the altar, as the most important interior element in their churches. Where they constructed new churches, they followed a longitudinal or centralized plan—shortening the distance between the congregation and preachers while increasing the proximity of the congregation to the Word.

Sources:

John T. Paoletti and Gary M. Radke, *Art in Renaissance Italy* (Upper Saddle River, N.J.: Prentice Hall, 1997).

Loren Partridge, *The Art of Renaissance Rome, 1400–1600* (New York: Abrams, 1996).

A. Richard Turner, *Renaissance Florence: The Invention of a New Art* (New York: Abrams, 1997).

Jane Turner, ed., *The Dictionary of Art* (New York: Grove, 1996).

## ART AND THE BODY

**Studying the Body.** Renaissance artists had little personal freedom in how they depicted the divine body, especially that of Christ. Pictorial tradition emphasized the need to demonstrate both the divine and human aspects of Christ's nature. Techniques that stressed Christ's smooth and serene forehead, upstanding carriage, and dignified demeanor influenced pictorial conventions of other religious figures. As artists mastered naturalistic canons, they ran the risk of creating religious images that awakened problematic emotions in the viewer. For example, the image of St. Sebastian, located in San Marco in Florence, was removed because of reports that the comely, seminude image had provoked women to sexual fantasies. Renaissance artists also glorified the human body and strove to master the perfection of form. Inspired by the canons of proportion, based on classical antiquity, they created idealized figures whose proportions and measurements internalized order and in turn exemplified Renaissance ideals of harmonious beauty. The Renaissance fascination with the sculptural idea of *contrapposto* (the shifting weight of limbs to suggest the natural poise of the still body) clearly manifests this ideal. At the same time, scientific interest in anatomical dissection allowed artists to draw from cadavers, stimulating a better understanding of muscular and skeletal structures so that artists could produce a more naturalistic representation of the human body. Classical medical authorities, such as the second-century Greek physician Galen, however, still remained the standards by which artists and scientists interpreted the functioning of the human body. Leonardo da Vinci's fascination with the way in which human character connected with physiognomy led him to create a series of graphic studies of cadavers, portrait caricatures, and scientific notes on the working of the human body. In Giorgio Vasari's *Vite de' più eccellenti architetti, pittori ed scultori italiani* (*Lives of the Most Eminent Painters, Sculptors, and Artists*, 1550, commonly known as *Lives of the Artists*), he recorded how da Vinci struggled in his *The Last Supper* (1495–1497) to depict the inner character of each disciple through external poses and bodily gestures and the ultimate challenge of creating compelling representations of Good and Evil in his portraits of Christ and Judas Iscariot.

**The Suffering Body.** The image of Christ as the Man of Sorrows was a key late-medieval devotional model for understanding heroic bodily suffering. The deep sorrows expressed by the Virgin Mary and Christ's disciples established how the viewer was to respond with pity and piety for Christ's sacrifice for mankind. Dominican friars had

The task of fashioning the young is made up of many parts, the first and consequently the most important of which consists of implanting seeds of piety in the tender heart; the second in instilling love for, and thorough knowledge of, the liberal arts; the third in giving instruction in the duties of life; the fourth in training in good manners right from the very earliest years. This last I have now taken up as my special task. For others as well as I have written at great length on the other aspects I have mentioned. Now although external decorum of the body proceeds from a well-ordered mind, yet we observe that sometimes even upright and learned men lack social grace because they have not been taught properly. It is seemly for the whole man to be well ordered in mind, body, gesture, and clothing. But above all, propriety becomes all boys, and in particular those of noble birth.

Thus, for the well-ordered mind of a boy to be universally manifested—and it is most strongly manifested in the face—the eyes should be calm, respectful, and steady: not grim, which is a mark of truculence; not shameless, the hallmark of insolence; not darting and rolling, a feature of insanity; nor furtive, like those of suspects and plotters of treachery; nor gaping like those of idiots. . . . For it is no chance saying of the ancient sages that the seat of the soul is in the eyes.

The nostrils should be free from any filthy collection of mucus, as this is disgusting (the philosopher Socrates was reproached for that failing too). It is boorish to wipe one's nose on one's cap or clothing; to do so on one's sleeve or forearm is for fishmongers, and it is not much better to wipe it with one's hand, if you then smear the discharge on your clothing. The polite way is to catch the matter from the nose in a handkerchief, and this should be done by turning away slightly if decent people are present. If, in clearing your nose with two fingers, some matter falls on the ground, it should be immediately ground under foot. . . .

To repress the need to urinate is injurious to health; but propriety requires it be done in private. There are some who lay down the rule that a boy should refrain from breaking wind by constricting his buttocks. But it is no part of good manners to bring illness upon yourself while striving to appear "polite." If you may withdraw, do so in private. But if not, then in the words of the old adage, let him cover the sound with a cough. Besides, why do they not rule in the same way that boys should not purge their bowels, since it is more dangerous to refrain from breaking wind than it is to constrict the bowels?

Source: Desiderius Erasmus, *The Civility of Childhood*, in *Collected Works of Erasmus*, volume 25, *Literary and Educational Writings* (Toronto & Buffalo: University of Toronto Press, 1985), pp. 273–275, 277–278.

such images in their cells and were encouraged to visualize this event while praying, reading, or meditating. The friars saw that the Virgin and her son looked back at them with a compassionate gaze. A half-length figure of Christ wearing a crown of thorns, arms crossed to display the nail wounds in his hands, became a popular image recollecting his suffering and burial. Such images were based upon the heavenly vision Pope Gregory the Great received while he was celebrating mass. Because his vision recorded a "vera icon," or true portrait, of the Man of Sorrows, all other models based on it were considered accurate. After Gregory's painting was relocated to the church of Santa Croce at Rome, the monks commissioned German artist Israhel van Meckenem to reproduce it as an engraving in the 1490s. His print recorded the history and image of the icon. The text stated that prayers recited before the icon gave remission from temporal punishments (Purgatory) after death.

**Taming the Body.** The forceful message of eternal damnation was a prominent theme in late-medieval art and prompted viewers to ponder their own mortality. Last Judgment scenes on church exteriors reminded those who entered of heaven and hell. Wall paintings at burial grounds depicted the skeletal dead leading mankind in a dance of death. Tomb portraits of the dead as decaying bodies recalled the brevity of life to the passersby. Preoccupation with worldly pleasures, especially depictions of the seven deadly sins, reminded viewers to mend their ways. The Netherlandish painter Hieronymus Bosch's *Tabletop of The Seven Deadly Sins and the Four Last Things* (1485) is a visual representation of the relationship between God, sin, and mankind. The center of the panel depicts the Eye of God with Christ standing in his tomb displaying his wounds. The Latin text cautions, "Beware, beware God is watching." At the outer ring the seven deadly sins (sloth, gluttony, avarice, envy, anger, pride, and lust) are illustrated in separate scenes. Bosch pays particular attention to the role of gender and class and the social repercussions of sinful behavior, but the key message is that the lack of self-control leads to universal human folly. For example, the scene of lust shows a noble couple courting in the presence of two fools. A brawl outside an inn takes place between two men and a woman whose actions are the folly of anger. At the outer edges of the panel, death, divine judgment, and heaven or hell await the sinners.

Hieronymus Bosch's *Tabletop of The Seven Deadly Sins and the Four Last Things,* 1485 (The Prado, Madrid)

**The Gendered Body.** Print culture commented on the folly of love and sensuality as well and clarified the differences between true and false love, lawful marriage and adultery, for the urban middle classes. Fifteenth-century municipal governments manifested similar concerns by enacting stricter legislation against adultery, prostitution, and illegitimacy. Classical and biblical conceptions of women as lustful seducers inspired many depictions of the "power of women" theme. Print series that recorded the downfall of male biblical heroes such as Samson, Solomon, and David, who lost their strength, wisdom, and piety to feminine wiles, were displayed in town halls and on decorative objects. In humanist circles the theme of Aristotle and Phyllis added new dimensions to the depiction of women as lustful seducers. Elite viewers recognized the story of the great philosopher, Aristotle, who chastised his pupil Alexander the Great about his excessive devotion to the youthful Phyllis. In visual representations Phyllis wreaks her revenge by reducing him to a beast of burden. Classical images of Hercules at the Crossroads, choosing between virtue and vice represented by two women who woo him, also illustrated the dilemma of male desire.

**The Socialized Body.** Renaissance humanists emphasized that the duality of human nature and free will allowed human beings to develop their higher, divine nature by cultivating the mind or upper body and suppressing the desires of the lower body. In 1530 Dutch humanist Desiderius Erasmus penned a short etiquette manual intended for the instruction of children. Erasmus's *Manners for Children* begins with the premise that a disciplined body is as much a product of a liberal education as a well-trained mind. Learning how to blow one's nose, break wind, and urinate discreetly in public were seen as important steps toward social behaviors that disciplined the latent animality of human nature. Erasmus's emphasis on bodily discipline paralleled sixteenth-century reformers' efforts to impose new standards of moral behavior upon the general European populace and contributed to the popularity and proliferation of etiquette manuals as a literary genre. Writing about his experience at the ducal court in Urbino, Italian writer Baldassare Castiglione articulated the emergence of a new code of noble behavior in his *Il cortegiano* (*The Courtier*, 1528). For Castiglione, *sprezzatura* (grace), the ability to conceal physical exertion as well as inner feelings, was the guiding principle of courtly demeanor. It permitted courtiers to manipulate patronage systems at court and control their social identities by distinguishing themselves from their peers. The control of bodily gestures, facial expressions, and carriage gradually came to be envisioned as an index of civil and Christian society. This ideal was readily manifest in the field of courtly portraiture, where the conventions of self-representation focused on the decorum and dignity of the sitter. Raphael's painting of Castiglione (circa 1515) established a widely emulated standard for court portraits in the sixteenth century. The elegance of his clothing, refinement of his gestures, and overall restraint in demeanor exemplified the new mannered courtly ideal.

**Sources:**

Michael Baxendall, *Painting and Experience in Fifteenth-Century Italy: A Primer in the Social History of Pictorial Style* (Oxford: Clarendon Press, 1972).

Edward Muir, *Ritual in Early Modern Europe* (Cambridge & New York: Cambridge University Press, 1997).

Jane Turner, ed., *The Dictionary of Art* (New York: Grove, 1996).

Evelyn Welch, *Art and Society in Italy, 1350–1500* (Oxford & New York: Oxford University Press, 1997).

## THE ARTIST IN SOCIETY

**Artistic Training.** During the late Middle Ages artists were affiliated with craft guilds that regulated the education of apprentices and the entry of masters into the guild structure. An apprentice lived at his master's house for two to seven years while he received instruction in basic skills, such as grinding pigments and mixing them for paint. At his master's workshop he would be given more challenging tasks as his skills improved and finally be awarded a journeyman's certificate by the guild. Some journeymen, such as Albrecht Dürer, went on lengthy trips to improve their skills and visit other workshops. The production of a masterpiece for the guild was the final challenge before being allowed to set up an independent workshop as a master craftsman. Since much of the work created in the master's workshop was collaborative, the style of the work created had to be uniform. For this reason, paintings or sculptures of lesser quality are sometimes listed as a creation of the workshop rather than the master, as is the case with Dutch painter Hieronymus Bosch's *Tabletop of The Seven Deadly Sins and the Four Last Things* (1485). The primary concern of these guilds was to stay competitive, control outside competition, and ensure the quality of the work produced.

Albrecht Dürer's *Self-Portrait,* completed in 1500, when he was about thirty years old (Alte Pinakothek, Munich)

Prior to 1450 the artist was viewed as a skilled craftsperson, and the distinction between fine arts and the decorative arts was not made. Traditions among the workshops varied with the type of work produced, and there is little documentary evidence regarding the roles that women played in the fine arts.

**Medieval Workshop.** Monastic workshops were centers of book production, as well as painting, glassmaking, and metalwork—where resources and space were available. The copying and illustration of sacred texts was a spiritual discipline practiced by monks and, to a lesser degree, nuns. Monasteries and convents were also active in commissioning and producing inexpensive devotional images and votive prints for the pilgrimage trade and the broader lay market. They continued to stimulate the production of religious books and prints into the Renaissance. By the late Middle Ages, laymen also had established workshops in urban centers for the creation of religious and secular work. Many of these independent craftsmen, including playing-card makers, were designated in archival records as "Jesus makers." Wives and daughters often took part in craft and artisan activities within the family workshop and were especially prominent in the luxury trades, such as embroidery, bookbinding, goldsmithing, and silk-making. Over the course of the fifteenth and sixteenth centuries, however, guild ordinances increasingly restricted the economic participation of women, even within the family household workshop. By the end of the sixteenth century, women had virtually disappeared from these organizations.

**Social Position.** By the fifteenth century the artist's social position in Italy shifted with the association of painting, sculpture, and architecture with the liberal arts. Training included the study of the human body, classical antiquity, and life drawing. Patrons of the arts, such as Lorenzo de' Medici, newly conscious of these needs, made available their collections of antique and contemporary art to artists such as Michelangelo. Italian artists began to market themselves through the publications of manuals, commentaries, and treatises. Cennino Cennini's *Il Libro dell' Arte* (circa 1390) was an early handbook of workshop

---

## GIORGIO VASARI'S "LIVES OF THE ARTISTS" AND LEONARDO DA VINCI'S "LAST SUPPER"

Leonardo also executed in Milan, for the Dominicans of Santa Maria delle Grazie, a marvelous and beautiful painting of the Last Supper. Having depicted the heads of the apostles full of splendor and majesty, he deliberately left the head of Christ unfinished, convinced he would fail to give it the divine spirituality it demands. This all but finished work has ever since been held in the greatest veneration by the Milanese and others. In it Leonardo brilliantly succeeded in envisaging and reproducing the tormented anxiety of the apostles to know who had betrayed their master; so in their faces one can read the emotions of love, dismay, and anger or rather sorrow, at their failure to grasp the meaning of Christ. And this excites no less admiration than the contrasted spectacle of the obstinacy, hatred, and treachery in the face of Judas, or indeed, than the incredible diligence with which every detail of the work was executed. The texture of the very cloth on the table counterfeited so cunningly that the linen itself could not look more realistic.

It is said that the prior used to keep pressing Leonardo, in the most importunate way, to hurry up and finish the work, because he was puzzled by Leonardo's habit of sometimes spending half a day at a time contemplating what he had done so far; if the prior had had his way, Leonardo would have toiled like one of the laborers hoeing in the garden and never put his brush down for a moment. Not satisfied with this, the prior then complained to the duke, making such a fuss that the duke was constrained to send for Leonardo and, very tactfully, question him about the painting, although he showed perfectly well that he was only doing so because of the prior's insistence. Leonardo, knowing he was dealing with a prince of acute and discerning intelligence, was willing (as he never had been with the prior) to explain his mind at length; and so he talked to the duke for a long time about the art of painting. He explained that men of genius sometimes accomplish most when they work the least; for, he added, they are thinking out inventions and forming in their minds the perfect ideas which they subsequently express and reproduce with their hands. Leonardo then said that he still had two heads to paint: the head of Christ was one, for this he was unwilling to look for any human model, nor did he dare suppose that his imagination could conceive the beauty and divine grace that properly belonged to the incarnate Deity. Then, he said, he had yet to do the head of Judas, and this troubled him since he did not think he could imagine the features that would form the countenance of a man who, despite all the blessing he had been given, could so cruelly steel his will to betray his own master and the creator of the world. However, added Leonardo, he would try to find a model for Judas, and if he did not succeed in doing so, why then he was not without the head of that tactless and importunate. The duke roared with laughter at this and said that Leonardo had every reason in the world for saying so.

**Source:** Giorgio Vasari, *Lives of the Artists: A Selection*, volume 1, translated by George Bull (Baltimore: Penguin, 1965), pp. 262–263.

practices such as the art of tempera painting. Lorenzo Ghiberti's *Commentarii* (circa 1450s) discussed his new understanding of the relationship of sight to the structure of the eye. His book is the earliest surviving autobiography by an artist. In it he demonstrates his conscious awareness of his own place within Florentine history. Leon Battista Alberti, a humanist cleric who worked for the papacy, was a prolific writer whose Latin treatises engaged a humanist audience deeply interested in art. His works were circulated in Latin and in Italian. *De pictura* (On Painting, 1435) was the first known theoretical treatise on painting. His book included discussions of the principles of the pictorial arts such as composition, spatial perspective, and the reception of light. Alberti's treatise on architecture, *De re aedifictoria* (*Ten Books on Architecture*, 1435–1436) was highly influential for Renaissance city planning. He promoted Neoplatonic ideals about the perfection of the cosmos through geometrical forms, particularly for churches.

**Women in the Arts.** For female artists the access to these new skills was limited by the restrictive norms of gender roles in Renaissance society. A new emphasis on domesticity increasingly confined women across the social spectrum to the household. While humanists generally believed that upper-class women should be trained like their male counterparts in studies of Latin, classical literature, philosophy, and history, they still envisioned women primarily as wives regardless of their class and extolled modesty, silence, and discretion as female virtues. Well-educated aristocratic women applied their skills within the confines of the domestic household and court. Raised in a noble family where humanist educational ideals popularized in works such as Baldassare Castiglione's *Il cortegiono* (*The Courtier*, 1528) were influential, a female artist such as Sofonisha Anguissola (circa 1532–1625) was in many ways an exception. While her father encouraged her artistic development, even actively brokering her career as an artist, portraits, commissioned by nobles and princes, remained solidly within the established codes of courtly society.

**Markets for Art.** While private commissions and donors continued to drive artistic production throughout the Renaissance, some artists began to produce work on speculation for the open market by the end of the fifteenth century. Many lesser artists began selling their works at huge international fairs in northern European cities. New print technologies made it possible to produce relatively inexpensive works that could be stockpiled and sold at open-air stalls, print shops, or in a secondhand market regulated by a middleman. Artists such as German artist Albrecht Dürer became attuned to the broadening market for less expensive genres, such as woodcuts and engraving. His invention of a personal monogram (AD) allowed him to claim ownership of his creative designs, to create a name recognition that associated his work with high standards and quality, and to undercut other artists who appropriated his style.

**Connoisseurship.** The humanist reverence for antiquity dictated relatively rigid standards of taste. Rivalry between collectors often inflated prices. Many collectors were willing to pay premium prices for classical sculptures. Michelangelo may have deliberately buried his sculpture *Sleeping Cupid* (circa 1495) in order to have it unearthed and pronounced an antique by collectors. For princely connoisseurs art became an important arena in which to demonstrate their magnificence, individuality, and aristocratic distinction through artistic taste. By the late fifteenth century, collectors also began to accumulate prints in large numbers. The Nuremberg humanist scholar Hartmann Schedel collected and pasted prints into his books and manuscripts, suggesting a broadening respect for quality prints among some elite collectors who traditionally invested in more-prestigious objects, such as antique manuscripts, medals, and coins. Print artists, such as Marcantonio Raimondi, who were accepted as full members of humanist and courtly circles in Bologna, Rome, and other humanist centers, were indicative of the new status of the print as art form in Renaissance Europe. He also exemplifies the increasingly intimate relationship between artists and collectors, who were engaging in a mutual enterprise to develop a common vocabulary of critical response. From this exchange the Renaissance elite established a new canon of aesthetic taste.

**Production of Fame.** Most medieval craftsmen and artists produced their works in anonymity. By the late Middle Ages, however, they began to use various seals and markers to indicate responsibility for the quality of their product. Even though the fourteenth-century Florentine artist Giotto only signed two of his paintings, his name became synonymous with artistic achievement by the late 1300s, thanks to the attention his work was given by later writers and chroniclers. By the mid fourteenth century many artists in Italy began to be aware of the importance of promoting themselves and their memory, either writing about their lives or encouraging others to write about them. An increasing sensitivity to individual artistic talent, style, and achievement closely connected to humanist sanctions of fame, immortality, and wealth. Roman scholar Pliny the Elder's discussion in his *Natural History* of the status, wealth, and prestige that artists enjoyed in classical society became the model that was used to justify the growing prestige accorded to artists in the Renaissance. Intellectual and artistic exchanges between Italy and northern Europe helped promote and sustain this model north of the Alps. Dürer employed multiple strategies to promote the status of the artist and the elevation of the arts. As a young boy he began to draw and later paint a remarkable series of self-portraits that reflect an intense self-consciousness about his social position, artistic talent, physical health, and keen awareness of his own fate and mortality. In a striking portrait he painted at the age of twenty-six, in which he styled himself as a man of fashion, wearing fine doeskin gloves, the young Dürer recorded for posterity his upward movement in society. His upright posture, restrained comportment, and fine clothing were all important markers of status in Nuremberg society and Europe generally. From self-portraits to major commissioned altarpieces, such as the *Madonna of the Rosegarlands* (1506), Dürer remained acutely conscious of his posterity and the need to propagate his physical presence, memory, and talent for immortality.

Sources:

Michael Baxendall, *Painting and Experience in Fifteenth-Century Italy* (Oxford: Clarendon Press, 1972).

Jane Campbell Hutchison, *Albrecht Dürer: A Biography* (Princeton: Princeton University Press, 1990).

David Landau and Peter Parshall, *The Renaissance Print, 1470–1500* (New Haven: Yale University Press, 1994).

Wendy Slatkin, *Women Artists in History; From Antiquity to the 20th Century* (Englewood Cliffs, N.J.: Prentice-Hall, 1985).

Jane Turner, ed., *The Dictionary of Art* (New York: Grove, 1996).

Evelyn Welch, *Art and Society in Italy, 1350–1500* (Oxford & New York: Oxford University Press, 1997).

## HUMANISM AND THE ARTS

**Rebirth.** Beginning in the mid fourteenth century, many scholars and writers began to be concerned with the decline of the arts and the corruption of the Latin language after the barbarian invasions of the fourth and fifth centuries. Italian poet Francesco Petrarch (1304–1374), often considered the father of humanism, called upon his contemporaries to engage in new initiatives in the arts and education that would enable future generations to walk out of "the slumber of forgetfulness into the pure radiance of the past." Throughout the fourteenth and fifteenth centuries Italian scholars were most keenly aware of the distinctive juncture between the ancient world and medieval society, and they saw themselves as apostles of a new golden age that would usher in the *rinascità* (rebirth) of civilization by restoring the literary and artistic standards of classical society. These scholars vehemently attacked the relentless rationalism of scholasticism that dominated medieval universities and became ardent champions of a new educational program or curriculum that focused on the *studia humanitatis* (study of humanistic disciplines), such as grammar, rhetoric, poetry, history, and moral philosophy.

**Civic Humanism and Public Art.** The broad educational program advocated by fourteenth- and fifteenth-century humanists emphasized the moral responsibility of the educated elite to engage in civic service. This politics of engagement was particularly suited to the republican city-states of central Italy, where skilled humanists played a pivotal role in government. As chancellors, secretaries, and diplomats, humanists carried out extensive administrative duties as well as defended the republican ideals of the city-states they served, writing epic poems and patriotic histories, often in an eloquent Latin style accessible only to other members of the ruling elite. Scholars have paid particular attention to the links between the arts and politics in fifteenth-century Florence, where the ruling elite commissioned artists such as Lorenzo Ghiberti, Donatello, and Filippo Brunelleschi—working in the new vocabulary of classicism—to create visual monuments to republican idealism and civic pride throughout the city. By 1430 the construction or renovation of some important civic sites, such as the cathedral, Palazzo della Signoria (town hall), and Foundling Hospital testified to Floren-

---

### MARSILIO FICINO, "HOW THE SOUL IS RAISED FROM THE BEAUTY OF THE BODY TO THE BEAUTY OF GOD."

Consider this, dear guests; imagine Diotima addressing Socrates thus.

"No body is completely beautiful, O Socrates. For it is either attractive in this part and ugly in that, or attractive today, and at other times not, or is thought beautiful by one person and ugly by another. Therefore, the beauty of the body, contaminated by the contagion of ugliness, cannot be the pure, true, and first beauty. In addition no one ever supposes beauty itself to be ugly, just as one does not suppose wisdom to be foolish, but we do consider the arrange of bodies sometimes beautiful and sometimes ugly. And at any one time different people have different opinions about it. Therefore the first and true beauty is not in bodies. Add the fact that many different bodies have the same family name, 'the beautiful.' Therefore there must be one common quality of beauty in many bodies, by virtue of which they are alike called 'beautiful.' Therefore the single beauty of many bodies derives from some single incorporeal maker. The one maker of all things is God, who through the Angels and the Souls every day renders all the Matter of the world beautiful. Therefore it must be concluded that the true Reason of beauty is to be found in God and in His ministers rather than in the Body of the World....

The beauty of bodies is a light; the beauty of the soul is also a light. The light of the soul is truth, which is the only thing which your friend Plato seems to ask of God in his Prayers: *Grant to me, O God he says, that my soul may become beautiful, and that those things which pertain to the body may not impair the beauty of the soul, and that I may think only the wise man rich.* In this prayer Plato says that the beauty of the soul consists in truth and wisdom, and that it is given to men by God. Truth, which is given to use by God single and uniform, through its various effects acquires the names of various virtues. Insofar as it deals with divine things, it is called Wisdom (which Plato asked of God above all else); insofar as it deals with natural things, it is called Knowledge; with human things, Prudence. Insofar as it makes men equal, it is called Justice; insofar as it makes them invincible, Courage; and tranquil, Temperance."

**Source:** Marsilio Ficino, *Commentary on Plato's Symposium on Love*, translated by Sears Jayne (Dallas: Spring Publications, 1985), pp. 141–145, as cited in Kenneth R. Bartlett, *The Civilization of the Italian Renaissance: Sources in Modern History* (Lexington, Mass.: Heath, 1992), pp. 120–123.

Frontispiece for Charles de Bouelles's *Liber de Sapiete,* circa 1510 (British Library)

tines' willingness to shoulder expensive public-works projects that radically transformed the urban fabric of the city. Private citizens and guilds also commissioned artists to renovate parish churches, private chapels, and palatial residences in the latest style.

**Family Commissions.** Humanist treatises, such as Leon Battista Alberti's *Della famiglia* (*On the Family,* 1433), which defended marriage, the acquisition of wealth, and the pursuit of fame as fundamental to the survival of the republic, encouraged patrician families to erect permanent monuments to their family's power and status. To mark their political ascendancy in Florence, for example, the Medicis engaged in many building projects, including the renovation of the parish church of San Lorenzo. In 1442 Cosimo de' Medici agreed to assume the entire cost of renovating the church. In return for this generous gesture he demanded legal control of the main altar, the most sacred space in the church, and stipulated that no other family's coat of arms could appear in any guise in the building. Cosimo and his brother Lorenzo assured the imprimatur of their patronage would be prominently displayed in other

ways, hiring artists such as Donatello to design impressive funerary monuments for their parents and stucco reliefs of their own patron saints, Lawrence and Cosmas.

**Private Collections.** The Renaissance mania for collecting and even replicating ancient manuscripts, works of art, coins, and other artifacts was a natural outgrowth of the humanist reverence for antiquity. In the burgeoning and competitive market for antiquities, renowned artists such as Donatello were called upon to appraise the authenticity and value of newly discovered works. Skilled artists such as Michelangelo participated in the growing traffic in reproductions and forgeries that were created with and without the complicity of their clients. In some ways the antique coins, jewelry, and small objets d'art that comprised the collections of Renaissance princes and the wealthy elite were remarkably similar in composition to collections amassed by princely connoisseurs such as the duke of Berry a century earlier, but the essential spirit behind the enterprise was profoundly different. By surrounding themselves with classical artifacts and reproductions, humanists, wealthy collectors, and princely connoisseurs strove to form a clearer conception of the civilization whose ideals they wanted to reclaim and re-create in their private and public lives.

**A Golden Age.** By the late fifteenth century the artists and humanist scholars who gathered at the court of Lorenzo de' Medici were perpetuating a timeless and essentially romantic vision of antiquity. The idealized frescoes of a young golden-haired Lorenzo as one of the Magi, painted by Benozzo di Lese Gozzoli (circa 1421–1497) for the family's private chapel in Florence; the large-scale mythological works of Sandro Botticelli (1445–1510); and the Vitruvian villa that Guiliano da Sangallo (circa 1443–1516) built for Lorenzo at Poggio a Caino in the 1480s, employed a language that was strikingly different from the naturalistic and narrative conventions embraced by artists of the early fifteenth century. Even the Neoplatonic love poetry written by Lorenzo and his close associates reflects the emergence of a new courtly style consonant with his princely ambitions.

**Neoplatonism and Human Creativity.** While Renaissance humanists and artists admired and imitated ancient models closely, many of the works they produced were cultural hybrids that strongly reflected their Christian training and orientation. Late-fifteenth-century humanist scholars, such as Marsilio Ficino (1433–1499) and his disciples at the Florentine Platonic Academy, were strongly drawn to study Plato and second-century Neoplatonic philosophers in part because their writings upheld the superiority of the spiritual world over the material. His most famous works, *Platonic Theology* (1482) and *On Christian Religion* (1474), reflected his desire to synthesize pagan philosophy with Christianity. Like his most famous disciple, Giovanni Pico della Mirandola (1463–1494), Ficino attributed superhuman potential to human beings, made in God's image with the unique capacity to mediate spiritual reality. Through the study of ancient and arcane texts Ficino believed that scholars could uncover the hidden sympathies that existed between the spiritual and corporeal worlds and learn to command all created beings, even the celestial intelligence or stars, to do their bidding. For Ficino the creative powers harnessed by the scholar-magician, through the study of arcane texts, belonged naturally to artists, who were gifted with the divine vision to replicate beauty and thus approach the very mind of God. In his *Commentaries on Plato*, Ficino described how physical images of beauty directed the human mind and spirit toward the revelation of True Beauty or God. Not surprisingly, Michelangelo, Botticelli, and other fifteenth-century artists were drawn to Neoplatonism and its reverence for the creative powers of artistic genius.

**Christian Humanism.** By the 1500s the term "humanism" described an increasingly ambitious enterprise to reform the fundamental features of medieval society, including the Church itself. Northern scholars were deeply attracted to the Neoplatonic studies of Ficino and his circle which corresponded to their own interests in spiritual reform. The literary efforts of Northern humanists such as Jacques LeFebvre d'Etaples (1450–1536) in France, Desiderius Erasmus (circa 1466–1536) in the Netherlands, and Cardinal Francisco Jiménez de Cisneros (1436–1517) in Spain were largely directed toward biblical scholarship, religious reform, and education. Like the Italian humanists, many northern humanists envisioned the rebirth of a golden age, but one that was profoundly Christian: a *pax christiana* where justice, peace, and civility would transform civil society. The artistic and literary program of transalpine humanism also proved useful to the political and cultural agenda of the princely elite in the north, where humanists serving as royal secretaries, historiographers, and librarians became architects of royal power and the new culture of courtliness and civility.

Sources:

Charles G. Nauert Jr., *Humanism and the Culture of the Renaissance* (Cambridge & New York: Cambridge University Press, 1995).

John T. Paoletti and Gary M. Radke, *Art in Renaissance Italy* (Upper Saddle River, N.J.: Prentice Hall, 1997).

Donald J. Wilcox, *In Search of God and Self: Renaissance and Reformation Thought* (Boston: Houghton Mifflin, 1975).

## PRINCELY COURTS AND PATRONAGE

**Princely Magnificence.** For Renaissance princes and monarchs, both north as well as south of the Alps, huge and costly public-works programs, palatial residences decorated in the latest style, extensive libraries, and collections of classical artifacts were the natural corollary of rulership. Fifteenth-century humanists rediscovered a classical ideal that envisioned great private wealth as a prerequisite of civic virtue. They expressed this ideal, in part, by the lavish expenditure of money for the public good as well as private pleasures. In purportedly republican city-states, such as Florence, merchant dynasties sometimes had to counter charges of princely ambition by downscaling their architectural projects. Such concerns probably prompted Cosimo de' Medici to accept the more modest design for renovation of the palace proposed by Michelozzo di Bartolomeo instead of the imposing architectural plans drawn up by Filippo Brunelleschi. In princely states of northern Italy, lavish expenditures on art, architecture, and ceremony were rarely curbed by concerns about republican virtue, familial rivalries, or public censure. Humanist propagandists employed by princely houses defended extravagant artistic commissions as the purest expression of *magnificentia,* that search for majesty and immortality that inspired Roman imperial and senatorial elites to engage in grandiose building programs whose vestiges reminded Italians of the glories of the Roman Empire more than a thousand years later. In Machiavelli's now classic redefinition of princely power, *The Prince* (1532), the Florentine writer argued that the defining characteristic of a successful ruler was the ability to command the obedience and assent of his subjects through the judicious mix of fear, clemency, and majesty. In his treatise, *De re aedifictoria* (*Ten Books on Architecture*, 1435–1436), Leon Battista Alberti urged humanist princely patrons to demonstrate their majesty by employing classical motifs, such as temple porticos, triumphal arches, and friezes, to impart noble or superior attributes to their architectural commissions. Princes and patricians often went a step further and inscribed public buildings and private residences with their personal emblems, initials, and coats of arms.

**Chivalry.** Princes from smaller Italian states, such as Urbino and Ferrera, often enhanced their financial and political fortunes by hiring themselves out as *condottiere* (mercenaries) to larger, principally Italian, foreign powers. Military prowess thus remained an important expression of aristocratic authority in northern Italy, and chivalric romance literature continued to be fashionable among Italian nobles. Nonetheless, the highest praise of the age was reserved for princes who were accomplished men of letters as well as military leaders. Pedro Berruguete's *Portrait of Federico da Montefeltro and his son Guidobaldo* (1476–1477), which depicts Federico, the duke of Urbino, seated and solemnly reading at a lectern, incongruously dressed in full armor, clearly reveals the dual concerns with humanist learning and chivalric honor. A rich red tunic trimmed in ermine is draped over Federico's armor, a reference to the chivalric Order of the Garter and Order of the Ermine to which the duke belonged. Poised on the lectern is a jewel-encrusted Persian hat that recalls Federico's pivotal response to the Persian call for an international crusade against the Turks. At Federico's knee is his young son, Guidobaldo, holding a golden scepter in his right hand as a sign of the duke's victorious battle to secure dynastic control of Urbino. An endemic rivalry with the sumptuous courts of northern Europe, especially France and Burgundy, also encouraged northern Italian princes to commission works that employed the visual language of chivalry as well as of classical Rome. Italian princes continued to admire and collect French ivory miniatures and Flemish tapestries. They also employed artists trained in the International Gothic style, which often made the content of their art collections virtually indistinguishable from their northern counterparts. Leonello d'Este, who governed the small principality of Ferrara, for example, was an avid patron of the Flemish artist Rogier van der Weyden and owned Passion tapestries and a Deposition from the Cross by the artist. He especially admired the moving piety and elegant lines that defined the Flemish artist's style.

## ISABELLA D'ESTE'S COMMISSION OF LOVE AND CHASTITY TO PERUGINO, 19 JANUARY 1503

Our poetic invention, which we greatly want to see painted by you, is a battle of Chastity against Lasciviousness, that is to say, Pallas and Diana fighting vigorously against Venus and Cupid. And Pallas should seem almost to have vanquished Cupid, having broken his golden arrow and cast his silver bow underfoot; with one hand she is holding him by the bandage which the blind boy has before his eyes, and with the other she is lifting her lance and about to kill him. By comparison Diana must seem to be having a closer fight with Venus for victory. Venus has been struck by Diana's arrow only on the surface of the body, on her crown and garland, or on a veil she may have around her; and part of Diana's raiment will have been singed by the torch of Venus, but nowhere else will either of them have been wounded. Beyond these four deities, the most chaste nymphs in the trains of Pallas and Diana, in whatever attitudes and ways you please, have to fight fiercely with a lascivious crowd of fauns, satyrs and several thousand cupids; and these cupids must be smaller than the first [the God Cupid], and not bearing gold bows and silver arrows, but bows and arrows of some baser material such as wood or iron or what you please. And to give more expression and decoration to the picture, beside Pallas I want to have the olive tree sacred to her, with a shield leaning against it bearing the head of Medusa, and with the owl, the bird peculiar to Pallas, perched among the branches. And beside Venus I want her favorite tree, the myrtle, to be placed. But to enhance the beauty a fount of water must be included, such as a river or the sea, where fauns, satyrs, and more cupids will be seen, hastening to the help of Cupid, some swimming through the river, some flying, and some riding upon white swans, coming to join such an amorous battle. On the bank of the said river or sea stands Jupiter with other gods, as the enemy of Chastity, changed into the bull which carried off the fair Europa; and Mercury as an eagle circling above its prey, flies around one of Pallas's nymphs, called Glaucera, who carried a casket engraved with the sacred emblems of the goddess. Polyphemus, the one-eyed Cyclops, chases Galatea, and Phoebus chases Daphne, who has already turned into a laurel tree; Pluto, having seized Proserpina, is bearing her off to his kingdom of darkness, and Neptune has seized a nymph who has been turned almost entirely into a raven.

I am sending you all these details in a small drawing, so that with both the written description and the drawing you will be able to consider my wishes in this matter. But if you think that perhaps there are too many figures in this for one picture, it is left to you to reduce them as you please, provided that you do not remove the principal basis, which consists of the four figures of Pallas, Diana, Venus and Cupid. If no inconvenience occurs I shall consider myself well satisfied; you are free to reduce them, but not to add anything else. Please be content with this arrangement.

**Source:** D. S. Chambers, ed., *Patrons and Artists in the Italian Renaissance,* translations by Chambers (London: Macmillan, 1970), pp. 136–137.

Sandro Botticelli's *Portrait of a Young Man*, circa 1480
(Galleria degli Uffizi, Florence)

Nonetheless, echoing the sentiments of Quattrocento humanists, Italian nobles and the princely elite believed that the urbanity of Italian Renaissance culture rendered it superior to the essentially rural and rustic character of aristocratic life in the north.

**Self-Representation.** Portraiture was of pivotal importance in humanist and princely circles. Like gifts of books, the presentation of one's own likeness was charged with profound moral, social, and political significance. The elite exchanged portraits as an act of friendship, as a bid for political authority, and as a guarantee of immortality. Renaissance portraits were more than representations of specific likenesses; they were also fundamental to the construction of social identities and the perpetuation of personal and dynastic power. Princes, popes, and patricians commissioned artists to reproduce their likeness in commemorative medals, plaquettes, portrait busts, and death masks, as well as in paintings. Commemorative medals were widely admired for their associations with classical antiquity and imperial prerogative, and were widely repro-

duced and given as gifts to favorites and visiting dignitaries from the mid fifteenth century onward. Sandro Botticelli's *Portrait of a Young Man* (circa 1480), which depicts a handsome and courtly young man holding a commemorative medal with the profile of Cosimo de' Medici, is a cunning marriage of the two most popular genres of Renaissance self-representation.

**Gender.** Portraits of women generally conformed to established literary conventions and gender roles. Artists were sent to foreign courts to render lifelike portraits of potential brides so suitors could deem their aesthetic suitability. Feminist scholars have shown how aristocratic portraits from the fifteenth-century courts of northern Italy represented their female subjects in profile, with a distant or lowered gaze, often dressed in clothes embroidered with heraldic symbols, all of which reinforced women's traditional reproductive and domestic role in the perpetuation of family power and lineage. By the late fifteenth century, the growing popularity of female portraits, where the sitter directly faced the viewer, often represented extremely idealized images of female beauty based on the values of Petrarchan love poetry and Neoplatonism.

**Artists and Patrons.** Profound concerns about honor and decorum prompted aristocratic patrons to work in unusually close concert with artists. Patrons stipulated the quality of artistic materials to be used in commissions. They also specified themes and sometimes even the compositional structure of the commission. When Isabella d'Este, marchioness of Ferrara, decided to commission a painting titled *Love and Chastity* from the Italian artist Perugino, she detailed a complex iconographic program that tied the artist to a nearly impossible task. The ease with which she described the battle between Pallas, Diana, Venus, and Cupid revealed her familiarity with classical mythology and its allegories. The theme of love and chastity itself fit within the larger courtly tradition of genteel virtue. Isabella's reputation as a connoisseur was enhanced by her ability to attract Perugino, considered the most famous artist of his generation, into her service and demonstrated her keen attention to the reciprocity of fame. By the mid fifteenth century, artists were often given permanent positions at court, where they were sometimes given honorific titles as valets in the inner household and sometimes even granted titles of nobility. They enjoyed these rewards, however, at a considerable loss of personal and artistic freedom. Talented artists remained extremely mobile, marketing their skills to several patrons. This traffic in artistic talent assured the rapid dissemination of the newest techniques and classical motifs throughout the courts of Europe.

**Popes as Patrons.** After the political and moral challenges to papal authority during the Avignon Papacy (1304–1377) and Great Schism (1378–1417), Renaissance popes were determined to reestablish Rome as the undisputed center of Latin Christianity. Envisioning Rome as the heart of a *pax romana* and *pax Christi*, the papacy affirmed its supreme temporal and spiritual power through classical history and myth. In his 1455 deathbed speech Pope Nicholas V described his vision for the urban renewal of Rome as a celestial Jerusalem seemingly made by the hand of God. Through such programs the power of the Holy See would be exalted and the authority of the Roman Church presented at its greatest throughout Christendom. The unlettered and weak of faith would be moved by such extraordinary sights and confirmed in their beliefs. Subsequent popes carried forward his vision in the form of expansive building programs of churches, palaces, and villas, as well as the urban renewal of city streets and squares according to classical principles of design. What some scholars have deemed the "imperial style" flourished most fully under Julius II (r. 1503–1513) and the Medici Popes, Leo X (r. 1513–1521) and Clement VII (r. 1523–1534). Bold commissions, such as the St. Peter's Basilica allowed Renaissance popes to underscore the historic continuity of the papacy as well as conflate imperial and ecclesiastical power. Funerary monuments, such as the tomb that Julius II commissioned Michelangelo to design, reveal more temporal desires to achieve a measure of personal immortality. Michelangelo's original plans, which were never fully executed, called for a massive three-story mausoleum with allegorical representations of victories that would recall Julius's military campaigns and statues of the most heroic figures of Christian tradition, notably Moses and Paul. Julius planned to have his tomb strategically placed near the relics of St. Peter, from whom the popes claimed their authority by apostolic succession, in the new basilica.

Sources:

Alison Cole, *Virtue and Magnificence: Art of the Italian Renaissance Courts* (New York: Abrams, 1995).

Ralph Goldthwaite, *Wealth and the Demand for Art in Italy, 1300–1600* (Baltimore: Johns Hopkins University Press, 1993).

Catherine E. King, *Renaissance Women Patrons: Wives and Widows in Italy, c. 1300–1500* (Manchester & New York: Manchester University Press, 1998).

Loren Partridge, *The Art of Renaissance Rome, 1400–1600* (New York: Abrams, 1996).

Paola Tinagli, *Women in Italian Renaissance Art: Gender, Representation, Identity* (Manchester & New York: Manchester University Press, 1997).

## PRINT CULTURE

**Literacy and Class.** In early modern Europe the ability to read and write was a mark of social distinction and authority. For most of the Middle Ages, literacy was a skill largely confined to the clerical elite, and in medieval parlance usually referred to the ability to read and write Latin, the language of the Church, not the vernacular. The proliferation of pious images of aristocratic patrons reading, especially devotional manuals and prayer books such as Books of Hours, suggests that many upper-class women as well as men probably could read by the fourteenth century. Many merchants and tradesmen possessed a kind of functional literacy that allowed them to carry on correspondence and keep account books necessary for business. By the sixteenth century both humanists and reformed-minded theologians, Catholic and Protestant, encouraged city fathers across western Europe to set up grammar schools, which, as the name suggests, educated the sons of the urban elite in the rudiments of Latin, and sometimes Greek, grammar and literature. While humanists also sponsored some schools for girls, literacy rates remained higher for men than women throughout the early modern period. The humanist-based curriculum differed from that of the medieval period, but it largely replicated the Latin bias of medieval education and perpetuated class distinctions based on access to the printed word and classical elitism.

**Advent of Print.** The invention of the movable-type printing press by Johannes Gutenberg in the mid fifteenth century created the possibility of mass literacy. Many of the most-famous print shops established in the fifteenth and sixteenth centuries, however, initially targeted elite audiences. Aldus Manutius, founder of the renowned Aldine Press in Venice, for example, devoted himself almost entirely to the publication of texts in Greek and Latin. The few texts that he published in the vernacular were intended

Israhel van Meckenem's *Dance at the Court of Herod*
(National Gallery of Art, Washington, D.C.)

primarily for patrician collectors. Recent scholarship has shown that even his decision to produce smaller octavo editions, rather than the large folio editions favored by some collectors, was for the convenience of the scholar-diplomats who comprised his clientele, not the masses. In northern Europe many of the first print shops directed tremendous energies toward the publication of esoteric biblical works and projects. Printmakers and printers competed with artists and illuminators for the attention of a small and sophisticated market of collectors, many of whom remained dubious about the aesthetic value of printed materials. Federico da Montefeltro, whose library at Urbino was considered to be one of the best in Europe, prided himself on the fact that he had not succumbed to the growing practice of buying printed books. In response to such attitudes many of the most renowned booksellers in late-fifteenth-century Italy, such as Vespasiano da Bisticci, dealt only in the manuscript volumes so prized by elite collectors.

**Marketing Prints.** During the late fifteenth century, however, printing shops and a printmaking trade emerged, geared toward a broader, middle-class market. Nuremberg printer Anton Koberger, who had the largest printing establishment in Europe, recognized the potential market for luxury books in northern Europe. Nonetheless, even his famous *Die Schedelsche Weltchronik* (1493), a lavishly illustrated history of the world, was, in Koberger's words, "not meant for students of antiquity, but for the delight of the general public." Moreover, the bulk of his publications were pitched toward the popular market for biblical and devotional texts, which still comprised approximately 85 percent of the book and print trade north and south of the Alps. The German printmaker Israhel van Meckenem even more fully exploited the commercial possibilities of printmaking in the late fifteenth century. Considered something of a plagiarist because he purchased and reworked plates that he reissued under his own name, Meckenem was also an entrepreneurial genius who pioneered marketing strategies that would become key features of the commercial print trade in the sixteenth century. He developed print cycles that could be marketed separately or together, explored the market for anecdotal and satirical prints dealing with secular themes, and experimented with strategies that linked text and image. The popularity of Meckenem's bootlegged engravings of indulgences (which he issued without papal approval) and his *pestbilder* (religious prints that promised to protect buyers against the plague) testify to the lively commerce in northern Europe generally in devotional images and texts, which often also extended to more tangential realms of supernatural experience, such as prophecy and astrology. Printmakers and printers also exploited the burgeoning interest in exploration and science, producing maps, illustrated herbals, anatomies, and technical manuals that revolutionized the exchange of information in western society. Even classic scientific texts, such as those by second-century Greek physician Galen

Oh woe, oh woe is me, poor fool

How I must work to pull this cart!

And why? Because I took myself a wife.

Would that the thought had never crossed my mind!

A shrewish scold has come into my house;

She has taken my sword, my pants, and my purse.

Night and day I have no peace,

And never a kind word from her.

The woman behind him replies:

Hey, dear boy, what you say is true,

But be quiet or I'll hit you over the head.

If you want a beautiful and pious little wife

Who obeys you at all times,

Then stay at home in your own house

And stop carousing about.

. . . If you will not work to support me,

Then you must wash, spin, and draw the cart

And be beaten on your back.

Source: Keith Moxey, *Peasants, Warriors, and Wives: Popular Imagery in the Reformation* (Chicago: University of Chicago Press, 1989), pp. 108–109.

and Alexandrian astronomer Ptolemy, were revitalized by print illustrations that rearticulated the crucial link between the printed word and printed image. By 1550 the proliferation of print had encouraged the development of self-conscious intellectual communities, actively exchanging ideas, images, and texts and establishing new canons of human understanding.

**Reproductive Prints.** In the late fifteenth century, artists also began exchanging prints as a way of disseminating new techniques and propagating their fame among their colleagues. Sometimes they marketed prints themselves, but they also used the services of colporteurs, the early modern equivalent of traveling salesmen, who were crucial agents of the new print culture in rural and urban society. Raphael, for example, employed several printmakers, including the highly skilled artist Marcantonio Raimondi, to reproduce engravings of his works of art for sale and as gifts. By the early sixteenth century there is evidence to suggest that many engravers began to reproduce prints independently of the artist, changing models and even marketing the work under their own names. By the 1530s and 1540s "reproductive" prints became an important genre in printmaking; their reduced portfolio size and cost opened up art collecting to a broader middle-class audience.

**Cheap Print and the Masses.** The evangelical impulses of Reformers encouraged many printers to broaden their publishing strategies and target the semiliterate and illiterate populace with cheaply produced single-sheet woodcuts and engravings. While book ownership remained within the reach of only a small minority of artisans, merchants, and professionals for most of the sixteenth century, single-sheet prints of biblical scenes or devotional images were purchased by a broad cross section of consumers, who prized the images for their decorative value as well as their pious nature. This type of a cheap print often presented information in "hybridised" fashion, using a combination of image and text to communicate an edifying message. An English broadside of "fyne gloves devised for newyeres gyftes" (1559) illustrates the way in which print culture often appropriated the devices of oral culture. Virtuous resolutions, such as "to do all things only for the love of God," were printed on each fingertip, presumably to be memorized and suitably applied by the young girls who were the intended recipients of this "New Year's gift."

**Text and Image.** Cheap woodcuts and engravings often dealt with explicitly secular themes, such as the war between the sexes, in ways that reinforced Reformed ideology concerning gender and marriage. Sixteenth-century reformers advocated marriage as the best antidote to concupiscence among laity and clergy alike and championed the social value of households in which wives and children modeled appropriate deference to patriarchal authority. Printers often departed from the sober tone of Lutheran and Calvinist sermons on the subject. In sixteenth-century Nuremberg, playwrights, artists, and printers worked in concert, producing satirical prints captioned by moralizing little rhymes that illustrated the perils of female insubordination. The poem, *There is no Greater Treasure Here on Earth than an Obedient Wife* (1533), for example, accompanied a woodcut by Erhard Schön that showed a well-dressed bourgeois housewife beating her husband and forcing him to pull a cart loaded with laundry like a lowly beast of burden. German poet Hans Sachs frequently wrote rhymes for all kinds of illustrated broadsheets, including Hans Schaüffelin's highly popular 1536 print *Diaper Washer*, which satirized the dangerous consequences of the inversion of gender roles within the family by showing a husband beating a diaper clean with a mallet while his wife stands guard with a stick in her hands.

**The Spoken Word.** In the sixteenth century, Reformed theology was communicated as much through the spoken word as through print. While literacy rates steadily rose over the course of the sixteenth century, Martin Luther and his fellow reformers abandoned their insistence that every Christian should be able to read the Bible and focused instead on the oral transmission of religious tradition by trained ministers of the Word. By the 1530s and 1540s Sunday sermons and catechism lessons became the key methods of religious instruction and indoctrination in Protestant churches. Religious instruction was also carried on at home during family devotions over which the father

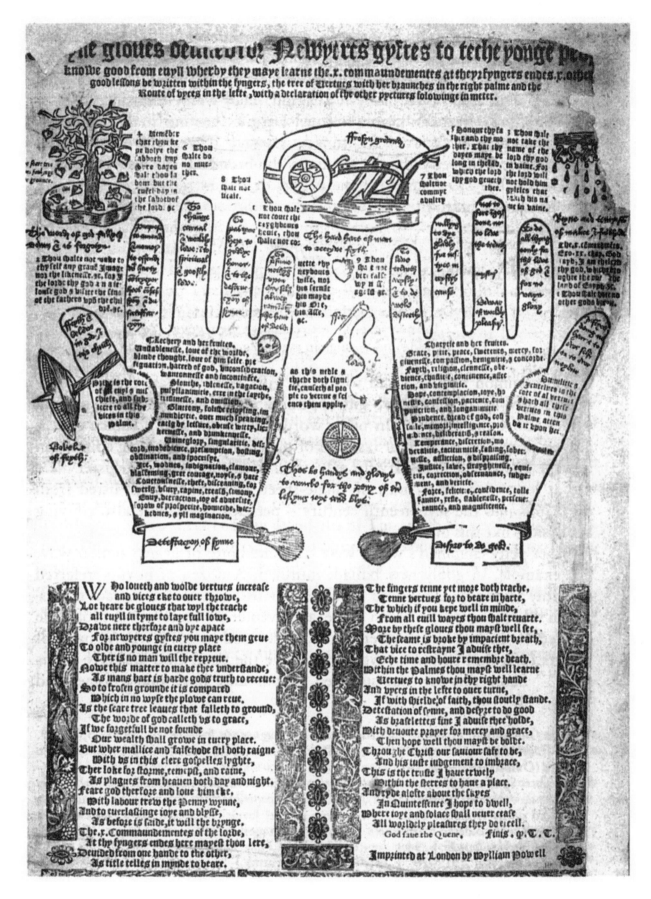

William Powell's metaphorical broadside, circa 1560, with sins on the left palm, virtues on the right, and resolutions on the fingers (Huntington Library, San Marino, California, RB 18343)

usually presided. In an exercise that reinforced paternal as well as divine authority, fathers convoked the entire family, including servants, morning and evening, to sing songs and read from the Bible. For most Protestants, Bible reading remained a communal, oral activity until the later seventeenth century. Even outside the home most people experienced the printed word by someone reading aloud in the workshop, in a confraternity or craft guild, or in a religious assembly.

Sources:

Roger Chartier, *The Cultural Uses of Print in Early Modern France,* translated by Lydia G. Cochrane (Princeton: Princeton University Press, 1987).

Chartier, ed., *The History of Private Life,* volume 3, *Passions of the Renaissance* (Cambridge, Mass.: Belknap Press of Harvard University Press, 1989).

Elizabeth L. Eisenstein, *The Printing Press as an Agent of Change: Communications and Cultural Transformations in Early Modern Europe* (Cambridge & New York: Cambridge University Press, 1979).

David Landau and Peter Parshall, *The Renaissance Print, 1470–1500* (New Haven: Yale University Press, 1994).

Bob Scribner, *For the Sake of the Simple Folk: Popular Propaganda for the German Reformation* (Cambridge: Cambridge University Press, 1981).

Tessa Watt, *Cheap Print and Popular Piety, 1550–1640* (Cambridge & New York: Cambridge University Press, 1991).

## THE REFORMATION

**Printed Propaganda.** In their desire to make the Bible the primary medium of spiritual understanding and experience, Protestant reformers presented a profound challenge to visual arts and to the livelihood that many artists drew from ecclesiastical commissions. At the same time, reformers were extremely adept at using new print technologies to popularize their ideas and win adherents to their cause. Cheaply produced woodcuts and broadsheets allowed Reformers to disseminate evangelical theology to a marginally literate populace. In Germany, Martin Luther worked directly with artists sympathetic to Reformed theology, such as Lucas Cranach the Elder (1472–1553), to create didactic prints that explained theology through text and image. One popular format presented contrasting images of Catholic and Protestant practices and beliefs, usually with Catholic practices on the left (or sinister side) and Protestant on the right.

**Stock Images.** Catholic polemicists quickly took up the counteroffensive, using printed pamphlets and broadsheets to expose the dangerous errors of Protestantism. Both Catholic and Protestant artists satirized the religious practices, beliefs, and ringleaders of the opposition by drawing on popular cultural codes and iconographic traditions that required little textual explanation and could be readily comprehended by illiterate as well as literate viewers. Hydra-headed monsters and dragons dressed in papal regalia, which recalled the apocalyptic drama recounted in the book of Revelation, allowed Protestant propagandists to identify the Pope with the Antichrist. Polemicists on both sides of the religious divide used grotesque figures, such as slack-jawed demons and she-devils devouring (or sometimes defecating on) figures dressed in clerical garb, to

## LUTHER DISCUSSES IMAGES AND ICONOCLASM

I approached the task of destroying images by first tearing them out of the heart through God's word and making them worthless and despised. This indeed took place before Dr. Karlstadt ever dreamed of destroying images. For when they are no longer in the heart, they can do no harm when seen with the eyes. But Dr. Karlstadt, who pays no attention to matters of the heart, has reversed the order by removing them from sight and leaving them in the heart. . . .

I have allowed and not forbidden the outward removal of images, so long as this takes place without rioting and uproar and is done by the proper authorities. . . . And I say at the outset that according to the law of Moses no other images are forbidden than an image of God which one worships. A crucifix, on the other hand, or any other holy image is not forbidden. Heigh now! you breakers of images, I defy you to prove the opposite! . . .

Thus we read that Moses' Brazen Serpent remained (Num. 21:8) until Hezekiah destroyed it solely because it had been worshiped (II Kings 18:4). . . .

However, to speak evangelically of images, I say and declare that no one is obligated to break violently images even of God, but everything is free, and one does not sin if he does not break them with violence. One is obligated, however, to destroy them with the Word of God; that is, not with the law in a Karlstadtian manner, but with the Gospel. . . . Beyond this let the external matters take their course. God grant that they may be destroyed, become dilapidated, or that they remain. It is all the same and makes no difference, just as when the poison has been removed from a snake. . . .

Nor would I condemn those who have destroyed them, especially those who destroy divine and idolatrous images. But images for memorial and witness, such as crucifixes and images of saints, are to be tolerated. This is shown above to be the case even in the Mosaic law. And they are not only to be tolerated, but for the sake of the memorial and the witness they are praiseworthy and honorable, as the witness stones of Joshua (Josh. 24:26) and of Samuel (I Sam. 7:12).

**Source:** Wolfgang Stechow, *Northern Renaissance Art, 1400–1600: Sources and Documents* (Englewood Cliffs, N.J.: Prentice-Hall, 1966), pp. 129–130.

defame and demonize the rival faith. Images that elided the human form with animals relied on a complex matrix of literary conventions from low and high culture for their potency. Popular proverbs and fables provided models for anticlerical satires, often showing a fox or wolf in clerical

*Devourers of the Dead in the Jaws of Hell,* an engraving depicting a she-devil with priests and nuns in her mouth
(Staatliche Museen, Preussischer Kulterbesitz, Berlin-Dahlem)

garb preaching to geese or hens. Humanists' aversion to any gesture, feature, or image that exposed the animal side of human nature made these images a particularly potent form of debasement. Printmakers also devised ingenious visual strategies to ridicule the opposition. In the folding print a soberly dressed theologian, clearly identifiable as Luther, was literally undressed when viewers lifted the tab to reveal the illustrious reformer urinating. Scatological prints such as this one were extremely popular and effective polemical tools that reduced revered figures to the lowest common denominator—what the literary theorist Mikhail Bakhtin called the "material bodily principle."

**Iconoclasm and Social Disorder.** Most mainstream Protestant reformers were vehement in their denunciation of the veneration of relics, images, and liturgical objects that lay at the heart of medieval devotion, but they rarely supported popular efforts to purify religious space by removing, breaking, or defacing idolatrous images such as statues, paintings, or stained glass in local churches. In a tract titled *Against the Heavenly Prophets in the Matter of Images and Sacraments* (1525), Luther denounced the iconoclastic excesses of his colleague Bodenstein von Karlstadt (Andreas Rudolf Boden-

stein). He defined his view on the question of images to the great relief of artists, such as Albrecht Dürer, who were otherwise drawn to Reformed teachings. In characteristic fashion Luther drafted a response which emphasized that the war against idols was to be waged by words on the battlefield of the heart and not in the streets and churches of German villages and towns. Later reformers, such as Huldrych Zwingli and John Calvin, were more radical in their denunciation of saints' images, but they still condemned iconoclastic violence as the most egregious expression of social disorder.

**Ritual Violence.** Clerical censure did little to stem the groundswell of popular fury against the idols of the old faith. For many iconoclasts all objects in Catholic churches, from altar lamps and eucharistic chalices to freestanding sculptures and crucifixes, were cultic objects that perpetuated false idols and therefore needed to be purged from the church. Iconoclastic riots, however, were rarely random acts of violence. Most emulated elaborate ritual forms, deeply embedded in the vocabulary and symbolism of popular culture. Carnival-like processions and inversion rituals, which mocked the liturgical traditions of the medieval church, stripped religious artifacts and images of their sacred power. In sixteenth-century Germany and Switzerland crucifixes as well as saints' relics and images were smashed, dismembered, and in one instance even smeared with cow's blood, to demonstrate that they were merely human creations of wood, metal, or stone. Sometimes, in rituals that mocked judicial rites of judgment, icons were condemned, mutilated, and then executed for their many crimes against the Christian community. In Switzerland and Germany, rioters expressed their frustration with the spiritual economy of medieval Christianity when they explained that the statues they smashed were voracious idols that consumed financial resources that should have been directed toward the sustenance of the poor rather than material maintenance of the Church.

**Musical Traditions.** In their desire to elevate the Word, Protestant reformers also opposed the rich musical traditions of the medieval church. The highly ornamented, contrapuntal motet perfected by Renaissance composers juxtaposed voices against each other, obscuring the text in favor of spectacular vocal splendor and beauty. Moreover, medieval and Renaissance church music was composed in Latin to be sung by trained singers or clerics as part of a liturgy that many Protestant reformers rejected. Sixteenth-century Reformers favored hymns in the vernacular, often drawn directly from biblical texts such as the Psalms. They were often set to popular drinking songs and lullabies so everyone could easily sing them. Singing, along with sermons, became one of the identifiable features of Reformed liturgy. For more sober Calvinists, the popular provenance of Lutheran hymns and melodies rendered them somewhat suspect. The Psalms of David at the heart of the Calvinist psalter or songbook were a powerful vehicle of the Protestant faith, expressing the certainty of divine protection and providence.

Sources:

Carlos M. N. Eire, *War Against the Idols: The Reformation of Worship from Erasmus to Calvin* (Cambridge & New York: Cambridge University Press, 1986).

Craig Harbison, *The Mirror of the Artist: Northern Renaissance Art in its Historical Context* (New York: Abrams, 1995).

Edward Muir, *Ritual in Early Modern Europe* (Cambridge & New York: Cambridge University Press, 1997).

Bob Scribner, *For the Sake of the Simple Folk: Popular Propaganda for the German Reformation* (Cambridge: Cambridge University Press, 1981).

Lee Palmer Wandel, *Voracious Idols and Violent Hands* (Cambridge: Cambridge University Press, 1995).

## RITUAL AND SPECTACLE

**Art and Spectacle.** During the late Middle Ages, urban ceremonies impressed public events upon the collective memory of the inhabitants of a city. They included processions, royal visits, plays, liturgical celebrations, tournaments, and coronations. Rituals marking pivotal events in the life cycle such as births, marriages, or death bridged the domains of public and private life. These activities defined urban relations, creating social solidarity by reinforcing hierarchical order through gender and social norms. They also often created tensions, making public those who were excluded based upon issues of class, gender, age, or noncitizenship. Rituals modeled behavior, just as courtesy books did, in outlining proper behavior at a meal. During the royal entry of a king into a city the ritual procession mirrored his place in society as he saw it. The plays and art that the city government and social institutions devised, however, could conflict with this representation. Ceremonies required correct performance for ritual efficacy, but control of its representations was difficult to manage and could inflame social discord.

**Church Festivals.** By the fourteenth century public interest in urban events and participation in such spectacles expanded. Their initiators recognized the power, prestige, and economic benefits generated for the city through the employment of the arts, liturgies, and plays in public spectacles. One early example was the feast of Corpus Christi. Pope Urban IV authorized its addition to the church calendar in the thirteenth century. Juliana of Liege promoted this feast day as a result of her visions of the Eucharist, the bread and wine representing Christ's body and blood in the ceremony of the Catholic Mass. During this ceremony these material forms are consecrated, miraculously transubstantiated into Christ's body and blood, and consumed by the congregation. The sight of the consecrated host held up by the priest became a focal point of adoration. Public processions during this celebration (about 21 May to 24 June) grew into elaborate public spectacles and dramatic performances extending over several days. Symbols of power and well-being were created through the public carrying of the host under a canopy. Members of the clergy, craft guilds, and lay confraternities walked in procession together with reliquaries and banners. Figures clothed in costumes, placed before painted scenery on wagons, represented religious stories. The itineraries of these processions reflected spheres of influence, such as powerful family seats or village boundaries. Cycles of plays were frequently performed during this feast in England. Guild and confraternity members took part as actors in plays based upon biblical stories and the lives of the saints. These dramas assisted in the transformation of church ritual from its focus on the mystical body of Christ to public vernacular narratives that clarified the events of his life. The greater role of magistrates and guilds in organizing such events linked secular and sacred life.

**A Belgian Procession.** Festival church processions, known as *ommegangen* in northern Europe, conflated urban spectacle and religious ritual. The German Renaissance artist Albrecht Dürer recorded one such event held at Antwerp on 19 August 1520. His journal entry described the sights, sounds, and artistic creations that accompanied the Assumption of the Virgin procession from the Church of our Lady, as members of the church chapter carried statues of the Virgin Mary and Lord Jesus through the town. As an artist he focused upon beautifully executed biblical scenes, and the themes, costumes, and wagons used for the spectacle. Dürer affirmed the key status given to the guilds of goldsmiths, painters, and sculptors by noting their prominent place in the processional order. Dürer's comment that he could not mention all that he saw indicates how stimulated he was by the spectacle.

Gentile Bellini's *Procession of the Relic of the True Cross*, 1496 (Accademia, Venice)

**Triumphal Entries.** Secular rulers used the symbolic value of saints' feast days in their own processions. In the following example, however, the city of Ghent borrowed these strategies from triumphal entry celebrations. The inhabitants were anxious to win political concessions from Philip the Good, who had recently defeated the city in military engagement. On 23 April 1458, St. George's Day, Philip entered the city. The extensive four-hour program of *tableaux vivant* (silent plays) was devised to gradually induce his favor as he moved from site to site, rather like a chess piece. Painted and woven decorations for such entries were temporary and often did not survive, but in this instance the city based one of their *tableaux vivant* on an extant painting still located in the Church of St. Jan at Ghent. *The Adoration of the Mystic Lamb* (1432) was an altarpiece created by the Flemish artist Jan van Eyck as a private commission for a local family chapel altar. The painted interior of the altarpiece represents a model of an earthly and heavenly paradise with images of God the Father, Christ, and Mary above, and the mystic lamb (Christ) below. The lamb is surrounded by figures representing different social classes, including Christian knights and just judges. By using this image the city suggested a new golden age would occur under the duke's realm. Each knight represented virtues the duke admired and his own role as a defender of the faith. Although their efforts were not successful in thawing the duke's anger, their program became a model for most triumphal entries thereafter. The pageant represents an unusual documentation of how existing art could be used for civic political agendas.

**Urban Celebrations.** Civic festivals in urban cultures, such as in Florence, developed strong associations with local history. The feast day of San Giovanni (St. John the Baptist) on 24 June was gradually transformed into a communal celebration of the republican government. Their rituals were derived from feudal practices and included jousts, dances, and horse races over a period of days. Male brigades participated in competitive equestrian races, known as *armeggerie*, honoring their families and the city government that relied on them. Feudal displays demonstrated the family's wealth and encouraged social alliances and rivalries. Bartolomeo Benci and his four hundred supporters, for example, processed to the home of Marietta degli Strozzi, pulling a contraption twenty yards tall showing the triumph of love under the Benci and Strozzi coats of arms. A more generalized display of power and wealth occurred when the merchants were required to publicly display their priceless things in honor of the saint. Male representatives from each Florentine family were expected to participate in ritual processions honoring the saint. The city streets were filled with people dressed in their fineries. Confraternities (lay organizations of secular men) celebrated the survival of the city from military threat or its peaceful state by making music and dressing as angels as they marched in procession. Feast days such as San Giovanni enabled the government to order city life and maintain its continuity in ritual.

**Print and Pageantry.** The Holy Roman Emperor Maximilian I used the symbolic language of pageantry to immortalize his family and assure the lasting fame of his deeds. Under his instructions, court advisers devised programs for two large series of woodcut prints. He intended to distribute them to members of the urban educated elite. *The Arch of Honor* (circa 1515) woodcut series was designed by Jörg Kölderer and produced at Nuremberg in Albrecht Dürer's workshop. This paper pageant depicted a large triumphal arch based upon Roman architecture, although it was never actually built. Dürer devised ornamentation for it using the symbolic language of Horus Apollo's Greek text (fifth century B.C.E.), translated by the artist's humanist friend Willibald Pirkheimer. Both of them worked on a second project, a *Great Triumphal Chariot*, for a woodcut triumphal procession series that

Item: On the Sunday after Our Lady's Assumption [August 19 1520] I saw the Great Procession from the Church of Our Lady in Antwerp, when the whole town of every craft was assembled, each dressed in his best clothes according to his rank. And all the ranks and guilds had their signs, by which they might be known. In the intervals great costly pole-candles were carried, and their long, old Frankish silver trumpets. There were also in the German fashion many pipers and drummers. All the instruments were loudly and noisily blown and beaten.

I saw the Procession pass along the street, the people being arranged in rows, each man some distance from his neighbor, but the rows close behind one another. There were the goldsmiths, the masons, the painters, the embroiderers, the sculptors, the joiners, the carpenters, the sailors, the fishermen, the butchers, the leatherers, the clothmakers, the bakers, the tailors, the shoemakers—indeed, workmen of all kinds, and many craftsmen and dealers who work for their living. Also the shopkeepers and merchants, and their assistants of all kinds were there. After these came the shooters with guns, bows, and crossbows, and the horsemen and footsoldiers also. Then followed the Watch of the Lord Magistrates. Then came a fine troop all in red, nobly and splendidly dressed. Before them, however, went all the religious orders and the members of some Foundations very devoutly, all in their different robes. A very large company of widows also took part in this procession. They support themselves with their own hands and observe a special rule. They were dressed all from head to foot in white linen garments, made especially for the occasion, very touching to see. Among them I saw some very stately persons. Last of all there came the Chapter of Our Lady's Church with all their clergy, scholars, and treasurers. Twenty persons carried the Virgin Mary with the Lord Jesus, adorned in the costliest manner to the honor of the Lord God. In this procession many delightful things were shown, most splendidly got up. Wagons were drawn along decorated like ships and other traveling stages. Behind them came the company of Prophets in their order, and scenes from the New Testament, such as the Annunciation and the Three Holy Kings on big camels and other rare animals, very well arranged. Also how Our Lady fled to Egypt—very devout, and many other things, which for shortness I omit. At the ends came a great Dragon with St. Margaret and her maidens led by a girdle; she was especially beautiful. Behind her came St. George with his squires, a very handsome knight in armor. In this host also rode boys and maidens most finely and splendidly dressed in the costumes of many lands, representing various saints. From beginning to end the Procession lasted more than two hours before it was gone past our house. And so many things were there that I could never write them all in a book, so I let it alone.

Source: Jane Campbell Hutchison, *Albrecht Dürer: A Biography* (Princeton: Princeton University Press, 1990), pp. 137–138.

was never completed. Pirkheimer's letter and Dürer's presentation drawing outlining their plans suggest that they relied on the medieval literary genre known as the *Mirror for Princes* that described the ideal virtues of a ruler. Maximilian's death prevented the completion of the second project, but the *Arch of Honor* was produced and distributed by his grandson Archduke Ferdinand.

Sources:
Barbara A. Hanawalt and Kathryn L. Reyerson, eds., *City and Spectacle in Medieval Europe* (Minneapolis: University of Minnesota, 1994).

Richard C. Trexler, *Public Life in Renaissance Florence* (Ithaca, N.Y.: Cornell University Press, 1980).

Barbara Wisch and Susan Scott Munshower, *Art and Pageantry in the Renaissance and Baroque*, volume 1, *Triumphal Celebrations and the Rituals of Statecraft* (University Park: Pennsylvania State University, 1990).

## SACRED ART

**Monastic Communities.** During the late Middle Ages, monastic communities brought the devout closer to images of salvation by revealing paths to the discovery of God. These monasteries, friaries, and nunneries were indispensable centers of urban education. Through sermons and the liturgy, and the commissioning of religious art, they helped preserve religious norms and values. Monks and nuns were living examples of the personal struggle for perfection through prayer and meditation. The powerful stimulus of sacred images generated tension and ambiguity in their interpretation by the unlettered. For example, the second of the ten commandments prohibited the worship of images. Rather than serving as a permeable screen through which the divine was accessed, the image might be worshiped directly. According to Saint Thomas Aquinas these images instructed the ignorant and illiterate, stimulated devotion, and reminded one of the precepts of the church. As creators of religious art, painters knew what their objectives were. The viewer was encouraged to examine their life and reform it. During the fourteenth and fifteenth centuries the transformation of devotional culture stimulated the desire for intimacy with the divine by the laity. Prayers were directed to Christ, Mary, and the saints rather than to God the

One Good Friday, as the said creature beheld priests kneeling and other worthy men with torches burning in their hands before the Easter Sepulchre, representing the lamentable death and doleful burying of our Lord Jesus Christ according to the good custom of Holy Church, the memory of our Lady's sorrows, which she suffered when she beheld his precious body hanging on the cross and then buried before her eyes, suddenly filled the heart of this creature. Her mind was drawn wholly into the Passion of our Lord Christ Jesus, whom she beheld with her spiritual eye in the sights of her soul as truly as if she had seen his precious body beaten, scourged and crucified with her bodily eye, which sight and spiritual beholding worked by grace so fervently in her mind, wounding her with pity and compassion, so that she sobbed, roared and cried and, spreading her arms out wide, said with a loud voice, "I die, I die," so that many people were astonished at her, and wondered what was the matter with her. And the more she tried to keep herself from crying, the louder she cried, for it was not in her power to take it or leave it, but as God would send it. Then a priest took her in his arms and carried her into the Prior's Cloister to let her get the air, supposing she would not otherwise have lasted, her affliction was so great. Then she turned all blue like lead, and sweated dreadfully.

Margery Kempe sees a pieta at a church in Norwich.

There was also a lady who wanted to have the said creature to a meal. And therefore, as decency required, she went to the church where this lady heard her service, and where this creature saw a beautiful image of our Lady called a pieta. And through looking at the pieta her mind was wholly occupied with the Passion of our Lord Jesus Christ and with the compassion of our Lady, St. Mary, by which she was compelled to cry out very loudly and weep very bitterly, as though she would have died.

Then the lady's priest came to her, saying, "Woman, Jesus is long since dead."

When her crying had ceased, she said to the priest, "Sir, his death is as fresh to me as if he had died this same day, and so, I think, it ought to be to you and to all Christian people. We ought always to remember his kindness, and always think of the doleful death that he died for us."

Then the good lady, hearing what she had said, declared, "Sir, it is a good example to me, and to other people also, the grace that God works in her soul."

Source: Margery Kempe, *The Book of Margery Kempe*, translated by B. A. Windeatt (Harmondsworth, U.K.: Penguin, 1985; New York: Viking/Penguin, 1985), pp. 178–179, 186–187.

Father. Representations of the Virgin nursing, the *Madonna lactans,* emphasized her human qualities and accessibility to the laity's prayers.

**Visualizing Devotion.** In urban communities the mendicant orders played a critical role in making the divine tangible through their missions of preaching and conversion. The Franciscans and Dominicans exercised a more-prominent role locally by assisting at burials and hearing confessions. Local congregations responded with charitable donations enabling the construction of larger churches and monastic centers. Ties between the secular world and sacred time were constantly brought to mind by the bells calling people to prayer four times a day. Public preaching in the city square on important feast days renewed these ties. Lay confraternities—dedicated to penitence, prayers, and good works—dissolved the separation of religious and secular life as well. Paintings and prints of saints, such as Francis and Catherine of Siena, exemplified the devotional life for the devout. Both of these saints, through prayer and visions, had received the stigmata (visible signs of Christ's wounds in his hands, feet, and side) as marks of their piety and sanctity. Giovanni di Paolo's painting

*The Stigmatization of St. Catherine of Siena* (1461) represents the saint in her Dominican habit with a golden halo. Her direct mystic access to Christ is shown through her gaze directed toward the vision of the crucified Christ suspended over the altar. The stigmata she received affirmed her sanctity. The Catholic Church frowned upon representations of this event from her life, however, even after she was officially declared a saint. This policy suggests its concern about how her vision would be interpreted and modeled by female devotees. The potential for unmediated access to the divine was problematic for the institutional church.

**Convents and Patronage.** During the fifteenth century a growing population of nuns also petitioned for salvation of the lay community through their prayers. Like the monastic orders, they commissioned painting cycles and initiated building campaigns with gifts from the urban elite. Often daughters of these families were members of wealthier nunneries. Monasteries also cultivated patronage, allowing patrons such as Cosimo de' Medici to stay in guest housing available for spiritual retreats. Religious images—placed in chapter houses, eating halls, and cells for instruction and contempla-

Giovanni di Paolo's *The Stigmatization of St. Catherine of Siena,* 1461 (Metropolitan Museum of Art, New York, Robert Lehman Collection, 1975.I.34)

tion—supported the devotional life. These images were especially important in cultivating the culture of prayer, by helping the viewer to visualize withdrawal from the physical world. Fra Angelico (Guido di Pietro), a Dominican monk and Italian painter at the convent of San Marco, encouraged his fellow monks to mentally place themselves with recent saints, who were depicted beneath the crucified image of Christ in his frescoes.

**Church Spaces.** Cathedrals and parish churches were a focal point of urban life for the laity. The cathedral, as the bishop's administrative seat, included memorials and tombs dedicated to prominent members of the community such as poets, artists, and military leaders. The local parish church played a role as a place for guild and family chapels and confraternity meetings. Endowments for the construction and maintenance of these chapels led to a privatization of church space and decoration. A family had the power to have their own chaplain offer memorial services and place their coat of arms on the altarpiece—a public display of its wealth, piety, and reputation. Family tombs were often constructed before a person's death, but public rites of mourning

and memorial services renewed a family's obligations. As a record of the deceased's achievements and a reminder to pray for their soul, the appearance of the tomb reflected family honor. A good death was memorialized through the monument. Ceremonial burial requirements for women were not as elaborate, with emphasis placed on the woman's role as a good mother. Giovanni Tornabuoni, a Florentine banker, had his daughter-in-law—who died in childbirth—buried beside his own wife in their choir chapel at Santa Maria Novella. He commissioned portraits of both women for the embroidered altar cloth of the chapel, thus demonstrating their devout characters prominently.

**Mass and Ritual Devotion.** The church structure was divided into public spaces accessible to the laity, private spaces for families, and those reserved for the clergy's use. The central axis or nave was the main public space for the congregation. The priest celebrated the mass commemorating Christ's sacrifice for mankind at the high altar located at the east end of the nave. Painted or sculpted altarpieces placed on the altar formed the focal point of ritual devotion. Liturgical objects used by the priest clarified the events of the mass. The congregation viewed the ceremony while standing, kneeling, and reciting special prayers. Wealthy congregants could follow along in their prayer books, known as Books of Hours. Some pages depicted their owners attending mass while housed in temporary curtained structures near the altar, indicating their ability to access the divine. These structures sometimes included other works of art, such as a painted image of the patron kneeling before the image of Christ and Mary. Public fascination with witnessing the miracle of transubstantiation (when the host is transformed into the body of Christ) led religious leaders to write about proper decorum in partaking of the Eucharist. For instance, Church officials frowned on the behavior of following the service from church to church to witness the transubstantiation.

**The Church Calendar.** During the liturgical year ritual ceremonies taught the congregation the key religious events of Christ's and the Virgin Mary's life. The emotional impact of these rituals was recorded by Margery of Kempe after her visit to the Easter Sepulchre at St. Margaret's Church. The ritual enactment of Christ's burial and resurrection in some instances included a figure of Christ that could be taken down from his cross and placed in the tomb. Margery spoke of her emotional response to Christ's passion through her "spiritual eye," but on other occasions she mentioned the vivid effects that the visual images had on her emotions and memory. Although churchgoers were directed to give their primary attention to God and Christ, the wealth of images, liturgical objects, and monuments created an environment of overwhelming effect, allowing the devout to model their own patterns of religious devotion.

Sources:

Henk van Os, and others, *The Art of Devotion in the Late Middle Ages in Europe, 1300–1500*, translated by Michael Hoyle (Princeton: Princeton University Press, 1994).

Evelyn Welch, *Art and Society in Italy, 1350–1500* (Oxford & New York: Oxford University Press, 1997).

## SCULPTURE

**Workshops.** Sculpture workshops were operated by independent masters or as part of a larger building campaign for structures such as cathedrals. Thus, training practices, in which an apprentice learned under a master, focused upon developing a uniform style of production. The types of work produced could vary greatly in material (stone, wood, terracotta, wax, or bronze) and in scale. They included such figures as life-size statues of saints, equestrian monuments of military leaders, crucifixes, tomb effigies, portrait busts, and altarpieces. Small objects such as commemorative metals, statuettes, decorative works, or inexpensive religious objects were also produced in certain shops.

**Stone Carving.** Artists worked in stone that had been quarried and shipped as a rough stone block to their workshops. Their assistants began the process of shaping the block by studying a three-dimensional model, drawing, or print provided by the master. A series of points marked on the figure model would be transferred to the large block for orientation. As the figural form emerged, the sculptor changed tools from drills and pointed chisels to those that helped him subtly refine the form. Application of pumice smoothed the stone surface, which was then polished to a smooth luster.

**Wood Carving.** Wood sculptures were carved from the trunks of trees. To stabilize the changes in moisture and humidity of the carved form, sculptors sometimes hollowed out the back of the figure. They also worked carefully with the grain of the wood. Some sculptures were painted or polychromed to create lifelike effects, after preparing the surface with gesso or gesso painted over fine linen material. Artists such as Dutch sculptor Claus Sluter sometimes added realistic details such as metal spectacles or a leather belt to his Old Testament prophet figures. Wooden sculptures of Christ that included movable arms were used in church rituals reenacting his burial and resurrection from the dead. By the sixteenth century the debates about the relationship between religious art and idolatry led in Reformation Germany to the abandonment of polychromy in new altarpieces, which left the limewood material exposed.

**Changing Status.** In Italy, sculptors were initially connected with the role of crafts or the mechanical arts. For instance, in Nanni di Banco's relief for the Wood and Stone Workers' Guild at Or San Michele in Florence (circa 1416), the sculptor's studio depicts craftsmen working on designing capitals and columns as well as a nude figure. The gradual evolution in the status of sculptors was tied to the development of theoretical treatises that associated sculpture with the liberal arts. Leon Battista Alberti's *De Statua* (circa 1464), composed in Latin, established a theoretical foundation by examining the motivations for the creation of likenesses in three-dimensional forms. Alberti drew a distinction between modelers who added or took away material and sculptors who revealed the figure hidden within the marble block. A debate about which art was most admirable among painting, poetry, music, and sculpture continued throughout the Renaissance. Although Leonardo da Vinci was both a painter and a sculptor, he concluded that sculpture was a mechanical art rather than a science. For Michelangelo, who was deeply influenced by Neoplatonist philosophy in his art and poetry, a gulf always remained between spirit and matter with the artist's struggle to release the image contained within.

Sources:

John T. Paoletti and Gary M. Radke, *Art in Renaissance Italy* (Upper Saddle River, N.J.: Prentice Hall, 1997).

Michelangelo's *Pietà*, commissioned in 1497 and completed around 1500 (St. Peter's Basilica, Vatican City)

Rudolf Wittkower, *Sculpture: Processes and Principles* (London: Allen Lane, 1977).

## THEATER

**Church and Spectacle.** For most of the later Middle Ages the church was an important locus for theatrical performance. Celebration of the Eucharist, the centerpiece of Catholic liturgy, was itself a kind of theater that dramatized the miracle of transubstantiation for the faithful. During the high holy days of the Christian calendar, choirboys, novitiates, and monks often staged processions and plays. In the French city of Beauvais, for example, choirboys staged plays at Christmastide, replete with fanciful singing and dancing sequences reminiscent of the riotous processions led by young novices during Feast of Fools and May celebrations. While medieval bishops protested from time to time about such "*inhonesti ludi*" (dishonorable plays) and pastimes, they did little to stop theatrical performances, which remained an integral part of the festal culture of Europeans until the Reformation. Lay performers also staged plays, invariably about religious themes, in churches and churchyards. Between 1399 and 1550 the most popular play performed in Lincoln Cathedral in England was titled "The Coronation of the Virgin."

**Guilds and Corpus Christi Plays.** Medieval and early modern townspeople were treated to a whole range of theatrical spectacles from royal entries to Corpus Christi processions of the host, which celebrated the conflation of the body, sacred and social. In northern England, towns with strong governments and trade guilds also sponsored Corpus Christi play cycles, which related the biblical history of the universe from Creation to the Day of Judgment. Guilds and confraternities laid claim to particular biblical stories, which were performed on a mobile stage or pageant wagon along traditional processional routes at prearranged stops or stations. Throughout much of northern Europe, mystery-play cycles were an important feature of the religious and civic life of urban communities. During the six Sundays leading up to Easter some towns staged Passion plays. Local townspeople acted in the plays and designed costumes and sets. In the French city of Orléans, a surviving text of the play "The Siege

A Corpus Christi procession depicted in a late-fifteenth-century manuscript (National Szecheny Library, Budapest)

of Orléans" commemorated the redemption of the French from the English during the Hundred Years' War (1337–1453). Although it is not clear if this play was ever actually performed, it was common practice for playwrights to mix religious narrative and local history. In the mid sixteenth century Corpus Christi or mystery-play cycles fell out of fashion, especially in Protestant regions where reformers abolished the Corpus Christi feast and attacked popular festivities that had been a vibrant part of medieval religious culture.

**Household Productions.** Aristocratic and royal households were also an important locus of dramatic productions. Court artists, such as Leonardo da Vinci, were drafted to stage theatrical entertainments, masques, and spectacles. Other household retainers were also pressed into service as entertainers. Chaplains were often literate musicians and singers who helped stage entertainments for their aristocratic patrons. Female actors, forbidden on the public stage, had the freedom to perform in masques at court, where courtiers and even royals themselves disported on stage for entertainment. Most household productions were ephemeral stage pieces, making use of local history, topical events, and figures to amuse elite audiences, and few actual scenarios have survived. By the sixteenth century some household troupes in England began to tour, dressed in livery of their patron. Between 1530 and 1580 at least fifty theatrical troupes toured England under the aegis of a noble patron. Many of the leading patrons of touring companies in mid-sixteenth-century England—such as the Duchess of Suffolk and the Earl of Leicester—were keen advocates of Protestantism who used their troupes to win popular consent for religious reform.

**Humanism and the Theater.** Influenced by their humanist training, many early reformers embraced drama as a medium of religious instruction, edification, and pro-

paganda. Humanist-educators, such as the Dutchman Desiderius Erasmus and the Spaniard Juan Luis Vives, regarded drama as an important adjunct to the academic disciplines of rhetoric and oratory, which cultivated persuasive skills needed for leadership in the reformed Christian state. One of the most eloquent expressions of this pedagogical interest in drama can be found in the German theologian Martin Bucer's treatise on social and educational reform, *De Regno Christi* (1551), dedicated to the young Edward VI of England. In a chapter titled "De Honesti Ludis," Bucer defended drama as an effective tool to promote piety and moral character as long as the dramatists were themselves religious men whose plays promoted "faith in God." Bucer's inspiration may well have been the many Protestant ministers-cum-playwrights in England, who were linked to a nationwide system of Protestant patronage. Under Thomas Cromwell's patronage, John Bale, a former Carmelite friar, wrote more than a dozen virulently anti-Catholic plays (as the title, *The Knaveries of Thomas Becket,* suggests) promoting the Crown's religious policies and performing them with his own troupe. Lesser playwrights such as Thomas Ashton, a Protestant schoolmaster from Shrewsbury, wrote moralistic plays that drew audiences of some ten thousand people.

**Reformation Opposition.** By the mid sixteenth century growing opposition to the theater in Calvinist circles coincided with growth of the commercial stage. In London the new public playhouses, situated beyond the jurisdiction of municipal authorities, were increasingly associated with moral degeneracy, social disorder, and disease. At the same time, religious reformers engaged in a potent critique of the public theater as a kind of antichurch that encouraged the faithful to profane the Sabbath and gratify their senses. The common practice of boys playing female roles was attacked as a dangerous blurring of sexual distinctions that bordered on transvestitism. In some English cities, funds, which had been set aside for civic religious drama, were diverted toward preachers and prophecy conferences. In Catholic countries and missions, the Jesuits continued to use drama as an instrument of moral instruction and religious training.

**Commedia dell'Arte.** Until the fifteenth century, theatrical entertainers employed by the princely courts in Italy combined songs with satirical verses and jokes, much like modern vaudeville. The rediscovery of the plays of Titus Maccius Plautus, Terence, and other Roman playwrights prompted humanists to reintroduce classical standards of drama that relied much more heavily upon a narrative structure and plot. This *commedia erudita* (elite comedy) found ready patrons among the cultured and princely elite in Ferrara, Urbino, and Venice. It also influenced, and was in turn influenced by, popular theater, such as *commedia dell'arte,* an improvisational form of theater that snubbed authority by exposing the implicit paradoxes of the rigid social codes of society. Professional troupes composed plays from a stock of scenarios or commonplace books of soliloquy and witty exchanges while adapting plays to target local audiences and current events. The actors' improvisations followed precise social and literary codes that allowed the spectators to identify generic characters, such as the archetypal master, often christened Pantalone, and his canny servant, Zani. Many of the actors also wore masks in imitation of Roman drama. This device allowed some actors to double parts, but most actors developed an expertise for playing one particular character. *Commedia dell'arte* often positioned young lovers (traditionally unmasked) against the marital designs of their fathers. Like modern musical theater (and Greek and Roman farces on which *commedia dell'arte* was based), actors were expected to entertain audiences with juggling and acrobatic routines and musical and balletic interludes. Exported in the seventeenth century to northern Europe, Italian drama—high and low—profoundly influenced the dramatic structure employed by the seventeenth-century court playwrights such as Molière.

Sources:

Richard Andrews, *Scripts and Scenarios: The Performance of Comedy in Renaissance Italy* (Cambridge & New York: Cambridge University Press, 1993).

John D. Cox and David Scott Kastan, eds., *A New History of Early English Drama* (New York: Columbia University Press, 1997).

Paul Whitfield White, *Theatre and Reformation: Protestantism, Patronage, and Playing in Tudor England* (New York: Cambridge University Press, 1993).

## WOODCUTS

**Printed Images and Books.** Most histories of printed images begin with Johannes Gutenberg's invention of the printing press in the fifteenth century, but printing textiles from woodblocks was a technique that dates back to the sixth century. In the later Middle Ages woodblocks were widely used to reproduce religious images that were hand-colored and sold to the public. Fourteenth- and fifteenth-century woodcuts were usually single-sheet prints, but the production of picture books known as block books were an important craft in

A a scene from the Annunciation in the fifteenth-century Dutch block book *Biblia Pauperum* (Bible of the Poor; British Library)

the Lowlands. One of the most popular block books was the *Biblia Pauperum* (*Bible of the Poor*) in which New Testament scenes were inscribed in the middle of an architectural frame surrounded by Old Testament images and explanatory text. Eleven editions of the *Biblia Pauperum* were printed in the fifteenth century. Members of the minor clergy were often the intended audience for such editions. Other block books include manuals on the art of dying, the Apocalypse, and medieval parables. In Germany, woodcut prints were also used on cards expressing New Year's wishes.

**Printing Techniques.** Woodcuts were produced by a relief process in which a drawing traced on smooth wood was carved away to leave the dominant lines of the figure being depicted. The block was inked and printed with a reverse image. The sturdy qualities of this technique allowed for large quantities of prints to be produced. Printers employed professional block-cutters to produce these images in wood. Graphic artists usually supplied the designs. Nuremberg artist Albrecht Dürer produced many inexpensive religious woodcuts with traditional medieval markets in mind. In the late 1490s he revised the images devoted to the traditional subjects of the Passion and Apocalypse with new techniques and stylistic innovations that created greater pictorial effect through large-scale prints. These woodcuts were intended for a less literate audience, and his thematic choices recognized popular interests. He pioneered new technical innovations in the intaglio proc of engraving on metal plates as well. These engravi

were directed at a highly educated humanist audience that was developing an interest in collecting prints.

**Innovations and Technology.** In the late fifteenth century, artists such as Israhel van Meckenem and Martin Schongauer were developing reputations as skilled engravers. Engraved prints required more careful work than the woodcut. Both material and labor costs were more demanding and expensive. Engraved work by goldsmiths and artisans on such items as plates, armor, and mortuary monuments were related to intaglio practices. Early engravings competed with manuscript illuminations for collectors' attentions. Sometimes they were pasted in books in place of manuscript illuminations. In a similar fashion, woodcuts were an inexpensive substitute for paintings and were pasted on walls and domestic furnishings. In the fifteenth and sixteenth centuries woodcuts remained a popular medium of book illustration, but the technological potential of engraving for printing illustrated books advanced the communication revolution inherent in the invention of the press. This advance was another major feature in the internationalization of artistic language and humanist culture.

Sources:

Charles D. Cuttler, *Northern Painting From Pucelle to Bruegel: Fourteenth, Fifteenth, and Sixteenth Centuries* (New York: Holt, Rinehart & Winston, 1968).

Jane Campbell Hutchison, *Albrecht Dürer: A Biography* (Princeton: Princeton University Press, 1990).

John Rowlands and Giulia Bartrum, *The Age of Dürer and Holbein: German Drawings 1400–1500* (Cambridge & New York: Cambridge University Press, 1988).

# SIGNIFICANT PEOPLE

## PIETER BRUEGEL THE ELDER

### CIRCA 1524-1569
### PAINTER

**Early Activities.** Pieter Bruegel the Elder was born circa 1524 in the vicinity of Breda, the Netherlands. His activities as a painter and draftsman may be dated to 1551 when he became a member of the Antwerp Guild of St. Luke. His initial training was in the workshop of Pieter Coeck van Aelst, whose daughter he later married. Bruegel's paintings reflect his familiarity with Jan van Amstel's work, particularly in the technique of painting with diluted colors that allowed the underpainting of the canvas to show through. Shortly after becoming a master in the St. Luke's Guild, Bruegel traveled to Italy (circa 1551–1554), perhaps with the painter Maerten de Vos. Scholars have attempted to identify their travel route based upon Bruegel's landscape studies that appear to include scenes of southern Italy. By 1555 he returned to Antwerp to create drawings for a print series known as the Large Landscapes, which was published by Coeck. These naturalistic depictions of alpine and Netherlandish landscape scenes gave new prominence to this subject. From 1555 to 1563 Bruegel created more than forty drawings for diverse prints produced at Coeck's shop, "At the Four Winds."

**Religious Scenes.** After his marriage Bruegel moved to Brussels, where he spent the remainder of his career until his death in 1569. The earliest paintings of his extent work include the *Netherlandish Proverbs* (1559), as well as the *Battle between Carnival and Lent* (1559). Bruegel's interpretations of folkloric traditions had a strong impact on later Flemish painting. In the *Battle Between Carnival and Lent*, for instance, two scenes from carnival plays are included. The "Wedding of Mopsus and Nisa," also known as the "Dirty Bride," reappears in an unfinished woodblock intended for a separate woodcut print on this same theme. Bruegel's religious and political views may not be directly expressed in his work, although scholars have applied such meanings to his later paintings, such as *Dulle Griet* or *Mad Meg* (circa 1562) and *The Triumph of Death* (circa 1562). One reason is that his patrons included wealthy collectors such as merchants, businessmen, and scholars with divergent views. Cardinal Granville, Archbishop of Mechelen and councillor to Margaret of Parma, owned *The Flight into Egypt* (1563). Abraham Ortelius, a cartographer and humanist friend of the painter, owned *The Death of the Virgin* (1574). Ortelius, like the Antwerp printer Christopher Plantin, may have been a member of the Family of Love, a secret semireligious organization that promoted peace among people of diverse faiths. Antwerp banker Nicolaas Jonghelinck's collection of Bruegel works included a series painted for his residence. The five surviving paintings depict peasants at labors specific to the seasons and the shifting light and colors of northern landscapes. The *Wheat Harvest* (1565), located at the Metropolitan Museum of New York, is one such example.

**Peasant Paintings.** During the last four years of his life Bruegel also produced paintings of peasant celebrations. The *Peasant Dance* (1568) and *Peasant Wedding* (circa 1568) have been the focus of discussion about the painter's response to peasant culture and the accuracy of his depiction of it. Karl van Mander's *Lives of the Illustrious Netherlandish and Germanic Painters* (1604) is the primary biography of Bruegel's life. The author created an anecdotal portrait of the painter by mentioning his visits to peasant weddings and fairs and praising his ability to copy nature. A representative understanding of his career has been hampered by the fact that two-thirds of his surviving work (approximately thirty paintings) were created during the last six years of his life. Van Mander mentioned that Bruegel had his wife destroy many drawings out of remorse or fear of repercussions because of the sharp tone of their inscriptions.

Sources:

Maryan W. Ainsworth and Keith Christiansen, eds., *From Van Eyck to Brueghel: Early Netherlandish Painting in the Metropolitan Museum of Art* (New York: Metropolitan Museum of Art, 1998).

James Snyder, *Northern Renaissance Art: Painting, Sculpture, and the Graphic Arts from 1350 to 1575* (New York: Abrams, 1985).

Jane Turner, ed., *The Dictionary of Art* (New York: Grove, 1996).

# DONATELLO

## CIRCA 1386-1466
### SCULPTOR

**Early Career.** Donatello, born in Florence around 1386, was the son of a wool-carder. A leading sculptor in the early Renaissance, his work was noted for its versatility in conveying human drama. He was a friend of the humanist theorist Leon Battista Alberti and architect Filippo Brunelleschi. Donatello traveled to Rome with Brunelleschi, but the date of their trip is disputed. Both men had a strong interest in classical antiquity. Donatello's work demonstrated his understanding of Roman portrait sculpture as well as the heroic nude. Donatello was trained as a goldsmith in the workshop of Lorenzo Ghiberti, where the bronze reliefs for the doors of the Florence Baptistery were being developed. His early work included commissions of guild saints for San Michele in Florence (1411–1414). Among these was a statue of St. Mark for the Linen Drapers' Guild and a statue of St. George for the Armorers' Guild. The poses of these figures created a sense of animation through their weight shift and gestures. The marble St. George wore a metal helmet and sword provided by the guild. The finely carved relief, showing the slaying of a dragon by St. George, marked new developments in conveying the optical experience of distance. Donatello also began carving marble statues of two prophets for the bell tower niches of the Cathedral of Florence in 1415. These figures were based upon antique statues of Roman senators. The gilt bronze reliquary (a container for sacred relics) for the head of St. Rossore, an early Christian martyr, was cast for the friars of Ognisanti in Florence in 1422. This soldier-saint had been decapitated for his faith. Donatello's interpretation gave the sculpture of the saint a distinct personality, derived from the traditions of the Roman portrait bust. Many of his sculptures demonstrated his ability to reinvent classical forms or to challenge conventions of representation by fresh interpretations of standard subject types.

**Classical Interpretations.** Donatello's influence spread beyond Florence. He worked in Pisa, Rome, and Padua as well. The large bequest of funds from a merchant enabled the friars of the Santo (the basilica of St. Anthony) to commission a new high altar in bronze (1447–1448). This elaborate altar included six life-size standing figures of patron saints surrounding the Virgin and Christ Child. Several of the bronze relief scenes record the *Miracles of St. Anthony*. In one instance, a man's donkey is shown kneeling in adoration of the host as the saint celebrates mass. In another, St. Anthony reattaches the foot that a son had cut off in penance for insulting his mother. These examples encouraged lay devotion by choosing events from hagiography rather than the Bible. While at Padua, Donatello made a bronze equestrian statue of Erasmo da Narni, the former captain-general of the Venetian army. The general's wife and son sponsored the commission (1447–1453) for the public square outside the Santo. Donatello based his interpretation of the general on horseback from the tradition of public Roman equestrian monuments. Erasmo, known by his nickname *Gattamelata,* was shown as a model warrior rather than an individual personality. The general's gesture of authority and his control over his horse modeled the ideal of a military leader.

**Civic Statues.** Two commissions Donatello executed for the Medici family in the 1460s represented the civic virtues that formed part of the Florentine ethos. The dating of the bronze *David* has been disputed because the work is undocumented, but it was displayed on a pedestal in the Medici palace courtyard for the wedding of Piero de' Medici's son in 1469. Donatello's *David* is the first freestanding bronze nude of the Italian Renaissance. Its use of nudity for a biblical hero is also rare. Scholarly opinions have linked the work with Florentine traditions, where David was a symbol of the city; others have suggested it is more closely related to the Neoplatonic ideals of the Medici philosophical academy. David's nudity represented the ideals of heavenly love. The bronze statue of *Judith and Holofernes* (1455–1460) may have been intended as a fountain sculpture for the Medici garden. A lost but recorded inscription by Piero de' Medici stated, "Piero, son of Cosimo, had dedicated the statue of this woman to that liberty and fortitude bestowed on the republic by the invincible and constant spirit of its citizens." Cosimo, the father of Piero, was a generous patron to Donatello and ensured that he would receive a pension from the family in his old age. He also requested that the artist be buried in the Medici family tomb at San Lorenzo near Cosimo.

Sources:

Bonnie A. Bennett and David G. Wilkins, *Donatello* (Oxford: Phaidon, 1984).

Roberta J. M. Olson, *Italian Renaissance Sculpture* (London: Thames & Hudson, 1992).

Joachim Poeschke, *Donatello and His World: Sculpture of the Italian Renaissance,* photographs by Albert Hirmer and Irmgard Ernstmeier-Hirmer, translated by Russell Stockman (New York: Abrams, 1993).

Jane Turner, ed., *The Dictionary of Art* (New York: Grove, 1996).

# ALBRECHT DÜRER

## 1471-1528
### PAINTER AND PRINTMAKER

**German Roots.** Albrecht Dürer was born on 21 May 1471 in Nuremberg, the third of eighteen children. He began his training as a goldsmith in his father's workshop but persuaded his father to allow him to apprentice with Michael Wolgemut, a local painter and designer of woodcut book-illustrations. Wolgemut's shop created works for Anton Koberger, Dürer's godfather, and a prestigious printer and editor. After completing his apprenticeship, Dürer traveled (1490–1494) and visited notable artists and publishing centers at Colmar, Basel, and Strasbourg, while employing his skills as a print designer. He married Agnes Frey, the daughter of a local well-to-do artisan, upon his return but left several months later when the plague broke out in Nuremberg. During that trip to Venice (1494–1495) he created some of the first autonomous watercolors depicting landscapes and architectural settings. Upon his return he concentrated on the production of woodcuts and engravings. Dürer acted as his own publisher for the *Apocalypse* series, produced in 1498, using the typefaces of Kolberger. The combination of the printing press and oil-based ink had made books more widely available to upper-middle-class readers during Dürer's lifetime, and he was able to shape the tastes of his public and to select his images and subject matter with great freedom.

**Commissions.** A second trip to Venice from 1505 to 1507 resulted in a commission to paint *The Madonna of the Rosegarlands* (1506) for the German merchants of the Confraternity of the Rosary. Dürer writes of the new respect he obtained from the Venetian community in letters to his humanist friend Willibald Pirkheimer. He recognized the elevated status that artists had in Italy and wished to obtain these benefits in his home country. His choice of subjects, such as Adam and Eve, enabled him to incorporate his understanding of the classical nude in his engravings. Dürer's choice of themes and medium (woodcut or engraving) reflected his awareness of his audience and their resources in the marketing of his prints. He painted portraits of the emperors Charlemagne and Sigismund for the Nuremberg city council around 1510–1513. These works were located in a room of a house where the imperial relics and jewels of the Holy Roman Empire were displayed to the citizens. Dürer's altarpiece *The Assumption of the Virgin and Her Coronation by the Holy Trinity*, commissioned by Jakob Heller of Frankfurt am Main, survives only in a copy, but the letters he wrote to his patron record the conflicts he encountered about the cost of his work and his time. He received several major commissions from Emperor Maximilian I, including a multiple-block print series of *The Triumphal Arch* (1515–1517) and *The Triumphal Procession* (1516–1518). In 1520–1521 he traveled with his wife to the Netherlands, recording his experiences in a journal and sketchbook. He devoted his subsequent time to preparing a series of theoretical treatises on human proportion and measurement, which was published in 1527–1528.

**The Artist's Role.** Dürer's position within a nascent print culture functioned at the nexus of developments in which oral and scribal culture both existed. His work expresses some self-consciousness about the role of the artist in the newly developing consumer market among the nobility and educated burghers. He was a member of the humanist circle of Konrad Celtis, the imperial poet laureate. He also frequented a religious study group organized by Martin Luther's mentor, the Augustinian monk and theologian Johann von Staupitz. Dürer had a substantial collection of Luther's writings (1517–1519), which has led to scholarly investigations that attempt to place his work within specific theological views. The fact that Dürer created work for such diverse patrons as Desiderius Erasmus of Rotterdam and Cardinal Albrecht of Brandenberg documents that his personal views did not enter into these arenas.

**Sources:**

Anja-Franziska Eichler, *Albrecht Dürer, 1471–1528,* translated by Fiona Hulse (Cologne: Könemann, 1999).

Jane Campbell Hutchison, *Albrecht Dürer: A Biography* (Princeton: Princeton University Press, 1990).

Joseph Leo Koerner, *The Moment of Self-portraiture in German Renaissance Art* (Chicago: University of Chicago Press, 1993).

# ISABELLA D'ESTE

## 1474-1539
### PATRON OF THE ARTS

**Female Connoisseur.** Isabella d'Este, a notable patron of the arts and collector of antiquities, established the first known *studiolo* (study) created for a woman. The daughter of Ercole d'Este and Eleonora of Aragon, she came from an eminent family of patrons and collectors of art. Giovanni Battista Guarino and Mario Equicola served her as tutors; the latter taught her Latin and became her secretary in 1508. She was an accomplished player on the lute and viol, abilities considered desirable for court ladies. Isabella's marriage to Francesco il Gonzaga, Marchese of Mantua, took place when she was sixteen years old. She bore him seven children, including an heir (Federico II) and a son (Ercole) who became a cardinal. Isabella established her own apartments in the ducal palace, commissioning works for it from notable Italian painters and sculptors. Her studiolo and grotta (treasure chamber) contained a library, marble statuary, paintings, coins, bronzes, and antique gems. As a woman she was exceptional in her ardent competition for antiquities within the public arena. Her apartments and collections were visited frequently during her lifetime and were mentioned often in sixteenth-century guidebooks. Using court practices of patronage, Isabella devised multiple strategies to establish a distinct social personality. This maneuvering allowed her to negotiate the boundaries of gender and social process. One such example may be found in the domain of fashion.

**Fashionable Attire.** Nicolosa Sanuti, a Bolognese aristocrat, disputed the imposition of sumptuary laws establishing dress codes for women in 1453. She argued for the positive values that clothing provided by their differential mark of status and value. Using their creative skills women were able to establish a social personality distinct from the collective identity assigned to wives. Within a patrilineal culture, customs such as the trousseau were means to establish natal or marital ties through the *imprese* (familial symbols) women wore on their public garments. Fashion could be a form of social negotiation setting women apart. D'Este's inventive fashion style was well known. Letters exchanged with her sister, Beatrice d'Este, convey an astute awareness of how clothing facilitated a court lady's self-fashioning. Her agents were instructed to search abroad for the finest quality cloth and to relate new fashion innovations they saw. Francis I requested that she send to Paris a doll clothed in her latest fashions for his court ladies to see. According to Giangiorgio Trissino's *Ritratti* (*Portraits*) of 1524, the gorgeous attire of such ladies was a mark of liberality by which their riches were shared. Physical beauty, in keeping with Platonic ideals, was an outward manifestation of virtue.

**Self-Portraits.** Isabella's portraits, like those of other court ladies, documented her social persona and made the absent present. She rewarded poets and writers with a gold medal depicting her portrait. An inscription on the 1498 medal stated, "for those who do her service." A gem-studded copy was kept on display, together with an antique cameo, in her grotta. Among her most notable portraits was a profile of her with book in hand, drawn by Leonardo da Vinci during his 1499 visit to Mantua. Her pleasure with it is evident from the fact that she had it copied several times—evidently to circulate among court circles. After 1516 she no longer sat for her portrait. Isabella was sixty when she commissioned Titian to paint her portrait in 1534, so he had to base it on earlier paintings. By this time she had moved to new quarters in the ducal palace, where she had a walled garden and a newly constructed studiolo and grotta on the ground floor.

**Courtly Roles.** Even though she was aristocratic, d' Este operated within the conventions and expectations of female rulers. Court ladies were to exemplify piety, learning, virginity or chastity, and fidelity to husband and family. These rules of decorum could result in potential conflict with the public exercise and display of wealth and power. Ladies of the court had their own income and entourage, enabling them to construct and support monasteries, nunneries, and chapels as well as to commission altarpieces, manuscripts, and tapestries. Isabella supported the canonization of local saints and promoted churches and monastic institutions. Desiring to be remembered for her chastity and marital fidelity, she commissioned paintings with themes of females who preserve their reputation and virginity. Although hampered by limited financial resources, she augmented them by purchasing works secondhand rather than commissioning them. In addition, she began to control her own contemporary and posthumous reputation through her patronage of writers, such as Baldassare Castiglione, as well as musicians and artists. In the 1490s she commissioned her court artist, Andrea Mantegna, to

design a monument dedicated to the classical Roman poet Virgil. Unfortunately, the work did not proceed beyond the preliminary stages, but the commission would have made a public statement about her humanist interests.

**Art Collections.** Isabella wanted Mantegna to paint several works for her studiolo as well. The poet Paride da Ceresera and the Venetian humanist Pietro Bembo devised the *invenzione* (programs) for these classical allegories. The artists she chose were not always pleased with the limitations imposed by such detailed programs, but it was not uncommon within her family's Ferrarese patronage traditions. Mantegna produced the *Parnassus* (1497) and *Pallas Expelling the Vices* (circa 1499–1502) before his death. A record of the correspondence and commission for *The Battle of Love and Chastity* (1505) by Pietro Perugino still survives. Isabella's own collection of classical antiquities accorded well with the classical themes of the studiolo paintings. Cesare Borgia gave her an antique statue of Venus and a *Cupid* by Michelangelo executed in an antique style. An antique Greek statue of *Cupid* (circa 330 B.C.E.), attributed to the Athenian sculptor Praxiteles, was purchased from Pope Julius II and displayed with them. She commissioned from the noted sculptor Antico (Pier Jacopo Alari Benacost, circa 1460–1528) copies of antique statues such as the *Apollo Belvedere* (fifth century B.C.E.) by the noted sculptor Antico. The extent and quality of her collection was exceptional for a court lady. An inventory made in 1542 listed 1,620 items, including coins, gems, medals, and vases, as well as more than two hundred books. Her studiolo and its contents attest not only to her abilities to shape the qualities of virtue and magnificence required of a court lady, but also her commitment to self-fashioning her image and reputation.

Sources:

Alison Cole, *Virtue and Magnificence: Art of the Italian Renaissance Courts* (New York: Abrams, 1995).

Diane Own Hughes, "Regulating Women's Fashion," in *A History of Women in the West*, volume 2, *Silences of the Middle Ages*, edited by Christiane Klapisch-Zuber (Cambridge, Mass.: Harvard University Press, 1992), pp. 136–158.

Evelyn Welch, *Art and Society in Italy, 1350–1500* (Oxford & New York: Oxford University Press, 1997).

# LEONARDO DA VINCI

## 1452-1519
### PAINTER, SCULPTOR, AND SCIENTIST

**Court Artist.** Born in the Tuscan town of Vinci, Leonardo da Vinci was the illegitimate son of Ser Piero da Vinci, a notary who eventually established a successful career in Florence. As a child da Vinci was raised in his paternal grandfather's household. Sometime in his late teens he was admitted to the painters' guild in Florence, where he was apprenticed to the sculptor Andrea del Verrocchio (circa 1467–1477). While in Florence he received several civic commissions and began his lifelong studies of mechanics and the natural sciences, which he recorded in his famous notebooks. In the 1480s, da Vinci sought the patronage of Ludovico Sforza, ruler of Milan, whose attention he attracted largely as a consequence of his interest in military engineering and inventions. For the next twenty years Leonardo enjoyed a period of fertile creation in the Sforza court, where the princely ambitions of his patron gave him greater latitude to express his varied interests in the arts, engineering, and science. Like many court artists, he worked on projects that enhanced the political and dynastic program of his patron. He helped stage court spectacles, decorated apartments at the princely residence, the Castello Sforza, and completed an equestrian monument that memorialized Francesco Sforza, the founder of the dynasty. He also collaborated with other court artists and humanists, including the mathematician Luca Pacioli, and drew illustrations for Pacioli's *De divina proportione*, published in Venice in 1509. Da Vinci's first extant notebook, the Codex Trivulziano, dates from this period and reveals his insatiable curiosity in scientific and technical questions as well as humanist pursuits. Three of his most famous paintings were completed during this tenure in Milan. Da Vinci was commissioned by the Confraternity of the Immaculate Conception to paint *The Virgin of the Rocks* (1483). In the 1480s he also began to experiment with wall paintings and completed *The Last Supper* (1495–1497) for the refectory of Sta. Maria delle Grazie. His enigmatic *Portrait of a Lady with an Ermine* (circa 1490) is probably a portrait of Sforza's mistress, Cecilia Gallerani.

**Travels.** In 1499 the French royal army invaded Milan and claimed the duchy for French monarchy, forcing da Vinci to seek refuge briefly in Mantua before returning to Florence to reestablish his career. While in Mantua he drew a portrait of Isabella d'Este, who doggedly pestered him to produce a more formal piece for her collection. He refused to do so. He spent the next eight years working in Urbino, Florence, and other central Italian cities. The painting that is regarded as the central product of these years is the *Mona Lisa* (1503–1506), a portrait of Lisa del Giocondo, the wife of an important figure in the Florentine government. In 1508 the French governor of Milan petitioned the Florentine government to release da Vinci from various civic commissions so that he could continue his career as the most famous court artist in Milan. From 1508 to 1513 he worked in Milan and helped establish the legitimacy of the French regime. His fame as an inventor earned him the attention of Pope Leo X, for whom he completed several military commissions in Rome.

**French Patronage.** It may have been in this capacity as an artist/engineer at the papal court that he attracted the attention of the new king of France, Francis I, who negotiated the Concordat of Bologna with the pope in 1516. A year later da Vinci became "first painter and engineer" to

Francis I, lodged at royal expense at the manor house of Clos-Lucé in Amboise. Shortly after arriving in France, da Vinci suffered a stroke that paralyzed his right side, but his notebooks reveal his unflagging curiosity in science and continuing involvement in courtly entertainments and spectacles. Some art historians have argued that his compositions of a half-length female nude may have influenced the erotic paintings attributed to the school of Fontainebleau. He died in 1519 and was buried in Amboise. Da Vinci's wide-ranging interests in drawing, painting, sculpture, philosophy, mathematics, engineering, and the natural sciences have become synonymous with the term "Renaissance man." Although many of his projects remained unfinished, da Vinci's achievements in several domains simultaneously confirmed the new status of the artist as creative genius in Renaissance society.

Sources:

David Alan Brown, *Leonardo da Vinci: Origins of a Genius* (New Haven: Yale University Press, 1998).

Vincenzo Labella, *A Season of Giants: Michelangelo, Leonardo, Raphael, 1492–1508* (Boston: Little, Brown, 1990).

John T. Paoletti and Gary M. Radke, *Art in Renaissance Italy* (Upper Saddle River, N.J.: Prentice Hall, 1997).

Jane Turner, ed., *Dictionary of Art* (New York: Grove, 1996).

## LIMBOURG BROTHERS

### 1380s-1415

### ILLUMINATORS

**Noble Service.** Renowned for their skill as manuscript illuminators, the Limbourg brothers—Paul, Jean, and Hermann—are most famous for their illuminations in the *Très Riches Heures,* a lavish Book of Hours or prayer book produced for their patron, Burgundian duke and collector Jean de Berry. As young men the Limbourg brothers followed their father, a wood sculptor of some note, and uncle, a painter attached to the French and Burgundian courts, into the artistic trades. It was probably their uncle who influenced the brothers to enter the service of the duke of Burgundy in the early fifteenth century. Between 1405 and 1415 the Limbourgs advanced in the duke's service and eventually were given honorary positions as *valets de chambre* in de Berry's household. Their respected position in the household is clear from the various gifts (jewelry, money, and possibly even a house in Bourges) that they received from the duke. While in the duke's service, the Limbourgs engaged in several artistic projects, including the *Très Riches Heures.* Stylistic evidence suggests that Paul and Jean illustrated a beautiful, illuminated Bible in the duke's possession, and they may have painted panels and frescoes at one of de Berry's castles outside of Paris. They probably also produced many illuminated manuscripts for the duke, whose extraordinary collection of books included fourteen Bibles, sixteen psalters, and fifteen Books of Hours. Unfortunately, few of these works, with the exception of the *Très Riches Heures,* seem to have survived.

**Art of Devotion.** Books of Hours were an essential feature of the devotional lives of lay men and women in the later Middle Ages and Renaissance. Noblewomen, in particular, played a key role in the patronage of Books of Hours, which allowed them to replicate in part the spiritual experience of the cloister or convent without embracing its constraints. By the thirteenth century, Books of Hours were generally composed around a sequence of prayers to the Virgin Mary that were to be recited throughout the course of the entire day in imitation of the daily round of prayers, or Divine Office, recited by priests, monks, and nuns. Calendars, prayers, psalms, and masses for various holy days were also included. These prayers allowed laymen as well as laywomen to access divine power without the mediation of the clergy, protected them from potential physical and spiritual dangers, and sanctified their daily activities. Private and public prayers were an integral feature of courtly life and ritual and encouraged an extensive traffic in the production of Books of Hours. Between 1250 and 1550 more Books of Hours were produced, both by hand and by the printing press, than any other type of book, including the Bible. The popularity of Books of Hours meant that often they were the only kind of art the middle classes owned.

**Personalized Books.** Until the late fifteenth century, when the printing press made it possible to produce inexpensive imitations (in some cases in the vernacular rather than Latin) for the wealthy urban elite, Books of Hours were almost exclusively commissioned and collected by noblemen and women, who prized these illuminated manuscripts for their aesthetic as well as religious value and function. Aristocratic patrons proudly demarcated their ownership of Books of Hours in various ways. Coats of arms, initials, monograms, and personal emblems were engraved in the bindings and incorporated into illuminations. By the fourteenth century recognizable portraits of the donor became an important element in the genre. De Berry had his personal image and sumptuous residences incorporated in various places in his prayer books. In this way Books of Hours became profoundly personal emblems of aristocratic power and prestige.

**Stylistic Choices.** Chaplains, confessors, and priests helped plan the text and illustrations for Books of Hours, but artists and patrons had considerable freedom to tailor prayer books to reflect their own program of religious devotion and interests. The peripatetic de Berry, for example, had the Limbourgs incorporate a special prayer for a safe journey into three of his prayer books. The *Belles Heures,* also attributed to the Limbourgs, contained several pictorial cycles drawn from the golden legend and the story of St. Bruno, the founder of the Carthusian monastic order, which reflected the duke's own interest in monastic devotion. Many of the stylistic and thematic choices that the Limbourgs made in the execution of the *Très Riches Heures* also demonstrate that they were familiar with the work of Italian artists such as Simone Martini, Taddeo Gaddi, and the Lorenzetti brothers at a time when most northern artists were still primarily working from medieval models. Some figures in the *Très Riches Heures* reveal the artists' interest in classical antiquity, which may have been stimulated by the duke's growing collection of medieval and contemporary copies of Roman coins and medals. The Limbourg brothers, however, are primarily known for their mastery of psychological expression and naturalistic detail, clearly revealed in their illuminations for the calendar, in which peasants and nobles carry out the daily and festive activities associated with rhythms of the agricultural year. Considered keen exemplars of the courtly International Style, the Limbourgs' careers were brought short by the plague, which in 1415 killed all three siblings before they were thirty years old.

**Sources:**

Jane Turner, ed., *The Dictionary of Art* (New York: Grove, 1996).

Roger S. Wieck, *Painted Prayers: The Books of Hours in Medieval and Renaissance Art* (New York: Braziller, 1997).

Wieck, ed., *Time Sanctified: The Book of Hours in Medieval Art and Life* (New York: Braziller, 1988).

# MARGERY OF KEMPE

## CIRCA 1373-CIRCA 1440
## LAYWOMAN AND AUTOBIOGRAPHER

**A Fulfilled Life.** Margery of Kempe wrote the first English-language autobiography, commonly known as *The Book of Margery Kempe* (1436–1438), which relates the spiritual aspirations of a bourgeois laywoman through her mystical experiences, pilgrimages, and travels to the Holy Land, Italy, Spain, and Germany. Kempe was born circa 1373 at King's Lynn in Norfolk, England, of middle-class parents. Her father was locally active as mayor of Lynn. She married John Kempe around 1393. By the age of forty she had given birth to fourteen children and negotiated a joint vow of chastity with her husband thereafter. She was active in commercial society, having organized public work, invested capital, and run a brewing business. The last references to her occur in 1438 when she was admitted to the prestigious Guild of the Trinity, and she is mentioned again the following year. The original manuscript of her life has been lost, but it was available at Mount Grace Priory, Yorkshire, in the late Middle Ages, where several local monks added their individual comments in the margins of the text. In 1501 Wynkyn de Worde published excerpts of her book in pamphlet form. The British Library holdings include a fifteenth-century copy of her manuscript.

**Visions Interpreted.** Recent scholarship has revitalized understanding of her text by placing it within fifteenth-century devotional practices that focused upon corporal images of Christ. These images derived from the visual arts and drama. Margery's visions reflected habits of mind that evoked such representations as a form of devotional theater. They showed a pervasive verbal and typological indebtedness to the *Meditationes vitae Christi,* translated by Nicholas Love in 1410. This evidence refutes scholarly opinions that her experiences were aberrant or pathological. Her visions paid tribute to popular late-medieval texts, images, and relics as well as folk ritual magic found in mystery plays. Margery's visions included themes of conception and childbirth. In one she offers to assist St. Anne in the care of the infant Mary. When Mary wrapped her own son, Christ, in swaddling clothes, Margery received permission to do so as well. The associations between Christ's birth and death were made clear to Margery when she saw that Mary used the swaddling clothes to wrap Christ's nude body at his crucifixion. These domestic experiences are made real through Margery's visit to the Lower Church of St. Francis at Assisi where she saw the relic of the Virgin Mary's veil. Further ties with folk ritual practice are evident in her story of a woman traveling to Rome with two Franciscan friars. The woman placed an image of the Christ child on the lap of respectable wives who dress and kiss it, at which Margery was seized with sweet devotions and meditations. This female ritual evoked fruitfulness and protection from the dangers of childbirth through meditations on the events of the Nativity. These examples demonstrate how popular piety and gender informed the creation of and response to religious art.

**Validating Life.** Margery's text has generated scholarly discussion about its relation to the English mystical tradition and saints' lives narratives. More recently, studies have emphasized how her autobiography relates to a search by the urban middle class for a positive and powerful identity in the late Middle Ages. Margery's narrative represents this profound dilemma of searching for spiritual validation while remaining an active member of mercantile society. It also reveals how religious authorities expressed diverse and competing views about female spirituality. Her text provided its own authorization of her claims to sanctity, evading the Church's attempts to control religious experiences. It provided a place for the female laity's experiences to be heard. Ecclesiastical and aristocratic ideologies that privileged withdrawal from the active life were challenged by lay literacy as well as religious and political reform. Margery's behaviors (such as her loud weeping) and the assertive positions outlined in her text are resolved through the affirmations she receives in her conversations with Christ and his mother. These dialogues reinterpret social and religious conventions in ways that reflect the needs of lay piety validating the active life as a means to holiness.

**Mysticism and Hagiography.** The book begins with an account of her spiritual crisis after the birth of her first child, the visions she receives of Christ and the Virgin Mary, and her conversations and interactions with them. Descriptions of her pilgrimages refer to the distrust of orthodoxy she encountered from religious authorities, churchgoers, and pilgrims. The historical figures she met, and their conversations, create a fascinating picture of fourteenth-century English religious culture. For instance, Margery visited the English mystic and recluse Dame Julian of Norwich, to inquire anxiously whether her own experiences were genuine. Her knowledge of the lives of other female mystics, such as Blessed Angela of Foligno (1249–1309) and Dorothea of Montau (1347–1394), clarify their place as role models. Margery's vocabulary demonstrates familiarity with popular fourteenth-century mystic

texts. Throughout the autobiography her descriptions of encounters with ecclesiastical figures and the responses of the priest who served as a scribe for her words affirm that the work is a self-consciously calculated hagiographic text. As a primary source document of a self-proclaimed visionary and mystic her book represents a rare opportunity to study the interaction of popular piety and gender.

**Sources:**

Kathleen Ashley, "Historicizing Margery: The Book of Margery Kempe as Social Text," *Journal of Medieval and Early Modern Studies,* 28 (Spring 1998): 371–388.

Gail McMurray Gibson, *The Theater of Devotion: East Anglican Drama and Society in the Late Middle Ages* (Chicago: University of Chicago Press, 1989).

Margery Kempe, *The Book of Margery Kempe,* translated by B. A. Windeatt (Harmondsworth, U.K: Penguin, 1985; New York: Viking/Penguin, 1985).

# MICHELANGELO

## 1475-1564
### SCULPTOR, PAINTER, ARCHITECT

**Early Years.** Michelangelo, whose full name was Michelangelo di Lodovico Buonarroti Simoni, was born on 6 March 1475 in Caprese and died on 18 February 1564 in Rome, Italy. He was active as a sculptor, painter, architect, and poet during his lengthy career. His initial training was in the workshop of the painter Domenico Ghirlandaio. As a member of Lorenzo de' Medici's household Michelangelo was introduced to the family's antique sculpture collection and the circle of Neoplatonic humanists active there. The *Bacchus* (1496) demonstrates his study of the male nude figure and classical sources. In 1497 Cardinal Villiers gave him a commission for a tomb sculpture. The *Pietà,* or Mary mourning over the death of her son Christ, was uncommon in Italian art. When Michelangelo returned to Florence in 1501, he created a nude figure of the biblical hero *David* (1504). The statue was placed in front of the town hall at Florence as a symbol of civic virtue.

**Religious Art.** In 1505 Michelangelo returned to Rome to work on the tomb of Julius II for St. Peter's Basilica. This work was never completed, as Michelangelo refocused his attention on painting the Sistine Chapel ceiling at the Vatican (1508–1512), a complex thematic program that illustrates the creation cycle in Genesis. The restoration and cleaning of the Sistine ceiling, completed in 1989, led to a major reevaluation of Michelangelo's career as a painter, as scholars reexamined his methods of creating three-dimensional forms with the fresco technique. He completed the papal chapel with a fresco of *The Last Judgement* (1534–1541) located over the main altar. Michelangelo, influenced by the Italian poet Dante, included the figure of the mythological King Minos as the judge of the dead. A self-portrait of Michelangelo can be found on the facial features of a flayed human skin held by St. Bartholomew in the frescoe.

**Architect.** Michelangelo's architectural commissions included several projects in Florence. He designed the funerary chapel for Pope Leo X's Medici ancestors (1519–1534) but was unable to finish the project. Idealized figures of two Medici dukes represented the Active and Contemplative Life; reclining figures of the times of day were placed below. In addition, Michelangelo designed the Laurentian Library for the Medici family's manuscript collection housed at the San Lorenzo cloister. The vestibule, with its unique staircase design, was completed in 1559. These works challenged the stylistic conventions of Renaissance art and are linked to Michelangelo's contribution to the development of Mannerism. By 1546 Michelangelo was appointed chief architect of St. Peter's, his most ambitious architectural project at Rome. He refined and reintegrated the architectural plan of the church into an organic structure.

**Later Years.** During the last decades of his life he returned to the theme of the pietà. The *Duomo Pietà* (circa 1547–1555) was intended for Michelangelo's own tomb, but was completed by others and placed in the Florence Cathedral. According to Italian painter and art historian Giorgio Vasari, the standing figure of Nicodemus, placed behind the collapsed figure of Christ, represented a self-portrait of Michelangelo. His prolific activities in the visual arts had a great impact during the sixteenth century and beyond.

Sources:

George Bull, *Michelangelo: A Biography* (London & New York: Viking, 1995).

Anthony Hughes, *Michelangelo* (London: Phaidon, 1997).

Joachim Poeschke, *Michelangelo and His World: Sculpture of the Italian Renaissance,* photographs by Albert Hirmer and Irmgard Ernstmeier-Hirmer, translated by Russell Stockman (New York: Abrams, 1996).

Jane Turner, ed., *The Dictionary of Art* (New York: Grove, 1996).

# GIORGIO VASARI

## 1511-1574

### PAINTER, ARCHITECT, AND ART HISTORIAN

**A Life of Art.** Giorgio Vasari was born in 1511 in Arezzo, Italy, into a family of tradesmen. He studied in Florence briefly with Michelangelo in 1524 and subsequently trained with Andrea del Sarto. He returned to Florence to work for Duke Cosimo I de' Medici in 1555 and assisted in the foundation of the new art academy, the Academia del Disegno, in 1563. The duke commissioned the architectural design for the Uffizi in 1560 as a building to house all the civic offices, guilds, and Medici court artists. Vasari and his pupils also furnished paintings for the studiolo of Francesco I de' Medici. Located in the Palazzo Vecchio, it was dedicated to the scientific interests of Cosimo's son and successor. Vasari is best known for his *Vite de' più eccelenti architetti, pittori ed scultori italiani* (*Lives of the Most Eminent Painters, Sculptors, and Artists*) published in 1550, and in an enlarged and revised edition in 1568. The book, also identified as *The Lives,* supposedly originated at a dinner party of Cardinal Alessandro Farnese, where Vasari agreed to assist the art collector and biographer Paolo Giovio in writing a treatise on the lives of illustrious artists. Giovio eventually gave Vasari sole responsibility for the text. Vasari used anecdotes or literary conventions (*topoi*) throughout his biographies to illustrate his points. His biographies affirmed the place of virtue in the rise and decline of an individual's fortune. Using anecdotes and epigrams, Vasari created the life of an artist as a moral exemplar. The dedication of *The Lives* to Cosimo acknowledged Vasari's obligation to his patron.

**Artistic Models.** The goal of his book was to raise the status of the artist and establish Tuscany as an artistic center of excellence. The first edition traced the history of art through the individual biographies of artists from antiquity to Michelangelo. Based upon a model of historical progress, his biological cycle of the arts creates three stages of development: childhood, youth, and a golden age. This model precluded emphasis on social and political circumstances related to artistic production. The assessment of quality, style, patronage, sources, and documentation was the criteria for evaluation of art. Vasari's personal collection of drawings, the *Libro di disegni,* provided some of the evidence he used to judge the excellence of individual artists or their place within the stages of development.

**Artistic Paradigms.** In the first stage of Vasari's model, the conquest of representation, or truth to nature, defined artistic quality. Subsequent improvements meant greater accuracy and ease in depicting the figure in space. Understanding and application of antique forms was a second standard; it denoted excellence particularly in the second and third stages. In his text Vasari mapped the progress of art by recording the innovations of outstanding artists in the fourteenth, fifteenth, and sixteenth centuries. Artists such as Giotto, Donatello, and da Vinci served as paradigms for their eras. Progress was a rebirth (*renascità*) through which forms were increasingly perfected and art itself moved closer to the divine. Giotto revived the art of design and thus reflected the creation of God. One of Vasari's anecdotes recorded how Giotto's skills in re-creating nature surpassed those of his own teacher, Cimabue. According to Vasari, Giotto painted a fly on the nose of one of Cimabue's figures. His teacher noticed the fly and attempted to brush it away. This incident demonstrated that Giotto's abilities rivaled nature itself, a topos frequently found in ancient accounts of artists' lives.

**Second Era.** According to his developmental outline the artists of the fifteenth century, or second era, were much better. Their compositions were more lifelike with richer ornamentation. Brunelleschi aided in the Renaissance rediscovery of classical rules and measures applied to architecture. For Vasari, Donatello's sculptures most closely resembled antiquity because they were so full of grace and design. Donatello's figures of prophets for the bell tower of Santa Maria del Fiore in Florence married lifelike representation and classical models of virtue. *Il Zuccone,* the bald-headed prophet, was believed to represent Giovanni di Barduccio Cherichini, a contemporary Florentine citizen. Vasari stated that Donatello would speak urgently to the sculpture while constructing it—demanding that it speak to him. The topos of a figure coming to life derived from classical literary models. The prophet's duty to employ his rhetorical skills recollected the Florentine citizen's obligations to speak persuasively and be involved in the active life.

**Third Era.** In the third era, or Golden Age, Vasari claimed that artists achieved the highest perfection in the creation of art. They copied the most beautiful things of nature and combined them with the best of antiquity. He credited da Vinci with originating this "modern period." His work showed robust draughtsmanship, subtle repro-

duction of nature, and an inspired sense of grace. His figures were said to have moved and breathed for these reasons. The beauty, grace, and talent of artists such as da Vinci exemplified the harmony between the creator and created. The inspired ability to create, rather than an artisan's manual skills, determined the artist's new place in society. Vasari even used the term "divine" in association with Michelangelo's artistic reputation. He was the only major living artist whose biography appeared in Vasari's first edition of *The Lives.* In his second edition of *The Lives* (1565), Vasari added material based upon a trip to north Italy. He also included twenty more biographies. He died in 1574. His work forms an integral part of the repertoire of sources on the history of art and theory.

**Sources:**
T. S. R. Boase, *Georgio Vasari: The Man and the Book* (Princeton Princeton University Press, 1979).

E. C. Fernie, *Art History and Its Methods: A Critical Anthology* (London: Phaidon, 1995).

Patricia Lee Rubin, *Giorgio Vasari: Art and History* (New Haven: Yale University Press, 1995).

Giorgio Vasari, *Lives of the Artists: A Selection,* volume 1, translated by George Bull (Baltimore: Penguin, 1965).

# DOCUMENTARY SOURCES

Leon Battista Alberti, *De pictura* (*On Painting,* 1435)—A pioneering treatise on Renaissance theories of art and representation rooted in humanist interests in the liberal arts and classical theories of beauty and proportion.

Baldassare Castiglione, *Il cortegiano* (*The Courtier,* 1528)—This Renaissance dialogue examines the ideal characteristics of genteel or courtly behavior within the context of the new princely courts of northern Italy and Europe. For Castiglione, courtliness was an essential noble virtue that required the suppression of inner feelings (honest dissimilation), and the strict control of bodily gestures and impulses (decorum), and physical grace. An important text for understanding the emergence of the courtly culture and civility, it was widely imitated in sixteenth-century etiquette manuals.

Desiderius Erasmus, *Encomium moriae* (*The Praise of Folly,* 1511)—A biting satire that reveals Erasmus's keen wit and eloquent style. This highly readable medieval critique of medieval devotional practices and religious institutions provides a clear understanding of the growing dissatisfaction of the humanist elite with the per-

ceived corruption of western Christianity in both its institutional and popular expressions.

Margery Kempe, *The Book of Margery Kempe* (1436–1438)—The earliest autobiography written in English. It is significant as the portrait of a middle-class woman who records her travels, pilgrimages, and mystical visions in language that reflects patterns of female piety. The impact of late-medieval saints' lives, mystic literature traditions, as well as pageantry and religious art, inform her spiritual life while providing eyewitness material to understand popular devotional practices.

Giovanni Pico della Mirandola, *De hominus digitate oratio* (*Oration on the Dignity of Man,* 1486)—An Italian nobleman and talented mentor of the Florentine Academy, Mirandola clearly articulated in his nine hundred theses the humanist enthusiasm concerning human potential and creativity.

Francesco Petrarch, *Canzoniere* (*Songbook,* circa 1327–1374)—Some of the most vivid expressions of the courtly, platonic ideal of love in Western literature. These poems, written in Italian, are good examples of the growing popularity of vernacular idiom among fourteenth-century poets and writers.

François Rabelais, *Pantagruel* and *Gargantua* (1532; 1534)—A rollicking romp through the French countryside with two giants, father and son, whose adventures allow Rabelais to satirize contemporary society, and in particular, the foibles of the Catholic clergy.

Giorgio Vasari, *Vite de' più eccelenti architetti, pittori ed scultori italiani* (*Lives of the Most Eminent Painters, Sculptors, and Artists*, 1550, commonly known as *Lives of the Artists*)—A comprehensive study of the history of Italian art written by an Italian painter, architect, and theorist. Vasari's book created a biological model tracing the development of the arts using the life cycle from childhood to a golden age. He generated principles for the evaluation of art based on standards of quality and connoisseurship that are still fundamental to the analysis of art.

St. Peter's Basilica in Vatican City, Rome (1546–1564), which was designed by Michelangelo. The dome was completed by Giacomo della Porta and Domenico Fontana.

Italian artist Titian's *Assumption of the Virgin*, 1516–1518, painted for the altar of Sta. Maria dei Frari in Venice (Ca'd'Oro [House of Gold] Venetian Palace, Venice; SEF/Art Resource, New York)

# COMMUNICATION, TRANSPORTATION, AND EXPLORATION

by NORMAN J. WILSON

## CONTENTS

*Sidebars and tables are listed in italics.*

**1360**
- Henry de Vick builds the first mechanical clock with an hour hand for the royal palace of King Charles V.

**1366**
- *The Travels of Sir John Mandeville* is published. Written anonymously, it describes the faraway regions of China, India, and Tibet and is consistent with Marco Polo's geographic locations. *The Travels* also helps perpetuate the myth of Prester John, the Christian ruler of an island kingdom.

**1375***
- Geoffrey Chaucer begins writing *The Canterbury Tales,* narrated by a group of pilgrims on their way to a religious shrine. The work is unfinished when Chaucer dies in 1400.

**1386**
- A clock is built at Salisbury Cathedral and is the oldest surviving clock in England. Unlike the clock at Wells Cathedral, the Salisbury version strikes the hour as opposed to the quarter hour.

**1396**
- Byzantine scholar and diplomat Manuel Chrysoloras lectures in Florence and begins a trend toward the revival of Greek texts in Renaissance Italy.

**1400***
- The first domestic clocks appear in Europe. Most of them have no cases or means of protection from dust. (Forms of cover such as glass do not appear until the seventeenth century.) They usually stand on pedestals with apertures to accommodate the weights.
- Fibonacci's *Liber Abaci* (originally published in 1202) popularizes the use of Hindu-Arabic numerals.
- *The Book of Sir Marco Polo* (1298), the memoirs of the famed traveler to Asia, is widely read by Renaissance scholars. By 1500 there are at least twenty-four editions of this book.

**1419**
- Prince Henry of Portugal becomes governor of the province of Algarve. He establishes a residence at Sagres, Cape St. Vincent, where he begins to sponsor exploring expeditions of the West African coast. By 1446 his ships have sailed as far south as the mouth of the Gambia River, about 15° north of the equator.

**1438**

- Johannes Gutenberg, a German craftsman and inventor, agrees to a five-year business contract with three Strasbourg businessmen, Hans Riffe, Andreas Dritzehn, and Andreas Heilmann. When Dritzehn dies on Christmas Day, his heirs attempt to circumvent the terms of the contract by demanding to be made partners. They lose the suit, but not before discovering that Gutenberg is working on a printing invention.

**1455**

- Gutenberg perfects his invention, a printing press with movable type, and produces the first printed book, the *Forty-two-Line Bible,* before the end of the year. Meanwhile, he loses a suit to Johann Fust, a Mainz financier and goldsmith, and is forced to pay the sum of 2,020 guilders. Fust also gains control of the type for the Bible and for Gutenberg's second book, a *Psalter,* as well as some of the printer's equipment.

**1457**

- The first printed book in Europe to bear the name of its printer is a Psalter completed by Fust and Peter Schöffer, Gutenberg's son-in-law and former employee who testified against the printer in his 1455 trial.

**1474**

- William Caxton's *The Recuyell of the Historyes of Troye* is the first book printed in English.

- The Florentine geographer Paolo Toscanelli dal Pozzo reports to King Afonso V of Portugal that the distance from Europe to China is approximately five thousand nautical miles. (The distance is actually double).

**1488**

- Portuguese navigator Bartholomeu Dias sails around the Cape of Good Hope into the Indian Ocean.

**1492**

- Christopher Columbus, an Italian mariner in the service of Spain, discovers the New World by landing on an island he calls San Salvador. He conducts three other voyages to the New World in 1493, 1498, and 1502.

**1497**

- The Italian explorer John Cabot, sailing under the English flag, sights what is now believed to be Newfoundland.

- Vasco da Gama sails around the Cape of Good Hope and trades on the Malabar coast of India. He returns to Portugal in 1499 with a cargo of spices worth sixty times the cost of the voyage.

**1500\***

- Iberian shipwrights design the caravel and *nao,* two types of vessels capable of carrying large cargoes on long transoceanic voyages.
- The German locksmith Peter Henlein begins to make the first portable timepiece. It is driven by springs and possesses an hour hand only (minute hands do not appear until 1670).
- Portuguese sailors identify the Southern Cross, the equivalent to the North Star, in the Southern Hemisphere.

**1500**

- Portuguese explorer Pedro Cabral arrives in Brazil after trying to find a westerly route to India.

**1501**

- Amerigo Vespucci, an Italian navigator, sails along the coast of Brazil and concludes that Columbus had discovered a new continent.

**1513**

- Vasco Núñez de Balboa sights the Pacific Ocean and claims it for Spain.

**1515**

- The first printed edition of Ptolemy's *Almagest* appears in Europe.

**1516**

- Desiderius Erasmus's edition of the Greek New Testament appears.

**1522**

- A four-year-long expedition led by Ferdinand Magellan finishes circumnavigating the world.

**1529**

- Mexico City becomes the capital of the viceroyalty of New Spain.

**1533**
- The conquistador Francisco Pizarro conquers Cuzco, the Incan capital.
- In *Cosmographia*, Peter Apian explains triangulation, a mathematical method for drawing accurate maps by using the known distances between two points.

**1534**
- The Frenchman Jacques Cartier discovers the St. Lawrence River.

**1536**
- The Spanish, under Pedro de Mendoza, arrive in Argentina.

**1543**
- Portuguese ships arrive in Japan.

**1544**
- Lima becomes the capital of the viceroyalty of Peru.
- Sebastian Münster writes *Cosmographia Universalis* (General Description of the Known World), which includes chapters on the New World. An extremely popular book, it goes through forty-six editions and is written in six languages before 1644.

**1550**
- Spanish discoveries and conquests in the New World are reported in Francisco Lopez de Gomara's *Historia de las Indias y conquista de Mexico.* Two years later Bartolome de Las Casas writes *History of the Indies.*

**1551**
- Erasmus Reinhold publishes the *Prutenic Tables,* a collection of astronomical charts based on Copernicus's theorems. Publication of these tables contributes to the reform of the Julian calendar.

**1569**
- Christophe Plantin publishes the first volume of *Biblia polyglotta* (Polyglot Bible), written in Latin, Greek, Hebrew, and Chaldaic (ancient Semitic). By 1572 there are eight volumes.

**1571**
- The Spanish conquer the Philippine Islands.

**1580**
- In *Travel Journey*, Michel Eyquem de Montaigne describes inns and dining habits in various European countries, including Italy, Germany, and Switzerland.

**1582**
- Pope Gregory XIII proclaims the New Style, or Gregorian, calendar as a replacement for the Old Style, or Julian, calendar, which has been in effect since 46 B.C.E. The Gregorian calendar restores the vernal (spring) equinox to 21 March. The change is effected by advancing the calendar ten days after 4 October (the following day becomes 15 October). This calendar also has no century year as a leap year unless it is exactly divisible by 400 (for example, 1600 or 2000).

**1583**
- The Italian states, Portugal, Spain, and the German Catholic principalities adopt the Gregorian calendar. The Protestant nations change over gradually; England and its colonies do not make the transition until 1752.

**1584**
- Sir Walter Raleigh sends an expedition to present-day Roanoke Island, North Carolina. Two attempts to colonize the site end in failure.

**1587**
- Spanish ships arrive in Japan.

# OVERVIEW

**Sign of the Times.** In the thirteenth century, a Franciscan friar named Roger Bacon sent an appeal for calendar reform from England to the Pope in Rome. Bacon correctly calculated that the calendar was incorrect. His appeal was denied and the erroneous calendar continued to be used throughout Europe. Three centuries later, Pope Gregory XIII corrected the calendar in Catholic Europe by deleting ten days. Had the correction been ordered in Bacon's day, a papal adjustment of the calendar would have been accepted without question across Europe, but by 1582 Europe was religiously divided and Rome was no longer the focal point of European authority. Calendar reform in Europe was not universally embraced because Protestant Reformers and the Eastern Orthodox Church refused to accept the papal correction.

**Promises of Trade and Riches.** Sixty years after Bacon's death, a new and deadly disease, the bubonic plague, decimated Europe's population. Known as the Black Death, the plague swept Europe between 1347 and 1351. The devastation wrought by the plague resulted in a shift of mood, or mentality, throughout Europe from one of optimism to one of cynicism. The economy, population, and cultivated land all shrank. Furthermore, western Europe's political orientation shifted from a universal Christian commonwealth under a strong papacy to autonomous kingdoms and principalities. The Church fared poorly as the Avignon papacy (1304–1377) evolved into a Great Schism (1378–1417) where rival popes ruled from Avignon and Rome. Dynastic struggles became long civil wars that further stifled economic development. Yet, within one hundred years of the Great Schism, strong monarchies centralized power and then began to compete with each other for trade and riches. Developments in maritime technology and navigation allowed this competition to extend beyond the European shores. Voyages of exploration and colonization created a New World that was much larger than the world of medieval geographers. The voyages also shifted the focal point of Europe from Rome and the Mediterranean Sea to the Atlantic Ocean.

**Quantitative Thinking.** The origins of this shift are to be found in a complicated mixture of economic reality, technological possibility, and human perceptions. Bacon's calendar reforms fell on deaf ears in the thirteenth century, but they were recognized as valid three hundred years later. This change was in part a product of a new quantitative mentality that emerged in late-medieval and Renaissance Europe. Mathematical precision became a defining character of music, painting, and education. A vivid example of quantification is the introduction of town clocks that brought a new regularity to urban life. Clocks, calendars, artistic perspective, and advances in accounting practices are vivid examples of a burgeoning Renaissance mind-set that was moving away from qualitative thinking and toward a more reasoned, mathematical, quantitative approach. This shift had important ramifications in science, technology, and geography. For instance, mariners began to calculate latitude with complicated abstract mathematical equations, whereas earlier they had relied on visual observation. Geographers began to construct new maps that were mathematically accurate, and astronomers began to consider new ways of explaining the mathematical precision of the universe. These developments had profound effects on Renaissance and Reformation Europe.

**Literary Culture.** During the period of the Renaissance and Reformation, there was also a shift from an oral culture to a literary one. The spread of literacy went hand in hand with the rise of vibrant literature written in local dialects instead of the traditional Latin. The rise of regional languages, the vernacular, stimulated the shift from verbal to written communication and created national consciousness. It did so because the vernacular fostered localism as a wider audience of readers came to be interested in local issues rather than the universal issues of Christianity. Increased literacy and the rise of local literature increased demand for reading material and encouraged the pursuit of technological innovations in manuscript preparation. The resulting printing revolution re-created a universal audience and simultaneously codified the vernacular languages by creating a printed standard form of each language.

**Revolution.** The transition from manuscript culture to that of books printed with movable type was part of a broad revolution in communication that involved more than simple technological innovation. In the centuries before Johannes Gutenberg used movable type, the market of potential readers grew because of the thirteenth-century rise of urban universities, the fourteenth-century development of scholars known as humanists, and the growing number of literate urbanites. Readers of printed books were now certain that their counterparts in other parts of Europe were reading the same text, something that could not be taken for granted in manuscript culture. Printers developed elaborate marks, the origins of the modern trademark, in order to verify the accuracy of editions. Printing also changed the role of scholars and village storytellers. Scholars had become famous for the ability to recall texts from memory and then comment on them; now the scholar needed to create new texts. And village storytellers soon found their role replaced by people of less gifted oratorical skills who could simply read to the others. Early printed texts were frequently in Latin, but by the end of the sixteenth century those Latin texts were frequently translated into the vernacular. The success of the Protestant Reformation hinged in part on the ability of the presses to circulate religious ideas in the vernacular at a reasonable price. Ultimately, the communications revolution created a stronger national consciousness, but it also created small cosmopolitan audiences of individuals within fields such as astronomy, physics, and cartography.

**Travel Literature.** Printing and the communications revolution fostered the cross-cultural exchange of knowledge and allowed remote scholars the opportunity to contemplate a wider range of written works. One of the most popular genres of printed material was travel literature. Travel literature found eager audiences among pilgrims, merchants, geographers, and, perhaps most importantly, cartographers and explorers. Travel accounts written by Christians such as Marco Polo and John Mandeville fostered dreams of economically prosperous adventure. *The Travels of Sir John Mandeville* (1366) perpetuated the existing myth of Prester John, a Christian ruler on a remote island. Christian explorers could hope to find a Prester John and use his support to convert or conquer non-Christians. With the rise of movable type in the fifteenth century, published copies of the earlier travel literature found a much broader audience. Europeans were devouring the travel literature at an unprecedented level on the eve of European voyages to Asia and the Americas.

**Voyages of Discovery.** The crusading spirit of Medieval Christians, the quest for contact with Asia, the Renaissance pursuit of knowledge, innovations in the construction of ships, and cartographers' search for better methods of mapping were all factors in the late-fifteenth-century increase in voyages of exploration and discovery. Printing provided explorers with a wide range of theories, standardized navigational charts, and an avenue to spread information about their discoveries. Technological advances in ship construc-

tion and riggings allowed the Portuguese to explore the coast of Africa. Their findings forced cartographers to reconsider the usual depiction of the world and thereby opened the horizons of what was possible. Bartholomeu Dias's 1488 voyage around the Cape of Good Hope, the southern point of Africa, dispelled the Ptolemaic belief that the Indian Ocean was a landlocked sea. While the Portuguese mariners were seeking a passage to Asia via a south-easterly route, the Spaniards were searching in a westerly and southwesterly direction. In 1492 the Spaniards sent a Genoese mariner named Christopher Columbus with three small ships west across the Atlantic.

**Motivations.** Explorers frequently mentioned two motives for exploration: to serve God and to become rich. These motives created conflicts between Christian Spain and Christian Portugal over what areas each country should control. The conflicts were resolved in 1494 when the Treaty of Tordesillas divided the oceans into a western Spanish area and an eastern Portuguese area. Vasco da Gama was the first European to actually sail to Asia (1497–1498). He did so via an eastern route that went around the African Cape of Good Hope. During Columbus's lifetime, da Gama sailed a Portuguese fleet east to the Indies and Amerigo Vespucci sailed under Spanish and Portuguese flags to the southern of the two continents that bear his name (South America), but Columbus went to his grave with the mistaken belief that his Enterprise of the Indies had successfully brought him to Asia. These voyages had a dramatic effect on how one depicted the world, but they failed to establish exactly what the circumference of the world actually might be. Ferdinand Magellan, a Portuguese mariner sailing under the Spanish flag, circumnavigated the globe in 1519–1522 and thereby established a definitive answer to the size of the earth. Yet, even with the correct size of the earth, cartographers were unable to create maps that were both accurate and useful for navigation until the late sixteenth century, when Gerardus Mercator developed a system of projections in a method now called the "Mercator projection." Maps made in this manner remained the standard for navigation into the twentieth century.

**An Atlantic World.** The shape of the known world changed at an unprecedented pace at the end of the fifteenth century. By the mid sixteenth century, the focal point of Europe had shifted from the world of the Mediterranean Sea to that of the Atlantic Ocean. The convergence of literacy, printing, and exploration provided a wide audience of Europeans with new information about diverse civilizations and cultures. This new knowledge contributed to a revolution in science, but it also contributed to a century of religious conflicts and wars.

# TOPICS IN COMMUNICATION, TRANSPORTATION, AND EXPLORATION

## CLOCKS, CALENDARS, AND QUANTIFICATION

**Measurement of the Day.** Time plays a central role in the social organization of all cultures despite the fact that various cultures conceive of time differently. During the Renaissance and Reformation, cultural perceptions of time changed dramatically for urbanites but remained remarkably constant for the bulk of the population that lived outside of cities and large towns. The traditional peasant view of time was based on cyclical rhythms of nature such as spring, summer, fall, and winter, or dawn, noon, and sunset. Precise measurement of the hours in a day was neither available nor useful for the rural and peasant populations. Urbanites, on the other hand, came to understand and then live under a mechanical notion of time during the Renaissance and Reformation. Large urban clocks disciplined the passage of time and served as a constant reminder that it was also the passage of opportunities to acquire wealth. An urban preoccupation with precise measurement of the day's hours is evidence of a materialization of this social construction of time that eventually led to new moral issues such as punctuality and tardiness.

**Henry de Vick.** The English word *clock* is derived from the French word *cloche* and the German *glocke,* all words for bell. The bell regulated urban life long before Henry de Vick designed the first mechanical clock with an hour hand in 1360. De Vick's clock was built for King Charles V of France and was situated in his royal palace in Paris. Dante mentioned clocks in his writings, which suggests that large mechanical clocks were widespread in Italy by the early fourteenth century. Mechanical clocks were first located on cathedrals and later on city halls. Huge urban clocks appeared in Germany in the 1330s, England by the 1370s, and France by the 1380s. These clocks measured time in equal hours regardless of the season, whereas rural measurements of time fluctuated with longer mornings in June and shorter mornings in December. Urban clocks were also complicated machines that required regular maintenance by skilled mechanics. The town clock was a complicated machine that constantly reminded citizens of uniform time. Clocks brought a new regularity to urban life, and by the end of the sixteenth century, people began to carry pocket

A reconstruction of a fourteenth-century turret clock at Dover Castle in England (Science Museum, London)

watches. These developments in timekeeping were both a product of and a contributor to a new mind-set that viewed the world in visual and quantitative terms.

**Gregorian Calendar.** Urban clocks spread quickly once Europeans learned how to build them, but Europeans were slow to develop an accurate calendar despite the fact that they knew how to repair the ten-day discrepancy between solar reality and the Julian calendar. (The Julian calendar was introduced in Rome in 46 B.C.E., establishing the twelve-month year of 365 days, with each fourth year having 366 days and the months each having 31 or 30 days except for February, which has 28 days in regular years or

29 days in leap years.) Roger Bacon, a Franciscan friar in England during the thirteenth century, was the first to challenge the Church on the measurement of time. Bacon appealed to Pope Clement IV to correct an error in the calendar of roughly one day every 125 years. Clement died in 1268, and the next Pope, Gregory X, chose to ignore Bacon. Three centuries later, Pope Gregory XIII corrected the calendar by simply removing ten days and instituting leap years and a leap-century rule (the leap-century rule cancels leap years in three out of four new century years). The modern Gregorian calendar went into effect at the end of Thursday, 4 October 1582, and the beginning of Friday, 15 October 1582, when the calendar skipped ten days.

**Adherence to the System.** Had the Pope changed the calendar in Bacon's day, most of Europe would have probably accepted the change because thirteenth-century Europe was predominantly Roman Catholic. However, in 1582 Europe was a jigsaw puzzle of religious groups, most of whom were at odds with the papacy. Italy, Spain, and Portugal embraced the October 1582 changes, but France, Belgium, and Catholic states in the Netherlands waited until the end of the year. The Emperor of the Holy Roman Empire lacked the power to proclaim such a drastic change, so Catholic German states made the changes at their own discretion over the next two years. Protestants in Germany, Denmark, and Sweden did not switch to the Gregorian calendar until the eighteenth century. The Eastern Orthodox Church still retains the Julian calendar for calculating Easter (with the exception of the Orthodox Church of Finland, which is fully Gregorian).

**Need for Reform.** Calls for calendar reform increased between Bacon's time and that of Pope Gregory XIII for several reasons. The fall of Constantinople in 1453 forced intellectuals, including many mathematicians and astronomers, to flee to the West. Economic prosperity increased markets and created a growing number of literate urbanites with a quantitative mind-set. The printing press made calendars available for a large market that previously would not have been exposed to them. Advances in astronomy led to precise calculations of the flaws in the Julian calendar, and the efforts of the Council of Trent (1545–1563) to thwart the Protestant Reformation often included decrees involving the reissuing of mass books and breviaries that were related to the calendar. The 1582 Papal Bull that proclaimed the new calendar opened with claims of authority derived from Trent, rather than science, and thereby made it more difficult for Protestants to accept the change.

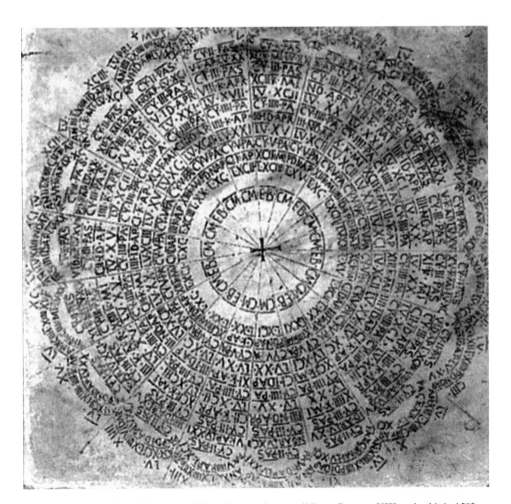

The Julian calendar, which was used from Roman times until Pope Gregory XIII revised it in 1582

**New Mind-Set.** European quantification of time, both with clocks and calendar reform, was part of a broad movement toward quantitative habits of thought that began a century before the Renaissance. Literacy, maintaining account books with double-entry bookkeeping, advances in the way cartographers mapped known bodies of water and newly contacted lands, astronomers' observations and constructions of mathematical models of motion, perspective in Renaissance art, and the mass production of books are examples of how Europeans evolved new visual and quantitative ways of perceiving time, space, and the physical environment. This new mind-set involved the ability to reduce things to something one can visualize and then measure. This visual and quantitative way of modeling thought offered a new way to examine, reason about, and even manipulate reality. The ability to bring mathematical theory and practical measurement together created habits of thought that enabled Europeans to advance swiftly in science and technology.

Sources:

Michael Baxandall, *Painting and Experience in Fifteenth Century Italy: A Primer in the Social History of Pictorial Style* (Oxford: Clarendon Press, 1972).

Alfred Crosby, *The Measure of Reality: Quantification and Western Society, 1250-1600* (Cambridge & New York: Cambridge University Press, 1997).

David Ewing Duncan, *Calendar: Humanity's Epic Struggle to Determine a True and Accurate Year* (New York: Avon, 1998).

## LITERACY AND THE RISE OF VERNACULAR LITERATURE

**Limited Skill.** Literacy, the ability to read and write, was a skill limited largely to clerical elites in Medieval Europe. These elites read and wrote Latin, the language of the church and the universities. The late medieval growth of cities and towns included a dramatic increase in the number of merchants, traders, and artisans. These townspeople maintained businesses that required the ability to write basic correspondence and maintain account books. By 1300 most European merchants were literate, and by 1500 many of their wives could also read and write. The growing numbers of functionally literate urbanites sought educational opportunities for their children as well. Townspeople broke the clerical monopoly on learning and created schools.

**Schools.** Italy, with four cities of populations about or more than one hundred thousand, led the way in education of urban boys and girls. Northern European schools served mainly to educate young boys for a career in the church. Similar schools existed in Italy, but Italian towns also had two other types of schools: Latin based "grammar" schools for boys from elite families, and arithmetic based "abacus" schools for the remainder of the boys. The "abacus" schools, named after the instrument for mathematical calculation, prepared boys for business with a curriculum of mathematics, accounting, and basic writing skills. The church and "grammar" schools taught students Latin, whereas abacus schools taught in the local dialects. Girls found their educational opportunities limited by gender as well as class. Girls were limited to elementary education unless the family hired private tutors or took an active role in home schooling. As a result, they were rarely taught Latin and had no access to the universities. Nonetheless, females constituted an active audience for the growing number of works published in the vernacular, or native spoken language of the region.

**Writing for an Audience.** In the fourteenth and fifteenth centuries, authors across Europe began to write popular works in the vernacular. Dante (Durante Alighieri), Francesco Petrarch, Giovanni Boccaccio, Christine de Pisan, François Villon, Geoffrey Chaucer, and a wave of others chose to bypass the language of the Church (Latin) and write works for a local audience. Latin was still necessary for authors seeking a European-wide audience of literate elites, but the vernacular provided a local audience of individuals more apt to share the sentiments of a regional storyteller. Vernacular authors drew on the twelfth- and thirteenth-century troubadour and courtly romance predecessors but also wrote for a broader, nonnoble audience. Vernacular literatures tended to include more romance and sensuality than the Latin literature of the period, while still maintaining the moral and ethical emphasis evident in the Latin literature.

*Divine Comedy.* Three Italian poets from Florence, Dante, Petrarch, and Boccaccio, turned their native Tuscan dialect into the standard Italian literary language. Dante's *Divine Comedy* (circa 1308–1321) is an allegorical trilogy that describes one man's journey through Hell, Purgatory and Paradise. Virgil, an antirepublican poet of Imperial Rome, guides Dante through Hell and Purgatory but is unable to proceed further because he is a pagan. Reason, represented by Virgil, can lead one only so far. Beatrice, the love of Dante's youth, leads Dante through Paradise. Dante's beloved Beatrice stands metaphorically for God's love. The poet utilized the logic of medieval theologians throughout the book. Hell is divided into levels, and the sinners are placed into a level that corresponds to the evilness of their sins. The work is a fine example of medieval scholasticism and its mathematical structure and reliance on reason and logic. The poem reflects many cultural issues such as the relationship between reason and faith, the tension between supporters of the emperor and those of the pope, and the psychological aspects of medieval religion. Dante offers poignant criticism of church authorities and a descriptive analysis of social and political problems within his profoundly Christian poem.

**Father of Humanism.** Petrarch's vernacular works are more secular than Dante's works. Petrarch's writings mark a clear shift from the medieval scholasticism evident in Dante to a new tradition known as Renaissance Humanism. Petrarch is known as the "Father of Humanism." He and the humanists who followed him studied and imitated classical forms as they revived classical culture and promoted an educational program based on rhetoric and philology. Humanism, or the *Studia Humanitatis*, was a curriculum that focused not on the mathematical logic and reason of the scholastics, but rather on the study of Latin and Greek texts. Humanists studied grammar, rhetoric, history, poetry, and ethics, whereas the scholastics studied arithmetic, astronomy, music, geometry, rhetoric, grammar, and logic. Early humanists, such as Petrarch, were frequently poets or orators. They were not bound to Scholastic traditions of logical analysis of recognized authorities. Rather than provide mere commentaries on previously written works, humanists created original literature in both the classical and the vernacular languages. As a young man, Petrarch wrote stunning love poetry in a fourteen-line format that has come to be known as the Italian, or Petrarchan, sonnet. His popularity is evident in the name of the sonnet form and in the fact that in 1341 he was crowned "Poet Laureate" in Rome.

**Influence of the Classics.** Petrarch and other Italian urbanites of the fourteenth century shared a kindred spirit with the great urban cultures of classical Athens and Republican Rome. Merchants and urbanites, steeped in the daily administration of Florence's republican government, found the call to political activity of the classics more pertinent than the contemplative life of the scholastic theologians. Petrarch studied classical Latin and learned some Greek. He read the classics, imitated their style, and was so indebted to the ancient authors that he published a collection of "Letters to the Ancient Dead" in which he carried on a correspondence with Cicero, Seneca, Horace, and Virgil. His enthusiasm for the classics was contagious, and twenty years after Petrarch's 1374 death the Florentines invited a Byzantine scholar and diplomat named Manuel Chrysoloras to lecture in Florence. In the decades following his visit, a revival of Greek studies and literature in Italy profoundly influenced science, astronomy, and philosophy. Petrarch's legacy to Renaissance humanism includes his efforts to revive classical Greek learning, his support of stoic ideas of virtue as "greatness of soul," his balance of the active and contemplative life, and his faith in human potential.

*Decameron.* Boccaccio, a countryman, friend, and student of Petrarch, assembled an encyclopedia of Greek and Roman mythology but never mastered Greek. His failings as a language student are largely forgotten because he was so successful at drawing on his interest in myths to tell a good story. He is best known for *Decameron* (1353), an innovative work full of lively and irreverent descriptions of Italians during the 1348–1351 plague. This collection of short stories recounts how seven women and three men fled Florence because of the plague. Their fear of the plague forced them to travel to remote villas in hopes of remaining healthy. On ten days of their adventure, each traveler told a short story to entertain the others. This situation amounts to one hundred short stories, filled with scatological humor and lively characters. Boccaccio's bawdy discussion of sex and his frank creation of ordinary and realistic characters distinguish *Decameron* from previous works. His characters are stock literary figures, but he shows none of the medieval contempt of the world evident in earlier works. Boccaccio's *Decameron* also differs from earlier works in the scope of his intended audience. The book was dedicated to a noblewoman, but the narrator opens by addressing an audience of bourgeois women: "Most gracious ladies." Boccaccio's social commentary on sexual, economic, and religious misconduct was written to a lay audience of women and men who shared his sympathetic perspective of human behavior.

**Female Readers.** The new audience of urban women readers became avid readers of two types of vernacular literature: works of devotion and romance. This dichotomy reinforced the late-medieval misogynist notion that women were destined to inferior positions. The church offered two extreme models: the temptress Eve, who ended life in the Garden of Eden, and the Virgin Mary, who gave birth to Jesus. The romance tradition was largely condemned as a potential corrupter of women because it encouraged contemplation of unregulated love. The temptress-virgin mother models of women evident in the devotional tradition found a new expression in the romance tradition when Jean de Meun revised the famous thirteenth-century *Romance of the Rose.* De Meun's fourteenth-century revision satirized human follies of the clergy and women. Moreover, he drew on a wide range of cultural beliefs (folklore, theology, and classical authors) to depict the vanity, depravity, and weakness of women.

**Pisan.** Of the many refutations of de Meun, Christine de Pisan's *The Book of the City of Ladies* (1405) stands out for its eloquence, its strong refutation of the medieval stereotypical woman, and the uniqueness of its author. Christine de Pisan was the daughter of an Italian physician and astronomer at the court of Charles V of France. She was educated at the French Court in Greek, Latin, French, and Italian literature. The death of her father and husband left her with limited resources and three small children. From 1389 until her death, Pisan supported herself by writing poems and books at the French Court. She wrote about love, religion, morality, and the role of women. *The Book of the City of Ladies* opens with the question of why so many male authors have depicted women so negatively. She maintains a dialogue with three celestial ladies: Reason, Prudence, and Justice. The solution is that women need to build a city of women where reason, prudence, and justice would protect women. This imaginary city was far away from the real settings of women's lives that she outlined in *The Book of Three Virtues* (1405), also called *Treasures of the City of Ladies.* The book describes three worlds of women: the court, the city, and the village. Unlike the early humanists, Pisan saw little reason to look for truth in the past. Pisan was an heir of the medieval world, yet she embraced a new set of attitudes.

**Villon.** This postmedieval mentality is evident in the realist poetry of another fifteenth-century French poet named François Villon. Duke Charles of Orleans organized a poetry contest in 1453 around the contradictory phrase, "I die of thirst beside the fountain." The Duke himself wrote a traditional medieval poem centered on

The opening page of the "Knight's Tale," from the Ellesmere manuscript of Geoffrey Chaucer's
*The Canterbury Tales* (Huntington Library, San Marino, California)

the sufferings of love. Villon wrote a poem from prison that emphasized the physical sufferings of the downtrodden. Villon was speaking from personal experience. He had studied at the University of Paris, but his poor upbringing rendered him out of place in academe. Villon was a tavern brawler who killed a man in a 1455 fight. Banished from Paris, he spent the remainder of his life wandering the countryside with a band of thieves. He is best known for *Grand Testament* (circa 1461), a bawdy string of bequests that reveal much about the life of the wandering poor. Villon used medieval verse for his poems but wrote them in the vernacular of the downtrodden. His psychological depth and the obvious message of social rebellion distinguish him from the medieval tradition. His celebration of the human condition, faith in the beauty of life on earth, and reliance on individual experience distinguish him from medieval poets such as Dante in Italy and Chaucer in England.

**Langland.** Fourteenth-century English literature emerged from a medieval tradition vastly different from that of the French and Italian literatures. The high nobility in England spoke and wrote French, so the English language lacked the courtly literature tradition. Early English authors relied heavily on their continental predecessors. William Langland and Chaucer were profoundly influenced by Boccaccio. Both followed Boccaccio in offering cultural criticism of a broad cross-section of society while still telling a good tale. Langland provided the perspective of the common person in *Piers Plowman* (circa 1370). His peasant hero criticized worldly injustice, the pain of plagues and wars, and the general poverty of the peasants. Langland used traditional medieval allegorical figures and forms, such as the dream vision, to comment on the evils of society. Like the Bavarian knight Wolfram von Eschenbach, who wrote *Parzival* in the late twelfth century or early thirteenth century, Langland remained tolerant toward Muslims at a time when most authors condemned them. For instance, Dante placed Muhammad near Satan in the ninth circle of Hell. Langland, Boccaccio, and Chaucer all wrote for a broad audience of literate urbanites, but Langland's heavy reliance on symbolism and allegorical language is more consistent with Dante and the medieval tradition.

**Canterbury Tales.** Chaucer followed Boccaccio's tradition of telling realistic and bawdy tales that offered critical analysis of contemporary society. Modeled on Boccaccio's *Decameron*, Chaucer's *Canterbury Tales* (circa 1375–1400) was supposed to consist of 120 stories told by several pilgrims making their way to Canterbury to visit the shrine of Saint Thomas à Becket. To pass the time, each pilgrim was to tell two stories on the way to Canterbury and two more on the return trip. When he died in 1400, Chaucer had completed only 22 of the tales, and therefore *Canterbury Tales* is an unfinished work. The storytelling device allows Chaucer to provide a wide range of perspectives and to address a rich panorama of the moral and social ills of fourteenth-century society. Chaucer's pilgrims share an ironic view of good and evil. Though pilgrims, and thus

Christians, they are also materialistic, worldly, and sensual. Chaucer and Boccaccio both tell realistic tales in the vernacular, which offer clear social and cultural commentary. Both expected their audiences to share common values and ideas that included criticism of the Church and contemporary society.

**Religion and Society.** Criticisms of the Church and social conditions were common themes in vernacular literature across Europe. In Prague, the Bohemian intellectual Jan Hus had sought church reform. His followers merged the religious issues with a political critique of German control of Bohemia. Their success is evident in the unique fact that the first book published in Bohemia was not a religious text, such as the Bible, but rather a secular text. Literary German, on the other hand, is based on the dialect used by Martin Luther in his German translation of the Bible. Vernacular German had been used in the many local chanceries for centuries, but rather than standardize the chancery dialects, printers usually employed the dialect of the local chancery. No attempts were made to create a uniform written language in all of the chanceries until the rule of Emperor Maximilian I in the early sixteenth century. Shortly thereafter, the language of the chancery of the electorate of Saxony in Wittenberg became the model for Luther's German Bible and thereby became the standard for vernacular German known as High German.

Sources:

William Anderson, *Dante the Maker* (London & Boston: Routledge & Kegan Paul, 1980).

Renate Blumenfeld-Kosinski, ed., *The Selected Writings of Christine de Pizan: New Translations, Criticism,* translated by Blumenfeld-Kosinski and Kevin Brownlee (New York: Norton, 1997).

Giovanni Boccaccio, *The Decameron,* translated by Guido Waldman, edited by Jonathan Usher (Oxford: Oxford University Press, 1998).

Nevill Coghill, trans., *The Canterbury Tales* (Baltimore: Penguin, 1977).

Robert Allan Houston, *Literacy in Early Modern Europe: Culture and Education, 1500-1800* (London & New York: Longman, 1988).

Robin Kirkpatrick, *Dante: The Divine Comedy* (Cambridge & New York: Cambridge University Press, 1987).

Sarah Lawson, trans., *Treasures of the City of Ladies* (Baltimore: Penguin, 1985).

Earl Jeffrey Richards, ed., *Reinterpreting Christine de Pisan* (Athens: University of Georgia Press, 1992).

François Villon, *Complete Poems,* edited and translated by Barbara N. Sargent-Baur (Toronto: University of Toronto Press, 1994).

Charity Cannon Willard, *Christine de Pisan: Her Life and Works* (New York: Persea, 1984).

## NAVIGATION AND CARTOGRAPHY

**The Earth.** Basic knowledge of the earth's geography survived the economic decline of the Western Roman Empire in the quadrivial subjects of astronomy and geometry, which delineated the climatic zones on the spherical earth. The classical Greek division of the habitable world into the three continents of Asia, Africa, and Europe, surrounded by ocean, is evident in the earliest medieval maps, and knowledge of the earth's sphericity was evident among the Vikings, who had been successfully navigating westward to Greenland and Nova Scotia by following fixed latitudes. However, efforts to map both land and sea

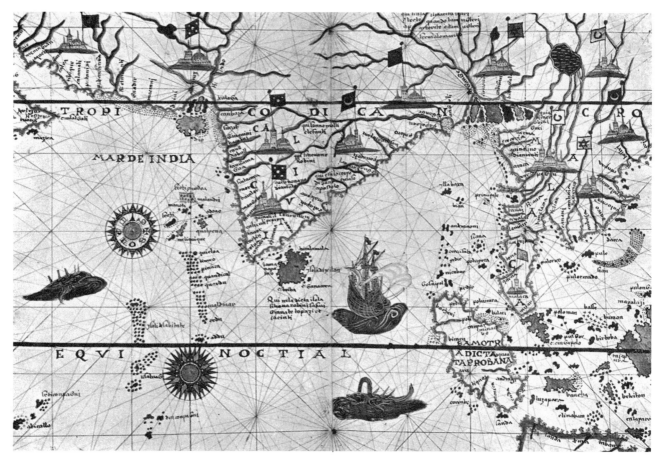

A sixteenth-century map of the Indies, drawn during the height of Portuguese power (British Library)

in a way that represented real distances and relations between places did not happen until the mathematical methods of the ancient scholar Ptolemy were rediscovered and used in conjunction with compass and triangulation during the Renaissance.

**Portolan and Compass.** Europeans became aware of the directional properties of the lodestone, a naturally occurring magnetic mineral, in the twelfth century and began to use magnetized iron needles for navigation in the thirteenth century. Previously, sailors piloted by landmarks and did not stray far from the coastline. On the rare occasions when they ventured out into the ocean, they followed fixed latitudes by measuring the height of the polestar with a simple cross-staff, or quadrant. Such simple methods permitted the Vikings to find and settle Iceland and Greenland, which were due west of Norwegian ports, and even to make their way to Vinland along the North American coast; but, generally speaking, sailing out of sight of land, or at least land birds, was fraught with danger and thus avoided. The introduction of the magnetic compass corrected this problem by permitting merchants to cross open sea on oblique directional headings, thus shortening travel times and enabling them to avoid pirate-infested coasts. This method was facilitated by the creation of a new kind of map, the portolan, which combined detailed knowledge of the coastal geography of Europe and North Africa with well-placed compass roses, radiating directional rhumb lines that intersected each other and ran to key ports. The fifteenth-century navigator could follow one magnetic heading to another and find his way with reasonable accuracy, but the maps were not suitable for long voyages at sea and did not give a realistic portrayal of distances. The limitations of such maps became increasingly evident as the voyages of discovery by Vasco da Gama and Christopher Columbus revealed new lands and aroused scientific curiosity about the surface of the globe and its inhabitants. Geographers did not doubt the sphericity of the earth but needed more data to determine its size and to map its lands.

**Accurate Representation.** The problem of accurate portrayal lay with the difficulty of representing a spherical section of the earth's surface on a flat map. Ptolemy had described methods for projecting a grid of latitudinal and longitudinal lines onto a conic surface, which could be unrolled flat, in his *Geography,* but this text was not rediscovered by Western scholars until the early fifteenth century. Printed in 1475, it quickly became a source for Peter Apian, whose *Cosmographia* (1524) was a basic textbook for sixteenth-century cartographers and mapmakers. One reader was Gerardus Mercator, who incorporated the latitudes of distant lands as they were reported by adventurers such as Columbus.

**Mercator Projection.** Mercator realized that Ptolemaic projections were of limited use to sailors, since

An illumination of a French mariner "shooting" a star to obtain his position, from Jacques Devault's
*Cosmographie,* 1583 (Bibliothèque Nationale, Paris)

lines of constant magnetic heading, called loxodromes, were represented by arcs, so he invented a new technique by which the globe's surface is projected onto a cylinder that is tangent at the equator. The resulting "Mercator projection" represented loxodromes as straight lines and permitted navigators to lay out courses with a straight edge, making them more useful than the portolans. Maps made in this way remained the standard for navigation into the twentieth century.

**Determining Longitude.** Mercator's teacher in mathematics and cartography, Gemma Frisius, introduced two new ideas to geography and navigation: triangulation and the determining of longitudes by using a portable clock to measure azimuthal passages of known stars. In theory, if one could observe an azimuthal passage (when a star or the Sun was at its highest point in the sky, passing through the observer's meridian) and compare the time of the observation with respect to when the passage should have occurred at a standard place, such as Greenwich, England, one would know how many hours east or west of the standard meridian one had traveled, and thus could determine the longitude by adding fifteen degrees for every hour. Unfortunately, using clocks in this way was not possible in the sixteenth century, and the pressing problem of finding longitudes remained unsolved until the technology was refined.

**Triangulation.** In the 1533 edition of Peter Apian's *Cosmographia,* Frisius explained how land maps could be accurately established by using two known points, a graduated arc to measure angles, and standard linear measures to locate a third point, which could then serve as one of the base points needed to locate a fourth, and so on. This method, called triangulation, was first applied on a large scale map by Tycho Brahe, who printed an accurate map of the island on which his observatory was located and pre-

cisely oriented it with respect to landmarks on the coasts of the Danish sound. In the generations that followed, cartographers and mapmakers produced beautiful maps of even greater precision, as printing and surveying became more technically sophisticated. Europeans were now armed with the tools to explore, map, and colonize the globe.

**Sources:**

Jerry Brotton, *Trading Territories: Mapping the Early Modern World* (Ithaca, N.Y.: Cornell University Press, 1998).

G. R. Crone, *Maps and Their Makers: An Introduction to the History of Cartography* (London & New York: Hutchinson's University Press, 1953).

J. B. Harley and David Woodward, eds., *The History of Cartography* (Chicago: University of Chicago Press, 1987-1994).

J. H. Parry, *The Age of Reconnaissance* (Cleveland: World, 1963).

J. R. S. Phillips, *The Medieval Expansion of Europe* (Oxford & New York: Oxford University Press, 1988).

## PILGRIMS, TRAVEL, AND TRAVEL LITERATURE

**Saints and Pilgrims.** Geoffrey Chaucer opens *The Canterbury Tales* (circa 1375–1400) with an agrarian calendar that defines months based on crops and other factors. At that time, the average person would have been more aware of saints' days than the months of the year. For instance, Chaucer defines April, the start of spring, as the month when people go on pilgrimages: "Then folks long to go on pilgrimages, and palmers to visit foreign shores and distant shrines, known in various lands." Pilgrimages were religious journeys that sinners would take as a form of penance, or repentance for sin. Just as warriors would go on a Crusade to win penance, so, too, ordinary people would journey to Jerusalem, Rome, or local sites such as the Shrine of Saint James of Compostela in Spain. Chaucer's pilgrims were headed to the most popular of medieval English pilgrimages, the Shrine of Saint Thomas à Becket in Canterbury. Becket was King Henry II's chancellor and later Archbishop of

A fourteenth-century manuscript illumination of adventurer Marco Polo departing from Venice in 1271 (Bodleian Library, Oxford)

Canterbury. He was murdered at Canterbury Cathedral in 1170, supposedly while kneeling in prayer. Becket was canonized and Canterbury became a popular pilgrimage destination. Pilgrimage sites usually contained relics, or what were believed to be the actual body parts of dead saints. Saints and their relics were believed to work miracles. The cult of saints developed into a significant manifestation of popular piety and official doctrine in late-medieval Europe.

**Cult of the Saints.** The tragedy of the Black Death (1347–1351) was an impetus for the veneration of saints and served to move them from the monastery into the world. All saints were holy men and women who sought a personal, direct, and extraordinary relationship with God. Saints canonized in the fourteenth and fifteenth centuries frequently had employed innovative forms of piety that could be critical of the Church, whereas saints chosen in the sixteenth century tended to have been mil-

itant defenders of Catholicism, such as Ignatius of Loyola and Francis Xavier. Throughout the entire period, saints were people who had renounced worldly concerns in favor of religious goals. An individual became a saint when the church recognized unusual religious piety and evidence of miracles. Saints were held in such high esteem because the degree and quality of their religious zeal was so different from their contemporaries. The cult of saints was a recognition of the individual devotion and unique heavenly focus of a saint.

**Worldly Horizons.** Pilgrims were not always models of individual devotion and heavenly focus. In fact, they were frequently accused of being simple tourists or worse, of wandering in search of immorality away from the watchful eyes of local authorities and neighbors. Even devout pilgrims were frequently models of a group mentality and a focus on worldly concerns that was the antithesis of the saintly model they supposedly sought.

## SAINTS' BIRTHPLACES

| Place | 13<sup>th</sup> Century | 14<sup>th</sup> Century | 15<sup>th</sup> Century | 16<sup>th</sup> Century |
|---|---|---|---|---|
| British Isles | 10 | 2 | 2 | 54 |
| Scandinavia | 1 | 3 | 0 | 0 |
| Low Countries | 6 | 1 | 2 | 3 |
| Holy Roman Empire and Switzerland | 22 | 7 | 4 | 1 |
| France | 24 | 11 | 7 | 4 |
| Iberia | 12 | 3 | 9 | 16 |
| Italy | 79 | 74 | 53 | 33 |
| Eastern Europe | 4 | 5 | 4 | 4 |
| Non-European | 1 | 1 | 2 | 1 |
| TOTAL | 159 | 107 | 83 | 116 |

Source: Donald Weinstein and Rudolph M. Bell, *Saints and Society: The Two Worlds of Western Christendom, 1000-1700* (Chicago: University of Chicago Press, 1982), p. 167.

Pilgrims often looked for the most popular pilgrimages where they could join the largest crowds. Large crowds proved the significance of a site and guaranteed the potential for great miracles. Pilgrims flocked to saints' relics in pursuit of worldly favors. The cult of the saints encouraged travel to pilgrimage sites where a pilgrim would see clear reminders of even more remote locations. This practice offered a rare opportunity for Europeans, especially women, to participate in acceptable travel over long distances. The European-wide pilgrimage movement during the Renaissance contributed to an awareness of a world that, while Christian, was far removed from local life.

**Islamic Travel Literature.** Ibn Battuta and Ibn Khaldun were two Muslim writers from northern Africa whose fourteenth-century works provided Europeans with a perspective on the world beyond Christianity. Ibn Battuta, a native of Ceuta, left northwest Africa in 1325 and traveled for almost thirty years. He went through the Mamluk kingdom of Egypt to Arabia and Mecca, then further to Delhi, Ceylon, Bengal, and China. He returned to Ceuta in 1349 and then traveled to Granada in Spain and the kingdom of Mali. He obviously exaggerated his responsibilities in the courts of foreign rulers much the same way that his Christian counterpart, Marco Polo, had done. Ibn Battuta's *Rihlah* (Travels, 1353) is consistent with a genre of Arab travel stories that are similar to the autobiographical, picaresque novel. The resulting mixture of fact and fiction is quite different from the more factual works of Ibn Khaldun. Ibn Khaldun was a politician, legal scholar, and historian. His family had joined the Muslim conquest of Spain before settling in Maghreb (the Arab-dominated

section of Northwest Africa). He later moved to Algeria and began writing *Al-Ibar* (1406). He continued to revise the *Al-Ibar* in Egypt, where he settled after a pilgrimage to Mecca. Ibn Khaldun was famous among historians for constructing a logical methodology for historical accuracy by questioning historical errors. The method was similar to that employed by Lorenzo Valla, a mid-Renaissance Italian humanist who disproved the *Donation of Constantine* in 1440. The *Rihlah* and *Al-Ibar* became important sources for Europeans to consider history, geography, and the late-medieval world.

**Marco Polo.** The so-called silk road was a network of overland travel that connected Asia and Europe. The most famous western merchant to travel the silk road was Marco Polo, who traveled with his father and uncle across Asia from 1271 to 1295. Polo lived in Asia for seventeen years before returning to Italy. Historians debate whether Polo was motivated by commercial motives or simple curiosity and the quest for adventure. He was certainly a refugee who spent many years traveling the caravan routes of the Great Mongol Empire. His account offers a unique perspective because he was clearly accepted by the Mongols. He possessed knowledge of Asia that was unprecedented in Europe.

**Influence on Geographers.** Polo dictated his memoirs while he was in a Genoese prison. *The Book of Sir Marco Polo* (1298) is a cultural geography of a Christian's travels in China and across Asia. Initially, his accounts were disregarded as being mythical stories. The book became extremely popular in the fourteenth and fifteenth centuries among Renaissance humanists. These humanists were fascinated with geography but were forced to rely largely on ancient accounts because of the lack of Chris-

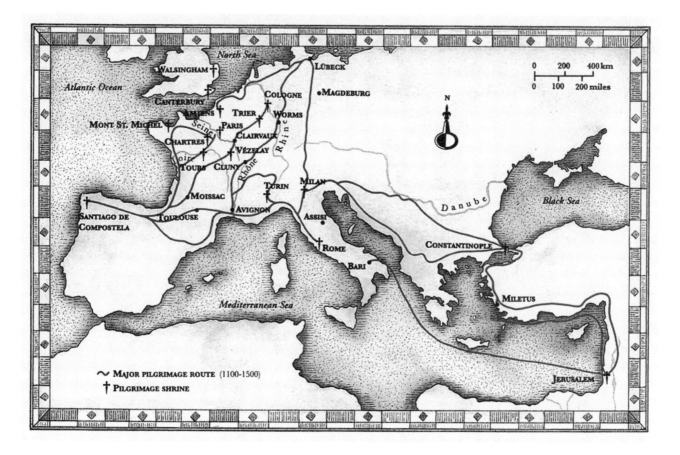

The routes taken by pilgrims throughout Europe and the Near East (from James Harpur, *Revelations: The Medieval World*, 1995)

tian geographers. A Christian perspective, such as that of Polo, was held in high esteem. Mapmakers and explorers relied on his account for centuries. The fifteenth-century rise of printing in Europe made the book available to a much wider audience. Printed copies of *The Book of Sir Marco Polo* became extremely popular: at least twenty-four printed editions were published in the sixteenth century in several different languages. Prior to printing, relatively few people could afford handcopied manuscripts of the work. Henry the Navigator's brother Pedro went to great lengths to obtain a manuscript of Marco Polo's account for Portugal, and King Peter III obtained one for Aragon.

**Prester John.** Peter III of Aragon and his son Jafuda did not stop with the Polo account. They also obtained Odoric of Pordenone's *Travels* (circa 1314–1330) and a work by an unknown author titled *The Travels of Sir John Mandeville* (1366). Mandeville's *Travels* differs considerably from the other two books because it, like Ibn Battuta's *Rhilah*, is full of obviously fictional stories. However, Mandeville's *Travels* also argues for the sphericity of the earth and discusses locations that were consistent with Marco Polo's locations, despite the fact that the author apparently did not use Polo's book. The author, in the persona of an English knight, tells of his travels to diverse places, usually "islands" such as Cathay (China), India, and Tibet. Chapter XXX of the book describes an island ruled by Prester John, a powerful Christian ruler. The Prester John legend was not new, having first appeared in an 1145 work by Otto of Freising, but Mandeville gave new impetus to the myth. Prester John was a medieval ruler who was baptized and lived in an amazing palace in the delightful city of Susa. The legend was sufficiently enticing to attract Europeans to seek the Island of Prester John. The fact that he lived on an island was significant because the myth spread at the moment when Iberian sailors were exploring Atlantic islands off the coast of Africa. When it became obvious that Prester John was not to be found in Asia, the Portuguese began seeking him in Africa. *The Travels of Sir John Mandeville* was a popular geographical romance that influenced how Renaissance Christians viewed the non-Christian world. The book's sphere of influence is evident in the 250 known medieval manuscripts and the 80 editions published between 1478 and 1592. Europeans were eager to read what they believed was the actual travel account of an English knight. *The Travels of Sir John Mandeville* became an important part of late-medieval travel literature that encouraged a mentality of chivalric adventure and foreign exploration.

Sources:

Ross E. Dunn, *The Adventures of Ibn Battuta, a Muslim Traveller of the Fourteenth Century* (Berkeley: University of California Press, 1986).

Iain M. Higgins, *Writing East: The "Travels" of Sir John Mandeville* (Philadelphia: University of Pennsylvania Press, 1997).

## SAINTS' PROFESSIONS

| Category | 13th Century | 14th Century | 15th Century | 16th Century |
|---|---|---|---|---|
| Popes and Cardinals | 4 | 2 | 3 | 4 |
| Bishops and Archbishops | 28 | 8 | 7 | 1 |
| Abbots, Abbesses, Priors, and Prioresses | 26 | 14 | 20 | 12 |
| Lesser Clerics | 35 | 32 | 18 | 53 |
| Tertiaries | 8 | 15 | 5 | 9 |
| Lay People | 58 | 36 | 30 | 37 |
| TOTAL | 159 | 107 | 83 | 116 |

Source: Donald Weinstein and Rudolph M. Bell, *Saints & Society: The Two Worlds of Western Christendom, 1000-1700* (Chicago: University of Chicago Press, 1982), p. 204.

John Larner, *Marco Polo and the Discovery of the World* (New Haven: Yale University Press, 1999).

Donald Weinstein and Rudolph M. Bell, *Saints and Society: The Two Worlds of Western Christianity, 1000-1700* (Chicago: University of Chicago Press, 1982).

## PRINTING

**Profound Impact.** A communications revolution took place in the mid fifteenth century. Few technological innovations had as dramatic an influence on the communication of ideas as the introduction of movable type. Thousands of identical pages could be produced in the fraction of the time that it took a scribe to hand copy a manuscript. As works published on presses replaced hand-copied books, the prices of books fell dramatically. The successes of the Protestant Reformation hinged in large part on the ability to circulate printed religious and political ideas widely and inexpensively. Printing changed written communication, created a new role for the author, restructured communities of readers, provided new notions of libraries and the preservation of knowledge, fostered cross-cultural exchanges of ideas, and influenced the local knowledge of uneducated Europeans. The world of the uneducated masses altered when the functionally literate villager gained a degree of respect and attention previously reserved for the village storyteller. The transition from script culture to print culture required more than simple technological innovation. Heightened demand for books encouraged a wide range of innovations in the mechanical aids for scribal production. Increased production of handcopied books fed this audience and created a culture receptive to written knowledge. An audience and a message preceded the technological transformation.

**Technological Innovations.** Printing was not really invented; it evolved over time as the increased demand promoted a range of innovations in manuscript production. Johannes Gutenberg is usually credited with the first use of movable type in Europe circa 1454, but aspects of printing originated in several places. Printing required basic technological innovations such as inexpensive substances suitable for taking printed impressions (such as paper); ink that could be applied to metal surfaces and then transferred to paper; a press that would firmly press the paper to the inked metal; and a metal alloy appropriate for creating movable type. Printing words onto paper is quite similar to printing patterns onto textiles, an industry that flourished in Europe long before the first printing press. The rise of printing required that technological innovations corresponded to increased demand for written texts. This demand for books was fueled by the thirteenth-century rise of urban universities, the fourteenth-century rise of humanism with its focus on philology and textual analysis, and the fourteenth- and fifteenth-century rise of a literate urban audience that read the growing body of vernacular literature. The broad audience differed in profound ways but also shared a cultural approach of qualitative thinking and the insistence on accurate record keeping that was prerequisite to quantitative thinking.

**Market Demands.** Books, whether handcopied or printed, were commodities that were bought and sold. The earliest printed books (called incunabula) were essentially manuscripts in print. Early printers and their customers had all learned to read from handwritten manuscripts and thus they preferred books such as the 1457 *Mainz Psalter* that looked exactly like a handwritten manuscript. Perhaps the greatest difference between early books and manuscripts involved economic considerations. Scribes responded to buyer demand by taking orders to copy books. They rarely copied books in anticipation of finding buyers, with the exception of some scribes in university towns who would anticipate which books students might need. Printers, on the other hand, needed to print a large number of unordered books in order to turn a profit. Printers were thus forced to create a market for the books they printed and to print a number of titles simultaneously to hedge against a low-selling volume. This situation produced economic and intellectual issues. In a manuscript culture, the role of the scholar was to memorize, letter-perfect, key texts and comment on them. With printed books, the texts were readily available and the role of the scholar shifted to the creation of new texts. The economic issues involved raising sufficient capital to publish a number of titles and the ability to market what one printed. Combined with the changing role of the scholar, it becomes obvious that printers became more interested in printing books by known intellectuals than in printing books by aspiring scholars.

**Subject Matter.** Initially, printing presses were used to make the Bible accessible both in Latin and the vernacular to a wider audience of readers, supply university teachers and students the main texts under study, provide prayer books for church services and daily prayer, and make devotional works involving practical piety and mysticism for the lay society. The growing humanist interest in classical literature resulted in a wide range of Latin language textbooks and other works from classical antiquity and early church theologians such as Jerome and Augustine. Latin books outpaced vernacular books and scientific works in the fifteenth century. Some historians estimate that between 150–200 million books were published between 1500 and 1600. Early in that period, religious works outpaced Latin, Greek, and humanist works, but that trend was reversed later in the century. Moreover, vernacular translations of classical works began to appear in large numbers in the sixteenth century.

**Conquering the Old World.** In the 1450s a small group of printers worked in a handful of workshops in Mainz, Germany. The 1462 sack of Mainz in the so-called Bishop's War is frequently offered as an explanation for the spread of printing. (Whether printers immigrated to other parts of Europe because of the war or simply to exploit economic opportunities elsewhere is open to debate.) During the 1460s, printing expanded rapidly in Germany because of the high number of skilled metal workers, the abundance of wealthy urban merchants, and the familiarity of trade connections with the German-speaking Mainz artisans. Some Germans moved to Italy in the 1470s, and by the 1480s more than 110 towns in Western Europe had printing presses. Mainz ceased to be as significant, and the Italians grew in importance because of the better quality of their paper, the introduction of Roman type, and the humanist demand for classical texts. Spain and England relied largely on imported books, but in France a dramatic increase occurred in printing because of developments in Paris. Germany, Venice, and France were the main centers of printing at the end of the fifteenth century, but Antwerp and Basel quickly became important sites for European-wide distribution. Every major town in Germany, Italy, France, and the Low Countries (present-day Netherlands, Belgium, and Luxembourg) had a press by the early sixteenth century and every large town in Portugal, Spain, and Poland had one by the mid sixteenth century. In England,

A modern reconstruction of Johannes Gutenberg's printing workshop in Mainz

on the other hand, government restrictions limited presses largely to London.

**New World Secrets.** Portuguese voyages of exploration were kept fairly secret. Christopher Columbus's famous letter describing his first voyage was printed simultaneously in Barcelona, Rome, Basel, and Paris in 1493, reprinted in Basel in 1494 and Strasbourg in 1497, and was quickly purchased across Europe. Portuguese voyages of exploration in the East Indies had been intentionally kept fairly secret until Peter Martyr wrote *Libretto* in 1503. Other than the Columbus letter, the geographic discoveries and the imperial conquests of Spain and Portugal were not known beyond a comparatively small circle of scholars, merchants, and courtiers until about 1550. However, Sir John Mandeville's *Travels* was reprinted many times in a wide range of languages during this same period. The *Cosmographia Universalis* (General Description of the Known World) by Sebastian Münster was published in Basel in 1544 and was extremely successful, with forty-six editions in six languages in its first century in print. Shortly after Münster's work, a number of groundbreaking books on the New World were published for a wide audience. This dissemination began in Spain in 1550 when Francisco Lopez de Gomara (Hernán Cortés's secretary) published *Historia de las Indias y conquista de Mexico* and the Dominican priest Bartolome de Las Casas published *History of the Indies* in 1552. In Portugal, Joao de Barros's *Decades* appeared in 1552 and Afonso de Albuquerque's *Commentaries* were edited and published by his son in 1557. By the 1560s, an avalanche of books

William Caxton, the first printer in England, writes in the preface to his translation of Virgil's *Aeneid* about the use of the vernacular.

I confess I am not learned nor knowing the art of rhetoric, nor of such gay terms as are in these days now used . . . having no work in hand, I was sitting in my study where many diverse pamphlets and books laid, it happened that to my hand came a little book in French, which of late was translated out of Latin by some noble clerk of France . . . which book I saw over and read therein . . . in which book I had great pleasure, by cause of the fair and honest terms and words in French, which I never saw the like before, nor none so pleasant or well ordered . . . and when I had advised me in this said book, I deliberated and concluded to translate it into English. And forthwith I took a pen and ink and wrote a leaf or two, which I oversaw again to correct it. And when I saw the fair and strange terms therein I doubted that it should not please some gentleman which of late blamed me, saying that in my translations I had over curious terms which could not be understood by common people, and wanted me to use old and homely terms in my translations. And then would I satisfy every man, and so to do took an old book and read therein, and certainly the English was so rude and broad that I could not well understand it. And also my Lord Abbot of Westminster did show me of late certain evidences written in old English and to reduce it to our English now used, and certainly it was written in such a way that it was more like Dutch than English. I could not reduce it nor bring it to be understood. And certainly our language now used varies far from that which was used and spoken when I was born. For we English men are born under the domination of the moon, which is never steadfast, but ever wavering, waxing one season and waning and decreasing in another season. And that common English that is spoken in one shire varies from another. Insomuch that in my days it happened that certain merchants were in a ship in Tamyse for to have sailed over the sea into Zelande, and for lack of wind they tarried at Foreland, and went to land to refresh themselves. And one of them named Sheffeild, a mercer, came in to a house and asked for meat, and especially he asked after "egges." And the good wife answered that she could speak no French. And the merchant was angry, for he also could not speak French, but would have had "egges" and she did not understand him. And then at last another said that he would have "eyren," then the good wife said that she understood him well. Now what should a man in these days now write, "egges" or "eyren?" Certainly it is hard to please every man because of diversity and change of language. For in these days every man that is in his country will utter his communication and matters in such manners and terms that few men shall understand them. And some honest and great clerks have been with me and wanted me to write the most curious terms that I could find. And thus between plain, rude, and curious I stand abashed. But in my judgement the common terms that are used daily are lighter to understand than the old and ancient English.

Source: Douglas McMurtrie, *The Book: The Story of Printing & Bookmaking*, third revised edition (New York & London: Oxford University Press, 1962).

on the New World flooded the market and dramatically influenced how Europeans viewed non-Europeans.

**Standardization and Cross-cultural Interchange.** Printing altered written communications in many ways. Cross-cultural interchange expanded greatly with access to identical copies of a wide range of books. Readers were certain that they shared the same text as their counterparts in other areas. This degree of standardization and dissemination was not possible in a script culture because scribal mistakes inevitably crept into handcopied manuscripts. The inherent corruption of manuscripts was compounded as scribes inserted further mistakes into already tainted texts. The use of movable type did not prevent all errors, but it ensured that any errors were shared by all readers of an edition. Errors that crept into handcopied books could be changed further.

**Fixity and Certainty.** The ability to overcome scribal mistakes created a permanence of canonical texts that formed a new foundation for certainty. Tycho Brahe provides a clear example of how the new certainty could influence scientific thought. Brahe was an autodidact, or a self-taught scholar. At his remote island workshop, Brahe assembled a collection of works from a wide range of commentators in astronomy, a task that was inconceivable prior to movable type. Printing allowed him to acquire the newest theories from around the world and even to place multiple editions of a wide range of astronomers' works side by side. Brahe experienced a previously impossible opportunity to observe the heavens and simultaneously monitor various theories. He was also able to oversee the printing of his ideas and thus could be certain that accurate accounts were disseminated. Brahe possessed a certainty that was inconceivable before printing; namely, his sources were accurate and his ideas would be spread accurately.

**Piracy.** A problem inherent in the new technology of printing emerged quickly. Brahe's control over the printing of his ideas contrasts sharply with Galileo's experience one generation later. Piracy of Galileo's work was rampant because the church officially forbade the open publication of his works. As a result, circulated copies of Galileo's famous phases of the moon were largely erroneous for decades. The maintenance of accurate texts shifted from communities of clerical and lay scribes to self-serving entrepreneurs when centers of book production shifted from monasteries, university towns, and aristocratic courts to urban commercial centers.

**Skepticism.** People's skepticism of printed books changed as communities of readers came to experience written knowledge in new ways. Initial skepticism centered on the remarkable number of books that could be produced. Contemporaries commonly attributed the new output to either God or the Devil. Early printers began to use a "printer's mark" to identify whose movable type had been used to print the book. (No such producer's marks were used by scribes for their handcopied books.) The printer's mark evolved into the modern trademark. In the sixteenth century, entrepreneurial printers began to include the firm's name and the location of their shop on the front page of the books, thereby creating the title page. Fifteenth-century books, both hand and machine produced, placed this information at the end of the book in what was called a colophon. Although a colophon did not always include the title and name of the author, the movement to a title page became a method for selling books as authors such as Desiderius Erasmus and Martin Luther came to achieve celebrity status in society. Consequently the celebration of the author as cultural hero reinforced the growing national consciousness that vernacular literature had helped to create. Written knowledge thus created communities of conscious readers during the Reformation who bought and collected written texts at a pace and in a manner that was not possible in the early Renaissance.

Sources:

Roger Chartier, *The Order of Books: Readers, Authors, and Libraries in Europe between the Fourteenth and Eighteenth Centuries,* translated by Lydia G. Cochrane (Stanford, Cal.: Stanford University Press, 1994).

Elizabeth L. Eisenstein, *The Printing Press as an Agent of Change: Communications and Cultural Transformations in Early Modern Europe,* 2 volumes (Cambridge & New York: Cambridge University Press, 1979).

Lucien Febvre and Henri-Jean Martin, *The Coming of the Book: The Impact of Printing 1450-1800,* translated by David Gerard, edited by Geoffrey Nowell-Smith and David Wootton (London: N.L.B., 1976).

Douglas McMurtrie, *The Book: The Story of Printing & Bookmaking,* third revised edition (New York & London: Oxford University Press, 1962).

## TRANSPORTATION AND SHIPPING

**Trade Routes.** European trade followed two "urban belts" that stretched east-west along the Mediterranean Sea and south-north from Italy to the Netherlands. The Italians played a central role in both trade networks and held almost monopolistic control of the southern east-west axis. Mediterranean trade was lucrative because of the high number of luxury items from Asia, such as spices and silk, that flowed through Italy. These items were carried overland across Asia and placed on Italian ships in the eastern Mediterranean area known as the Levant. Venetian and Genoese merchants dominated Mediterranean trade as far west as Cadiz and Lisbon. The Italians used the Iberian ports to sell eastern goods and to purchase textiles from northern Europe. The Italians also played a major role in the south-north trade routes by shipping items north to England and Flanders or transporting them overland across France or through Alpine mountain passes. Overland travel was costly and thus was limited mainly to luxury items such as the vibrant spice trade. The northern end of the south-north axis consisted of cities with access to the North Sea. They also controlled a third, and less lucrative, trade axis that went west-east from the ports of the North Sea and the Baltic to the rivers stretching into the European Great Plain (Poland and Russia).

**Political and Geographical Limits.** The location and geography of the Italian peninsula favored shipping more than land transportation. In the early Renaissance, Italian territories and city-states were frequently in protracted wars that were often decided by battles fought at sea. The necessity of a strong navy and the lower cost of shipping by sea meant that resources were turned toward the sea and shipping as opposed to the development of overland routes. The Iberian peninsula on the far western shore of Europe was also better situated for sea than land travel. The Pyrenees, a mountain range that separated the peninsula from the rest of Europe, forced merchants in Iberia to turn to the seas for trade. North of the Alps and Pyrenees, the northern monarchs fought several long dynastic wars with neighboring rulers in the early Renaissance that discouraged overland trade. For instance, the Hundred Years' War (1337–1453) between England and France disrupted trade and discouraged rulers from devoting money to the development of road networks. In Germany, the Holy Roman Empire was a jigsaw puzzle of local princes and lesser nobles who were more interested in personal gain than in the well-being of the empire beyond their own territories. Free Imperial Cities in the empire did form leagues to promote trade, but they were forced to travel through vast territories that were not participants in the confederations. The most famous of these leagues was the Hanseatic League or Hansa, a group of German and Baltic cities that dominated the northern trade until the sixteenth century, when Dutch merchants slowly gained dominance in the region.

**Overland Transportation.** Overland transportation was severely limited by the political realities of feudal society. There were few incentives for rulers to devote their limited finances to the development of road networks. Overland routes frequently followed the old Roman roads, but they were in a condition much worse than they had been during the Roman Empire. During the Renaissance, powerful dynastic families unified vast territories and created a potential for governments to invest in infrastructure such as roads. Instead, they

A model of Christopher Columbus's caravel *Niña*
(from Angus Konstan, *Historical Atlas of
Exploration*, 2000)

late-Roman times divided shipping between a long ship, or galley, and a round ship. Galleys relied on human power to row the boat and thus had less room devoted to cargo. They were used for the military and to ship luxury goods in the Mediterranean but were unsuitable for the Atlantic. Round ships, on the other hand, relied on winds and thus had a smaller crew. They were the main cargo ship in the Mediterranean. Virtually all Mediterranean ships had curved keels that were well suited for a sea without tides. The Mediterranean ships experienced rough sailing on the waves and strong winds of the Atlantic Ocean. The cog, a northern ship developed on the ports of the Baltic Sea, had a straight keel that provided more stability. Cogs were built with overlapping planks that were frequently strengthened by internal frames. They were steered with an axial stern rudder and powered with a single square sail. Clumsy and slow, the cogs were also able to carry an extremely large cargo with a small crew. They immediately caught the eye of sailors when they first arrived in the Mediterranean Sea.

**Riggings.** The square sails of the Baltic cogs prevented ships from sailing into a head wind, whereas the lanteen sails allowed sailing with less favorable winds. Most Mediterranean ships had rectangular sails until the Arab lanteen sail was introduced. The lanteen provided maneuverability and the ability to sail into partial head winds by tacking, or zigzagging, back and forth. The lanteen sail also prevented ships from putting about, but the size of the sail was limited because it was difficult to control. Mediterranean sailors increased the number of masts to three, but they eventually turned to the square sails of northern ships to remedy the problem. Initially they used square sails on two masts and a lanteen sail on a third mast, but later they combined the sails into complicated riggings on three-mast ships.

**Caravels and *Naos*.** Iberian mariners wisely combined the best aspects of northern and southern seafaring traditions and created two boats that could carry a large cargo, steer well, and sail in either the Mediterranean or the open seas: the caravel and *nao*. Caravels were developed in Portugal for use along the West African coast. Three or four masts carried a complicated rigging on ships with one deck. The caravels were rather small and cabin space was limited. *Naos* were larger than caravels and functioned as square-rigged cargo carriers. Columbus brought one *nao* and two caravels on his initial journey across the Atlantic. *Naos* armed with cannons were used during voyages of exploration to carry extra supplies and, later, colonists.

**Galleons and *Fluyts*.** The combination of northern and southern rigging and shipbuilding culminated in the military galleons and the cargo-carrying *fluyts* of the sixteenth century. Longer and narrower than the caravels and *naos*, the three-masted galleons were developed by the Italians. The ships were capable of transoceanic travel but had limited cargo space. The Spanish, English, and Dutch built large fleets of galleons for use as specialized warships. The

devoted their resources to the military and the construction of facilities for shipping. The Protestant Reformation polarized Europe and further stifled overland transportation. European governments did not construct strong networks of roads until changes in the military dictated a necessity for better overland transportation. Renaissance rulers who were reluctant to invest in a network for land transportation were quick to devote money and prestige to shipping and maritime trade.

**Shipbuilding.** The century after the Black Death (1347–1351) was a time of extensive innovations in the design of European ships. By the end of the fifteenth century, shipbuilders across Europe were constructing similar types of ships. The convergence of northern and southern styles of ship construction corresponded with a convergence of northern and southern methods of rigging. The resulting ships (caravels and *naos*) were designed to satisfy the commercial and military needs of the day, but they proved to be suitable for blue-water voyages across the ocean. Transoceanic voyages became possible when maritime explorers sailed Iberian caravels and *naos* on the famous early voyages to the Americas and India. The two vessels of discovery continued to dominate shipping throughout the sixteenth century when the rulers who supported exploration turned to conquest and colonization.

**Galleys and Cogs.** Mediterranean ships had rudders, which allowed precise handling of the vessels, and three-sided sails (lanteen sails) that allowed ships to utilize wind from any direction. Mediterranean navies since

Dutch *fluyts*, or flyboats, used innovative hull design to create long ships with fairly flat bottoms. They became a vital part of the late-sixteenth-century expansion of Dutch trade. The galleon was a precursor to frigates and ships of the line, whereas the *fluyt* was a precursor to commercial freighters.

**Warships.** By 1450 the differences between Atlantic and Mediterranean ships were insignificant because the northern and southern styles had merged into the caravels and *naos*. Yet, Atlantic navies did develop a different notion of how a ship could be used in warfare. Mediterranean navies since late Roman times split shipping between a "round ship" and a "long ship." The long ship, or galley, was equipped with oars and used as a warship, whereas the "round ship" depended on sail to carry cargo. The Venetians developed the galleass, or "great galley," a hybrid that combined oars and sails. Galleasses became popular but still required a crew that could row them. The large crew of the galleasses made them more expensive to operate and limited their operational range. The galleys remained the most common Mediterranean war vessel until the seventeenth century. However, these galleys were not suitable for the choppier and windier Atlantic Ocean. Atlantic war fleets were forced to modify their sailing ships for military purposes. Henry VII of England built two sailing ships manned with guns in 1487 and King John II of Portugal simultaneously experimented with cannons on small caravels. This new approach allowed Atlantic navies to replace rowers with sails and guns. The shift from human energy to wind power on warships provided Europeans with sufficient protection to turn their sails to the most distant seas. Sixteenth-century developments with the galleons and *fluyts* allowed Europeans to expand maritime trade to a global scale.

Sources:

Carlo Cipolla, *Guns, Sails, and Empires: Technological Innovation and the Early Phases of European Expansion, 1400-1700* (New York: Minerva, 1965).

Jan Glete, *Warfare at Sea, 1500-1650: Maritime Conflicts and the Transformation of Europe* (London: Routledge, 2000).

J. H. Parry, *The Age of Reconnaissance* (Cleveland: World, 1963).

J. R. S. Phillips, *The Medieval Expansion of Europe* (Oxford & New York: Oxford University Press, 1988).

William D. Phillips Jr. and Carla Rahn Phillips, *The Worlds of Christopher Columbus* (Cambridge & New York: Cambridge University Press, 1992).

Geoffrey Vaughan Scammell, *The First Imperial Age: European Overseas Expansion, c.1400-1715* (London: Unwin Hyman, 1989).

Roger C. Smith, *Vanguard of Empire: Ships of Exploration in the Age of Columbus* (New York: Oxford University Press, 1993).

Richard W. Unger, *The Ship in the Medieval Economy, 600-1600* (London: Croom Helm, 1980).

## VOYAGES OF EXPLORATION: PORTUGAL

**Ceuta.** King John I of Portugal was a popular ruler who defeated neighboring Castile in 1411 and temporarily ended a long string of wars between Portugal and Castile. He had a politically beneficial marriage to Philippa of Lancaster, the daughter of John of Gaunt, with whom he had six children: Edward, Pedro, Henry, Isabel, John, and Ferdinand. In 1414, the three oldest sons were at the age to make a name for themselves on the battlefield, but Castile was no longer a threat. Instead, they planned an attack on the North African city of Ceuta, a Moorish city strategically located south of the Straits of Gibraltar at the western entrance to the Mediterranean Sea. The plan was based in part on youthful pursuit of adventure, greed for the wares of Ceuta, and a crusading mentality that encouraged Christians to attack the Muslims. Ships were outfitted in the summer of 1415 when, on the eve of the scheduled departure, Queen Philippa died unexpectedly of the plague. Four days later, hundreds of vessels set sail in order to fulfill the queen's purported death wish of conquering the Ceuta infidels. Bad winds and a severe storm scattered the fleet and caused some to question the wisdom of sailing so soon after the queen's death. The remaining ships regrouped and finally reached their destination one month after setting sail. Ceuta fell in one day.

**Henry the Navigator.** Prince Henry, better known to modern readers as Henry the Navigator, participated in the capture of Ceuta. However, his more important contribution to exploration is that he purportedly gathered scholars, navigators, and mapmakers at Sagres, on the peninsula of Saint Vincent overlooking the Atlantic. Henry did not actually establish a "school of navigation" at Sagres, but he certainly perpetuated the image of scientific navigation by overseeing Portuguese exploration along the West African Coast. Under Henry's supervision, Portuguese sailors were the first Europeans on record to reach the Atlantic islands of Madeira (1418) and the Azores (1427). Henry's captains led the way down the western coast of Africa: Gil Eanes rounded the dangerous Cape Bojador (1434); Nuno Tristão sighted Cape Blanc (1442), discovered the mouth of the Senegal River (1444), and explored the mouth of the Gambia River (1446); Dinis Dias reached Cape Verde and explored Palmas Island (1444); Ca'da Mosto was perhaps the first to land on the Cape Verde Islands (1456); and Pedro da Sintra sighted and named Mount Auriol in Sierra Leone (1460). Modern historians have been critical of Henry's role in Portuguese exploration, but they cannot deny that the Portuguese made tremendous advances in shipbuilding and exploration during his lifetime.

**Gomes Eanes de Zurara.** The fourteenth-century Portuguese chronicler Gomes Eanes de Zurara wrote both a history of Ceuta and a chronicle of Portuguese exploration. The chronicle of exploration opens with praise for "that most glorious conquest of the great city of Ceuta." He clearly believed that the conquest of Ceuta was the defining origin of Portuguese expansion. According to Zurara, Ceuta was the catalyst for exploration and Henry was the most influential person in Portugal's voyages of discovery. Zurara outlines six factors that motivated Henry: (1) curiosity about lands beyond the Canary Islands; (2) opportunity to profit from trade; (3) knowledge of the extent and power of the "infidels"; (4) discovery of Christian rulers who could support Henry in the war against non-Chris-

A glazed earthenware bowl depicting a high-decked *nao*, which was superior to Spanish caravels for ocean voyages
(British Museum)

tians; (5) conversion of people to Christianity; and (6) the desire to fulfill the predictions of Henry's horoscope. The "heavenly wheels" were aligned such that Henry "should toil at high and mighty conquests, especially in seeking out things that were hidden from other men." Zurara offers the portrait of Henry as a medieval man hoping to serve God, grow rich, and fulfill his astrological potential.

**Motives.** God and greed were two obvious motives for most Renaissance explorers. Crusading zeal, the quest to find the legendary kingdom of Prester John, an appetite for Guinea gold, the acquisition of African slaves, and the pursuit of spices were clearly motives for the Portuguese. Portuguese exploration was also motivated by several political, economic, and geographical factors that distinguish it from other early exploration. Politically, Portugal was united during the fifteenth century, whereas most European territories were involved in dynastic wars. The Portuguese Crown encouraged, financed, and protected both those sailing on the voyages and those who invested in the voy-

ages. The Crown supported exploration for new trade routes in part because the expanding Ottoman Empire was limiting European access to Indian spices. The Portuguese wanted to bypass the Muslim traders and deal directly with India. Their location on the Iberian peninsula left them particularly vulnerable to fluctuations in Muslim trade. The Iberian peninsula was geographically well placed for European overseas expansion in general, and Portugal was well situated for sailing down the West African coast because that is the direction of the prevailing winds that blow down the West African coast, toward islands in the Atlantic, and eventually across to Brazil. Moreover, the westerlies, winds that blow from west to east across the Atlantic Ocean, were easily caught in the Americas and comfortably sailed back to Portugal.

**Technology and Innovations.** Portugal's unique geographical location allowed the Portuguese to monitor maritime inventions from the northern Baltic to the Levant in the eastern Mediterranean Sea. This knowledge fostered the invention of new maritime technologies and, more importantly, the employment of innovations practiced elsewhere. The most famous adaptations include: placing a central rudder on the stern post of the keel (Scandinavians), utilizing a magnetic needle and compass (Arabs), using a three-sided lanteen sail (Levanters), and navigating from portolan charts with compass and rhumb lines (Italians).

**Modifications.** In the mid fifteenth century, Portuguese shipbuilders combined Baltic and Mediterranean construction and rigging in the caravels and *naos*. Caravels were further modified with complicated combinations of square and lanteen sails in order to simplify return voyages from Guinea. The ability to sail in the open seas also forced innovations in navigation. With the exception of the Gulf of Guinea, the West African coast follows a north-south direction that forced navigators to calculate latitude. The Pole Star, or North Star, was used as a reference point and a simple quadrant was used to calculate latitude. By the death of Prince Henry in 1460, Portuguese ships were as far south as Sierra Leone and the Pole Star was barely visible above the horizon.

**Southern Cross.** Astrolabes, a sighting instrument perfected in the Muslim East for calculating celestial coordinates, were used to measure latitude based on the height of the sun. King John II appointed a commission in 1484 to improve the necessary calculations and to draft tables of declination suitable for Portuguese travel. These charts were effective only if the sun was visible at noon. By 1500, Portuguese mariners were aware of the Southern Cross, the Southern Hemisphere's equivalent to the North Star. Vasco da Gama employed an Arab pilot for his voyage across the Indian Ocean and Portuguese captains after da Gama were eager to employ native navigators to help them sail and chart foreign seas. The flexibility to adapt technology and techniques allowed the Portuguese to develop a major presence in eastern trade routes.

**Fortified Trading Posts.** Historians debate where Columbus exactly landed on his first voyage, but there is little debate about the locations of Portuguese landings. The Portuguese kept meticulous records of landfall and left wooden crosses, and later stone pillars, to mark the spots. King John II established the practice of marking landfall as a sign of possession and superiority in the early 1480s. In the fifteenth and sixteenth centuries, the Portuguese accumulated a tremendous amount of information about navigation and trade routes. They used this information in a different manner than the other major European nations of exploration. Nations with greater populations, such as France and England, signed treaties and created colonies, whereas the Portuguese preferred to establish "factories," or trading stations. The establishment of forts to protect trading stations evolved into the creation of *feitorias,* or fortified trading posts. Portuguese explorers sought defensible points that were strategic for military or trade purposes. They then established as small a force as was necessary to hold the fort. In some areas of the Indian Ocean they avoided any actual settlement and opted instead to control a trading point on a nearby island. The control of the Indian city of Gao and other key points allowed the Portuguese to profit from trade without incurring the tremendous cost of military occupation. This successful strategy proved to be a weakness in the seventeenth century, when the Dutch and English began to capture Portuguese forts and dominate trade.

**Bartholomeu Dias.** Bartholomeu Dias rounded the Cape of Good Hope in 1488 and dispelled the Ptolemaic belief that the Indian Ocean was a landlocked sea. Prior to 1488 the Portuguese had gained control of several islands off the African coast. These islands were financially rewarding as locations of actual production, as trading bases, and as centers for the growing slave trade, but they offered no new trade routes to India. Dias's voyage suggested that the Portuguese could reach India by sea. Moreover, Dias sailed correctly around dangerous Cape Agulhas, south of the Cape of Good Hope. He found a route to India and the safest way to round the extremely treacherous southern point of Africa. The journey was also revolutionary in that it proved that the South Atlantic wind system was symmetrical with the known pattern of the Northern Hemisphere. Prince Henry the Navigator's motives were remarkably similar to those of Dias, who claimed that he had sailed "to give light to those who are in darkness and to grow rich."

**Sea Route to India.** The Portuguese gave the southern cape of Africa the name *The Cape of Good Hope* "for the promise it gave of the finding of India." The idea of a sea route to India was further supported by a written report based on overland travel to Eastern Africa. The same year that Dias had departed for his famous voyage, King John II sent two Arabic-speaking Portuguese on separate land journeys to Abyssinia (Ethiopia) and India. Pero da Covilhã visited the Malabar Coast of India, the Persian Gulf, the Red Sea, and the eastern coast of Africa. On his return trip, he stopped in Cairo and sent a written account to Portugal in 1492. The sea report of Dias combined with the overland report of Covilhã offered solid evidence that the Portuguese could sail south and then east to India.

**Treaty of Tordesillas.** The same year Covilhã's account was written, a Genoese captain named Christopher Columbus sailed under Spanish colors on a voyage on which he claimed had reached islands off the eastern coast of Asia. The Crowns of Castile and Portugal found themselves in a heated competition to claim rights to newly discovered areas. The 1494 Treaty of Tordesillas solved the debate by dividing the world into a western area for Castile and an eastern area for Portugal. John II and his advisers began planning an eastern voyage to India that would pass the Cape of Good Hope.

**Christians and Spice.** In 1495 Manuel I became king of Portugal and inherited the plans for da Gama to sail to Asia. Two well-armed ships were built specifically for the voyage and two other ships were modified for the trip. In 1497 Gama departed with four ships on a two-year voyage. For the first ninety-six days Gama sailed beyond the sight

## MOMBASA

In the following excerpt from "The East Coast of Africa," the Portuguese government official Duarte Barbosa describes the African town of Mombasa around 1518 and the resulting effect of Portuguese influence on it.

Further on, an advance along the coast toward India, there is an isle hard by the mainland, on which there is a town called Mombasa . . . this Mombasa is a land very full of food. Here are found many very fine sheep with round tails, cows and other cattle in great plenty, and many fowls, all of which are exceedingly fat. There is much millet and rice, sweet and bitter oranges, lemons, pomegranates, Indian figs, vegetables of diverse kinds, and much sweet water. The men are often times at war . . . but at peace with those of the mainland, and they carry on trade with them, obtaining great amounts of honey, wax, and ivory.

The king of this city refused to obey the commands of the King our Lord, and through his arrogance he lost it, and our Portuguese took it from him by force. He fled away, and they slew many of his people and also took captive many, both men and women, in such sort that it was left ruined and plundered and burned. Of gold and silver great booty was taken here, bangles, bracelets, earrings, and gold beads, also great store of copper with other rich wares in great quantity, and the town was left in ruins.

Source: *The Book of Duarte Barbosa: An Account of the Countries Bordering on the Indian Ocean and Their Inhabitants*, 2 volumes, edited by Mansel Longworth Dames (London: Hakluyt Society, 1918–1921).

that would allow the Portuguese to achieve naval supremacy in the Indian Ocean.

Sources:

C. R. Boxer, *Four Centuries of Portuguese Expansion, 1415-1825: A Succinct Survey* (Johannesburg: Witwatersrand University Press, 1961).

Felipe Fernández-Armesto, *Before Columbus: Exploration and Colonisation from the Mediterranean to the Atlantic, 1229-1492* (Houndmills, U.K.: Macmillan Education, 1987).

J. H. Parry, *The Age of Reconnaissance* (Cleveland: World, 1963).

J. R. S. Phillips, *The Medieval Expansion of Europe* (Oxford & New York: Oxford University Press, 1988).

A. J. R. Russell-Wood, *A World on the Move: The Portuguese in Africa, Asia, and America, 1415-1808* (New York: St. Martin's Press, 1993).

Geoffrey Vaughan Scammell, *The First Imperial Age: European Overseas Expansion, c.1400-1715* (London: Unwin Hyman, 1989).

### VOYAGES OF EXPLORATION: SPAIN

**Trends.** The Italian explorer Christopher Columbus lived during the convergence of several long-term trends that contributed to maritime exploration: the crusading spirit of Medieval Christians; the quest for contact with Asia; the Renaissance pursuit of knowledge and glory; innovations in the construction of ships; and cartographers' search for better methods of mapping. Since the twelfth century, Europeans had sought new routes to the Far East. Columbus's voyages combined that quest with a militant Christian mentality that had been launched centuries earlier in the crusades. He lived in an age of Renaissance developments in printing, literacy, engineering, and shipbuilding that vastly changed the mental horizon. Printing provided Columbus with access to a broad array of notions about the earth's size and shape. Moreover, technological advances in ship construction and riggings allowed the Portuguese to explore the coast of Africa.

**Western Route.** The Portuguese voyages forced cartographers to gradually reconsider how they mapped Africa and the world. Fifteenth-century world maps tended to follow the Ptolemaic conception of the world as three large land masses surrounded by smaller bodies of water. Columbus was one of many fifteenth-century navigators and geographers who believed that the Atlantic Ocean was actually a fairly narrow body of water. The idea derived from a thirteenth-century Franciscan named Roger Bacon and gained impetus in the early fifteenth century, when Pierre d'Ailly revived the study of Ptolemy. Columbus and Nuremberg geographer Martin Behaim applied Marco Polo's land distances to Ptolemy's erroneous estimate of the earth's size. In 1474 the Florentine geographer Paolo Toscanelli dal Pozzo had written to the king of Portugal that one could sail roughly five thousand miles west from Portugal to China with stops at islands along the way. Toscanelli's theories were well known on the Iberian Peninsula in the decade before Columbus sailed. Columbus believed that he could sail west from the Canary Islands and would reach Japan after only 2,400 nautical miles (the actual distance is 10,600 nautical miles). He presented the idea of a western passage to Asia, his so-called

of land. The decision to stay away from the African Coast after he reached Sierra Leone allowed him to make landfall less than one hundred miles northwest of the Cape of Good Hope. It also opened his voyage with what was at that time the longest European voyage out of sight of land (nearly three times as long as Columbus's near-mutinous sailors had experienced). The fact that he could continue without mutiny is evidence of the seafaring abilities of the Portuguese. Da Gama rounded the Cape and headed north along the African coast until Malindi. At Malindi he employed Ahamad-Ibn-Madjid, an Arab pilot who was familiar with the Indian Ocean. Ibn-Madjid sailed da Gama straight to Calicut, a major trade center, where the Portuguese were surprised to find North African merchants who spoke their language. When asked what had brought them to Calicut, the Portuguese responded "Christians and spices," the same duo that had motivated Prince Henry almost a century earlier. After a three-month stay in Calicut, Gama returned home. Only two of the four ships made it back to Portugal and they carried only small amounts of spices. Yet, the ships also carried a treasury of knowledge

Enterprise of the Indies, to King John II of Portugal in the early 1480s. John II refused to support Columbus's proposal but shortly thereafter supported at least two other westward expeditions in search of new islands.

**Spanish Support.** Columbus moved to Spain in 1485. Spain may have been a better candidate for patronage because Columbus planned to turn west at the Spanish-controlled Canary Islands. Two 1479 treaties between Portugal and Castile had essentially barred Spanish mariners from African trade beyond the Canary Islands. Moreover, Portugal was also pursuing a possible sea route to Asia around the southern tip of Africa at that time. Columbus made a proposal that the Spanish royal family compensate for Portugal's control of western Africa by supporting his project to open a new trade route to Asia. The proposal also revealed religious motives that were consistent with the Spanish Inquisition (in 1492, the recently unified Spaniards defeated the Muslims at Granada and expelled them from Spain). After several rejections, Castile finally agreed to fund Columbus and grant him significant benefits for any land he might claim for the Spanish crown. He was given a *nao*, or cargo ship, called the *Santa Maria* and two smaller caravels called the *Pinta* and *Niña* (the *Niña* was actually named the *Santa Clara* but was referred to as the *Niña* because its owner was Juan Niño). The owners of all three ships joined the expedition, but Columbus had problems finding a crew until a local shipowner named Martin Alonso Pinzón and his younger brother Vincente Yáñez Pinzón agreed to captain the *Pinta* and *Niña*.

**Discovery.** On 12 October 1492 Columbus landed on present-day San Salvador in the Caribbean Sea and thereby became the first European to voyage to the Americas with a written record of the voyage. He named the people he encountered *Indians* because he believed he was near India. He soon realized that Asian traders were not in the vicinity and that the available luxury items were limited. Columbus searched further until he reached Cuba, which he mistakenly believed was part of the mainland. He did not find gold in Cuba, but he did note in his diary the abundance of pine trees that were both suitable for shipbuilding and the sites with sufficient water power to run sawmills. Historians have found in those comments the origins of a shift from the Portuguese trading-post model of exploration to the Spanish and English model of settlement and colonization. Columbus may not have given up his dream of finding gold, but he did shift the focus of his diary to descriptions of fertile lands and industrious people. When the *Santa Maria*, the larger *nao*, ran aground and broke apart, Columbus was forced to abandon his flagship and any hope of bringing a sizeable cargo of treasures back to Europe. Thirty-nine men remained in a fort constructed from the wrecked ship. Columbus turned the shipwreck into a sign from God that he should found a settlement.

An Aztec depiction of the Spanish at the Great Temple in Tenochtitlán, 1576 (British Library)

**Indians.** In a letter written six months after landing in the Caribbean, Columbus also used the shipwreck to rationalize the paucity of goods. In the letter he attempted to convince a broad audience that better provisions should be supplied for a future trip. He also suggested that settlement and colonization were the best way to profit from the Indies. Columbus even outlined how the Indians might be converted to Christianity. To facilitate these conversions, Columbus had found it imperative to prevent the other Europeans from cheating the Indians with unfair trades. He thereby rationalized his efforts to monopolize all trade with the Indians. These restrictions may have motivated Martin Pinzón to take the *Pinta* and leave the other two ships one month before the shipwreck of the *Santa Maria*. Two days after Columbus had left thirty-nine men behind, and forty-six days after the *Pinta* had sailed away from the other ships, the *Pinta* chanced to encounter the *Niña*. The two captains reconciled and the two ships sailed together again. Shortly thereafter, the Europeans faced their only

With financial support from Queen Isabella of Castile, Italian explorer Christopher Columbus set sail in 1492 in search of a new sea route to China. Trade had been disrupted due to Muslim conquests along the traditional Mediterranean route, and Columbus was searching for an alternate route. The following letter was written six months after Columbus landed in the Caribbean. It was intended for a wide audience and was one of the most widely printed documents from the voyages of discovery.

Knowing that it will afford you pleasure to learn that I have brought my undertaking to a successful termination, I have decided upon writing you this letter to acquaint you with all the events which have occurred in my voyage, and the discoveries which have resulted from it. Thirty-three days after my departure from Cadiz I reached the Indian Sea, where I discovered many islands, thickly peopled, of which I took possession without resistance in the name of our most illustrious monarch, by public proclamation and with unfurled banners. To the first of these islands, which is called by the Indians Guanahani, I gave the name of the blessed Saviour (San Salvador) relying upon whose protection I had reached this as well as the other islands; to each of these I also gave a name. . . .

Thus they bartered like idiots, cotton and gold for fragments of bows, glasses, bottles, and jars; which I forbade as being unjust, and myself gave them many beautiful and acceptable articles which I had brought with me, taking nothing from them in return; I did this in order that I might the more easily conciliate them, that they might be led to become Christians, and be inclined to entertain a regard for the King and Queen, our Princes and all Spaniards, and that I might induce them to take an interest in seeking out, and collecting, and delivering to use such things as they possessed in abundance, but which we greatly needed. . . .

In all these islands there is no difference of physiognomy, of manners, or of language, but they all clearly understand each other, a circumstance very propitious for the realization of what I conceive to be the principal wish of our most serene King, namely, the conversion of these people to the holy faith of Christ. . . .

Finally, to compress into a few words the entire summary of my voyage and speedy return, and of the advantages derivable therefore, I promise, that with a little assistance afforded me by our most invincible sovereigns, I will procure them as much gold as they need, as great a quantity of spices, of cotton, and of mastic (which is only found in Chios), and as many when for the service of the navy as their Majesties may require. I promise also rhubarb and other sorts of drugs, which I am persuaded the men whom I have left in the aforesaid fortress have found already and will continue to find; for I myself have tarried no where longer than I was compelled to do by the winds, except in the city of Navidad, while I provided for the building of the fortress, and took the necessary precautions for the perfect security of the men I left there. Although all I have related may appear to be wonderful and unheard of, yet the results of my voyage would have been more astonishing if I had had at my disposal such ships as I required.

But these great and marvelous results are not to be attributed to any merit of mine, but to the holy Christian faith, and to the piety and religion of our Sovereigns; for that which the unaided intellect of man could not compass, the spirit of God has granted to human exertions, for God is wont to hear the prayers of his servants who love his precepts even to the performance of apparent impossibilities.

Source: Christopher Columbus, *Letters*, translated and edited by R. H. Major (London: Hakluyt Society, 1847), pp. 1-17.

significant military encounter with the Indians. Columbus then decided to return to Spain.

**Second Voyage.** Columbus wrote Luis de Santángel a letter that was meant for wide circulation. The letter does not correspond with his diary, apparently because he wanted to create an image of the Indies that would encourage further support. Columbus was made "Admiral of the Ocean Sea" and "Viceroy and Governor" of the new lands. He was instructed to select the best caravels and crews for a return voyage that would establish a royal monopoly over trade in the area. Rather than create a Portuguese-style trading post, Columbus was to begin a process of settlement and colonization. He set sail in September 1493 with seventeen vessels, including three heavily loaded *naos*. Upon returning to the Caribbean, he faced heated combat with the natives. He also learned that the thirty-nine Europeans who had stayed in the Caribbean on the first voyage were all dead. Columbus's propaganda backfired during the second voyage, and he had to face the reality that he was unable to accumulate spectacular amounts of gold and silver in a short period of time. The second voyage did provide some slaves for Spain but few riches. From a financial perspective, the voyage was a disaster because the rewards did not cover

The following account describes from the native's perspective the brutal Spanish destruction of the Aztec capital Tenochtitlán in 1519.

Spanish conquistador Hernán Cortés provides the Spanish perspective of the destruction of Tenochtitlán in an excerpt from one of his letters, written on 12 August 1521.

The greatest evil that one can do to another is to take his life when [the victim] is in mortal sin. This is what the Spaniards did to the Mexican Indians because they provoked them by being faithless in honoring their idols. [The Spaniards], catching [the Indians] enclosed [in the courtyard] for the feast [of Huitzilopochtli], killed them, the greater part of whom were unarmed, without their knowing why.

When the great courtyard of the idol, Huitzilopochtli, god of the Mexicans, was full of nobles, priests, and soldiers, and throngs of other people, intent upon the idolatrous songs to that idol, whom they were honoring, the Spaniards suddenly poured forth ready for combat and blocked the exits of the courtyard so that none could escape. Then they entered with their weapons and ranged themselves all along the inner walls of the courtyard. The Indians thought that they were just admiring the style of their dancing and playing and singing, and so continued with their celebration and songs.

At this moment, the first Spaniards to start fighting suddenly attacked those who were playing the music for the singers and dancers. They chopped off their hands and their heads so that they fell down dead. Then all the other Spaniards began to cut off heads, arms, and legs, and to disembowel the Indians. Some had their heads cut off, others were cut in half, and others had their bellies slit open, immediately to fall dead. Others dragged their entrails along until they collapsed. Those who reached the exits were slain by the Spaniards guarding them; and others jumped over the walls of the courtyard; while yet others climbed up the temple; and still others, seeing no escape, threw themselves down among the slaughtered and escaped by feigning death.

So great was the bloodshed that rivers of blood ran through the courtyard like water in a heavy rain. So great was the slime of blood and entrails in the courtyard and so great was the stench that it was both terrifying and heartrending. Now that nearly all were fallen and dead, the Spaniards went searching for those who had climbed up the temple and those who had hidden among the dead, killing all those they found alive.

Source: "The Destruction of Tenochtitlan," in Bernardino de Sahagun, *The Conquest of New Spain,* translated by Howard F. Cline (Salt Lake City: University of Utah Press, 1989), pp. 76-78.

On leaving my camp, I had commanded Gonzalo de Sandoval to sail the brigantines [ships] in between the houses in the other quarter in which the Indians were resisting, so that we should have them surrounded, but not to attack until he saw that we were engaged. In this way they would be surrounded and so hard pressed that they would have no place to move save over the bodies of their dead or along the roof tops. They no longer had nor could find any arrows, javelins, or stones with which to attack up; and our allies fighting with us were armed with swords and bucklers, and slaughtered so many of them on land and in the water that more than forty thousand were killed or taken that day. So loud was the wailing of the women and children that there was no one man among us whose heart did not bleed at the sound; and indeed we had more trouble in preventing our allies from killing with such cruelty than we had in fighting the enemy. For no race, however savage, has ever practiced such fierce and unnatural cruelty as the natives of these parts. Our allies also took many spoils that day, which we were unable to prevent, as they numbered more than 150,000 and we Spaniards were only some nine hundred. Neither our precautions nor our warnings could stop their looting, though we did all we could. One of the reasons why I had avoided entering the city in force during the past days was the fear that if we attempted to storm them they would throw all they possessed into the water, and, even if they did not, our allies would take all they could find. For this reason I was much afraid that your Majesty would receive only a small part of the great wealth this city once had, in comparison with all that I once held for your highness. Because it was now late, and we could no longer endure the stench of the dead bodies that had lain in those streets for many days, which was the most loathsome thing in the world, we returned to our camps.

Source: "We Could No Longer Endure the Stench of Dead Bodies," from Hernándo Cortés, *Letters from Mexico,* translated and edited by Anthony Pagden (New Haven: Yale University Press, 1986), pp. 261–262.

the great cost of the initial fleet and of relief ships that had been sent. In 1496 Columbus returned from his second voyage to a royal family that was no longer interested in elaborately funding colonization.

**Third and Fourth Voyages.** Columbus eventually persuaded Ferdinand and Isabella to fund eight ships on a voyage that was to create a self-sustaining colony. Authorization was given to bring three hundred men and thirty women as new colonists, but only two hundred and twenty-six could be found. Columbus returned to the Caribbean in the summer of 1498 to find chaos that was beyond his control. In October 1500, Columbus and his two brothers were arrested and sent home in chains. The king and queen received Columbus well upon his return but they refused to let him serve again as viceroy and governor. On a fourth and final voyage in 1502, Columbus and his entire crew were shipwrecked. After being rescued, Columbus returned to Spain in late 1504 and died two years later, still convinced that he had sailed west to islands off the eastern coast of Asia.

**The Americas.** Spain clearly agreed with Columbus's assessment that he had found a new sea route to Asia because the government created a Council of the Indies. Another Italian, Amerigo Vespucci of Florence, made a voyage to Venezuela under the Spanish flag in 1499–1500. Vespucci's second voyage (1501–1502), this time under the Portuguese flag, forced geographers to reassess their conception of the world. Vespucci knew that Pedro Cabral had sighted Brazil while leading a Portuguese fleet along a route similar to that of da Gama's famous voyage around the Cape of Good Hope. Vespucci used this information to chart the Brazilian coast along a south-southwest route that he believed crossed the 1494 Treaty of Tordesillas's line dividing Spanish and Portuguese areas. Vespucci correctly surmised that South America was a new world distinct from Asia. His first name, *Amerigo,* became the basis for cartographers adapting the name *America.* Vasco Nunez de Balboa's crossing of Panama in 1513 simply supported Vespucci's claims of a new land mass.

Christopher Columbus landing in the New World, a 1493 woodcut from Giuliano Dati's *La lettera dell'isole che ha trovato nuovamente il re di Spagna* (New York Public Library)

**Revised Perceptions.** Geographers were unable to calculate the circumference of the earth until Ferdinand Magellan, a Portuguese mariner sailing under the Spanish flag, circumnavigated the globe. Magellan died in the Philippines in 1521 but his Basque assistant, Juan Sebastián del Cano, completed the three-year journey in a ship appropriately named *Victoria*. Magellan correctly planned to sail past the demarcation line of the Treaty of Tordesillas and on westward to the Spice Islands. Although Portuguese by birth, he sailed with the Spanish because they stood to benefit from his prediction that the Pacific was sufficiently narrow to warrant a western route to Asia. Columbus miscalculated the width of the Atlantic Ocean and Magellan miscalculated the width of the Pacific Ocean, but their voyages forced cartographers to make drastic revisions in how the world was depicted.

**Conquering the New Land.** Conquest of the New World tended to follow the model of colonization that Columbus had started, as opposed to the Portuguese model of fortified trading posts. Contact and colonization had a profound influence on the indigenous populations and on the Europeans. Devastating diseases swept the New World, whereas only one main disease from the Americas, syphilis, spread across Europe. Diets on both sides of the Atlantic changed as corn, potatoes, and various fruits made their way to Europe, while European pigs spread throughout the New World. Coffee and sugar became popular in the New World, and tobacco and cocoa found eager consumers in Europe. The nature of European trade shifted in two key respects: the items that were actually traded shifted from expensive luxury goods traded in small amounts to inexpensive goods traded in large quantities, and the focal point of trade shifted from the Mediterranean Sea to the Atlantic Ocean.

**Conquistadores.** Europeans did encounter two prosperous empires in the New World: the Aztecs in Central Mexico and the Incas in Peru. Both civilizations were brutally destroyed by opportunistic military leaders known as conquistadores. The actions of Hernán Cortés against the Aztec population and, specifically, the main city of Tenochtitlán in 1519–1520 are well known because of the unusually thorough documentation from surviving eyewitnesses. Bernal Diaz of Castile provided the perspective of a foot soldier in his account of the atrocities. Cortés landed with a force of six hundred soldiers and immediately removed the possibility of desertion by destroying his ships. Cortés conquered the Aztec center of government and used the city as his base. His army slaughtered Aztecs and zealously destroyed native temples. The Aztec population fell from twenty-five million to just two million. Francisco de Pizarro was equally brutal to the Incas in Peru during his 1530-1531 campaign. Cortés and Pizarro conquered populated areas, established Spanish cities, and found productive silver mines. They and other conquistadores had funded their own campaigns in hopes of reaping great rewards. Private military leaders were soon replaced by royal appointees once the Spanish Crown realized that the conquistadores were a potential threat to royal power in the New World.

**Sources:**

Felipe Fernández-Armesto, *Before Columbus: Exploration and Colonisation from the Mediterranean to the Atlantic, 1229-1492* (Houndmills, U.K.: Macmillan Education, 1987).

J. H. Parry, *The Age of Reconnaissance* (Cleveland: World, 1963).

J. R. S. Phillips, *The Medieval Expansion of Europe* (Oxford & New York: Oxford University Press, 1988).

William D. Phillips Jr. and Carla Rahn Phillips, *The Worlds of Christopher Columbus* (Cambridge & New York: Cambridge University Press, 1992).

Geoffrey Vaughan Scammell, *The First Imperial Age: European Overseas Expansion, c.1400-1715* (London: Unwin Hyman, 1989).

# SIGNIFICANT PEOPLE

## CHRISTOPHER COLUMBUS

### 1451-1506
### EXPLORER

**Crossing the Atlantic.** Christopher Columbus, a Genoese merchant mariner sailing for the Spanish government, departed from Palos in Southern Spain on 3 August 1492. He sailed south along the coast of Africa to the Canary Islands and then turned west until he reached an uncharted island (present-day San Salvador). Columbus believed that he was somewhere to the east of Cathay (China) and the west of Japan. He mistakenly believed that he was close to his originally projected destination of India, and thus he called these islands the Indies.

**Enterprise of the Indies.** He had planned his Enterprise of the Indies for several years and had made pleas to the kings of Portugal and Spain. Both turned him down, but Isabella, the queen of Spain, had sufficient confidence in Columbus to underwrite a three-ship fleet: two caravels of seventy feet each, the *Niña* and *Pinta*, and a larger flagship named the *Santa Maria*. At one point the crew of the *Santa Maria* purportedly demanded that Columbus turn the boats around, but he negotiated two more days of sailing. Land was sighted on the second day. Columbus had reached the uncharted Caribbean Islands that lie between eastern North and South America, but until his death he believed that he had sailed to Asia.

**Return Voyage.** Columbus traveled as far west as Cuba before tacking north along the western edge of the Sargasso Sea, a vast track of the Atlantic Ocean filled with seaweed due to the circular pattern of currents. Columbus sailed north of the Sargasso Sea and then turned east toward the Iberian Peninsula. He was uncertain of his exact location until he reached the Azores that are west of Portugal. Columbus had little status and importance when he moved from Genoa to the Iberian Peninsula, but this one voyage transformed him into a powerful celebrity.

**Family and Personality.** At the conclusion of his first journey across the Atlantic Ocean, Columbus returned to Spain. Later that year (1493), he set out with his brother Diego on a second voyage to America. Columbus was accompanied by Diego and his other brother, Bartholomew, on his third voyage (1498–1500). Ferdinand, Columbus's fourteen-year-old son, accompanied the three brothers on a fourth and final voyage (1502–1504). Columbus's family was eager to sail with him, but other sailors were frequently disgruntled with his leadership. On the third voyage the three Columbus brothers were arrested and returned to Spain as prisoners, and on the fourth voyage Columbus lost all of his ships due to careless seamanship. Columbus's loyalty to his Genoese family has prompted some historians to label him a self-serving family man whose loyalty to the Spanish Crown was questionable. He was well known for his persistence, a trait that did not endear him to his crew or even his patrons (reportedly Ferdinand and Isabella were eager to be rid of him before the fourth voyage in 1502).

**Round versus Flat Earth.** Contrary to popular belief, Columbus and his sailors did not think they might sail off the edge of the world. In the Renaissance, navigators and sailors were relatively certain that the world was round. Columbus, however, did err in his calculation of the circumference of the globe. Like his contemporary, the Nuremberg globemaker Martin Behaim, Columbus appears to have calculated the circumference based on Marco Polo's land distances and Ptolemy's erroneous estimate of the earth's size. Behaim and Columbus agreed on the earth's circumference, but their views were not shared by the various committees that reviewed and ultimately rejected Columbus's proposal in January 1492. Shortly thereafter, Queen Isabella rapidly accepted the plan because powerful friends intervened on his behalf.

**Navigator.** Columbus made up for his weak sailing and interpersonal skills by proving to be an outstanding navigator. Having spent his young adulthood in Portugal and Spain, he had an opportunity to learn the best navigation techniques of the Iberian Peninsula. He also knew the Atlantic islands off of Africa, as he had lived on Madeira after his 1479 marriage. On his first voyage, Columbus was able to turn his familiarity with Mediterranean and Atlantic shipping to good use. He chose what was perhaps the best route to the West and, more remarkably, the best route back. Columbus headed south to the Canaries and then took the trade winds across the Atlantic on his outbound voyage. He was obviously aware of the winds off the western coast of Africa. On the return voyage, he turned northward and caught the westerlies (winds that blow from west to east) to the Azores. Columbus's successful voyages reveal a keen awareness of navigation techniques along with a familiarity of winds to the south and west of the Iberian Peninsula. He may have held wildly inaccurate views of the earth's size, but he understood the oceanic wind patterns.

**Naming the New Land.** Several years after Columbus, another Italian sailor named Amerigo Vespucci sailed to South America and correctly identified that he was on a new continent. A mapmaker named Martin Waldseemüller adopted the name *America* for South America in 1507 and twenty-one years later Gerardus Mercator used the name *America* for South and North America; hence, Vespucci's name identifies what Columbus mistakenly called the Indies.

**Legacy.** Columbus transformed himself from a self-interested Genoese merchant mariner into a Spanish national hero. He may not have been the first to sail to the Americas, but he was the first to construct a written record of his journey across the Atlantic. The record shows his mistaken ideas about a narrow Atlantic and the location of the islands that he chartered. History also reveals a man of questionable personality traits, whose lack of political skills produced a good deal of animosity. Columbus and his contemporaries viewed his voyage as a contribution both to the expansion of European trade and an extension of the militant Christianity that had begun with the Crusaders' assaults on Islam years earlier. Columbus's perseverance helped turn his erroneous quest for Asia into a voyage that changed the way Europeans viewed the globe. Historians may never agree on Columbus's intentions and merits, but they continue to recognize the fact that Columbus forced cartographers to reconsider how they mapped the world. Columbus's legacy lies in the convergence of the European quest for contact with Asia and the gradual mapping of the Atlantic Ocean.

Sources:

Alfred W. Crosby, *The Colombian Exchange: Biological and Cultural Consequences of 1492* (Westport, Conn.: Greenwood Press, 1972).

Felipe Fernández-Armesto, *Before Columbus: Exploration and Colonisation from the Mediterranean to the Atlantic, 1229-1492* (Houndmills, U.K.: Macmillan Education, 1987).

Samuel Eliot Morison, *Admiral of the Ocean Sea: A Life of Christopher Columbus* (Boston: Little, Brown, 1942).

William D. Phillips Jr. and Carla Rahn Phillips, *The Worlds of Christopher Columbus* (Cambridge & New York: Cambridge University Press, 1992).

Peter Rivière, *Christopher Columbus* (Stroud, Gloucestershire, U.K.: Sutton Publishing, 1998).

# HENRY THE NAVIGATOR

## 1394-1460
### PRINCE OF PORTUGAL

Henry, the Duke of Viseu, is best known for the somewhat inaccurate name *Henry the Navigator*. The title *Navigator* was added to Prince Henry of Portugal's name in the nineteenth century by an admiring English scholar. This title has stuck despite the fact that Henry himself was not a famous navigator. He is credited with gathering navigators, scholars, and cartographers around him at Sagres, on the peninsula of St. Vincent overlooking the Atlantic Ocean. He used his wealth and influence to sponsor Portuguese voyages to the West Coast of Africa between 1419 and 1460. On these voyages the Portuguese made significant advances in navigation, and they began to sail a type of ship called the caravel. Caravels were perfected during Henry's lifetime in order to combat head winds and contrary currents on the return voyage of Portuguese ships from Guinea. Sailors learned to sail the caravels west-northwest into the open sea until they spotted the Azores and then turned east to Portugal. Henry did not invent the caravels, but his sponsorship moved them into the forefront of open-sea sailing on the eve of the famous voyages of Bartholomeu Dias, Christopher Columbus, Vasco da Gama, and Ferdinand Magellan.

**Motives.** Prince Henry was the third son of King John I, a successful and long-ruling monarch. As a young man, Henry participated in the 1415 Portuguese defeat of the Moors at Ceuta (on the African Coast to the south of Gibraltar). The mixture of commercial and religious motives are evident in most of Henry's undertakings. Contemporaries of Prince Henry emphasized his personal piety and fascination with the idea of crusading, while also acknowledging his quest for financial gain. Gomes Eanes de Zurara, the best-known contemporary chronicler of Prince Henry, offers a long list of motives behind the exploration of the Western coast of Africa. Zurara starts with basic curiosity but emphasizes that commercial factors were evident. He suggests a basic medieval formula of serving God and growing rich, but he also claims that the strongest motive was Henry's aspiration of fulfilling the predictions of his horoscope.

**Commercial Gain.** Modern historians debate the degree to which Henry the Navigator was motivated by attempts to combat Muslims and convert heathens to Christianity, but virtually all concede that Henry had monetary aspirations. Henry maintained commercial control over all territories claimed by early Portuguese voyages. He used the Atlantic islands along the coast of Africa to establish monopolies on fishing, soap making, and dye making.

Unlike royal patrons of later voyages, Henry was not interested in claiming vast amounts of ungovernable territory. He focused instead on the strategic and pragmatic monopolization of trade at key ports and islands. Portuguese cartography from his era provided functional records of Henry's trade network that stand in sharp contrast to the grandiose and distorted maps created for the sixteenth-century royal patrons of exploration and cartography.

**Impact.** Henry has been credited with establishing Portugal's maritime empire and transforming Portugal into a world power. Contemporary chroniclers certainly contributed to this reputation, as did Portuguese nationalists. More recent assessments suggest a complex man who has been given more credit than he deserves. Henry did not establish a "school of navigation," and there is no evidence that he read the main Arabic and classical works on geography. He certainly did not lead any expeditions, something that a man of his status would never have done in the fifteenth century. His support of expeditions along the African coast were more likely motivated by the value of slaves than in idealistic pursuit of navigation. Henry frequently led Portugal into nearly ruinous wars in his many attempts to claim the Canary Islands. Yet, he was also a man of sincere religious faith and deep loyalty to those who supported him. After his death, the Crown was willing to encourage exploration but was unwilling to invest in it. Henry had been eager to take financial risks, as well as to motivate others to take personal risks sailing on Portuguese caravels.

Sources:
Jerry Brotton, *Trading Territories: Mapping in the Early Modern World* (Ithaca, N.Y.: Cornell University Press, 1998).

Peter Russell, *Prince Henry "the Navigator": A Life* (New Haven: Yale University Press, 2000).

Geoffrey Vaughan Scammell, *The First Imperial Age: European Overseas Expansion, c.1400-1715* (London: Unwin Hyman, 1989).

# FERDINAND MAGELLAN

## CIRCA 1480-1521
### EXPLORER

**Circumnavigation.** Ferdinand Magellan, a Portuguese sailing for the Spanish, is credited as the first person to circumnavigate the globe, despite the fact that he did not complete the journey. His voyage was not the first one seeking a water passage through America into the Pacific Ocean. The water route that he successfully navigated around the southern tip of South America bears his name: The Straits of Magellan. While in the Philippines in 1521, Magellan intervened in a civil war and was killed, but one of his five ships (*Victoria*) did sail around the world. Juan Sebastián del Cano, Magellan's Basque assistant, completed the journey in 1522 and thus became the first to actually circumnavigate the globe. The three-year journey was a crucial voyage for cartographers, who could finally correct Christopher Columbus's miscalculation of the earth's circumference.

**Portuguese Experience.** Magellan's name is well known in the English and Spanish versions (Ferdinand Magellan and Fernando de Magallanes, respectively), but his actual Portuguese name (Fernão de Magalhães) is relatively unknown. Like many other Portuguese explorers, his Portuguese roots are often overlooked. In fact, the first published account of his journey, written in French by an Italian squire, attributed the voyage to the Spanish (*Le Voyage et navigation, faict par les Espaignolz es Isles de Mollucques*). Magellan sailed under the Spanish flag, but his navigational skills were developed sailing for the Portuguese navy. He had been a page in the service of the queen and then served King Dom Manuel. Prior to becoming a well-known navigator, Magellan had a distinguished military career: between 1505 and 1511, he served as a soldier in India; he went on expedition to Sofala and Kilwa in East Africa; he fought against the Egyptian-Gujarati force at Diu; and he served at the 1511 conquest of Malacca. He continued to sail and serve Portugal until 1517 when he moved to Seville and began working for King Charles I of Spain (Charles is better known as Emperor Charles V of the Holy Roman Empire, a title he acquired shortly after Magellan sailed).

**Spanish Support.** Magellan solicited and won Charles V's support for an expedition around the southernmost point of America. The logic behind the expedition was based on mirroring the Portuguese route to India around the southernmost point of Africa. If the Portuguese could sail east to India and the Molucca Islands, then the Spaniards could sail west to the Moluccas. The Treaty of Tordesillas (1494) had divided the world into an eastern zone of exploration (Portuguese) and a western zone of exploration (Spanish). The Portuguese claimed the Moluccas and showed no interest in ceasing their eastern expansion. The circumference of the earth was unknown, so it was impossible to tell how far east the Portuguese zone actually spread. Like Columbus, who had underestimated the width of the Atlantic Ocean, Magellan underestimated the width of the Pacific Ocean. Magellan correctly calculated that the southwesterly trend of the Brazilian coast continued across the Treaty of Tordesillas line, and thus southern South America was in the Spanish zone. While Charles V supported the idea of a western route, he allocated limited resources of five older ships because he feared that Magellan could actually be sailing into the Portuguese zone.

**Eyewitness Account.** Antonia Pigafetta, an Italian participant on the voyage, wrote a descriptive chronicle of the voyage that included praise for Magellan's leadership. Like Columbus, Magellan was a foreigner leading a crew on a risky voyage. After clearing the Straits of Magellan, they sailed for three months and twenty days without obtaining any provisions. They saw only two small and uninhabited islands during that period. They named the islands the Unfortunate Islands because they offered no provisions for the sailors. Nineteen sailors reportedly died from scurvy, a gum disease that frequently plagued sailors who did not receive enough vitamin C in their diet. Pigafetta describes his desperation at that stage of the journey: "And if our Lord and his blessed Mother had not given us such good weather we should all have died of hunger in this very vast sea. I believe of a certainty that no one will ever again make such a voyage."

**Significance.** Magellan opened the southwest passage around the southernmost promontory of the South American continent in 1520. The passage still bears the name Magellan's Strait. No logbook has survived for this journey and thus it, like Bartholomeu Dias's opening of the southeast passage around the Cape of Good Hope, lacked the precise records that were available for contemporaries of most other voyages. Seven years after Columbus's first voyage, da Gama sailed a Portuguese fleet from India into Lisbon, thereby finding the true "Indies" that Columbus had sought. The actual size of the Pacific Ocean remained a mystery until Magellan crossed the Pacific from South America to Asia. Magellan's circumnavigation of the globe was a crucial voyage for cartographers because it allowed them to understand both the geographical location of South America and the size of the earth.

Sources:

Tim Joyner, *Magellan* (Camden, Me.: International Marine, 1992).

Charles M. Parr, *Ferdinand Magellan, Circumnavigator* (New York: Crowell, 1964).

J. H. Parry, *The Age of Reconnaissance* (Cleveland: World, 1963).

Edouard Roditi, *Magellan of the Pacific* (London: Faber & Faber, 1972).

A. J. R. Russell-Wood, *A World on the Move: The Portuguese in Africa, Asia, and America, 1415-1808* (New York: St. Martin's Press, 1993).

# ALDUS MANUTIUS

## 1449-1515

### SCHOLAR, EDITOR, PRINTER

**Beginnings.** The founder of the famed Venetian Aldine Press, Aldus Manutius was born in the village of Bassiano near Rome in 1449. Little is known of his early life, but records from the archives of the Roman princely family of Caetani, lords of Bassiano and the surrounding duchy of Sermoneta, suggest that the young Manutius probably came from a family of some means with sufficient connections to princely and clerical elite. He studied in Rome, where he was trained in the Latin classics by the renowned humanist, Gaspare da Verona, and

probably attended the lectures given by another famous scholar from Verona, Domizio Calderini.

**Sojourn in Ferrara.** A promising scholar and philologist, Manutius was drafted into papal chancery, enjoyed a brief career as a university lecturer, and in 1472 entered the service of the antiquarian and collector, Cardinal Bessarion. In the mid 1470s, Manutius left Rome for the duchy of Ferrara, which had become one of the leading centers of Hellenist studies in Renaissance Italy. In Ferrara, Manutius perfected his skill in Greek under Battista Guarini, whose formidable talents attracted students from all over Italy. Manutius's sojourn in Ferrara proved pivotal, both because it established his lifelong commitment to Hellenistic students and humanist education and because it introduced him to the network of aristocratic patrons whose financial support and cultural capital would become an essential feature of his later success as printer-scholar. By the late fifteenth century, the court of Ercole d'Este, Duke of Ferrara, was an important center of humanist study as well, and Manutius probably became acquainted with the duke's daughter, Isabella d'Este, who later became an assiduous patron of the Aldine Press.

**Other Connections.** Manutius also met Giovanni Pico della Mirandola, one of the most influential figures in the Platonic Academy in Florence. Manutius's friendship with Pico led to an appointment as tutor to Pico's two nephews, the princes Alberto and Lionello Pio, lords of Carpi, from 1480 to 1488. In this capacity, Manutius continued his own studies in philology, drafted and edited several Greek and Latin grammars that would become stock publications of the Aldine Press, and continued to forge connections with illustrious quattrocento (fifteenth-century) humanists, such as Angelo Poliziano and Ermalao Barbaro. Fully embracing the Hellenistic convictions of the late quattrocento, Manutius was convinced that mastery of the Greek language and literature was the key to excellence in every field of learning. At the age of forty, he was prompted by his belief to establish the first printing press in all of Europe to specialize specifically in the publication of Greek texts.

**Venetian Aldine Press.** In either 1489 or 1490, Manutius moved to Venice, where he joined forces with a resident printer, Andrea Torresani (whose daughter he later married), and founded the press that eventually bore his name. From 1495 to 1515, Manutius assembled one of the most impressive teams of print-artisans and humanist-scholars to have ever collaborated in early modern print shops. In so doing, he transformed the reception of printed books and the image of the publishing trade among elite collectors.

**Elite Objections.** In late-fifteenth-century Europe, resistance to the world of printed books, especially among the aristocratic collectors and humanist-scholars who drove the market for classical texts, was problematic. Aristocratic collectors were still highly attracted to handwritten and illuminated manuscripts, which were considered aesthetically superior to and a sounder capital and cultural investment than printed books. Even humanists, who certainly had occasion to champion the printing press as the antidote to the errors and ignorance of medieval copyists, were ambivalent about the rapid diffusion of the sometimes hastily edited texts, commentaries, and abridged editions produced by commercially driven print shops.

**Reputation for Excellence.** Manutius's reputation as a classicist of some talent and his connections to respected humanists in Rome, Florence, and northern Europe challenged the prevailing perception that printers were merely skilled artisans. Manutius also deftly countered elite objections to printed material by employing skilled technicians to create types in Greek and Latin cursive that closely resembled the italic script favored by humanists and collectors. His interest in placement of print on the page reflects Renaissance aesthetics and concerns with beauty, proportion, and the essential classical canons of form. Finally, Manutius employed a stable of scholars to proof his texts, including the English humanist Thomas Linacre. His reputation for accurate scholarship attracted clients, such as Desiderius Erasmus, who insisted upon publishing the second edition of his *Adages* in 1508 with the Aldine Press and even oversaw final copyediting himself.

**Harsh Employer.** Erasmus's somewhat unflattering account of his experiences in the Aldine workshop, where he was pressed into service as a copyeditor on several other projects, reveals that Manutius was a harsh taskmaster and shrewd businessman who demanded excellence from the fifteen-odd artisans comprising his workshop. Later generations of scholars have criticized Manutius for his extensive use of Greek and Latin cursive type rather than the more simplified Roman type, which he sometimes adopted for vernacular publications, such as Francesco Colonna's *Hypnerotomachia Poliphili* (1499), a story about an ill-fated romance involving two Latin lovers, Polia and Polifiloa. However, as Martin Lowry has argued, Manutius was more widely revered by his contemporaries for his Greek editions and for the cursive type he invented, which appealed to the aesthetic sensibilities of wealthy collectors. Even his decision to adopt a smaller format (the octavo for his books), it now seems, favored scholar-diplomats who disliked the cumbersome and larger folio editions.

**Achievements.** During his career as a printer, Manutius engaged in an ambitious publishing program. Rough estimates suggest that the Aldine press in Venice was responsible for a total output of between 100,000 to 120,000 books, many of which found their way into the libraries of princely and royal collectors as well as humanists. Although he never fulfilled his grand project to publish the entire corpus of Aristotle's works, Manutius nonetheless completely dominated the publication of Greek texts in the late fifteenth and early sixteenth

centuries and helped reconstitute the literary heritage of the Greeks, recovered by fifteenth-century scholars.

**Later Years.** By the early sixteenth century, the fame of the Aldine Press and its editions drew Manutius even more firmly into the circle of northern humanists and collectors and prompted him to envision the establishment of his own academy, closely imitating Florentine and imperial models. His friendship with the German humanist Conradus Celtis may even have encouraged him to consider an abortive scheme to reestablish his printing house in Vienna under the patronage of Emperor Maximilian I. The failure of these grand designs, and financial difficulties exacerbated by endemic political instability in Renaissance Italy, frustrated Manutius in his later years, and he died a melancholy and unhappy man in 1515. His impact and influence, however, continued after his death, and the revolutionary image which he created of the print shop as the locus for scholars and printers, united by the desire to diffuse learning and literacy, was perpetuated by northern printers, such as Johann Froben in Basle and Christophe Plantin in Antwerp.

Sources:

Helen Barolini, *Aldus and His Dream Book: An Illustrated Essay* (New York: Italica Press, 1992).

Martin Davies, *Aldus Manutius: Printer and Publisher of Renaissance Venice* (Tempe, Ariz.: Arizona Center for Medieval and Renaissance Studies, 1999).

Martin Lowry, *The World of Aldus Manutius: Business and Scholarship in Renaissance Venice* (Oxford: Blackwell, 1979).

# GERARDUS MERCATOR

## 1512-1594
### CARTOGRAPHER

**Education.** Gerhard Kremer was born in Flanders to German parents. He Latinized his family name to Mercator (Latin for Kremer, "merchant") when he matriculated at the University of Louvain in 1530. There he studied philosophy and theology, but also became interested in cartography and the then state-of-the-art technology for printing illustrations called copper-plate engraving.

**Famed Mentor.** After graduation he studied mathematics and astronomy privately with Gemma Frisius, a renowned humanist geographer and maker of terrestrial globes for navigation. In 1529 Frisius edited and revised Peter Apian's *Cosmographia* (1524), a description of Earth that was based on Ptolemy's *Geography*. He then published his own *Gemma Phrysius de principiis astronomiæ et cosmographiæ* (Principles of Astronomy and

Cosmography, 1530). Frisius added to Apian's work a description of how to apply the method of triangulation to mapmaking, which was later used by Danish astronomer Tycho Brahe, and suggested that longitude at sea could be determined by using portable clocks. The calculation of longitude posed serious problems for open-sea navigation, and Frisius's solution was eventually adopted, but not until sufficiently accurate chronometers were invented in the eighteenth century.

**Mapmaking.** Mercator collaborated with Frisius in preparing a globe in 1536, a process that involved printing tapered map pieces called gores that can be glued onto a sphere to produce an accurate representation. He published his first flat maps in 1537—a map of Palestine and a folio-size map of the world, which popularized the name *Amerigo* for the lands of the new world. Mercator produced his own terrestrial globe in 1541, to which he added loxodromes, or lines of constant bearing, to make them more useful to navigators. Globes were generally too small to be of practical use in navigation, however, and Mercator's reputation rests rather on his work as a mapmaker and instrument maker.

**Mercator Projection.** In 1552 Mercator left Louvain for Duisburg, Germany, where he was appointed cosmographer to the Duke of Cleves. There he undertook compiling the first modern maps of Europe and in 1578 publishing a new edition of Ptolemy's *Geography*. His greatest achievement is a 1569 world map titled "New and Improved Description of the Lands of the World, Amended and Intended for the Use of Navigators." It was based on a new kind of projection, which has become known as the Mercator projection. This technique charts the surface of the globe onto a cylindrical map that is tangent to it at the equator, resulting in the parallels of latitude being represented as parallel lines on the surface of the cylinder, which is flat when cut and unrolled. Such a map progressively distorts the shapes of land masses the farther they lie from the equator. For instance, Greenland is dramatically larger on Mercator's map than lands at the equator. Land masses are distorted but the maps preserve one consistency which permits navigators to lay out constant headings with a straight edge. The ability to plot compass courses as a straight line on a map is one reason why Mercator's projection is still in use.

**Last Project.** The culmination of Mercator's life's work was a cosmography taking in the entire world and its history, a kind of study in praise of the Creator's design that is called natural theology. He died before he could complete this massive project, but his son published a shorter, one-volume version under the title *Atlas sive cosmographicæ meditationes de fabrica mundi et fabricati figura* (Atlas, or Cosmographic Meditations on the Architecture of the World and the Form of the Creation, 1595). It is from this work that the term *atlas* is used to refer to a collection of maps.

Sources:

Phillip Allen, *The Atlas of Atlases: The Mapmaker's Vision of the World* (New York: Abrams, 1992).

A. S. Osley, *Mercator* (London: Faber & Faber, 1969).

John N. Wilford, *The Mapmakers* (New York: Knopf, 1981).

# CHRISTOPHE PLANTIN

## CIRCA 1520-1589
### BOOKBINDER, PRINTER, AND PUBLISHER

**Renown.** Christophe Plantin, head of the large Plantin publishing house in Antwerp, was the most famous publisher of the sixteenth century despite the fact that he offered no real innovations in terms of book or type design. His fame rested on the ability to tap financial resources, to exploit political connections to King Philip II of Spain, and to organize production of books along industrial lines. His famed Bible won him a monopoly of sales in all lands under the rule of the Spanish king. Plantin capitalized on his unique opportunities to create what French historians Lucien Febvre and Henri-Jean Martin have called "the most powerful book manufactury to exist before the nineteenth Century."

**Antwerp.** Plantin built his huge publishing empire without the aid of private fortune. He was born about 1520 in France, and he learned printing and bookbinding in Caen, Rouen, and Paris. Plantin left Paris in 1548 and settled in Antwerp the next year. Initially he worked as a bookbinder and decorator of jewel boxes until an injury to his arm forced him to return to printing. In the 1550s he began to print and publish a wide range of works in many languages. His only significant publication prior to 1562 was printed at the expense of the state and titled *Account of the Funeral Ceremonies of Charles V.* In 1562, church censors searched his shop for publication of an unorthodox prayer book and forced him to flee Antwerp. After nearly two years, Plantin returned to find all his possessions sold, but his decision to come back was fortuitous. Years later, in a letter to Pope Gregory XIII, Plantin explained his reasons for choosing Antwerp: "Access to the city is good," the market squares have representatives from "many different nations," materials for "the art of printing" are available, workers "in any of the crafts" are abundant, and "finally there flourishes the University of Louvain."

**Rebuilding His Business.** In 1563 Plantin found financial backers in Antwerp and ordered new type from the best punch cutters in Europe. Plantin was a member of a religious group called "The Family of Charity." He used these connections to form a syndicate of publishers funded by some of the city's wealthiest residents. The syndicate ended after five years, but it had published 260 works and put Plantin back in control of a thriving publishing office.

**Philip II.** Plantin used his connections to cultivate ties with influential churchmen and with Gabriel de Cayas, secretary to Philip II. As a result, he received legal and financial support from the Spanish Crown. Plantin eventually was granted papal permission to monopolize the publication of liturgical books used in all lands that fell under the rule of the Spanish king. The king of France and the duke of Savoy attempted to persuade him to move to Paris and Turin, but he opted to stay in Antwerp and publish for Spanish lands.

**Polyglot Bible.** Plantin's initial fame derived largely from an eight-volume *Biblia polyglotta* (Polyglot Bible, 1569–1572). The Bible included Latin, Greek, Hebrew, and Chaldaic (ancient Semitic) texts printed in columns with a brief summary at the bottom of each page. The project was funded with a cash advance from the king of Spain that was to be repaid with copies of the completed book. One thousand two hundred and twelve copies were printed with five prices, contingent on the quality of the paper or vellum used. The Polyglot Bible was an exercise in diplomacy as well as printing because the king refused to allow publication without preapproval from Pope Pius V. The Pope rejected the offer and Plantin sent an editor to Rome to petition papal reconsideration. After the death of Pius V, the new pope, Gregory XIII, finally consented, but the work remained under Church suspicion. The Inquisition examined the books for many years after publication and prevented circulation until 1580. The delay strained Plantin's resources but final approval greatly enhanced his reputation.

**Labor and Constancy.** A good deal is known about Plantin through his connections and the mass of papers, records, and correspondence that he left. His shop had as many as two dozen presses running at the same time and more than one hundred employees. He maintained outlets in major commercial centers across Europe. Despite the huge scale of his operations, he had severe fluctuations in his fortune. Spanish troops mutinied in Antwerp in 1576 and disrupted business. In 1581 he was forced to sell his collection of books in Paris for half its value. The next year, he passed the business over to his sons-in-law, and he died eight years later. Plantin's printer's mark, the small symbol that printers used to identify their works, has a hand coming down from the clouds to mark a circle with a compass. The words "By the Labor and Constancy" appear on the mark. Plantin's ability to rebound from defeats, to tap Antwerp's financial resources, to win the Spanish monarchy's support, and to gain papal authorization allowed him to turn a small printing shop into a major publishing house.

Sources:

Colin Clair, *Christopher Plantin* (London: Cassell, 1960).

Lucien Febvre and Henri-Jean Martin, *The Coming of the Book: The Impact of Printing 1450-1800*, translated by David Gerard, edited by Geoffrey Nowell-Smith and David Wootton (London: N.L.B., 1976).

Saul Marks, *Christopher Plantin and the Officina Plantiniana* (Los Angeles: Plantin, 1972).

Douglas McMurtrie, *The Book: The Story of Printing & Bookmaking*, third revised edition (New York & London: Oxford University Press, 1962).

# DOCUMENTARY SOURCES

Pierre d'Ailly, *Imago mundi* (Image of the World, 1410)—French cardinal's early geography claims that a westward voyage from Europe to Asia was possible. Based on Ptolemy's work, as well as biblical and Muslim sources, the text was read by Christopher Columbus. A slightly later work, *Compendium Cosmographiae* (1414), was written after d'Ailly had read the 1410 translation of Ptolemy's *Geography*.

João de Barros, *Década* (1552)—An account of Ferdinand Magellan's circumnavigation of the earth.

Ibn Battuta, *Rhilah* (1353)—The autobiographical adventures of a Muslim from Ceuta, who travelled as far east as China. Many of the stories are obvious exaggerations, but the work offered Europeans information about the history and geography of the Muslim world.

Giovanni Boccaccio, *Decameron* (1353)—A collection of short stories providing a lively account of life at the time of the Black Plague. The work is a vernacular example of early Italian humanism.

William Caxton, *The Recuyell of the Historyes of Troye* (1475)—The first book printed in English. In Book III of this text, Caxton tells how he "practised and learnt" to use a printing press after his "pen became worn, his head weary, his eye dimmed" from handcopying so many manuscripts.

Geoffrey Chaucer, *The Canterbury Tales* (circa 1375–1400)—Modeled on Boccaccio's *Decameron* (1353), this English work has pilgrims telling stories that address the moral and social ills of the period.

Christopher Columbus, *Letter to Luis de Santángel* (1493)—Columbus's account of his first voyage to the Caribbean was modified by royal officials and then published. It circulated widely throughout Europe.

William Langland, *Piers Plowman* (circa 1372–1386)—Early English criticism of society from the perspective of the peasant.

Bartolomé de Las Casas, *Historia de las Indies* (1527–1559)—A descriptive account of the Americas written by a Dominican monk known as the "Apostle to the Indians." Las Casas relied on his own experiences in the Americas as well as firsthand accounts such as Christopher Columbus's own writings and family papers. Las Casas also wrote two scathing attacks on the European treatment of Amerindians: *Apologetic History of the Indies* (1551), and *Short Account of the Destruction of the Indies* (1552).

Francisco Lopez de Gomara, *Historia de las Indias y conquista de Mexico* (1552)—Account of the Spanish defeat of the Aztecs written by Hernán Cortés's secretary.

Sir John Mandeville, *The Travels of Sir John Mandeville* (1366)—The author pretends to be an English knight in this geographical romance. The work popularized the existing Prester John myth and supported many of Marco Polo's claims. The immense popularity is evident in the eighty editions published in eight languages between 1478 and 1592.

Facanzano da Montalboddo, *Paesi novamente retrovati* (1507)—The first great collection of eyewitness descriptions of the early transoceanic voyages. The book contains real and forged accounts including Amerigo Vespucci's voyages to South America.

Abraham Ortelius, *Theatrum orbis terrarum* (Epitome of the Theater of the Worlde, 1570)—The first atlas in the modern sense of the word, that is, a collection of maps intended to describe the world. Mapmaking in early modern Europe was one of the means that political authorities had of staking and maintaining territorial claims and was therefore an important part of the European expansion and hegemony process.

Luca Pacioli, *Summary of Arithmetic* (1494)—The volume that popularized the practice of double-entry bookkeeping is an example of the growth in quantitative perception among urban Europeans.

Christophe Plantin, *Biblia polyglotta* (Polyglot Bible, 1569–1572)—Written in Latin, Greek, Hebrew, and Chaldaic (ancient Semitic).

*Regimento do astrolabio e do quadrante* (1509)—King John II of Portugal appointed a committee to draft written tables of declination so navigators could accurately calculate latitude with astrolabes and quadrants.

Erasmus Reinhold, *Prutenic Tables* (1551)—These astronomical tables, based on Copernicus's mathematical astronomy, are tangible evidence that Copernicus's work was being read and used, even if those who were using it remained unconvinced of the reality of the heliocentric hypothesis.

Plate for the month of September from the prayer book *Tres Riches Heures* (1413–1416) by the Limbourg Brothers (Musee Conde, Chantilly)

A model of Christopher Columbus's flagship, the nao *Santa Maria* (Mariners' Museum, Newport News, Virginia)

## CHAPTER FIVE

# SOCIAL CLASS SYSTEM AND THE ECONOMY

by JOHN THEIBAULT

## CONTENTS

*Sidebars and tables are listed in italics.*

**1350**

- The European population is approximately seventy-four million people, the vast majority of whom live in rural areas. The largest cities are Venice, Florence, Paris, Milan, Bologna, Genoa, London, Ghent, Siena, and Palermo.

**1358**

- A French peasants' revolt known as the *Jacquerie* occurs in reaction to heavy taxation.

**1378**

- Following a period of economic decline, *ciompi* (cloth workers) and other propertyless laborers revolt against the merchant oligarchy and powerful guilds who rule Florence.

**1381**

- Wat Tyler, Jack Straw, and others lead a peasants' revolt in England. They demand commutation of servile dues, disendowment of the Church, and abolition of game laws. Richard II represses the insurrection after the murder of Tyler.

**1397**

- The Medici bank is founded in Florence, specializing in foreign bills of exchange and commodities of all kinds. Medici family members soon become the official bankers and fiscal agents of the papacy and develop extensive operations in the international cloth trade.

**1415**

- The Portuguese capture the port city of Ceuta from the Moors and begin to build a flourishing trade in African spices, ivory, gold, silver, monkeys, and parakeets.

**1427**

- The Florentine Catasto, an early census document, is compiled.

**1429**

- Cosimo de Medici becomes head of the Medici bank and establishes branch offices in Pisa, Milan, Avignon, Bruges, and London. He also controls three cloth-manufacturing facilities in Florence.

**1430**

- Philip III the Good, Duke of Burgundy, establishes the Order of the Golden Fleece. Its first members include the sovereign duke as grand master and twenty-three knights. This organization is founded to defend the Roman Catholic faith and to uphold the ideals of chivalry. The actions of the members are open to review by the order, and the knights have the right to trial by their compatriots on charges of rebellion, treason, or heresy.

**1440**

- Prince Henry of Portugal begins to introduce sugar cultivation and African slaves in the Canary Islands, the Madeiras, the Azores, and the Cape Verde Islands.

**1455**

- The Madeira Islands produce almost two hundred thousand pounds of sugar; by 1500 this figure increases twentyfold.

**1487**

- The Fugger family establishes an international bank in Augsburg, which quickly rivals the Medici financial institution.

**1492**

- An Italian sailor in the pay of Spain, Christopher Columbus conducts his first voyage of discovery to the Americas, opening the Western Hemisphere to European exploration and colonization.

**1494**

- Luca Pacioli writes *Summary of Arithmetic*, which popularizes the practice of double-entry bookkeeping.

**1498**

- The Portuguese mariner Vasco da Gama successfully sails around the Cape of Good Hope and reaches India. When he returns home, he brings a cargo of pepper and precious stones worth sixty times the cost of the voyage.

**1510**

- The Portuguese establish factories at Goa and Calcutta on the Malabar Coast of India, successfully challenging the Arabs and Venetians for control of the European spice trade.

**1516**
- Baldassare Castiglione writes *The Book of the Courtier,* an important guide for noblemen.
- In response to the social problems of his day, the English humanist Sir Thomas More writes *Utopia,* a satire that describes an idealistic society on an imaginary island.

**1524**
- The Peasants' War begins in Swabia and Franconia. The year-long insurrection is in protest of the social and economic inequalities of German feudalism.

**1545**
- The Spanish discover rich silver deposits at Potosí, in present-day Bolivia, and within one year the value of precious metal imports into Europe quadruples.

**1568**
- Hans Sachs writes *The Book of Trades,* which describes the different occupations of the era.

**1571**
- A bourse, or stock exchange, is founded in London for the sale and purchase of securities such as shares, stocks, and bonds.

**1573**
- Thomas Tusser writes *Five Hundred Good Points of Husbandry,* an early type of farmers' almanac.

**1576**
- Following the revolt of their provinces in the Netherlands, the Spanish retaliate by sacking the port city of Antwerp, the commercial and financial capital of Europe.

**1591**
- Cyriacus Spangenberg writes *Mirror of Nobility,* a long, rambling description of the Three Orders: clergy, nobility, and general populace.

## 1600

- The English East India Company is chartered. Shares in the company are transferable, and policy control is vested in a board of directors elected by stockholders. Because of its government charter, the East India Company has monopolistic privileges and quickly becomes a successful financial entity.

- There are eighty-nine million people in Europe, with 75 to 90 percent of the population living in the countryside. The largest cities are Paris, Naples, London, Venice, Seville, Prague, Milan, Palermo, Rome, and Lisbon.

An illumination showing financial trading, circa 1470–1480 (Bibliothèque Nationale, Paris)

# OVERVIEW

**A Hybrid Economy.** The period between 1350 and 1600 laid the foundation for the rise of Europe to economic predominance in the world. However, for much of the period, the actual economic progress of Europe was slow and inconspicuous. The economy was a hybrid of medieval and modern capitalist practices. The most important transformations often took place in the ordinary segments of the economy, such as in the organization of farming. The perception of society also remained fairly static throughout the era. Social and political power was in the hands of the nobility, who claimed their authority from service to society and superior "blood." Below this surface image of order there were tensions between the interests of the nobility and the "Third Estate," which included wealthy merchants and professionals, ordinary artisans, and the peasantry. Thus, the most significant economic and social events of the era are often far more obvious in retrospect than they would have been at the time.

**Population Change.** One example of an inconspicuous process with far-reaching consequences was population change. It was perhaps the single most important factor for all aspects of the economic development of Europe. The impact of population change was direct: the more people, the more goods and services created and consumed; the fewer people, the fewer goods and services created and consumed. This trend persisted because productivity per person changed little during the era. Between 1347 and 1351 the Black Death carried off almost one-third of the population. After that period, population change was less dramatic. For most of the fifteenth and sixteenth centuries, population steadily increased. Europe had 20 percent more people in 1600 than it had had in 1350. By 1600, the effects of that population increase were apparent to all, and there were many comments about overpopulation.

**Agricultural Production.** One of the main forces fueling population growth was people's dependence on agriculture. The overwhelming majority of the population lived in the countryside. Food production was easily the largest sector of the economy. The agricultural activity of the majority of the population was necessary to allow a small minority to do all the other activities of society. Agricultural production was so shaped by the basic elements of nature that some historians used to describe rural life as unchanging.

Yet, even though there were no dramatic changes in the basic conditions of life for the rural population in this era, there were many subtle changes demonstrating that agricultural production was shaped as much by human decisions as by the forces of nature.

**Land Ownership.** Agricultural production was shaped by the system of land ownership and the techniques farmers used to plant and harvest their crops. In much of Europe, the main system of land ownership was seigneurialism, wherein a lord formally owned the land, but a peasant farmer owned the right to work on the land and could pass on that right to his children. The landlord, or seigneur, controlled the peasant farmer to some extent because of his formal ownership of the land, but if a peasant farmer fulfilled the expectations of the traditional contract with the lord, he had a fair amount of personal control over what actually happened on the land. This system proved effective for distributing the produce of the land to market, but it did not encourage increases in productivity.

**Communal Limits on Farming.** In many parts of Europe, the peasant farmer who wanted to innovate ended up being more constrained by fellow peasant farmers than by the landlord. The technique of three-course crop rotation (one field in every three is purposely not planted with crops so the soil can replenish itself) helped to shape a collective approach to work in the fields. Village traditions determined when and how fields would be planted and work divvied up. By the end of the sixteenth century, some changes in the three-course system, such as "enclosure" of scattered fields, began to increase the yields of grains on some estates. However, in general, food production continued to be limited because of adherence to traditional practices.

**Urban Economy.** The town economy was different from the rural economy. Though much smaller in terms of numbers employed, it was by far the more conspicuous area of economic activity. Towns took advantage of their legal position as markets and their traditions of self-government to monopolize manufacturing. The organizing structure of the town economy was the guilds, which regulated the production process, quality, and prices of goods in most industries. The guilds also often shaped the political life of towns. However, guilds were not agents of economic change. They had an incentive to shield against any kind of economic change in order to protect their members. Instead, the most conspicuous changes in economic activity in the towns were those signaled by the great fortunes gained by merchants and bankers. These two groups consolidated a European-wide network of trade that enabled the largest towns in Europe to grow substantially during the era.

**A Money Economy.** The economic life of the towns was connected to the productivity of the village by another subtle process that became nearly completed in this era: the shift to a money economy. In the Middle Ages (500–1500), much local commerce could be carried out with barter transactions. Already by 1300 there was a bustling circulation of silver and gold coins. Most were minted for small regions, so bankers and merchants developed procedures for exchanging the different local varieties. The need to pay attention to the abstract value of money and goods meant that new accounting techniques developed, which, in turn, reinforced a tendency to "calculate." By the end of the era, new economic tools, such as stock markets, had been developed, which facilitated the development of a capitalist mindset.

**Atlantic Economy.** Contemporary commentators did not take as much notice of changing business practices as they did of the discoveries of the Americas and maritime trade routes to the Indian Ocean. These discoveries provided the European economy with new products and a large influx of precious metals. In the major port cities of the Atlantic, the high visibility of luxury products from Asia and the Americas demonstrated the degree of economic change. They generated fabulous wealth for a few merchants. However, less exotic products such as salted fish, wheat and rye, and timber from the Baltic region formed an equally powerful long-distance trade network that helped make the Netherlands, rather than Spain, the economic powerhouse of Europe by the end of the sixteenth century. The Baltic trade, the Atlantic luxury trade, and small changes in production in the towns and countryside all contributed to a significant shift in the economic balance of Europe, from the Mediterranean to the Atlantic.

**Society of Orders.** Changes in the economy had no immediate effect on the perceptions of how society was organized. Throughout the period, the preferred image of society was of three "orders" or "estates," which fulfilled their individual niches to fit within a hierarchically organized universe. According to that image, the clergy was the First Estate, the nobility was the Second Estate, and everybody else was the Third Estate. Each Estate had distinct social roles and privileges. Though formally the Second Estate, the nobility had most of the power and status in society. People were supposed to remain content in whatever Estate they belonged and not to strive to change Estates.

**Cracks in the Ideal.** However, even in 1350 that idealized image of contentedness did not correspond with reality, and by 1600, the picture seemed even less appropriate. First of all, it was obvious that members of a given Estate were not all equal in status. Even among nobles there were great differences between the richest and the poorest. In the Third Estate, the differences were massive. Some bankers, merchants, lawyers, and officials gathered fortunes that rivaled those of all but the greatest of the nobles. At the other end of the Third Estate were masses of poor laborers and peasants, who teetered on the brink of starvation.

**Different Approach.** The relatively huge size of the Third Estate in comparison to the First and Second Estates meant that it made sense to think of other ways of identifying social distinctions. The nobility continued to be a social group by itself. It emphasized its distinctiveness by using "blood" or descent as the primary identifying characteristic of the group. The different lifestyles of town and countryside meant that the Third Estate consisted of at least four distinct subgroups: two of which were urban, one of which was rural, and one of which was both urban and rural.

**Urban Social Groups.** The two main social groups in the towns were the patriciate and the artisans. The patriciate was the urban elite. Especially in the largest cities, the patriciate remained as socially distinct from the rest of the town's inhabitants as the nobility did. Members of the patriciate married among themselves and dominated the offices of the town government. The artisans, on the other hand, were the mainstays of the guild economy. Some master artisans could become quite wealthy, but few achieved more than modest wealth. In fact, by the later sixteenth century, the percentage of artisans who could aspire to become independent masters of their own shop had declined sharply. Social tensions emerged between masters and the journeymen who did much of the work in most shops.

**The Peasantry.** In the countryside, the social distinctions between the elite and the rest of the population were less striking. Some peasants were able to raise enough food to support themselves comfortably, while others had to supplement their incomes with additional work as field laborers or craftsmen. In the course of the sixteenth century, population pressures reduced the percentage of "full" farmers in relation to small landowners and the landless. Since large farmers tended to dominate the internal government of villages, even within the comparatively socially homogeneous village population, social tensions between haves and have-nots became apparent.

**The Poor.** The final important social fact about the social order of Renaissance and Reformation Europe was that there were an enormous number of poor people. Perhaps 30 percent of the population could have been considered poor. There were poor people in both the towns and the countryside. In the idealized model of the Society of Orders, these people were not even part of the Third Estate, since they had no socially acceptable niche. Yet, in fact, they could contribute to the economy in many ways. In the countryside, poor people were those without land, so they could not support themselves by growing food as a peasant could. Some survived by working as day laborers on the farms of peasants. Others subsisted on the margins of the community, getting occasional alms from the parish and undertaking the least desirable tasks in the community. In the towns, the poor also took on day laboring tasks and more marginal social activities such as prostitution. Contemporaries often commented on the concentration of poor people in the cities. The most desperate poor alternated between town and countryside as beggars, and sometimes as criminals.

**Emergence of Capitalism.** Overall, the Renaissance and Reformation era was a time of subtle changes in both the economy and ideas about society. People became increas-ingly aware of the significance of wealth and occupation as marks of social distinction because of these changes, but there was no sudden break where one could say a new economy or social order had emerged. Throughout the period, the wealthiest members of the Third Estate tried to buy their way into the Second Estate to increase their social status. However, while noble social ideas dominated on the surface of European society, modern capitalist economic practices were becoming more ingrained at all levels of society. People may not have recognized them at the time, but those practices would eventually transform the European economy during the Industrial Revolution of the eighteenth century.

# TOPICS IN SOCIAL CLASS SYSTEM AND THE ECONOMY

## AGRICULTURAL PRODUCTION AND THE RURAL ECONOMY

**Food Production.** The overall structure of the European economy was shaped by food production; other economic activities ceased if there was too little food to go around. The absolute importance of food production in the late medieval economy can be demonstrated in many ways, but the most obvious one is that between 75 percent to 90 percent of the total population lived in the countryside and between 75 percent to 95 percent of those people would consider agricultural production to be their primary occupation. In most of Europe, the main activity in agricultural production was growing a grain crop such as wheat or rye, which was the staple of the diet of nearly everyone.

**Patterns.** Most food was perishable and bulky. It had to be consumed close to where it was produced because the costs of transporting it were too high. As a result large cities developed in areas that produced lots of surplus food or had easy access to supplies on major trade routes. Though almost every city was surrounded by fields tended by city residents, the vast majority of grain came from the countryside, grown by peasants living in villages. Even small towns depended on nearby villages to sustain them. The supply pattern was interconnected: one small town was supported by several villages; one larger town was supported by several small towns and their local villages; the largest towns were supported by a network of large towns. This pattern meant that there were at least three distinct economic units in Europe: the countryside, the small town, and the large city. In the countryside, the village was more prominent than the freestanding farmstead for organizing grain production. At least three-quarters of the European workforce had to grow food to make it possible for the remaining quarter to do anything else.

**Basic Agricultural Practices.** The basic conditions of agricultural production did not change much in the Renaissance and Reformation eras. In the Mediterranean area, the triad of wheat, olive oil, and wine dominated the rural economy, just as it had since ancient times. Soils were light and could be worked by a scratch plow and planted in grains in alternating years. North of the Alps, heavier soils favored cereal crops such as wheat, rye, oats, and barley, as well as livestock. The basic production technique was three-course crop rotation, in which one of three fields remained fallow to replenish the lost nutrients every year.

**Three-course Crop Rotation.** The three-course crop rotation system had been perfected early in the Middle Ages and was little changed in 1350. Its demands and rhythms influenced rural life in many ways. It favored production in small- to medium-sized villages rather than in isolated family farms, because different people's lands could be worked simultaneously side by side in a village. Livestock raising was closely connected with three-course crop rotation because draft animals had to pull the heavier plows better suited to the richer soils, and the manure from the

Agricultural work, as depict in a late fifteenth-century manuscript (from Franco Cardini, *Europe 1492*, 1989)

animals was vital to the replenishment of the fallow land. In fact, work and manure, not meat and dairy products, were the main contributions that cattle and horses made to the economy. However, raising livestock complicated the land-use pattern of the village. The fallows did not produce enough by themselves to feed the livestock, so some area around the village had to be turned into pasture for grazing or meadow for hay production. Often meadows and pastures were not owned by individual villagers but were communal property of the entire village, with complex regulations about whose animals would be allowed to graze them and when.

**Scattered, Small Plots.** Not everyone in a village could afford to keep draft animals or a heavy plow with yoke and harness. The nature of three-course crop rotation made it less necessary for each individual villager to be completely independent and self-sufficient in that manner. The division of the fields into three rotations was done on a village-wide basis, not on the basis of individual landowners. Individual owners did not have one big chunk of land in one of the three fields; instead, they had lots of smaller pieces scattered among all three of the fields.

**Insurance against Risk.** Ownership of scattered property provided a kind of insurance against the tricks of nature. If all of one's lands were planted in wheat the year a wheat blight came through, it would be two more years before one would have a chance to recoup that loss; but if only a third of one's land was in wheat that year, one could start recouping one's losses the next year, and maybe one's oats crop would thrive. The scattering of small parcels of land made it more efficient to organize work in the fields in teams covering several different people's plots, instead of one individual's plots. Those villagers without cattle or plows could "trade" their services in weeding or harvesting for the plowing of their plots.

**Seasonality of Work and Profits.** The fact that the fields of the village were organized around the key crops also imposed seasonal rhythms on production. Labor was particularly intense at sowing and harvesting time. At other times of the year, less had to be done and peasant labor was idle. This situation affected wage rates for agricultural laborers, which would be high in peak season, but low in the off season.

**Price Fluctuations.** The fact that nearly all the grain from a village went to market at the same time meant that prices were depressed at harvest time and then rose as supplies diminished. The poor usually had to sell as soon as the crops were harvested, when the price was lowest, because they needed money to pay debts. Only those villagers who produced a significant surplus could hope to profit from price fluctuations. Yields from the leading crops were fairly small, often just four or five times the seed sown. With a yield of five times the seed sown, peasants had to save 20 percent of their crop every year for next year's seed. After paying rents and taxes, villagers might only store one-half or less of their harvest to tide them over to the next year.

**Influence of the Towns.** From the perspective of the economy as a whole, there was a problem with the village-based production of grain used to support the rest of society. Most villagers, if they had been given the choice, might have organized themselves in completely self-sufficient units, providing enough food to feed themselves, along with clothing and other products to satisfy their needs. How, then, were townspeople to get any of the food? A couple of factors contributed to "loosening up" some of the grain in the village and making it available to towns. First was the system of actual landownership. That system forced villagers to give up a portion of their produce as rent for the land. Second was the rights that towns were able to exert over the making of products other than grain and livestock. Some villagers might have been eager to spend their spare time in the slack agricultural seasons producing the other necessities of life such as clothing, implements, and furniture. However, towns generally insisted on, and could enforce, regulations preventing villagers from doing anything but the most routine manufacturing. Towns had a market right over the surrounding countryside, forcing villagers to sell agricultural products in the town and spend that money on crafts produced in the town.

**Ownership of the Land.** The land tenure system had a profound effect on the rural economy. A system that evolved in the Middle Ages, it had developed an enormous number of variations by the Renaissance and Reformation. Its theoretical basis was encapsulated in the French expression *nulle terre sans seigneur,* "no lands without a lord." All land in a territory belonged ultimately to the king. However, over time, the king had supposedly given some of that land to other nobles in exchange for their support in defending the kingdom. Those nobles, in turn, kept some of the land as their personal domain, to be farmed according to their own rules, but turned over the rest of the land to farmers, who could farm it according to their own needs, in cooperation with the rest of the village. For all practical purposes, the farmers "owned" that land: they could sell bits of it to other farmers or pass it down to their children. Yet, what they actually owned was the usufruct, or right to use the land. The farmer-owners had to recognize the overlordship of the landowner by paying clearly defined rents and acknowledging various other prerogatives of lordship. These payments were set by local custom and, while they could not be adjusted at the whim of the lord, they could be burdensome.

**Crop Payments.** Village grain thus came on the market in the local towns because it was siphoned off as rents by local lords. In some areas those rents might be a fixed percentage of a year's harvest, but most of the time they were a fixed amount that was due no matter how good or bad the harvest had been. The obligations could be paid in a wide variety of crops. It was common for peasants to have to provide their lords with a goose at Christmastime, a chicken at Michaelmas, a carton of eggs at Easter, and a bucket of tallow, along with a few bushels of wheat or rye. In some areas these various obligations were converted into a cash equivalent sometime during the Middle Ages. Over time, the value of that cash equivalent diverged in relation to the underlying product. Peasants either benefited or suffered because of the conversion to cash, depending on the inflation rate.

**Innovations in Land Management.** In the course of the sixteenth century, some of the underlying assumptions of village-based three-field crop rotation began to be challenged. A split developed between Western and Eastern Europe. In Eastern Europe, farming became organized in large noble-run farms. Unlike the more subsistence-oriented village economy, these large farms produced grain primarily for export. Grain would be shipped downriver to Baltic seaports, where it would be transported through the Danish sound to Antwerp. (Later in the seventeenth century Amsterdam became the main destination instead of Antwerp.) Though owned by nobles, these farms were more "capital-

ist" in character than feudal because they relied on the international export market.

**Enclosure.** A similar capitalist spirit became apparent in the Western European countryside as well. Some villagers broke free from traditional communal agriculture and focused on intensifying production for the grain market. The most conspicuous way that innovative land management happened was through the phenomenon of enclosure. Prosperous villagers used their preferred position in local administration to acquire the scattered bits of land of different peasant owners and draw them together into larger units. These larger farms operated more efficiently by using paid labor from landless villagers than through the cooperative labor of small landholders. Enclosure became a major concern in England, where it even became a target of criticism from the humanist writer Sir Thomas More in his novel *Utopia* (1516). In France, by contrast, village institutions and customs remained stronger and inhibited the building of unified farms. Some attribute the growing prosperity of England in relation to France to this difference in the organization of agricultural production, which made it possible for England to become more open to entrepreneurial ideas.

**Low Countries.** By the end of the sixteenth century, the new pattern of Baltic trade meant that Dutch cities no longer had to rely on the surrounding countryside to support their basic needs. The Low Countries (present-day Netherlands, Belgium, and Luxembourg) thus became the first area to develop extensive specialization in nongrain crops to supplement the main dietary needs. Various kinds of vegetable farming, called garden farming, provided the main new crop. However, another notable innovation was in nonconsumable products like flowers. In the seventeenth century, Holland got caught up in a speculative frenzy over rare varieties of tulip. That excitement was made possible not only because of the differences in Holland's markets but also because land was no longer needed to raise wheat and rye and could be put to other uses.

Sources:

Marc Bloc, *French Rural History: An Essay on Its Basic Characteristics,* translated by Janet Sondheimer (Berkeley: University of California Press, 1966).

Carlo M. Cipolla, *Before the Industrial Revolution: European Society and Economy, 1000–1700,* third edition (New York: Norton, 1993).

Mark Overton, *Agricultural Revolution in England: The Transformation of the Agrarian Economy, 1500–1850* (Cambridge & New York: Cambridge University Press, 1996).

## IDEAS ABOUT SOCIETY

**Society of Orders.** During both the Renaissance and Reformation, people did not usually use wealth or occupation as the main determinants of social stratification. The most common social model, which embodied the underlying assumptions about human nature, was that society was made up of "Orders," or "Estates." These Orders were determined not by wealth, but by social function. People assumed that society was divided into Three Orders: the clergy, the nobility, and the populace. The clergy was the

First Estate because its function brought it closest to God. It was responsible for teaching the other two orders about truth and morality. The nobility was considered the Second Estate, even though it held most of the real power in society. Its primary function was to protect the other two orders and ensure that laws were made and enforced. The Third Estate produced everything that was needed to keep themselves and the other two orders supplied.

**Public Function.** There were several assumptions about society that went along with this three-part division of society. First of all, social inequality was assumed to be a natural part of society. It was acceptable, or even desirable, to have distinctions between rich and poor. Inequality was derived from a sharp distinction between the "public" and "private" realms of activity. People did not define public and private exactly as they are known today. Public activity was activity that affected how government was run, while private activity was dedicated only to improving oneself and one's family. All forms of business were considered "private" in this sense. The modern word *economy* is derived from the ancient Greek word for "household," which underscores the idea that the economy was a private matter. Nobles were a higher Estate than merchants because their role was public, not private. They had no choice but to participate in government because of their obligation to protect society. At least, that is what the ideal of the society of orders implied.

**Society of Privileges.** The other side of the obligations that went with the public/private distinction is that one's social position entailed privileges. During the Renaissance and Reformation, privilege did not just mean having an advantage; it was an almost legal term designating things just because of the social group one belonged to. A privilege could be an exemption from an obligation that other people in society had; for example, nobles were usually exempt from taxation. On the other hand, a privilege could

Illumination depicting a feast at a lord's house, from a fifteenth-century Flemish manuscript for *Histoire d'Olivier de Castille* (Bibliothèque Nationale, Paris)

One Fourth of a cloth factory . . . Bartolomeo Corbinelli operated this shop and paid a rent of 42 florins, but he didn't want to pay that much and he left on March 6, 1425. Since then, the shop has been closed.

Taxable value 150 florins.

One half of a cottage, which I inhabit, with . . . orchard in the parish of San Michele a Castello.

Taxable value 0.

An adjoining vineyard in the same parish. The vineyard is cultivated by Fede di Domenico . . .

Taxable value 64 florins.

One house with vineyard in the same parish. . . . I receive a rent of 9 florins.

Taxable value 128 florins 11 soldi.

One peasants' cottage in the same parish with vineyard . . .

Taxable value 163 florins 8 soldi.

In Tunis, I commissioned Piero de Ser Naddo to arrange for the shipment of 204 bales of wool to Pisa on the ship owned by Giovanni Uzzino. But this wool was never loaded and it remained at the port. It was a total loss, and was valued at 600 florins or more. I have not yet been able to investigate the cause of this loss. . . . Since my return from Tunis, I have been unable to pursue this matter on account of the litigation in which I have been involved . . .

Taxable value 0.

Also, this Piero de Ser Naddo received 150 florins from Bernardo di Caccione which he was obligated to give me in Tunis but did not. I believe that Bernardo paid him that money without any letter or instruction from me. I have not yet legally demanded the return of the money but have only made an oral request. . . . I don't know how this will end. When this business is settled, I will inform the authorities.

Taxable value 0.

Also, Marco di Messer Forese Salviati and company owe me 100 florins or thereabouts, the price of leather which I sent him from Tunis. . . . This debt is not yet settled, but I fear that I will not be repaid, and I don't expect to win a lawsuit against them since they are very influential.

Taxable value 0.

Holdings in the Monte di Pieta.

Taxable value 65 florins.

Commercial and personal debts.

Taxable value 115 florins.

Personal exemptions:

Francesco, aged 56 200 florins

Monna Ginevra, his wife, aged 50 200 florins

Antonio, his son, aged 27 200 florins

Bernardo, his son, aged 24 200 florins

Michele, his son, aged 21 200 florins

Gabriello, his son, aged 7 200 florins

Total estimated value of Giovanni's taxable assets 572 florins 7 soldi

Total debts and exemptions 1315 florins.

Source: Gene A. Brucker, ed., *The Society of Renaissance Florence: A Documentary Study* (New York: Harper & Row, 1971), pp. 8–10.

be a right to do something that other people in society could not; for example, nobles were permitted to carry swords at all times, while members of the Third Estate were not.

**Sumptuary Laws.** From the modern perspective, some privileges were obviously more important than others. It made more difference to the well-being of a nobleman that he was exempt from paying taxes than that he was allowed to wear a sword. Yet, in the process of social definition, all of the different privileges were taken into account. People would actively defend any given privilege because to lose it might indicate a loss of the social status to which the privilege pertained. The most visible sign of this commitment to the symbolic side of privilege can be seen in the sumptuary laws passed in major cities. Sumptuary laws were laws that prohibited people of a certain class from wearing clothing or jewelry that was reserved for people of higher status. As commoners became wealthier, they had access to fine fabrics. They began to engage in conspicuous consumption, which threatened the status and economic well-being of noblemen who came to the towns. The enforcement of noble privileges reduced that threat.

**Political Power.** The prominence of the idea of the Three Estates as an organizing principle for society was reinforced by political institutions. In many territories in the late Middle Ages, princes turned to consulting bodies called Estates to help them in governing. The most famous of these bodies were the Estates General of France, which met several times in the fifteenth and sixteenth centuries, but stopped meeting after 1614 until the French Revolution in 1789. The three Estates were the three main interest groups in any territory. Each Estate would first meet together to deliberate their own needs, then the three Estates would meet together with the prince's representatives to offer support and negotiate concessions. In almost all territories, the Second Estate, the nobility, had the commanding role in the meetings of the Estates. Nobles came to view participation in the meetings of Estates as a kind of substitute for their medieval obligation to raise troops to defend the territory.

**Problems with the Theory.** There were obvious limitations to the society of orders as a system of social classification that even people at the time recognized. First, anywhere from three-quarters to 95 percent of the population belonged to the Third Estate. The model was discriminating at one end of the scale and quite indiscriminate at the other end of the scale. However, equally troubling was the fact that each of the three Estates had tremendous variations of wealth and power of individuals within them. This situation was most obvious in the Third Estate, which included merchants and lawyers with close ties to kings and princes throughout Europe. In regard to lifestyle, some of them were better off than others, but the most prominent nobles had to fear that a sudden reversal of fortune would ruin them and they would not have status to fall back on. There was also a large middle strata of members of the Third Estate in the towns, and an even larger number of peasants. The Third Estate theoretically included the urban and rural poor, though those people rarely had any kind of political representation for their own interests.

**Strata.** Social stratification was also noticeable within the First and Second Estates. At the beginning of the Renaissance, all of the First Estate was Catholic, which meant legally that they were celibate. Every member of the Estate had to be recruited from either the Second or Third Estate because it was impossible to be "born into" the Estate. Thus, the social attitudes of the First Estate were shaped by the Estates from which members were recruited. The Pope, Cardinals, archbishops, and bishops were at the top of the First Estate. These people lived lives much like those of the most prominent nobles. Most of the staffing of the church, on the other hand, was by members of the Third Estate. In remote rural corners of Europe, the lifestyles of parish priests were not much different from those of the peasants they served on Sundays and religious holidays. In Protestant Europe after 1520, clergy could marry and have their sons join the clergy, too (for only males were allowed to become pastors). Noblemen generally were less attracted to the clerical lifestyle of Protestantism than they were to the upper echelons of the Catholic Church hierarchy, so the Protestant clergy adopted a social role more like other professions under the banner of the Third Estate.

**Nobles.** The nobility was perhaps the most unified social group within the society of orders model, but even it was subject to wide variation. In remote corners of Europe there were people who were technically noble, but whose lifestyle was scarcely different from that of the peasants who lived around them. Often this segment of the nobility was most vocal in emphasizing the social distinction between nobility and Third Estate. They strained to maintain the outward privileges of nobility despite their poverty. At the other extreme, the rulers of the most powerful states in Europe were nobles. They possessed vast wealth and power. Within the wealthiest countries, such as France, some nonroyal nobles had personal estates as large as the independent states in Germany or Italy. They lived in an entirely different social environment from the rural nobleman.

**Alternate Models.** Though the society of orders model was the most widespread ideal of social organization, most people also had a more pragmatic view of society that fit more closely with day to day reality. The social distinction between nobility and commoners was maintained in almost all models, but most models made more explicit gradations in status within the Third Estate, and dropped the clergy as a distinct social group. The Englishman William Harrison, for example, in 1577 divided the population into four categories: gentlemen, citizens, yeomen, and laborers. The first group corresponded roughly to the nobility; the second, to the politically active urban groups; the third, to the leading figures in the rural community who were not noble; and the fourth, to the poor farmers and ordinary workers in both town and countryside. In alternate models of social organization there was a greater willingness to recognize that different social groups sometimes had conflicting interests and society was not just a harmonious whole. For every social group there were books and pamphlets that both extolled the virtues and complained about the vices of the group.

Sources:

Jonathan Dewald, *The European Nobility, 1400–1800* (New York: Cambridge University Press, 1996).

George Huppert, *Les Bourgeois Gentilhommes: An Essay on the Definitions of Elites in Early Renaissance France* (Chicago: University of Chicago Press, 1977).

Peter Kriedte, *Peasants, Landlords, and Merchant Captialists: Europe and the World Economy, 1500–1800* (Cambridge & New York: Cambridge University Press, 1983).

## LONG-DISTANCE TRADE

**Luxury Products.** Because of the difficulty of transport, the luxury trade was the most conspicuous part of long-distance trade in medieval Europe. Traders had to expect large profits for the things they imported or there would be little point in assuming the risks. There were two varieties of luxury trade in Europe in the fourteenth century. The first variety was internal to Europe itself. A few regions specialized in high-quality manufacturing in traditional European products. The most notable were the woolens and silk industries in the towns of Northern Italy and the Low Countries (present-day Netherlands, Belgium, and Luxembourg). This internal European luxury trade made cities such as Bruges and Florence prosperous beyond the usual standards of manufacturing centers. The second variety of luxury trade was in products that were not manufactured in Europe. This long-distance trade was the most visible in creating great wealth.

**World System.** The European economy was already linked to the economies of other parts of the world in the Middle Ages. For example, Marco Polo's famous journey to China began around 1270. He traveled a familiar route for merchants between the Middle East and China, though one that was seldom used by Europeans. Spices were the most desirable products from Asia because they were comparatively easy to transport and were in demand. Pepper was in particularly high demand because it added variety to a monotonous diet and helped preserve meats that had started to spoil. It has been estimated that up to a million pounds of pepper entered the European market in some years. Europe had comparatively little of luxury value other than gold and silver to offer China and India in return for their products, so there was a considerable trade imbalance.

**Levant Trade.** At the beginning of the Renaissance, the key to long-distance trade was in the Mediterranean. Access to the Chinese and Indian markets passed through Muslim lands controlled by either Arabs or

Seeschiff vom Ende des 15. Jahrh., halb vor dem Winde segelnd.
Aus Bernh. v. Breydenbach, Peregrinationes. Mainz 1486.

A German ship with a square sail and stern rudder, engraving from *Peregrination of Brendenbach* (1486)

Turks. Europeans called all of the trade that flowed from that direction the Levant trade, their term for the Middle East in general. The situation made shipments precarious, since Christians and Muslims had been fighting in the Middle East since the Crusades in the eleventh century. Until 1450, there was only one Christian outpost in the eastern Mediterranean, Constantinople (now Istanbul). When that city fell to the Ottoman Turks in 1453, many Europeans feared that they would be permanently cut off from important luxury goods.

**Venetians.** On the European side, the primary carriers of the Mediterranean trade were the Venetians. The city-state of Venice was noted for its strong naval power and astute merchants. In the fifteenth century, there were 42,000 seamen and shipbuilders in the city. In the 1370s, the rival merchant city-state Genoa tried to break Venice's dominance of the Eastern Mediterranean trade but was defeated and forced to turn its attention westward. As the Turks were subduing Constantinople, the Venetians were cementing control over a network of islands in the Aegean, right up to the gates of Constantinople, as well as extending their control in the Italian peninsula. Thus, Venice had one of the greatest concentrations of wealth in all of Europe. It was a crossroads of trade and had a reputation for both the positive and negative attributes that this implied: it was exciting, at the cutting edge of culture, and prosperous; but it was also filled with price-gougers, thieves, and prostitutes, offering nearly any vice that could be imagined. In the second half of the fifteenth century, Venice fought against the Turks to maintain its privileged position in the eastern Mediterranean.

**Portuguese.** Venice's near monopoly of the luxury trade in the Mediterranean made it the object of envy and competition from other parts of Europe. In 1415 a small principality took the first step toward trying to break that monopoly. King John of Portugal captured the Moroccan fortress of Ceuta, just across the Strait of Gibraltar, from the Arabs. This act began a century of exploration and economic expansion westward and southward. In the 1430s Portugal, now ruled by Prince Henry the Navigator, began to settle the Atlantic islands of Madeira and the Azores. The Portuguese used these islands as staging areas for voyages along the African coast. The Spanish kingdom of Castile, not wishing to be outdone, occupied the Canary Islands. The immediate goal of such exploration was to find a way to the source of African gold in the Senegambia, which, up to that point, was available only from long routes run by Muslim merchants through the Sahara Desert. Prevailing wind conditions, sail technology, the desolation of the African Sahara coast, and complete ignorance about what the South Atlantic might be like all made exploration dangerous. However, by 1446 the Portuguese had reached the mouth of the Senegal River and had begun to set up trading posts. The explorations proved profitable and gold began to flow back to Portugal. Africans also grew a kind of pepper, which, while not as coveted as East Indian pepper, formed an adequate substitute and created competition

for the Venetian spice merchants. In addition the Portuguese began to cultivate the Atlantic islands to produce cash crops such as sugar. In the 1430s, Henry the Navigator authorized Portuguese shippers to trade for slaves on the African coast. Some of these slaves were transported to Madeira and the Azores to work in plantations, and this slave trade was the beginning of what was to become a big business in later centuries.

**Sea Route to India.** Portuguese success in exploring the west coast of Africa opened the possibility for an even greater source of profit. The African trade was still not as lucrative as the spice trade that flowed through the Indian Ocean, but perhaps it was possible to sail to the Indian Ocean around Africa. For the rest of the fifteenth century, Portuguese explorers sailed down the African coast, hoping to find a route to India. All the while, they set up new trading posts, drawing more of Africa into the European trade network. When Bartholomeu Dias rounded the Cape of Good Hope in Southern Africa in 1488, he proved that a sea route to the Indies was possible. The decline of the Mediterranean economy was set in motion.

**Discovery of the Americas.** The shift from the Mediterranean economy to an Atlantic economy became even more pronounced with the discovery of the Americas by Christopher Columbus in 1492. Although Europeans were intrigued by new products discovered in the Americas, such as tobacco, potatoes, and maize, those products had relatively little impact on the European economy before 1600. The most important import from the Americas in the first decades was gold. Conquistadores captured centuries of accumulated gold from the Aztec and Inca empires as plunder. Not long after that initial influx of precious metals, the Spanish established silver mines in present-day Mexico and Bolivia, which became the main source of revenues from colonies for the rest of the sixteenth century.

**Baltic Trade.** The gold and silver of the Americas flowed into Spanish ports, bringing wealth to one strata of merchants, but Spain was often just a way station in the circulation of wealth. The reorientation toward an Atlantic economy created a new crossroads for merchants and goods: the city of Antwerp in the Low Countries. Gold and silver flowed into Antwerp to support another long-distance trade in bulkier commodities throughout northern Europe.

**Herring Merchants.** In the late Middle Ages, control of the Baltic trade in timber, iron ore, and grain had been in the hands of an association of German towns called the Hanseatic League. By 1500 the towns of the Low Countries had taken over leadership of that Baltic trade, with Antwerp gaining the most from that dominance. Dutch towns could rely on a steady supply of wheat and rye shipped from Prussia and Poland. In exchange, Dutch traders sent woolen cloth and fish to the East. They perfected their shipbuilding techniques for merchant vessels operating in the northern environment. In the North Atlantic, fishing banks proved to be dependable sources of profit, as were the silver mines of Spanish America. The

Below is an account taken from Tome Pires's *Suma Oriental* (1515). Pires was *contador* (accountant) of the royal factory at Malacca and is generally recognized as the best early Portuguese observer of East Indian trade.

China is a profitable voyage, and moreover whoever loads up . . . sometimes makes three for one, and in good merchandise which is soon sold.

And because this loading of the junks is a very profitable matter, as they sail in regular monsoons, the king of Malacca derived great profit from it. They gave the king one third more than they give to others, and the king made the man who dealt with his money exempt from dues, so that it was found that from this loading of the junks a great store of gold was brought in, and it could not be otherwise. And here come the kings of Pahang, and Kampar, and Indragiri, and others, through their factors, to employ money in the said junks. This is very important for anyone with capital, because Malacca sends junks out, and others come in, and they are so numerous that the king could not help but be rich. And the said merchant who dealt with the king's money had a share; he got pride and freedom, and they welcomed him gladly and paid him in due time. For this the king had officials to receive the merchandise and grant the said rights, and this was attached to the custom house, in charge of Ceryna De Raja, the Bamdara's brother.

If when the time is up the said merchant has no gold to pay with, he pays in merchandise according to the vale in the country, and when he pays in merchandise it is more profitable for one settled there. This is the custom if you have not contracted to be paid in gold. But the merchant prefers merchandise to gold, because from day to day the merchandise goes up in price, and because trade of every kind from all parts of the world is done in Malacca.

And should anyone ask what advantage to his exchequer the King our Lord can derive from Malacca, there is no doubt that—once the influence is finished that this ex-king of Malacca still exercises, and also once Java has been visited, to win the confidence of the merchants and navigators, and of the kings who still trust the false words of the king of Bintang, who does more mischief among relatives in one day than we can undo in a year—there is no doubt Malacca is of such importance and profit that it seems to me it has no equal in the world.

Anyone may note that if someone came to Malacca, capable of sending each year a junk to China, and another to Bengal, and another to Pulicat, and another to Pegu, and the merchants of Malacca and for the other parts took shares in these; if a factor of the King our Lord came to tax money and merchandise so much per cent as aforesaid; and if someone else with officials came to take charge of the custom house to collect dues; who can doubt that in Malacca bahars of gold will be made, and that there will be no need of money from India, but it will go from here to there? . . . Malacca should be well supplied with people, sending some and bringing back others. It should be provided with excellent officials, expert traders, lovers of peace, not arrogant, quick-tempered, undisciplined, dissolute, but sober and elderly. . . . Courteous youth and business life do not go together; and since this cannot be had in any other way, at least let us have years, for the rest cannot be found. Men cannot estimate the worth of Malacca, on account of its greatness and profit. Malacca is a city that was made for merchandise, fitter than any other in the world. . . . Wherefore a thing of such magnitude and of such great wealth, which never in the world could decline, if it were moderately governed and favoured, should be supplied, looked after, praised and favoured, and not neglected. . . . And it is true that this part of the world is richer and more prized than the world of the Indies, because the smallest merchandise here is gold, which is least prized, and in Malacca they consider it a merchandise. Whoever is lord of Malacca has his hand on the throat of Venice. As far from Malacca, and from Malacca to China, and from China to the Moluccas, and from the Moluccas to Java, and from Java to Malacca and Sumatra, all is in our power.

Source: J. H. Parry, ed., *The European Reconnaissance: Selected Documents* (New York: Walker, 1968), pp. 109–122.

Dutch were disparaged as "Herring Merchants," but their prosperity became the envy of the rest of Europe. Antwerp's position declined in the course of the Dutch Revolt (1568–1648), to be replaced by Amsterdam as the pivot of the North Atlantic and Baltic trade.

**Networks.** By 1600 there were three distinct trade networks that were beginning to become interconnected. The Baltic and North Atlantic trade was dominated by the Dutch, but the English and French also began to take an active interest in it, which led to the settling of North

American colonies in the 1600s. The Caribbean trade was dominated by the Spanish, but in the course of the Dutch Revolt, the Dutch became serious rivals because of privateering. The Indian Ocean trade also passed from the hands of the Portuguese to the Dutch, who took the initiative in establishing colonies in modern Indonesia. The full implications of the Dutch role in all three of these trade circuits would only become apparent in the seventeenth century, when the Netherlands were widely recognized as the wealthiest part of Europe.

Sources:

Fernand Braudel, *Civilization and Capitalism 15th–18th Century*, 3 volumes, translated by Siân Reynolds (New York: Harper & Row, 1982–1984).

James D. Tracy, ed. *The Rise of Merchant Empires: Long Distance Trade in the Early Modern World, 1350–1750* (Cambridge & New York: Cambridge University Press, 1990).

Immanuel Wallerstein, *The Modern World-System*, volume 1: *Capitalist Agriculture and the Origins of the European World-Economy in the Sixteenth Century* (New York: Academic Press, 1974).

## MONEY

**Gold and Silver.** Money is used to provide equal exchanges of value for unlike products. During the Renaissance and Reformation, money came either in the form of gold and silver coins, or in promises to supply gold or silver coins by people whose credit was acceptable. Coins were minted with the approval of the king or some other ruler, but the actual number and placement of the coins was determined by bankers and the open market. There was no such thing as a monetary policy directed by governments.

**Coin Sizes, Weight, and Fineness.** In general, large gold coins such as ducats and florins were used to finance major projects of governments and individuals, while most daily business was carried out with silver or copper coins. The latter would usually only have value within a local economy where they could be readily used again. The value of the gold and silver coins depended on their weight and fineness. A favored pastime of those who wanted to get illicit profits from coinage was to slightly scrape, or "clip," some of the gold or silver from a number of coins and remint the clippage as a new coin. Over time the clipping of coins led to their devaluation because the weight no longer measured up to expectations.

**Local Varieties.** There was no universal standard for coins. Local varieties of coinage were complicated. Making the situation even more confusing was the fact that governments often created another kind of artificial money, called money of account, that they used for their own books. For example, Italian fiscal records of the fourteenth and fifteenth century are recorded in *lire* and *soldi*, though there were no actual coins by that name. In the sixteenth century, the German territory of Hessen had a coin called a *gulden* valued at twenty-six *albus*. However, in fiscal accounts, there was a money of account called a *gulden* that was valued at twenty-seven *albus*. These local variants meant that people who handled money frequently had to be extremely careful about valuation of coins. A few large coins, such as Venetian ducats and Florentine florins, were so sufficiently widespread in commerce that they could be used in international trade.

**The Advance of Monetization.** Even the countryside had developed contact with money during the course of the Middle Ages. Rents and other payments that were initially designated to be paid "in kind" (meaning with bushels of wheat or dozens of eggs and the like) had often been transformed into cash payments during the Middle Ages. On the one hand, it was easier to collect a few pennies from a peasant than to have them drop off poultry, which might spoil before it could be eaten. On the other hand, coinage was sometimes in short supply. Because gold and silver were universal signs of value, they were often hoarded instead of kept in circulation. For that reason, barter continued to play a major role in the economy. Often barter transactions used moneys of account to indicate the real money value of the exchange, so that even barter was "monetized" by the Renaissance era.

**Double-Entry Bookkeeping.** This era also had other innovations that fostered economic development. First, the process of keeping accounts was rendered much more logical and complete by the introduction of double-entry bookkeeping by Luca Pacioli at the end of the fifteenth century. The double-entry system gave a businessman an overview of both his assets and debts in a relatively simple format. Though the system was not adopted universally, it marked a clear rationalization of economic practice that made "capitalist" systematization more manageable.

**International Banks.** Another innovation involved more complex and efficient ways of raising money to support new businesses. Banks existed in the Middle Ages. Christian theology formally rejected the idea of charging interest for loans, calling any interest charge "usury." Some money-lending activity was handled by Jews, who were tolerated in some places because they performed a needed service. Nevertheless, most of the moneylending in the Middle Ages was done by Christians. Christian bankers either received dispensations to allow them to lend at interest, or, more commonly, covered their interest-based lending by charging for other services. In the thirteenth century, international banks with offices in different cities were a major economic power. To minimize the risks of transporting large quantities of gold coins through robber-infested woods, international banks developed something called the bill of exchange. The bill of exchange was a written agreement between bankers and their clients in two different locations that allowed for the balancing of money holdings in both places. In the sixteenth century, people began to realize that a bill of exchange was as good as money because it represented a legal obligation to give money. It became more common for the designated payee to endorse the bill as a check and use it for payment to third parties. As long as there was confidence that the designated payer would be able to pay, this paper money was fully negotiable.

**Public Deposit Banks.** In the course of the sixteenth century, international merchant banks had to compete with a parallel institution: the public-deposit bank. Local

Now I shall discuss the best way to invest money: whether it should be all in cash, or all in real estate and communal bonds, or some in one and some in the other. Now it is true that money is very difficult to conserve and to handle; it is very susceptible to the whims of fortune, and few know how to manage it. But whoever possesses a lot of money and knows how to manage it is, as they say, the master of the business community because he is the nerve center of all the trades and commercial activities. For in every moment of adverse fortune, in times of exile and those disasters which occur in the world, those with money will suffer less than those who are well provided with real estate. . . . I would not wish to deny, however, that real estate is more secure and more durable than money, although occasionally it has been damaged and even destroyed by war, by enemies with fire and sword. Real estate holdings are particularly useful for minors and for others who have no experience in banking. . . . There is nothing easier to lose, nothing more difficult to conserve, more dangerous to invest, or more troublesome to keep, than money. . . . The prudent family head will consider all of his property , and will guard against having it all in one place or in one chest. If war or other disasters occur here, you might still be secure there; and if you are damaged there, then you may save yourself here. . . .

Let me warn you again that in our city Florence, wealth is conserved only with the greatest difficulty. This is due to the frequent and almost continual wars of the Commune, which have required the expenditure of great sums, and the Commune's imposition of many taxes and forced loans. I have found no better remedy for defending myself than to take care not to gain enemies, for a single enemy will harm you more than four friends will help. I have always remained on good terms with my relatives and neighbors and the other residents of the district, so that whenever the taxes have been assessed, they have befriended me and taken pity on me. In this business, good friends and relatives are very useful. . . . So guard against making enemies or involving yourself in quarrels and disputes. And if someone with gall and arrogance tries to quarrel with you, you should treat him with courtesy and patience. . . .

With respect to good, honest, and virtuous friends, I again counsel you to serve them and be liberal with them. Lend to them, give to them, trust them. . . . And while being liberal and generous to friends, one should occasionally do the same to strangers, so that one will gain a reputation for not being miserly, and also will acquire new friends.

I have told you, my sons, how I have treated good friends, and also how I have treated the swindlers and beggars who daily petition me. Now I must tell you how to respond when, as happens every day, your close relatives make demands on you. It seems to me that one is obligated to help them, not so much with money, as with blood and sweat and whatever one can, even to sacrificing one's life for the honor of the family. One must know how to spend money and acquire possessions. He who spends only in eating and dressing, or who does not know how to disburse money for the benefit and honor of his family, is certainly not wise. But in these matters, one must use good judgment, because it makes no sense to destroy one's own fortune in order to save that of a relative. . . .

Of necessity, the rich man must be generous, for generosity is the most noble virtue that he can possess, and to exercise it requires wisdom and moderation. Whoever wishes to be regarded as liberal must spend and give away his wealth, for which trait the rich are much liked. . . . But who gives beyond his means soon dissipates his fortune. But if you wish to acquire a reputation for liberality, consider well your resources, the times, the expenses which you must bear, and the qualities of men. According to your means, give to men who are in need and who are worthy. And whoever does otherwise goes beyond the rule of liberality, and does not acquire praise thereby. Whatever you give to the unworthy is lost, and whoever disburses his wealth beyond measure soon experiences poverty.

Source: Gene A. Brucker, ed., *The Society of Renaissance Florence: A Documentary Study* (New York: Harper & Row, 1971), pp. 24–27.

deposit banks grew in cities with lots of free-floating capital such as Venice. Like international banks, deposit banks could handle much of their accounting as paper transfers in the account books rather than physically moving gold coins around. The innovation that deposit banking allowed was for lenders to lend more money than they actually had on hand at any given time. As long as there was sufficient reserve to handle any immediate call for coins from a given depositor, the banker could make use of the depositor's coins for his own profit. In the Middle Ages, these deposit banks were private. Beginning with the Taula de Canvi (exchange bank) in Barcelona in 1401, government officials created their own banks to serve the same function. Other parts of

A boxed coin scale, with weights and coins from various European countries, circa 1600
(American Numismatic Society, New York)

Europe were slow to follow the Spanish lead, but by the seventeenth century, public banks were becoming a common feature of European commerce.

**Merchant Exchanges.** The other important innovation that provided capital for economic growth during the Renaissance and Reformation was the rise of merchant exchanges, or bourses. Again, the roots of these institutions in the Middle Ages were in the main commercial towns of Italy. An exchange was a way for a merchant to gather support for large risky undertakings, such as overseas trade. As the system developed in the sixteenth century, it became the primary way in which English and Dutch adventurers financed their colonial ventures in the Atlantic and Indian Oceans. In the seventeenth century, full-fledged stock markets developed in Amsterdam for all sorts of businesses. Even ordinary investors got caught up in periodic waves of speculative frenzy in the markets, most notoriously in the tulip mania of the 1630s.

**Inflation of the Sixteenth Century.** The other notable monetary feature of the sixteenth century was a steady price inflation in agricultural products. In the century after the Black Death, prices had been low, relative to wages, because of the severe population decline. Two factors probably contributed to the rise in prices after 1500. The first was renewed population growth, which increased demand for food and goods. The second was the influx of gold and silver from the new world, which increased the amount of money in circulation. More money available to spend on the same amount of goods tends to drive the price of those goods upward.

**Price Revolution.** The inflation pressure of the sixteenth century was slow and steady rather than abrupt and disruptive. Over time, however, the gap between prices and wages began to be quite noticeable. By 1600, prices were two to three times higher than they had been in 1500, while wages were essentially stagnant. Though not dramatic in the short term, these trend lines were powerful enough in the long term to prompt economic historians to speak of a "price revolution" in the sixteenth century.

Sources:

Carlo M. Cipolla, *Before the Industrial Revolution: European Society and Economy, 1000–1700* (New York: Norton, 1976).

Lisa Jardine, *Worldly Goods: A New History of the Renaissance* (New York: Doubleday, 1996).

Harry A. Miskimin, *The Economy of Early Renaissance Europe, 1300–1460* (Englewood Cliffs, N.J.: Prentice-Hall, 1969).

## THE NOBILITY

**Definition.** According to the society of orders model, nobility was a status acquired by service in the defense of society. The battle chiefs and knights of the Middle Ages were, according to this idea, the true exemplars of nobility. By the late fifteenth century, this notion ran into the inescapable fact that most people who called themselves nobles were no longer primarily soldiers. Two other, partly contradictory, definitions of nobility merged with the model from the society of orders. The first harked back to the ancient philosopher Aristotle, who argued that the aristocracy consisted of the most talented people, who should use their tal-

ent to rule society. Nobles defended society not just by fighting wars, but by taking the lead in local administration of all kinds. The second argued that nobility was in the blood. The surest sign of nobility was to have been born into a noble family. In theory, the society of orders model and Aristotle's model assumed that nobility was a result of personal accomplishments, while the blood model assumed that it was innate. Nobles reconciled the contradiction by arguing that pedigree was the best determinant of who actually had talent. A long genealogy of military service supposedly predisposed nobles to act in a virtuous, noble manner. Discussions of the idea of nobility in the era tended to focus on the issue of noble ancestry, though sometimes they criticized current nobles for failing to live up to their ancestors.

**Gradations.** Different segments of the nobility reacted to the various elements of the definition of nobility in different ways. At the peak of the nobility was a small group of the highest nobles. They were known as the peerage in England and *Ducs et pairs* in France. Though few in number, they wielded enormous authority because of their wealth and the traditional respect due their lineage. Comparisons across countries can be complicated. There were dukes in France who were under the King of France, while in Germany, dukes generally ran their own countries, though they were supposedly subordinate to the Holy Roman Emperor. The great nobles generally took their close access to kings for granted. They ultimately determined the ideals of nobility for the territory.

**Middling Level.** Below the peers was a layer of regionally important nobles that formed the backbone of noble representation in the territorial Estates. In the political affairs of the kingdom, these regional nobles often aligned themselves as part of the cliental network of a peer. At the same time, these nobles could be particularly vocal defenders of the privileges of the nobility against the claims of the king. Their wealth could come from two distinct sources, and social tensions within the nobility were caused by the two sources. Some nobles relied almost exclusively on the revenues from their extensive landholdings. A substantial proportion of their estates would actually be owned by peasants, with the usual rent payments. The rest would be the personal domain of the noble, who could farm it or rent it out on shorter-term leases, depending on how he wanted to run it. These nobles derived their status primarily from a long line of ancestors who had controlled specific pieces of land. Other nobles derived a lot of their income from occupying administrative posts in local government. The nobles who relied primarily on their lands were known as the nobility of the sword, because their estates were theoretically derived from their military service to earlier kings. The nobles who relied primarily on their offices were known as the nobility of the robe, because of the judicial robes often worn by high government officials. In 1516, the Italian nobleman Baldassare Castiglione published a book called *The Courtier*, which had a profound influence on the self-understanding of this middling level of nobles.

The Burgundian court, circa 1480 (from Neville Williams, *Expanding Horizons*, 1970)

**Minor Nobles.** The lower reaches of the nobility were often the most concerned about maintaining the importance of blood as a sign of nobility. Some could trace their genealogies far back into the medieval era, but their landed estates were small, for any variety of reasons. Most had little money left to finance significant political roles, even in regional affairs. They were usually deferred to by the peasants who happened to live near their estates but were looked down upon by the more active nobles in the region. For most, the only reliable source of income was the rents from their estates, which could no longer cover the costs of either maintaining a cavalry unit or "living nobly."

**Living Nobly.** Between 1350 and 1600 the distinctiveness of the nobility as a social group became stronger rather than weaker. Regulations governing how far back one had to be able to demonstrate noble ancestors were enforced more strictly. The specific conditions under which a nonnoble family could become ennobled were spelled out. Some noble families purchased forged documents to prove long-standing noble status. Other poor noble families who may have had a long noble genealogy lost their status because they had no documents that proved their heritage. The process of losing noble status was called "derogation." Some obvious failings, such as treason or murder, might cause derogation of an individual nobleman, but a whole lineage might also be lost for failing to live nobly. Living nobly meant adhering to a broad set of noble values and actively competing with other families for honor and reputation. Nobles were forbidden to learn a manual trade or become a merchant, because such activity was considered inappropriate to living nobly. Living nobly thus created a real contradiction for nobles. It required lots of money to exhibit the conspicuous consumption that honor and reputation demanded, but it did not allow nobles to earn money in any straightforward fashion, except by farming or fighting. As a result, many nobles were in serious debt. When they were unable to pay, their family also faced derogation.

**Chivalry.** In northern Europe, and especially in France, the era of the early Renaissance corresponded with the flowering of a particularly medieval noble ideal: chivalry. This model for social behavior stressed valor, loyalty, and attention to personal honor as the key signs of high social status. The ideals of chivalry were expressed in new genres of writing, such as romantic poetry and adventure novels. Many elements that would be considered "typically medieval" about the behavior of knights actually became widespread only during the Renaissance and Reformation. Two of the most notable examples were participation in elaborate tournaments and duels of honor.

**Women.** Despite the modern connection of the idea of chivalry with romance, "true love" played a minor role in the lives of most noblewomen. The importance of genealogy for noble status meant that most noblewomen's careers were preordained by family considerations. A few would be destined to marry, usually into another noble family determined by clientage networks. Many would remain unmarried, either joining a religious order, serving in the entourage of some more prominent noble, or staying home with their parents to help run the estate. The cost of a dowry was often a major barrier to marriage for noble daughters. Many noble families focused their attention on the dowry for one daughter and the inheritance portion for one son. Other children would have to accept whatever was leftover. Among the lower levels of nobility, the wife of a nobleman had much the same role as in third estate households: she ensured that the house and its staff were run efficiently. In the great noble families, household administration was in the hands of courtiers. Often the wives of great nobles played important diplomatic roles as representatives of their original family in the entourage of their new family. In rare instances, a noblewoman would gain political power herself: some queens came to power through genealogical claims, such as Elizabeth I of England, and a few more became regents, such as Catherine de Medici. A noblewoman and other mothers of underage sons exerted influence by a combination of shrewd management of courtiers and close connections to their sons. On the whole, though, it was rare for noblewomen to have a public role.

Sources:
Jonathan Dewald, *The European Nobility, 1400–1800* (New York: Cambridge University Press, 1996).

Anne J. Duggan, ed., *Nobles and Nobility in Medieval Europe: Concepts, Origins, Transformations* (Woodbridge, Suffolk, U.K. & Rochester, N.Y.: Boydell Press, 2000).

George Huppert, *Les Bourgeois Gentilshommes: An Essay on the Definition of Elites in Early Renaissance France* (Chicago: University of Chicago Press, 1977).

### PATRICIANS AND ARTISANS

**Urban Elites.** The citizenry of the towns consisted of the patriciate and the artisans. Almost every town had a relatively small group of families that had the largest fortunes and controlled most of the political offices of the town. These individuals represented the patriciate. Most men in the patriciate belonged to one of two clusters of occupations: they were either merchants and bankers or they belonged to one of the learned professions, primarily the law. They emulated the nobility by not actually making anything, but by controlling the activities of those who did make things. Also like the nobility, patricians preserved their social distinctiveness by blocking upward social mobility for all but a few nonmerchants, or professionals. Elite families forged multiple links by marriage and made various deals to ensure that they were represented politi-

Two woodworkers trying to qualify for mastership, illumination from a fifteenth-century Flemish codex (from Franco Cardini, *Europe 1492*, 1989)

cally in urban policy. Occasionally, one patrician family came to exercise such a powerful role in the city that they became de facto rulers of the city. In free city-states such a concentration of power might lead to a showdown in which either the powerful family was driven into exile, or it would overthrow the institutions of self-government and turn itself into a principality. Other than that, there were comparatively few differences in the social attitudes or position of the patriciate in either free city-states or ordinary towns, though the former did have more authority over their surrounding countryside.

**Guild Cycle.** The term *artisan* refers to all people involved in basic manufacturing requiring any special skill or technique. The life of the artisan was shaped by the craft guilds, which ran the trade in any given city. Though the specifics of guild organization could vary greatly from one town to another and one craft to another, there was a general life cycle that virtually all guilds imposed on their members. A person learned a craft first as an apprentice in a master's shop. After some period of apprenticeship, the craft member would become a journeyman. After serving a period as a journeyman, the member would become eligible to become a master, with his own shop. For the most part, girls were excluded from the usual artisan training cycle. If they learned the techniques of a particular craft, it was in the shop of their own parents or husbands, rather than in the traditional craft route. Usually, only masters had a say in how the guild was run. Apprentices and journeymen were subject to the authority of masters both in the individual shops and in the general regulations that the guild promulgated.

**Apprenticeship.** Children began their artisanal careers at an early age. It was common for parents to make a contract for their sons to become apprentices at the age of six or seven. The contract specified the length of service, support, and conditions of the child's initial training. For all practical purposes, the apprentice then became a member of his new master's household. Most apprentice positions were achieved through connections. The oldest son of a master in a particular craft would be apprenticed to a prominent master in that same craft. Other sons might apprentice in a different craft or the same craft, but without the assurance that they could eventually inherit their father's shop. The apprentice would live and work in the house of the master. Initially, his responsibilities would be menial. He would clean up scraps, sweep the floors, and bring materials to the other workers in the shop. In most cases, he would learn the craft first by observing, and then by introduction from the master and the other workers in the shop. After a few years, he would have learned enough about the craft to be able to contribute to any shop. At that time, he would leave the security of his hometown and, bearing a letter of introduction from his hometown guild, he would undertake the next stage of his training as a journeyman.

**Journeymen.** Journeyman status was complicated by the fact that it consisted of two distinct groups of people. In the guild model, apprentices became journeymen to learn more of the tricks of the craft so that they would become qualified to be masters. But only some journeymen could reasonably aspire to become masters. After all, it was not in the interest of the other guild masters to allow too many guild shops in any given town. They might lose business to the newcomers. The guilds themselves deliberately limited the opportunities to open a shop in order to assure that masters could earn a living wage. Usually only the journeymen whose fathers already ran a master's shop that they could inherit would be assured of becoming masters some day. They set out on their wanderings in their mid to late teens, going from town to town in order to learn nuances of the craft that they might not have learned by staying in one shop. The other group of journeymen may or may not have begun their travels in the hopes of eventually becoming masters, but over time they discovered that their path to advancement was blocked, no matter how much skill they may have acquired. They became perpetually locked into journeyman status. They provided the bulk of the labor for the larger master's shops in the towns. So journeymen were, on the one hand, a group of late adolescents and young adults who were just learning the more refined techniques of their trade, and, on the other hand, older men whose career ladder had peaked.

**Lifestyle.** Like the apprentices, journeymen mostly lived and worked in the household and shop of a master. Yet, unlike the apprentices, journeymen did not have family-backed contracts that regulated their roles with the masters. Instead, their interactions were regulated by the local guilds. The process of finding work was straightforward. The journeyman carried a letter from his hometown guild, demonstrating that he had passed apprentice status. When he came to a new town, he would go to the guildhall of his guild and present his letter. At the guildhall, he would be informed if there were any masters looking for workers. If so, he would be directed to the master's shop and work would be arranged. If not, he would be lodged at the guildhall for a brief period of time, perhaps given a small sum of money, and sent on to the next town. The journeyman would continue wandering from town to town until he found temporary or permanent work with a master.

**Associations.** The shared lifestyles of journeymen created a distinct culture. In order to represent their interests against the masters of the guild, journeymen also created their own organizations to back up their culture. Even more than the guilds, these associations were reminiscent of a modern trade union. They would negotiate the terms of employment for all journeymen in a town's guilds and punish those who refused to accept the terms. For example, in the hat-making trade of France, journeymen steadfastly refused to make more than two hats a day. If masters tried to increase their workload they would go on wildcat strikes to enforce their preset limit. They also forced masters to recognize periodic holidays when the journeymen would be exempt from work. Among the more notable customs was "Blue Monday," which was a day off to recuperate from excessive drinking on Sundays.

**Masters' Shops.** A master's shop was both his business and his home. In general, the master made all decisions about what was to be produced and who would produce it within the shop. He also had parental control over the lives of his apprentices and journeymen. He would be accountable if they violated town rules, and, in turn, was allowed to enforce household discipline on them. Masters and journeymen all ate at the same table. Guilds preferred that masters be married men. Masters' wives could help in running the shop, both by looking after the apprentices and journeymen and by assisting in sales or some parts of production. A married couple was also considered a better source of moral guidance for the journeymen and apprentices than a bachelor would be.

**Gaining Master Status.** As noted above, the path to master status was often restricted. In general, the first goal of the guild was to ensure that all masters had a chance to earn enough to live on. Guilds restricted the number of masters so there would not be excessive competition for customers. When a potential new master applied to open a shop, he would have to produce a masterpiece to prove that he was competent in the skills of the trade. The masterpiece was a certification of competence, not a test of merit. The mere fact that one could produce the best or most elaborate masterpiece did not mean that one would be accepted as a master. That decision was left up to the guild

1. No master shall henceforth enter into any association, fraternity, league or combination with any journeyman or other worker, nor shall journeymen and workers make any common laws or regulations except with the express approbation of masters and council of the city.

2. All employed persons, whether indentured to knights, artisans, or burghers, and all journeymen residing in this city shall, furthermore, swear an oath of obedience to masters and council, pledging themselves to advance the interest and honor of the city and do nothing to cause it harm or injury as long as they shall serve this city and reside in it. . . .

3. No journeyman or other employed person shall from now on have a common room or house, nor any place, house, or garden in which to congregate for talk of common affairs or negotiation on conditions of work, nor shall they be permitted to form any kind of association for banding together. . . .

4. Journeymen shall not prevent a master from employing, for whatever reason, whomever he wishes to employ, for no employed person has the right to negotiate with a master or with another journeyman concerning conditions of employment. All such negotiations shall take place before the guild and nowhere else. . . .

5. Journeymen shall hold their funeral processions on holidays only, and not on working days.

6. No journeyman or other employed person shall henceforth carry a sword, foil, or long knife, nor any other weapon save a common bread or cutting knife not to exceed one span in length. . . .

7. No three journeymen or other employed persons shall wear identical hats, coats, trousers, or other identifiable marks.

8. Whoever violates any of the above stated points or articles shall not be given work by any master in this city. . . .

9. No city that has become a signatory to these articles shall alter them in any way without prior consultation with all the other signatory cities.

## Response of the Journeymen Furriers of Strasbourg, 1470

Wise and honorable sires: Concerning the recent troubles between masters and journeymen of the furrier's guild in Strasbourg, we have heard that the master furriers are asking your worships to compel journeymen furriers to accept employment procedures dictated by your command and intervention, which, though customary among tailors and some other trades, are an unheard of innovation in the furrier's craft and never before encountered in German lands. Surely you know that our craft has long possessed the liberty of negotiating its own conditions of employment. We cannot condone an infringement on this liberty, whether it be attempted in Strasbourg or elsewhere. We do not doubt that your worships have due regard to this liberty of ours, which was granted to us by your forefathers and predecessors and was affirmed and sealed by the city of Strasbourg itself. We feel certain that you will wish to leave us secure in our just liberties and that you will do nothing to destroy our fraternity and our freedoms. . . .

## Response of the Journeymen Furriers of Willstaett, 1470

Our friendly greeting, dear journeymen of the furrier's craft in Strasbourg. Dear journeymen, we pray that you now cease all work in Strasbourg until your masters shall have decided to respect once again our old traditions, privileges and seals. No honest journeyman will wish to work under the conditions now prevailing. We therefore caution you against allowing yourselves to be persuaded by your masters to act contrary to the interests of all good journeymen by accepting improper and illicit conditions. A man who submits to masters against our cause shall not be forgiven for ten or twenty years. May God help you to conduct yourselves toward us as you would wish us to behave toward you. The new order which our masters are now attempting to impose upon us is unheard of in Germany, in Latin lands, and even among the pagans.

Source: Gerald Strauss, ed., *Manifestations of Discontent on the Eve of the Reformation* (Bloomington: Indiana University Press, 1971), pp. 130–137.

---

based on its own criteria, which rarely made skill a top priority. The most effective way to become a master was to be the son of a master and inherit the business from the father. Another effective way was to be wealthy and buy one's way into the guild. Both of these approaches minimized the chances that the new master would fall into poverty and thus bring disgrace to the guild.

**Social Distinctions.** The fact that guilds were interested in reducing competition among masters does not mean that all artisans led comfortable lives or that all masters were equal. There was, in fact, a fairly substantial gap between the richest masters in a guild and the poorest. In some industries, such as weaving, most masters were quite poor. In the course of the sixteenth century, the distinctions between masters also became more pronounced. Some guilds began to lose control over the artisans of the surrounding countryside, so the pressures of competition became more acute. By 1600 guild production in smaller towns was on the defensive, and the framework for new forms of production was coming into place.

**Women and Artisanal Work.** The basic model of the guild economy did not foster women's participation in the world of work. The main way in which guilds encouraged women's work was to allow the wives of masters to work in their husband's shops, usually as the sales clerk. Yet, there were many women engaged in artisanal work, despite the apparently limited opportunities. The most successful women artisans tended to be the widows of master artisans. Their experiences within their husbands' shops enabled them to run the business even after their husbands' deaths. Such women were highly desired as wives by young artisans, because they represented a fast track to master's status. However, widows were often reluctant to remarry, precisely because they would lose their newfound financial independence. Usually guilds tried to discourage widows from running independent shops for too long by forbidding them from hiring new journeymen or taking on apprentices, but they were reluctant to remove a shop from a widow's control.

**Women's Work.** There were also some trades which came to be viewed as "women's work." Some of the women engaged in these trades were married to men in other lines of work. Others were single women who needed a trade to support themselves. The three most prominent areas in which women found work were in health care (as midwives, hospital attendants, or working in public baths), sales (primarily as market vendors and peddlers), and domestic workers (as maids and servants). Though some women could prosper in these trades, most workers were poorly paid and marginal in their communities. Over the course of the period 1350–1600, women's work became increasingly marginal. The trend of the era was for more patriarchal control of women's work, not less.

Sources:

Martha C. Howell, *Women, Production, and Patriarchy in Late Medieval Cities* (Chicago: University of Chicago Press, 1986).

Richard Mackenney, *Tradesmen and Traders: The World of the Guilds in Venice and Europe, c.1250–c.1650* (Totowa, N.J.: Barnes & Noble, 1987; London: Croom Helm, 1987).

Merry E. Wiesner, *Working Women in Renaissance Germany* (New Brunswick, N.J.: Rutgers University Press, 1986).

## PEASANTS

**Social Distinction.** Historians use the term *peasant* rather than *farmer* to refer to the villagers of the medieval and early modern era because the latter term implies a greater commitment to the market and less of a commitment to self-sufficiency than was found at the time. Peasants could not avoid participating in the grain market, but their first objective was to produce grain for their own consumption and then to sell only the surplus above what they produced for themselves. If ever there was a group where one would expect to find uniformity in social status and wealth, it would be the peasantry. Indeed, in terms of lifestyle there was not a lot of difference between the most exalted peasant of the village and the poorest, except that the rich peasant might eat a lot more meat than the poor peasant. Nevertheless, there were social distinctions within the peasantry that mattered considerably within village society.

**Freedom versus Serfdom.** Within the legal system of classification of the society of orders, the most important distinction within the peasantry was between "freedom" and "serfdom." Slavery, though it still existed in some parts of Europe, was too rare a practice to have any impact on the economy. A free peasant was one who could buy and sell land, move about freely, and basically control his or her identity in the village. A serf was a peasant whose identity was legally tied to the piece of land where he or she was born and was, therefore, directly under the rule of the lord that owned that land. If a free peasant did not like the conditions of lordship on the land, he could abandon the land and move someplace else, though he rarely did so. A serf had no choice about whether he or she wanted to move because he or she was "owned" by the land.

**Practice.** The basic characteristics of serfdom followed from that identity of the individual with the land. Serfs were more subject to arbitrary changes in the rents for the lands they inhabited. It was much easier for a lord to demand labor services on his own domain for one or more days of the week under serfdom, though it was not uncommon for labor services to be part of the rents of free peasant land as well. More important, lords were in a position to directly affect the life decisions of their serfs because they had an interest in how those decisions affected the tie between the individual and the land. Serfs could only move from their land with the permission of the lord. Some serfs did, of course, try to leave without permission, but lords would sometimes hire bounty hunters to forcibly return them. Serfs also had to get their lords' permission to marry. Lords did not want their serfs marrying nonserfs and then trying to become exempt from serfdom because of the alleged freedom of the spouse. If they did permit a serf to marry a free peasant, they often did so with a contract that demanded all children be counted as serfs. (This practice may be the origins of the notorious *ius primus noctis*, in which the noble lord was supposedly allowed to have intercourse with a serf's wife on the first night of their marriage. Though much commented on as an example of the abuse of noble power, there is no evidence that it was actually practiced anywhere in Europe.) Again, as a sign of the control that the lord held over the land, serfs usually had to make substantial payments at the moment of inheritance to the next generation. All of these restrictions rankled the serfs and made their status undesirable.

A detail from *Village Wedding* by Pieter Bruegel the Younger, early seventeenth century (Ghent Museum, Belgium)

**Eastern Europe.** By the fifteenth century, serfdom was actually a rather rare status in most of Europe. The term was more often invoked as a kind of complaint by free peasants about ill treatment by their lords, along the lines of: "You are trying to turn us into serfs!" However, in the sixteenth century, serfdom started to make a comeback in an area that had originally been settled by free peasants: the northeastern frontier of Europe, Prussia, and Poland. Lords began to exercise their collateral powers as landlords to bind peasants to specific bits of land and then increase the required labor services for those residents. By the end of the sixteenth century, clearly a "second serfdom" had taken root in the East that was qualitatively quite different from medieval serfdom. It was designed primarily to help lords run large *latifundia,* single-crop farms producing primarily for export rather than local consumption.

**Wealth Strata.** Within the village, differences in how one related to one's lord and whether one was a serf or not made far less difference to social standing than a pragmatic consideration: how much land one had. Most villages could be broken into three broad social strata. The first stratum was those peasants who held sufficient land to produce enough to supply the family and have a surplus for sale. This amount of land was the standard unit for measuring land in many parts of Europe. A "rich" peasant family would have "one" or more units.

The second stratum was those who held some considerable amount of land, but not enough to regularly supply the family or produce a surplus. These peasants were partly self-sufficient but still had to generate some income by a route other than their own fields. The third stratum was those who owned little or no land. They would produce what they could for the sake of self-sufficiency, but even in the best of years they would not be able to be self-sufficient from agriculture. They were dependent upon either wage labor or the charity of others within the village. The different categories of peasants were familiar in all parts of Europe, where they would be known by localized names. In one part of Germany, for example, full peasants were called *Hufner,* after the unit of land and courtyard sufficient to support a family; half peasants were called *Koetner,* after the cottage with no courtyard that they owned; while the land poor were called *Brinksitzer,* because they lived literally on the brink. In a nearby region, those same categories were labeled "horse peasant," "cow peasant," and "goat peasant" after the most valuable animal that a peasant could afford to support on the land he or she owned.

**Population Growth.** Not surprisingly, the relative proportions of these three strata in the village changed depending on population growth. In the fifteenth century, the number of "full" peasants was fairly large while the number of "half" peasants and marginal peasants was small, because population pressures were light. In the sixteenth century, as population pressure increased, the number of "half" peasants and marginal peasants began to increase. Villages came to depend on crafts and day labor to support the large proportion of land-poor peasants.

**Wealthy Villagers.** Among the most wealthy stratum of villagers, most of the wealth was bound up in the land that people owned. Rich peasants were primarily farmers. Some crafts, however, were essential in the countryside and provided an alternate source of wealth. Millers were often among the wealthiest inhabitants of any village. To run a mill required a large capital investment, and so local lords usually granted a monopoly to one or two millers and required villagers to use their services, rather than to try to mill their grain at home. The millers' ability to monopolize a basic service allowed them to skim off a considerable amount of any harvest, though the fees they were allowed to charge were regulated. There were often tensions between poorer peasants and millers, with the peasants accusing the millers of taking more than their share in the milling process (it could, in any case, be quite a shock to see how much less the volume of flour was than the volume of grain that was sent to the mill).

Sources:

Peter Kriedte, *Peasants, Landlords, and Merchant Captialists: Europe and the World Economy, 1500–1800* (Cambridge & New York: Cambridge University Press, 1983).

Thomas Robisheaux, *Rural Society and the Search for Order in Early Modern Germany* (Cambridge & New York: Cambridge University Press, 1989).

Werner Rösener, *Peasants in the Middle Ages,* translated by Alexander Stützer (Urbana: University of Illinois Press, 1992).

### THE POOR

**Perennial Problem.** Europe was close enough to being a subsistence economy that poverty was a constant presence. Almost no one believed that the elimination of poverty was a sensible social goal. Instead, social policy centered on how to minimize the negative effects of poverty both for its victims and for society at large. There were, in fact, two distinct layers of the poor within European society. Some families and individuals were completely incapable of supporting themselves from farming or wages. Even in the best of times, they had to rely on alms, or charity, to survive. Still others were capable of working but were close enough to the margins of existence that the slightest food shortage would plunge them into crisis. The proportions of both of these groups could be very high. In one city in the late-sixteenth century, it has been estimated that 15 percent of the population was completely dependent on alms for survival. Probably 65 percent of the population was vulnerable to economic crises and would fit the second definition of the poor.

**Perceptions.** The poor were "always among us," but that does not mean that people did not distinguish between the deserving and the undeserving poor. It was widely recognized, for example, that an injury to the principal laborer in the household, usually the father, could push a family into desperate economic circumstances. Formal disability insurance was unknown, but friends, relatives, and even town or village leaders would step in to try to help families who were thrown into poverty by an unfortunate accident. At the other extreme, however, were those who "chose" to be poor, rather than submit to the social confines of town or village life. Critics complained about the swarms of beggars that accosted people in the towns and migrated through the countryside. It was widely understood that some of these beggars had no other way of earning a living because they were blind or crippled, but that others were fakers, who hobbled about to gain sympathy. For that reason, officials often insisted that beggars obtain begging licenses to prove that they were genuinely desperate. The trickery often associated with begging also meant that there was a fine line between general vagrancy and crime. In towns, some vagrants earned their living from pickpocketing or robbery. In the countryside, bands of beggars frequently joined together to undertake highway robbery. Indeed, most officials assumed that unlicensed beggars and criminals were equivalent.

Hieronymus Bosch's drawing of beggars, most of whom are physically deformed (from Franco Cardini, *Europe 1492,* 1989)

The honorable city council has been informed often and emphatically, fully and credibly that some beggars and beggaresses live a life without fear of God, even lives that are unseemly and unbecoming. Also that there are some who come here to Nuremberg for alms, demanding and taking them, even though they are not needy. And because alms, when they are given, are a particularly praiseworthy, meritorious, virtuous and good work, and because those that take alms without need or falsely are thereby burdened by a heavy and manifest wrong, the above-named our councilors, to the praise of God but also from necessity, undertake to prevent such dishonesty and danger from swindling whereby poor, distressed persons are deprived from their support by alms. To this end they desire to establish and earnestly command that the following ordinance, avoidance of which shall incur the herein contained penalties, shall be enforced and kept, according to which everyone is to comply:

First, our councilors direct, establish, and command that neither citizens nor visitors—men or women—in this city of Nuremberg may beg either day or night, unless permission to do so is granted by the appropriate person appointed by the honorable council.

And whoever has received such permission shall not beg unless they openly wear the beggar's badge that is given them. Whoever begs without permission and the badge shall remain a year and a mile away from this city.

Beggars and beggaresses who are ashamed to beg by day and desire to beg only at night will be given a special badge. In the summer, they are to beg no longer than two hours in the night, and in the winter no longer than three hours, and not without a light according to the law of the city ordinance.

Then each beggar and beggaress, before being given permission and the badge, shall inform in an appropriate manner the lords chosen by the council the truth of their condition, their health, whether married or single, and number of children in order to determine whether they are dependent or not on begging. Whoever holds back the truth shall remain a year and a mile outside the city. In addition, even if begging is necessary to such a person, permission will not be granted unless he brings at least every year from his father confessor a statement that he has at least confessed and received absolution.

Beggars will not be permitted to beg if they have children with them among whom one is eight years old and without disability because they could very well earn their own bread. However, if a man or woman beggar has four or five children, all under seven years, and also a child over eight to watch the rest, then the elected lords shall be entitled to make an allowance.

The names of such beggars' children who are over eight and are healthy and would not be helped by their parents to work, shall be indicated to the bailiff. This is in order to be able to pick them up, make note of them, and determine whether they can be helped to employment here or in the countryside.

Source: Carter Lindberg, *Beyond Charity: Reformation Initiatives for the Poor* (Minneapolis: Fortress Press, 1993), pp. 179–182.

**Occupations.** The lives of the poor were different in the towns than in the countryside. In the countryside, the poor were those who had little or no land of their own and had to earn a living by supporting the agricultural economy in some way. Most were day laborers who assisted in the plowing or harvesting of the fields during the peak seasons. In between, many developed additional talents that made them potentially valuable, but also potentially dangerous, members of the community. Poor women sometimes supported themselves by becoming midwives or mastering herbal remedies. Villagers sometimes suspected that those women inflicted spells on members of the community. Poor men might find jobs tending animals or cleaning out toilets and cesspits. Such positions often were considered dishonorable, making the men who performed them outcasts in their own communities.

**Servants, Prostitutes, and Soldiers.** In towns, there were a greater array of tasks that the poor might undertake, but most of the poor subsisted on wages from day laboring. An honorable route to employment would be as a servant or maid in a citizen's household. Women who were unable to find other employment might become prostitutes in the licensed brothels of the towns. Some men became soldiers, who were generally recruited from the most desperate sectors of society. Pay was haphazard and discipline extremely violent, but there was the occasional opportunity to strike it rich by plunder or the ransoming of captives.

**Poor Relief.** Individual almsgiving was probably the most common way that Renaissance society provided for the poor. There are no statistics to indicate just how much money circulated because of money placed by villagers and townspeople in beggars' cups. Catholic religious ideals favored individual almsgiving as a form of good works. But often, charity was focused in larger religious organizations. In Italy, in particular, urban confraternities ministered to the poor. Confraternities were not made up of priests, but of ordinary citizens who wanted to increase their merit in the eyes of God by performing acts of mercy such as caring for the sick, almsgiving, and burying the dead. In some cities, these organizations were large and diverse enough to handle the main load of poor relief. In the Spanish town of Zamora, for example, there was one confraternity for every fourteen households in the town.

**Community Chests.** Partly under the influence of the Protestant Reformation, poor relief came to be viewed more as a civic responsibility than a religious obligation. Protestant theology undermined the rationale of confraternities, and instead urged the creation of "community chests" that would be available to minister to the poor of a specific neighborhood or village. Protestants maintained and even deepened the distinction between the deserving poor and the idle and dangerous beggars. Territorial rulers used poor-relief measures to intensify social control to the best of their abilities. However, in the end, poor-relief policies in either Catholic or Protestant lands had little measurable effect on the numbers of poor or idle, undeserving poor, which were determined much more by broad demographic and economic forces than by social policy.

Sources:

George Huppert, *After the Black Death: A Social History of Early Modern Europe* (Bloomington: Indiana University Press, 1986).

Robert Jütte, *Poverty and Deviance in Early Modern Europe* (Cambridge, U.K. & New York: Cambridge University Press, 1994).

Carter Lindberg, *Beyond Charity: Reformation Initiatives for the Poor* (Minneapolis: Fortress Press, 1993).

## POPULATION TRENDS

**Growth.** The beginnings of the Renaissance coincided with one of the greatest social and economic tragedies in history. The population of Europe grew steadily through the Middle Ages and seemed to be accelerating at the dawn of the fourteenth century. Between 1250 and 1300 it grew by more than 40 percent to around seventy million people, an annual percentage rate gain of 0.41 percent. However, in 1315 a devastating famine hit

*The Foundlings Being Taken in and Nursed and the Marriage of the Foundlings* (1440), a fresco by Domenico di Bartolo in a Siena hospital (from Franco Cardini, *Europe 1492,* 1989)

It was the year of the bountiful Incarnation of the Son of God, 1348. The mortal pestilence then arrived in the excellent city of Florence, which surpasses every other Italian city in nobility. Whether through the operations of the heavenly bodies, or sent upon us mortals through our wicked deeds by the just wrath of God for our correction, the plague had begun some years before in Eastern countries. It carried off uncounted numbers of inhabitants, and kept moving without cease from place to place. It spread in piteous fashion towards the West. No wisdom or human foresight worked against it. The city had been cleaned of much filth by officials delegated to the task. Sick persons were forbidden entrance, and many laws were passed for the safeguarding of health. . . . Almost at the beginning of the spring of that year, the plague began to reveal, in astounding fashion, its painful effects.

It did not work as it had in the East, where anyone who bled from the nose had a manifest sign of inevitable death. But in its early stages both men, and women too, acquired certain swellings, either in the groin or under the armpits. Some of these swellings reached the size of a common apple, and others were as big as an egg, some more and some less. The common people called them plague-boils. From these two parts of the body, the deadly swellings began in a short time to appear and to reach indifferently every part of the body. Then, the appearance of the disease began to change into black or livid blotches. . . . And just as the swellings had been at first and still were an infallible indication of approaching death, so also were these blotches to whomever they touched. In the cure of these illnesses, neither the advice of a doctor nor the power of any medicine appeared to help and to do any good. Perhaps the nature of the malady did not allow it; perhaps the ignorance of the physicians (of whom, besides those trained, the number had grown very large both of women and of men who were completely without medical instruction) did not know whence it arose, and consequently did not take required action against it. Not only did very few recover, but almost everyone died within the third day from the appearance of these symptoms, some sooner and some later, and most without any fever or other complication. This plague was of greater virulence, because by contact with those sick from it, it infected the healthy, not otherwise than fire does, when it is brought very close to dry or oily material.

Source: Boccaccio, in *Medieval Culture and Society*, edited by David Herlihy, (New York: Walker, 1968), pp. 351–358.

northern Europe, a sign that the fortunate circumstances producing population growth were coming to an end. After the famine ended in 1322, the population again began to creep upward, but at a slower annual percentage rate of 0.14 percent. By 1350, there were around seventy-four million Europeans, probably the greatest number there had ever been.

**The Black Death.** In 1347 that upward trend came to a sudden halt when the bubonic plague came to Europe from the Middle East. Unlike the famine of 1315–1322, the plague did not reap its horrible harvest and then disappear. Instead, a wave of epidemics crashed over Europe. Outbreaks hit Italy, for example, in 1347–1350, 1360–1363, 1371–1374, 1381–1384, 1388–1390, and 1398–1400. As a result, the population gains of the previous century disappeared in just two generations. There were around fifty-two million Europeans in 1400, a drop of about 30 percent in sixty years, and an annual percentage rate decrease of 0.59 percent.

**Importance.** The number of people had a direct impact on the most basic categories of the economy: production and consumption. In simplest terms, expanding population was possible only if there were economic resources available to support it. The slowdown of population growth after 1300 and the severe contraction of population between 1347 and 1400 were not just because the weather turned bad and diseases struck. They were also caused by the fact that Europe had reached the limits of productivity given the economic system it had inherited from the Middle Ages. Europe was overpopulated in 1340. It would have to make some adjustments to its economic structure if it were to grow even larger.

**Population Theory.** At the end of the eighteenth century, the basic dilemma of population was explained by English social scientist Thomas Malthus. He described a notion of a "Malthusian trap": natural population can grow exponentially, as parents can have many children who, in turn, have many children, and so on, but foodstuffs can only grow arithmetically, as each bit of unused land is brought into cultivation until all of the arable land is taken up. Unless one comes up with a way of increasing the productivity per acre of land, population will have to fall. There is a great deal of evidence that late-medieval Europe was experiencing just this kind of Malthusian trap. Marginal lands, the ones that were least likely to generate large harvests, had been brought into cultivation in the 1300s because all of the most productive land was already in cultivation. By 1400 when the population fell, the marginal lands were abandoned by farmers and reclaimed by the woods. In some parts of Europe, whole villages disappeared, never to return. The fact that European population seemed to adjust itself in accordance with the basic principles of ecological balance has led historians to speak of an "auto-regulatory system" of population. Birth and death rates would each adjust to ensure that population did not exceed the capacity of production.

**Economic Impact.** This point, however, also indicates the silver lining in the terrible tragedy that befell Europe between 1350 and 1400. For those people who managed to survive the Black Death, and the generation that followed, there were favorable opportunities to accumulate wealth. Land was relatively abundant and labor was hard to find, so wages went up for the average worker and agricultural productivity per person increased. Once the shock of the demographic crisis was over, there was room for optimism. The basic principles of the Malthusian cycle began to take root again. More abundant food and better wages encouraged parents to have more children. More children meant increasing pressure on the job and land markets, which increased the likelihood of another catastrophe unless further adjustments in the economic system took place.

**Trends after the Black Death.** The impact of this new cycle can be seen in the population trends of the 1400s and 1500s. During the 1400s, European population began to increase again, faster than it had done in the first half of the fourteenth century, but much slower than it had at the end of the thirteenth century. By 1500, the population had increased by almost 30 percent to sixty-seven million, an annual percentage rate increase of 0.25 percent. (Note that even though the increase from 1400 to 1500 and the decrease from 1340 to 1400 are both 30 percent, that does not mean that the population was the same in 1500 as it was in 1340. The decrease in 1340–1400 was 30 percent of seventy-four million, while the increase in 1400–1500 was 30 percent of just fifty-two million.) After 1500, the growth accelerated slightly more, to an annual percentage rate of 0.29 percent. There were already complaints about overpopulation in some parts of Europe. By 1600, Europe had surpassed its late-medieval population peak and had about eighty-nine million people. The "extra" fifteen million people in Europe in 1600 in comparison to 1340 indicate that some adjustments in the economic and social structure had taken place since the tragedy of the 1350s. Yet, the population trends also showed that Europe was once again coming to the limits of its economic capacity. There was no major demographic catastrophe to compare with the Black Death in Europe after 1600, but the population basically stopped growing. The annual percentage increase in population was just 0.07 percent for the seventeenth century.

**Visual Image.** A graph of the population pattern for Europe during the Renaissance and Reformation would look vaguely like a square root symbol. First, there was a short but steep downward slope, the collapse caused by the Black Death. Then, there was a longer, but slightly less

steep, upward slope, the recovery of the fifteenth and sixteenth centuries. Finally, at the end of the Reformation, there was a leveling off at a plateau, the stagnation of the seventeenth century.

**Changing Center of Gravity.** The numbers for Europe as a whole tell one story about the relationship between population and the economy for the period from 1350 to 1600; but there is an even more-striking story if the numbers are examined in a little more detail. Population statistics between 1350 and 1600 mirrored a fundamental shift, in Europe's economic center, from a Mediterranean to an Atlantic economy. The economic and cultural hub of Europe from ancient times through the Middle Ages was the Mediterranean. In 1200, almost 75 percent of Europe's population lived south of the Alps. More people lived in Italy than lived in Germany, Britain, the Low Countries, and Scandinavia combined. Both southern and northern Europe suffered from the effects of the Black Death, but southern Europe suffered more. Despite the Black Death, Northern Europe's population experienced accelerating growth between 1200 and 1500, while Southern Europe's growth decelerated.

**Leading Sector.** Even in 1600, more than half of Europe's population still lived south of the Alps, but the balance was much more even than it had been in the Middle Ages. Northern Europe had grown to be an equal economic partner with the Mediterranean. Most of the most important economic transformations of the Renaissance and Reformation made the Atlantic economy the leading sector of the economy.

Sources:

Michael W. Flinn, *The European Demographic System, 1500–1820* (Baltimore: Johns Hopkins University Press, 1981).

Douglass C. North and Robert Paul Thomas, *The Rise of the Western World: A New Economic History* (Cambridge: Cambridge University Press, 1973).

James D. Tracy, *Europe's Reformations, 1450–1650* (Lanham, Md.: Rowman & Littlefield, 1999).

## THE URBAN ECONOMY

**Types of Towns.** The economic division of labor between town and countryside meant that towns were different entities from villages, even when they were sometimes almost the same size as a village. It makes sense to think of two distinct types of towns during the Renaissance and Reformation. The vast majority of towns functioned as regional market centers for the surrounding villages. They might range in size of up to perhaps ten thousand inhabitants, though most had fewer than five thousand. They were large enough to have a variety of trades among their citizens, but small enough that everyone who lived there knew his or her neighbors. Conversely, the few larger towns were dedicated primarily to fostering long-distance trade and making products available to a small stratum of wealthy people. They were too large for there to be a sense of neighborliness among all inhabitants. Instead, there were more pronounced social tensions between the "haves" and "have-nots," who sometimes encountered one another and sometimes existed in different orbits. From 1350 to 1600, the largest cities in

Europe grew from just 100,000 inhabitants to more than 250,000 people. However, even in 1600, any city with more than 20,000 inhabitants would have been considered large.

**Corporate Body.** The basic distinction between a town and a village was a legal one: towns had market rights and villages did not. Yet, in most cases, the visible symbol of the difference between town and countryside was the town wall. In medieval times town walls acted as a defensive system against invaders, but by the Renaissance only towns in war-torn regions could afford the complicated fortification systems that would protect them against modern siege techniques. Nevertheless, even old-fashioned walls created a distinct social space that emphasized separation from the outside world. Most towns used their walls as a way of regulating who came in and went out. At night, the gates of the town would be closed and guards posted to check on who wanted entry. During the day, the gates formed a useful checkpoint for wagons bringing their produce in to market.

**Self-Government.** Towns were also distinctive for their tradition of self-government. Citizenship was jealously protected because it was the prerequisite to political participation. The towns usually had elaborate and distinctive constitutions that regulated internal politics. Small towns were deliberately quite insulated from the migration of the neighboring countryside. New residents were only permitted with the approval of the town council, and if someone tried to sneak in, it was not usually long before they were discovered and told to leave. Furthermore, permission to reside in the city was not the same thing as gaining citizenship. To become a citizen one usually had to demonstrate a certain level of wealth, pay a substantial fee, be nominated by someone who was already a citizen, and swear an oath of allegiance to the town.

**Large versus Small.** In larger cities the same regulations existed in theory, but it was harder to drive hangers-on away. Large cities received a greater number of "foreign" visitors (meaning from a different town, not a different nation) who could blend in with visitors and immigrants from local villages. In times of war and local dearth, a fortified major city was a logical destination to escape the turmoil. The elites of large cities were thus more tolerant of long-term residents who had no claim of citizenship. There were also more menial tasks that had to be taken care of in the cities, and thus a mobile underclass who could fill in when necessary was tolerated.

**Immigration.** Life could be hard and dangerous in the largest European cities of the era. Most grew considerably larger during this era, but they did so primarily from immigration, not from natural Malthusian growth. In fact, for most cities, the death rate far exceeded the birthrate, and population would have gone down were it not for the even larger number of immigrants.

**Guilds.** The most common way that economic activity took place in the urban economy was through an organization known as the guild. Like towns, guilds were self-governing bodies with a defined area of jurisdiction. Yet, what they governed was a specific industry, not a geographical area. There were guilds for almost every common craft of the era, such as tailors, weavers, carpenters, shoemakers, and coopers. There were also guilds for more obscure industries, such as spurmakers, armorers, and gold-foil beaters.

**Conflicts of Interest.** There were several built-in tensions, or conflicts of interest, in guild organization. First of all, guilds regulated the entire production process of any given craft. They set the quality standards for finished products, the prices that could be charged for those products, and the mechanisms for punishing people who violated those standards. At the same time, they were an advocacy group for the craft and its members, defending it against encroachment from other crafts. Though they sometimes posed as protectors of consumers because they guaranteed a specific quality level from producers, their primary loyalty was to the guild members themselves. Production was usually in the workshop of a guild master, which was within his home. Only in rare instances would a shop employ more than about fifteen workers. There was no incentive to develop larger-scale industrial production because of the dominance of guild masters in the guild organization.

**Dual Orientation.** Guilds had a dual orientation. On the one hand, they were located within towns and participated in the social and political life of the town. Guild members were generally among the most politically active groups in any city. On the other hand, guilds also had ties to members of the same guild in other towns. For the sake of their craft, they had to be aware of trends in other regions. The traditional learning stage of production in a guild was known as "journeyman" because it was based on wandering from guild town to guild town, learning techniques at various locations.

**Manufacturing in Larger Cities.** Guilds were active in large cities just as they were in smaller towns. Even in cities such as Paris, London, or Florence, most production took place in the small shop. However, there were more gradations in the kind of guilds that might be active in the largest cities. In Florence, for example, there were guilds of merchants as well as of craftsmen. Some of the most specialized guilds, such as goldsmiths and sculptors, were only present in the largest towns where there would be sufficient commissions from patrons of the arts to support them. Thus, in a typical large town like Frankfurt, which had about twelve thousand inhabitants at the start of the sixteenth century, there were 130 different guilds.

**Government.** In some cities the guilds played a major role in town government. Seats on the council would be reserved for guild masters, and guild members would vote as a bloc to achieve their political goals. In other cities, such as Nuremberg in Germany, guilds were excluded from the town government, and a merchant patriciate ran the city alone. In either case, there were usually significant social tensions between the guilds and the merchants.

**Specialized Industries.** Even in the largest cities, guild regulations usually made it impossible to set up a large factory for manufacturing. The concentration of industry

The marketplace in Antwerp during the late sixteenth century (Musées royaux des beaux-arts de Belgique, Brussels)

depended more on the connections between artisans and merchants than it did on the need to be where the natural resources were. Nevertheless, some cities were noted for their excellence in a specific industry, even without large-scale factories or dominance over raw materials from the immediate neighborhood. For example, Florence was renowned throughout Europe for fine woolen textiles. The most prominent exception to the predominance of small shops was the shipbuilding industry, which flourished in large factories in Venice and Amsterdam. The most famous "factory" of the Renaissance was the Venetian Arsenal, or shipyards, which employed more than five thousand workers.

**Patterns of Urbanization.** Large towns were not evenly spaced across the European landscape. Instead, there was an "urban belt" running along the Mediterranean and north-south from Italy to the Netherlands where towns were numerous, and a "rural belt" extending to the east and west. Before the Black Death, the largest cities were the independent city-states of Italy. The ten largest European cities before 1350 were Venice, Florence, Paris, Milan, Bologna, Genoa, London, Ghent, Siena, and Palermo. Most of these cities shared a diverse base of manufacturing for international export, along with a significant merchant-banker segment.

**Largest Cities in 1500.** Even after the Black Death and the shift to an Atlantic economy, Italy continued to be home to half of Europe's largest cities. In 1500, the largest European cities were Paris, Venice, Naples, Milan, Ghent, Moscow, Florence, Prague, Genoa, and Bruges. The presence of Moscow and Prague on the list is a sign that the economic geography of Europe was beginning to change and even the "rural belt" was developing major urban centers.

**Largest Cities in 1600.** The change in urbanization was even more apparent by 1600. Now the largest cities in Europe were Paris, Naples, London, Venice, Seville, Prague, Milan, Palermo, Rome, and Lisbon. With the exception of Milan, all of these cities were either capitals or major ports of larger European principalities. The presence of Seville and Lisbon underscores the importance of the Atlantic trade for population growth.

**New Kinds of Towns.** During the Renaissance and Reformation, a new type of town began to develop in northern and western Europe in both a small and large format—the court city. Before the 1400s and even into the sixteenth century, most kings and princes lived a mobile lifestyle. They had castles in the countryside and spent much of their time traveling from one part of the kingdom to another, bringing the entire court with them. The "capital" of any country was wherever the king happened to be. Over time, more and more of the regular functions of the court began to be carried out at an urban "home base," which had a central royal palace that was the seat of government. In the largest kingdoms, a great city with traditional ties to the monarchy became the capital of the country, such as London in England or Paris in France. In the case of Vienna in Austria and Madrid in Spain, a relatively small city immediately became a major center because a powerful monarchy set up permanent residence there. In lesser dukedoms and principalities, a less substantial city had to become the focus, and so that city grew in order to serve the needs of the court. The most dramatic changes were in cities such as Munich and Berlin, which were minor urban centers in 1400, probably less important than neighboring towns such as Ingolstadt or Stendahl. Once the courts of Bavaria and Brandenburg became fixed in those cities, however, they grew to be the major urban centers of their regions.

**Needs of the Nobility.** A court city had to be different from an ordinary market center or international merchant center because the needs of the nobility so clearly dominated its social life. Only rarely would those nobles become citizens of the town, so there was a real split between court and citizenry in jurisdiction. On the other hand, nonnoble officials who contributed to the territorial administration more often did become citizens of the town, becoming locally prominent administrators as part of the urban patriciate.

Sources:
Philip Benedict, ed., *Cities and Social Change in Early Modern France* (London & New York: Unwin Hyman, 1989).

Alexander Cowan, *Urban Europe, 1500–1700* (London & New York: Arnold, 1998).

Christopher R. Friedrichs, *The Early Modern City, 1450–1750* (London & New York: Longman, 1995).

# SIGNIFICANT PEOPLE

## THOMAS BETSON

### DIED 1486

### ENGLISH MERCHANT AND TRADER

**Obscure Origins.** Thomas Betson was a merchant in the wool cloth trade between England and France in the middle of the fifteenth century. His date of birth is not known, and almost nothing is known of his early life, but his activities became much easier to follow as he engaged in correspondence with his suppliers and fellow merchants in the 1470s.

**Merchants of the Staple.** It is quite common to associate merchants in early modern Europe with cities, because generally only cities had the privilege of engaging in trade, especially important international trade such as the manufacture and export of woolen cloth. Wool was produced in England and woven into fine cloth in Flanders, leading to close commercial and political ties between the two regions. This trade generated so much revenue to the governments of both realms that the English kings, wishing both to protect and control it, designated certain towns as "staples," centers of distribution for nearly all raw materials for export. For much of the period the staple town was Calais, an English possession on the coast of modern France. The incorporated group of merchants who dealt in wool for export were known as Merchants of the Staple. They had a monopoly on the wool trade, in return for which they paid heavy customs duties to the Crown; they were also responsible for guaranteeing the quality of their wool. As a Merchant of the Staple, Betson had a regular place of business in Calais, as well as in London, and he traveled to Bruges, Ghent, and other Flemish cities in a regular circuit throughout the business year.

**Procurement.** Yet, the trade that could only be carried out in duly privileged towns began each spring in the heart of English country districts such as the Cotswolds and Yorkshire with the annual sheepshearing. The first task of the Stapler, as members of the trading company were called, was to inspect and purchase wool, either from individual farmers or from local dealers. This was a large-scale enterprise: a single Stapler might purchase several thousand sacks of wool in one consignment. Generally they did not pay in cash, but with bills which they were bound to pay in six months. Once purchased, the goods had to be packed and shipped according to the strict regulations of the government and the Fellowship of the Staple itself. All wool and skins had to be packed in the county in which they were purchased and sealed by officials appointed by the Crown. They were then packed on horses for the overland trip to London. En route, customs officials carefully noted the name of the merchants with the quantity and description of the wool they shipped. Once in London, the wool was stored in warehouses, then packed and shipped across the English Channel to Calais. Such a cargo made a tempting prize for the many local seamen up and down the coasts who supplemented their income with piracy, and the Staplers often traveled in convoy with their own hired guards.

**Business Deals.** Betson generally traveled across the Channel with the wool to see it safely arrived, unpacked, inspected, then repacked and resealed, ready to be sold. If possible, he tried to sell it right off the boat to Flemish merchants, who would in turn resell it to cloth manufacturers. Any wool left would be taken to the Flemish fairs, held on a regular schedule throughout the year. In the summer he would return to his dealers in the Cotswolds and elsewhere to purchase more wool from the summer sheepshearing, and he would return again in the fall to purchase sheepskins, called fells, after the annual sheep killing. Each would, in turn, be packed, sealed, transported to London, shipped to Calais, and sold as quickly as possible. Much of the leverage in these transactions remained with the Staplers, who had the raw materials the Flemish manufacturers needed, and this leverage is reflected in regulations set by the Fellowship of the Staple. For example, "old wool," defined as wool from the summer shearing which still remained unsold the following April, was much less desirable than new wool, but Fellowship regulations required Flemish merchants to purchase one allotment of old wool with every two of new, thus ensuring Staplers were not left with last year's wool on their hands.

**Settling the Accounts.** However much leverage the Fellowship might have when formulating its regulations, its members still faced the age-old difficulties of merchants when it came to collect their money. Often cloth merchants paid for their wool with bills, which the Staplers had to collect when they came due, and they, like all other early modern merchants, accepted payment in many different currencies and from English, Flemish, Italian, and Spanish banking families. Only after foreign accounts were settled would Betson and his colleagues be able to pay their own bills to their wool suppliers, packers, shippers, and the government. The number of transactions, the need for careful accounting, and the many possibilities for legal wrangles made the business highly specialized. Yet, it was also highly lucrative, with revenues of the Fellowship regularly augmented by loans to the English Crown. Betson became a wealthy man.

**Personal Affairs.** Thomas Betson wrote a series of charming love letters to his fiancée, whose family had important trading connections, when she was fourteen, exhorting her to eat well so she might grow quickly and they could be married. They had five children in seven years of marriage before his death in 1486.

Sources:

Peter J. Bowden, *The Wool Trade in Tudor and Stuart England* (London: Macmillan, 1962).

Alison Hanham, *The Celys and Their World: An English Merchant Family of the Fifteenth Century* (Cambridge & New York: Cambridge University Press, 1985).

Eileen Edna Power, *Medieval People*, tenth edition (London: Methuen, 1963; New York: Barnes & Noble, 1963).

# COSIMO DE MEDICI

## 1389-1464

### FLORENTINE BANKER

**Famous Family.** One of the greatest families of the Italian Renaissance was the Medici family of Florence. In the course of the sixteenth century, Medicis became popes (Leo X and Clement VII), queens of France (Catherine de Medici and Marie de Medici), and the grand dukes of Tuscany when Florence's republican constitution was overthrown. However, the Medicis did not start out as nobles—their rise to power rested on their role in creating a more modern system of international banking. A pivotal figure in that rise to power was Cosimo de Medici of Florence.

**Papal Connections.** The Medici bank was founded by Giovanni di Bicci de Medici in the late fourteenth century in Rome to lend money to papal projects. The association with Rome was to be an important part of the Medicis' success. Under Pope John XXIII, the Rome office of the Medici bank became depository general of the Apostolic Chamber. Giovanni became the richest citizen in Florence and exerted considerable political influence in the city. In the 1420s he turned over day-to-day control of the bank to his son Cosimo, who became director after Giovanni's death in 1429.

**Branch Offices.** The fortunes of the Medici bank grew all the more under Cosimo's leadership. Branch offices were established in Pisa, Milan, Venice, Geneva, Lyon, Bruges, and London. Unlike Florentine banks of the medieval period, which had extremely centralized investment structures, each of these branches was granted a great deal of autonomy in lending. They could keep a large share of the profits of their lending activity, but also were insulated against the losses from other branches. This system prevented a repeat of the banking crisis that had brought down the three largest Florentine banks of the 1340s.

**Ruler of Florence.** The Medicis' role as bankers also enabled them to play a major role as patrons for others. They had connections at the papal court and sometimes managed to get church appointments for their clients. Cosimo's primary activities in patronage were for his clients within Florence, and he was able to place allies in prominent positions in the Florentine government, making himself ruler of Florence in everything but the title. Indeed, he was so successful at this that his rivals tried to break his influence by driving him into exile. This attempt backfired. When a pro-Cosimo administration was selected in the next elections, the Pope himself intervened to allow Cosimo to return. From that point on, the Medici family set the tone for political life in Florence, though the republican constitution remained until 1494.

**Patron of the Arts.** Cosimo's patronage not only influenced the distribution of political power in Florence and Rome, but also affected Renaissance cultural life. He promoted the literary pursuits of humanists such as Marsilio Ficino and the artistic work of Donatello and Benozzo Gozzoli. He was particularly active in various important building projects around Florence. The parish church of San Lorenzo became the centerpiece of Medici family activity. Cosimo supported the project to rebuild it entirely in Renaissance style. His supporters then began to pay for chapels built in the new style, which reinforced the association of the church and family. The Palazzo Medici, started in 1445, set the standard for a Florentine building boom. It guaranteed the predominance of the Renaissance architectural style. In all of these things he, as patron of the arts, set standards that would persist for his successors.

**Spiritual Concerns.** Cosimo's interest in church projects was partly prompted by his worries about how his moneylending would affect his salvation. He became strongly attached to monastic life as a counterpoint to the excesses of banking. In the convents and monasteries he patronized, he made sure there was a monastic cell available for him to retreat to for contemplation. He took special pains in his burial arrangements, insisting that the ceremony be simple, but that he be buried in front of the high altar at the church of San Lorenzo. The great sculptor Donatello was chosen to create his tomb.

**Collapse of the Bank.** The bank of the Medici began to falter after Cosimo's death in 1464. His son Piero proved to be at best a mediocre administrator. Yet, more important, the Medicis began to focus more on their political and patronage roles. Piero's son Lorenzo acquired the nickname "the Magnificent," but that had nothing to do with how he ran the bank, which went into an even steeper decline after 1478. Instead, Lorenzo became an active behind-the-scenes ruler of Florence and a major patron of the arts. He forged dynastic alliances with the leading families of Rome and set the stage for the Medicis' rise into the nobility. Thus, even when the Medici bank collapsed in 1494, two years after his death, the standing of the Medici family no longer depended on its resources.

**Impact.** With the collapse of the Medici bank, new families stepped in to take the lead in international finance. The most prominent sixteenth century international bankers were the Fuggers of Augsburg. Nevertheless, the close relationship between private bankers and the needs of governments and the papacy was to remain a defining feature of the Renaissance and Reformation.

Sources:
D. V. Kent, *Cosimo de' Medici and the Florentine Renaissance: The Patron's Oeuvre* (New Haven: Yale University Press, 2000).

Raymond de Roover, *The Rise and Decline of the Medici Bank, 1397–1494* (Cambridge, Mass.: Harvard University Press, 1963).

# THE PAPPENHEIMER FAMILY

## FLOURISHED 1600

## BAVARIAN BEGGARS

**Marginal People.** There are few records of the people living on the bottom margins of society because most could not read or write, and they were too unimportant for anyone to want to read or write about them. The only time the lives of such marginal people were recorded was when they got in trouble and were jailed and brought to trial. Under sad circumstances the hard lives of the Gämperl family, known as the Pappenheimers, were brought to light.

**Background.** At the time of their trial in 1600 in Munich, in the duchy of Bavaria, the family consisted of Paulus, aged 57, Anna, aged 59, and their three sons, Gumprecht (22), Michel (20), and Hänsel (10). Anna was the daughter of a gravedigger in the Franconian town of Ansbach, an occupation which, though necessary, was deemed dishonorable. More respectable residents spoke to her father only when his services were needed, and Anna could not associate with other girls in the town, even marginal ones such as servants. Without a dowry or connections, she had difficulty finding a husband until she met Paulus, a day laborer in the town brickyard. He was from Swabia and had had an even worse childhood than Anna because he was illegitimate and had been constantly teased and abused at home. He ran away many times before the age of fourteen, when he finally left for good, earning his living by going from one village to another doing any odd jobs he could find. It is possible he did some stealing during this time, though he was never caught. He was eighteen when he married Anna, and the marriage gave them their first prospect of future security, for Paulus became assistant gravedigger with the likelihood that he could take over his father-in-law's job in time.

**"Deserving Poor."** In fact, that did not happen, though it is not known why. When Anna's father died some eighteen years after their marriage, the family left Ansbach to seek their fortune in Nuremberg. It is not clear what work they intended to find, but they ended up, like many others, as beggars. Begging was carefully regulated in most towns in Germany: generally permits to beg were given to the town's own indigent population who fit the category of "deserving poor." In the 1580s, Nuremberg had about seven hundred registered beggars. The Gämperl family, like the many other "outsiders" from the countryside, were unlicensed and therefore illegal. That fact did not stop them begging for a month or so, until the city authorities caught up with them and evicted them. The same situation was repeated several times, until Paulus and Anna purchased counterfeit "begging letters" written by a traveling schoolteacher and purporting to certify that they were beggars duly licensed by the authorities. After about a year of traveling from town to town as beggars, though, Paulus learned of another opportunity. He met a man who, though also a wanderer, had steady employment as an emptier of privies. This profession was another necessary though dishonorable one. Privies, with cesspits, were a relatively recent innovation in personal hygiene in the sixteenth century, a great improvement on the practice of using chamber pots and throwing the contents out of the window. Paulus became the privy-emptier's assistant, then his successor. Since "Pappenheimer" was the local name for his profession, Paulus and his family became known as the Pappenheimers.

**Odd Jobs.** The family continued to travel from place to place in search of work, which, however, was always forthcoming. Paulus and his sons used buckets on ropes to remove the contents of the cesspit, which were either spread on fields as a form of manure or, where possible, dumped into running water. They generally worked in cold weather, and at night, to minimize the offensiveness of the activity. In the summer, when the water table was low and emptying cesspits was both more offensive and unhygienic, the Pappenheimers would take on other odd jobs, mending windows, pots, and other implements. Anna occasionally worked as a maid, and Paulus carried a portable gambling table and set up a game to earn some money. In bad times the family might turn to begging again, but in good times they might earn enough to be able to pay for meat and beer. Over the course of the twenty years at this kind of work, they established a regular "beat," staying with friends or at illegal but cheap lodging houses (legal lodging houses had to be registered and cost more to maintain).

**Show Trial.** After twenty years of scraping by on the margins of legality without attracting much attention from government authorities, the Pappenheimers were arrested, having been denounced as "murderers of seven pregnant women" by a thief with whom Paulus may have quarreled. There was no evidence to support this accusation, but the Pappenheimers were clearly a family of vagrants, and the normal juridical procedure would have been to evict them from the territory after a fairly uncomfortable period in jail. Unfortunately for them, the accusation came at a moment when official and popular fear of witchcraft was reaching a peak, so instead of receiving the rough, but predictable, treatment of the vagabond, they became caught up in a show trial. The Pappenheimers, bewildered, were brought to Munich, accused of witchcraft and murder, and tortured until they confessed to unspeakable, and completely unsubstantiated, crimes. Their confessions led to the arrest of some of their friends and associates, who were also arrested, accused, and tortured until they confessed. At a public execution attended by thousands, Paulus was tortured with red-hot pincers, broken on the wheel, then impaled; Michel and Gumprecht also were broken on the wheel. Since breaking on the wheel was proscribed for women, Anna simply had her breasts cut off. All four were then burned alive. Hänsel, horrified, was required to watch it all before being executed by burning with other accused witches at a second public execution several months later. There might have been more executions, but the remaining accused were more-respectable residents with influential friends. The government hurriedly issued a spate of pamphlets allegedly proving their case against the Pappenheimers, and then dropped the matter. All that remained was the transcript of the trial, with its detailed account of the lives, and deaths, of those on the margins in early modern Europe.

Sources:

De Lamar Jensen, *Reformation Europe: Age of Reform and Revolution* (Lexington, Mass.: D. C. Heath, 1981).

Michael Kunze, *Highroad to the Stake: A Tale of Witchcraft* (Chicago: University of Chicago Press, 1987).

# MAGDALENA (1555–1642) AND BALTHASAR (1551–1600) PAUMGARTNER

## NUREMBERG MERCHANTS

**Family Business.** One of the characteristic activities of the patriciate of Central European cities was as a general merchant of luxury goods. This type of business was carried out by Balthasar Paumgartner of Nuremberg, with the able assistance of his wife Magdalena. Scholars know about their lives from a series of letters they wrote between 1582 and 1598. Both were from established merchant families, and though their marriage was almost certainly arranged by their parents, they made an affectionate as well as profitable team.

**Three Essential Skills.** Since generations of men on both sides of his family had been merchants, Balthasar was educated for the same occupation as a matter of course. As a boy, he learned the three essential skills for a mercantile life—reading, writing, and arithmetic, probably including bookkeeping—and then spent six or seven years apprenticed to his uncle, an established merchant. He completed his apprenticeship about the age of twenty-one. The family enterprise was based in Nuremberg, but maintained a commercial presence in the Italian city of Lucca, where they purchased Italian products to ship to Nuremberg and to Frankfurt for the fall and spring fairs. Their standard products were consumer goods for well-to-do urban dwellers: expensive materials such as damask and velvet, Italian and Dutch cheeses, wine, and oil. Balthasar was obliged to spend much of the year away from Nuremberg, in the Lucca offices, in Frankfurt, or on the established merchant routes between cities, traveling in convoys as protection from attacks from highwaymen. Within ten years he was firmly established as an independent merchant and could marry and establish his own household in Nuremberg.

**Wife and Partner.** From the time of their betrothal in 1582, Magdalena became Balthasar's confidante, bookkeeper, and chief Nuremberg distributor. She was twenty-seven years old and had received a sound education, again in the merchant essentials of reading, writing, and accounting. Her job was to supervise the arrival of the packing crates, open them, inspect them for damage, and check for quality, including tasting the wine to make sure it had not gone sour. She then arranged for them to be delivered to their purchasers and collected payment. In addition to selling to their urban customers, the Paumgartners also sold cutlery and other cheap manufactured goods to the local peasants, and this distribution, too, was in Magdalena's hands, though if she had difficulty collecting money, she sent for Balthasar's brothers. She acted as a stand-in for her husband at important social functions, an activity she always enjoyed, and watched out for Balthasar's interests in family disputes. It is clear from their letters that Balthasar regularly consulted with her on business matters and respected her judgment. However, it is also clear that Magdalena thought of her "business activity" as an extension of her role as good wife, mother, and household manager. In her letters, family and commercial news are mingled with endearments and complaints that Balthasar does not write often enough. She always signed her name "Magdalena Balthasar Paumgartner." Also, though she often offered Balthasar her advice, it was always with deference due to the head of the household.

**Piety and Work Ethic.** Magdalena and Balthasar were Lutheran, and their piety was infused into all of their activities. They thanked God for business success, and their letters were full of prayers for their own continued well-being and that of their friends and family. They believed that God would reward hard work, not high living, and though they dealt in consumer goods, they restrained themselves from what they considered undue luxury. When their only child, their son Balthasar, died at the age of ten, a heartbroken Magdalena turned to God as well as to her husband: "I must now accept these facts: that we had him for so short a time, that he has not really been ours but rather God's. . . . "

**Sense of Accomplishment.** The Paumgartners' financial success, and that of their extended family, gave them an enviable standard of living. Yet, Balthasar never liked the mercantile life. Its one advantage, he believed, was that the hard work kept him from the temptation caused by his great love of drinking, and he felt that it was God's great mercy that he had become a merchant instead of a drunkard. However, he hated being on the road all the time, he never had confidence in his ability to make difficult decisions, and he dreaded above all the constant haggling over goods, payment, and exchange rates that was an essential part of commercial life. The constant traveling took its toll on his health, too. By the age of forty-seven, he had finally acquired the financial resources to purchase a small estate and to retire from commerce to the more-settled life of a country gentleman collecting rents on his estate. He died three years later. Magdalena lived for another forty-two years. She never remarried, and little is known about her life as a widow, for any letters she may have written have not survived. Likely, though, she remained busy and actively involved in family affairs.

Sources:

Magdalena Balthasar Paumgartner, *Magdalena and Balthasar: An Intimate Portrait of Life in 16th-Century Europe Revealed in the Letters of a Nuremberg Husband and Wife,* compiled by Steven Ozment (New Haven: Yale University Press, 1989).

Jeffrey Chipps Smith, *Nuremberg: A Renaissance City, 1500–1618* (Austin: University of Texas Press, 1983).

# GILLES PICOT, SEIGNEUR DE GOUBERVILLE

## 1521-1578
### FRENCH NOBLEMAN

**Rare Insight.** Though the nobility was the elite of the early modern era and much is known about the various kings, queens, and dukes, it is surprisingly difficult to know much about the lives of minor noblemen. For every great noble there were hundreds of lesser nobles, living on and running their own estates. Because their activities were so mundane, such country gentlemen rarely left extensive records that have survived through the generations. One ordinary nobleman whose life story survives is Gilles Picot, Seigneur de Gouberville. His journal recounts the daily life of a nobleman in the Normandy countryside in the 1540s and 1550s.

**Estate Management.** Gilles de Gouberville did not keep his journal to record his hopes, dreams, feelings, and emotions, but instead as an aid to other records in running his estate, centered on a manor house equidistant from three villages. The two-story manor house was de Gouberville's living quarters, which included several bedrooms, a separate kitchen and outbuildings, and a private chapel. More important, it acted as the growing and processing center for agricultural resources, including sheep, cattle, and apple orchards, as well as the implements for sheepshearing, butchering, and pressing apples into cider. Made of local stone, the manor house required constant repair, from the kitchen chimney to the outer walls. The roads extending within the seigneurie also needed regular maintenance. The point of "living nobly" was to live without having to work, but Sire de Gouberville's journal makes clear just how much work was involved in the life of nobility in the country. The routine agricultural labor was carried out by his peasant tenants, outside his immediate purview, but anything more complex, from repairs to the estate buildings, to constructions of new roads, was carefully supervised. De Gouberville's special care was his fruit trees and nursery garden, though again he left routine care to his most trusted workmen. De Gouberville also held the royal appointment of Lieutenant of Waters and Forests for the region, requiring him to carry out periodic inspections, see to the removal of fallen trees and other potential hazards, and guard against poachers—in its way, another kind of estate management.

**Demeanor.** However active Gilles de Gouberville was, though, he lacked military experience. De Gouberville never held a commission in the king's army, and he was not even particularly martial in temperament, preferring compromise to aggression even in legal disputes. His closest contact to chivalric ideals of knighthood was his enthusiastic reading of *Amadis de Gaul,* a popular novel of the period.

**Lineage.** His life also demonstrates the vulnerability and anxiety caused by the need to live nobly. In 1555 he was part of an investigation into patents of nobility carried out by royal officials. Nobility was a distinct legal category, which carried with it definite legal privileges, among them exemption from certain kinds of taxation to be paid to the king. Since the Crown was always strapped for money, royal officials were authorized from time to time to investigate claims to noble status. On the day before the hearing, de Gouberville was up until midnight preparing documents demonstrating his legal claim to being a noble, documents in which the nobility of his ancestors was duly certified. The decision was in his favor: though he was not, apparently, judged to be of truly ancient—and most prestigious—noble lineage, the nobility of his family was at least traced back more than a hundred years to 1463. That infor-

mation was enough to confirm his privileges, and five years later he was given the additional privilege of legal right to use the surname "de Gouberville," from the title of his estate, rather than his original surname "Picot." Yet, the lineage "de Gouberville" ended with Gilles's death, for though he had three illegitimate daughters, he had no legitimate son to carry on his noble name.

Sources:

Jonathan Dewald, *Pont-St-Pierre, 1398–1789: Lordship, Community, and Capitalism in Early Modern France* (Berkeley: University of California Press, 1987).

Madeleine Foisil, *Le Sire de Gouberville: Un Gentilhomme Normand au XVIe Siècle* (Paris: Aubier Montaigne, 1981).

Kristen B. Neuschel, *Word of Honor: Interpreting Noble Culture in Sixteenth-century France* (Ithaca, N.Y.: Cornell University Press, 1989).

# DOCUMENTARY SOURCES

Baldassare Castiglione, *The Book of the Courtier* (1516)—the most influential guide to how noblemen ought to behave in their dealings with other noblemen. It was written in the form of a dialogue, rather than as a work of nonfiction. Nonetheless, the characteristics exhibited by the characters became the norm expected of ambitious noblemen everywhere.

Desiderious Erasmus, *Colloquies* (1526)—a series of dialogues written in Latin that serve as an introduction to the social and intellectual environment of the sixteenth century. The colloquies express Erasmus's observations on current issues, institutions, ideas, customs, and even individuals. Collections of the *Colloquies* were enormously successful and became standard textbooks for students of Latin in the sixteenth and seventeenth centuries.

Conrad Heresbach, *Four Books on Husbandry* (1577)—A friend of Melanchton and student of Erasmus, Heresbach uses the dialogue format to present his ideas on successful farming. The work is divided into four main topics: husbandry and land leases; gardens, orchards, and woods; feeding, breeding, and curing of cattle; and poultry, fowl, fish, and bees.

Charles Loyseau, *Treatise on the Orders and Dignities* (1610)—this work is the classic formulation of the idea of the Society of Orders. It was designed both to explain how the system worked and to justify it as the natural social order.

Sir Thomas More, *Utopia* (1516)—Written as an ironic comment on the English social order, *Utopia* was designed as an exposure of the evils afflicting men who were obliged to live under the rule of tyrants. It touches on a wide range of political, social, and cultural factors that characterize the Renais-

sance, such as the consolidation of absolute monarchy, the role of the community, the decline in power and prestige of the Catholic Church, and the triumph of humanism. More coined the term *utopia* ("no place") in recognition of the fact that no ideal society actually exists.

Luca Pacioli, *Summary of Arithmetic* (1494)—the volume that popularized the practice of double-entry bookkeeping, turning it from a practice known to only a few Italian merchants to an important tool in the development of capitalism.

Hans Sachs, *The Book of Trades* (1568)—a poem that described more than one hundred different occupations that one could find in the towns and countryside of the era. Its purpose was more for entertainment and moral instruction than for social analysis, but it is a good introduction to the kinds of work people did.

Cyriacus Spangenberg, *Mirror of Nobility* (1591)—a massive and rambling description of the three orders and the importance of the nobility within them. It was written to combat antinoble sentiments in the popular German literature of the time.

Thomas Tusser, *Five Hundred Good Points of Husbandry* (1573)—the English version of a popular genre of the era: the farmers' almanac. In its pages were covered most of the pragmatic issues of agricultural production, such as how to look after animals and when to plant various crops. It also offered guidance on the general running of a household. Tusser produced an earlier prose version of the work, but this work was in poetry. Authors such as Johannes Coler in Germany and Etienne Liebault in France produced prose almanacs.

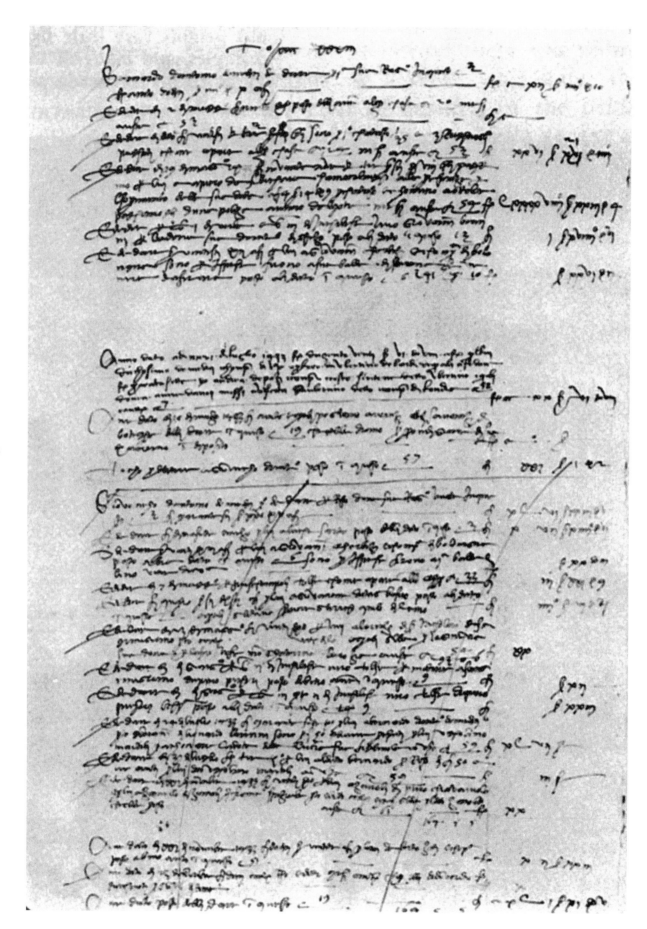

A Medici family business ledger, circa 1444 (Baker Library, Harvard University, Ms. 499)

CHAPTER SIX

# POLITICS, LAW, AND THE MILITARY

by FREDERIC J. BAUMGARTNER and NORMAN J. WILSON

## CONTENTS

*Sidebars and tables are listed in italics.*

## 1350

- A naval war breaks out between Genoa and Venice over navigation in the Black Sea. After three years the Genoese are defeated and sue for peace.

- John II (the Good) succeeds Philip VI as king of France.

## 1351

- In response to the ravages of the Black Death, several English acts are established, including the Statute of Provisors, which puts restrictions on foreign clergy, and the Statute of Labourers, which tries to maintain wages and price levels.

- Zurich joins the Swiss Confederation, originally made up of the cantons of Uri, Schwyz, and Unterwalden that had united against the Habsburg intrusions in 1291.

## 1352

- The Swiss canton of Zug (and possibly Glarus) joins the Swiss Confederation. Bern joins the next year.

## 1353

- Ivan II (the Red) becomes the Grand Duke of Moscow and serves for six years, until his death in 1359.

## 1354

Nov.    A Venetian fleet under the command of Marino Falier is destroyed by the Genoese during the third naval conflict between the two city-states. Falier is executed the next year for allegedly conspiring to assassinate some nobles and make himself the ruler of Venice.

## 1355

- King Edward III's troops raid the French countryside near the port of Calais, which had been captured by the English in 1347.

## 1356

- English troops fight the Lothians in southeastern Scotland in the "Burned Candlemas" expedition. Edward de Baliol, who had ruled since 1332, formally surrenders Scotland to Edward III.

10 Jan.    Holy Roman Emperor Charles IV issues the Golden Bull, the constitution for the German empire that establishes the election procedures for the sovereign. The bull blocks papal prerogatives in determining the leader.

| | | |
|---|---|---|
| | 19 Sept. | Edward III's son and namesake, known as the Black Prince, defeats French troops at the Battle of Poitiers. King John II of France is captured (and imprisoned until 1360) and forced to accept peace. Military defeats, and the ravages of undisciplined troops in the countryside, help weaken the status of the French nobility. The Estates General insists on representation and influence over royal matters. |
| **1357** | • | The Estates General meets and passes measures designed to supervise levies, taxes, and poor relief, but does nothing to directly confront the powers of the king. |
| **1358** | • | French popular leader Etienne Marcel gives his allegiance to the king of Navarre and leads an uprising in Paris. His mob storms the palace and kills several officials, but Marcel is assassinated before he is able to open the city to invasion. The Parisians are eventually defeated at Meaux. |
| | 21 May | Peasants in Compiègne (known as Jacquerie) revolt, destroy castles, and kill members of the nobility. Led by Guillaume Cale, the peasant soldiers march to Paris to join Marcel, but they are defeated at Clermont-en-Beauvais in June. |
| **1359** | • | The Treaty of London forces the French to cede territory to the English, but the area is so vast that the French resist its implementation. Edward III besieges Reims and attempts to take the French Crown. Although his army marches through Burgundy and Paris, he is unsuccessful in gaining the throne. He accepts the Treaty of Calais (1360), which renounces his claim, but gains for the English the area of Aquitaine in southwestern France. |
| | • | Nine-year-old Dmitry Donskoy, the son of Ivan II, becomes the Grand Duke of Moscow. |
| **1360** | • | John II is allowed to return to France under provisions of the Peace of Brétigny, but he fails to raise the required ransom (three million gold crowns). He is returned to England and dies there in 1364. |
| | • | Adrianople, between the southwest portion of the Black Sea and the Mediterranean, is captured by the Turks. |
| **1361** | • | Danish king Valdemar IV Atterdag conquers Gotland, an island in the Baltic Sea, initiating a war with the Hanseatic League, or Hansa (a commercial confederacy of Baltic cities). |

**1362**
- A Hansa fleet is destroyed by the Danes at Helsingborg.

**1363**
- David II of Scotland, who had been king since 1329 and was released in 1357 after a nine-year imprisonment, comes to peace with England, but then faces an internal revolt from Robert II and the Scottish parliament.

**1364**
- Charles V, the son of John II, becomes king of France. He rules his country wisely, regains territories lost to England, reorganizes the navy, and serves as a patron of the arts.

**1365**
- In an attempt to neutralize the mercenary soldiers ravaging central France, Charles V has them sent to Spain, where many of them are killed in four years of fighting in support of Henry of Trastámara (later Henry II).

**1366**
- Lionel, the Duke of Clarence and governor of Ulster, pushes through the Statute of Kilkenny, which forbids the intermarriage of Irish and English settlers.

**1368**
- Troops of Valdemar IV Atterdag of Denmark are defeated by a coalition of forces of the Hanseatic League, Sweden, Mecklenburg, Holstein, and Jutland.

**1369**
- Charles V of France repudiates the Treaty of Calais and wins back Aquitaine from the English.
- Peter the Cruel, King of León and Castile, is captured and killed by Henry of Trastámara, who with the aid of France is attempting to gain control of Spain. Henry also invades Portugal.

**1370**
- Valdemar IV is forced to accept the Treaty of Stralsund, which grants commercial privileges in the Baltic trade to merchants of the Hanseatic League.
- The French city of Limoges is sacked by English troops.

**1371**

- David II of Scotland dies and is replaced as king by Robert II.

**1372**

- Ferdinand of Portugal allies with John of Gaunt, provoking another invasion by Henry II, who takes Lisbon and forces Ferdinand to renounce the alliance.

- The Spanish win temporary control of the English Channel after defeating an English fleet off La Rochelle, France.

**1373**

- John of Gaunt's troops march through France from Calais to Bordeaux, but John returns home in 1374 with little to show for the effort. A year earlier, Edward III tried to land troops in France, but was thwarted by poor weather. Edward is forced to make a truce with the French in 1375.

**1375**

- Valdemar dies and is succeeded by his grandson, Olaf, who rules with his mother, Margaret, as his regent of Denmark.

**1376**

- The "Good" Parliament removes the influence of John of Gaunt upon the king and impeaches his followers. John will regain his standing after Prince Edward dies in June; he overthrows the acts against him upon the death of Edward III the following year.

**1377**

- Ten-year-old Richard II, son of the Black Prince and grandson of Edward III, takes the English throne.

**1378**

- Wencelas, king of Germany and Bohemia, becomes the Holy Roman Emperor. He is unable to control relations among the nobility or respond to the demands of the commoners; he is deposed in 1400.

22 July
- An insurrection of the lower classes in Florence, led by the Ciompi (wool carders), defeats government forces and places Michele di Lando in office. Although the new government is more democratic, a counterrevolution led by the major guilds defeats the upstarts, and the victors abolish the Ciompi guild.

**1379**

- Henry II of Spain dies.

**1380**

- Charles V's son, Charles VI (or the Well-Beloved), takes the French throne upon the death of his father. A minor when he assumes the throne, he will suffer from insanity (1392).

- The alliance between England and Portugal is reestablished.

- Margaret of Denmark, who is still serving as regent for her son Olaf, gains the regency of Norway as well upon the death of Haakon VI.

- The military prestige of the Tartars is broken by the army of Grand Duke Donskoy at the Battle of Kulikova, although they remain a potent and dangerous force in Russia.

**1381**

- A peasant revolt breaks out in England, under the leadership of Wat Tyler, in response to oppressive poll taxes and wage freezes. The participants call for an end to serfdom and restrictions on trade. The peasant army, which grows to around one hundred thousand men, kills some Flemish merchants and beheads two government officials in London, but the revolt is put down by Richard II, and Tyler is killed in June. Although the rebellion fails to change manorial relations, it stops the imposition of the poll tax.

- Despite an initial defeat at Pula on the Adriatic Sea and an invasion of the Venetian settlement at Chioggia, the Genoese fleet is blockaded and trapped by the Venetians. After many attempts to break the blockade, the starving Genoese are forced to surrender and accept the Peace of Turin, giving the victors control of trade routes.

**1382**

- Workers in Ghent rebel and gain supporters in nearby towns, but the uprising is put down by royal forces at Roosebeke. Charles VI uses this victory to gain royal control of other French municipalities, including Paris.

**1383**

- João Fernandes Andeiro, Count of Ourém, is killed by John of Aviz, who overthrows the sitting regent and defends Portugal against a Castilian invasion.

**1384**

- Jadwiga, the daughter of Louis the Great of Hungary, is elected queen of Poland and serves until her death in 1399. During her reign she marries the Lithuanian grand duke Jagiello in 1386, and the two countries form a union.

**1385**

14 Aug. John I of Castile is defeated by John of Aviz at Aljubarrota. Aviz is crowned king of Portugal and becomes John I, and the independence of Portugal is established.

**1386**

9 May     An alliance between Portugal and England is secured with the Treaty of Windsor, and John I marries the daughter of John the Gaunt.

9 July     An army of soldiers from the Swiss Confederation and Swabian League defeat a force of Austrians led by Leopold III at the Battle of Sempach. Two years later Albert of Austria will attack the Swiss again, but his forces will lose the Battle of Näfels.

**1387**

•     Margaret seizes the thrones of Norway and Denmark when Olaf dies. She proves an effective ruler of the Scandinavian countries, increasing the power of the monarchy over that of the nobles.

**1388**

19 Aug.     A Scottish army, despite the death of their leader on the field of battle, defeats an English army during a night engagement at the Battle of Otterburn in Northumbria, England.

**1389**

•     The Serbs, under Prince Lazar Hrebeljanovi, are defeated by Turkish troops under Murad I at the battle of Kosovo.

•     Danish and Swedish troops, fighting to seat the Norwegian and Danish queen Margaret on the Swedish throne, defeat and imprison Albert of Mecklenberg. It takes another eight years to conquer Sweden.

•     Vasily I succeeds his father, Donskoy, as the ruler of Moscow.

**1390**

•     Robert II is crowned king of Scotland upon the death of his father Robert II (he had ruled for his father since 1384).

**1391**

•     Around four thousand Jews are massacred in Seville.

**1394**

•     Richard II invades Ireland.

**1395**

•     Albert II succeeds his brother Rudolf IV as leader of Austria.

**1396**

- Richard II of England and Charles VI of France reconcile and establish a twenty-eight-year peace between their realms.

25 Sept.
- An army of around ten thousand European knights and soldiers led by John the Fearless, on a crusade to evict the Turks from the Balkans, is destroyed by Bayezid I's forces at Nicopolis on the Danube River.

**1397**

- Denmark, Sweden, and Norway form the Union of Kalmar, with the monarch to be Danish. The first king is Margaret I's grandnephew, Erik of Pomerania.

- Richard II forces the English Parliament to soften its demands for financial accounting, obtains a lifetime income, and seats members favorable to him.

**1399**

- Henry of Bolingbroke, Duke of Hereford (son of John of Gaunt, and later known as Henry IV), who had been banished a year earlier from England, returns and defeats Richard II, who is deposed and imprisoned. Henry is proclaimed king and he puts down resistance from remaining followers of Richard.

**1400**

- Henry defeats a rebellion in support of Richard II, who dies (possibly murdered) in prison.

**1402**

- A Scottish invasion of ten thousand men, led by Archibald Douglas, enters England and sacks the town of Durham. The English, led by Henry Percy, surprise the returning Scots at Homildon Hill, cutting down the invaders with effective archery.

**1403**

21 July
- Troops under Percy, now a supporter of Scottish king Robert III and fighting with Douglas, are defeated by the forces of Henry IV at the Battle of Shrewsbury. Percy is killed while Robert and Douglas are captured.

**1404**

- King Albert IV dies and is replaced on the German throne by his son Albert V.

**1406**

- Florence captures Pisa, which will remain under its control into the sixteenth century, except for a brief interlude from 1494 to 1509.

**1407**

- A civil war erupts among the French nobility.

**1410**

15 July    Polish and Lithuanian troops, along with Bohemian, Russian, and Tartar mercenaries, defeat a force of Teutonic Knights at the Battle of Tannenberg in northeastern Poland. Many Prussian cities are forced to surrender, and the expansion of the Teutonic order is halted.

**1411**

- Following their loss to the Poles and Lithuanians, the Teutonic Knights sign the Peace of Thorn.

**1412**

- Queen Margaret I dies and is replaced by her grandnephew, Erik of Pomerania, who had been dominated by Margaret. His favoritism toward the Danes angers his other Scandinavian kingdoms.

**1413**

- Henry V, who had defeated the Welsh rebellions, succeeds his father, Henry IV, to the throne of England.

- Sir John Oldcastle is arrested by Henry V and convicted of heresy for his support of the Lollards, who are anticlerical and anti-Catholic religious reformers. He escapes and plots a rebellion against the king, which is brutally countered by Henry.

- Merchant Simon Caboche leads a revolt in Paris, forcing Charles VI to accept the elections of councillors and other government reforms. The revolt is later put down and the concessions are withdrawn.

**1415**

25 Oct.    The Spanish enclave of Ceuta in northern Morocco is captured by the Portuguese.

- Ten thousand English troops under the command of Henry V, who hopes to gain control of the French throne, defeat a larger French army under Charles VI at the Battle of Agincourt, leading to the recapture of Normandy.

**1416**

- Henry V allies with the Holy Roman Empire.

**1417**

- Although Oldcastle initially avoids detection, he is caught and executed by Henry V.

**1419**

- The Hussites, followers of the martyred Jan Hus, present King Sigismund of Hungary and Bohemia with the Four Articles of Prague, which call for freedom of religion, a communion of bread and wine, reduction in church finances, and punishment of several individuals. Sigismund answers by proclaiming a crusade against the Hussites, who defeat him and repel two other attacks on Prague.

**1420\***

- European foundries begin producing cast-bronze cannons.

**1420**

- After marrying Catherine of Valois, the daughter of the deranged Charles V, Henry V is recognized under the Treaty of Troyes as the regent and heir to the French throne. The treaty blocks Charles VI's son from the French succession, but Charles VII assumes the title nonetheless upon his father's death (1422). He will reorganize French politics, dividing the country into provinces for easier control.

**1421**

- Henry V dies and is succeeded by his son, Henry VI, who is only one year old. His uncle, the Duke of Gloucester, serves as regent. At the age of ten he is then crowned the king of France.

**1423**

- James I of Scotland, who was captured in 1406, is released from his imprisonment in England.

**1424**

- Bohemian general, former Polish mercenary, and Taborite leader Jan Zizka dies. He had designed new ways to use field artillery and baggage trains and had commanded troops to several victories in 1420 to 1422, during the Hussite Wars.

**1425**

- Vasily II (the Blind) becomes Grand Prince of Moscow, but his reign is marked by general anarchy and by infighting among the nobility.

**1427**

- Florence initiates a form of income tax called the *catàsto*, which will be replaced by the Medicis with one that lowers the burden on the poor.

**1429**

- Philip III (the Good), Duke of Burgundy, founds the Order of the Golden Fleece, a knighthood dedicated to the Virgin Mary and St. Andrew. Its purpose is to defend Roman Catholicism and the code of chivalry.

May
- With the help of Joan of Arc, Charles VII raises the English siege of Orléans. The English are also defeated at the Battle of Patay. Meanwhile, the French march to Reims, where Charles is coronated.

**1430**

- Joan of Arc is captured by the Burgundians at Compiègne and turned over to the English.

**1431**

30 May
Joan of Arc is burned at the stake after being convicted of witchcraft.

**1433**

- Edward I, the son of John I, becomes king of Portugal; he will reign for only five years.

**1434**

- Swedish nationalist Engelbrekt Engelbrektsson and the Council of Aristocrats start a rebellion to weaken the power of the Danish king Erik of Pomerania without toppling the Union of Kalmar. Stockholm is captured in 1436, but Engelbrektsson is killed that same year.

- Banker Cosimo de' Medici returns to Florence from an exile and dominates Florentine politics and arts for the next thirty years.

- Jagiello's ten-year-old son Vladislav VI succeeds him to the throne of Poland.

**1435**

- John of Lancaster, the most accomplished English field commander, dies. The English lose Burgundy as an ally when Charles VII and Philip of Burgundy arrange a peace, the Treaty of Arras, which establishes Charles as the supreme ruler in France. Charles gradually regains most territory lost to the English, except for Calais.

## 1437

- The Portuguese, in an attack promoted by Prince Henry the Navigator, fail to capture the Moroccan port city of Tangier. The defeat will slow, but not stop, Portuguese expansion.

## 1438

- Alfonso V becomes king of Portugal.

- Albert II is crowned the king of Hungary, Bohemia, and Germany. He institutes political reforms, but his reign is short, as he dies in battle against the Turks in 1439. All succeeding emperors, except Charles VII and Francis I, belong to the House of Hapsburg.

7 July    Charles VII issues the Pragmatic Sanction of Bourges, a decree that restricts the rights of the Pope in France.

## 1439

- The French army establishes uniform rules for strength of contingents, discipline, and pay of soldiers. This development is a necessary step in creating a standing army capable of defending the country from enemy invasions.

- Erik of Pomerania is succeeded by Christopher of Bavaria on the Scandinavian thrones, but he proves to be a weak monarch who is dominated by the Hanseatic League.

## 1440

- The Praquerie conspiracy, a coalition of nobles attempting to overthrow the French king, is put down.

- Milan is defeated by a united Florence and Venice.

- Frederick III becomes king of Germany.

## 1442

- János Hunyadi, the son of King Sigismund and pupil of Francesco Sforza, defeats the Turks in Transylvania. He breaks the Ottoman hold on the Balkans.

## 1444

10 Nov.    Hunyadi's Hungarian army, without the support of a promised Venetian fleet, is defeated by Turkish troops at the Battle of Varna, blocking his attempt to protect Constantinople. The Hungarian king Ulászló and Polish king Vladislav are killed in the battle and Hunyadi is forced to withdraw; the Turks are free to reduce the Greeks and capture Constantinople.

**1445**

- The first permanent French army, consisting of twenty companies of cavalry, is established.

**1446**

- Alfonso V issues the *Ordenaçoes Affonsinas,* the first true law code for Portugal.

**1447**

- The Visconti family, who has ruled Milan continuously since 1277, falls from power and is replaced by the Sforzas three years later.
- Vladislav VI's brother Casimir IV takes the Polish throne. He limits the power of the nobles and the clergy in favor of the gentry.

**1448**

- The French establish a militia of foot soldiers armed with bows, the "free archers," which will help defeat the incursions of the English.

**1449**

24 May — A conflict over what branch of the Portuguese ruling family will control the young king Alfonso V erupts into battle when the forces of the Duke of Bragança, the illegitimate son of João I, face those of Pedro, who are marching on Lisbon. Pedro is defeated and killed, and the House of Avis achieves ascendancy.

**1450***

- The arquebus, a smoothbore matchlock weapon fired from the shoulder, is invented in Germany.

**1450**

- Francesco Sforza occupies Milan and founds the Sforza dynasty.
- John Cade leads a rebellion of lesser property owners in Kent, England. Around thirty thousand men join Cade in the fight against high taxation. His force defeats an army of Henry VI at the Battle of Sevenoaks and later enters London, where he seeks the execution of several government officials. His forces are defeated at London Bridge and he is captured and killed.

15 April — French forces defeat the English at the Battle of Formigny, killing approximately five thousand men. Many of the English archers fight to the death rather than have their fingers cut off, a common penalty imposed upon their kind. The way is now open for the French recovery of Normandy.

**1452**

- Frederick III is elected the Holy Roman emperor, a position he holds until 1493; he is crowned in Rome.

**1453**

- An English army under John Talbot, Earl of Shrewsbury, is decimated by French field artillery at the Battle of Castillon. Talbot is killed and his garrison surrenders; though a minor engagement, it signals the end of the Hundred Years' War.

29 May
- Sultan Mehmed II captures Constantinople and renames it Istanbul, ending the Byzantine Empire.

**1454**

- Prussian nobles and town dwellers, with help from the Poles, revolt against the Teutonic Order.

9 Apr.
- Francesco Sforza is recognized as the ruler of Milan and hostilities are concluded with Venice by the Peace of Lodi. Both sides had desired an end to the war because of the threat to their trade posed by the Turks; they establish a mutual defense league among Italian municipalities.

**1455**

- The War of the Roses, a power struggle between the houses of Lancaster and York in England that will last for thirty years, begins. Richard, Duke of York, defeats the forces of the Duke of Somerset (who is killed).

**1456**

- Joan of Arc's verdict is overturned.

**1458**

- George of Podebrady, a Hussite leader who captured Prague (1448) and defeated the Habsburgs, is elected the king of Bohemia after the death of King Ladislav (1457), for whom George had served as regent. He persecutes members of the Bohemian Brotherhood, which advocates greater democracy and separation from religious control from Rome.
- Matthias Corvinus (Mátyás Hunyadi) becomes the king of Hungary.

**1459**

- Ludovico III of Mantua calls a "congress of princes" to counter Turkish advances. Proposed by Pope Pius II, the action fails.

**1460**

- Prince Henry the Navigator of Portugal dies.

**1461**

- Louis XI, the son of Charles VII, becomes the king of France, despite having made several attempts to unseat his father and having served an exile in Flanders. He overturns the Pragmatic Sanction of Bourges.

17 Feb. Henry VI is defeated by the Yorkists at the second Battle of St. Albans and is deposed (4 March) and imprisoned. On 29 March the Lancastrians, in retreat from London, are attacked by Yorkist troops under the Neville brothers, Edward and Richard, near the village of Towton. In a driving snowstorm the bloodiest engagement of the War of the Roses is fought, resulting in a rout and massacre of Lancastrian troops. The Duke of York is proclaimed Edward IV.

**1462**

- Ivan III (the Great) becomes Grand Prince of Moscow; during his reign he eliminates foreign control of his country, expands its territory, and promotes the Orthodox religion. He increases the power of the monarch, taking the title *Czar*.

**1464**

- The League of Public Weal, led by Charles the Bold, Duke of Burgundy, revolts against Louis XI.

**1465**

- Burgundian prince Charles the Bold recaptures lands controlled by Louis XI at the Battle of Montl'héry.

**1466**

- Poland obtains an outlet to the Baltic Sea and peace with the Teutonic Order with the Second Peace of Thorn.

**1468**

- Philippe de Commynes negotiates a truce between Charles the Bold and Louis XI.

**1469**

- Lorenzo de' Medici (the Magnificent) and his brother, Giuliano, begin their rule of Florence.

- Isabella I, the daughter of John II of Castile, marries Ferdinand V of Aragon. Together they will unify Spain, reform the clergy, expel non-Catholic elements, and recapture Granada.

**1470**

- The Earl of Warwick and Duke of Clarence lead a rebellion in support of Henry VI, but they are defeated at the Battle of Stamford. Henry will be murdered in the Tower of London in 1471.

**1471**

- Casimir IV's son Vladislav becomes the king of Bohemia and later is crowned Ladislas II, king of Hungary (1490).

**1474**

- Isabella I becomes queen of Castile.

**1475**

- The English invade France, but Charles the Bold is bought off by Louis XI, leaving Edward IV without support, and peace is secured through the Treaty of Picquigny.

**1476**

- Swiss Confederation troops defeat Burgundian forces (under Charles the Bold) at the battles of Grandson (2 March) and Morat (22 June). In the latter engagement nearly one-third of Charles's forces are slaughtered.

- The Portuguese, who move to attack Castile, are defeated by the Spaniards at the Battle of Toro. Forces of the two nations will continue to skirmish along their common border.

**1477**

- Charles the Bold is defeated by troops from Switzerland, Lorraine, and Austria, and is killed near Nancy, France. The Swiss use pikes against the Burgundian cavalry. Charles's daughter, Mary of Burgundy, marries Maximilian of Austria.

**1478**

26 Apr.  The Pazzi family, aided by Pope Sixtus IV, attempt to overthrow the rule of the Medicis in Florence. While some conspirators try to take over the government, an assassination attempt is made on Giuliano and Lorenzo de' Medici while they attend mass. The former is killed, but the latter escapes; support arises in the city in favor of the Medicis, and many of the conspirators are massacred. A two-year war with the Vatican erupts, but Lorenzo is able to consolidate and extend his power at home.

**1479**

- Alfonso V renounces his claim on Castile in the Treaty of Alcáçovas.

**1480***

- The French begin mounting cannon on specially adapted carriages for land use.

**1480**

- An Ottoman fleet captures Otranto, an Italian city on the peninsula jutting out into the Adriatic Sea.

**1481**

- John II becomes king of Portugal upon the death of Alfonso V.

22 Dec.  A civil war among the states of the Swiss Confederation, largely over the political strength of rural as opposed to urban members, is avoided at the Diet of Stans. The members allow two cities to join (one of which is the first French-speaking area) and strengthen the federal alliance.

**1483**

- Louis XI of France dies and is succeeded by his son, Charles VIII.
- The Duke of Gloucester becomes King Richard III, after the son of the recently deceased Edward IV is declared illegitimate. Henry's two sons are then murdered. Richard suppresses a rebellion led by the duke of Buckingham.

**1484**

- The Estates General is convened by Charles VIII.

**1485**

22 Aug.  Richard III is killed by the Earl of Richmond at the Battle of Bosworth Field. The earl becomes Henry VII (Henry Tudor), progenitor of the house of Tudor.

**1487**

- Henry VII forces Parliament to allow him to establish the Star Chamber, a court that could hear trials of powerful nobles. In the 1700s it will become more repressive and secretive.

16 June  Supporters of Lambert Simnel, who claims to be the Earl of Warwick and opposes Henry VII, are defeated at Stoke-on-Trent. The pretender is captured and forced to work in Henry's kitchen.

## 1488

**11 June**  James III of Scotland is murdered by nobles who resist his pro-English policy; he is succeeded by James IV, who takes an anti-English stance.

## 1489

* Hans Waldman, who as the burgomaster of Zürich supplied mercenaries for many European countries, dies.

## 1492

* Lorenzo de' Medici dies and is replaced by his son, Piero.
* Russia invades Lithuania.

**2 Jan.**  Granada, the center of Moorish strength in Spain, falls to the forces of Ferdinand and Isabella. Spanish Jews are also exiled from the country in this year.

## 1493

* Archduke Maximilian, the son of Frederick III, becomes the Holy Roman emperor as Maximilian I. He is intent on reestablishing Habsburg control over the Swiss.

## 1494

* Charles VIII of France invades Italy. He is supported by Ludovico of Milan, though his state will be seized by the French in 1499.
* Poyning's Law (Statute of Drogheda) limits legislation in the Irish Parliament and firmly places English law over that of Ireland.

**7 June**  The Treaty of Tordesillas between Portugal and Spain establishes a line 1,185 miles west of the Cape Verde Islands as the demarcation between areas to be controlled by each country, with Portugal getting the area east of the line (Africa and Brazil), and Spain the west (North and South America). Other European countries choose to ignore this division of the world.

## 1495

* The Duke of Beja, who becomes Manuel I, succeeds John II to the throne of Portugal.
* Pope Alexander VI, Holy Roman Emperor Maximilian I, and Ferdinand II, as well as the leaders of Venice and Milan, form the Holy League against Charles VIII.
* Another imposter and rival to Henry VII's throne, Perkin Warbek, who claims he is the Duke of York, invades England with the help of James IV of Scotland. He will be executed in 1499.
* Constitutional reform is undertaken in Germany at the Diet of Worms.

**1496**

- The Holy League forces the French out of Italy.

**1497**

- Manuel I forcibly expels Jews from Portugal, many of whom had been welcomed into the country when they left Spain. Many Jews are forced to convert to Catholicism.

- A tax revolt breaks out in Cornwall, England, but the insurrection is put down at the Battle of Blackheath (22 June). Its leaders—including Lord Audley—are executed.

**1498**

- Charles VIII dies while planning another Italian invasion and is replaced on the throne by Louis XII, who takes up his predecessor's invasion plans.

**1499**

25 Aug.    War breaks out between Venice and the Ottomans; a Venetian fleet is defeated at Sapienza.

22 Sept.   The Swiss Confederation achieves independence, with the signing of the Treaty of Basel, after defeating the forces of the Holy Roman Emperor Maximilian I at the Battle of Dornach.

6 Oct.     Louis XII's troops occupy Milan.

**1500**

- The Treaty of Granada partitions Naples between Louis XII and Ferdinand II.

8 April    Ludovico attempts to liberate Milan, but his forces are defeated by the French at Novara.

**1501**

- Naples falls to the French.

- Basel joins the Swiss Confederation.

**1502**

- A peasant conspiracy emerges in the bishopric of Speyer, Germany. The peasants call for the confiscation of church property and an end to the power of the nobility. The budding revolt is betrayed and many of the conspirators are killed.

**1503**
- Spain captures Naples; the Spanish control the city for the next two hundred years.
- Russia obtains much of its Baltic borderlands after concluding a peace with Lithuania.

**1504**
- The Treaty of Lyons divides Italy between France and Spain. France gains control of Milan in the Treaty of Blois.
- Isabella of Castile dies.
- Henry VII places English guilds and trade companies under supervision of the Crown.

**1505**
- Louis XII renounces his claim to Naples in favor of Spain.
- Maximilian I begins the reformation of the Holy Roman Empire.

**1506**
- Philip I (the Handsome), who rules for less than a year as the king of Castile, dies. Despite his short reign, he establishes the Habsburg dynasty in Spain.
- A riot breaks out in Lisbon and many *conversos* (Jewish converts) are massacred by the crowd. Manuel I issues protections and allows many of the survivors to emigrate.

**1508**
- Ludovico Sforza dies while a captive of the French.
- 10 Dec. Pope Julius II, Holy Roman Emperor Maximilian I, Louis XII, and Ferdinand II form an alliance, the Holy League of Cambrai, against Venice in hopes of dividing its lands.

**1509**
- Henry Tudor dies and is succeeded by his son, Henry VIII.
- 14 May French troops defeat the Venetians at Agnadello, east of Milan. The Vatican recovers cities in Romagna; the Holy Roman Empire gains Verona, Vicenza, and Padua; and Spain is ceded lands in Apulia, including Brindisi.

**1510**
- The Holy League of Cambrai collapses when Pope Julius joins with Venice in hopes of forcing the French out of Italy; Ferdinand takes a neutral stance.

## 1511

- England joins the Holy League; Pope Julius also unites Spain with Venice in the anti-French league. The Holy Roman Empire, Swiss Confederation, and Milan are also members.

- An ordained priest, Thomas Wolsey rises through the ranks of Henry VIII's government to the position of privy councillor, directing war activities in France. He serves as lord chancellor (1515–1529).

## 1512

- The kingdom of Navarre, after its rulers participate in fomenting a schism in the Catholic Church, is invaded and conquered by the forces of Ferdinand II.

**11 April** The French defeat the Holy League at the Battle of Ravenna. The French are, however, driven from Milan.

## 1513

- Italian philosopher Niccolò Machiavelli writes *Il principe* (The Prince), which will be published in 1532.

**6 June** Swiss troops defeat a combined French and Venetian army at the Battle of Novara.

**16 Aug.** English and German troops are victorious over the French at the Battle of the Spurs and enter the city of Théroanne. The Holy League is disbanded.

**9 Sept.** During an invasion of England, Scottish troops—supported by the French—are defeated, and their leader James IV is killed by troops led by the Earl of Surrey at Flodden Field.

## 1514

- A peace is brokered between England and France.

## 1515

**13–14 Sept.** A French and Venetian force under Francis I defeats Swiss mercenary troops protecting Milan at the Battle of Marignano, which leads to a peace treaty between France and the Swiss Confederation. The Swiss abandon expansionist policies and declare neutrality, although some of their troops become palace guards for the Vatican.

## 1516

- Ferdinand of Aragon dies and is succeeded as ruler of the Spanish Kingdoms by his grandson, Charles I.

- Francis I and Pope Leo X negotiate the Concordat of Bologna, which establishes relations between the Vatican and France, giving the king the right to nominate church officers in France.

**29 Nov.** France and Switzerland sign the Treaty of Fribourg.

**1518**

- Thomas More joins Henry VIII's council. Wolsey negotiates a peace between France and England in the Treaty of London.

**1519**

- Emperor Maximilian I dies and is succeeded by Charles V, who now controls a vast empire, including Spain, Austria, Naples, Sicily, the Low Countries, and colonies in America.

**1520**

- Henry VIII and Francis I meet at the Field of Cloth of Gold, where Francis tries to convince Henry to support his attempt to gain dominion over the Holy Roman Empire.

- A league of Spanish cities rebel against Charles V and receive French support, but they are defeated at Villalar the next year.

- About one hundred anti-Danish nobles are killed by the newly crowned Christian II, a Dane, in what becomes known as the Bloodbath of Stockholm. The Swedes rise up under Gustavus Vasa and invade Denmark. He becomes King Gustavus I of Sweden in 1523.

**1521**

- France and Spain are at war again over French support of the comuneros revolt.

    ly Roman Empire.

- Henry VIII, after a secret agreement with the Spanish king, launches "The Great Enterprise," with Charles V, against France. Charles, aided by Pope Leo X and Henry VIII, recaptures Milan in November.

22 Apr.    Francis I declares war on the Holy Roman Empire.

**1522**

- The Hospitalier Order of the Knights of St. John of Jerusalem heroically defends Rhodes from a Turkish invasion, but the knights are finally defeated and dispersed. Many of the surviving knights will resettle in 1530 on the island of Malta.

- The French are expelled from Milan by the Spanish.

**1523**

- Christian II of Denmark is deposed.

- John II, the son of Manuel I, becomes king of Portugal.

- Thomas More, Speaker of Commons, petitions successfully for freedom of debate.

- Sweden leaves the Union of Kalmar.

24 June    Charles V defeats the French at the Battle of La Bicocca, gaining most of Lombardy.

**1525**

24 Feb.    A French army of twenty-eight thousand troops, under Francis I, is defeated by troops under Habsburg emperor Charles V at the Battle of Pavia, south of Milan; Francis is taken prisoner.

**1526**

14 Jan.    Francis I is forced to agree to the Treaty of Madrid in order to obtain his freedom and cedes his claims to Italy.

22 May    Francis I forms the League of Cognac (England, Venice, Florence, and the Vatican) to oppose Charles.

29 Aug.    At the Battle of Mohács, the Turks under Süleyman I kill Hungarian king Louis II along with about two-thirds of his troops. The Turks occupy Belgrade.

**1527**

•    Charles V's troops, which include German mercenaries, sack Rome and take Pope Clement VII prisoner.

**1528**

•    Andrea Doria forces through a new constitution and restores the Genoese doges, led by an oligarchy of noble merchants. He ends the allegiance to France and allies Genoa politically with Spain in an attempt to gain access to the new empire in the West.

•    Naples is besieged by the French, but an epidemic of typhus weakens the invaders, forcing them to end their attack.

**1529**

•    The Turks attack Vienna from their stronghold in Hungary. Although beaten back, the Turks will remain a constant threat to the Viennese.

3 Aug.    The Peace of Cambrai is signed between Francis I and Charles V. Both France and the Holy Roman Empire are exhausted from warfare and deadlocked over who will control Italy. The peace is negotiated between Louise of Savoy, mother of Francis, and Margaret of Austria, aunt of Charles. The Pope makes a separate peace with Charles in the Treaty of Barcelona.

25 Oct.    Sir Thomas More is appointed lord chancellor by Henry VIII, after Wolsey fails to obtain from the Pope a divorce for the king. More is the first commoner to achieve this post.

3 Nov.    Henry VIII calls the "Reformation Parliament," which renounces papal authority in England. It holds seven sessions until 1536.

**1530**

•    The Hospitalier Order of the Knights of St. John of Jerusalem takes over Malta, officially as a fiefdom of Charles V.

**1531**

- Ferdinand of Habsburg is elected king of Germany.

- The Lutheran states of the Holy Roman Empire—including Hesse, Saxony, Brunswick, Anhalt, Magdeburg, Bremen, Strasbourg, and Ulm—form a defensive alliance, called the Schmalkaldic League, to counterattacks by Charles V.

**11 Oct.** Swiss Protestant reformer Ulrich Zwingli, defending Zurich from an invasion of Catholic Swiss, is killed in battle near Kappel. After a second defeat, the Protestant army is forced to accept a peace on 23 October that blocks Zwingli's planned reforms for the Catholic cantons.

**1533**

- Henry VIII secretly marries Anne Boleyn. She will be charged with adultery in 1536 and beheaded.

**1534**

- Henry VIII obtains the Act of Supremacy, separating the English Church, its clergy and property, from control by the Pope. More, who refuses to acknowledge the new arrangement, is executed in 1535. Also passed is the Treason Act, which makes it a crime to deny royal titles.

**1535**

- Francesco Maria Sforza of Milan dies.

- Charles V defeats the pirates of Tunis.

**1536**

- Turkish fleets attack coastal cities along Italy, aiding the French in their capture of Turin.

**1–12 Oct.** In opposition to Henry VIII's reforms, heavy taxation, and the enclosure movement, a rebellion is sparked in Lincolnshire when government officials arrive to close the monasteries and seize the taxes. The uprising collapses, but an even larger rebellion arises in York under the leadership of Robert Aske. Believing he had obtained his objectives, Aske releases his troops in December. The English government will later capture and kill around two hundred of the conspirators, including Aske.

**1537**

- Italian mathematician Niccolò Tartaglia writes *Nova scientia*, a treatise on gunnery tactics.

**1538**

- Francis I and Charles V meet at Aigues-Mortes to confirm the Truce of Nice.

**1539**

- An uprising against Charles V emerges in Ghent. The revolt is put down, Ghent's privileges ended, and troops are stationed in the city.

12 Jan.    Francis I and Charles V sign a treaty for combined action against Henry VIII.

**1540**

- The English Privy Council is reformed to combine deliberative and executive functions.

**1541**

- Charles V grants the Protestants concessions in the Diet of Regensburg.

**1542**

- Charles V issues the New Laws of the Indies, an attempt to correct inadequacies of previous edicts for the administration of the New World colonies. One of the things he attempts to change is the level of cruelty inflicted upon native populations. The measure sparks widespread protests among the Spanish settlers.

24 Nov.    Scottish troops, fighting for James V and under the command of Oliver Sinclair, are defeated by the English at the Battle of Solway Moss. Despite having a much larger army, the Scots are disorganized and hemmed in by marshy ground. James is broken by the loss, although he was not present, and it may have contributed to his death less than a month later.

**1543**

- The English perfect a process that allows them to cast iron cannon, which are cheaper and heavier than bronze cannon.

**1544**

- Scotland is invaded by the English, who are intent on enforcing the Treaty of Greenwich, which betrothed the six-month-old Mary, Queen of Scots, to six-year-old Edward, Prince of Wales.

- Charles V invades France and reaches Soissons. The English occupy Boulogne. Charles and Francis sign the Treaty of Crépy.

**1546**

Sept.    Protestant German princes refuse to attend the Diet of Regensburg, and Charles V uses this event as a reason to go to war with the members of the Schmalkaldic League.

## 1547

- Henry VIII dies and is succeeded by his son Edward VI.
- Francis I dies and is succeeded by Henri II.
- Ivan IV (the Terrible) is proclaimed the Grand Duke of Moscow.

**24 Apr.** Charles V defeats the Schmalkaldic League at the Battle of Mühlberg, capturing the wounded John Frederick I, who is forced to accept territorial losses.

**10 Sept.** In hopes of uniting the Scottish and English crowns—through a forced marriage between Mary, Queen of Scots, and King Edward VI—Edward Seymour, Duke of Somerset, employs a sixteen-thousand-man army in Scotland, meeting a force of around twenty-six thousand. Both armies employ a range of weaponry and tactics, many of them modern, such as guns. Seymour's men defeat a pike charge by the Scots and win the day. This engagement is the last formal battle between Scottish and English national armies.

## 1549

- Robert Kett leads a rebellion aimed at the enclosure movement—the fencing of common lands—as rioters destroy the fences of landholders in Norfolk and march on Norwich. The Duke of Somerset sends the marquis of Northampton at the head of an English army, staffed largely with mercenaries, to put down the rebellion. He fails and a larger army is dispatched, and this time they get the upper hand, killing more than three thousand rebels in one engagement. Kett is captured and later executed.

## 1550*

- The musket is invented.

## 1551

- Edward Seymour, Duke of Somerset, who had served as regent for Edward VI, is executed after the Duke of Northumberland, John Dudley, convinces the king that Somerset has conspired against him.

## 1552

- A short-lived truce of religious disputes is achieved in Germany with the signing of the Treaty of Passau by Ferdinand (Charles V's brother) and the elector of Saxony, Maurice.

## 1553

**6 July** Edward VI dies. Lady Jane Grey is declared queen of England, after the Duke of Northumberland induces the king to change the order of succession, but the conspiracy collapses. The duke is executed and Mary Tudor (Bloody Mary) is put on the throne. She attempts to reestablish Catholicism in England and persecutes Protestants.

## 1554

**12 Apr.** Mary of Guise becomes regent of Scotland for her twelve-year-old daughter.

**25 July** Mary I marries Philip II of Spain. She accuses her half sister Elizabeth of complicity in Wyatt's Rebellion and has her imprisoned.

## 1555

**25 Sept.** Lutheranism and Catholicism are recognized in Germany in the Peace of Augsburg.

## 1556

• Charles V abdicates and gives the throne to his son, Phillip II, and his brother, Ferdinand I. Phillip signs the Truce of Vaucelles with Henri II. France and Spain are at war.

## 1557

• Three-year-old Sebastian, the grandson of John III, becomes ruler of Portugal upon the death of the king.

**10 Aug.** French troops are defeated by the Spanish at the battle of Saint-Quentin and are forced out of Italy.

## 1558

• Elizabeth I, daughter of Henry VIII, takes the English throne upon the death of Mary I.

• Charles V, who had retired to a monastery, dies.

**7 Jan.** The French take Calais, the last English foothold on the Continent.

## 1559

• Henri II dies after suffering a fatal head wound during a tournament. He is replaced by his infirm son Francis II, who rules for less than a year.

**3 Apr.** The Treaty of Cateau-Cambrésis ends the wars between France and Spain over control of Italy, leaving the Habsburgs dominant in Italy, where they will remain so for another century and a half. The French are unable to continue the struggle because of domestic religious struggles and financial difficulties.

## 1560

• Charles IX, who is Henry II's second son, becomes king of France upon the death of his brother, Francis II. His mother, Catherine de' Medici, serves as regent.

• Mary of Guise dies.

**6 July** The Treaty of Edinburgh forces a French withdrawal from Scotland.

**1561**

- Mary, Queen of Scots, returns to Scotland.

**1562**

- The Wars of Religion (Huguenot Wars) begin in France, which last until 1598. The conflict is initiated by the Duke of Guise, who orders a massacre of Huguenots (French Protestants) at Vassy.

4 Oct.
- The English, under Sir Adrian Poynings, enter Le Havre, France, a port that had been taken over by Huguenots.

19 Dec.
- The Huguenots are defeated at the Battle of Dreux.

**1563**

- Elizabeth I obtains from Parliament an extension of the Act of Supremacy, strengthening the Protestant faith in England.

25 Mar.
- A short truce in the French Religious Wars is achieved with the Peace of Amboise, which allows Protestants to worship and return to their homes and forbids harassment on the basis of religion.

27 July
- Le Havre is recaptured by the French.

**1564**

- England gives up its claim to Calais in the Peace of Troyes.

- Antoine Perrenot de Granvelle, sent by Phillip II to be president of the council of state for Margaret of Parma, regent of the Netherlands, angers Dutch patriots by employing Spanish troops and persecuting Protestants, and is forced to retire.

- Emperor Ferdinand I dies and is succeeded by his son, Maximilian II.

- Cosimo de' Medici of Florence abdicates in favor of his son, Francesco.

**1565**

- A meeting between the Duke of Alba and Catherine de' Medici, the wife of Charles IX, sparks Protestant protests in France that eventually lead to several massacres of Protestants.

- The Hospitalier Order of the Knights of St. John of Jerusalem fight off an attack on Malta by the Turks under Süleyman I. The invaders number around forty thousand men, but the much smaller force of defenders avoids capture. The Turks continue their siege until early September, when they retreat.

**1566**

- The "Beggars," a group of nobles in the Netherlands, ask Margaret of Parma to relax religious persecution of Protestants, which she does.

**1567**

* The Netherlands provinces revolt against Spanish rule, especially that of the Duke of Alba, who attempts to restore Phillip's authority by leading an army into the Low Countries, forcing out or killing much of the opposition.

24 July    Lord Darnley, who is thirteen months old, becomes James VI when his mother, Mary, Queen of Scots, abdicates.

**1568**

* The English defeat the Scots at Langside, and Mary, Queen of Scots, who is Catholic and has escaped to England, is imprisoned. Activities on her behalf impel Elizabeth I to persecute Catholics.

**1569**

* Cosimo de' Medici becomes the Grand Duke of Tuscany.

* Poland and Lithuania unite into a single state with the Union of Lublin.

Nov.    The earls of Northumberland and Westmoreland foment a rebellion and restore Catholic worship at the cathedral in Durham, in what is known as the Revolt of the Northern Earls. The crown sends an army under the Earl of Sussex and the rebels withdraw.

**1570**

* The Peace of St. Germain-en-Laye ends the Third Religious War in France. An amnesty for Huguenots is declared, as well as freedom of worship granted.

* A revolt of converted Moslems, known as *moriscos,* in Spain is defeated; they will be expelled from the nation in 1609.

* Troops of the Ottoman leader Selim II invade Cyprus and Nicosia, sparking a response from Spanish and Italian leaders.

* The Ridolfi plot, which calls for an invasion of England by Spanish troops stationed in the Netherlands, is uncovered; the Duke of Norfolk is executed in 1572 for his part in the conspiracy, and Mary, Queen of Scots, is implicated.

**1571**

7 Oct.    A combined Venetian and Spanish fleet of around two hundred vessels captures an Ottoman fleet off the Peloponnesian coast in the Gulf of Patras in the Battle of Lepanto, temporarily blocking expansion of the eastern empire further into the Mediterranean. Spanish novelist Miguel de Cervantes, author of *El ingenioso hidalgo Don Quixote de la Mancha* (1605), is wounded in this battle.

## 1572

* William of Orange initiates the Dutch War of Independence against Spain. The Sea Beggars, fighting from foreign ports, harass the Spanish and capture the Dutch port city of Brielle (1 April), sparking a wider revolt in support of William. French support fails to materialize, however, and William is forced to retreat to the northern provinces. There he leads a resistance against Spanish invaders.

24 Aug.    Thousands of Protestant Parisian protestors are killed in the St. Bartholomew's Day Massacre, possibly in an attempt by the king to head off a new round of civil wars.

## 1573

* Cyprus falls to the Ottoman Empire. The Venetians are forced to accept Turkish domination in the eastern Mediterranean in the Peace of Constantinople.

## 1574

* Charles IX dies; Henri III of Anjou becomes king of France.
* Cosimo de' Medici, Grand Duke of Tuscany, dies in Florence.

## 1575

* The Prince of Transylvania, Stephen Báthory, is elected king of Poland; he is forced to put down a rebellion in Gdansk within two years.

## 1576

* Unpaid Spanish troops go on a rampage, known as the Spanish Fury, in Antwerp. They destroy property, loot buildings, and murder approximately six thousand citizens.
* The southern Netherlands provinces unite against Philip in the Pacification of Ghent and place William of Orange (the Silent) at their head.
* Emperor Maximilian II dies and is succeeded by his brother Rudolf II.

## 1577

* In response to Henri III repealing an edict of toleration, the Huguenots rebel and begin a sixth round of civil wars in France. The war ends with the Peace of Bergerac, which restores most provisions for freedom of worship.

## 1578

* Sebastian of Portugal, along with more than eight thousand of his troops, is killed during an aborted invasion of North Africa, at the Battle of the Three Kings near Alcazar. The Moors reportedly capture around fifteen thousand Portugese troops. Sebastian is succeeded by Henry, his uncle, who serves for only two years.

**1579**

- The northern Netherlands provinces unite under the Union of Utrecht.

**1580**

- Upon the death of Henry I, Philip II sends troops under the Duke of Alba into Portugal. Along with his rule over Spain, Philip becomes Philip I of Portugal.

**1581**

- The Estates General of the Netherlands issues the Act of Abjuration, declaring that Phillip II's tyranny meant forfeiture of his sovereignty over the country.

**1582**

- James VI is kidnapped by William Ruthven, Earl of Gowrie, and is forced to denounce the Duke of Lennox, a Roman Catholic who allegedly schemed to return his faith to Scotland.

**1583**

- Englishman Francis Throckmorton, along with a group of exiles, is involved in a plot to help France invade England and kill Elizabeth. He is captured, tortured, and then executed in 1584.

**1584**

18 Mar.   Ivan the Terrible dies and his son, Fyodor, succeeds, but he cedes power to Boris Gudonov.

10 July   William of Orange, who became the leader of the Union of Utrecht, is assassinated by Balthazar Gérard at the instigation of Philip II. He is succeeded by his seventeen-year-old son Maurice.

**1585**

- The Treaty of Nonsuch commits England to aid Dutch Estates against Philip II.

- The Treaty of Nemours bans Protestantism in France and requires all Protestants to renounce their faith or be exiled. In response a religious civil war breaks out among the forces of Henri of Guise and the revived Catholic League, Henri III of France, and Henri of Navarre (heir to the throne), called the War of the Three Henris. The two former kings are attempting to end Protestantism in France, but are opposed by the Protestant Henri of Navarre.

**1586**

- An alleged plot to kill Elizabeth I and her ministers, in a Catholic insurrection supported by the Spanish, is uncovered. The plot is named for Antony Babbington, a page and messenger for Mary Stuart; the plotters are captured and executed. Mary is tried for treason on 15 October and sentenced to death ten days later. Parliament finds her guilty and petitions Elizabeth to sign her death warrant.

**1587**

- The Battle of Coutras is a victory for Henri of Navarre over Henri III.

8 Feb.  Mary is beheaded at Fotheringhay on order of Elizabeth I.

**1588**

12 May  Parisians rise up against Henri III in the Day of the Barricades, but he manages to escape the city. In July he capitulates to their demands, making Henri of Guise lieutenant general of France. Henri is later assassinated, along with his brother Cardinal Louis II, by Henri.

Aug.  With the aid of a storm, the English defeat an invading Armada sent by King Philip. The Spanish experience supply difficulties and are outclassed by the English long gunners. Less than half of the original Spanish fleet makes it back to safety.

**1589**

- Henri III is assassinated by Jacques Clément, a Dominican monk. The Protestant Henry IV (Henry of Navarre) takes the throne, initiating the Bourbon reign. He renounces Protestantism in 1593. Henri IV takes the war to the Catholic League and defeats the army of the Duc de Mayenne at the Battle of Arques.

**1590**

- The army of Henri IV deals the Catholic League another setback at the Battle of Ivry. His army advances to Paris and begins its siege, but it is unsuccessful in taking the city. The Spanish help provide food to the besieged Parisians.

**1591**

- Aragon rebels against Phillip II in an attempt to protect Antonio Perez, Phillip's former secretary and an intriguer who had escaped from imprisonment.

- Polish attempts to control their numbers spark Cossack bands to rebel.

**1593**

- Emperor Rudolf II of Hungary initiates the Long War, which ends in 1606, against the Magyars, who had left the Catholic Church in favor of Protestantism.

## 1594

- Henri IV is crowned.

Aug.  An English force trying to supply a castle near Enniskillen, under siege by Irish rebels, is defeated at the Battle of the Ford of Biscuits, so named because of the scattered supplies on the battlefield.

## 1595

- Spanish troops, in support of Catholic factions in France, are defeated at the Battle of Fontaine-Française and driven from Burgundy.

## 1596

- The Articles of Folembray end the War of the Catholic League in France, stopping the attempt by the Spanish to deny Henri's claim to the throne.
- The Privy Council raises "Ship Money" from coastal regions for provision of the navy.

## 1597

- Irish discontent coalesces under the leadership of Hugh O'Neill, the Earl of Tyrone, who is attempting to regain control of Ulster, though he appeals to broader nationalist sentiments. O'Neill's army achieves a stunning victory over an English army under Sir Henry Bagenal at Yellow Ford in Ulster (1598). However, the victory is short-lived as the Irish forces, reinforced by Spaniards, are crushed at Kinsale in 1601, although Tyrone does not submit until 1603.

## 1598

- The Edict of Nantes grants political rights to French Protestants; the Wars of Religion in France are over.

2 May  The Peace of Vervins between Spain and France gives back lost French land.

13 Sept.  Philip II of Spain dies and is succeeded by Philip III.

- Fyodor I of Russia dies, and Godunov is elected czar by the national assembly.

## 1599

- The Polish king Sigismund III Vasa, a Catholic, is deposed by Swedes and Charles IX, who establishes Lutheranism as the state religion of Sweden.

## 1600

- A government charter is granted to the English East India Company. Shares in the company are transferable and policy control is vested in a board of directors elected by stockholders. The company soon monopolizes trade in the Indian subcontinent.
- Henri IV of France marries Marie de' Medici.

# OVERVIEW

**Holy Roman Empire.** In the Middle Ages the accepted form of government was the monarchy, in which one man had absolute authority, and the ideal was the universal empire, in which all the peoples of the world were subject to one emperor. The Holy Roman emperors claimed authority over all Christendom, but by 1350 the empire was called the Holy Roman Empire of the German Nation, indicating that it largely consisted of Germany. There were about three hundred territorial divisions that controlled their own local affairs. The emperor was elected by seven major lords of the empire. In 1438 Albert V, Duke of Austria, was elected, and the title stayed in the Habsburg family for the duration of the empire.

**Ottoman Empire.** The Turkish Ottoman Empire also claimed universal authority, although its mandate came from Islam. Osman I, its founder, had built a powerful state in Asia Minor by his death in 1326. His successors expanded their lands at the expense of the Byzantine Empire, completing the conquest when Constantinople was taken in 1453. By 1526 the Ottoman Turks controlled the Middle East, the Balkans, and Hungary.

**Elective and Joint Monarchies.** Imperial claims to universal rule infuriated kings who asserted their own sovereign power. There were several elective monarchies—Poland-Lithuania, Bohemia, and Hungary—in eastern Europe, where the rulers were chosen by the nobility. There were joint monarchies, such as Poland-Lithuania, in which two or more realms with separate governments had the same ruler. The Union of Kalmar (1397) created a joint monarchy for Denmark, Sweden, and Norway. The union endured until 1523, when Sweden seceded. The most-powerful joint monarchy came from the marriage of Ferdinand of Aragon and Isabella of Castile in 1469. Their realms remained two separate states until 1592, when their great-grandson Philip II united the two kingdoms with a central administration. Spain thus became a national kingdom, where the borders of the realm largely coincided with a dominant ethnic group from which came the ruler. France, England, Scotland, and Portugal were among the other national kingdoms in which hereditary succession determined the right to the throne.

**City-States and Confederacies.** Northern Italy was the home of city-state republics, including Venice, one of the major powers of Europe. Their form of government was the commune, in which the members of the merchant and artisan guilds had political rights. The number of city-states had been as large as eighty in 1350, but by that time the largest cities were rapidly expanding, taking over what had been independent cities. The best example was Venice, which built a large state on the Italian mainland. Milan and Florence also expanded, and both eventually became duchies. The commune was the form of urban government across Europe, but most of the cities had to answer to a royal authority. The exception was a group of mostly northern German cities that formed the Hanseatic League. It was organized in 1356 to control trade in the North and Baltic Seas. Until 1500 it was a major economic and political power in northern Europe, but the growing power of neighboring kings and competition from Dutch traders caused its decline. There were also two unique states in Europe. The pope was the ruler of lands that stretched across central Italy, but his authority over the Papal States was often limited. The Swiss Confederation was a loosely affiliated group of cantons. It was formed in 1291 when three cantons joined to oppose the outside claims to authority over them. By 1500 the confederation had reached largely the borders of modern Switzerland. In most respects the thirteen cantons were independent republics, but they did cooperate during wartime.

**Administration.** Government administration in 1350 was marked by amateurism; many officials had no formal training for their positions. Clergymen often became officials because they could read and write. Another feature was the small number of officials. The Italian city-states set the standard for effective administration. Their wealth enabled them to finance large bodies of professional officials, with the Venetian diplomatic service being the best example. By 1431 Venice was dispatching diplomats across Europe.

**Government Officials.** The other Italian cities retained elements of their earlier communes as did the cities of northern Europe. In the Holy Roman Empire the emperor appointed the imperial chancellor, the chief administrative officer. When matters concerning the entire empire needed to be decided, the Imperial Diet met. Its usual function was approving taxes for an imperial army. The growth of royal administration was a key characteristic in the national monarchies of the late Middle Ages. The principle of royal government was that the king embodied in himself all of the powers of government and handed out a share of it to others for the well-ordered governance of the realm. The English and French governments were highly similar. The chancellor was the chief officer of the realm under the king. He kept the great seal that was used on royal decrees, and he supervised the systems of justice and taxation. War was the major reason why kings raised taxes. In peacetime they were expected to live off their properties and feudal dues. In 1362 Edward III promised the English Parliament that the monarchy would not impose a new tax without its consent. With its two houses (Lords and Commons), Parliament avoided the problem of the bitter division between nobles and commoners found in the Estates General in France with its three estates (clergy, nobles, and commoners). The Estates General never gained a major role, because the French kings found that it was not helpful. Similar institutions were found in nearly every medieval realm. The Ottoman Empire's administration was far different. In a way that was never true in Europe, the sultan combined in himself supreme authority of both state and religion. The millions of Christians and Jews in the empire were allowed to govern themselves as long as they paid taxes. The sultans created an impressive administration for their vast empire that lasted into the modern era. The Spanish and Portuguese also were successful in building an effective administration for the overseas empires that they won after 1492.

**Changes in Warfare.** In 1350 the heavily armored knight still dominated the battlefields of Europe with his couched lance and broad sword. Against commoner foot soldiers, knights had held an enormous advantage for centuries, but by 1350 some infantry weapons were in use that reduced knightly superiority. Crossbow, longbow, and pike, when used correctly, were effective weapons against charging cavalry. In the long term the most-important new weapons were those using gunpowder, a Chinese invention that was carried westward by the Mongols in the thirteenth century. The first reliable mention of gunpowder weaponry in Europe is dated to 1326. Early gunpowder weapons were ineffective in battle, but with improvements they soon became formidable.

**Gunpowder Weapons.** Several innovations made effective handguns possible. Corned powder and the match appeared about 1420, and the matchlock, by 1460; together they created the arquebus. As a smoothbore weapon it was inaccurate, and it took over a minute to reload. The Spanish musket, a heavier firearm that used a larger ball, appeared about 1520. Its weight required the use of a fork for resting the barrel. Another new weapon was the pistol, which used the wheel lock mechanism. Its expense restricted its use to the nobles.

**English Victories.** Shortly before the Renaissance infantry had been victorious over armies of knights in two major battles—Laupen (1339) and Crécy (1346). A knight's proper opponent was another knight, not poorly armed and untrained infantrymen. Knightly disdain for fighting commoners was a major reason for the English victories in the Hundred Years' War (1337–1453), as the French knights largely ignored the commoner archers in order to battle the English knights. In a war with the Scots, the English developed the combination of longbow archers and dismounted knights that proved so effective against the French. During their conflict against the French, the English commanders were victorious when they chose the terrain for the battle—a hilltop where they placed their forces to wait for the French attack. What defeats the English suffered occurred when they could not dictate the terrain and battle tactics, such as at Orléans (1429), where they fought French forces led by Joan of Arc. In their last battles in the war the French effectively used small cannon against the English.

**Swiss Innovations.** For all of the victories won by English tactics, the Swiss system of pike and halberd proved more revolutionary. In the fourteenth century the Swiss defeated Austrian knightly armies and established their style of fighting. Their tactics were successful in the era before 1515, but their style of warfare became obsolete in the face of improved gunpowder weapons. The first army successfully to use them was Jan Zizka's forces during the Hussite revolt that broke out in Bohemia in 1415. Zizka's use of war wagons gave his untrained soldiers a stable platform from which to fire their gunpowder weapons against their mounted foes. By the time of the French invasions of Italy in 1494, both cannon and firearms had been improved sufficiently so that they could be used as effective weapons in the field. The Spanish captain Gonzalo Fernández de Córdoba introduced the combination of arquebus and pike. The slow reloading time and inaccuracy of the arquebus required pikemen to protect the handgunners as they reloaded. The infantry formation in which pikemen and handgunners provided mutual support became known as the Spanish Square. It was the dominant formation in European combat for the next century. As for the Turks, they continued to depend on a combination of light and heavy cavalry and infantry for victory until 1600.

**Naval Warfare.** Gunpowder also changed the nature of war at sea. In the fifteenth century, cannon and firearms began to replace catapults and bows onboard ship. Gun ports allowed the heavy guns to be placed lower on the ship and increased its stability. By 1540 the galleon, with up to forty heavy guns firing through gun ports, could project naval power far from its home waters. In the Mediterranean, the long naval war between Christians and Muslims reached its climax in the sixteenth century. The greatest battle in the history of galleys was the Battle of Lepanto (1571) off the Greek coast. The Christian fleet at Lepanto included several much larger galleasses, whose firepower played a major role in their victory. It led to a great increase in the size of galleys, which, however, made them slower and more vulnerable to the sailing ships from the Atlantic making excursions into the Mediterranean by 1600. The major conflict between Atlantic fleets involved the Spanish Armada. The failure of the Armada in 1588 was not the end of Spanish naval power, since Philip II rebuilt his fleet, but the episode convinced the English monarchy that it should build a powerful royal navy.

**Fortifications.** By 1350 the medieval fortification had reached its apex and changed little for more than a century, until the development of gunpowder artillery began to have an impact. The castle primarily served as the residence of a powerful lord. Typically, it had high stone walls with round towers surrounded by a ditch and a variety of other structures designed to aid the defenders in holding off attackers. The walls of towns were constructed little differently except for their far greater length. In 1350 a well-built castle or walled town defended by a small garrison of resolute men was capable of withstanding a siege even when it was the king's army that was besieging it. Over the next century the development of gunpowder artillery into effective siege weapons turned the advantage to the attackers. By 1453 the French had established the first effective royal artillery train. The development of the mobile gun carriage allowed heavy guns to be transported at about the same speed as the rest of the army. The major success of cannon in the fifteenth century was the successful siege of Constantinople (1453) by the Ottoman Turks. The superbly fortified city fell after a siege of a month. The crucial development in the late fifteenth century was the casting of bronze muzzle-loaders. Such cannon had a major role during the French invasions of Italy beginning in 1494. In a few days the French took Italian fortifications that the Italians expected would take them all summer to capture.

**Italian Trace.** The Italians, seeking ways to withstand the French artillery, developed the Italian trace. The key innovation was the bastion, which projected far forward of the wall to provide better flanking fire. The bastion was designed so guns at the flanks of a bastion could sweep every foot of the adjoining wall and the face of the neighboring bastion. As long as the architect's calculations were correct, the bastions could provide cover from fire all the way around the wall. By 1570 the offense again was catching up to the defense. Improvements in the casting of iron led to better iron cannons. Iron being cheap, the new method led to a vast increase in the number of guns that could do severe damage to fortifications. Military architects responded by designing ways to push the besiegers' heavy guns further from the walls by using outworks, which were developed extensively during the Dutch Revolt against Spain in the 1570s. The Europeans used the Italian trace successfully in their occupation of large parts of the world in the sixteenth century. The failure of the Ottoman Turks to keep up with European fortification design and siege craft was a factor in the decline of that empire's power in the late sixteenth century.

**Rise of Monarchies.** These military developments effectively ended the role of petty rulers in most parts of Europe. In 1350 a handful of resolute warriors could withstand sieges from even the king's army; hence, knights in Medieval Europe could openly defy their king. By the fifteenth century, developments in gunpowder artillery had reversed this advantage and kings won great advantages over the local knights. Monarchs strengthened their control and expanded their kingdoms at the expense of the petty rulers. The centralizing monarchs created more effective bureaucracies in their efforts to consolidate power.

**Legal Codes.** The monarchy also began to replace local customary laws with written codes based on Roman law. Roman law was a revival of a code from the ancient Roman Empire. The Roman Empire was ruled for more than six hundred years by emperors, and thus Roman law was a legal tradition favorable to monarchical rule. Kings were eager to employ a legal system that placed them at the focal point of the law. The eleventh-century revival of emperor Justinian's Body of the Civil Law began a revival of Roman law in Europe. Roman law evolved into a field requiring extensive university training. Law departments at the universities were divided into the study of Roman law and of a related law code, known as canon law. Roman law covered issues falling under the government's jurisdiction and canon law covered legal issues within the Church's jurisdiction, yet the two shared several procedural elements that had a profound influence upon the European legal tradition.

**Evolution of the Law.** The term *canon* was used by the early Christian Church to signify formal decisions of church legislation. This legislative process evolved into a system of ecclesiastical or church law that regulated the Church and issues of belief. Canon law was distinct from the customary laws of northern Europe and the written or Roman law of southern Europe. The revival of Justinian's Body of the Civil Law and the twelfth-century appearance of Gratian of Bologna's *Decretum,* or *Concordance of Discordant Canons,* set the stage for a Renaissance revival of Roman and canon law. Both systems evolved into highly specialized university disciplines. Moreover, both were employed across Christian Europe with the exception of England, Wales, and Ireland, where a system of case law was deeply entrenched. The Reformation split the legal profession because Protestant reformers broke with the Roman Catholic Church and thereby rejected the Church's system of canon law. Protestants expanded Roman law and gave it a role over marriage, divorce, and other areas that had previously fallen under canon law. Canon law declined in the sixteenth century, but many aspects of it remained because they had been assimilated into Roman law, such as the traditions of the Inquisition. By the end of the fifteenth century, the state could withhold from the accused the names and testimony of the witnesses. Courts began to function in secret and turned to trials as a public ceremony at the end of a secretive inquisition. Punishment and execution evolved into a public spectacle that legitimized the court by demonstrating the populace's consent to a sentence that they could no longer control.

**Crime and Punishment.** Centralization of power in the hands of a few monarchs and the imposition of Roman law codes contributed to a dramatic shift in the treatment and punishment of criminals in Renaissance and Reformation Europe. Rulers redefined crimes as attacks on the state and thereby created a new role for the courts. When the Fourth Lateran Council in 1215 eliminated ordeals, or the physical testing of oaths, rulers turned to inquistorial trial procedures that combined elements of Roman and canon law. Church inquisitional tribunals aimed at finding and stopping heresy. In the opinion of church and government authorities, heresy threatened all of society and thus justified drastic measures. Rather than wait for accusations, Inquisition courts took the initiative of starting hearings and collecting evidence. Potential heretics were presumed guilty until proven innocent. The accused did not know what the exact charges were and could not review evidence being used against them. Heresy was difficult to prove and Inquisitors frequently turned to torture as a means to obtain confessions. Common forms of torture included stretching body limbs with a rope or on a rack, water or fire torment, and sleep deprivation.

**State Models.** Inquisitional techniques became models for the state and torture became a common method of extracting confessions. Officials interrogated and tortured suspected criminals without allowing recourse to a defense attorney. Punishments could range from fines and disgrace to mutilations and death. Executions by burning, drowning, and burying alive were common because they allegedly purified the community. After 1600, hanging and beheading became more common. The church sentenced heretics in a public ceremony, known as an auto de fe, and then turned them over to the state for public punishment. The condemned were usually burned at the stake in the sixteenth century. The actual burning took place on feast days and in public squares to insure a large audience of leading officials and common people. The judicial system punished rather than rehabilitated, so punishments were usually public affairs.

**Prisons.** Precursors to the modern prison system were built in the late sixteenth century, but they were not used for criminals. City governments constructed these early houses of correction for the able-bodied poor. Workhouses, such as Bridewell in England, attempted to rehabilitate idle people by housing them in an environment where they were forced to work. By 1600 the judicial system remained punitive but notions of rehabilitation were evident in the emerging prison system.

# TOPICS IN POLITICS, LAW, AND THE MILITARY

## ADMINISTRATION: FORMS OF GOVERNMENT

**Universal Emperor.** The monarchy, in which one man had absolute authority received from God, was the accepted type of government during the Middle Ages. The ideal was the universal empire, in which all the peoples and kings of the world were subject to one emperor, following the example of the Roman Empire. It was based on the concept that all of humanity properly should have just one ruler. The divine sovereignty of one God over the world and one pope over the Church were models of the authority of the universal emperor.

**Holy Roman Empire.** The reality of government in Europe was far different, but there was an institution called the Holy Roman Empire, whose emperors occasionally voiced claim to authority over all of Christendom as God's viceroy on Earth. What power the emperor had was in fact limited and in steady decline. The concept of the Holy Roman Empire began with Charlemagne's coronation in 800. It took on its medieval form when the Pope crowned the German king Otto I emperor in 962. (Otto I had wanted the title in order to affirm his authority over northern Italy.) Thereafter until 1648, the Holy Roman Empire theoretically included Italy north of Rome, Switzerland, Austria, Bohemia, Germany, the Low Countries (present-day Netherlands, Belgium, and Luxembourg), and eastern France. Imperial authority over Switzerland and northern Italy was nonexistent after 1350, but the emperors maintained the pretense that they had sovereignty. In 1519, for example, Emperor Charles V declared war on French king Francis I, because Francis had taken over Milan without Charles's approval. By 1350 the empire was being called

In 1525 the peasants in Germany revolted in response to changes invoked by the feudal lords that restricted traditional social and economic freedoms. In response to these changes, the peasants made the following demands.

1. It is our humble petition and desire . . . that in the future . . . each community should choose and appoint a pastor, and that we should have the right to depose him should he conduct himself improperly. . . .

2. We are ready and willing to pay the fair tithe of grain. . . . The small tithes [of cattle], whether [to] ecclesiastical or lay lords, we will not pay at all, for the Lord God created cattle for the free use of man. . . .

3. We . . . take it for granted that you will release us from serfdom as true Christians, unless it should be shown us from the Gospel that we are serfs.

4. It has been the custom heretofore that no poor man should be allowed to catch venison or wildfowl or fish in flowing water, which seems to us quite unseemly and unbrotherly as well as selfish and not agreeable to the Word of God. . . .

5. We are aggrieved in the matter of woodcutting, for the noblemen have appropriated all the woods to themselves. . . .

6. In regard to the excessive services demanded of us which are increased from day to day, we ask that this matter be properly looked into so that we shall not continue to be oppressed in this way. . . .

7. We will not hereafter allow ourselves to be further oppressed by our lords, but will let them demand only what is just and proper according to the word of the agreement between the lord and the peasant. The lord should no longer try to force more services or other dues from the peasant without payment. . . .

8. We are greatly burdened because our holdings cannot support the rent exacted from them. . . . We ask that the lords may appoint persons of honor to inspect these holdings and fix a rent in accordance with justice. . . .

9. We are burdened with a great evil in the constant making of new laws. . . . In our opinion we should be judged according to the old written law. . . .

10. We are aggrieved by the appropriation . . . of meadows and fields which at one time belonged to a community as a whole. These we will take again into our own hands. . . .

11. We will entirely abolish the due called Todfall [that is, heriot or death tax, by which the lord received the best horse, cow, or garment of a family upon the death of a serf] and will no longer endure it, nor allow widows and orphans to be thus shamefully robbed against God's will, and in violation of justice and right. . . .

12. It is our conclusion and final resolution, that if any one or more of the articles here set forth should not be in agreement with the Word of God, as we think they are, such article we will willingly retract.

Source: Donald Kagan, Steven Ozment, and Frank M. Turner, *The Western Heritage*, sixth edition (Upper Saddle River, N.J.: Prentice Hall, 1998): p. 380.

the Holy Roman Empire of the German Nation, recognizing the fact that it largely consisted of Germany. Yet, the Golden Bull of 1356, which established the method of the emperor's election, called for the selection of someone who spoke Italian and Slavic as well as German.

**Principalities and Free Cities.** The sense of the term *emperor* as it was used in the Middle Ages included the expectation that there would be kings under his authority. The Holy Roman Empire included the king of Bohemia as well as various prince–bishops, dukes, and counts. Its territory was divided into three types of governmental units: church principalities, where the local bishop or archbishop served as the ruler as well as the church leader (for example, the archbishops of Cologne and Mainz); lay principalities, where rulers with a wide range of titles had power (for example, the duke of Saxony and the margrave of Branden-

burg); and sixty-five Free Imperial Cities, where the city councils exercised complete authority within the city walls (for example, Augsburg and Nuremberg). The church princes usually came from the powerful noble families, often for several generations in succession. There were in all about three hundred territorial divisions, including those outside of Germany. Each had local autonomy to control its own affairs.

**Elected Emperor.** The emperor was elected, although until the sixteenth century he could not use the title of emperor until the pope had crowned him. The Golden Bull of 1356 set the number of electors at four territorial princes and three archbishop-princes. With the principle of hereditary succession missing, the emperors were chosen from several families until 1438, when Albert II, from the Habsburg family and Duke of Austria, was elected, and the title stayed in that family. Maximilian I's marriage to Mary of Burgundy (1477) was the first in a series of marriages that passed the Habsburg and Burgundian inheritances and the Spanish kingdoms to his grandson, Charles. When Maximilian died in 1519, there was the first serious competition for the election in two centuries. Henry VIII and Francis I invested heavily in bribing the electors as did Charles, who had the advantages of having more money and being regarded as German. Charles V arranged in 1530 for the election of his brother Ferdinand as his successor, since his son Philip was then three years old. When the Reformation began, Charles could not prevent the division of the empire into Catholic and Lutheran lands. He was forced to accept the Peace of Augsburg (1555) by which the local rulers had the right to determine the religion of their lands. Worn out by his wars, Charles abdicated his titles, and the imperial title passed to his brother. While Philip received most of Charles's hereditary lands including Spain, Ferdinand was given the duchy of Austria to give him with a power base from which to rule as emperor. The Austrian Habsburgs were the emperors for the duration of the empire.

**Ottoman Turks.** The Ottoman Empire also claimed universal authority, although its mandate was based on being an Islamic state. Its name came from Osman I, the founder of the ruling dynasty. He was a Turkish warlord who succeeded in building a powerful state in northern Asia Minor before he died in 1326. Ottoman expansion depended greatly on the tradition that a new sultan had to prove himself worthy of rule by making a major conquest early in his reign. The Ottoman sultan was first of all the commander of the Turkish army. The dynasty had risen to power through military conquest and continued to hold it through the loyalty of the fighting men, who were more loyal than most European forces were to their rulers. The fighting men were amply rewarded with pay, lands, and plunder, but they were obliged to earn their rewards by conquest, which was another reason for the constant expansion of the Ottoman Empire until the late sixteenth century. When the expansion of the empire ceased, their loyalty declined as well. One requirement for soldiers was that they be Muslim; non-Muslim subjects who wished to join the army had to convert.

**Eliminating Rivals.** Osman's successors expanded their lands largely at the expense of the Byzantine Empire, conquering most of it before Sultan Mehmed II took Constantinople in 1453. Selim I conquered Egypt and the Middle East between 1514 and 1520. By becoming ruler of Arabia the sultan became the protector of the Muslim holy places and the leader of Islam. When his only son Süleyman I succeeded him in 1520, the Ottoman Turks controlled the Mediterranean coastline from Albania to Libya. In 1526 Süleyman conquered most of Hungary after winning the Battle of Mohács. Although he failed to take Vienna (1529) and the island of Malta (1565) after long sieges, he was one of the great rulers of the sixteenth century. At his death in 1566, the absence of a clear law of succession for the Ottoman sultanate began to create problems as Süley-

Ballot pouches used by Florentine officials during municipal elections (from George Constable, *Voyages of Discovery,* 1989)

man designated the young son of his favorite wife as his heir instead of one of his more mature and capable sons. (The sultans practiced polygamy on a large scale.) The practice of killing all of the new sultan's brothers and half brothers in order to eliminate any rivals to the throne appeared at this point, which increased the stakes in the competition for the succession. Selim II began a series of weak sultans, but he did conquer Cyprus from Venice (1571), the last significant Ottoman conquest.

**Elective Monarchy.** Both Christian and Islamic empires claimed universal sovereignty, but such claims were refuted by the presence in Europe of kings who asserted their own sovereign power. The fondest boast of the king of France, for example, was that he was "emperor in his own realm." The principle of elective monarchy functioned in eastern Europe, where the rulers of Poland, Bohemia, Hungary, Lithuania, and several smaller political units were chosen by the nobility. There was little sense that the man elected king had to be a native. In Bohemia, the election in 1363 of Wenceslas II from a German family was one cause of the Hussite Revolt. Bohemia passed permanently under Habsburg control in 1526, when Ferdinand I, brother of Charles V, was chosen as king after Louis II of Hungary, who also had been elected king of Bohemia in 1516, was killed at Mohács. Ferdinand gained the elective throne of Hungary at the same time. The Habsburgs kept the crowns of both Bohemia and Hungary from then on, although in theory they remained elective long after 1600.

**Poland-Lithuania.** The best known example of an elective monarchy was Poland-Lithuania. The Polish monarchy had been hereditary until 1386, when Duke Jagiello of Lithuania married Polish queen Jadwiga and was elected king of Poland. The hereditary Lithuanian throne then became elective also. The nobles of the joint monarchy chose members of the Jagellonian family as rulers for the next two centuries. When Sigismund II, the last male in

Ambrogio Lorenzetti's *Allegory of Good Government*, 1337–1339, fresco in the Palazzo Pubblico in Siena, Italy

the dynasty, died in 1572, the nobles turned to the French prince Henri of Valois, who dashed back to France to claim the French throne in 1574 when his brother died. The Poles then elected a Hungarian (Stephen Báthory) in 1576 and a Swede (Sigismund III) in 1587 as kings. These elective monarchies had two major problems. One was that the successful candidates usually had to make concessions to the nobles to get elected. The other was that the lack of continuity prevented the kings from building up royal power and passing it on their own heirs, a defect that became obvious in Poland-Lithuania after the Jagellonian dynasty ended and the monarchy slipped badly in both international power and internal authority.

**Joint Monarchs.** Poland-Lithuania was also an example of the joint monarchy, in which rulers from one ethnic background were accepted peaceably through marriage or election as monarchs in another realm. The Union of Kalmar (1397) created a joint monarchy for the three realms of Denmark, Sweden, which controlled Finland, and Norway, which ruled Iceland; the Danish prince Erik was elected king. His male descendents were to serve as king of the three realms; if his family died out, the kingdoms in the union were free to choose their own kings. The system never worked all that smoothly, but despite short periods of unrest, the union endured until 1523, when Swedish opposition to their Danish king Christian II because of heavy taxation and mistreatment of Swedish nobles erupted into violent rebellion. In short order the Swedes elected Gustavus I as king, who defeated Christian and established both Swedish autonomy and his family as the ruling dynasty. Norway remained part of the union with Denmark because the Danes ousted Christian and enthroned his uncle Frederick I as king later in 1523.

**Aragon and Castile.** The most important joint monarchy came out of the marriage of Prince Ferdinand of Aragon and Princess Isabella of Castile in 1469. Soon both had become rulers of their realms and worked together to strengthen them. When Isabella died in 1504, Ferdinand II secured control of Castile in the name of his insane daughter Joanna, who had married Philip of Habsburg, Emperor Maximilian I's son. When Ferdinand died in 1516, the Spanish realms passed to his grandson Charles of Habsburg, who ruled there as Charles I but is better known as Holy Roman Emperor Charles V. Under him Aragon and Castile remained two separate states with their own governments and officials. In 1592 Charles's son Philip II united the two kingdoms after a failed revolt in Aragon, using the Castilian government largely created by Isabella as the central administration for unified Spain.

**National Kingdoms.** Spain thus joined the small number of states for the era 1350–1600 that were national kingdoms, where the borders of the realm largely coincided with the dominant ethnic group and it was expected that the ruler would be a member of that group. Although modern people usually identify medieval government with that kind of monarchy, it probably is because France and England, along with Scotland and Portugal, were among the few national kingdoms in which blood-right determined the royal succession.

**France.** In one key respect France was most adamant about its status as a national kingdom, because its Salic law, which governed succession to the French throne, was invented before the Hundred Years' War (1337–1453) to keep England's Edward III off the throne. It required that the throne pass from father to oldest son or, in default of a son, to a male who could trace his ancestry in the direct male line to a royal ancestor common to him and the dead king. The law made it impossible for a woman or a foreign prince to gain the crown. It was a major factor in the relative stability of the French monarchy. Even in the anarchy of the French Wars of Religion, it ensured the succession of Henri of Bourbon to the French throne in 1589 after the assassination of Henri III despite being a distant cousin, although it is true that he had to convert to Catholicism to secure the crown. French writers pointed to the turbulent history of the English monarchy to emphasize the value of the Salic law.

**England.** During the century before Henry Tudor made good his claim to the crown in 1485, England experienced a bloody civil conflict called the War of the Roses (1455–1485) over the right to the throne. Even the Tudor dynasty came close to disaster when Mary I married Philip of Spain. Had they had a child, who would have inherited the crown, he or she would have been more Spanish than English, since Mary was half Spanish herself. Her half sister Elizabeth I avoided any such problem by not marrying, but that meant she had no children. When she died in 1603, James VI of Scotland, the grandson of Henry VIII's sister Margaret, became King James I. England and Scotland thus became a joint monarchy.

**Exceptions.** Scotland was a hereditary national monarchy, but its history demonstrated another problem with succession by blood-right. Five Scots rulers in a row were minors at the time of succession, including Mary, Queen of Scots, who was only a week old when her father died in 1542. That predicament disrupted the continuity of building royal power, and the Scots monarchy remained weak in respect to controlling its realm. In Portugal the lack of a law like the Salic law allowed Philip II of Spain to claim the throne of Portugal through his Portuguese mother, when the last male in the ruling dynasty (Cardinal Henry of the House of Avis) died in 1580. The union between Spain and Portugal was a joint monarchy, as Portugal kept its own government and officials. Even that was not enough to overcome a separate Portuguese identity, since they revolted in 1640 and regained their independence.

**Small Independent Realms.** As of 1350 there were many smaller principalities that were independent, in fact, if not always in legal status. Among them were the Kingdom of Navarre located in the Pyrennes between Spain and France, Muslim-ruled Granada in southern Spain, and several realms in the Balkans such as Serbia, which was conquered by the Ottoman Turks. Only a few avoided being absorbed into their larger neighbors by 1500. One that did was the Duchy of Savoy, tucked between France and Italy in the southern Alps. Its dukes on occasion emerged as significant players in international politics. The most important of these states was the Kingdom of Naples, which included Italy south of Rome and the islands of Sicily and Sardinia. Medieval politics had resulted in the royal families of Aragon and France having claims to its throne. After 1350 the Aragonese dynasty had the upper hand, but Charles VIII resurrected the old French claim when he led the first French invasion of Italy (1494). Ferdinand of Aragon responded to Charles's ousting of his cousin from Naples by sending forces to Italy. When the Spanish had driven the French out of the Kingdom of Naples, Ferdinand claimed it for himself instead of returning his relative to power. The Spanish monarchy ruled Naples for the next two centuries and through its position there dominated all of Italy.

**Italian City-States.** Northern Italy in the era 1350–1600 was the home of city-state republics, including Venice, which was one of the major powers of Europe. Theoretically part of the Holy Roman Empire, the Italian city-states had been independent since their victory over the emperor in 1176. Their form of government was the commune, in which those accepted as citizens, usually the members of the merchant and artisan guilds, had the right to participate in the meetings that determined policy and to be elected to public office. Participation in the communes ranged widely: from Venice, where the small number of elite families with power remained unchanged for centuries, to Florence, where over 10 percent of the adult males had some political rights. The number of independent republics had been large, perhaps as many as eighty in 1350. The city-states had always controlled the countryside and villages around them. None had ever been restricted to only the space within their walls, as was true for many cities outside of Italy, but by 1350 the territorial extent of the larger cities was rapidly expanding, taking over what had been independent cities. The best example was Venice, which built a large state on the Italian mainland that included Padua, with its esteemed university. As the trade center of Europe, Venice had also had extensive holdings in the eastern Mediterranean, including Crete and Cyprus. The Ottoman Turks, however, steadily captured the Venetian positions after the fall of Constantinople. Milan expanded its territory in the Po valley, to the point that it became a duchy in 1416. Florence also became a territorial power by conquering its neighbors, especially Pisa, which fell to Florence after a bitter siege in 1406.

**Condottieri.** The many wars that the expansion of the city-states touched off created a problem for the merchants and artisans who governed them. They were not eager to do their own military service, especially if it involved going out in the field for a long campaign; yet, they did not trust their own lower classes enough to arm them. Many cities had seen lower-class uprisings, of which the Ciompi Revolt in Florence in 1378 is the best known. They hired mercenary captains, called condottieri, to fight their wars for them. The captains often had the only armed force in a city-state and took advantage of the situation by seizing power, thereby becoming tyrants, a word used for someone who had taken control illegally. The principal example of a condottieri-turned-tyrant was Francesco Sforza, who declared himself duke of Milan in 1450. The jockeying for power among his descendents was one factor in bringing about the French invasions of Italy, as the French royal family also had a claim to Milan. Charles V intervened in 1519 after Francis I had himself proclaimed duke of Milan,

*The Holy Roman Empire* (1510). The Imperial Eagle carries the coats of arms of member nations on its wings (woodcut by Hans Burgkmair).

and Milan passed under Habsburg control after the imperial victory at Pavia (1525).

**The Medici.** Florence had a different kind of tyrant. A local family, the Medici, used its wealth and influence to dominate the city from behind the scenes. In 1531 Tuscany, Florence's region, was declared a duchy with a Medici as its duke. The only major city-state that retained its old form of government was Venice, which changed little before 1600.

**Hanseatic League.** The commune was the form of local urban governance across medieval Europe, but most of them also had to answer to the authority of king, duke, or bishop. The exception was a group of mostly northern German cities that formed the Hanseatic League, or Hansa. It was organized in 1356 to control trade along the coastlines of the North and Baltic Seas. At its height it numbered more than seventy cities, of which Bremen, Cologne, Hamburg, and Lubeck were the leaders; Lubeck was the center of the League where the assembly of members usually met once a year. It dominated trade in other cities that stretched from London to Novgorod in Russia. The League won a war against Denmark (1369–1370) to secure duty-free trade throughout Danish waters. For a century after, it was a major economic and political power in northern Europe, and its members were independent states, regardless of what larger political units might have claimed sovereignty over them. After 1500 the growing power of the Scandinavian kings and increasing competi-

tion from Dutch traders caused the League's decline, and by 1550 it had all but disappeared as a political power.

**Papal States.** There were also two unique states in Europe: the Papal States and the Swiss Confederation. The pope was the ruler of a group of territorial units that stretched from the coastline southwest of Rome across Italy to the Adriatic coast north of Bologna. Rome itself was administered separately from the rest of them. Since popes were elected, this monarchy was not hereditary; but in theory the pope was absolute ruler of these lands, although his authority over them was often limited, as it was during the period he resided in Avignon (1304–1377). A few popes tried to create a hereditary principality for their heirs out of the Papal States, and a major reason for Alexander VI's notoriety was that he came closest to achieving it for his son Cesare Borgia. His death in 1503 before Cesare had gained complete control and the subsequent election of Julius II prevented the dividing up of the Papal States. Julius, "the Warrior Pope," put great effort into regaining control over them, and at his death (1513) they were tightly under papal control.

**Swiss Confederation.** The Swiss Confederation was far different, although it too was a loosely affiliated group of political units. The Confederation was formed in 1291 when three cantons in central Switzerland came together to oppose the claims of the duke of Austria to authority over them. Their victory in the ensuing war persuaded other Swiss cantons and cities to join them, and by 1500 the Confederation had reached largely the borders of modern Switzerland. It can be described as an army without a state. It lacked a national leader or legislature and had no capital or common coinage. In most respects the thirteen cantons were independent republics. The only thing that the Swiss did in common was to wage war. When word came of an invasion (the Swiss rarely fought outside of their own borders), the fighting men of the cantons swiftly came together, and an assembly of the canton captains elected one of their own as commander and set the strategy for the conflict. It says a great deal about the nature of both government and warfare in the era 1350–1600 that for most of that period the Swiss army was probably the best in Europe.

Sources:

Christopher Allmand, ed., *The New Cambridge Medieval History, vol. VII, 1415–1500* (Cambridge & New York: Cambridge University Press, 1998).

Ernst Breisach, *Renaissance Europe, 1300–1517* (New York: Macmillan, 1973).

John H. Elliott, *Imperial Spain, 1469–1716* (New York: St. Martin's Press, 1964).

De Lamar Jensen, *Reformation Europe: Age of Reform and Revolution* (Lexington, Mass. & Toronto: D. C. Heath, 1981).

Jensen, *Renaissance Europe: Age of Recovery and Reconciliation* (Lexington, Mass. & Toronto: D. C. Heath, 1981).

Garrett Mattingly, *Renaissance Diplomacy* (Boston: Houghton Mifflin, 1971).

J. H. M. Salmon, *Society in Crisis: France in the Sixteenth Century* (New York: St. Martin's Press, 1975).

J. H. Shennan, *The Origins of the Modern European State, 1450–1725* (London: Hutchinson, 1974).

Daniel Waley, *The Italian City-Republics* (New York: McGraw-Hill, 1969).

## ADMINISTRATION: OFFICES AND INSTITUTIONS

**Amateurism.** Government administration in the era 1350–1600 was marked by amateurism. A large portion of government officials had no formal training for their positions. If they were nobles, it was expected that they were qualified by birth to undertake the business of government without any professional training or experience. It was marked also by clericalism; the word *clerk* came from the fact that the medieval clerks were clerics. Since they could read and write and calculate, clergymen often became officials, although that practice declined dramatically after 1517 in those lands that became Protestant. A third feature of administration was its small size. The number of officials and bureaucrats was amazingly small, even taking into consideration the smaller size of states and the population in that era. Around 1500 the French monarchy, which had the largest bureaucracy, had eight thousand to twelve thousand officials, about one per twelve thousand to sixteen thousand persons.

**Italian City-States.** The powerful Italian city-states were models of effective administration. Their wealth enabled them to finance large bodies of officials, who could be drawn from the bourgeois families with an interest in educating their sons in the skills necessary for administra-

tion. The ability to write the important documents in classical Latin became ever more highly valued as the Renaissance progressed, and the desire of cities to have famous humanists on the payroll helped to stimulate the growth of humanism. The spread of Roman law in Italy also stimulated the growth of bureaucracies, since the codes of Roman law took for granted the existence of officials in the extensive Roman bureaucracy and described their functions and responsibilities.

**Venice.** The increasing amount of record keeping demonstrated bureaucratic instincts of Italian urban officials. Venice set the standard in that respect, as it did in most aspects of administration, but it should be noted that the Church and its institutions had long been efficient record keepers. The Venetian archives are a treasure trove of information. In 1484 the Florentine chancellor ordered the recopying of the important records from its archives to be kept in a separate place should the originals be destroyed by fire. One reason for increased record keeping was the growing specialization of the officials; a small group of men was no longer in control of the affairs of government and knowledgeable about them. Separate offices for finances, justice, military affairs, and diplomacy were organized,

## RULE BY FEAR

The sixteenth-century Italian political philosopher Niccolò Machiavelli believed that a successful ruler must instill fear in his subjects. The following selection is from his *Il principe* (The Prince, 1513).

Here the question arises; whether it is better to be loved than feared or feared than loved. The answer is that it would be desirable to be both but, since that is difficult, it is much safer to be feared than to be loved, if one must choose. For on men in general this observation may be made: they are ungrateful, fickle, and deceitful, eager to avoid dangers, and avid for gain, and while you are useful to them they are all with you, offering you their blood, their property, their lives, and their sons so long as danger is remote, as we noted above, but when it approaches they turn on you. Any prince, trusting only in their words and having no other preparations made, will fall to his ruin, for friendships that are bought at a price and not by greatness and nobility of soul are paid for indeed, but they are not owned and cannot be called upon in time of need. Men have less hesitation in offending a man who is loved than one who is feared, for love is held by a bond of obligation which, as men are wicked, is broken whenever personal advantage suggests it, but fear is accompanied by the dread of punishment which never relaxes.

Source: Niccolò Machiavelli, *The Prince* (1513), translated and edited by Thomas G. Bergin (New York: Appleton-Century, 1947), p. 48.

A kneeling courier delivering a royal dispatch, illumination from *Historie romaine* (circa 1350) by Pierre Bersuire
(Bibliothèque Nationale, Paris)

which was a process that appeared later in the other European states as well. The best example of the creation of a professional body of officials was the Venetian diplomatic service. By 1431 Venice was dispatching trained diplomats to the major governments of Italy and northern Europe. Part of their duties was to pick up any information that might have an impact on Venice and especially its commerce with those places and report it promptly. When an ambassador was called home, he had to produce a lengthy report providing as much information as possible about the government, key officers, condition of the military and the economy, and prospects for war and peace in the place where he was posted. Those reports are today truly valuable historical sources.

**Doges and Councils.** Venice was the envy of Europe with its excellent administrative service and its internal stability. The head of the government was the doge (duke), who was elected for life, usually at fairly advanced age. His power declined after 1350, and by 1600 he was little more than a figurehead. Real authority resided in the Great Council, which was made up of all male members of the great families over the age of twenty-five; they totaled

about 2 percent of the city's population. Since it met only on Sundays, in order to carry on routine government business it elected a council of three hundred, which was known as the Senate. It received and sent out ambassadors, appointed the governors for its holdings in the Mediterranean and on the mainland, and named the committees that supervised the city. In times of war and other crises, a Council of Ten made the urgent decisions. Venice was thus an oligarchy; the vast majority of the people had no voice in the government. The oligarchy, while quick to watch out for its own interests, worked to ensure the well-being of all of the residents and was sufficiently successful that there were none of the violent uprisings that marked most other Italian cities. While hardly free of crime, Venice was the safest place in Europe as well as the most prosperous, and credit belonged largely to its oligarchy.

**Florence.** The other Italian cities maintained at least some elements of their earlier communal government; tensions that this situation created were responsible in part for frequent revolts. Florence retained more of the form of its commune than most, which seems to have been a factor in the social unrest that marked the fourteenth century, culminating in the major revolt of the laborers in the cloth industry in 1378 called the Ciompi Revolt. The Florentine elite responded by changing the government more in their favor, and it then remained unchanged until the creation of the duchy of Tuscany in 1531. Members of all the guilds were subject to the scrutiny, which determined if they were eligible to hold office. The scrutiny usually went against members of the lesser guilds, leaving the names of merchants and the wealthier artisans to be placed in a lottery for selection to the *signoria* for a two-month term. The eight-man *signoria* served as the executive council to supervise the government officials, but it had to take major decisions such as declarations of war to a council of all the citizens for approval. The *signoria* appointed the members of the chancery, whose first secretary was chief administrative officer for the city. It was this position that Niccolò Machiavelli held when he was ousted from power in 1512.

**The Medici.** The post-1378 Florentine system, especially the scrutiny, was open to manipulation by powerful politicians, and none did it better than the Medici, a wealthy banking family. In 1434 Cosimo de' Medici gained control of the city, and three generations of Medici dominated it until 1494, despite rarely holding public office. They ran a political machine that ensured their supporters were chosen for the *signoria*. The Medici were ousted in 1494 but returned to power in 1512. In 1531 Florence was transformed into a principality with a Medici becoming its duke.

**Holy Roman Empire.** The cities of northern Europe had governments largely similar to Florence's, although few had anything similar to the scrutiny. Only a handful had the kind of independence Florence did. The others answered to a superior power, usually a king or the emperor. Those cities in the Holy Roman Empire took part in what limited administration there was for the empire as a whole. The emperor appointed the imperial chancellor, who was the chief administrative officer. His staff of clerks and diplomats was considerably smaller than those for the other major states of Europe. When matters that concerned the entire Empire needed to be decided, such as a foreign war or the issue of religion during the Reformation, a meeting of the Imperial Diet was held. Its usual function was approving new taxes to allow the emperor to field an army. About 150 princes and great nobles, 100 bishops, and 65 towns had the right to send delegates to the Diet; not all attended every meeting. The northern Italian states and the Swiss refused to attend the Diet, which was therefore largely a German institution. Besides presiding over meetings of the Diet, the emperor's authority extended largely to directing the foreign policy of the Holy Roman Empire. He sent and received ambassadors, signed treaties, and declared war. On occasion he also served as supreme judge in matters of concern to the entire Empire. For a century after 1350, there were still imperial councils where proceedings were carried on in secret. Bitter complaints about them persuaded the emperor to curtail

their jurisdiction, and local administration thereafter was almost entirely under the control of the local political unit.

**England and France.** The growth of royal administration was a key characteristic in the national monarchies of the late Middle Ages. Since much of English administration was created by the Anglo-Norman kings after 1066, there were many similarities between the English and French governments. The basic principle of royal government was that the king embodied in himself all of the powers of government and handed out a share of it to others to ensure the well-ordered governance of the realm. The king could not do all of the business of the government, even if he wanted to, and most kings preferred to spend time hunting or with the army at war rather than deal with the details of finance or justice. Royal officials were the king's "creatures," although his ability to remove them was often stymied by the lifetime tenure that some had, such as the chancellor in France. The kings had always surrounded themselves with close friends, who gave him advice. By 1350 they formed a formal council called the privy council in England and the secret council in France. There was also a much larger council, the great council, made up of the powerful nobles and royal officials. Major decisions were made first in the privy council and then confirmed by the great council.

**Great Seal.** The chancellor, in England called the lord chancellor, was the chief officer of the realm under the king. His most important duty was keeping the great seal, which had to be used on royal degrees for them to be valid. He could object to sealing a degree on the grounds that it was contrary to the laws of the realm, which usually caused the king to reconsider it, although he could also formally order the chancellor to seal it and make it law. He also supervised the system of justice and served as the chief of the law courts; in France he was automatically the head of the high court called the *Parlement*.

**Finances.** In England all royal financial matters were handled in the Exchequer, headed by the lord treasurer. The French system was divided into a chamber of accounts, which was responsible for accounting, and a treasury, which collected and dispensed royal revenues. The French monarchy had three types of taxes: the largest was the taille, originally a war tax that appeared during the Hundred Years' War (1337–1453), which was collected only from commoners on the grounds that the nobles served the king with their blood; the gabelle was a tax on salt; and the *aide,* a sales tax and the oldest of the three, developed out of the practice by medieval kings to ask for aid for war. In addition, the king had revenues from royal properties, tolls on commerce, and his role as head of the feudal system. The English tax system was more complicated, as the king collected a large variety of taxes, including the old danegeld, which had been first imposed by Alfred the Great to fight the Vikings.

**Military.** War was the major reason why kings raised taxes. In peacetime they were expected to live off of their properties and feudal dues. The king was the commander-in-chief of the army, and in England it rarely fought without him in command. On the few occasions when he was not present, a prince took his place. In France there was a larger military establishment. The constable was the king's lieutenant in the field when the king was not present with the army, which was fairly often, and he also had extensive duties in seeing to the army's maintenance during peacetime. He was also a major figure in the king's councils. By 1500 his responsibilities at the court frequently prevented him from commanding in battle, and the marshals, whose original task was to keep order in the army as it marched, often took command. By 1600 there were four marshals in the French army. The admiral was responsible for coastal defense; he rarely commanded a fleet at sea. The French army that fought in the Hundred Years' War, except for its mercenary Italian crossbowmen, was made up largely of the feudal levy. Nobles who held fiefs were obliged to provide military service for them. The English fighting men were almost all paid for their service in that war. The English monarchy had replaced feudal service with a tax called scutage that replaced military service for much of the English nobility. France did not get a professional army until 1445, when Charles VII created fifteen royal cavalry companies. They were paid out of the taille, which the king had been given the right in 1439 to collect for the duration of the war with England. Like nearly every war tax in history, it continued to be collected after the war.

**Parliament.** In 1362 Edward III promised the English Parliament that the monarchy would not impose a new tax on wool without its consent. It was the first time that the king committed himself to consulting Parliament about raising taxes. For more than a century the English kings had been calling meetings of the major men of the realm because they found it easier to raise money if they had the consent of those who had to pay. By 1362 Parliament was organized into two houses: Lords, which included the bishops and the greater nobles; and Commons, which had representatives from the lesser nobility and the towns. By joining the petty nobles with the bourgeoisie from the towns, the English system avoided the problem of the bitter division between nobles and commoners found in France. The kings found that they usually could get what they asked for from the Parliament and called it to assemble often. It became an important part of the English system of government. When Henry VIII asked it to approve of his degrees for breaking the ties of the English Church with the papacy in 1531, it created another important precedent for the steadily increasing authority of the Parliament.

**Estates General.** In France a similar institution was called the Estates General. It was composed of three estates: the churchmen or First Estate, the nobles or Second Estate, and the commoners, usually townspeople, or Third Estate. The final vote on an issue was done by the whole estate, that is, a total of three votes. On issues such as taxation, the Third Estate usually found itself outvoted two to one. The commoners were far less likely to accept a new tax imposed on them than was true in England, where there was a greater sense that their representatives had approved of it. The Estates General, therefore, never developed an important role in French government, because the kings found that it did not prove helpful and did not call it often. Unlike England, there were provincial estates in France, which were easily bent to the king's will, and the French king found it easier to raise taxes from them than the Estates General.

**The Cortes.** Similar institutions were found in nearly every medieval realm. In the Spanish kingdoms they were called the Cortes, which also had three estates as in France. In Aragon the Cortes gained extraordinary power to supervise the king and his officials, and in the century before the union with Castile it was the most powerful in Europe. The Spanish monarchs after 1469 preferred the Castilian system of a weak Cortes, and by 1592, when Philip II formed a unified Spanish government, the Aragonese Cortes had lost most of its power.

**The Sejm.** In Poland-Lithuania, the representative institution, the Sejm, gained power to the detriment of the king's authority in the sixteenth century. Every nobleman was eligible to attend along with delegates from a large number of towns, and even Jews sent deputies representing their communities. In 1505 King Alexander pledged that the king could decide nothing without the consent of the Sejm. Once the Polish monarchy became truly elective after the Jagellonian dynasty ended in 1572, the Sejm steadily increased its powers through concessions demanded from the successful candidates, and it changed from being a valuable check on royal power to becoming an obstacle to effective government in Poland-Lithuania.

**Castile, Austria, and the Papal States.** The other monarchies of western and central Europe were administered largely as France and England were. Their governments had developed from much the same institutions and practices, and France in particular served as a model for other realms, especially for those on its borders. Castile's administration was a smaller version of France's. The principalities of the empire had even smaller administrations, although that of Austria grew in size and sophistication after the Habsburgs became entrenched as emperors. Among the most poorly administered realms before 1500 were the Papal States. Despite the impressive advances in administration that the popes made for governing the Church, they made little effort to improve the governing machinery for their Italian lands until the reign of Pope Julius II (1503–1513).

**Ottoman Empire.** While the Christian states had administrations that were largely similar across Europe, the Ottoman Empire's was far different. The sultans took over the administration of the Byzantine Empire they conquered, but it too was different from the Western style of government. The Byzantine emperor had been the absolute despot of his empire in matters of state and religion, and the sultan easily took over the same role. As the absolute head of Islam he protected its holy places, inter-

Château de Chambord, built by order of Francis I, king of France, in 1519

preted its law, which served as civil law in Muslim states, and led its fighting men in war against the infidels. In a way that was never true in Western Christendom with its competition between pope and rulers, the sultan combined in himself supreme authority of both state and religion. The sultan also ruled millions of Christians and Jews who lived in his empire. The sultan did appoint the patriarch of the Greek Orthodox Church and the chief rabbi of the Jews, but as long as those subjects paid their taxes, which were heavier than for Muslims, and did not rebel, they were allowed to govern themselves in what were called *mullets*. The most unusual feature of the relationship between the Ottoman state and its non-Muslim subjects was the practice of taking boys from Christian families as part of their tax and raising them as Muslims and soldiers. They formed the Janissaries, whose fanaticism in battle and loyalty to the sultan became legendary. They often gained high government and military positions, although they officially were the sultan's slaves. The practice led to many conversions to Islam among the Christians of the Balkans, creating the Muslim population that is still present in many Balkan states.

**Sultan's Household.** Since the sultan was the absolute despot of his empire, his household was the center of administration. That had been true earlier in the Middle Ages in the West, but it had disappeared by 1350, although many of the royal offices had emerged out of the royal household. Part of the household was the harem, which included all of the women at the court. Muslim law requires the seclusion of women, and the harem was guarded from prying eyes by a corps of eunuchs (emasculated men). The sultan's mother was the most powerful member of the harem. Beginning with Selim II's succession in 1566, she was usually young when her son succeeded to the throne, and she maintained power and influence over him for a long time. In theory she was less powerful than the grand vizier, but often she had greater influence than he did. The grand vizier was the chief administrative officer of the empire. He received the sultan's seal upon gaining the post and had the right to make nearly all decisions and appointments for the sultan, although he needed to clear the major ones with his ruler. When the seal was taken from him, it was the signal that he had been dismissed from office; his execution frequently followed.

**Change.** After Selim II became sultan, the independence of the grand vizier increased significantly. One official who answered directly to the sultan and not through

A fifteenth-century Flemish miniature of Charles the Bold presiding over a Burgundian court
(Osterreichische Nationalbibliothek, Vienna)

the grand vizier was the treasurer, who had complete authority over the imperial fiscal system. Another was the commander of the Janissary corps, who usually rose through the ranks and in the later empire, sometimes to the office of grand vizier. This method of advancement meant that the major officials of the Turkish state often came from Christian families, but they were Muslims by the time they gained office, as all officials had to be. The admirals of the Ottoman fleet usually were also former Christians, but they were renegades who came into Turkish service as adults. By bringing some of their subject peoples into government service, the Ottoman sultans were able to overcome the problem of the relatively small numbers of ethnic Turks in their empire, bind the subject peoples more tightly to their rule, and create an impressive administration for their vast empire that lasted into the modern era.

**Colonies.** The effective administration of vast overseas colonial empires was also a problem for the Spanish and Portuguese after 1492. In the East the Portuguese were content to build up an empire of trading posts without directly ruling more than a handful of people, but in Brazil they faced much the same situation as the Spanish, and there the administration was largely the same. Already in 1503 the Spanish government established the Board of Trade in Seville to control completely all trade and travel to and from the New World. In 1524 it created the Council of the Indies, which oversaw all appointments in the colonies, created and implemented policy there, and controlled the military. Once the Inca Empire had been conquered in 1529, Spanish-ruled America was divided into two kingdoms, New Spain (Mexico) and Peru (most of South America), and Spanish viceroys (vice-kings) were appointed to rule them. They had most of the authority and privileges of the king but only for a three-year term. While they were the heads of the royal courts in the colonies called the *audiencia*, the other judges could appeal to the king in Madrid, which was a major check on the viceroy's power. Another check was royal appointment of the captains of the captaincies-general into which the large colonial kingdoms were divided. All of the major officers in the Spanish colonies came from Spain, and most intended to return home after their terms were up and their fortunes made. This situation prevented them from becoming well entrenched in their colonial posts and too sympathetic to the colonial-born Spaniards, the Creoles. The Spanish kings were amazingly successful in appointing men who remained loyal, and they also established a loyal administration for their vast empire that lasted until 1800.

Sources:

Christopher R. Friedrichs, *The Early Modern City, 1450–1750* (London & New York: Longman, 1995).

Denys Hay, *Europe in the Fourteenth and Fifteenth Centuries* (London & New York: Longman, 1989).

De Lamar Jensen, *Reformation Europe: Age of Reform and Revolution* (Lexington, Mass. & Toronto: D. C. Heath, 1981).

Jensen, *Renaissance Europe: Age of Recovery and Reconciliation* (Lexington, Mass. & Toronto: D. C. Heath, 1981).

David Nicholas, *The Transformation of Europe 1300–1600* (New York: Oxford University Press, 1999).

Eugene F. Rice Jr. and Anthony Grafton, *The Foundations of Early Modern Europe, 1460–1559* (New York: Norton, 1994).

## COMBAT

**Transition.** In 1350 European warfare was beginning the transition from the medieval style, in which the knight or heavily armored cavalryman dominated the battlefield, to early modern warfare, in which infantrymen reigned supreme. Shortly before 1350 there had occurred two major battles in which foot soldiers had been victorious over cavalrymen—Laupen (1339), where Swiss infantrymen wielded pikes and halberds, and Crécy (1346), where English longbowmen were supported by dismounted knights. The English longbow archers' successes in the Hundred Years' War (1337–1453) are far better known, but the Swiss use of the pike and halberd had the greater impact, since it remained a powerful factor in warfare until well into the sixteenth century.

**Knights.** A knight's proper opponent was another knight, not the poorly armed and untrained infantrymen who accompanied medieval armies. Knightly disdain for fighting dismounted peasant levies was a major reason for the English victories in the Hundred Years' War. Knights spent little time drilling together. Imbued with the old Germanic tradition that the best warrior led the others into battle, the knights competed to be the first to close with the enemy, making it difficult for their commanders to get them to wait for simple tactical maneuvers, such as flanking an opponent's position. Despite such deficiencies, knights were for three hundred years nearly invulnerable to the weapons used by European infantrymen. The advent of pikes and longbows caused knights to use plate armor for themselves and their horses, which were more likely to be killed in battle than the riders. Despite the increased protection it offered, plate armor created problems. It was too expensive for the less-wealthy nobles, and the number of fully armored knights declined. Its weight required larger and more costly warhorses, which were slower and less maneuverable, allowing the knights to do little more than make a straight-ahead charge. Despite being defeated by infantrymen in various battles after 1350, the armored

horsemen remained a potent element in war, especially in the French army, until the mid sixteenth century.

**English Innovations.** Having learned of the longbow from the Welsh in the thirteenth century, the English fought a war with the Scots (1295–1333) in which they developed the combination of longbow archers and dismounted knights that proved so effective against the French in the Hundred Years' War. At Crécy and the nearly identical battle at Poitiers (1356), the English commanders, Edward III and Edward the Black Prince, respectively, were able to choose the terrain for the battles—hilltops where they placed their forces to await the French attacks. Both commanders dismounted most of their knights to form two divisions and placed archers between them and on the flanks. Meanwhile, the commander stationed himself with a mounted reserve, ready to strike at an opportune time. At Crécy the French attack began when crossbowmen were sent forward first to inflict what casualties they could on the English and to disorder their lines. The English archers, having greater range and firing from the high ground, easily drove the crossbowmen back. The French knights, cursing the footmen as cowards, charged up the hill without waiting for them to clear the ground. As a result, the momentum of the horsemen slowed as they charged through the retreating bowmen, and they became easy targets for the English archers. Few made it through the hail of arrows to exchange blows with the English dismounted knights at the top of the hill. At Poitiers, the French king, John II, decided the lesson to be learned from Crécy was that the English had won because they had dismounted their knights. It was a valid decision because horses had been the principal victims of the archers at Crécy, but John ordered his knights to dismount too far from the English lines. They were nearly exhausted by the time they had made it up the hill, and they were thrown back after a bloody fight. John then led his mounted reserve into the battle and was captured. The enormous ransom the English demanded for him nearly depleted French royal coffers and created popular unrest for a decade after.

**French Reactions.** For the remainder of the Hundred Years' War the English used the identical formation and tactics for pitched battles with constant success. At Agincourt (1415), Henry V had to fight in a soggy plowed field rather than on a hilltop, but the result was the same. What defeats the English suffered occurred when they did not have the opportunity to dictate the terrain and battle tactics. At Orléans (1429), they lost partly because Joan of Arc had restored French morale but also because they had to defend their siege lines and could not form up in their usual style. The boost Joan gave the French continued after her death in 1431, and the English were put on the defensive until their army in northern France was forced to fight at Formigny (1450). They took their usual formation at the top of a hill, but the French had finally found a way to deal with the English combination of archers and dismounted knights. They brought up four small cannon that fired on the archers on the flanks of the English line.

On 19 September 1356 an English army, led by Edward, The Black Prince, defeated French forces under John II at the Battle of Poitiers. The late-fourteenth-century chronicler Jean Froissart, a Frenchman who later served as personal secretary to the wife of Edward III, began writing about the battle a year after it occurred, although he would continue revising his history until his death around 1405.

The fighters on both sides endured much pain: king John with his own hands did that day marvels in arms: he had an axe in his hands wherewith he defended himself and fought in the breaking of the press. Near to the king there was taken the earl of Tancarville . . . and a little above that under the banner of the capital of Buch was taken sir Charles of Artois and divers other knights and squires. The chase endured to the gates of Poitiers: there were many slain and beaten down, horse and man, for they of Poitiers closed their gates and would suffer none to enter; wherefore in the street before the gate was horrible murder, men hurt and beaten down. . . .

Then there was a great press to take the king, and such as knew him cried, "Sir, yield you, or else ye are but dead." There was a knight of Saint-Omer's, retained in wages with the king of England, called sir Denis Morbeke, who had served the Englishmen five years before, because in his youth he had forfeited the realm of France for a murder that he did at Saint-Omer's. It happened so well for him, that he was next to the king when they were about to take him: he stept forth into the press, and by strength of his body and arms he came to the French king and said in good French, "Sir, yield you." The king beheld the knight and said, "To whom shall I yield me?" Where is my cousin the prince of Wales? If I might see him, I would speak with him."

Denis answered and said: "Sir, he is not here; but yield you to me and I shall bring you to him." "Who be you?" quoth the king. "Sir, I am Denis of Morbeke, a knight of Artois; but I serve the king of England because I am banished from the realm of France and I have forfeited all that I had there." Then the king gave him his right gauntlet, saying, "There I yield me to you."

The same day of the battle at night the prince made a supper in his lodging to the French king and to the most part of the great lords that were prisoners. The prince made the king and his son, the lord James of Bourbon . . . to sit all at one board, and other lords, knights and squires at other tables; and always the prince served before the king as humbly as he could, and would not sit at the king's board for any desire that the king could make, but he said he was not sufficient to sit at the table with so great a prince as the king was. But then he said to the king, "Sir, for God's sake make none evil nor heavy cheer, though God this day did not consent to follow your will; for, sir, surely the king my father shall bear you as much honour and amity as he may do, and shall accord with you so reasonably that ye shall ever be friends together after. And, sir, methink ye ought to rejoice, though the journey be not as ye would have had it, for this day ye have won the high renown of prowess and have passed this day in valiantness all other of your party. Sir, I say not this to mock you, for all that be on our party, that saw every man's deeds, are plainly accorded by true sentence to give you the prize and chaplet." Therewith the Frenchmen began to murmur and said among themselves how the prince had spoken nobly, and that by all estimation he should prove a noble man, if God send him life and persevere in such good fortune.

Source: G. C. Macauly, ed., *The Chronicles of Froissart*, translated by John Bourcher, Lord Berners (London: Macmillan, 1904), p. 201.

Unwilling to take the artillery fire for long, the archers broke ranks to rush the cannon. They overran the guns, but by breaking ranks they made themselves vulnerable to a French cavalry charge. After eliminating the archers the French turned their attention to the dismounted knights and crushed them. Three years later the French again used cannon effectively to defeat the English forces in Gascony and drive the English out of Bordeaux, their last stronghold in the southwest. The conclusion of the Hundred Years' War did not end the use of the archer-dismounted knight combination. During the War of the Roses, the civil war that wracked England from 1455 to 1485, both sides used the same formation and virtually identical tactics against each other.

**Swiss Tactics.** The archer-dismounted knight tactics won many victories for the English in the Hundred Years' War, yet these tactics could not be adopted outside of England because of the lack of archers in other lands. The Swiss system of pike and halberd proved more revolutionary, because it could be easily adopted across Europe, especially by German foot soldiers who became known as *landsknechts*. The pike and halberd were not new weapons, but in the hands of sturdy Swiss mountainmen they proved effective against knights. In a series of battles in the fourteenth century the Swiss defeated Austrian and Burgundian cavalry forces and established both their style of fighting and the independence of Switzerland. At Sempach (1386), while fighting Austrian cavalrymen, the

*The Battle of Poitiers*, 1356, illumination from a fifteenth-century manuscript (Bibliothèque Nationale, Paris)

Swiss came up with the formation and tactics that became their trademark. When news of an invasion came, the Swiss assembled quickly and marched toward the enemy already in the formation they would take on the battlefield, that is, in three columns, with the lead column in the center flanked by a column on each side. The pikemen were at the head of each column with the halberdmen behind them. At the rear were soldiers armed with either crossbows or firearms. When the lead column, often well ahead of the others, spotted the enemy, it would move immediately to the attack. As the lead column engaged the enemy's center, first one flanking column, then the other, would strike the enemy on his flanks. The center of the field would remain clear for the lead column to fall back if it needed to without the disruption of the sort that ruined the French at Crécy. This formation was always successful in the era before 1515 whenever the Swiss fought an army close to theirs in size. On several occasions small units of Swiss faced much larger forces. They then formed a circle of pikemen bristling with pike in every direction, called the "hedgehog," and fought to the last man. The enormous number of casualties they inflicted earned them a reputation for inordinate bloodshed. Their bloody reputa-

tion was further enhanced by that fact that the Swiss, unaffected by chivalry and the practice of taking prisoners for ransom, killed any captives they took.

**Battle of Grandson.** The best example of the Swiss style in action occurred at the Battle of Grandson (1476). Duke Charles the Bold of Burgundy had invaded Switzerland with his forces of Burgundian knights, Flemish pikemen, Italian crossbowmen, and German handgunners along with the best artillery train of the era. The size of his force was about 14,000 men, while a surviving muster roll puts the Swiss army at exactly 18,113. Charles chose the terrain for the battle, a broad plain well suited to cavalry charges and artillery fire. Nonetheless, the Swiss moved immediately to the attack upon sighting their enemy. They repulsed the Burgundian cavalry charge, dashed through the field of cannon fire, and smashed into Charles's infantry, which quickly broke ranks and ran. Charles, an energetic commander, regrouped his army and fought two more major battles with the Swiss. In the Battle of Nancy (1477), he was killed, "cleaved from crown to chin" by a halberd blow to the head.

**War Wagons.** The Swiss were fortunate that during their period of military superiority they did not have to face an enemy as strong in missile fire as the English army that fought the French. Soon after 1500, their style of warfare became obsolete in the face of the continuing development of gunpowder weapons. They suffered their first major setback at Marignano (1515), where French cannon fire made them vulnerable to a cavalry charge. Although gunpowder weapons appeared in Europe early in the fourteenth century, they had little impact on combat for a century. The first army to use them successfully was Jan Zizka's Hussite forces during the revolt that broke out in Bohemia in 1415. The Hussites were mostly Czech-speaking peasants inspired with a combination of nationalistic zeal against the German dynasty that ruled Bohemia and religious fervor against the Catholic Church that was seen as corrupt and too dominated by German prelates. Zizka's manpower was made up of untrained foot soldiers who could not be expected to stand up against the German knights that constituted the enemy's forces. His solution was the use of war wagons. He placed a squad of men in each wagon; half of them had a variety of edged weapons, and the others had handcannon. The Hussites also had wagons on which small cannon were mounted. Although gunpowder weapons of that time were both highly inaccurate and slow to reload, the wagons, which were drawn up in a line, gave the Hussites a stable platform and a defensive position from which to fire them against the large target presented by their mounted foes. Zizka gained victory after victory using this tactic. His death in 1424 did not eliminate the Hussite advantage, but success led to a split within the Hussite movement between moderates and radicals and a bloody civil war between the two factions. At the Battle of Lipany (1434), the moderates crushed the radicals and then negotiated favorable peace terms with the German king.

**Spanish Square.** The Hussite war wagon had no impact outside of Bohemia, and gunpowder weapons had only a limited effect on war over the next sixty years. By the time of the French invasions of Italy, which began in 1494, both cannon and firearms had been improved sufficiently that they could be used as effective weapons in the field. Using an artillery train of eighty large cannon on mobile carriages, French king Charles VIII had great success in taking Italian fortifications. At the Battle of Seminara (1495) the French army crushed a combined Spanish-Italian army. Faced with the need to reform his army after its crushing defeat, Ferdinand of Aragon decided to concentrate on the infantry and introduced the combination of firearms and pike that became known as the Spanish Square. By then the first effective firearm, the arquebus, had been developed, but it still took at least a minute to reload, probably longer in the disorder of the battlefield, and was highly inaccurate. Foot soldiers using the arquebus would be quickly overrun by a charging enemy, especially if it was cavalry, before they could reload. The solution was to use pikemen to protect the handgunners as they reloaded and to charge an enemy line if the arquebus fire had broken it. At the Battle of Cerignola (1503), Gonzalo Fernández de Córdoba, the

Spanish commander, dug trenches in front of his lines to further shield his troops. Over the next twenty years the Spanish infantry was victorious as long as it had the time to dig entrenchments, and the French and their Swiss mercenaries relied on frontal assault on the enemy lines. At the Battle of Pavia (1525), the combination of arquebusiers and pikemen in Holy Roman Emperor Charles V's army formed up without entrenchments and defeated the French. The Spanish Square was the dominant formation in combat for the next century across Europe.

**Ottoman Turks.** The major military power of the sixteenth century that did not adopt the Spanish Square was the Ottoman Empire. The Turkish army continued to depend on the combination of light and heavy cavalry and infantry that had served it so well since the early fourteenth century. Ottoman horsemen used a short bow which remained the principal weapon of the Turkish army until 1600. The Ottoman sultans also created a force of armored horsemen similar to the knights. It always remained small in size but was highly effective when used in coordination with the light cavalry. The most notorious part of the Ottoman army was its infantry, known as janissaries. They were soldiers who had been taken as small boys from Christian subjects of the sultan and raised in the barracks as Muslims. They constituted an elite corps of infantrymen totally loyal to the sultan. The early janissaries used the bow but adopted the arquebus by 1500. This change demonstrated that the Turks were abreast of weaponry developments in that era, although they fell behind by the late sixteenth century. The Turks also had been quick to develop a strong artillery train, which served them well at the siege of Constantinople (1453).

**Battle of Mohács.** The major campaign for the Turks after their victory over the Byzantine Empire in 1453 was the conquest of Hungary. In 1526 Sultan Süleyman I (the Magnificent) gave battle to an Hungarian army at Mohács. The Hungarian force was made up largely of heavy cavalry, and the battle began when the Hungarians charged into the lines of Turkish light cavalry. In what may have been a planned tactic, the Turkish horsemen fled from the field only to expose the Hungarians to devastating fire from janissaries and artillery pieces. The Turks had chained cannon together to prevent the Hungarians from breaking through their line. At the same time, the Ottoman heavy cavalry charged into the Hungarians from the flanks, while a large detachment of light cavalry, which had been sent on a wide flanking movement, crashed into the Hungarian rear. The Hungarians suffered enormous casualties, including their king, and Suleiman marched to Budapest and took it without resistance. In 1529 he brought his army to the walls of Vienna. The well-defended city withstood the Turkish siege, and Austria remained in Christian control.

**Naval Warfare.** Perhaps because of his defeat at Vienna, Süleyman turned his attention to the naval contest in the Mediterranean Sea. Christianity and Islam, the two rival religions that divided the lands bordering the sea, had been involved in a naval war for nearly a thousand years, but it reached its climax in the sixteenth century. Warfare in the Mediterranean still was a matter for rowed galleys because the winds on the sea were too light and unpredictable for sailing ships of that era to use under battle conditions. Despite the two-thousand-year history of galley warfare, large-scale fleet actions were relatively uncommon. The greatest battle in the history of galleys was the Battle of Lepanto (1571) off the western Greek coast. The Muslim fleet was manned by the Ottoman Turks and North African corsairs, while the Christian flotilla consisted of ships from Spain, Venice, Genoa, and Malta. The two fleets had more than two hundred galleys each, and the manpower, including the rowers, in each fleet was about eighty thousand men. Naval combat was still largely like combat on land. The basic tactic was for galleys to form up in a long line opposite one another and charge toward the foe. They fired the few cannon they carried, placed at the bow, at as close a range as possible to do damage to the defenders of the enemy ship before the ships grappled. Armed men then dashed onto the enemy's deck to seize control of the ship in hand-to-hand combat. The Christian fleet at Lepanto had something of a secret weapon, however. The Venetians had developed a much larger rowed ship called the galleass, which was capable of carrying more cannon and handgunners than the smaller galleys. The heavy firepower from the galleasses played a major role in the overwhelming Christian victory. Three-quarters of the Ottoman fleet was captured or destroyed; twenty-two thousand Turks were killed or taken prisoner; and as many as fifteen thousand Christian galley slaves were freed. Despite the overwhelming Christian victory, they failed to follow up on their success, as the Christian alliance quickly fell apart. The principal result of Lepanto was a great increase in the size of galleys, building on the example of the galleasses. Their larger size, however, made them slower and less maneuverable and more vulnerable to the broadside-firing sailing ships from the Atlantic that were making excursions into the Mediterranean by 1600.

**Spanish Armada.** The most significant conflict between Atlantic fleets before 1600 was the Spanish Armada. Stung by English pirate attacks on Spanish shipping and English support for Dutch Protestant rebels, Philip II decided that it was necessary to invade England and replace Queen Elizabeth I with a Catholic ruler. In 1588 he ordered his fleet to sail into the English Channel to take control of it so that his army in the Low Countries fighting the Dutch could cross over to England without interference from the English navy. The Armada consisted of 123 ships, including thirty-five galleons, manned by 8,000 sailors. Philip had assembled the Armada from all of the resources available to him, which included many ships from the Mediterranean to serve as transports for the 19,000 soldiers. They were not built for the storms and rough waters of the North Atlantic, and several had to be left behind. Disease spread quickly among the seasick soldiers crowded below the decks.

Late-sixteenth-century parade armor belonging to Alessandro Farnese, Duke of Parma (from Felipe Fernandez-Armesto, *The Spanish Armada*, 1988)

**Protestant Wind.** The Armada reached the western English coast and sailed eastward along it toward Belgium. The English ships came out from their ports and followed the Armada as it passed, but it maintained a tight defensive formation and lost no ships to English attacks during this stage of the voyage. When the Spanish reached the Belgian coast, they found that there was no harbor large enough to accommodate the entire fleet. They were forced to put down anchors in the open sea. The next night the English set several old ships on fire and sent them into the Armada's anchorage. In a near panic the Spanish captains cut their anchors to get away from the fire ships, and the wind scattered them northward into the North Sea. The next morning the Armada's galleons formed a defensive line against the English fleet to protect the scattered transports, and the only significant fighting, called the Battle of Gravelines, occurred. The English innovations in creating a new style of fighting at sea were successful, especially the use of retractable gun carriages, which allowed for quicker reloading. The Spanish apparently did not have them and were forced to reload their guns while their muzzles were fixed outside the hull. One galleon was sunk by a line of English ships that sailed along it firing broadsides, and several more had to be beached. With the "Protestant wind" continuing to blow to the north, the English broke off, and the Armada soon was blown far into the North Sea. Unable to return the way it had come, the Armada was forced to sail around Scotland and Ireland to get back to Spain. Many of the ships, battered by battle and violent storms, either sank or were forced to put into shore, where most wrecked because of the lack of anchors. Eventually sixty-four ships made it home, but even they had heavy casualties, so only about one-third of the Armada's manpower survived. The failure of the Armada was not the end of Spanish naval power, since Philip II rebuilt his fleet along the English model in the next years. Its most important impact was convincing the English monarchy that it should invest in building a substantial royal navy that would dominate the seas by the end of the next century.

Sources:

Larry H. Addington, *The Patterns of War through the Eighteenth Century* (Bloomington & Indianapolis: Indiana University Press, 1990).

David Eltis, *The Military Revolution in Sixteenth Century Europe* (London and New York: I. B. Tauris, 1995).

John Keegan, *The Face of Battle* (New York: Viking, 1976).

Geoffrey Parker, *The Military Revolution: Military Innovation and the Rise of the West, 1500–1800* (Cambridge & New York: Cambridge University Press, 1988).

## CRIME AND PUNISHMENT

**Medieval Origins.** The English epic *Beowulf* is a tale of bravery and vengeance. The evil monster Grendel periodically kills Hrothgar's warriors until the hero Beowulf arrives. In a heated battle, Beowulf tears Grendel's arm off and forces the mortally wounded monster to flee. Peace is briefly restored, but Grendel's mother soon appears seeking blood vengeance for the death of her son. She kills Hrothgar's favorite adviser and thus the vendetta continues. Eventually, Beowulf kills Grendel's mother, and the feud ends because Grendel has no living relatives.

**Transition.** The unwritten code of the blood feud demanded vengeance whenever kin or a knightly retainer was killed. These contests could end when one side was eliminated or when a killer paid *wergild*, or the price of a man, to the family of the victim. The money served as an example that the dead man's kin had acted correctly by defending him. The use of wergild was an early step in the transition from blood feud to the modern court system. Medieval crimes were viewed as attacks on an entire family, and thus the family was required to pursue justice. Blood feuds were replaced with civilized court cases in the twelfth

century because territorial lords had sufficient power to legislate kinship vengeance. Rulers redefined crimes as attacks on the state instead of mere attacks on the individual. These changes contributed to the distinction between criminal cases and civil cases. Individuals could still pursue civil cases, but the state became responsible for criminal cases. Twelfth-century changes in the notion of crime evolved over the course of the Renaissance and Reformation into new forms of justice, new beliefs about immorality, and new ways of handling perpetrators. These changes contributed to the origins of the modern prison system.

**Refinement.** Urban officials were also seeking ways to end private vengeance within their walls at the same time that powerful territorial rulers redefined the role of the courts. William Shakespeare's *Romeo and Juliet* (1594–1595) is a story of family vengeance that tears a city apart and creates unnecessary strife. Similarly, cities and territorial princes transferred the burden of justice from the family of the person wronged to the state: families ceased to accuse someone of wronging them and the state began to inquire into criminal activities and eventually to bring charges against criminals. This shift from accusatory justice to inquisitorial justice did not happen at the same time across Europe, and some areas never adopted inquisitorial trials. Yet, the rise of juries in accusatory systems, such as in England, corresponded with the rise of inquisition processes in areas that combined Roman and canon law traditions.

**Ordeals.** These changes originated in 1215 when the Fourth Lateran Council of the Roman Church outlawed ordeals from church courts and thus effectively eliminated them from secular courts as well. The ordeal was a way to test whether a person was telling the truth. An accused person would offer an oath certifying the honesty of testimony and then the person was physically tested, usually with hot water or hot irons. The ordeal was a natural development of the blood-feud mentality of Beowulf's age: Beowulf fought three main battles, or ordeals, where he proved that God was on his side by killing his opponent. The shift from actual battle to the battle of oaths included a Christian component: oaths were sacred and it was believed that God would intervene and determine the guilt or innocence of the accused. The Fourth Lateran Council prohibited priests from participating in ordeals and thus the ordeal disappeared from church and state judicial processes. However, one remnant of the ordeal was the belief that torture was an acceptable form of extracting a confession. The ordeal was, after all, a form of torture meant to persuade the guilty to confess.

**Marian Statutes.** The elimination of the ordeal as a viable judicial process forced rulers across Europe to develop suitable replacements. The methods tended to develop along two lines: accusatory justice with trials in England, and inquisitorial trials based on a mixture of Roman and canon law for the rest of Europe. English accusatory trials were based on someone bringing an accusation against another person. If the accused was imprisoned, then the accuser was also usually imprisoned. The entire process attempted to be fair to both parties. To maintain impartiality, the trial was a public event with both sides sharing access to the evidence. Accusations were brought before a justice of the peace, a title that first appeared in the 1360s, a decade after the onset of the Black Death. Justices were usually local gentry who were initially called upon to deal with vagrancy and other local problems. Over time, they became responsible for all pretrial procedures. Justices of the peace would try minor criminal cases but more serious crimes were tried before juries. Jurors were initially citizens who came forward as witnesses before the monarch's judges. By the fourteenth century, jurors assumed their modern role as evaluators of the case. Grand juries were used to hand the accused over to the court for trial and petty juries of twelve jurors rendered verdicts. After Henry VIII broke with the Roman Church, the crown attempted to use criminal law as a tool for enforcing conformity to the Church of England. The Court of Star Chamber (criminal cases) and the Court of High Commission (ecclesiastical law and doctrinal cases) sat without juries and adopted the inquisitorial methods of Continental legal systems. The two courts were highly partisan and were finally abolished in 1640 when Parliament gained sufficient power to do away with them. In 1554–1555, the Marian Statutes, named after Queen Mary, established the procedures upon which the modern English system of justice was built. The Marian Statutes demanded that justices of the peace examine suspects and witnesses, make a written record of any testimony, and certify that record to a trial court. Historians debate whether these developments were adapted from the Continental Roman–canon law tradition or if they were a natural progression of the English system. The exact degree of Continental influence may never be determined, but virtually all historians agree that the Marian Statutes established the foundation for a legal system in which the individual ceased to bring accusations, and the government began to replace the local community as the source of justice.

**Burden of the State.** After the Fourth Lateran Council, Continental Europe tended to follow the Roman law tradition while incorporating a strong dose of canon law. The resulting Roman-canon law system employed inquisitorial trials that were quite distinct from the open jury trials of the English accusatory model. This tradition evolved out of efforts at the Fourth Lateran Council to reform the Church and society. The Council attempted to control the beliefs and actions of the laity, reform the clergy, stifle heresy, deal with non-Christian minorities within society, and to institutionalize a process of church inquisition. The first four goals combined to provide a new impetus for the creation of inquisitional practices. In order to monitor belief and stop heresy, the Church needed a severe legal system that could sniff out and destroy heresy. Since heresy was the equivalent of treason against God, it was punished by death. The Roman-canon law tradition allowed the Church and the state to progress through inquisition trials that involved the authorities initiating legal procedures without actual accusations. Courts took the initiative and

began investigations by collecting evidence and arresting suspects. The authorities ceased to be bystanders at trials and became the force of the trial. Communal self-regulation based on communal deliberations were replaced with a system of prosecution exerted from above. Moreover, the inquisitorial model called for two eyewitnesses or a confession; hence, torture became an accepted method of extracting confessions. Vengeance became a burden of the state.

**Inquisition.** In 1231 Pope Gregory IX gave a convent of Dominicans the right to form an inquisitorial tribunal. This right came directly from the papacy and was part of a trend in the Roman Catholic Church. The inquisition was not one uniform movement, rather it was a series of court proceedings aimed at destroying heresy. In the fifteenth century, territorial princes realized the political potential of inquisitions and used them to attack political enemies. For instance, Joan of Arc convinced the French dauphin that God had chosen her to save France, and subsequently the French rallied to her side. Her activities changed the course of the Hundred Years' War (1337–1453), yet the king of France did not intervene on her behalf when she was caught by Burgundians and sold to the English. While she was held by the English, French churchmen tried her as a heretic and witch. She was burned at the stake on 30 May 1431. Joan of Arc's military career was unique, but she was one of many who were condemned and executed in the name of the Inquisition.

**Auto-de-fe.** The auto-de-fe was the public sentencing of heretics by the Inquisition. After sentencing, the convicted were turned over to the government for punishments that included public burning. The government was obliged to wait at least twenty-four hours but not more than five days. Heresy alone was not sufficient reason for burning at the stake. One needed to be obstinate in his or her belief, thus only relapsed or unrepentant heretics were burnt. While tied to the stake, the condemned usually had the opportunity to repent, and thus be strangled before being burned, or they could choose to remain obstinate and be roasted alive. The Church convicted a person of heresy, and then turned the person over to the state, so the Inquisition was not actually responsible for the burning. The church thus avoided pollution of the clergy by the shedding of blood. Burning was used in order to annihilate, or completely destroy, the person. This event exterminated forever any memory of the shameful person or the evil deeds and thus purified the community. Ultimately, the community would avoid God's wrath against it by destroying all memory of the deeds. The auto-de-fe originated as a religious act of penitence and justice, but it evolved into a public spectacle. Bernard Gui held several famous auto-de-fe in early-fourteenth-century France. In all of these ceremonies, he was careful to exact an oath of obedience from royal officials and local magistrates. By the time the Spanish Inquisition held its first auto-de-fe in 1481, such oaths were not necessary because the state was part of the Inquisition.

**Spanish Inquisition.** In the mid sixteenth century, the auto-de-fe became a public ceremony of the Spanish Inquisition. The ceremonial auto-de-fe was developed by Inquisitor General Fernando de Valdés in response to the discovery of Protestant heretics in Spain in 1558. The first new-style auto-de-fe was in May 1559 in Valladolid. The presence and patronage of the royal court legitimized the procedures, which were incorporated two years later in the inquisitorial *Instructions.* The actual burning took place on large scaffolds in public squares. They occurred on feast days with an audience of leading officials and the public. Many spectators frequently traveled long distances to attend. For instance, thirty thousand people attended the 1610 Logroño auto-de-fe despite the fact that the town had only four thousand residents.

**Procedures.** Inquisitors usually would arrive in an area and announce a grace period where all could confess sins. Males over age fourteen and females over age twelve were required to offer personal confessions and to report any indiscretions in the community. The resulting atmosphere of suspicion would continue as the grace period was recalculated. Inquisitors then incarcerated potential heretics without offering explicit charges and without explaining who the accusers were and what they had said. Heretics were presumed guilty until proven innocent and thus lost all rights, including control over their own property. If heretics did not confess, then the inquisitors would show them the tools of torture and explain what would happen if they did not cooperate. Ecclesiastical inquisitors viewed heretics as the worst possible threat to society and thus they altered procedures in significant ways: names and testimonies of witnesses were withheld, the defendant's access to counsel was limited, testimony from questionable witnesses was accepted, and the accused was offered false promises of leniency in attempts to win confessions. These changes were significant because government courts turned to the Inquisition as a model for actions. As a result, torture became a standard procedure in most of Europe.

**Torture.** The Roman-canon legal tradition called for two eyewitnesses or a confession. With the shift to ex officio cases, where the state brought charges against an individual, it was frequently difficult to find two eyewitnesses. Torture was not a means of proof, but rather of obtaining confession. If the court decided that a confession could be obtained, then the accused was given religious encouragement to confess. As in the case of the church investigations, a display of the instruments of torture would be made in order to encourage the accused to confess. Inquisitorial manuals of the late fifteenth century standardized when and how torture would be applied. Prior to that, judges turned to torture as a last recourse in the pursuit of truth. Only acceptable forms could be applied and only after appropriate protocol had been followed. Authorities frowned on innovations in torture and insisted that no blood be shed and that no permanent injury be inflicted. By the end of the fifteenth century, a person of any social class could be tortured, and thus torture served to make each individual equal under the law.

**Forms of Torment.** The most-common form of torture was the strappado, a pulley system whereby the hands of the accused were tied behind the back and a rope was placed through a pulley or over a beam. The accused was then lifted into the air. Weights were occasionally attached to the feet in order to increase the strain on the shoulders. Children, women, and everyone charged with less severe crimes would simply have their hands tied tightly, then

Acts of public punishment, as depicted by Pedro Berruguete in the late 1400s
(from Franco Cardini, *Europe 1492,* 1989)

released and tied again. Other tortures included sleep deprivation and fire torture, where the feet were doused in grease or another flammable substance and then fire was applied to the soles. A victim could also be stretched on a rack or subjected to the water torture. Water torture involved restraining the accused and forcing the person's mouth open. A piece of linen was placed in the mouth to conduct water down into the throat. The accused had trouble breathing and could die if blood vessels in the neck ruptured. In the sixteenth century, printed handbooks outlined procedures and clarified legal principles of torture. After 1600, more mechanical methods became popular, such as thumb screws and leg screws that were tightened to the point of crushing bones. Once a confession was obtained, the tortured person was given one day of rest and then asked to repeat the confession without further torture. Recanting was useless because the authorities simply reapplied torture, this time with the conviction that a confession was inevitable because one had already been made.

**Court Proceedings.** Suspected criminals were taken to criminal courts of the local city or territory. They were placed in jails that served both as places of detention and physical suffering. Suspects were interrogated and encouraged to confess immediately. Those who did not confess were tortured, and not surprisingly, most suspects confessed at this point. These events occurred without recourse to a defense attorney. The pursuit of justice had become the concern of local authorities, but sentencing was public and thus differed from community to community. Two main factors contributed to the sentencing: the deterrence of future crime and the appearance of merciful courts. Courts were eager to show the mercy of a judgment and they forced the guilty to swear "oaths of truce" stating that the guilty would not seek revenge for the decision. Those sentenced to death were given three days to prepare for death. Those not sentenced to death were usually punished in the part of the body that committed the offense, or they were banished from the community.

**Actual Punishments.** Mutilations, branding, and flogging were the most common forms of bodily punishment and they were frequently combined with social disgrace such as the pillory. Fines and church punishments involving penance were also issued. One historian has outlined four main levels of punishment: (1) church punishment that allowed the repentant to remain in the community; (2) disgrace that diminished one's social standing in the community; (3) mutilations that marked one as dead within the community or actual banishment from the community; and (4) death. The last was always a ritualized ceremony. Executions by burning, drowning, and burying alive were common ways to purify the community because they destroyed all traces of the evil person. The bodies of those executed in these manners could not be buried in a churchyard and thus the corpses did not exist from the community's perspective. In the seventeenth century, these purifying rituals began to disappear when beheading and hanging replaced burning, drowning, and burying alive as the most common forms of execution. Executions were public affairs that sent a message to the community. The community also participated by witnessing the execution and thereby showing communal consent. Residents who lacked strong social connections were treated more harshly because they lacked public support at the sentencing stage of trials.

**Witchcraft.** Individuals on the margins of the community were frequently the targets of witchcraft accusations. Charges of heresy were more common than charges of witchcraft, but after 1550 witchcraft became more common. Women who were neither married nor in a household with a male head were especially susceptible to charges of witchcraft. These women frequently were not witches, but they became scapegoats for all types of natural disasters or communal tribulations. Two Dominicans, Jacob Sprenger and Heinrich Cramer, wrote *Malleus Maleficarum* (The Hammer of Witches), a 1486 manual for witch-hunters that included theories about witches and steps for secular courts. Pope Innocent VIII commissioned the work at the same time that he issued a papal bull giving inquisitors license to stamp out witchcraft. Witchcraft was punishable by death according to the 1532 *Constitutio Criminalis Carolina* law code, but only in cases where harmful magic was documented. Few trials took place until the end of the sixteenth century, by which time legal scholars had redefined all witchcraft as a pact with the devil and thus punishable by death. Most witch trials were inside the Holy Roman Empire or in bordering regions such as France, Bohemia, Poland, and Switzerland. Relatively few trials occurred in areas with a strong inquisition presence such as Spain and Italy. Witchcraft was perceived as so serious a threat that political theorist Jean Bodin claimed that "one accused of being a witch ought never to be fully acquitted and set free" unless the person's innocence is "clearer than the sun." Bodin opposed any princely pardons of witches.

**Le Stinche.** In 1297 the city of Florence began construction of a public prison called Le Stinche. Florence also issued criminal statutes at that time and again in 1355 and 1415. The statutes regulated criminal justice and set guidelines for the prison. Children were occasionally placed in Le Stinche, but all inmates were divided by age, gender, degree of sanity, and the seriousness of the offense. The name *Le Stinche* became so common in Italy that other citizens of other cities,

such as Siena and Pistoia, used *Le Stinche* as a slang term for their prisons. In 1559 Venice commissioned construction of a prison with four hundred cells for individuals whose capital sentences were commuted to life in prison. This shift toward punitive imprisonment was not consistent with Roman law, but it did share striking similarities with canon law. Royal courts across Europe had looked to Italian legal scholars for guidance when imposing new legal codes and by the end of the sixteenth century they turned to Italian models of punitive imprisonment.

**Birth of the Modern Prison.** Le Stinche was in many ways a large medieval jail that was also used for confining undisciplined adolescents. Other medieval forms of imprisonment included monasteries that were known to physically restrain monks who wished to leave; hospitals that housed the terminally sick; leper communities; and places of forced labor. The galleys were a common form of forced labor in the Mediterranean area, and across Europe forced labor was used on public building projects, such as fortifications and city walls. Simple banishment was more widespread than imprisonment until the late sixteenth century. The earliest prisons were built after 1550 in areas that did not have galleys, such as England, the Netherlands, North Germany, and Baltic towns. Bridewell was a prison in London, England, that was completed in 1555. Located outside the city walls, it has a prison for undeserving poor. Its mission was clearly punitive as inmates were forced to work to support themselves. Houses of correction established in other English towns frequently used the name *Bridewell* as a generic title. On the Continent, punitive prisons were constructed in the 1580s and 1590s for able-bodied poor who were forced to work. People were imprisoned for bad habits, such as laziness, instead of specific acts, such as burglary. Urban officials in the sixteenth century began to take control of what had been church charity programs. They were less tolerant of begging than the church and thus wrote elaborate ordinances regulating poor relief. Noncitizens who begged were removed from the city and able-bodied citizens, those deemed capable of working, were prohibited from begging. Idleness became intolerable and beggars were put to work. Early European prisons were not places for hardened criminals, but rather places where authorities could monitor and control people who preferred not to work.

**Sources:**
John K. Brackett, *Criminal Justice and Crime in Late Renaissance Florence, 1537–1609* (Cambridge: Cambridge University Press, 1992).

Henry Kamen, *The Spanish Inquisition: A Historical Revision* (New Haven: Yale University Press, 1998).

John Langbein, *Prosecuting Crime in the Renaissance: England, Germany, France* (Cambridge, Mass.: Harvard University Press, 1974).

Petrus Spierenburg, *The Prison Experience: Disciplinary Institutions and Their Inmates in Early Modern Europe* (New Brunswick, N.J.: Rutgers University Press, 1991).

Spierenburg, *The Spectacle of Suffering: Executions and the Evolution of Repression, from a Preindustrial Metropolis to the European Experience* (Cambridge: Cambridge University Press, 1984).

Laura Ikins Stern, *The Criminal Law System of Medieval and Renaissance Florence* (Baltimore: Johns Hopkins University Press, 1994).

The walls of Constantinople, dating from the Turkish siege of the mid 1400s

Gerald R. Strauss, *Law, Resistance and the State: The Opposition to Roman Law in Reformation Germany* (Princeton: Princeton University Press, 1986).

Richard van Dülmen, *Theatre of Horror: Crime and Punishment in Early Modern Germany,* translated by Elisabeth Neu (Cambridge, Mass.: Blackwell, 1990).

Jonathan W. Zophy, ed., *The Holy Roman Empire* (Westport, Conn.: Greenwood Press, 1980).

## FORTIFICATIONS AND SIEGE CRAFT

**Types.** By 1350 medieval fortification design had reached its apex. Little change would take place for more than a century, until the development of gunpowder artillery began to have an impact. Medieval fortification had three major functions. The most-common one was serving as the fortified residence of a powerful lord, which is the proper meaning of the word castle. Fortifications were used also to defend towns and cities. The third type of fortification, royal forts with small garrisons to defend the frontiers of a realm, was fairly uncommon. There often was overlap between the basic types, such as the well-fortified city of Carcassonne in southern France, which served to block the key invasion route from Spain, or the royal forts built during the English occupation of Wales in the thirteenth century, which became the castles of nobles in the following century.

**Castles.** The typical castle was the residence of a baron, whose place in the feudal system ensured him of enough wealth to build a small castle and garrison it. It had stone walls thirty to forty feet high surrounded by a ditch. There were several round towers, usually at the four corners of a small square castle, that projected both above the wall and in front of it to provide flanking fire. Both the wall and the towers had long, narrow windows, small enough that a man could not crawl through, but large enough to allow bowmen to fire at attackers. At the top of the wall and the towers was the checkerboard pattern of crenellations and merlons that provided both protection for the defenders and spaces for shooting at besiegers. Along the outside top edge was a projecting galley built into the stone of the wall with holes in its floor. Called a machicolation, its function was to allow the defenders to shoot or drop objects straight down to the base of the wall at any enemy sappers without exposing themselves by leaning over the top of the wall. A set of towers called a barbicon defended the gate of the castle, without which the gate was the weakest point of the castle. The barbicon projected forward of the gate, creating a short tunnel in front of the gate. Holes in the ceiling of the tunnel allowed defenders to rain objects down on attackers who tried to batter down the doors. The doors were usually massive wooden structures reinforced with iron bars and covered with leather to prevent fire; they took several minutes to close and secure. To deter a surprise attack that might catch the doors open, the gate had an iron portcullis that could be dropped with the yank of a rope to temporarily shut off the entrance. If the castle had a moat around it, it had a counterweighted drawbridge designed to swing up rapidly to forestall a sneak attack. A large fortification with a substantial garrison had small postern doors hidden from the sight of those outside the castle designed to allow sallies against the attackers. Kings had large castles, such as the Tower of London or Vincennes outside of Paris, that served as their residences as well as strongholds to defend their capitals.

**Sieges.** A well-built stone castle outfitted with most of the above features and defended by a small garrison of resolute men was capable of withstanding a siege. Most mechanical siege machines did not throw objects of enough weight to do much damage to the masonry, nor were they accurate enough to hit the same spot twice and create a multiplying impact on the masonry to cause the wall to collapse and open up a breach. Mining was another option, which involved digging a tunnel under the wall. Once directly under the wall, the miners filled the tunnel with combustibles and set them on fire to burn away the supports of the tunnel's roof and crack the masonry of the wall above. If all went well, the tunnel would collapse and with it part of the wall above. Mining, however, was slow and difficult and subject to the countermining efforts of the defenders, who often succeeded in forcing the miners to give up. Consequently, a passive siege intended to starve the defenders out was the most common method. This type of operation usually required months or even a year. However, the spread of disease and boredom among the besiegers, the cost of keeping a siege army in place for months at a time, and the possibility of the arrival of a relief army meant passive sieges were not successful against a well-stocked castle with strongly motivated defenders. It was this lack of success that allowed many feudal nobles to openly defy their kings during the Middle Ages.

**Towns and Frontier Forts.** The walls of towns and frontier forts were constructed little differently than castles. City walls, of course, could run for a mile or more, requiring towers every one hundred yards or so and barbicons for several gates. In Italy the towers tended to be even with the top of the wall and be broad in diameter. These squat-looking structures were called drum towers. The defenders of the urban walls consisted of the urban militiamen, recruited from among artisans and merchants who formed the ruling class of medieval cities. They did not trust the poor residents of their cities enough to put weapons in their hands, so they were forced to provide the defense of their cities themselves, despite the time it took away from their businesses. Because the urban militiamen lacked military training, they sought weapons they could use effectively from the walls with only a little practice, such as the crossbow and later the handgun when it became available. The major differences between a frontier fort and a castle were the absence of a relatively comfortable apartment for the lord of a castle and the presence of more of the spartan living quarters for the larger garrison used in a fort.

**Advantages of the Besiegers.** In most respects the defenders of a fortified place had the advantage over the attackers in 1350. Over the following century, the development of gunpowder artillery into effective siege weapons turned the advantage to the attackers. Defenders could use cannon atop the walls against attackers or through gun loops opened in the walls and towers and hookguns, which were handguns designed to hook onto the wall to absorb the recoil. They could not, however, overcome the defects of late-medieval fortification in the face of powerful cannon. While early cannon had problems of inaccuracy, slow reloading time, and a tendency to burst, they were still more effective than the traditional mechanical siege machines in breaching walls. Cannon had a somewhat better chance of hitting close to the same spot on the wall, improving the odds of crushing the masonry. More important, the flat trajectory of cannon shot meant that the balls would strike low on the high and relatively thin walls. When they did crush the masonry and cause the wall to collapse, the breach that was opened was close to the ground and easier for the besiegers to assault than a breach high on a wall. The rubble from a high wall collapsing was also more likely to fill in the moat, making it easier for the attackers to cross it. In the final two decades of the Hundred Years' War (1337–1453), the French used cannon to take English-held towns and castles in rapid succession, playing a major role in the final ousting of the English from France. By the end of the war the French king had appointed the Bureau brothers as masters of the royal artillery train. They continued to develop better cannon and had a major role in creating the mobile gun carriage that allowed heavy guns to be transported at about the same speed as the rest of the army moved. Commanders no longer had to wait for days before the artillery would arrive for use in a siege or a battle. The major success of cannon in the fifteenth century was the siege of Constantinople (1453) by the Ottoman Turks. The Turks used huge bombards against the ancient but still powerful walls of the Byzantine city. Some of the Turkish bombards were so large that they were forged on the spot where they were fired, so that enormous effort would not have to be expended to move them into place. Constantinople, which had withstood dozens of major sieges since its walls had been built in the fifth century, fell after a siege of one month.

**Bronze Cannon.** The crucial development in the late fifteenth century was the use of bronze for casting guns. High-quality bronze muzzle loaders called culverins were capable of using iron or lead balls rather than the stone balls used in iron cannon. Metal balls struck the wall with a great deal more force than stone ones and did not shatter upon impact as stone balls frequently did. Traditional fortifications were more vulnerable than ever before. With the demise of the medieval castle, nobles and kings began to change the style of their residences. Abandoning any hope of being able to combine defense and residence in one structure, they built luxurious palaces and chateaux that were pleasant places to live and to show off their wealth and culture. Since bronze was expensive compared to iron, only the kings could afford to put together a large artillery train of bronze culverins. This situation gave the kings a great advantage over their nobles, whose ability to defy the king by holding out in their castles was eliminated. It was a major step toward the European monarchs taking effective control over their kingdoms. Cannon played the major role in the victory of Ferdinand of Aragon and Isabella of Castile over the Moors, the final step in the Christian Reconquista of the Iberian Peninsula. The Spanish monarchs had an artillery train of eighty heavy guns that successfully brought the siege of the great fortress of Granada to an end in 1492.

**Italian Trace.** The excellent French artillery train played a major role during the first French invasion of Italy that began in 1494. King Charles VIII's forces quickly took fortifications that the Italians expected would take them all summer to reduce. The conquered places were subjected to the traditional three days of sack, plunder, and rape that was the fate of the residents of fortified places that resisted, and their garrisons were executed. The ease with which the French took those places and the dire fate of the people within them persuaded the Italians to offer no further resistance, and Charles marched on south to Naples, his primary goal. The Italians, however, responded to the humiliation of the easy French victories by searching for new ideas to improve fortification to withstand the onslaught of the French artillery. The best minds of the time, including Leonardo Da Vinci and Michelangelo, set to work to design better fortifications, but the most successful ideas came from lesser known men such as the Sangallos, a family of military architects, and Fra Giovanni Giocondo. Their solution to the problem of designing fortification capable of withstanding cannon became known as the Italian trace. They had to deal with the problem that high walls were vulnerable to cannon fire, yet to lower them increased the risk of scaling. Their solution dropped the wall down into a deep ditch usually filled with water, so that a cannonball could hit only the top of the wall, yet there was twenty to thirty feet of wall to make scaling difficult. Crenellations and merlons were removed from the top of the wall, which was made rounded so that a cannonball was likely to bounce up and over it without striking at the full impact of a right angle hit. A space of up to one thousand feet was cleared of every building, tree, and bush to provide a clear field of fire for the defenders. It would often be laid with masonry to make tunneling up through it more difficult. This feature became known as the glacis. The bastion with gun openings, called casemates, was introduced; it projected farther forward of the wall than the medieval tower did in order to provide better flanking fire.

**Bastion Improvements.** Some early bastions were rounded on the assumption that cannonballs would glance off them. Albrecht Dürer, a military engineer as well as an artist, designed forts with round bastions for Henry VIII on England's south coast. Fortunately for the English, they were never tested by a siege, since the round bastions probably would have been found vulnerable as those built in

The siege of Rhodes, 1480, as depicted in a Latin codex of the period (Bibliothèque Nationale, Paris)

Italy were. The principal problem was that the round bastion had a dead space in front of it that could not be covered from the main wall, now called the curtain wall, or from other bastions. The Sangallos solved the problem by using triangular bastions for the fort at Nettuno (near Rome) they began in 1509. It was a small square fort with a triangular bastion at each corner. It was designed so that guns at the flanks of a bastion could sweep every foot of the adjoining curtain wall and the face of the neighboring bastion. The cannon on the neighboring bastion did the same for it, and so on around the fort, leaving no spot on the exterior line of defense unprotected. Protruding shoulders protected the men and guns on the flanks of the bastions from hostile fire. Soon cities began to strengthen their walls by placing bastions at regular intervals on the long expanses of wall. As long as the architect did his geometry correctly, the bastions could provide covering fire for neighboring bastions all the way around the city. The Italian engineers also began to put masonry on the counterscarp, the opposite side of the ditch from the wall, and cut casemates into it, so that anyone who came down into the ditch was caught in a murderous cross fire. A walkway was often placed a little less than a man's height from the top of the counterscarp. Defenders used this covered way to fire at the attackers with firearms or small cannon.

**Stalemate.** As the Italian trace spread across Italy and into northern Europe after 1525, besiegers found themselves stymied by the new style of fortification. Sieges no longer could be successfully ended in a matter of days as in 1494. An Italian trace bristling with its own heavy guns made it highly dangerous to try to batter the walls from as close a range as had been true in the late Middle Ages. Nonetheless, the offense soon found a way to catch up to the defense. Trenches had to be dug from beyond the effective range of the defender's heavy guns up the glacis to the top of the counterscarp. These trenches had to zigzag, so the defenders could not get a clear shot down them. A cannonball fired down a straight trench could roll for a long distance, killing or maiming a large number of men if they happened to be standing in it. The diggers were also protected by using gabions, cylindrical structures made of sticks and stakes bound together and filled with dirt, which were placed on the upper edges of the trench. Once the attackers' trenches reached the top of the counterscarp, the attackers would drag their heavy gun up and fire point blank (without any elevation to the gun) into masonry of the opposite wall or bastions, using the gabions to protect the gunners and the guns. At that range, perhaps twenty yards, cannon fire could open a breach quickly, with the rubble falling into the ditch, and the attackers would bring up material as well to fill it in. Then an assault took place. If the neighboring bastion was still held by the defenders, it could provide a murderous fire into the assault troops as they worked their way across the rubble in the ditch and into the breach, where the defenders had also posted troops. Frequently the assault was driven back, perhaps again and again, and the besiegers had to resort to a passive siege of trying to starve out the defenders. The result was a decline in the speed of war, since sieges again took perhaps an entire campaigning season, and the quick sieges and battles that had marked the era of the French invasions of Italy became a thing of the past.

**Palmanova and Philippeville.** When an army arrived to besiege a well-fortified city, it rarely had the capacity to lay siege lines around the entire defensive perimeter. Instead the military engineers would decide which side would be most vulnerable or easiest to approach and concentrate the guns there. Once it was clear where the attackers were concentrating their efforts, the defenders moved guns and supplies to the bastions under attack from the others. It was often difficult, however, to move the gun carriages and their large horse teams through the narrow and crooked streets of a medieval town and up and down steep inclines. When governments decided to build entirely new fortified towns, as they did in several instances, the design of the new towns took into account that problem. Wide streets were laid out in a straight line that led to a central plaza, where the gun carriages could easily wait their turns to go to the bastions under attack. Inclines were made as gradual as possible. The Venetians, for example, built Palmanova northeast of their city in 1593 to protect it against Turkish attack from Hungary. They made it a real city in hope that

the commerce attracted to it would help pay for the extensive and expensive fortifications that would be built. The enormous expense of the defensive works in the Italian-trace style forced the Venetians to reduce the number of bastions from twelve originally planned to nine. Cities such as Palmanova or Philippeville, which the Spanish began in 1555, reveal the precise geometry and symmetry of the Italian trace, especially when it was not complicated by the presence of existing defensive structures.

**Other Improvements.** By the late sixteenth century the offense again was catching up to the defense. In the 1540s German gunmakers working for Henry VIII discovered a better way to cast iron culverins. Iron being so much cheaper than bronze, the new method led to a dramatic increase in the number of quality guns that were capable of doing severe damage to fortifications. Steady improvements in siegecraft responding to the Italian trace reduced the initial advantage it had given to the defenders. Military architects responded by designing ways to push the besiegers' heavy guns further from the fortifications by using outworks. The first outwork to appear was the ravelin. When attackers struck at a simple Italian trace, they usually concentrated their efforts on the curtain wall, not the bastions, which were far more solid and difficult to breach. The ravelin was a detached triangular bastion placed in front of the curtain wall. It appeared early in the development of the Italian trace but became a standard part of fortification only by 1580. Outworks developed further during the Dutch revolt against the Spanish (1566–1648). The primary theater of this long war was the border between the Netherlands and Belgium, a comparatively level but marshy region. It was difficult to dig deep ditches but it was easy to build extensive outworks in the area. Fortifications in this region began to use demilunes, which were smaller bastions placed in front of the main bastions, and horn and crown works that were built in front of the ravelins and demilunes. A fine example of the extended outworks that marked Dutch fortifications especially was Coevorden, designed by Maurice of Nassau, who was both an excellent military architect and a siegemaster. The inner line of defense consisted of the curtain wall and its bastions surrounded by a ditch 180 feet wide. Then came a line of ravelins and demilunes fronted by a ditch thirty feet wide. The outer line of defense was a set of horn and crown works with another ditch in front of them. Next came a glacis that extended for five hundred feet. When an enemy had finally worked his way up the glacis and dragged his heavy guns to the edge of the counterscarp of the ditch in front of the outer line, they were still more than eight hundred feet from the main defensive line, out of effective range for cannon of that era. Such a fortification required a great number of men to defend, but it also required that a besieging army have a far greater number. A siege also took a long time to win. It took the Spanish a constant siege of three years to take the Dutch-held port of Ostend on the coast of Belgium, partly because it was supplied by sea, which the Dutch controlled.

**Significance.** The Italian trace was a significant factor in the military successes of the European powers in the sixteenth century. It was particularly true of the Portuguese, who built and defended a vast trading empire with few men by using the new style fortification to defend their trading posts in the East, where they faced more powerful local forces than the Spanish did in the Americas. In India in 1571, a Portuguese fort with a garrison of about 1,100 men withstood a siege conducted by the local ruler with more than 100,000 men. Once the Spanish began to build similar forts to defend their ports in the Caribbean, the attacks by English pirates against port cities such as Havana were far less successful than they had been previously. On the other hand, the failure of the Ottoman Turks to keep up with European fortification design and siegecraft was a significant factor in the eventual decline of that empire's power in the late sixteenth century.

Sources:

Christopher Duffy, *Siege Warfare: The Fortress in the Early Modern World 1494–1660* (London: Routledge & Kegan Paul, 1979).

Simon Pepper, *Firearms and Fortifications: Military Architecture and Siege Warfare in Sixteenth-Century Siena* (Chicago: University of Chicago Press, 1986).

Richard A. Preston, and others, *Men in Arms: A History of Warfare and Its Interrelationships with Western Society* (Fort Worth, Tex.: Holt, 1991).

The trial of Mary Queen of Scots in 1586, as depicted in a sketch preserved among the papers of Robert Beale, Clerk of Council of Elizabeth I (British Library, Additional MS 48027)

## LAW AND ORDER

**Complications.** *Utopia*, the wildly successful humanist satire of 1516, describes the imaginary island of Utopia, an ideal world of perfect justice where lawyers do not exist. Sir Thomas More was himself a practicing lawyer when he wrote his novel, yet he provided no place for lawyers in Utopia. Conduct in Utopia was governed by simple rules that were natural and obvious to all. Lawyers would complicate things and thereby alienate ordinary citizens who merely wanted to live free from arbitrary constraints. *Utopia* was More's scathing attack against the evils afflicting men who live under the rule of tyrants, yet he saw no role for legal scholars who might protect those citizens. Animosity toward lawyers was especially high in More's age because the heightened professionalism of law made it difficult to pursue legal avenues without employing a lawyer.

**Case Law v. Code Law.** More's England had a system of common law that was based on royal decrees and older customs. Decisions in English courts were made relative to the precedent of prior court cases. Case law, as this system is called, requires vast knowledge of previous court cases and a familiarity with how the court actually functions. Lawyers in England were trained at common-law courts where they could watch the deliberations of legally decisive cases. The Inns of Court began as housing for students who wished to follow the Westminister court sessions, but over time they evolved into formal schools. In contrast to England's case-law system, legal disputes on the Continent were settled by law professors and legal scholars who interpreted a written code. Code law required careful analysis of the actual written laws instead of the precedent of prior cases. Other than in England, Wales, and Ireland, code law had become the basis of European legal systems by the sixteenth century. The written law codes in these areas were products of Roman law, which was a system of laws that had modified and supplemented customary law in most of Europe. Roman law was a product of the ancient Roman Empire where legal matters were controlled by the emperor instead of the people. Roman law had become a university discipline, first in medieval Italy and then France. Medieval rulers replaced the role of local custom with a written law code that required academically trained lawyers who were versed in Latin. This language became a prerequisite for lawyers, and thus lawyers spoke a jargon that the average person could not fully understand.

**Roman Law.** Written Roman law dominated southern Europe and customary law was more common in northern Europe until Roman law was revived in the Middle Ages. Roman law returned to prominence in the eleventh century with the revival of a text known as the Justinian law code, or Body of the Civil Law. Emperor Justinian I was a successful Byzantine emperor of the sixth century C.E. who reconquered Western provinces lost to the Barbarians and rebuilt Ravenna and Constantinople. He is best known for

On 15 March 1579 Phillip II of Spain offered generous rewards to potential assassins of William of Orange, who had initiated in 1572 the Dutch War of Independence against Spain. The fanatic Catholic Balthazar Gérard, on 10 July 1584, succeeded in carrying out the order by shooting and mortally wounding William.

It is well known to all how favorably the late emperor, Charles V, . . . treated William of Nassau. . . . Nevertheless, as everyone knows, we had scarcely turned our back on the Netherlands before the said William . . . (who had become . . . prince of Orange) began . . . by sinister arts, plots, and intrigues . . . to gain [control] over those whom he believed to be malcontents, or haters of justice, or anxious for innovations, and . . . Above all, those who were suspected in the matter of religion . . . With the knowledge, advice, and encouragement of the said Orange, the heretics commenced to destroy the images, altars, and churches. . . . So soon as the said Nassau was received into the government of the provinces, he began, through his agents and satellites, to introduce heretical preaching. . . . Then he introduced liberty of conscience . . . which soon brought it about that the Catholics were openly persecuted and driven out. . . . Moreover he obtained such a hold upon our poor subjects of Holland and Zeeland . . . That nearly all the towns, one after the other, have been besieged. . . .

Therefore, for all these just reasons, for his evil doings as chief disturber of the public peace . . . we outlaw him forever and forbid our subjects to associate with him . . . in public or in secret. We declare him an enemy of the human race, and in order the sooner to remove our people from his tyranny and oppression, we promise, on the word of a king and as God's servant, that if one of our subjects be found so generous of heart and desirous of doing us a service and advantaging the public that he shall find the means of executing this decree and of ridding us of the said pest, either by delivering him to us dead or alive, or by depriving him at once of life, we will give him and his heirs landed estates or money, as he will, to the amount of twenty-five thousand gold crowns. If he has committed any crime, of any kind whatsoever, we will pardon him. If he be not noble, we will ennoble him for his valor; and should he require other persons to assist him, we will reward them according to the service rendered, pardon their crimes, and ennoble them too.

Source: James Harvey Robinson, ed., *Readings in European History,* volume 2 (Boston & New York: Ginn, 1904–1906), pp. 174–177.

the law code that bears his name. The Justinian code was not written by Justinian, rather it was the compilation of laws into a single coherent body. The Justinian code was a product of almost six hundred years of the Roman Empire under the rule of an emperor. The senate had controlled the legal system in the Roman Republic, but the emperor was the source of law in the Roman Empire. Roman law therefore supported strong centralized governments ruled by an emperor, king, or prince. European rulers intent on centralizing power were eager to modify a code that would allow them to be the focal point of the law. The revival of Roman law was also influenced by an 1140 compilation of church law by Gratian of Bologna known as *Decretum,* or *Concordance of Discordant Canons.* European customary law became written law due to the convergence of the Roman tradition with a Christian tradition known as canon law.

**Canon Law.** Ancient Greek construction workers used a measuring rod called a *kanon.* The early church used the term to define an approved standard such as the canon of books that the church deemed divinely inspired and thus part of the Bible. By the fourth century, church discipline had moved from local custom to formal regulations, or canons, that were legislated at synods. The legislation of councils thus began a legal tradition of ecclesiastical or church law that came to be known as canon law. The 325 Council of Nicaea was called in part to deal with early heresy. The Council of Nicaea created twenty canons dealing with everything from church structure and liturgy to the treatment of schismatics. The eleventh-century papal reform movement and Peter Abelard's twelfth-century dialectical method of textual criticism had important implications for canon law. These and other attempts to collect and rationalize church law culminated in Gratian's *Decretum.* Gratian reconciled contradictions in church law by applying Peter Abelard's dialectical method to church decrees. In so doing, Gratian established canon law as a field of study. The *Decretum* and the rise of formal study of law fostered the creation of law faculties across Europe. The growing number of legal scholars resulted in increased petitions to Rome to settle contested interpretations. In 1234 Pope Gregory IX compiled the *Decretals,* an official collection of papal decrees that were given specifically to settle legal disputes. Four other collections of decretals were released between 1298 and 1500. Gratian's *Decretum* and the five later collections of decretals were published together as *Corpus Iuris Canonici* in 1503. Fourteen years before Martin Luther posted the Ninety-five Theses, a universal law code for Roman Christianity was printed and circulated. Canon law was recognized by virtually all of Europe from the time of Gratian's *Decretum* until the Protestant Reformation.

**Role.** Canon law fulfilled a special role that was distinct from governmental laws. Canon law legislated the clergy, who were separate from the rest of society because of their vows, as well as issues for the laity that were related to belief and the sacraments, such as heresy, marriage, and divorce. Discipline in canon law was administered by the bishops who were expected to correct moral transgressions,

L'edit siege honnozablement.

Comment erles anglops

The burning of Joan of Arc at Rouen, France, in 1431, illumination in *Les Vigiles de Charles VII* (from John Holland Smith, *Joan of Arc*, 1973)

whereas the state punished criminal transgressions. Bishops could not seek the same avenues of punishment as the secular rulers because their ultimate goal was to correct evil and lead people to salvation. Church courts were not allowed to utilize any punishment that resulted in death, mutilation, or the shedding of blood. Canon law required penitential punishment. The emphasis of canon law on the correction and improvement of the perpetrator became a model for European systems of discipline that shifted from public punishment, such as the scaffold, to personal rehabilitation, such as the prison system.

**Demise.** Protestant reformers rejected the authority of the Roman Church and thus greatly curtailed the role of canon law in European society during the sixteenth century. Because Protestant reformers rejected the validity of canon law, they were faced with the task of creating legislation to regulate marriage and other aspects of canon law. Most followed one of three approaches: secular authority appointed members to consistories in Lutheran areas; church courts were eliminated and replaced by democratic bodies in Reformed areas; and the king placed everything under royal control, as in the case with England. The 1577 Formula of Concord maintained Luther's distinction between gospel, which can save someone, and law, which can only condemn. Canon law was thus reduced to human law that could not bind Christian conscience. The Formula of Concord did acknowledge the validity of the law for

political (maintain order), theological (make people aware of sins), and educational ends (guidelines for Christian life). The Roman Church responded to Protestant reformers' demands at the 1545–1563 Council of Trent. The council forbade anyone from publishing interpretations of canon law and thus ended a long tradition of legal commentaries and glosses. The *Corpus Iuris Canonici* was reviewed at the council and in 1582 an official edition was published. The Pope forbade any changes to the official edition and thus effectively ended the study of canon law by stifling any pursuit of improved interpretations of the law. The combination of Protestants turning to state legal systems and the papacy forbidding reinterpretation doomed canon law, but it left its mark on Europe because legal scholars who revised Roman law had relied heavily on the academic tradition of canon law.

**Convergence.** Canon law evolved in the tradition of Roman law and thus the two shared many structural similarities. Yet, when Roman law was revived, legal scholars turned to canon law as a model for reviving important procedural issues. Roman law adapted a rigid hierarchy of proofs that included a role for eyewitnesses and for confessions. In the fourteenth century the state became prosecutor in trials and the state began to withhold from the accused the names of witnesses and even their testimony. As a result, the accused had no right to question and evaluate the evidence. Procedures of the Inquisition made their way into Roman law and courts began to conduct most parts of a criminal trial. The open adversarial procedures that allowed public evaluation of evidence simply disappeared. The courts also had the ability to initiate the cases that were being prosecuted without public recourse to the evidence. This approach was not always popular with the general public who resented being forced to go to court for an offense that two parties might have reconciled. In 1532 Charles V issued his *Constitutio Criminalis Carolina,* a criminal code that attempted to safeguard the innocent from inquisitorial methods. However, the *Carolina* limited actual trials to a public ceremony at the end of the state's secretive inquisition. Trials were separate from the execution of punishment, but the actual deliberations were a secret matter controlled by the authorities. Punishment and execution were turned into public spectacle that validated the nonpublic courts. Public executions served to demonstrate that the people consented to a sentence that they could not control.

**Holy Roman Empire.** Rulers who sought to impose Roman law faced harsh opposition because it eliminated local traditions, customs, and statutes. This situation was especially true in the Holy Roman Empire, where lawyers had studied at foreign universities such as Bologna. New laws and foreign-trained lawyers who employed strange proceedings were common complaints of German grievances during rebellions such as the Poor Conrad (1514) and the Peasants' War (1525). Roman law took on a new role in the Holy Roman Empire in 1495 with the creation of the *Reichskamergericht* (Imperial Chamber Court). The Imperial Chamber Court was a supreme court of the empire and yet not of the emperor. The court was based on written law and thus contributed to the end of customary law in the Holy Roman Empire. The court also forced residents of the empire to hire a trained specialist or lawyer. Residents of the empire resented the new law code because they thought it was unfair when in fact it was less arbitrary than customary law. Not only was Roman law written, it also emphasized valid evidence and notarized documentation. Contracts needed to be drawn by a government certified official in a manner that gave the state an expanded role in all transactions.

**Law and Sovereignty.** The Renaissance conciliar movement was an attempt to shift church power from the hands of the popes to the hands of church councils. The presence of two popes during the Great Schism (1378–1417) threatened the authority of canon law because two different supreme judges were capable of making contradicting decisions. The conciliarists believed that the pope was obligated to obey the council. Ecclesiastical law, like civil law, was thus based on the authority of existing statutes: the canon law of the church council and the Roman law of the historical past. Tyranny in either arena could be resisted by appeal to a written legal code. Law remained a source of legitimacy until Niccolò Machiavelli and Martin Luther offered a different alternative. The two were at polar extremes on most issues, but both agreed that law and tyr-

anny went hand in hand. Luther believed that active resistance against a tyrant was always wrong, yet he broke with the Pope because he considered him a tyrant. Machiavelli argued that a tyrant was nothing other than a prince. For both men, law was a human creation. Jean Bodin offered a solution at the end of the sixteenth century. Like Luther and Machiavelli, he agreed that there was a huge difference between legality and legitimacy. Luther trusted faith and Machiavelli trusted politics as a means to bridge legality and legitimacy, but Bodin turned to the law itself. Rulers should have absolute power to establish order and law. Bodin's notion of the king as lawgiver contrasted with the medieval notion that law had always existed. The sovereign was the one to decide the laws. In the end, law that was approved by a sovereign was good law. The king, however, was in theory bound by natural law, divine law, and the fundamental laws of the realm. Yet, divine law and natural law were valid only if the sovereign accepted them. Whatever the sovereign accepted was valid for all subjects.

Sources:

Hans J. Hillerbrand, ed., *The Oxford Encyclopedia of the Reformation* (New York: Oxford University Press, 1996).

David Nicholas, *The Transformation of Europe 1300–1600* (New York: Oxford University Press, 1999).

Steven W. Rowan, *Law and Jurisprudence in the Sixteenth Century: An Introductory Bibliography* (St. Louis: Center for Reformation Research, 1986).

Laura Ikins Stern, *The Criminal Law System of Medieval and Renaissance Florence* (Baltimore: Johns Hopkins University Press, 1994).

Gerald R. Strauss, *Law, Resistance and the State: The Opposition to Roman Law in Reformation Germany* (Princeton: Princeton University Press, 1986).

Jonathan W. Zophy, *The Holy Roman Empire* (Westport, Conn.: Greenwood Press, 1980).

## WEAPONRY

**Knights.** In 1350 the heavily armored cavalryman known as the knight still dominated the battlefields of central and western Europe, as he had since the Battle of Hastings (1066). He was identified by his horse, armor, and weapons. Although it was not a violation of the knightly code to fight on foot, to be a true knight was to be on horseback, wear armor, and engage in hand-to-hand combat using couched lance, broadsword, and other shock weapons such as maces. By 1350 the knights had adopted plate armor replacing the chain mail of earlier centuries because of improvements in infantry weapons. It doubled the thirty-pound weight of chain mail and was more than twice as expensive. After 1350, armor was often placed on horses. The increased protection given by plate armor required that the knight's weapons be made stronger.

**Lance.** The lance was wooden with a metal point, nine or ten feet in length and held under the armpit in the right hand, which was used to direct the point against a foe. It was fitted with a conical device at the butt end fitted against the user's body to prevent it from sliding under the arm when it struck the foe. A lance, when properly wielded, combined the weight of man,

War flails used by Taborite soldiers during the Hussite War of the mid fifteenth century (National Museum, Prague)

**Crossbow.** For centuries, the knights had held an enormous advantage over ordinary infantry or foot soldiers, who usually lacked no armor and had mediocre weapons, often simply sharpened farm tools. By 1350, however, some infantrymen were carrying weapons that significantly reduced knightly superiority. One was the crossbow, which had been in use for more than two centuries but had reached its final, most powerful form by the period under consideration. A bow was attached at the end of a stock, which had a trough in it where the bolt, usually a foot long with a quadrangular iron head, was placed. A cord was attached to the bow and pulled back to catch on a nut at the opposite end of the stock. When the trigger was pulled, the nut turned and released the cord, which propelled the bolt forward with great force. The strength of the bow had steadily been increased, some being made of steel, so that a mechanical device rather than the hand had to be used to pull the cord back. A bolt from such a crossbow had tremendous impact at a distance of twenty or thirty yards, capable of piercing even plate armor, but it was not accurate at a greater range. The principal shortcoming of the crossbow was the length of time it took to get off a second shot, over a minute for the more powerful ones. Charging enemy cavalry would reach the bowmen before they could get off a second shot, so they had to have other fighting men around them to protect them against a charge. The crossbow's principal advantages were that it was cheap and easy to make and it did not require much training to use effectively. These factors made the crossbow the favorite weapon for urban militiamen, who defended the walls of their cities, where the slow reloading time was far less a problem than it was in the field.

**Longbow.** The longbow, which was over five feet long (about twelve inches longer than typical bows of the era), appeared later than the crossbow. The Welsh had used it in the course of their long struggle against the English in the thirteenth century. The most powerful type had a draw of up to 150 pounds, and it could kill an unarmored person at a range of 250 yards, although its penetration range for plate armor was far less. Longbowmen, who could be amazingly accurate when competing in contests, did not take the time to aim in battle but depended upon their experience and rate of fire to put a large number of arrows into a small space in a short period of time. A good archer could fire up to ten arrows a minute for several minutes until he tired. A company of archers truly could create a rain of arrows. A longbow required much skill to make, including the ability to identify the right piece of wood, the best being from yew trees. The effective use of the longbow also took years to develop. Only those who had been training since childhood were likely to become capable archers. England and Wales alone had the necessary social structure to encourage commoner boys to become good archers. Attempts to create archer companies on the Continent failed, because they tried to train adult men into longbow users. The longbow in the hands of a skilled English archer remained an effective weapon for a long time after

horse, and armor to drive its point through shield and armor and into the enemy.

**Broadsword and Mace.** The broadsword was about three feet long. It had been a one-handed weapon previously, but plate armor required an increase in weight, which made some swords two-handed after 1400. A knight usually carried a dagger and some sort of club such as a mace or a morning star, a ball-like device with sharp points attached to a chain.

**Cavalry Tactics.** The usual knightly tactic was the frontal charge. The horsemen formed a line and rode toward the enemy with their lances pointed outward, reaching a full gallop some thirty to forty yards before colliding with the foe's line. They used their lances to try to kill or at least unseat their opponents. If a foe was badly inferior in numbers or morale, allowing his line to be broken, hand-to-hand combat ensued in the melee after the two lines collided, in which swords and clubs were used. The individual combatants were usually identical in equipment, strength, and training. However, after 1350 the cost of the steadily increasing amount of plate armor resulted in the wealthier knights having an advantage in the quality and amount of armor.

firearms were developed, and the English army did not make the official changeover to muskets until the late sixteenth century.

**Pike.** A third infantry weapon that significantly reduced the cavalry's advantage over the infantry was the pike. The pike was a shaft of wood fifteen to twenty feet long with an iron tip. When enemy cavalrymen charged pikemen, the latter placed the butt end of their pikes in the ground and braced them with their right feet. The pike was held at an angle to the ground so that its point would be at a horse's chest level, placing the point of contact perhaps fifteen feet away from the pikeman. The goal was to have the horse impale itself on the pike as the knight charged, throwing the rider. The pikeman or another infantryman attached to the company then stepped forward with a sword or another weapon to kill the knight floundering on the ground. Against other infantry the pike was held overhand and driven down at an angle into the chest of the foe. An age-old weapon used so effectively by Alexander the Great's infantry, the pike required highly disciplined soldiers, especially when they had to face armored horsemen charging at them. That kind of discipline had disappeared in the Middle Ages and was only beginning to reappear as of 1350. The Swiss, who established their reputation as the best infantrymen of the late Middle Ages in using the pike, combined it with the halberd, a battle-ax on an eight-foot pole. After a pikeman had knocked a knight to the ground, another infantryman could dispatch him with a powerful swing of the halberd.

**Gunpowder.** The late Middle Ages are known in military history primarily as the era of the development of gunpowder weapons. Gunpowder is a Chinese invention that dates to before 1000 C.E. Gunpowder weapons were in widespread use in China by 1280. They apparently had the three essential elements of true gunpowder weapons: a metal barrel, an explosive substance such as black powder, and a projectile that filled the barrel in order to take full advantage of the propellant blast. The consensus among historians is that the Mongols carried gunpowder westward from China in the thirteenth century, but there is no agreement whether gunpowder weapons also came to Europe with the powder.

**Early European Use.** The first European mention of gunpowder has been dated to 1267. A reference to the making of gunpowder artillery found in a 1326 document from Florence is widely accepted as the first reliable mention, but an illustrated English manuscript from the next year provides more information. It shows a large potbellied vessel lying on its side on a table with a bolt projecting from its mouth, which is aimed at the gate of a walled place. Behind the device stands an armored man with a heated poker, which he is about to put to its touchhole. As the illustration reveals, these early gunpowder weapons were largely associated with sieges. The first definitive mention of them in action came from a siege in 1340.

**Handcannon and Bombards.** In field warfare these early gunpowder weapons lacked the technical quality to allow them to compete effectively with the other weapons in use. The weight, unreliability, inaccuracy, and slow rate of fire made early gunpowder firearms, called handcannon, inferior to traditional weapons until the early fifteenth century. In sieges, however, these defects were far less a problem, and early cannon soon became an effective weapon for attacking fortified places. The flat trajectory of the cannonball meant that the projectile would strike low against the high walls of medieval fortifications and open a breach. The first known instance of gunpowder artillery bringing a siege to a successful end occurred in 1371. Soon the size of gunpowder artillery increased greatly. Bombards, so called because the stone balls they used buzzed like bumblebees when fired, were short-barreled with large muzzles and could reach up to twenty tons in weight. At the siege of Constantinople in 1453, the Turks used a bombard that fired a one-thousand-pound cannonball. Nevertheless, bombards were extremely difficult to move, and the amount of gunpowder they required was expensive and difficult to find.

**Handguns.** Several innovations were necessary before the first effective handguns could be developed. Corned powder, which provided greater explosive power than earlier serpentine powder, appeared about 1420. Corned powder produced higher muzzle velocities, which meant that it could fire balls that were capable of penetrating the plate armor of knights. Higher muzzle velocity, however, required a longer barrel than the handcannon had. By 1450 gunsmiths had found the right compromise between ballistic performance and weight for handcannon by fitting them with barrels about forty inches in length. The first known illustration of a long-barreled firearm shows it being used for duck hunting. Another innovation that was necessary to create an effective firearm was the match—a piece of string soaked in saltpeter that burned slowly but hot enough to touch off gunpowder. The match was developed around 1420 and replaced the clumsy and unreliable burning stick. The match, however, created the same problem for its users as did the burning stick: It had to be held in a hand and touched down into the chamber to fire the powder. That meant only one hand could be used to hold the weapon, which was butted up against the chest, not the shoulder. Too large a charge of powder could result in a broken breastbone. The solution was the matchlock.

**Matchlock.** As it evolved in Germany, the matchlock brought together springs, a trigger, and a clamp for holding a smoldering match so that when the trigger was pulled, its burning tip was thrust into the powder and touched it off. After the shoulder stock, borrowed from the crossbow, was added to reduce the impact of the recoil from the greater muzzle velocity, the firearm was made up of the proverbial lock, stock, and barrel.

**Flash in the Pan.** Another innovation was the pan. The users of the matchlock device found that the match often failed to touch off the powder if the powder was too coarse, yet the use of fine powder to fire the ball created too much recoil. The problem was solved by placing a small pan

Viennese artillery piece from the late fifteenth century (Heeresgeschichtliches Museum/Militarwissenschaftliches Institut, Vienna)

behind the chamber of the barrel into which fine powder was placed, while coarse powder was put in the chamber. The match touched off the fine powder in the pan, blowing flame through a small hole into the chamber, igniting the coarser powder there, and firing off the ball. Often, however, the powder in the pan ignited without touching off the powder in the chamber, leading to another proverbial saying: "A flash in the pan."

**Arquebus.** The arquebus, as the first matchlock firearm was called, was developed by 1460, but its impact on the battlefield was slow to appear. As a smoothbore weapon it was inherently inaccurate. As the ball tumbles down a smoothbore barrel, what spin it has as it leaves the muzzle is imparted by the last point on the barrel it touches. The user has no idea of what direction the spin will cause the ball to take. Balls fired from smoothbore weapons will never follow the same trajectory. Consequently, the arquebus was accurate for only a short distance, before the uncontrolled spin took over. The impact of the ball on the foe, even an armored cavalryman, was deadly at close range, but that advantage was largely negated by the long time it took to reload an arquebus. If the arquebusier missed a charging foe with his first shot or if he had a misfire, common with the arquebus, the enemy would reach him before he could reload. Before the seventeenth-century invention of the paper cartridge that combined a ball and measured amount of powder, reloading an arquebus under the best conditions took over a minute. In the confusion and disorder of a battlefield, especially with knights with their lances and swords bearing down, it is easy to see why many arque-

busiers never reloaded and fired a second time. Compared to longbows, the early arquebus performed poorly in respect to reliability, rate of fire, and accuracy, but it was competitive with the crossbow. The arquebus found its first niche as a siege weapon, where it replaced the crossbow as the favored weapon for urban militiamen. They did not require much training to learn to use effectively on walls, and although they were more expensive than crossbows, the artisans and merchants who comprised the urban militia could afford them.

**Advancements.** While the arquebus first served as a useful weapon for defending fortifications, improvements in gunpowder artillery quickly overwhelmed what advantage it gave the defenses. Because late medieval iron casting produced a poor product, barrels made of cast iron frequently burst, killing the gun crews. Better quality pieces were made through forging iron rods formed into circles, which were banded by hot metal hoops that tightened down as they cooled. These hooped bombards were the weapons first associated with the name *cannon*, which came from a Latin word for tube. Small cannon often were equipped with breech pans, which were loaded in advance and set in the piece for firing in rapid succession.

**Bronze Cannon.** Another solution to the poor quality of cast iron pieces was the use of bronze. Europeans were familiar with casting bronze bells, and the technology was easily transferred to making weapons. Using bronze allowed the gunmakers to manufacture long-barreled pieces with small muzzles, called culverins from a French word for serpent, which were capable of using iron or lead balls.

Reconstruction of a Taborite war wagon used during the Hussite War in the mid fifteenth century (National Museum, Prague)

**Cannon Shot.** Metal balls caused far more damage to the masonry of a fortification than did the stone balls, which often splintered when they hit their target, reducing their impact. Cannon shot remained solid until the nineteenth century because of the lack until then of a reliable fuse to explode shells packed with explosives.

**French Innovations.** The French led in developing high quality culverins along with the gun carriage with the high wheels and long tail that defined artillery pieces until the nineteenth century. The culverins had loops cast on to the barrels by which they were attached to the gun carriage. The guns could be freely swung up or down, allowing for their proper elevation to provide the right trajectory for the ball. The gunners used a device called the gunner's quadrant to determine the correct elevation. Using an artillery train of some eighty bronze culverins on mobile carriages, French king Charles VIII had great success in reducing Italian fortifications during the initial phase of the French invasions of Italy (1494–1525). In the Battle of Fornovo (1495) the French artillery also played a significant role as an effective field weapon against the forces of the League of Venice.

**Spanish Square.** During the wars in Italy after 1494, field armies also began to include handgunners with arquebuses. The slow rate of fire, however, continued to retard their use, until the Spanish fighting the French for control of Italy developed a combination of pikemen and arquebusiers in which they provided mutual support for each other. Called the Spanish Square, it remained the dominant infantry system until the Thirty Years' War (1618–1648). Using the arquebus as a field weapon resulted in a reduction in its weight to make it easier for the handgunner to carry, but it then fired a lighter ball that reduced its ability to penetrate armor. A heavier weapon, called the Spanish musket, appeared about 1520 and used a larger ball. It was so heavy that soldiers often dropped the barrel down before they fired, hitting the ground in front of the enemy. The solution was the introduction of the fork on which the end of the barrel rested. Although putting the fork in place added another step to the process of reloading, it improved accuracy enough that the fork became used for the arquebus as well. By the end of the sixteenth century the differences between the two weapons had disappeared, and any firearm was called a musket.

**Drilling.** During the Dutch Revolt against Spain (1565–1648), the Dutch commander Maurice of Nassau made his musketmen more effective by extensive drilling, which had great success in improving their rate of fire. He broke down the process of loading and firing a matchlock firearm into forty-two steps; each step had a word of command shouted by the sergeant. Drill books showing the steps and providing the words of command spread across Europe, resulting in a significant increase in the effectiveness of firearms in battle.

**Pistol.** Another new weapon that also was developed by 1520 was the pistol. The first datable illustration of the wheel-lock mechanism used for it appeared in a German manuscript of 1505. The wheel-lock mechanism involved pieces of iron pyrite placed on a small wheel that was attached to a spring. When it was cocked and the trigger pulled, the spring spun the pyrite against steel, dropping sparks into the gunpowder in the pan. It was a delicate device, yet it still had to be sturdy enough to be used in the field. The wheel-lock pistol was far more expensive to make than the arquebus, and its expense restricted its use to those who could afford it—the nobles. The pistol was well out of the price range of the common soldier, for whom the arquebus was better anyway, being more reliable and firing a larger ball more accurately. For cavalrymen, the absence of the glowing match, which frightened their horses, was an important advantage. Earlier armies had mounted handgunners, but they were ineffective from horseback, so they usually dismounted to fire. The arquebus required two hands to use, whereas the pistol left one hand free for the reins. By allowing the pistol-carrying cavalryman to ride a smaller and cheaper horse and wear less armor, the several pistols a pistoleer carried reduced the financial burden on the users.

**Battlefield Use.** With a loaded pistol in his right hand and others in his boots and saddles, a pistoleer would approach his foe and fire his pistols at close range, around ten yards. This distance put him just short of the point of an infantryman's pike or a cavalryman's lance. He would fire as he wheeled about to the left, return to the rear of his company, and wait his turn to come forward again. A smoothbore pistol fired off a moving horse is an inaccurate weapon, but at close range it hit its target often enough and generated enough muzzle velocity to penetrate armor. The first mention of pistols on the battlefield dates to 1544 during the war between Charles V and the French.

The speed of the pistoliers was a major factor in their use; they were especially good for pursuing a fleeing enemy. During the French Wars of Religion (1561–1598), pistoleers came to make up most of the French mounted troops, and the knights disappeared.

**Naval Changes.** Gunpowder weapons also dramatically changed the nature of war at sea. In the fifteenth century, cannon and firearms began to replace catapults and bows on board ship. Combining improvements in sails, ship design, navigation, and the placement of cannon on the decks, the Portuguese were the first to develop a ship that was capable of making voyages across the oceans and effectively defend itself. Around 1500 the French came up with gun ports, which placed the heavy guns on a ship's lower decks and increased its stability. By 1540 the Spanish were using the galleon to protect its treasure ships returning from the newly conquered Americas. With as many as forty heavy guns firing through gun ports and soldiers with firearms posted on high castles built on the main deck, the galleon was capable of projecting naval power a long distance from its home waters. English pirates adopted the galleon to prey on Spanish shipping, but they found that the high castles reduced their speed and maneuverability, crucial elements for a successful pirate. They cut down the castle and created the "race-built galleon." The pirates also preferred not to close with a well-defended Spanish treasure ship and fight hand-to-hand on its decks to seize control of it, but to stand off and fire cannon at it, raking it with broadsides from their medium-weight cannon, until they forced it to stop and surrender. By the time of the voyage of the Spanish Armada (1588), the essential elements of the standard warship as it would last until the nineteenth century were in place.

Sources:

Larry H. Addington, *The Patterns of War through the Eighteenth Century* (Bloomington & Indianapolis: Indiana University Press, 1990).

Bert S. Hall, *Weapons and Warfare in Renaissance Europe: Gunpowder, Technology, and Tactics* (Baltimore: Johns Hopkins University Press, 1997).

Jaroslav Lugs, *Firearms Past and Present: A Complete Review of Firearm Systems and Their Histories*, 2 volumes (London: Grenville, 1973).

Richard A. Preston, and others, *Men in Arms: A History of Warfare and Its Interrelationships with Western Society* (Fort Worth, Tex.: Holt, 1991).

# SIGNIFICANT PEOPLE

## JEAN BODIN

### 1530-1596
### POLITICAL PHILOSOPHER

**Humble Beginnings.** The son of a tailor, Jean Bodin was born in the French city of Angers. It is possible that he had a Jewish mother from a family that had been expelled from Spain, which would explain his knowledge of Hebrew and deep interest in Judaism. He entered a monastery as a teenager, but left after five years and studied law at the University of Toulouse. He taught law there for a time after receiving his master's degree. In 1561 he arrived in Paris, where he served in the royal court. His knowledge of law and humanist learning caught the attention of Henri III, who appointed him the royal attorney in the city of Laon in 1576. Bodin had just arrived there when he was selected as a deputy for the Third Estate at the 1576 meeting of the Estates General, which met at Blois. There he was elected speaker for the Third Estate, which gave him a platform for appealing for religious toleration for the French Protestants. This stance marked him as a *politique*, one of those Frenchmen who argued that religious toleration was necessary for the good of the kingdom. He successfully opposed the efforts of the Catholic League to require the king to use force against the Protestants. He also succeeded in opposing Henri III's request to sell off royal lands to help pay the enormous royal debt. Bodin argued that it was a fundamental law of the realm that royal lands must remain in royal hands.

**Advocate of Freedom.** Bodin's advocacy of religious toleration was greatly expanded in his *Colloquium of the Seven about the Secrets of the Sublime*, which he finished in 1588 but was not published until long after his death. Three of the seven speakers who participate in the dialogue on religion and morality are a Jew, a Muslim, and a follower of natural religion, who criticize both sides of the religious split in France. They suggested that religious truth might be found outside of Christianity and that there might exist a universal moral code on which all religions could agree. Bodin seemed to hint at the need to tolerate not only different Christian churches but also Judaism and Islam. Yet, Bodin joined the Catholic League about the same time as he finished the Colloquium. The League was determined to prevent the Protestant prince, Henri of Bourbon, from taking the throne after Henri III's assassination in 1589. Bodin probably agreed with the League that French tradition required that the king be Catholic; he supported the claim to the throne of Henri of Bourbon's uncle, a cardinal in the Catholic Church. Bodin was quick to recognize Henri as king after the monarch converted to Catholicism in 1593.

**Economic and Social Philosopher.** Bodin also made a mark with two other books. His *Réponse aux paradoxes de M. de Malestroit* (Response to the Paradox of Monsieur Malestroit, 1568) called for free trade and dealt the problem of inflation at a time when no one had any idea that there could be such a thing. Since the early sixteenth century the European economy had seen a steady increase in prices, which averaged 1 to 2 percent annually until about 1550, then increased to 2 to 3 percent. Jehan Cherruyt de Malestroit, an adviser to the king, had blamed it on the greed of merchants who were gouging their customers. Bodin found the cause to be largely the great increase in the amount of gold and silver coinage in circulation coming from the Americas through Spain. He also placed some blame on the royal practice of debasing coinage, that is, reducing the amount of precious metal in coins and replacing it with lead, making them worth less. Bodin's book is generally regarded as the first work of economic theory. The other book was *De la demonomanie des sorciers* (On the Demonology of Sorcerers, 1580), which he wrote to oppose a handful of skeptics who were challenging the reality of witchcraft. In it he justified the use of judicial torture and execution for sorcery, on the grounds that it was real and evil. He had spent a great deal of time as a judge at witch trials and heard the confessions of the accused. The confessions were undoubtedly extracted by torture, but he and most contemporaries had no doubts about the value of torture to gain confessions. Anyone who had made a pact with a spirit to do evil was a traitor toward God and humanity. No toleration was to be permitted for such persons. Yet, the rationalism that shows itself in his other books comes through in this one as well, as he was eager to reform the legal procedures for witch trials, arguing that many judges were quick to convict on too little or questionable evidence.

**An Ideal State.** Bodin's major work was *Six livres de la République* (The Six Books of the Republic), published in 1576. He did his own Latin translation ten years later. The purpose of the work was to answer the question of how the king should deal with the anarchy of the French religious wars, which had been dragging on since 1562. Bodin believed it necessary to find a natural basis for the source of royal authority in order to replace religion, which no longer was adequate. Religion was a cause of the civil war and therefore was creating anarchy, not preventing it. Many French political thinkers of the era were arguing for a mixed constitution in which power would be shared between the king and the Estates General. Bodin believed that such thinking was partly responsible for the anarchy. His solution was to place all political authority in the hands of the king; only a king who had absolute power could reestablish law and order. Bodin argued that the absolute king depends on no one for power, makes and enforces the law for everyone, and has the right to command his subjects and take a reasonable part of their property as taxes for the common good. Bodin's discussion of the king as lawgiver was novel, since the medieval concept of law was that it had existed from time immemorial and the king "found it in his breast." The king, however, was bound by natural, divine, and fundamental laws of the realm. Bodin carefully hedged the authority of the monarch, who was not to be a despot in the way that Europeans believed the Ottoman sultan was. Despite that caveat, *The Republic* provided theoretical underpinnings for the development of French royal absolutism in the seventeenth century.

Sources:

Julian H. Franklin, *Jean Bodin and the Rise of Absolutist Theory* (Cambridge: Cambridge University Press, 1973).

J. P. Mayer, ed., *Fundamental Studies on Jean Bodin* (New York: Arno, 1979).

Paul Lawrence Rose, *Bodin and the Great God of Nature: The Moral and Religious Universe of a Judaiser* (Geneva: Droz, 1980).

# CHARLES V

## 1500-1558

### HOLY ROMAN EMPEROR

**A Royal Inheritance.** One of the most significant political figures of the sixteenth century, Charles V was emperor of the Holy Roman Empire (1519–1556) and, as Charles I, king of Spain (1516–1556). A member of the Hapsburg family, Charles was the son of Philip I the Handsome, the Duke of Burgundy and ruler of the Netherlands, and grandson of Emperor Maximilian I and Mary of Burgundy. His mother, Joan the Mad, was the daughter of Ferdinand I of Aragon and Isabella of Castile. He was raised by his aunt, Margaret of Austria, who was regent of the Netherlands. Upon the death of his father in 1506, Charles inherited the Netherlands, Luxembourg, and the Franche–Comté. When his maternal grandfather died in 1516, and his mother was deemed mentally unsound, he became king of Castile, as well as of the Indies, Aragon, Navarre, Sicily, Sardinia, and Naples. When his paternal grandfather died in 1519, Charles inherited the House of Austria and was elected Holy Roman Emperor. The total amount of land under Charles's direct and indirect control was staggering—placing him at the center of two conflicts that defined his life: dynastic struggles with Francis I of France and religious controversies stemming from the teachings of a resident of the Holy Roman Empire, Martin Luther.

**Spanish Connections.** Charles's political career began and ended in Spain, despite the fact that he spoke no Spanish when he first traveled there in 1517. Although Charles claimed his inheritance, the Spaniards were not happy to be ruled by an Austrian who was surrounded by Burgundians. The *comuneros,* a group of Castilian cities that opposed the government and were led by Juan de Padilla, revolted from 1520 to 1521 while Charles was in Germany. The uprising was put down, the leaders were executed, and Charles's authority was reestablished. After receiving his crown as emperor and presiding over the condemnation of Luther at the Diet of Worms (1521), Charles returned to Spain in 1522 and stayed for seven years. He learned Spanish and began to place Castilians in advisory positions formerly held by Burgundians. Charles established a new Council of the Indies, which controlled colonial policy for all of Spain's New World possessions. He put into place a law code for the Americas (*New Laws: Ordinances for the Government of the Indies and Good Treatment and Preservation of the Indians*) that, although unenforceable, sought to legislate control and protect subjects. Charles became well respected by his Spanish subjects, who reportedly joked that Charles spoke French with his diplomats, Italian with his lovers, German with his grooms, but Spanish with God.

**Struggles with France.** Charles's career was largely defined by conflicts with Francis I of France. This Valois versus Habsburg rivalry was inherited by both men as the two dynasties fought over control of territories in Italy. France had invaded Italy in 1494 and again in 1499. Italy bore the brunt of fighting between Charles and Francis until the Treaty of Combrai, signed in 1529, finally settled the conflict. The animosity between the two rulers was also fueled by the fact that both had attempted in 1519 to be elected emperor of the Holy Roman Empire. The competition was expensive, as both men attempted to bribe the seven electors. Charles won, thanks to his grandfather's anticipation of the election and funding from the Fuggers, a banking family that lived in Augsburg. Other rulers in Europe feared that either candidate would consolidate too much power in one family's hands. From the French perspective, the Habsburgs were attempting to encircle France and limit its power. The French went so far as to make alliances with the non-Christian Turks who were threatening Habsburg lands. Henry VIII and Francis I were at war with each other during most of their reigns. The king of England and the papacy used this rivalry to bolster their own power by supporting first one and then the other side of the conflict.

**Luther and the Protestants.** Charles was a deeply religious man who sought above all to protect the Roman Catholic faith. He supported the Inquisition in Spain and attempted to introduce it into his other territories. When he went to Spain in 1522 he apparently believed that his condemnation of Luther would stifle the spread of the reformer's teachings. Charles returned to the Holy Roman Empire seven years later, but he was greeted with the Augsburg Confession (1530), which clarified Lutheran beliefs and solidified a Protestant opposition to his policies—manifested in the newly formed Schmalkaldic League. Moreover, he had missed the Knight's Revolt of 1523 and Peasants' War of 1525, two defining moments in the history of Germany. Further hampering his anti-Protestant wishes, war with Francis I kept him from Germany from 1532 until 1541, by which time Protestantism was a formidable force. Conflicts between Protestants and supporters of Charles clashed for another decade until the league of German princes pushed his troops from Germany in 1552. Later that year the Treaty of Passau attempted to establish a religious division of the Holy Roman Empire, based on a principle whereby the local prince could determine the religion in his territory. This treaty led to the Peace of Augsburg on 25 September 1555, which divided his lands into Catholic or Protestant. Charles found this agreement unacceptable and considered it a personal failure. He began to withdraw from politics immediately thereafter.

**Medieval View of Empire.** Before Charles had reached the age of twenty-one, he had obtained a lifetime of experience in diplomacy in the Spanish unrest and the religious conflict in the Holy Roman Empire. Charles's youthful reliance on his Burgundian advisers almost cost him control of Spain, and his early experiences with Luther undoubtedly influenced his lifelong efforts to maintain Catholicism. Charles left several treatises on statecraft and a memoir of the first fifty-one years of his life. In 1532 he issued the *Constitutio Criminalis Carolina,* an imperial criminal code that safeguarded the rights of the innocent. The *Carolina* standardized criminal procedures and strengthened the role of central government. His *New Laws* attempted to control the Spanish colonies and protect his subjects, particularly native populations, abroad. Despite these two law codes, Charles's views were more medieval than modern. For instance, Charles challenged Francis I to personal combat to determine control of Burgundy and Milan, and he offered Luther a promise of safe-conduct to and from Worms (Emperor Sigismund did not honor a similar promise to Jan Hus at the Council of Con-

stance in 1415). His medieval mind-set was broader than mere chivalry, however, as he believed that world peace could be maintained only through a strong emperor. Charles may not have wanted a universal monarchy—he certainly did not view Spanish colonies on the same terms as his European lands—but he wanted a strong Holy Roman Empire that was based on Roman Catholicism. Humiliated and disgusted that he had not been able to maintain the Catholicism in his empire, he refused to accept the legal recognition of Protestantism and opted instead to abdicate.

**Last Years.** In 1555 Charles turned the Netherlands over to his son Philip and the next year he abdicated to Philip the kingdom of Spain, his Italian lands, and the colonies. Philip proceeded to have a glorious reign as Philip II of Spain. Charles retired to a country home near a remote Hieronymite monastery at San Jerónimo de Yuste. There he continued to monitor political developments, went fishing, and pursued his religious devotion until his death two years later.

Sources:

Manuel Fernández Alvarez, *Charles V: Elected Emperor and Hereditary Ruler,* translated by J. A. Lalaguna (London: Thames & Hudson, 1975).

Karl Brandi, *The Emperor Charles V: The Growth and Destiny of a Man and of a World-Empire,* translated by C.V. Wedgwood (London: Cape, 1939).

Jonathan W. Zophy, *The Holy Roman Empire: A Dictionary Handbook* (Westport, Conn.: Greenwood Press, 1980).

# ELIZABETH I

## 1533-1603
### QUEEN OF ENGLAND

**The Good Queen.** Elizabeth I, known as the Virgin Queen or Good Queen Bess, was the reigning monarch of England from 1558 to 1603. A shrewd, calculating, manipulative woman, she instilled deep loyalty in her subjects with her grave majestic poise. She preserved the English nation against internal as well as external threats, and during her forty-five-year reign the island kingdom emerged as a world power. It is because of her influence that the latter half of the sixteenth century in England is known as the Elizabethan Age.

**Early Years.** Elizabeth was born on 7 September 1533, the daughter of Tudor king Henry VIII and his second wife, Anne Boleyn. Because Henry VIII had defied the Pope and married Boleyn in the hope of producing a male heir to the throne, he was bitterly disappointed in the birth of a second daughter. Before Elizabeth was three, the king had her mother beheaded and their marriage declared invalid. Although now considered an illegitimate child,

Elizabeth was still third in line to the throne (after her half brother Edward and half sister Mary). She received tutoring from leading Renaissance scholars who noted the child's intellect and seriousness. The humanist Roger Ascham wrote: "Her mind has no womanly weakness, her perseverence is equal to that of a man, and her memory long keeps what it quickly picks up." In time she became fluent in Greek, Latin, French, and Italian.

**Court Intrigue.** Upon his father's death in 1547, Edward VI became king of England; when he died in 1553, Elizabeth's older sister assumed the throne. Mary Tudor, wife of Philip II of Spain and a devout Catholic, did not endear herself to her Protestant subjects. Consequently, many nobles as well as commoners saw Elizabeth as their savior. As for the queen's sister, she professed her own Catholicism in order to avoid suspicion, but in 1554 she was arrested for plotting to overthrow the government and narrowly escaped execution.

**Accession.** On 17 November 1558 Mary died and Elizabeth became queen of England. One observer of her coronation procession into London noted: "If ever any person had either the gift or the style to win the hearts of people, it was this Queen, and if ever she did express the same it was at that present, in coupling mildness with majesty as she did, and in stately stooping to the meanest sort." Elizabeth quickly surrounded herself with experienced and loyal advisers, including William Cecil (afterward Lord Burghley) who served the queen for forty years as secretary of state and lord treasurer. She followed a policy of avoiding conflict with Parliament and curtailing state expenditures, although she did see the need for a strong navy.

**A Woman's World.** During her years as monarch, Elizabeth refused to compromise her power by taking a husband, although arranged marriages to various foreign as well as English noblemen were proposed to her at times. Nonetheless, some evidence suggests that she did develop romantic attachments to two men, Robert Dudley, Earl of Leicester, and Robert Devereux, Earl of Essex. The notion of Elizabeth as the Virgin Queen wedded to her kingdom gradually developed. The powerful personal image she engineered was one of female authority and regal magnificence combined with extravagant dress and rich jewels.

**Religious Issues.** Under Elizabeth, England was restored to Protestantism. In 1559 Parliament passed the Act of Supremacy, which revived the statutes of Henry VIII proscribing Catholicism and declared the queen supreme governor of the Church. Some Catholic aristocrats protested these measures, and in 1569 Elizabeth brutally suppressed a rebellion in northern England. Two years later informers uncovered the Ridolfi Plot, an international conspiracy against her life. Possible links to Mary Stuart, Queen of Scots, the granddaughter of Henry VIII's sister Margaret and the nearest heir to the throne, soon surfaced. (Mary had been driven from Scotland in 1568 and had taken refuge in England.) English Protestants reviled the Catholic Mary and saw her as a serious threat, especially since Elizabeth had not produced a male heir.

**Eliminating Mary.** In 1580 Pope Gregory XIII proclaimed that there was no sin in killing the heretic Elizabeth, who had been excommunicated by Pope Pius V ten years earlier. Tensions with the Papacy increased after the English sent a small military expedition to assist Dutch Protestant rebels. When the Babington Plot against the queen was uncovered in 1586, secret correspondence in Mary's handwriting was intercepted. In February 1587 Elizabeth caved into the outcry against the Queen of Scots as a menace to the realm and had Mary beheaded.

**Diplomacy.** An astute observer of international affairs, Elizabeth played a diplomatic game with England's two chief rivals, France and Spain. However, persecution of Mary's adherents at home and a foreign policy of strengthening Protestant allies abroad ensured the wrath of the Roman Catholic nations, especially Spain. Privateers led by Sir Francis Drake and others raided Spanish shipping and ports, and by the mid 1580s it became clear that war was inevitable between the two countries. When Philip II launched the ill-fated Spanish Armada in 1588, the English navy quickly defeated it.

**Successor.** In her last years Elizabeth suffered much from ill health. Her principal counselor, Sir Robert Cecil, the son of Lord Burghley, secretly corresponded with the likeliest claimant to the throne, James VI of Scotland. Elizabeth supposedly indicated James VI as her successor before dying quietly on 24 March 1603.

Sources:

John Bennett Black, *The Reign of Elizabeth, 1558–1603* (Oxford & New York: Oxford University Press, 1994).

Christopher Coleman and David Starkey, eds., *Revolution Reassessed: Revisions in the History of Tudor Government and Administration* (Oxford: Clarendon Press; New York: Oxford University Press, 1986).

Christopher Haigh, ed., *The Reign of Elizabeth I* (Athens: University of Georgia Press, 1985).

Jasper Ridley, *Elizabeth I: The Shrewdness of Virtue* (New York: Fromm International, 1989).

# GONZALO FERNÁNDEZ DE CÓRDOBA

## 1453-1515
### GENERAL

**Military Genius.** Gonzalo Fernández de Córdoba was born on 1 September 1453 in Montilla, a city in the province of Córdoba, Spain, into a noble family with a long tradition of military service to the Castilian monarchy. Fernández de Córdoba rose in the favor of Queen Isabella for his service during the civil war and the Portuguese invasion that complicated her succession as queen of Castile in 1474. He was a combatant in the ten-year war with the Moors that ended with the conquest of Granada in 1492, marking the completion of the Christian *reconquista* (reconquest) of Spain. In 1495 Ferdinand of Aragon, Isabella's husband, gave him command of the forces dispatched to southern Italy to repulse the French, who had ousted Ferdinand's cousin, King Ferrante, from the throne of the Kingdom of Naples. On 28 June 1495 at Seminara, Fernández de Córdoba gave battle to the French, whose strength lie in their heavy cavalry and Swiss pikemen. His forces, mostly light cavalry and infantrymen carrying sword and shield, were badly beaten; it would be his only defeat. Fernández de Córdoba, whose strongest attribute as a commander was his ability to learn the lessons taught him by the enemy, set about to reform his army. He recognized the tactical advantage of small-arms fire, but also saw the need to defend the handgunners as they reloaded, which was a slow process with firearms of that era. He introduced the arquebus and pike to his infantrymen and formed them up in large squares in which the two types of weapons provided mutual support.

**Innovator.** By 1503 Fernández de Córdoba was ready to test his new army against the French. At the Battle of Cerignola in April of that year, his new infantry force, which included most of his seven thousand men, took the brunt of the fighting. Fernández de Córdoba had dug a set of fieldworks, behind which he posted his artillery and infantry. Despite the loss of most of his guns when a powder magazine exploded, he successfully used his arquebusiers to halt the charge of the French heavy cavalry and Swiss pikemen, killing the French commander. His pikemen then drove the enemy off the battlefield. This battle demonstrated the superiority of his combination of pike and arquebus over French tactics. The French rushed reinforcements to Naples, which he met at the Garigliano River. For three months the two armies faced each other across Garigliano, until late December, when Fernández de Córdoba, using the cover of darkness, had a pontoon bridge thrown up across the river. The Spaniards caught the French by surprise and routed them. The French retreated to the fortress of Gaeta on the coast north of Naples, which lacked the supplies to feed the thousands of soldiers who stumbled in after their defeat. On 1 January 1504 Gaeta surrendered. Over the next year Fernández de Córdoba cleared the French out of southern Italy, and a treaty in 1505 passed sovereignty over the Kingdom of Naples to Ferdinand. The Spanish crown ruled Naples for the next two centuries.

**Disappointment.** Fernández de Córdoba served as viceroy in Naples until Ferdinand, frightened by his popularity and success, recalled him in 1507. Hurt by Ferdinand's ingratitude, he retired from service, although he was offered another command in 1512 after the Spanish were defeated at the Battle of Ravenna. He died at Granada, Spain, in 1515. The officers who served under him in southern Italy commanded the Spanish army for the next thirty years with great success and helped spread his ideas. His system of combining pikemen and handgunners in large square formations became known as the Spanish

Square. It was the dominant infantry formation across western and central Europe until late in the Thirty Years' War. He earned such a reputation as a successful commander that he was called the "Great Captain."

**Sources:**

Gerald de Gaury, *The Grand Captain: Gonzalo de Cordoba* (London & New York: Longmans, Green, 1955).

Francesco Guicciardini, *History of Italy, from the Year 1490, to 1532,* translated by Austin Parke Goddard, ten volumes (London: J. Towers, 1753–1756).

Mary Purcell, *The Great Captain: Gonzalo Fernández de Córdoba* (Garden City, N.Y.: Doubleday, 1962).

F. L. Taylor, *The Art of War in Italy, 1494–1529* (Cambridge: Cambridge University Press, 1921; reprint, Westport, Conn.: Greenwood Press, 1973).

# NICCOLÒ MACHIAVELLI

## 1469-1527
### HUMANIST, DIPLOMAT, AND POLITICAL THEORIST

**Perfect Timing.** Born into a prominent, though a somewhat poorer branch of a Florentine family, Niccolò Machiavelli became a noted civic humanist. He was classically educated and applied this background to his work as a public servant for the city of Florence. Machiavelli was politically active at an exciting time for humanists. The Medici family had recently been expelled from Florence (1494), and the city reverted to a Republican form of government. This change meant that humanists had an opportunity to apply their theories of good government. Machiavelli participated on many diplomatic missions and was able to observe leading figures of Italian politics such as Cesare Borgia and Pope Julius II. During this time much of Italy was under siege because the king of France on two occasions marched huge armies through the small Italian territories en route to conquering Naples in southern Italy. Although the Italians were more advanced in their humanist studies and political theories, they were no match militarily for the vast northern armies. Machiavelli responded to the confusion and strife in Italy by focusing his writings on political liberty and military matters.

***The Prince.*** Machiavelli's reputation hinges in large part on a small book titled *Il principe* (The Prince, 1513). In this work, he completely rejected the moral principles of Christian rule that had been the focus of medieval and Renaissance treatises on government. Machiavelli claimed that he drew up "an original set of rules." New rules were needed because he sought to "represent things as they are in real truth, rather than as they are imagined." Prior treatises had envisioned a moral ruler who set an example for his subjects, but Machiavelli assumed that humans were evil and thus the prince must "know how to do evil, if that is necessary" in order to gain power. The prince who is capable of evil will be able to see evil in his subjects and also to be evil in stopping them. If power is the goal, then evil must be used but only when necessary. The prince must be capable of acting like "a fox in order to recognize traps, and a lion in order to frighten off wolves." Machiavelli's ideas have been summarized as "the end justifies the means," but he never wrote such a thing. However, he believed that people judge results and assume that power is an end in itself. At the same time, he condemned Agathocles, an ancient king of Syracuse, for the use of unnecessary cruelty. Much of *The Prince* is devoted to discussing military issues. For instance, Machiavelli strongly opposes the use of mercenaries, as well as the use of auxiliary or foreign troops, that might not be loyal to the prince. Machiavelli's advice is aimed at the ultimate goal of a strong state with a strong and loyal army.

**Advice Books.** Early "civic" humanists were actively engaged in Republican governments. They wrote advice books that were directed at the entire body of citizens. This interest in good government changed with developments in the political landscape. By the late fifteenth century, Italian humanists shifted to advice books directed at special groups of individuals such as Baldassare Castiglione's *Il cortegiano* (The Book of the Courtier, 1528) and Machiavelli's *The Prince*. Machiavelli had spent his entire career in politics and, from 1498 until 1512, he had served as secretary in the chancellory of the restored Florentine Republic. When the Medici returned to power in 1512, the Republic collapsed and Machiavelli found himself out of work. He wrote a draft of *The Prince* at that time and planned to give it to Prince Giovanni de' Medici in hopes of securing a job. In a letter to a friend he explicitly states that he hopes the book will persuade the Medici that he should be given a government position. Before sending the work, the man to whom it was dedicated died. Machiavelli simply changed the dedication to honor the new ruler, Lorenzo de' Medici. The book failed to win him an appointment, but it became an important model for the genre of advice books for princes.

**Republican *Discourses*.** Machiavelli began to write his *Discorsi sopra la prima deca di Tito Livio* (Discourses on the First Ten Books of Livy, circa 1518) after he realized that he had little chance of being employed by the Medici. The *Discourses* include many references to *The Prince* but offer a radically different outlook on government. In *The Prince* the focus is on the security of a prince's domain, whereas the *Discourses* are about political liberty. Perhaps because he was not given a role in maintaining the prince's state, Machiavelli turned to a critique of princely government. He argued that liberty involves the power to self-govern without a monarch or prince. His comments about Casear are suggestive of his

personal situation after the Medici had rejected the advice of *The Prince:* "nor should anyone be deceived by Casear's renown when he finds writers extolling him before others, for those who praise him have either been corrupted by his fortune or overawed by the continuance of the empire which, since it was ruled under that name, did not permit writers to speak freely of him."

**Legacy.** Interpretation of Machiavelli has changed dramatically over time. Sixteenth-century contemporaries viewed him as an evil man who encouraged immorality, but Italians during the nineteenth-century unification of Italy viewed him as a nationalist who simply wanted a strong ruler protecting Italy. Modern thinkers tend to view him either as a political realist with an accurate assessment of power or as an opportunistic, but unemployed, diplomat who desperately wanted a position in the Florentine government. Machiavelli believed in strong government and that a republic would best protect individual liberty. He never extrapolated this theory of legitimate evil from princes and republican leaders to the general public. For Machiavelli, the moral principles governing rulers are not the same as those governing individuals, because rulers need to secure peace.

Sources:

Gisela Bock, Quentin Skinner, Maurizio Viroli, eds., *Machiavelli and Republicanism* (Cambridge & New York: Cambridge University Press, 1990).

Sebastian de Grazia, *Machiavelli in Hell* (Princeton: Princeton University Press, 1989).

Niccolò Machiavelli, *The Discourses*, edited by Bernard Crick and translated by Leslie J. Walker and Brian Richardson (Harmondsworth, U.K.: Penguin, 1970).

Machiavelli, *The Prince*, translated by George Bull (Harmondsworth, U.K.: Penguin, 1968).

Quentin Skinner, *Machiavelli* (Oxford & New York: Oxford University Press, 1981).

# MAURICE OF NASSAU

## 1567-1625
### GENERAL AND POLITICIAN

**Royal Son.** Maurice of Nassau was the second son of William the Silent, Prince of Orange, who led the early stages of the Dutch Revolt against Philip II of Spain. Maurice was born in the German principality of Nassau on the border of the Netherlands. His older brother had been taken to Spain as a hostage and spent the rest of his life there. Maurice was educated at Leiden University, making him one of the first prominent military commanders in Europe to have a college education. He did not receive a degree, however, because his education ended shortly after his father was assassinated in 1584. Maurice took his place as *stadtholder* of the province of Holland and captain-general of the army of the seven provinces that made up the Dutch Republic, which had declared its independence from the Spanish king in 1581. Maurice had a keen interest in mathematics and military history and used both to promote new ideas in warfare. He used as his principal sources the fourth-century A.D. Roman Flavius Vegetius Renatus's *Rei militaris instituta* (Military Institutions of the Romans), Italian Niccolò Machiavelli's *Dell'arte della guerra* (The Art of War, 1521), which was largely an updating of Vegetius's book for the early sixteenth century, and the Flemish professor Justus Lipsius's *De militia romana* (On Roman Military Service, 1595), which did the same for the late sixteenth century.

**Copying the Romans.** Lipsius, who was on the faculty at Leiden when Maurice was a student there, had said that whoever restored the Roman art of war in his own army would rule the world. Maurice did not come close to ruling the world, but in close cooperation with his cousin, John William of Nassau, he made a strong effort to restore the Roman military style. Since the Romans had dug their own entrenchments for fortifying their camps, Maurice insisted that his men also do their own digging instead of depending on forced labor of local civilians. Soldiers of that era regarded such manual labor as beneath them, but he ensured that his men did it by paying them extra. Not only were the field fortifications and siege trenches dug by Maurice's troops superior to those of other armies, the work also kept his men busy, greatly reducing idle time in camp. Maurice's key inspiration was that extensive drilling of the infantrymen as the Romans did would vastly enhance their effectiveness. In 1594 his cousin persuaded him that Roman military prowess depended as much on their use of missile weapons as the sword, and that the musketmen in his army could duplicate the continuous hail of javelins and slingshot the Romans had achieved. The long reloading time of the musket, which then was as long as two minutes, made it difficult to maintain any kind of constant fire. Maurice recognized that if his musketmen were drawn up into long ranks and each rank fired in unison and then retired to the rear of the company to reload while the next rank stepped forward, he could achieve continuous fire. He quickly discovered that when a rank had fired a volley and was retiring to reload, they bumped into the men behind them, disrupting the following volleys. When they reached the rear, the soldiers were disorganized and unable to get off an effective second volley. The solution was constant drilling in the process of reloading and stepping forward and backward with one's rank through the company, which led to a dramatic improvement in the rate of fire. Maurice invented words of command for the sergeants to shout for each step of the process of loading and firing, and John William devised a drill book that had illustrations that showed both the steps and commands. Maurice could not dispense with the pikemen who supported the musketmen, because charging cavalry was still capable of reaching the lines of musketeers and cutting them to pieces, but he required them to drill with the musketmen so they could act more effectively together. The result of these innovations was an infantry force that produced a great deal more firepower from the same number of men, finally allowing firearms to attain their full potential.

**New Ideas.** The Dutch system required not only a large number of sergeants but also more and better trained officers to make the infantry companies act in close coordination on the battlefield. Another cousin, John of Nassau, worked with Maurice in creating what is regarded as the first military academy for training young officers. Maurice may also have been the first person to use the telescope for military purposes. For all of the long-term impact of his innovations, he had little opportunity to use his army in battle. The Dutch Revolt in the years after 1590 was largely a matter of fort building and sieges. Maurice in his day was best known as both the designer of excellent fortifications and a master at siegecraft, not as a general.

**Determined Opponent.** Politically, Maurice was a hard-liner in respect to the war with Spain. When Philip III suggested negotiations in 1607, Maurice fiercely objected, still hoping to seize the southern provinces (modern Belgium) from Spanish control. When the Twelve Year Truce was signed in 1609, over his objections, he worked to undermine it and discredit the men who had supported it. When the truce ended in 1621, Maurice prevented it from being extended, and the war was resumed. He died in 1625, well before the Dutch Republic gained recognition of its independence in 1648. He had never married, although he had many illegitimate children, so his titles passed to cousins and nephews.

Sources:

Hans Delbrück, *History of the Art of War Within the Framework of Political History,* translated by Walter J. Renfroe Jr., volume 4, *The Modern Era* (Westport, Conn.: Greenwood Press, 1985).

Geoffrey Parker, *The Military Revolution: Military Innovation and the Rise of the West, 1500–1800* (Cambridge & New York: Cambridge University Press, 1988).

Marco van der Hoeven, ed., *Exercise of Arms: Warfare in the Netherlands, 1568–1648* (New York: Brill, 1997).

# JAN ZIZKA

## CIRCA 1360-1424
### GENERAL

**Plebian Roots.** Called the "only military genius of the Middle Ages," Jan Zizka was born at Trutnov (located in the modern Czech Republic), which was known in the Middle Ages as the kingdom of Bohemia. Zizka means "one-eyed" and refers to the injury he received as a young man. His family name was apparently Trocnov. He came from an impoverished noble family and had to make his own way through military service. For a time he served Wenceslas IV of Bohemia, who came from a German dynasty. Wenceslas's father was Holy Roman Emperor Charles IV, who secured the Bohemian throne for his son, but his rule was constantly under challenge—one of which came from his brother Sigismund, who became emperor in 1410. Thus, Zizka gained a great deal of experience in war and political intrigue serving his king. About 1405 he left royal service and served as a mercenary in an extensive range of lands and wars across eastern Europe. He fought with the Poles against the Teutonic Knights at the Battle of Tannenberg in Prussia (1410).

**Hussite.** Zizka returned to Prague and probably to royal service by 1414, the year he bought a house there. In Prague he heard the sermons of John Hus, a Czech theologian who advocated extensive changes in the Catholic Church, one of which involved giving the cup of wine as well as the bread to the laity in the sacrament of the Eucharist. Hus's followers became known as Utraquists from the Latin word for "both." Hus also denounced the authority of the papacy and the domination of High Church offices in Bohemia by German clergymen. His program for reforming the Church became wrapped up in Czech opposition to the ruling German dynasty and the large percentage of nobles and wealthy merchants in Bohemia who were German. Hus was called to the Council of Constance (1414) to answer charges of heresy; despite the guarantee of safe conduct he was captured, convicted, and executed in 1415 with another Czech theologian.

*Wagenburg.* Bohemia immediately erupted in revolt. Zizka seems not to have joined the revolt until Wenceslas died in 1419. The dead king's brother Sigismund, who was already emperor, claimed the Bohemian throne and brought in German knights to help secure it. Zizka quickly emerged as the best captain available to the Utraquists. His personal beliefs took a more radical turn, as he joined a group of Utraquists who believed that Christ's Second Coming would soon occur on a Bohemian hilltop that they renamed Mount Tabor. These Taborites were convinced that they had to help in bringing about Christ's return through violence, by ridding the world of sinners. At the Battle of Sudomer (1420), Zizka for the first time used the *wagenburg,* a line of wagons on which were placed infantrymen armed with edged weapons and a few crossbows and handguns. The wagons provided a defensive position for the untrained peasants who served as Zizka's infantrymen, which enabled them to hold their position against the charge of German knights. Essentially the *wagenburg* mimicked a fortress, in which poorly trained fighting men frequently had held off knightly forces elsewhere in Europe. Zizka's shocking victory persuaded him of the value of the tactic, which he may have learned from the Russians, and he rapidly developed it further. He increased the number of handgunners, so that the twenty or so men on each armor-plated wagon were about equally divided between those with firearms and with edged weapons. Soon he also had wagons that carried small cannon, which were fired out of gunports cut into the sideboards. Later in 1420 he won his greatest victory at Vitkov, over a German knightly force three or four times the size of his own.

**Victories.** In a matter of only months, Zizka had formalized the tactics that brought him victory after victory over larger and better-equipped armies. When word came to the Taborites that the enemy was on the march, they would drive their wagons to an appropriate spot on the road over which the enemy was coming. The wagons were placed in a line across the road, and dirt was thrown under them to prevent any one from crawling underneath. Handgunners waited with their hookguns, attached to the wagons' sideboards, which absorbed much of the recoil. Charging knights and their horses presented a large target that even the highly inaccurate handguns of the time were capable of hitting at close range. Then the men with edged weapons dashed out and killed the knights who had been thrown to the ground. What cavalry Zizka had was posted on the flanks of the *wagenburg,* ready to charge into the enemy's line once the men on the wagons had brought it to a halt. In two years Zizka, despite having become completely blinded by an arrow in his good eye, had driven out Sigismund's forces and was taking the war into Germany. The religious turmoil unleashed by the Hussite Revolt, however, led to more radical extremes than even the Taborites could tolerate, such as the Adamites, who proclaimed they were living like Adam and Eve in the new Garden of Eden—naked and sinless. Claiming that they owned all the goods of the earth, they raided Czech villages from an island in a river. In 1421 Zizka was forced to use his army to destroy the Adamites, whose leader had promised them that God would blind their enemies. The moderate Utraquists and Taborites also fell to fighting as the external threat dissipated. As long as Zizka lived, the Taborites had the upper hand, but his death in 1424 from illness passed the advantage to the Utraquists. They won a major victory over the Taborites in 1434 and soon after negotiated favorable terms with the emperor and the Pope, which allowed the Utraquist Church to survive in Bohemia until the next century. Other than introducing the hookgun to the Germans, whose word for it probably was the source of the term "arquebus" for the first effective musket, Zizka's ideas had little impact on military men beyond Bohemia, and the *wagenburg* itself had died out even there by 1450.

Sources:

Thomas A. Fudge, *The Magnificent Ride: The First Reformation in Hussite Bohemia* (Aldershot, U.K. & Brookfield, Vt.: Ashgate, 1998).

Frederick G. Heymann, *John Zizka and the Hussite Revolution* (New York: Russell & Russell, 1955).

Howard Kaminsky, *A History of the Hussite Revolution* (Berkeley: University of California Press, 1967).

# DOCUMENTARY SOURCES

Jean Bodin, *Six livres de la République* (The Six Books of the Republic, 1576)—The author determines that the only way in which to maintain law and order is through recognition of the sovereignty or absolute power of the state. He identifies three types of political systems: monarchy, aristocracy, and democracy. Bodin prefers a monarchy that is kept informed of public needs through a representative assembly such as a parliament.

Charles V, *Constitutio Criminalis Carolina* (1532)—An imperial legal code compiled by the Holy Roman Emperor that curbed the inquisitorial methods of the Church but not the state. It standardized criminal procedures but at the same time limited public trials until after the state conducted its own investigation and rendered a judgment.

Charles V, *New Laws: Ordinances for the Government of the Indies and Good Treatment and Preservation of the Indians* (1542)—A failed attempt to regulate the legal administration of the Spanish New World colonies.

*Corpus Iuris Canonici* (1503)—A collection of papal decrees on canon law. It was revised by the Council of Trent (1545–1563) and an official edition was published in 1582.

Justus Lipsius, *Demilitia romana* (On Roman Military Service, 1595)—A treatise by a Flemish scholar who maintained that the Roman system of discipline and training is the key to victory on the battlefield. Lipsius taught History and Law at the University of Leiden when Maurice of Nassau, the famous Dutch general, attended that institution.

Niccolò Machiavelli, *Dell'arte della guerra* (The Art of War, 1521)—A commentary on Flavius Vegetius Renatus's highly influential *Rei militaris instituta* (Military Institutions of the Romans, circa fourth century C.E.).

Machiavelli, *Discorsi sopra la prima deca di Tito Livio* (Discourses on the First Ten Books of Livy, circa 1518)—A description of political liberty, the ability to self-govern without a ruler. As in *Il principe* (The Prince, 1513), Machiavelli makes a distinction between political virtue (needs of the state) and moral virtue (needs of the individual).

Machiavelli, *Il principe* (The Prince, 1513)—Dedicated by Machiavelli to the Florentine ruler Lorenzo de' Medici in a vain attempt to receive an office. Machiavelli is regarded as the inventor of the "reason of state," although that expression did not appear for the first time until the late 1540s. *Il principe* won much acclaim with its concise and blunt maxims about government and practical statecraft, although many have been taken too literally by readers.

Sir Thomas More, *Utopia* (1516)—The term *Utopia* is a Greek name invented by More and comes from the phrases *ou-topos* ("no place") and *eu-topos* ("good place"). *Utopia* is a popular novel written for a select audience of humanists and public officials. In it, More describes a pagan and communist-like state entirely governed by reason.

# LEISURE, RECREATION, AND DAILY LIFE

by JAY GOODALE

## CONTENTS

*Sidebars and tables are listed in italics.*

**1350**

- Herring begin to disappear from the Baltic Sea because of overfishing. Meanwhile, William Beukelszoon discovers a rapid method of gutting and salting the fish.

- For the next two hundred years, Europeans enjoy, on the whole, a relatively favorable standard of living, as far as diet is concerned. Most of the average European's caloric intake comes from meat.

- The style of men's clothing changes, and the short tunic begins to replace the knee-length version.

**1393**

- The recipe book *To Be Domestic in Paris* is published.

**1400**

- Tapestries become popular throughout the homes of wealthier Europeans, and in Italy the elite begin to favor intricately carved furniture.

- Hops is introduced in England, where it is used to impart a bitter flavor to malt liquors. Meanwhile, beer becomes popular in the Low Countries (modern-day Belgium, Luxembourg, and the Netherlands), Germany, Bohemia, Poland, and Russia.

**1457**

- The Roman aqueduct in Paris is repaired to increase the water supply to the city.

**1460**

- The senate of Venice passes sumptuary laws limiting who could hold expensive feasts in the city.

**1492**

- Christopher Columbus witnesses New World natives smoking tobacco.

**1500**

- The turkey, potato, tomato, and haricot bean are introduced throughout Europe from the New World. Meanwhile, asparagus, spinach, lettuce, artichokes, peas, and melons gain popularity as food staples in Southern Europe.

- The first mention of coffee, originally from Arabia, is made in Istanbul.

- The acceptance of the spoon as an eating utensil spreads throughout Europe at different rates, and it becomes fashionable to provide individual glasses for each dinner guest.

- Techniques for distilling hard liquor develop, and throughout Europe the number of suburban taverns increases dramatically, as does drunkenness.

- There are 11,000 registered prostitutes in Venice and 6,800 in Rome. In Valencia, Spain, prostitutes are housed in a special district of the city, and their doorways are illuminated by candles.

- Public baths close in many cities for fear of syphilis.

- Spanish missionaries in North Africa learn to distill seawater with an apparatus called an alembic.

- Among European elites, the Spanish style of clothing is the accepted manner of dress (black costumes, sober design, short capes, and high collars).

- Ceramic floor tiling becomes the standard in wealthy homes.

- The shortage of wood becomes more severe, and as a result more-efficient fireplace technologies and designs develop.

## 1517

- Antonio de Beatis reports that the muddy streets of Paris are so narrow and crowded with carts that they are dangerous for pedestrians.

## 1519

- Jews are expelled from the city of Regensburg in the Holy Roman Empire.

## 1520

- Chocolate is introduced in Spain from Mexico.

- Glazed earthenware heating stoves start to appear in European homes.

- Sugarcane is successfully introduced in Brazil, and this event marks the beginning of sugar as a New World cash crop.

- The average merchant's home in an English city houses eight people. In Moscow, a merchant or minor noble lives in a residence surrounded by a high fence. It is a self-sufficient home, with its own kitchens, bakeries, smokehouses, stables, and servants' quarters.

## 1521

- Brandy, an alcoholic beverage distilled from wine or fermented fruit juice, first appears in Antwerp.

## 1526

- A pump is developed in Toledo, Spain, to raise the level of the Tagus River and to supply the city with water.

## 1530

- German clerics label the fork a "diabolical" instrument.

- Desiderius Erasmus publishes *Manners for Children,* a guidebook for proper eating methods and table etiquette.

- For elites, the Italian style of dress—low-cut bodices, high sleeves, gold and silver embroidery, figured brocades, and velvet caps—is in vogue. Crimson is the color of choice, and velvet and satin are the preferred materials.

## 1534

- François Rabelais writes *Gargantua,* describing the meals, dining habits, and fashion for an idealized king and his young son.

## 1541

- Wine grapes are successfully introduced in the Spanish colonies of Chile and Argentina.

## 1547

- Houses are built so close together in early-modern cities that the risk of fires is great. Moscow suffers several large fires during this period and Troyes, France, is nearly destroyed when a fire breaks out.

## 1548

- A pump is developed in Augsburg, Germany, to raise the level of the Lech River and supply the city with water.

## 1550

- Alcoholic cider becomes popular among the poorer classes.

- Ortensio Lando publishes a travel guide for gourmet eating in Italy.

- A significant decline in meat consumption occurs throughout Europe following a period of population growth, inflation, and unemployment. Moreover, the poor no longer eat roasted or boiled meat but instead consume smoked or salted meat. The largest part of the poor's diet is now made up of grains.

- Peasants use "locked-chests" to safeguard their money and other valuables. These large wooden lockers or wardrobes are constructed from wooden planks with iron bands nailed across them and locks fashioned to the fronts.

## 1558

- Tobacco is cultivated in Spain and Portugal, where it is used initially as snuff.

**1560**

- Peasant homesteads vary by region throughout rural Europe. In northern Germany the average peasant family inhabits a longhouse, with stalls at one end, a kitchen and bedrooms at the other end, and a hearth in the center. The interior of such a structure is quite smoky, the roof frequently leaks, and the windows are simple wooden shutters. (Most English peasants at this time have installed pane-glass windows in their homes.) Stone is the predominant building material in Southern Europe, while in Russia it is pine logs. In villages, many peasants live in two-story frame houses, where they store grain on the second floor.

**1567**

- Tea, originally brought back to Europe from China, is mentioned for the first time in Russia.

**1570**

- In Wernigerode, Germany, court etiquette demands that male guests at the lord's table should refrain from urinating in front of ladies or windows. The court of Brunswick passes a similar resolution in 1578, prohibiting guests from urinating or defecating in closets or on stairs.

**1574**

- In Nuremberg, more than seven hundred beggars are officially registered with the municipal authorities, making begging, by far, the largest "occupation" in the city.

**1575**

- Sugar beets are mentioned in Europe for the first time.
- Heinrich Knaust publishes a book describing all types of beers and listing the medicinal qualities attributed to each of them.

**1580**

- Michel Eyquem de Montaigne's *Travel Journey* describes inns and dining habits in Italy, Germany, and Switzerland.

**1590**

- A European-wide famine occurs and is followed by decades of extremely high cereal prices.
- Sumptuary laws limit the types of clothes Parisian bourgeoisie can wear.

## 1600

- In England and France, the poor spend up to 80 percent of their incomes on fresh foodstuffs. If meat is eaten, it is usually served rare. Meanwhile, tarragon, basil, and thyme replace saffron, ginger, and cinnamon as the spices of choice.

- Kitchen cupboards become a popular means for storing pots, pans, candlestick holders, and other items.

- The elites of Europe begin wearing the bright-colored French style of clothing.

- Brick houses begin replacing wooden houses in Amsterdam.

The winter season, with women seated by the fire, as depicted by the Limbourg brothers in the calendar section of *Les Tres Riches Heures* (1413–1416)

# OVERVIEW

**Strategies.** Early-modern Europeans feared disorder, and every aspect of their society aimed at preventing, or at least curtailing, it. With this overriding objective, Europeans persecuted lepers and heretics with great fervor; permitted, after the successful consolidation of the Reformation, the practice of only one religion in any given area; burned women who violated social expectations by being witches; imprisoned pioneering intellectuals, such as Galileo; and maintained a rigid social hierarchy, a "society of orders," in which everyone—prince, bishop, priest, noble, merchant, scholar, artisan, and peasant—knew one's place and one's responsibilities. European culture, as expressed in the mundane practices and more complex rituals of its daily life, was, in essence, simply the manner by which this "society of orders" defined, regulated, and reproduced itself over generations in an often futile attempt to safeguard society from disorder.

**Social Hierarchies.** The topics discussed in this chapter all fit under the rubric of "practices of daily life." Upon examining the houses in which early-modern Europeans lived, in which city-neighborhoods they resided, the type and quantity of furniture they used, the clothing they wore or were allowed to wear, and the types of food they ate, one discerns a clear pattern. These expressions of daily life were articulated in such a way so as to enforce social differentiation and social hierarchies. Thus, certain members of society could, at dinner parties, serve more food and of a greater variety than other members of society. Some wore brightly colored clothes while others were permitted only to wear brown, black, or gray. The floor one occupied in a multistoried urban building conveyed one's status, as did the shape of one's dining table. While no one could deny that modern society uses particular commodities, such as sports cars, fancy watches and jewelry, or even designer clothes, to define one's social status, and while the possession of such items does serve to reflect social and economic inequalities, contemporary society is much different from that of early-modern Europe. For example, there are many different types of television sets, some of which may sell for under a hundred dollars and others for several thousand dollars. One might safely assume that wealthier people own, on average, better quality television sets than poorer people do. However, there is no law in present-day society that forbids poorer people from devoting a high proportion of their savings to purchase a high-quality television set, if that is how they choose to allocate their financial resources. Likewise, no social shame falls on those wealthy people who choose to own a small and inexpensive television set. This freedom differentiates present-day society from early-modern society. Even the development of manners emerged as a system by which the social elite could discipline those beneath them, a system that emphasized social hierarchies and the need for deference.

**Variables in The Rural World.** Practices of daily life—living conditions, types of food, work habits, and recreational activities—varied greatly from place to place, and certainly varied over time, as well. Many factors affected how peasants opted to organize their lives, and these circumstances shaped, to a large extent, the quality of those lives. It is important to remember that there was no single peasant lifestyle, house, or meal, and the topical subjects in this chapter present a panorama of rural life covering the huge distance between London and Moscow, and over several centuries. Peasant life was not as static as some historians argue, and changes in practices occurred. Crucial variables that determined practices of daily life included whether peasants owed their feudal lord annual dues in service-labor; in cash payments; as a fixed quota of farm produce, for example, 140 bushels of wheat per year, no matter how much was grown; or as a percentage of the total crop harvested, such as 12 percent. Generally, those peasants obligated to work the lord's fields were worse off, as they had to spend the optimal weeks of the year planting and harvesting another's land; as a result, the yield on their own fields would be lower. Peasants with an absentee lord were usually better off than those whose overseer was constantly around, looking over their shoulders. Population levels at a given time and place influenced, naturally, supply and demand rates for labor; where the labor was scarce, as in swamplands or marshes, peasants were treated much better by their lords. A great French historian, Marc Bloch, referred to the "Golden Age" of the western peasantry, a time that commenced shortly after the Black Death (1347–1351) wiped out anywhere from 30 to 40 percent of the European population. Given the shortage of peasant labor supply, the demand for this labor rose dramatically, and peasants who lived during the second half of the fourteenth century were granted privileges neither their ancestors nor their descendants would ever enjoy. Bloch also made clear that "freedom," as defined by the modern world, meant little to peasants of this era. It was much better, he argued, to be a bonded peasant on fertile land and with little dues to pay than to be a free peasant on infertile land. Conversely, a growing population and shortages of available land severely increased the supply of peasant labor during the sixteenth century and dramatically reduced the peasants' contractual standing with their lords. If 1350–1400 was a "Golden Age" for peasants, then 1450–1600 was surely its opposite. Finally, peasants in the West were much better off than peasants either in Russia, where serfdom ended only in 1861, or in central and eastern Europe (east of the Elbe River), where restrictions on peasants were severely increased over the course of the sixteenth century. Again, it is important to remember that at all times and in all places, inequalities served, ultimately and perhaps paradoxically, to reinforce social stability.

**The Rural World in General.** In *Leviathan* (1651), one of the great works of seventeenth-century philosophy, Thomas Hobbes described his view of the natural condition of man—that is, how man would live were there neither a government nor state to protect him. In a line that has since become famous, Hobbes wrote that natural man lived, before the advent of governments, under "continual fear, and danger of violent death," and that his life was, among other factors, "poor, nasty, brutish, and short." What Hobbes held true for mythic, "natural" man certainly can be said to have held true for the majority of peasants in early-modern Europe. Far from being an idyllic world of pristine beauty, of preindustrial environmental harmony, of hardworking communities where villagers chipped in to help one another in the fields by day and sang and feasted together by the hearth at night—as some contemporary representations suggest—the rural world during the Renaissance and Reformation was one of hardship, hunger, famine, disease, and death. Particularly in western and central Europe, rapid population growth between 1350 and 1600 created, gradually but decisively, severe land shortages, deforestation, an unfavorable alteration in diet, inflation at levels incomprehensible to the modern world, and social stratification within communities that tore apart already precarious communal bonds and loyalties. Some innovations were made, however, that partially offset these macrohistorical patterns: new types of frames allowed for sturdier houses and thus for the construction of second floors, on which food could more safely be stored; glass windows slowly replaced mere wooden shutters; in most peasant homes oakwood floorboards or even ceramic tile replaced dirt floors; New World crops rich in calories, such as the potato and haricot (a type of bean), were introduced throughout Europe; and, finally, distillation techniques rapidly advanced, greatly increasing alcoholic consumption, but, at the same time, providing the masses with a ready means of forgetting their troubles, pain, and toil. On the whole, however, the rural world was one of hardship and misery.

**The Urban World.** Like the rural world, urban life was quite varied. In the modern world there are considerable differences between the practices of daily life in the two largest U.S. cities: New York and Los Angeles. Some of these differences are caused by climate, structural planning (reliance on subways or roadways for transportation), the era at which fantastic growth occurred (the nineteenth or late twentieth centuries), and the focus of business (Wall Street or Hollywood). If two cities within the same country at the same time can be so different, how greatly over the course of several centuries must early-modern cities in Italy, France, Russia, and Spain have varied. Thus, any discussion of town and city life during the Renaissance and Reformation must necessarily be panoramic. It is important to stress that the overwhelming majority of the population in Europe between 1350 and 1600 was rural. Even in France (which by 1550 had the highest percentage of people living in towns and cities) only about 14 percent of the population resided in an urban milieu. In contrast, at the turn of the twenty-first century more than 50 percent of the world population was urban. There was also great disparity in the size of early-modern cities. Again using France as an example, in 1550 Paris had a quarter of a million inhabitants; Toulouse, the fourth largest city, had fifty thousand; while Troyes, one of France's ten largest cities, had only twenty-five thousand residents by 1600. Yet, some generalities existed for cities throughout Europe. Distinct from rural villages, all urban areas were noted for being walled-in and fortified. The urban social structure was, furthermore, characterized by a wider range of occupations, ethnic diversity, and services than existed in the rural world. And all contemporary accounts of urban life note the incredible noise; putrid smells; dark, narrow, and windy streets; and the sheer human density and overcrowding. City populations were also extremely fluid: an urban center attracted emigrants from the countryside during times of crop failure or prolonged warfare, and suffered waves of immigration to the countryside during times of plague or economic recession. This accordion-like movement, as one historian has called it, greatly affected the patterns of urban life. Finally, urban life during the Renaissance and Reformation maintained a highly stratified physiognomy; that is, there were, even in smaller towns, neighborhoods of great wealth and of great poverty. The splendid townhouses of the rich, replete with their golden facades, were built to face spacious squares and gardens, or were constructed along relatively broad, fashionable commercial boulevards. The poor, in contrast, lived in rat- and flea-infested garrets, in damp and fetid neighborhoods adjacent to the tanneries and slaughterhouses. Indeed, the neighborhood where animals were slaughtered was called, in early-modern England, the shambles; perhaps because the homes of the urban poor were there, the word has evolved to mean something rather dilapidated or disheveled in current usage. As in the rural world, however, such disparities were regarded as beneficial for maintaining the social order.

# TOPICS IN LEISURE, RECREATION, AND DAILY LIFE

### CLOTHING

**Sumptuary Laws.** The boundaries of social and political hierarchy were delineated by the clothes one wore, and throughout the early-modern period sumptuary laws tried to prevent economically successful peasants from dressing in styles that the nobles considered exclusive to their estate. The laws that established these guidelines were established as early as the thirteenth century, when nobles became alarmed that a growing number of the more-prosperous peasants were beginning to emulate their betters by wearing colorful clothes. Because clothing, more so than in present-day society, was an important status symbol, peasants were only allowed to wear certain colors, usually gray, black, or brown. Peasants also were limited in the type of fabric they could use. For instance, in parts of Germany peasant women were not allowed to wear coats or blouses trimmed with silk. And such laws did not only apply to peasants; in the late sixteenth century, French king Henry IV forbade the wealthier Parisian bourgeoisie from wearing silk clothes in order to safeguard the social standing of his often poorer nobles. The average peasant, however, probably would not have been able to break such a law even if he or she wanted to. Historians should thus be careful when analyzing either statutes that intended to curtail peasant luxury or commentators who assailed peasant extravagance. The cost of clothes was relatively high, and thus most peasants chose, of necessity, to produce their own clothing out of materials at hand—flax or hemp or wool. Indeed, studies of late medieval and early-modern family budgets in German-speaking cities reveal that poor families concentrated the greatest portion of their monetary resources on food, drink, fuel, and rent, and treated clothes and shoes as items that could be patched up and passed down.

**Peasants.** In general, peasant clothing was quite coarse, plain, and threadbare, and was often infested with fleas or lice. Remarking on the quality of peasant clothing, the French philosopher Michel Eyquen de Montaigne could write, in the early 1570s, that a greater difference existed between his way of dressing and that of a local peasant, than between the same peasant and a naked New World cannibal. In Western Europe many early-modern male peasants continued to wear the older style of tunic that had been in vogue among nobles between the eleventh and fourteenth centuries. This garment was so long that it came down almost to the knee. Although the nobility favored increasingly shortened tunics in the years following 1300, peasants, who had to toil in the fields, woods, and mines, found the longer tunic provided more protection, albeit a bit less flexibility. Yet, fashion is an aspect of culture that often defies common sense, and, in time, peasant men in

Three peasants dressed in tunics, woodcut by Albrecht Dürer, circa 1525 (Sachsische Landesbibliothek)

An English country squire, as depicted in an early-seventeenth-century manuscript (British Library)

Western Europe began to imitate their social betters by gradually shortening their tunics as well, revealing more of the breeches. Ultimately the tunic itself was discarded as peasants opted for the jerkin, which, with its buttons and laces, could fit more tightly around the upper body, combining adequate padding with flexibility. Records of church visitations to rural Saxon villages in the sixteenth and early seventeenth centuries testify to the consternation that reforming clerics felt, as they observed peasant men dancing at night in such "licentious" clothing. But such changes did not occur throughout Europe at an even rate. Shepherds in the Austrian Alps, for example, were still wearing the long tunic, stretched down to their knees, at the close of the sixteenth century, leaving their legs bare or covered with leather straps. While even most peasants probably had a "feast-day" set of clothes to wear on Christmas, Easter, or to celebrate a wedding, it was often of the same material, and was not much better than their work clothes. The fact that such attire was handed down between family members over the years suggests that most peasants could not respond to current fashions. Inventories are frequently filled with expressions such as "torn" or "old," revealing that even holiday clothes were worn and tattered.

**Footwear.** An aspect of clothing that clearly served to distinguish the peasant from his social betters was footwear. Peasant shoes were sometimes wooden, but were, more often, simple pieces of leather wrapped around the feet, made tight by lacing long thongs through loops attached to the leather strips. In fact, this *Bundschuh*, as it was known in German-speaking lands, became so associ-

ated with the peasantry that peasant rebels of the early 1520s adopted it as the icon by which they identified themselves during the series of uprisings now labeled the "Peasants' War."

**Urban Poor.** Like the peasants, the members of Western Europe's urban poor wore clothes of coarse wool or linen, and even, in the most miserable of cases, canvas. Masters sometimes gave their servants adequate clothing as part of their salary. Other urban workers had access to spinning wheels and made their own clothes. However, those who were not so fortunate had to rely either on "hand-me downs" or on theft. Trial records reveal that during the great plague of 1631, Florence's urban poor regularly violated both municipal statutes and health codes in order to prevent the clothes of relatives who had perished of plague from being burned. Inventories taken at death reveal that the urban poor, like peasants, did not own many pairs of clothes. One woman in Toledo left, upon her death in 1593, two small headdresses, an old shirt, pieces of an old blanket, and an old mantilla. Even these few items would have been worth about one-sixth of her annual salary. Because the urban poor were so scantily dressed, some cities, such as Basel, allowed charitable institutions to hand out charity gowns (*Luxrock*) to the native poor.

**The Wealthy.** By 1300 a change in men's fashion was under way: men's tunics, once indistinguishable from those worn by women, gradually became shorter and were often turned up, granting more flexibility. This change, which took more than one hundred years to catch on, illustrates well the speed at which fashion changed in the pre-modern

The first item is a contract that records the possessions (mainly clothes) that Giovanna Scandella, the daughter of a northern Italian village miller and carpenter, brought to her husband as a dowry in 1600. An orphan at the time of her wedding, her family had scraped by, even in difficult times, with the two mills which her father, at one time the village's mayor, had rented. The list therefore provides a good example of the clothes a better-off peasant might own. The second and third texts are excerpts taken from the 1578 correspondence between the son of a politically important and extremely wealthy Nuremberg family, Friederich Behaim VIII, and his mother, while he was a freshman at the nearby Altdorf Academy (an institution that could only confer the B.A. and M.A. degrees). The letters reveal that Friederich was more concerned with his clothes than his studies. His family's wealth permits him and his mother to take a much more nonchalant attitude toward replacing clothes than peasants could take. However, it is interesting to note that even his clothes are falling apart. The detail of the accounting in the dowry is explained by the fact that marriages were economic negotiations between families–not affairs of the heart–and the clothing listed represented a considerable portion of Giovanna's total worth.

Dowry (1600): One bed with a new mattress with a pair of linen sheets of half-length, and new pillow cases, pillows, and cushions; with a bed cover, which the aforesaid Stefano [her fiancé] promises to buy her a new undershirt. An embroidered shawl, with folds. A gray dress. A new linsey-woolsey with the bodice of reddish cloth. Another linsey-woolsey similar to the above. A gray dress of half-length. A white linsey-woolsey, bordered with white cotton and linen, with fringes at the feet. A blouse of half wool. A pair of cloth sleeves, light orange in color, with silk ribbons. A pair of sleeves of silver colored cloth. A pair of lined sleeves of heavy cloth. Three new sheets of flax. A light sheet (of flax) of half-length. Three new pillow cases. Six shawls. Four shawls. Three new scarves. Four scarves of half length. One embroidered apron.

Three shawls. One drape of heavy cloth. One old apron, one shawl, one of heavy cloth. One new embroidered kerchief. Five handkerchiefs. One mantle for the head of half-length. Two new bonnets. Five new undershirts. Three shirts of half-length. Nine silken ribbons of every color [sic]. Four belts of various colors. One new apron of thick cloth. A chest without a lock.

### Letter dated 13 October 1578, from Friederich

My trousers are full of holes and hardly worth patching; I can barely cover my rear, although the stockings are still good. Winter is almost here, so I still need a [new] lined coat. All I have is the woven Arlas, which is also full of holes. So would you have my buckram smock lined as you think best? I have not worn it more than twice.

### Letter dated 14 October 1578, from his mother

As for your clothes, I do not have Martin [an occasional household servant who could tailor] here with me now. . . but he has begun work on your clothes. He has made stockings for your holiday trousers, which I am sending you with this letter. Since your everyday trousers are so bad, wear these leather holiday trousers for now until a new pair of woolen ones can be made and sent to you, which I will do as soon as I can. Send me your old trousers in the sack I sent the pitcher in. As for the smock you think should be lined, I worry that the shirt may be too short and that it will not keep you warm. You can certainly wear it for another summer, if it is not too small for you then and the weather not too warm. Just keep it clean and brushed. I will have a new coat made for you at the earliest. . . . I am sending you some cleaning flakes for your leather pants. After you have worn them three times, put some on the knees. Since Martin is not around, I will have your old coat patched up and sent to you . . . [so that you can wear it] until a new one is made.

Sources: Carlo Ginzburg, *The Cheese and the Worms: The Cosmos of a Six-teenth-Century Miller,* translated by John and Anne Tedeschi (New York: Penguin, 1980), pp. 135–136.

Steven Ozment, *Three Behaim Boys* (New Haven: Yale University Press, 1990), pp. 105–108.

times. Certainly there were shifts to which the social elite had to respond; in the final quarter of the sixteenth century, for instance, Spanish-style high collars edged with basic fluting were replaced throughout Western Europe by the white ruff. Yet, generally speaking, fashionable whims affected only the smallest number of people prior to the eighteenth century. During most of the early-modern era, noblemen wore close-fitting breeches, preferably of linen, which covered their hips and thighs. These breeches also served as a type of suspender which held up the long stock-ings that were also in style. Obviously regional and tempo-ral differences existed. In 1575, for example, Paul Behaim, privileged son of a Nuremberg family, wrote his mother from Padua, where he was shortly to begin his legal studies, that "one should not live by German habits and customs in Italy. So having thought it over and consulted experienced people here, I have dressed myself . . . in the Italian man-ner." In Renaissance Italy, fashion favored low-cut bodices, high sleeves, gold and silver embroidery, and figured bro-cades. Crimson was the color of choice, and velvet and satin the preferred materials. The famed Venetian writer Pietro Aretino mentions such attire in his 1531 letter to Count Stampa, quite pleased with his velvet caps decorated with spangles of enameled gold. This Italian style was, in general, popular throughout Western Europe until the mid sixteenth century. François Rabelais dresses the young hero of his novel *Gargantua* (1534) according to an exaggerated Italian fashion: a linen shirt with square gussets put in at the armpit; a white satin doublet; light wool hosiery, slashed in the form of ribbed pillars, indented and notched behind (to provide air for the kidneys) and interspersed with blue damask; purple velvet shoes with pom-poms and leather soles; a blue velvet cape, embroidered with silver thread; a half-white and half-blue silk belt; and a white velvet hat enhanced by a blue feather plume and a gold-plated medallion. Gargantua also wears a codpiece, a fancy article resembling an athletic supporter and worn provocatively over the hosiery. Even in the early-modern era, fashion served vanity, and codpieces became so large that Rabelais jokingly has one character, Captain John, carry a large prayer book inside his. Gargantua also dons the attributes of the social elite—unconcealed weaponry (he wears a sword and dagger), and a purse (exotically made from the skin of an elephant's genitals). Weapons, like the codpiece and the money bag, suggested the potency and copiousness of the wearer, and, because these objects of fashion partly defined masculinity, municipal governments could shame reprobates by denying them the right to wear these items.

**Transition.** Slowly during the sixteenth century, the austere Spanish style that featured black costumes with close-fitting doublets, padded hose, high collars, and short capes began to predominate. In the seventeenth century the doughty French styles commonly depicted in movie versions of Alexander Dumas's *The Three Musketeers* (1844) emerged triumphantly. This outfit featured short, brightly colored breeches and large, down-turned collars made from linen or lace. Turks, noted the sixteenth-century Flemish diplomat Ogier Ghiselin de Busbecq, wore an ankle-length robe, covered their heads with a cowl, and wore a heavy silver gilt cone studded with stones and gems. In colder climates, such as in northern Germany, a gilded shirt might be worn under a fur wrap. Hooded coats with velvet borders were also stylish among the wealthy, as were camel-hair coats lined with fox fur. Finally, in Russia, nobles saved their finest clothes only for attending church, visiting or entertaining important people, and major public appearances. However, clothes were such an expensive commodity that even nobles had to take precautions, especially given the Russian climate: as soon as the appointment concluded, the noble would carefully remove his finest outfit and put on older clothes. Russian noblewomen were taught to store clothes carefully, to prevent them from smelling musty, and to dry them and brush them in certain ways. In fact, sixteenth-century guidebooks advise the mistress of the household always to keep the finer clothes locked in a chest to prevent theft. The dress of Russian noblemen was highly colorful and consisted of fine shirts and trousers,

and, interestingly, of several layers of taffeta or brocade caftans that were elaborately decorated with ribbons, feathers, furs, and various types of cloth. Often they wore four or five articles of clothing of increasing size over their shirt and trousers—*zipun, feriaz, okhaben* (a garment with long sleeves and a cape), *odnoriadka* (only worn outside), and, in winter, a fur coat on top of all. Men wore hats made preferably from the fur of the black fox. Both men and women wore *chetygi*, which were a series of linen cloths wrapped around the feet and which, like socks, were meant to keep the feet warm in winter.

**Female Attire.** Women's clothing consisted of a skirt, petticoat, mantle, apron, bodice, and corset. Over time, the style of the bodice became more close-fitting, and it was cut with a large décolleté. Generally, women's collars were open, but were turned down. Ruffs and headdresses varied regionally. Wealthier women wore silk clothes embroidered with gold ornaments, lace, and precious stones. In Russia, noblewomen wore knee-length coats made from the softest furs over jackets that were cut close to the figure and that had very long and wide sleeves. The overcoats often had fur hoods for protection against the winter cold. Because only maidens wore their hair loose, Russian noblewomen wore kerchiefs on their heads in summer and, in winter, a *kaptura,* a large beaver fur hat that covered the head and shoulders.

**Disease and Identity.** Early-modern Europeans, even peasants, changed their clothes occasionally, but at rates which would disgust most people today. Peasants and the urban poor, because they simply did not have many pairs of clothes, often wore the same articles for particularly long periods. For example, in the 1630s, a traveler to the Jura region of eastern France noted in his diary that a widow he encountered received from her husband's estate one new chemise every two years and a coarse cloth dress once every three. Moreover, water, one of the four fundamental elements of early-modern physics, was feared because of its ability to penetrate surfaces. For this reason, clothes in western Europe were cleaned by beating, dry scrubbing, and perfuming. Interestingly, Russian women were taught to wash clothes and boots frequently. Given such suppositions in the West, the wearing and regular changing of underwear was crucial to hygiene, but the possession of these garments was a luxury not all could afford. In consequence, many of Europe's lower orders suffered with skin diseases such as ringworm and scabies. Church-led investigations in sixteenth-century Saxony that aimed, in part, to determine whether or not villagers were still turning to "good witches" as healers—despite the prohibitions of the Lutheran reformers—discovered that the villagers contracted ringworm with such frequency that they refused to disavow their local healers. Urban beggars and other itinerants were forced to wear all their clothes at once, given their inability to store their possessions. Because of this practice, they were often resented and feared, sometimes with good reason, as carriers of plague and other dangerous diseases. Clothes were regarded as sites of contamination

Dame Prudence flanked by princesses in fashionable gowns, circa 1470 (Beinecke Rare Book and Manuscript Library, Yale University, MS 427, f. 16)

and odoriferous agents that spread potentially lethal miasma (vapors). Hence, guards posted at gates in city walls tried to prevent those wearing particularly decrepit clothes or many layers of clothes from entering, not simply to minimize the number of the indigent within the city, though that certainly was a concern of early-modern municipal governments, but also to preserve the health of the populace. During the plague that ravaged Florence in 1631, agents representing the municipal board of health arrested and detained those citizens who wore certain types of clothes as carriers of infection—an early-modern version of selective targeting of suspects.

**Concealment and Protection.** Clothes were not only regarded as articles that transmitted disease; they served to hide disease as well. The early-modern age lacked antibiotics and most people were themselves scarred, but extreme deformity, caused by pockmarks, burns, scars, boils, scurf, or festering sores, functioned as a sign that alerted the viewer to distrust or fear the disfigured individual. Rich and poor alike were obsessed with disfigurement. Judges identified witches by their blemishes or moles, and even kings were victims of this discourse: the hunchback attributed to England's Richard III exposed his nefarious inner nature. Deformed individuals thus had trouble entering cities as would-be immigrants, finding employment, or developing networks of social support. Clothing was therefore highly important as a tool of concealment, and this is a major reason that early-modern fashion covered almost all of the body's surfaces. In an age when wounds took a long time to

heal, clothing had to be designed in such a way that the body's flaws would be hidden. Also, clothing not only hid imperfections, it prevented them as well, which was important in an age when even the slightest of cuts could produce life-threatening infections. Montaigne, in his essay "Of the Custom of Wearing Clothes" (1572–1574), attributes Europeans' vulnerability to injury (as opposed to the sturdier condition he attributes to New World peoples and Moors) as an acquired characteristic made consequent by a culture that for centuries had demanded that the body be covered. As a result, clothes, in his mind, had become indispensable for the existence of many Europeans. Both of these functions (concealment and protection) became more important as cities became increasingly congested and "personal space" was reduced. It is not coincidental, then, that decorative gloves became popular among the wealthy who resided in those early-modern cities with rapid population increases, such as Paris and London. Early-modern fashion dictated that women of all classes covered their hair, just as wealthy men chose to wear wigs, in part to hide the effects caused by chronic malnutrition, by diseases such as smallpox, and by the scars and infections born of scratching lice infestations. In a related dynamic, the ruff became a popular style of the age because it highlighted the face, enabling those with relatively few facial blemishes to flaunt their beauty, and hence, their moral purity.

**Criminal Intent.** The absence of photographs and fingerprinting allowed criminals, vagabonds, and con artists to move from village to village and refashion themselves with relative ease. Clothing permitted criminals to hide certain identifying features, such as a peculiar scar, and, because certain styles of clothes were closely associated with certain professions, a change in outfit allowed those who wished to re-create themselves the ability to take on new personas. Recently discovered evidence regarding a skillful con artist and successful itinerant beggar who traveled with relative ease between northern German cities in the eighteenth century certainly would apply to the Renaissance and Reformation period as well. This contriver carried multiple sets of clothing with him, which, in times of real personal hardship, he could always sell. He wore a fine, respectable set of clothes as he approached a city wall to insure permission to enter. Once inside, he usually obtained a room in a quality hotel by appearing well dressed, and, once established as an honorable guest, he then slipped surreptitiously into his ragged begging attire to loiter around places, perhaps churches and upscale restaurants, where people were wont to give him their change. In a more famous incident, Martin Luther, after being condemned by the Diet of Worms, grew hair over his cowl and a beard, and replaced his monk's attire with more secular clothes. Under this guise Luther carried himself as the *Junker* Jorg, resident of the castle on the Wartburg. While historians debate how successful Luther really was in hiding his identity, the fact that a figure as famous as he resorted to such dissimulation is telling. It should not come as unexpected, then, to discover that early-modern plays and stories focus to a considerable extent on characters who disguise themselves to gain advantage. William Shakespeare's *The Merry Wives of Windsor* (1600–1601) revolves around the attempts of the impoverished knight Falstaff to swindle the burgher families by disguising himself in the clothes of a woman, while in *Henry V* (1598–1599), the title character disguises himself as a common soldier to ascertain the mood of his troops on the eve of the Battle of Agincourt. In addition, Margaret of Navarre's collection of tales depicting life at the French court of Francis I, the *Heptaméron* (1558), is filled with stories that center on how lecherous men and women disguise themselves as the spouses of others in order to seduce the would-be honorable objects of their affections.

**Social Deviants.** Clothing not only concealed; it also revealed. Social deviants were forced to wear distinctive articles of clothing that served as "signs" that publicized their presence to the accepted members of society, warning them of possible contamination. For example, an Italian miller, called Menocchio, was found guilty of heresy in 1584, and, though his life was spared, he was ordered to wear, for the remainder of his life, the *habitello*, a penitential garment decorated with a large cross that functioned solely to alert those with whom he came in contact that he had, like Nathaniel Hawthorne's Hester Prynne in *The Scarlet Letter* (1850), violated the laws and trust of the church. By the mid 1590s the miller had become obsessed with his symbol of exclusion, and neighbors testified at his later trial that he had wanted to visit the Holy Office to obtain permission not to have to wear the habitello any longer, as he was avoided because of it. During the time between his two trials he had actually discovered an interesting solution, and though he kept wearing the habitello, as he had sworn to do, he wore clothing over it, to conceal it for the sake of his business interests.

**Utopia.** Though Jews were not technically considered heretics, they were every bit as much "outsiders," and they too were forced to wear distinctive clothing. In sixteenth-century Worms, Jews, both men and women, wore large yellow rings affixed to the outer garment of their clothing, prominently placed over the left breast; this was known colloquially as the "Jewish badge." Diocesan synods in cities like Bamberg and Würzburg forced Jews to wear distinctive clothing as well. And finally, in his satire *Utopia* (1516), a book that condemned much of early Tudor England's public policy, Sir Thomas More argued that the Utopians' society was much more civil than the Europeans' because on Utopia the mere thought of having to wear humiliating articles as punishment for criminal behavior deterred all but a scant few from breaking any law.

Sources:

Fernand Braudel, *Civilization and Capitalism 15th-18th Century,* "The Structures of Everyday Life," translated by Siân Reynolds, volume 1 (New York: Harper & Row, 1979).

Giulia Calvi, *Histories of a Plague Year: The Social and Imaginary in Baroque Florence,* translated by Dario Biocca and Bryant T. Ragan Jr. (Berkeley: University of California Press, 1989).

*The Complete Works of Montaigne,* translated by Donald M. Frame (Stanford, Cal.: Stanford University Press, 1957).

Carlo Ginzburg, *The Cheese and the Worms: The Cosmos of a Sixteenth-Century Miller,* translated by John and Anne Tedeschi (Baltimore: Johns Hopkins University Press, 1980).

Robert Jütte, *Poverty and Deviance in Early Modern Europe* (Cambridge & New York: Cambridge University Press, 1994).

Steven Ozment, *Flesh and Spirit: Private Life in Early Modern Germany* (New York: Viking, 1999).

Ozment, ed., *Three Behaim Boys: Growing Up in Early Modern Germany* (New Haven: Yale University Press, 1990).

Margaret Pelling, "Appearance and Reality: Barber Surgeons, the Body and Disease," in *London 1500-1700,* edited by A. L. Beier and Roger Finlay (London: Longman, 1986), pp. 82–112.

Carolyn Johnston Pouncy, ed. and trans., *The Domostroi: Rules for Russian Households in the Time of Ivan the Terrible* (Ithaca, N.Y.: Cornell University Press, 1994).

Jacques Revel, "The Uses of Civility," in *A History of Private Life: Passions of the Renaissance,* edited by Roger Chartier, translated by Arthur Goldhammer (Cambridge, Mass.: Harvard University Press, 1989), p. 189.

Werner Rösener, *Peasants in the Middle Ages,* translated by Alexander Stützer (Urbana: University of Illinois Press, 1992).

Otto Ulbricht, "The World of a Beggar Around 1775: Johann Gottfried Kästner," *Central European History,* 27 (1994): 153–184.

# DRINK

**Water.** The sanitary quality of drinking water in early-modern Europe could not always be guaranteed. Even when one was sure that the water was pure, other problems, such as the illegal tapping of wells, spring and summer droughts, and winter freezes made it difficult to rely on water as a primary drink. Many early-modern cities thus devoted considerable finances and energy to providing a reliable drinking supply. For instance, in fifteenth-century Rome and Paris old Roman aqueducts were repaired, while the governments of sixteenth-century Augsburg and Toledo installed large hydraulic wheels to raise the levels of river water for their neighboring towns.

**Other Nonalcoholic Drinks.** Fruit juice was not an option for the overwhelming majority of Europeans at this time. Chocolate was brought from Mexico in the 1520s, tea was introduced to Western Europe from China in the 1610s (though evidence suggests that a few Russians were drinking tea by the 1560s), and coffee from Arabia reached the great cities of Western Europe by the early seventeenth century. These drinks remained far too expensive for all but the wealthiest of Europeans, and none of them became popular, even among the elite, until well into the eighteenth century. Although coffee had been used widely in Paris as a drug since 1643, the first stall in the city devoted to drinking coffee recreationally opened only in 1672. Furthermore, in 1648 Parisian doctors burned, in ridicule, the dissertation of a medical student that advocated the drinking of tea. Europeans certainly would have consumed milk in greater quantities than they did, but without selective breeding and chemically enhanced feed, cows in the early-modern era were unable to produce the levels of milk that cows today do. Secondly, milk was needed to make two staples of the common person's diet—butter and cheese—and so was not available for drinking. Most people contented themselves with drinking the whey that remained after a cheese had been made.

**Beer.** Europeans drank large quantities of alcohol, which meant beer, ale, or wine. One historian has estimated that the average adult in sixteenth-century England drank two pints of beer with every meal. Because of the frequency with which beer was consumed, it was generally brewed to be weak, especially in summertime, when large quantities were consumed by laborers toiling in the fields. Only the March and October beers (hence the famous Oktoberfests in Germany) were brewed to be kept year round and were thus stronger than the standard beer. It is important to remember, however, that beer was considered as much a food as it was a drink. Because it provided key nutrients and many calories, beer was truly a vital part of most poor people's diet. During the sixteenth century, when the price of barley in England increased sixfold, the availability of beer (which unlike ale could be brewed without barley) saved many a family from outright starvation.

**Wine.** The upper classes generally drank wine. In wine-producing areas in Germany, France, and Italy, the poor sold the wine they produced and contented themselves with drinking piquette, a mixture of water and the waste of wine production. Though the price of wine varied greatly with quality and availability, the cost of wine was generally quite high not only because one bad harvest could dramatically raise prices, but also because wine was difficult to preserve and expensive to transport. Early-modern wine spoiled quite easily, and, with the

Two drinkers, from a sixteenth-century carving by the Rigoley brothers in the church at Montreal-sur-Serein

The quality of one's wine, like one's clothes, conveyed social status. In the following letter, the famed journalist, gossip columnist, and raconteur of Venice, Pietro Aretino, writes to Girolamo Agnelli, thanking him for a gift of wine. Truly good wine, as suggested by Aretino's epistle, was valued above precious coins or silks. Renaissance Italians were obsessed with fame and with being remembered after they had died. Here Aretino ties such longings into his appreciation for the wine. Aretino was infamous for self-consciously spurning social convention; note he mentions giving this wine to prostitutes, so their kisses will taste better.

### Venice, 11 November 1529

I won't speak, dear brother, of the sixty beautiful crowns you have sent me on account of the horse; but I do want to say that if I were as famous for saintliness as I am for devilry, in other words if I were as much a friend of the Pope as I am his enemy, most certainly the people, at the sight of the crowds at my door, would think that I worked miracles, or that I was celebrating the Jubilee. This has happened thanks to the good wine you have sent me; because of it, not a single innkeeper is as busy as the members of my household. At dawn they start filling the flasks brought by the servants of as many ambassadors as we have here, not to speak of his grace the ambassador of France, who praises it as if he were the king himself.

As for me, I am quite puffed up with pride like those dreary little courtiers when their lord pats them on the shoulder or gives them some of his cast-off clothing. And I have every reason to put on airs, because every good fellow deliberately works up a thirst on purpose just to come and gulp down two or three glasses of my wine. Wherever people eat or sit or walk, the talk is only of my perfect wine, so that I owe my fame more to it than to myself. Had not this august liquor arrived, I would have been a nobody. And it's a great thing to my mind, that it is in the mouths of whores and drunkards for love of its sweet, biting kisses. And the little tear it brings to the eyes of those who drink it brings tears to mine as I write about it now; so you can imagine its effect upon me when I see it bubble and sparkle in a fine crystal cup.

In short, all the other wines you have sent me have in comparison lost all credit when I try to recall them. And I am indeed sorry that Messer Benedtto sent me those two caps of gold and turquoise silk, for I would prefer to have had wine such as this instead. Were I not afraid that Bacchus would go bragging about it to Apollo, I would dedicate a work to the cask it came from, where the devotions should be greater than at the tomb of the Blessed Lena. All that is left to say is that, despite my immortality, if you visit such dregs of your vines upon me at least once a year, I will truly become "divine."

**Source:** Pietro Aretino, *Selected Letters* (New York: Penguin, 1976), pp. 63–64.

---

exception of some of the stronger, sweeter wines from Southern Europe, turned sour, even under the best conditions, within a year. Early-modern wine was not a stable product, and it was for this reason that the sweeter wines were so highly praised. The best conditions for storing wine were rarely realized: glass bottles were not produced in quantity sufficient to store all of Europe's wine, so most wine was stored and shipped in wooden barrels that frequently let air in, thus spoiling the wine or even turning it to vinegar. Shipping wine took a great deal of time: it could take weeks for a shipment of wine from Southern France just to reach London. Any change in humidity or temperature spoiled early-modern wine. Because wine was so expensive, Europeans went to great efforts not to have to throw it out even after it went bad. Experts experimented with ways of preventing early-modern Spanish wine from turning in the first place, and suggested putting juniper chips into the wine while it was fermenting, or suspending a linen bag containing the flowers of hops and the seeds of rye into recently fermented wine. A common remedy in England to arrest the spoiling of white wine was to add, and then churn, several gallons of milk in the barrel. Another solution was to put a chunk of cheese in the wine and then to boil it. Honey, cloves, eggs, ginger, nutmeg, and sugar were all added according to various recipes. Indeed, the *Domostroi* (circa 1550–1580) devotes several chapters to the preservation of wine.

**Sources:**

Fernand Braudel, *Civilization and Capitalism 15th–18th Century,* "The Structures of Everyday Life," translated by Siân Reynolds, volume 1 (New York: Harper & Row, 1979).

Alison Sim, *Food and Feast in Tudor England* (New York: St. Martin's Press, 1997).

## FOOD

**Meat.** All social groups ate, by modern standards, a tremendous amount of meat, which was not a luxury item in Europe until the mid sixteenth century. Prior to that time Europeans—rich and poor alike—preferred their meat boiled or roasted, and the standards included beef, mutton, pork, poultry, pigeon, goat, and lamb. Game was regularly consumed: wild boar, hare, rabbit, stag, roe deer, as well as many types of birds that today would be considered rarities,

In many ways the diet of the poor in Eastern Europe and Russia was similar to that of the poor in Western Europe. Thought to have been written between 1550 and 1580 by a priest, Silvester, who served in one of the Kremlin cathedrals (Moscow), the *Domostroi* is a book that suggests the rules and manners by which Russian nobles and wealthy merchants ought to govern their houses. This passage provides detailed information on the diets of simple household servants and the nonresident poor who sought sustenance from their social betters. It is important to remember that the menus listed in the *Domostroi* are prescriptive; that is, they are recommendations only, and should not be regarded as definitive records of what the poor actually ate on a daily basis. Note how constructions of social status are highly connected to dining rituals.

When the [master's] table empties, you [the servants] must gather all the dishes and have them washed. You must go over all the food—meat, fish, chilled aspic, and soups—and [store them for future use]. On the evening following a feast, or even sooner, the master should check that all is in order. He should question the steward at length on what was eaten and drunk, on who received what. The steward should be able to account for every expense and every item. The steward should answer the master straightforwardly in every particular. If, God willing, all is in order, if nothing is broken or spoiled, the master may reward the steward. The same applies to the other servants: if the cooks and bakers have worked courteously and carefully and have not gotten drunk, then the master will feed them and give them drink. . . .

As everyday food servants receive rye bread, cabbage soup, and thin kasha [buckwheat groats simmered in broth] with ham. Sometimes they may have thick kasha with lard. This is what most people give their servants for dinner, although they vary the menu according to which meat is available. On Sundays and holy days servants sometimes get turnovers [small pies], jellies, pancakes, or other, similar food. At supper they eat cabbage soup and milk or kasha. On fast days the servants have cabbage soup with thin kasha, sometimes with broth, peas, or turnip soup. At supper on these days you may offer cabbage soup, cabbage, oatmeal, pickles, or fish and vegetable soup. On Sundays and holy days, for dinner [the main meal], give them various kinds of pies, barley-pease porridge, barley groats, or kasha mixed with herring or whatever God provides. For supper, serve cabbage, pickles, fish and vegetable soup, and oatmeal.

The serving women, aids, children, other kinfolk, and dependents [by "dependents" are meant non-resident beggars as well as non-relative members of the household, such as the stablemaster or the house carpenter] should get the same food, but with the addition of leftovers from the masters' and guests' tables. As for the better class of merchants [traveling salesmen], the master should seat these at his own table. . . .

Those who cook and wait at table eat after the meal; they also get leftovers from the table. The mistress honors seamstresses and embroiderers as the master does merchants: she feeds them at her own table and sends them food from her own dish.

Source: Carolyn Johnston Pouncy, ed. and trans., *The Domostroi: Rules for Russian Households in the Time of Ivan the Terrible* (Ithaca, N.Y.: Cornell University Press, 1994), pp. 160–162.

such as herons, egrets, wild swans, cranes, partridges, and larks. Turkeys became popular after they were introduced from the Americas in the first half of the sixteenth century.

**Availability.** Before the mid sixteenth century, the demand for meat rarely fell, and, even in times of famine, the poor were able to consume it. The size of the herds of cattle brought to sixteenth-century Germany's largest cattle fair, held in Buttstedt (near Weimar), commonly reached twenty thousand and testifies to the great supply of meat from Western Europe's mountains and countryside. Meat was so plentiful that the dukes of Saxony were able to issue an ordinance in 1482 that mandated that even simple craftsmen working on projects had to be fed at least two different types of meats at lunch and dinner, and at least one serving of fish at each meal on Fridays and fast days.

**Changing Pattern.** By the 1550s Europe's steady population growth had caught up with its preplague (1348–1349) levels. Land was becoming scarcer, unemployment was on the rise, real wages dropped, and prices rose dramatically. Additionally, long-established landholding patterns changed over much of Europe during the first decades of the sixteenth century, and many smaller, subsistence-level farms were displaced by larger-scale farms. Many smaller farmers were reduced to becoming landless day laborers, who had to hire themselves out for meager wages. Not surprisingly, patterns of food consumption among the poor in Europe changed accordingly, and a noticeable decline in meat consumption began that lasted until the mid nineteenth century. In general, the decline in meat consumption was greater in Southern Europe than in the north, where pasture fields were richer and more plentiful. However, even in the north, poorer workers and peasants had to alter their diets. Thus, in contrast to the Saxon craftsmen of the 1480s, workers in Saxony's copper mines in the early years of the 1600s could afford to eat only bread, gruel, and vegetables. Likewise, in 1601 elite journeymen weavers in the prosperous city of Nuremberg complained that, while they were due a serving of meat from their masters every day, they were receiving it only three times each week. Furthermore, the type of meat eaten also changed after the 1550s. No longer able to enjoy roasted or boiled meat, Europe's poor generally consumed smoked or salted meat during the remainder of the early-modern era. Salted beef and bacon became the standard type of meat eaten by the poor in Ireland and England, particularly during the winter months. According to one commentator on the English urban poor in the late seventeenth century, the Reverend Richard Baxter, the poor were happy to have a single piece of hanged bacon once a week. Peasants in France favored salted pork and bacon. Thus, the Republic of Venice's ambassador to France noted, during his stay in Paris in 1557, that "pork is the habitual food of the poor people, those who are really poor." In Italy and Germany, sausages were the predominant meat source of the poor. In the Venetian ambassador's native city, as in much of Southern Europe, offal, most usually tripe, was an everyday food for the poorer folk.

**Hospital Fare.** A recent study of the food served to those few among the poor who were fortunate enough to be admitted as patients to state-financed hospitals in Hesse, Germany, clearly reveals the transition of meat from a plentiful staple to a luxury item. An ordinance of 1534 specified that each patient was to receive, on Sundays, Tuesdays, and Thursdays, two separate meat dishes in the morning and a third in the evening. Though the prescribed diet also included plentiful portions of fish, cheese, pea soup, barley soup, and oatmeal, the average male patient was receiving an average of 3,556 calories per week from meat alone (while only eating meat three days a week!), as well as 1,015 and 833 calories per week from fish and cheese, respectively. The residents consumed 2,500 calories each day, and the proportion made up solely by meat, fish, and cheese was roughly 31 percent. Notable, however, is that this amount had become, within several decades, a cause for alarm and scandal, and, following investigations ordered at the highest levels of government in 1574, 1590, and 1621, efforts were repeatedly made to alter the weekly menus in Hesse's various hospitals. Officials were scandalized that patients were being served vast quantities of ox, calf, and cow meat, in addition to hogs, rams, lambs, goats, geese, and chickens. By 1590 daily servings of eggs, oatmeal, and honey had increased, while servings of meat, cheese, milk, and beer had been reduced, though not as much as the government wished.

**Eggs and Dairy Products.** Although meat did not remain a staple for Europe's poor throughout the entire early-modern era, other foods certainly did. Eggs, cheese, and milk served as the great sources of protein for the masses. In Turkey and in parts of the Balkans, yogurt, another milk product rarely consumed in other parts of Europe, comprised a large portion of the daily diet, and

was served with, depending on the time of year, cucumbers or melons, leeks or onions. Cheese was not considered a "gourmet food," and descriptions of, or recipes for, individual cheeses are conspicuously absent from pre-1700 cookbooks. All over Europe, peasants preferred cheese made from the milk of cows and ewes; goat cheese, a gourmet food today, was considered quite inferior. On the Continent, the more highly regarded cheeses included Roquefort, Parmesan, Swiss Gruyère, and *sassenage* (made from a mixture of cows', goats', and ewes' milk all boiled together). Milk was drunk in large quantities, but was of a somewhat different texture than the milk modern people drink, as it was commonly watered down both by the dairy farmers and by the larger-scale retailers. Butter, particularly salted butter—a form originally dictated by the lack of refrigeration which has, in present-day society, retained its popularity, though it is no longer necessary—was commonly consumed in Northern Europe, whereas Southern Europeans used lard, bacon fat, or olive oil. Eggs remained a fairly inexpensive commodity and were widely eaten as a good source of protein. Although eggs were an everyday food in most of Continental Europe, the French philosopher Montaigne was surprised to discover during his travels through Central Europe that the Germans seemed to eat only hard-boiled eggs, and then only in salads.

**Fish.** Because of the many religious fast days ordered throughout the year, fish was an important component in the diet of early-modern Europeans. Of course, in the years following the Reformation, subjects in Protestant lands were freed from observing many of these fasts. Yet, by the time most people had finally accepted their new religious freedom, the price of meat had risen exorbitantly, and so fish remained a staple in the diet of the peasants and urban poor in Protestant lands. In Catholic lands and in Orthodox areas, such as Russia, there were 166 days, including Lent, during which people could neither eat meat, eggs, nor poultry. Indeed, corrupt practices regarding the sale of *Butterbriefe* (documents that could be purchased and allowed a Christian to consume dairy products on fast days) were one of the specific catalysts that led Martin Luther in 1517 to write his Ninety-Five Theses and thus begin the Reformation. In such a religiously charged culture, the demand for fish, whether fresh, smoked, or salted, remained rather high. Since sea fishing was hardly sufficient to satisfy demand, Europeans, particularly those living far from a coast, turned to freshwater fishing. Another cause for this recourse to freshwater fish lies in the fact that fish spoils quickly in transit and becomes quite inedible. Seventeenth-century legislation stipulated that even the water which had been used to soak salted cod could be disposed of only during certain hours of the night. Thus, to combat the odors associated with spoilage, freshwater fish (that is, local fish) was introduced to the diets of central Europeans. No river, no stream, not even the Seine which flowed through Paris, was without an authorized group of fishermen. In fact, archival records throughout Germany and France between 1400 and 1600 reveal the conflicts that ensued when profit-hungry nobles flooded fields previously used by the peasants to graze their herds in order to establish artificial lakes for the breeding of carp. An inventory of ministerial revenues ordered by the Elector of Saxony in 1544 reveals that even in relatively small Thuringian towns, parishioners paid village pastors with hens, capons, cows' milk, and carp. Finally, though modern scientists recognize whales as mammals, whale meat and fat were consumed as "fish," particularly by poor people during Lent, when demand for fish was high among all social classes. Thus, whale fat was known, by the poor in seventeenth-century Italy, as "Lenten lard." The poor continued to eat whale meat and fat during Lent until the mid seventeenth century, when the commercial uses of whale fat—for oils, soaps, perfumes, and lighting products—rendered its use as a cheap food source economically untenable.

**Spices.** Because the food of the poor was often badly preserved, because the meat they ate was often far from tender, and because their diet was so monotonous, spices—predominantly peppers and salt—played a large role in the eating habits of early-modern Europeans. Westerners' contact with the Middle East during the twelfth-century Crusades reintroduced spices, such as cinnamon, cloves, nutmeg, and ginger, that had been forgotten since the Fall of Rome. Fourteenth-century cookbooks are filled with recipes for spicing meat, fish, jams and jellies, soups, dried fruits, and drinks. Of course, the laboring poor of Europe could not partake of these luxury spices as readily as could the privileged, but, after the Dutch in the mid seventeenth century had permanently established trade with the Indian subcontinent, the price of these "exotic" spices fell rapidly, and they began to appear less frequently on the food of the wealthy and more frequently on the food of the poor. Spices from the West Indies, in particular chili, were also consumed with gusto by the poor throughout Western Europe as quickly as they were introduced.

**Cereals.** Compared to other parts of the world, Europe had plenty of land relative to its population during the period 1350–1500, and a good deal of it was used to graze livestock. In order to feed all the people, however, especially during the population increases of the fifteenth and sixteenth centuries, an increasing amount of pasture land had to be converted to arable. This development occurred because a given amount of arable land will always produce, no matter how bad the quality of the soil or the agricultural technology, ten to twenty times as much food (measured in calories) as would be obtained by using the same land to graze animals for consumption. Thus, after 1500, grains made up the largest share of the lower-class diet. A study of early-seventeenth-century Genoa reveals that cereals alone comprised 53 percent of the daily calories in a noble's diet, but accounted for a whopping 81 percent of the daily calories for the institutionalized urban poor.

**Thomas More.** The need to transform pasture land to arable clarifies an otherwise obscure line located in a famous passage in Book One of Sir Thomas More's *Utopia* (1516). More realized that the conversions taking place in early-sixteenth-century England from arable land to stock-raising land (the opposite of what was happening, of necessity, elsewhere in Europe!) would create great hunger for the growing masses, and, fearing that from such hunger criminality and social disorder would arise, he wrote, "sheep that were wont to be so meek and tame, and so small eaters, now . . . become so great devourers and so wild, that they eat up, and swallow down the very men themselves." More's fears were based on the fact that grains were consumed in greater quantities in rural areas than in towns, and in greater quantities by the poor than by the rich.

**Dilemma.** The fact that wheat, like other winter cereals, requires careful manuring created somewhat of a dilemma, however. If productivity, and hence food supply, were to increase, more fertilizer (cow manure) would be needed. However, to obtain more manure, fields that ought to have been converted to arable had to remain as pasture for livestock. Sometimes peasants tried to solve this problem by grazing their livestock along the sides of roads, in hayfields, or even in forests.

**Maslin.** Wheat was considered the best quality of grain, but peasants usually mixed it with lesser grains such as rye due to its high quality and price. The mixture of wheat and rye was known as maslin, or "small corn." Peasants considered rye to be less nourishing than wheat and viewed it as a purgative. In Saxony in the 1540s, wheat was three times more expensive than oats, while rye was only twice as expensive as oats. In addition to growing wheat, peasants throughout Southwestern Europe also concentrated on barley, which was used for making beer, feeding pigs and horses, and making millet. A grass cultivated for its seed, millet could be stored for upwards of twenty years and was kept by municipal governments for emergency food supplies in case of military sieges and blockades. A traveler in the 1520s to Hendaye, a village located on the French-Spanish border, disparaged the local soil by claiming it was not much good for grains except for millet. In Northern Europe, peasants grew softer grains such as oats and rye. Regarding the English peasantry, William Harrison wrote in 1577, "they eat it [wheat] when they can reach unto the price of it. Contenting themselves in the meane time with bread made of otes and barlaie: a poore estate god wot!" Many standard recipes were based on coarser cereals as well. For example, in early-modern Spain polenta was a gruel that consisted of toasted barley, ground and then mixed with millet, while in the Brittany region of France peasants ate a gruel that consisted of buckwheat, water, and milk. Peasants in Britain ate porridge, a gruel made from oats, while kasha (a porridge made from buckwheat groats or toasted rye, simmered in broth) was a staple in Poland and Russia. This situation explains why Baltic merchants sold at least as much rye in Central Europe as they did wheat. In parts of Eastern France, and in the mountainous regions of Germany and Switzerland, peasants made bread from spelt.

Polish bakers at the bread oven, from Baltazar Behem's Codex, circa 1505 (Jagiellonian Library, Cracow)

**Distinctions.** Indeed the type of bread served to a guest or given as payment for a service was highly bound to notions of honor. Scores of grievance documents penned by sixteenth-century Saxony ministers inform us that peasants often tried to mitigate the economic hardship of the tithe, or church tax, by paying members of the local clergy with inferior breads. In fact, one way peasants could reveal their displeasure with a local cleric was to give him bread made from barley or millet rather than from wheat, as such a gift would quite literally label the cleric a "pig." White bread was a rarity and was quite expensive; perhaps only 4 percent of Europe's population ate it. Indeed, English peasants who ate white bread were taxed for it, and one of the mundane demands of the peasant rebels who participated in the religious uprising known as the "Pilgrimage of Grace" (1536–1537) was the abolition of this tax. White bread made from sifted flour and mixed with milk was a delicacy fit for royalty, and it was so favored by Maria de Medici, regent of France from 1610 to 1617, that it was known as "Queen's bread."

**Rice.** Introduced to Europe in antiquity, rice thrived in the Balkans and throughout Italy and Sicily. Like millet, it was inexpensive, and thus it is not surprising to find both of these grains on the inventories of poor-relief institutions in the sixteenth century. Rice was served to sailors on French military vessels and to soldiers in barracks, and was also distributed to the poor during times of famine, although even under these circumstances it might be mixed with mashed turnips, carrots, and pumpkins. In short, rice was a food for emergencies, and rarely did the rich ever have to eat it (and if they did, it was cooked in milk).

**Nuts and Beans.** The aforementioned grains alone did not suffice to feed the masses of Europe, as sudden, unexpected labor shortages following outbreaks of plague, or, at other times, increased cultivation led to rather drastic declines in cereal yields. To give just two examples, yields from one grain sown declined 27 percent in England between 1350–1399, and declined 18 percent in Germany between 1500–1599. Thus, consumption of chestnuts, buckwheat, acorns, and roots was generally higher than what one might suppose. Chestnuts were the popular supplement to grain until replaced by the potato in the nineteenth century. In the Auvergne, peasant farmers often lived on boiled chestnuts for several months each year. They ate them with a watery soup made up of cabbage, turnips, onions, and carrots. Likewise, lentils, beans, peas, and chickpeas were not valued as "honorable" foodstuffs in themselves, but were viewed only as supplements to the more traditional cereals. Peasants turned to pulses in those years when a wet spring dampened or mildewed the cereals, lest they eat grains which had become infested by ergot, a fungus which caused, in humans who digested it, lameness, necrosis of the extremities, and psychedelic hallucinations.

**The Rich.** The eating habits of the rich and privileged differed greatly from the eating habits of the bulk of Europe's population. Europe's poor bordered on chronic malnutrition, while the wealthy and privileged dined on elaborate feasts that competed with one another in terms of opulence and ostentation, and in which dozens of courses were served. During a typical banquet, royalty might dine on herb pastries; an assortment of salted and smoked meats and sausages; fricassee of small birds, minced with veal and egg yolk; veal, beef, pork, and mutton, roasted, as well as in pies and soups; chickens, pigeons, geese, and game pies; dishes with beans and peas; various servings of fish; and, for dessert, various cheeses, cakes, puddings, and seasonal fruits. The elite preferred to dine on birds no longer considered delicacies, such as swans, egrets, peacocks, and storks. Cooks would roast such birds without their feathers, but served them in dramatic poses with their original feathers reattached. In Venice and France, members of the royal courts ate foods sprinkled with gold dust, which was believed to be advantageous to the heart. Another distinguishing feature of the diet of the rich was its (relative) diversity. The majority of Europe's people could not afford imported exotic fruits, wines, or spices. Food grown locally was eaten day after day. The rich could afford luxuries such as chocolate and tropical fruit, and, unlike the poor, had the means to feed animals marked for slaughter throughout the winter, thus insuring themselves fresh meat whenever desired. Indeed, the eating of meat is a recurring theme in François Rabelais's novel *Gargantua* (1534), a source that reveals the eating habits of the French aristocracy and upper clergy in the early sixteenth century. The hero's mother, while pregnant with him, dines particularly on salted meat, hams, smoked ox tongues, chitterlings, sausages, beef pickled in mustard, and tripes. In fact, she is delivered of Gargantua specifically because she consumes so much tripe during a single meal. The novel is not completely absurd; diners at Henry VIII's court received 80 percent of their caloric intake from meat.

**New World Foods.** It is noteworthy that Europeans of the day, while embracing certain Asian and New World foods like the potato, were generally unwilling to eat non-European foods. The early eighteenth-century writings of Jean-François Foucquet, a Jesuit missionary who experienced a circuitous return to France after years in China, reveal that European settlers on islands in the Pacific and Indian Oceans chose to go hungry for weeks, waiting for the flour and rancid meat brought by supply ships, rather than to eat the monkeys and lizards which abounded in the jungles. Tobacco, however, was prized, both for its supposed medicinal value and aphrodisiac effects.

Sources:

Fernand Braudel, *Civilization and Capitalism 15th–18th Century,* "The Structures of Everyday Life," translated by Siân Reynolds, volume 1 (New York: Harper & Row, 1979).

Lorenzo Camusso, *Travel Guide to Europe 1492. Ten Itineraries in the Old World* (New York: Holt, 1992).

Natalie Zemon Davis, *The Return of Martin Guerre* (Cambridge, Mass.: Harvard University Press, 1983).

Robert Jütte, *Poverty and Deviance in Early Modern Europe* (Cambridge & New York: Cambridge University Press, 1994).

Susan Karant-Nunn, *Luther's Pastors: The Reformation in the Ernestine Countryside* (Philadelphia: American Philosophical Society, 1979).

H. C. Erik Midelfort, *A History of Madness in Sixteenth-Century Germany* (Stanford, Cal.: Stanford University Press, 1999).

Thomas More, *Utopia* (New York: Collier, 1910).

Alison Sim, *Food and Feast in Tudor England* (New York: St. Martin's Press, 1997).

Jonathan D. Spence, *The Question of Hu* (New York: Knopf, 1988).

## FURNITURE AND INTERIORS

**Floors, Ceilings, Doors, Windows.** The ground floor of the typical late medieval peasant's home might be no more than beaten earth, though by the early-modern era most peasants used lesser quality oakwood as floorboards or inlaid ceramic tiles, which were common in urban dwellings. Wealthier Europeans enjoyed the use of "leaded tiles," which were regular tiles covered with a graphite-based enamel. Ground floors, in peasant homes as well as in the palaces of the rich, were covered with straw in the winter and with herbs and flowers in the summer. Though this covering was theoretically to be changed, it often was not, and new straw or herbs were merely thrown on top of the old, creating, ultimately, a compressed mat of dirt and garbage. Rugs were rare, even in the homes of the wealthy, and certainly few peasants possessed them. Sir Thomas More affirmed his high social and political status by having Hans Holbein paint a portrait of his family with its members assembled on a large living-room carpet. By the seventeenth century, however, Europe's wealthy were covering their tables, chests, and cupboards with carpets. Walls in the homes of the rich were adorned with elaborate tapestries, while wealthier peasants and the urban poor relied upon wallpaper because it was inexpensive. As the aesthetic quality of wallpaper dramatically improved, it was no longer regarded as the poor man's decoration and, by the late seventeenth century, became prevalent even in Western Europe's finer homes. Sometimes, in lieu of wallpaper or tapestries, interior walls were covered with oak paneling for added insulation. Depending on the resources of the house, such paneling could be ornately carved, painted, or gilded.

Ground-floor ceilings, in those homes higher than one story, were merely the boarding of the second floor; second-floor ceilings were the boarding of the attic. These were simple and crude, though wealthier urban families, particularly in Italy, and after 1600, began to gild or paint their ceilings. In Russia the ceilings, even in the wealthiest nobles' homes, were extremely low in order to preserve heat. The outside doors of most homes were fairly narrow,

A painting of a seventeenth-century kitchen by Diego Rodríguez de Silva Velázquez (from Fernand Braudel, *The Structures of Everyday Life,* 1982)

and not simply because the houses themselves were narrow. Preserving heat in winter was a paramount concern, and so the doors of homes were designed to be as small as possible. Windows, when present, might even lack glass; in many homes, especially those of the peasants, windows were simply wooden shutters, which could open and close to let air in during the warmer months. The wealthier homes could afford glass windows, but the glass used throughout most of Europe until the seventeenth century was leaded, making it too heavy to move, not to mention exorbitantly expensive. It was not until the late-sixteenth and early-seventeenth centuries that transparent, movable glass windows were developed. These were introduced throughout Europe at widely different times. Thus, transparent windows were common even in peasant homes by the 1560s, but were still absent in southern France, Spain, and French-speaking Switzerland in the 1630s. In Russia, where glass was introduced in the seventeenth century, and in Scandinavia, many rooms in nobles' palaces remained windowless in order to conserve heat during the cold and prolonged winters, and the few windows present were extremely small. Ventilating and lighting one's home were, in general, problems shared by all Europeans.

**Peasant Furnishings.** The average peasant home did not possess nearly as much furniture as homes today do. Because wood was becoming an increasingly valuable commodity during this age and was the sole source for building, for heat, and for fuel with which to cook, peasants did not make furniture from newly cut timber, but from scrap wood. A great deal of the peasants' furniture was constructed from pieces of dismantled or collapsed wooden buildings, and rare was the household with many pieces. Specialized furniture makers and joiners did not even emerge from the generalized "carpenter" rank until the late sixteenth and seventeenth centuries, and so what furniture there was before that time tended to be very heavy, solid, and unsophisticated. Given that the *Domostroi,* a sixteenth-century guidebook for "better living," repeatedly mentions the need of Muscovite aristocrats to acquire pads, so as to make the hardwood furniture tolerable, one can only wonder at how the average peasant home was furnished.

**Beds.** In peasant Europe, beds were really nothing more than some sewn material filled with straw. The wealthier peasants had goose-feather or woolen mattresses. Generally, the beds were put along the walls of the one-room house in the dark corners to maximize what little privacy could be achieved. It seems to have been customary in rural Saxony for parents to let the children sleep on stuffed floor mattresses, while they themselves slept on *spanbetten,* which were wooden frames that lifted the mattress a bit off the floor, like a contemporary futon. Many peasants simply slept on straw laid out on the floor, and not too far, in winter, from their livestock. In winter, peasants who owned beds would place them in the kitchen if their home lacked a stove and was heated only by the kitchen hearth. Parents and younger children often slept together, as a means of keeping the family warm enough to survive frigid winter

The first item is excerpted from François Rabelais's novel *Gargantua* (1534). This passage describes the interior and exterior decoration of the Thélèmites' Abbey, a palace built and furnished by the novel's hero, Gargantua. Not a religious abbey in the usual sense, its decor represents an ideal to which the wealthiest nobles of France might aspire. Although drawings circulated widely, hardly anyone in Europe had seen living African animals. Thus, Rabelais believes the hippopotamus has a horn. The final two items, reproduced exactly as they were written, are carefully detailed inventories of the Lutheran pastors who served the Saxon town of Prettin in the 1530s and 1550s, respectively. The inventories provide good examples of what relatively well-off small town homes would contain. Given the detail, note the relative lack of furniture. The appraisers did not forget these items; the furniture simply did not exist. Note the difference in luxury between the residents of Rabelais's fictitious palace and the Saxon pastors. Note too that, aside from books, wall-hangings, and mirrors, this early-sixteenth-century ideal palace is also sparsely furnished by today's standards.

The ceilings were of Flanders plaster in circular patterns. The roof was covered in fine slates with a lead coping, which bore figures of grotesques and small animals, gilded and in great variety, and with gutters projecting from the walls between the casements, painted in gold-and-blue diagonals to the ground, where they flowed into great pipes, which all led to the river below the house. The said building . . . contained 9332 apartments, each one provided with an inner chamber, a closet, wardrobe, and chapel. . . . [There was] an internal winding stair(case), the steps of which were, some of porphyry, some of Numidian marble, and some of serpentine. . . . [There were] fine great libraries of Greek, Latin, Hebrew, French, Italian, and Spanish books, divided story by story according to their languages. . . . [There were] fine wide galleries, all painted with ancient feats of arms, histories, and views of the world. . . . [Inside the private rooms] were fine, long, spacious galleries, decorated with paintings, with horns of stags, unicorns, rhinoceroses, and hippo-

potami, with elephants' tusks and with other remarkable objects. . . . Every hall, room, and closet was hung with various tapestry, according to the season of the year. All the floors were covered with green cloth. The beds were embroidered. In each retiring room was a crystal mirror, set in a fine gold frame embellished all around with pearls, and it was large enough to give a true reflection of the whole figure.

Inventory of the pastor's homestead [1534]: six horses; seven cows; two oxen; one pony; three young calves; one sow; one male pig; sixteen suckling pigs; thirty hens and two roosters; three various-sized candlesticks; a locked-table and the keys to it; two iron barrels; one tin and one lead saltshaker; two cauldrons, one large and one small; four other cauldrons of different sizes, almost too damaged to be of any use; two fish pans, one iron and one copper; one mortar; one brass sieve; one wash tub; seven kegs with which to store drink; five kegs of beer and another keg containing sediment; five bushels of rye grain; five slabs of salted pork; a stocking partially filled with butter; some hard cheese and some soft; a bushel of rape-seed; four hides of land; an old wagon with two wheels; two chains, one long and one short; one large wooden peg; two harrows for ploughing.

Inventory of the pastor's homestead [1555]: three pigs; one sow; three kegs of beer; four cows, one of which was recently purchased; one ox; one cauldron with an iron ring and an iron hook [from which to hang it]; one copper fish pan; ten old kegs for storing beer, very poor quality; six old quarter kegs, little used; one copper blast-oven; one locked-table; three tin keys; [several] candlesticks; two saltshakers; one mortar; one copper sieve; one large copper wash basin; one copper lamp; one iron, three-legged pot; three iron barrels on legs; one iron mortar for making sausages; one wood-framed bed; one small tin measuring cup; cheese; twelve hens and a rooster; one bushel of rape-seed; six bushels of grain; seven bushels of straw; two cart-loads of hay.

**Sources:** Karl Pallas, ed., *Die Registraturen der Kirchenvisitation im ehemals sächsischen Kurkreise*, volume 3 (Halle, Germany: Hendel, 1906–1918), p. 16.

François Rabelais, *Gargantua and Pantagruel* (New York: Penguin, 1955), pp. 151–156.

nights. Unfortunately, this practice resulted in a substantially high number of infant deaths, as babies and younger children were frequently crushed to death during the night.

**Tables.** For eating tables, most peasants used the end of a barrel, which simultaneously stored their home-brewed beer. Others had long, narrow tables, which were placed in front of the open hearth, enabling the diners to sit on an equally long bench with their backs to the fire. The desire for warmth, as well as the absence of individual chairs (early-modern Europeans really preferred the bench) necessitated rectangular-shaped tables, which are still common today, even though the limitations that mandated their design have been overcome. Thus, the round table of Arthurian legend was special not only because it eliminated status hierarchies among the knights; it also symbolized the luxury of Camelot, for to enjoy such a table one would have to own many individual chairs as well as be able to heat a room from all of its sides.

**Chests.** Some peasants had a "locked-chest" to safeguard their money and any valuable document, such as a deed, that they might have. Surviving chests resemble large wooden lockers or wardrobes more than present-day chests of drawers. These chests were constructed from heavy, irregularly shaped planks that would be made to fit together with joints and with strips of iron nailed across them. Heavy iron locks were attached to the iron bands in the front. The chest was clearly a source of pride for the early-modern peasant home. In fact, in one famous trial from the 1550s, testimony about a family's chest served as a crucial piece of evidence. Two men had "returned" to a mountain village in southern France, both claiming to be the same individual who had left many years earlier. A dramatic part of the trial revolved around whether or not each man could identify what, exactly, his family stored in its chest. Many churches had these chests as well, and used them to secure communion wine, consecrated hosts (which were a valuable commodity on the black market, since people used them for medicine, good-luck charms, and as an ingredient in love potions), the weekly offerings, and important documents, like the baptism and wedding registers. It is thus in Europe's older churches that today's travelers have the best chance of seeing such a chest—the church of St. Sylvestri in Wernigerode, Germany, has an excellently preserved locked-chest. Those peasants who could not afford such a chest might own a "locked table," which, like a modern office desk, contained an underneath drawer in which valuables could be safely stored.

**Cupboards, Tubs, and Crates.** Many peasants also had cupboards hung on the kitchen walls, where they kept their tin and wood candlesticks, wooden plates, spoons, tankards, bowls, and iron knives, pots, pans, and kettles. (No forks, since knives served a dual function.) The cupboard, as a discreet piece of furniture, was originally no more than a series of small chests attached to one another, and in many homes the cupboards probably remained as such. The kitchen also would have had several wooden tubs and crates in which cheeses, lard, and various grains could be stored.

**Few Luxuries.** Though the house might contain a few stools, other pieces of furniture, such as card tables, buffet tables, night tables, soft armchairs, chests of drawers, and bureaus, were completely lacking; such possessions only became common in nonnoble houses during the first half of the eighteenth century. Indeed, visitors today to Martin Luther's home in Wittenberg may be surprised to see just how spartan the decor of even a famous university professor and best-selling author could be. In the Luther family parlor, exhibited as it appeared in the mid 1530s, one sees a room with a rather low wooden ceiling, with wooden planks making up the floor. A heating stove occupies one corner, and in the adjacent corner a rather narrow wooden bench is built into a wooden portion of wall. In front of the bench is a small table. Except for the area around the

bench, the walls are stone, and the room's one window is leaded and opaque. A small chest of drawers sits in front of the window. Such was the living room of a relatively highly paid scholar, who certainly enjoyed more comfort than the average peasant. But the peasant's home would be crowded enough, with all the stored grain, people, and animals under one roof.

**The Wealthy.** In Western Europe, beds became increasingly fancy, and, by the end of the early-modern era, included posts of elaborately carved wood, canopies, and tapestries or expensive serge curtains. Mattresses were stuffed with wool, and the pillows were down. The wealthy had more, and better quality, tables placed around their home than their peasant counterparts had. In the bedroom these tables, usually cloth-covered, kept candlesticks, books, powders and perfumes, and brushes and combs. Wealthy men might also have had a *studiolo* in the bedroom, a piece of furniture that resembled a modern secretary and had lockable drawers where important papers were secured. (The name also refers to a private and small study room.) Unlike peasants, Western Europe's wealthy enjoyed the use of mirrors, and their bedrooms were filled with dressers, built-in shelves, and screens for dressing. The wealthiest aristocrats had toilets in their private homes, located in antechambers adjoining the bedrooms, but these lacked running water and required periodic cleaning and disposal by socially dishonorable and little-paid cesspit-emptiers. In Russia, nobles' furniture was noted for being quite heavy. Carpets, pillows, throw rugs, and large cloths were thrown over the bulky pieces of furniture to make them more lavish. Beds, benches, tables, and chests were the main pieces; chairs were relatively scarce in early-modern Russia, and only the wealthiest of sixteenth-century nobles would even own one.

Sources:

Fernand Braudel, *Civilization and Capitalism 15th–18th Century*, "The Structures of Everyday Life," translated by Siân Reynolds, volume 1 (New York: Harper & Row, 1979).

Alain Collomp, "Families: Habitations and Cohabitations," in *A History of Private Life: Passions of the Renaissance*, edited by Roger Chartier, translated by Arthur Goldhammer (Cambridge, Mass.: Harvard University Press, 1989).

Natalie Zemon Davis, *The Return of Martin Guerre* (Cambridge, Mass.: Harvard University Press, 1983).

Susan Karant-Nunn, *Luther's Pastors: The Reformation in the Ernestine Countryside* (Philadelphia: American Philosophical Society, 1979).

Richard Marius, *Thomas More* (New York: Knopf, 1984).

Carolyn Johnston Pouncy, ed. and trans., *The Domostroi: Rules for Russian Households in the Time of Ivan the Terrible* (Ithaca, N.Y.: Cornell University Press, 1994).

## HOUSES AND INNS

**Building Materials.** With the exception of southern Mediterranean Europe, where stone predominated as building material, most houses in northern Europe, either in a city or in the countryside, were made completely of wood, while central European houses generally used a combination of both materials. The forests that dominated Europe's landscape, and which encroached upon the towns

The following is an excerpt from Erasmus's dialogue *Inns* (1523), which was one of a series of dialogues written originally in Latin and published as *Colloquia Familiara* (Informal Conversations). Though Erasmus was notoriously difficult to please and was given to bouts of melodrama, the following dialogue between Bertulf and William reveals the discomfort and lack of privacy most sixteenth-century travelers would have encountered while staying at an inn. Erasmus is usually regarded as a true cosmopolitan, as a "citizen of Europe," but this passage reveals his relative dislike for Germans, whom he generally considered rude. Note too the savage wit for which Erasmus is rightly famous.

*Bertulf:* Whether the method of treatment is the same everywhere, I don't know. I'll tell you what I saw [in Germany]. No one greets the arrival, lest they seem to be looking for a guest. For that they consider base and degrading, and unworthy of Germanic austerity. When you've shouted a long time, someone finally sticks his head out of the little window of the stove room [i. e., the one heated room in the inn] (where they spend most of their time until mid-summer) like a turtle from his shell. You must ask him if you may put up there. If he doesn't shake his head, you know there's room for you. . . . In [city inns] they furnish hay very reluctantly and sparingly, and it costs almost as much as oats itself. When the horse is provided for, you move into the stove room, with all your impedimenta—leggings, luggage, and mud. . . . In the stove room you take off leggings, put on shoes, change underwear if you like; rain-drenched clothing you hang beside the stove, and you move there yourself in order to dry out. If you want to wash your hands, water is brought out, but usually it's so clean that afterward you have to look for other water to wash it off with! . . . If you arrive at four o'clock, still you won't dine before

nine and sometimes ten. . . . There are often eighty or ninety men together in the same stove room: travelers afoot, horsemen, traders, sailors, carriers, farmers, young men, women, the sick. . . . One combs his hair, another wipes the sweat off, another cleans his rawhide boots or his leggings, another belches garlic. . . . The more [guests in the stove room that the aged servant] sees, the more energetically he fires up the stove, even though the weather is oppressively warm without it. Among these folk it's a principal part of good management to melt everybody in sweat. . . .

*William:* But nothing seems to me more dangerous than for so many persons to breathe the same warm air, especially when their bodies are relaxed and they've eaten together and stayed in the same place a good many hours. Not to mention the belching of garlic, the breaking of wind, the stinking breaths, many persons suffer from hidden diseases, and every disease is contagious. Undoubtedly many have [syphilis]. In my opinion, there's almost as much danger from these men as from lepers. Just imagine, now, how great the risk of plague.

*Bertulf:* [After the guests have dined, communally,] the uproar and tumult after they've all begun to grow heated from drink is astonishing. In short, it's completely deafening. . . . Often jesters mingle with the guests. . . . [The guests] sing, chatter, shout, dance, and stamp until the stove room seems about to collapse. You can't hear a word anybody else is saying . . . and you must sit there until midnight whether you want to or not . . . if someone tired out from travel wants to go to bed soon after dinner, he's told to wait until the others go, too. . . . Then everyone is shown his nest: actually a mere cubicle, for it contains only beds and nothing else you could use or steal.

Source: Erasmus, *Ten Colloquies,* translated by Craig R. Thompson (New York: Macmillan, 1986), pp. 14–21.

and villages, provided ready resources for construction. Because of the great risk of fire, municipal governments and village communes eagerly enacted legislation or coercive policies to force the introduction of stone and tile, at least for roofs, but the great expense of these materials prevented the fulfillment of this goal in the early-modern period. Population increases in sixteenth-century Europe led to a general clearing of forest land and its conversion into arable, thereby making wood even scarcer and forcing peasants to repair homes with earth, clay, and straw. The miscellaneous availability of building materials caused various styles of architecture to predominate throughout Europe. Timber-framed houses dominated English cities.

Such buildings, the originals of which can still be seen in most English towns, were made of black-framed beams in which white mortar was poured to fill all the spaces between the planking. Renaissance architects generally scorned wood as a building material, so stone and brick buildings were prevalent throughout much of Italy, both in town and country, while two-story stone farm buildings, influenced by the villas left by the ancient Romans, prevailed in southern France.

**Simple Peasant Homes.** Fragmentary knowledge of the northern-European peasant homestead can be derived from drawings and paintings, such as those by Breughel the Elder or by Albrecht Dürer, excavations of villages, and

A bourgeois woman being visited by an angel in a fifteenth-century southern German home, painting by an anonymous artist
(Kunstmuseum, Basel)

documentary evidence, such as regulations pertaining to where and how buildings were to be built. Because five large trees were usually required to build a peasant's house or barn, peasants would need permission either from their village commune or from the local lord to build a new house or to repair substantially an existing one. Indeed, many documents from sixteenth-century Germany reveal that teachers and ministers who settled in villages were often forced to alter their schedules and modify their pedagogical expectations to please those village communes that had initially refused to permit them to rebuild their houses or barns. From such varied sources, it appears that for most of rural Europe the peasant's home was more of a shelter than a house and was fashioned to meet only the barest requirements that sustained the life of the peasant's family and animals.

**Variations.** It is also important to remember that there was no "fixed" peasant home, and that the types of houses varied greatly not only because the peasantry was a socio-economic class comprised of many and quite differentiated elements, but also because regional variations, such as the production of grain, wine, or stock, influenced the design of the peasant homestead. In northern Germany, for instance, a one (and later, two) story longhouse commonly functioned as a "compact farmhouse." In such a structure,

the hearth was situated near the center, and around it the wife, and her servants or elder daughters, if she had any, worked. From this location, the wife kept an eye on the animal stalls that were located within the structure and that were built at one end, around two of the rectangular building's corners. A space existed between the two stalls called the hall or "fleet," where the family ate, where it threshed grain, and where it worked on all sorts of chores during the winter. At the other end of the structure, bedrooms were built around the remaining two corners. A small kitchen adjoined one of the bedrooms. A parlor filled the space between the bedrooms and extended out into the center of the building so that its outer wall was adjacent to the central hearth that heated the parlor, albeit with a good deal of smoke. Those peasants prosperous enough to own a heating oven, usually made of brick, enjoyed a smokeless parlor, for the oven's design allowed it to be stoked from the back, outside the parlor, and attached to a separate hearth located in the kitchen. The heated, smokeless parlor served as the place where wintertime dances and spinning bees were held, and it provided an appropriate place to entertain the solitary evening guest for card games or song. Because it not only provided a great deal more warmth than a hearth, but also functioned as the social space of the home (and, sometimes, of the entire village), the smokeless parlor was

A fourteenth-century moated manor house with gatehouse, Lower Brockhampton, Herefordshire, England

the most important room of the peasant house during the winter. In fact, a saying dating back to the eleventh century maintained that the three worst problems a homeowner could face were a nagging wife, a leaking roof, and a smoky house. The heating oven helped prevent fire as well, and therefore was common in areas where the winters were cold and the housing material consisted of wood. In such a home then, the peasants lived, worked, stored produce, and kept their livestock. By comparison, in southern Europe an open hearth provided heat sufficient in the milder climate, and, since the houses were usually made of stone, the advantages of the heating oven were considerably lessened. In Russia, the average peasant's house resembled somewhat an American pioneer's log cabin. Made of pine-tree trunks, the house was a simple square with split trunks fitting into each other at the corners and piled one row on top of each other. The house, which would be about six feet high and twelve feet wide, would have but two openings: a single window, fitted with glass, or, more likely, oiled paper, and a door. In one corner of the house a series of rods, interwoven with branches covered in clay, would be set up to serve as a catchment for the oven's smoke. Adam Olearius, who as ambassador to the duke of Holstein in the 1630s visited Moscow and its environs twice, described Muscovite peasant homes as "shoddy and cheap" and as containing few utensils or furnishings.

**Two-Story Peasant Homes.** The dampness and frequent rains that characterize much of northern and central Europe could cause stored grain to rot, threatening the survival of the village. The development of frame-constructed houses represented, therefore, a significant improvement over medieval building techniques. In such buildings, the supports which bore the weight of the house were no longer simply dug into the ground, but rather were fastened to stone foundations that made them more sturdy. With such a foundation, two-story homes became possible, allowing for a more effective and comfortable apportionment of storage space within the home. The grain stored in the peasant's house could henceforth be kept either in specially constructed enlarged roofs or in the newly developed second story. Because of this situation, peasants were extremely concerned with the condition of their roofs, as the aforementioned slogan makes clear. The hearth gave off enough heat, which rose and kept the stored grain dry. To permit loading wagons to drive into the fleet, a large gate was built at the end of the house, in between the stalls. These homes, though more dependably built, required additional features such as squares, braces, and nogging pieces to stabilize them, and were therefore slightly more sophisticated in design, forcing peasants to become a little more dependent on the village carpenter than they had been in the medieval era. Only the wealthier peasants possessed these two-story homes, which not only permitted their owners to maximize storage more efficiently, but also enabled them to display their wealth and status to all in the village during this crucial era when the forces of capitalism were beginning to creep into the village economy, creating wide ranks within the peasantry as a whole.

**Peasant Homestead.** The population explosion of the fifteenth and sixteenth centuries created the need for more grains, and, as a result, increased storage facilities. Thus, by the sixteenth century the wealthier peasants' (excluding cottagers, who owned little more than a cottage on some land, of course) homestead was no longer a compact farmhouse, but consisted of several small and fairly adjacent buildings—the peasant's home, a stable, and a barn with a threshing floor, or perhaps just a longer farmhouse which served as both stable and barn. These structures were surrounded by fences erected to keep the peasant's animals from wandering onto others' lands to graze, to provide protection against wild animals, and to prevent village traffic—wagons going to regional markets, shepherds leading their flocks out into the countryside—from despoiling one's yard. Documents from this period attest to the considerable importance of the fence. For example, when sixteenth-century Lutheran church officials visited Saxon villages in order to determine, in part, how well the local pastor was developing Reformation ideals, one of the first comments they recorded in their evaluations was whether or not the villagers were properly maintaining his fence for him. Within the enclosure, the peasant family's lodgings were in a small building at one end, containing perhaps two bedrooms, a small kitchen, and the heated parlor. The barn would adjoin the house, forming an "L." Adjoining the house at its other end would be a series of stables, thus forming a U-shaped central courtyard enclosed on three sides, or even a rectangularly shaped courtyard enclosed by buildings on four sides. In the colder parts of Europe, however, such as Britain, northern France, and in the Alps and Carpathians, the family's lodgings within this homestead might be considerably expanded so as to include stables, which were used during the winter months to protect livestock, particularly cattle, against the harsh weather. The separate stable buildings housed the animals in the warmer months and during the winter provided the great amount of storage needed to keep the animals' hay and straw dry.

**Urban Homes.** Cities throughout western Europe at this time were characterized by a prevalence of crowded, vertical houses, few of which looked alike. Some of these houses were pinched and narrow, and some were broad and rambling; some had bay windows, some had ornately painted façades, while some had neither windows nor decoration. Every house had a uniquely angled roof, and its own characteristic window shapes, gables, and turrets. The high cost of land within a city, exacerbated by the fact that whenever a city expanded a new series of walls had to be constructed at great cost, meant that most buildings were quite narrow, and relatively tall. When more space was needed it was cheaper to add a new story and most buildings had a depth extending away from the street three times their width. Windows were limited, and so only the barest light and air entered a home. In Renaissance Florence the wealthy addressed this disadvantage by developing covered terraces on the top floors that opened to the street, and by introducing small open courtyards on the ground floor. Both of these innovations enabled wealthy inhabitants to get some fresh air and light. Most houses did not look out from the front to the open street, but were narrow in the front and oriented toward the back alleys. The residential rooms in the homes of the wealthy did face the street, but these front rooms served as banquet halls,

salons, and what we today would call the "living room." Bedrooms were still placed toward the rear of the house. Homes of the wealthy also had a *studiolo*, or study. This room, usually lacking a fireplace and large windows, developed in Italy and was inspired by the medieval monk's cell. To this room the master of the house retired to read, study, or conduct the business of the family in private. Men usually put on clothes similar to clerical garb before retiring to their study, and this early-modern custom probably inspired the modern smoking jacket.

**Households.** Most buildings in a city were subdivided among several tenants, and generally the higher the lodger lived in a building the poorer he or she was. However, in cities with a great deal of canals that were prone to flooding, such as Amsterdam or Bruges, the poorest lodged in low houses or even in basements of buildings. Many of these buildings were not "apartments," in the contemporary sense, but dormitories that housed the owner's domestic servants and artisanal apprentices with their families. With the exception of dwellings in the Low Countries, the artisan's shop was generally on the ground floor, the master and his family lived on the second and perhaps the third floor, and the workers and apprentices were housed on the higher floors, or even in the building's attic, in an order commensurate with their experience. This entire group was considered a single "household." In nonartisanal houses, urban elites used the ground floor to store produce from the family's country farms. There was little notion of intrafamily privacy in early-modern Europe. The simple internal design of most homes, the widespread employment of resident servants, and the periodic presence of extended kin, who often lived with the nuclear family while trying to establish themselves in the city, meant that little privacy could be realized in the home. A detailed study of Coventry in the 1520s reveals that the average merchant's home, small and nestled in an overcrowded street, housed about eight people. In a Russian city like Moscow, a wealthy merchant's or noble's home consisted of a series of buildings surrounded by a high fence that awarded both privacy and security. Beside the master's family residence, the homestead would include stand-alone kitchens, bakeries, breweries, smokehouses, icehouses, drying rooms, granaries, stables, and servants' quarters. Much like an antebellum American plantation, the home would be rather self-sufficient, with servants who tended orchards and vegetable gardens, prepared the food, raised livestock, preserved food for use during the winter (remarkably, given the cold, food was never frozen), and performed artisanal tasks. It was common for such a homestead to number as many as 250 people. The main house contained ground-floor storerooms and exterior staircases, roofed to keep snow off the steps, that led to the upper floors, where the bedrooms and reception rooms were located; thus, visitors did not have to walk through the storerooms.

**Inns.** Like today, early-modern inns and public houses (hence the term *pubs*) varied in their quality. The better inns had a shingle advertising their names, but most were located by simply hanging a leafy branch or vine over the doorway. A famous inn in Bordeaux, the Red Cap, had stalls alone for two hundred horses, while other inns were little more than emptied barns with a single fireplace, where guests slept fully clothed on wooden benches or on the floor. A typical inn was two or three stories tall and had on the ground floor one large dining hall with long, communal tables, where the guests would dine (usually only on the food they had brought themselves), and later drink and converse. A guest spent the night in one of the several bedrooms that occupied the top floors. Corridors separating the rooms were absent from most inns. A picture in the French book *Cent Nouvelles* (circa fifteenth century) reveals the average sleeping arrangement in an inn: there are several beds per room, with several guests forced to sleep in each bed. Not surprisingly, travelers' diaries from this time frequently mention the bugs and fleas to which one was exposed in such rooms. In lieu of toilets, guests either shared the vase or pan provided for each bed or used, as seems to have been the custom in parts of France, the fireplace. The use of chamber pots did not really advance hygiene, as their contents were simply poured out the window.

**Sources:**

Samuel Baron, ed. and trans., *The Travels of Adam Olearius in Seventeenth-Century Russia* (Stanford, Cal.: Stanford University Press, 1967).

Fernand Braudel, *Civilization and Capitalism 15th–18th Century,* "The Structures of Everyday Life," translated by Siân Reynolds, volume 1, (New York: Harper & Row, 1979).

Gene A. Brucker, *Renaissance Florence* (Berkeley: University of California Press, 1969).

Lorenzo Camusso, *Travel Guide to Europe 1492. Ten Itineraries in the Old World* (New York: Holt, 1992).

Michael Kunze, *Highroad to the Stake,* translated by William E. Yuill (Chicago: University of Chicago Press, 1987).

Carolyn Johnston Pouncy, ed. and trans., *The Domostroi: Rules for Russian Households in the Time of Ivan the Terrible* (Ithaca, N.Y.: Cornell University Press, 1994).

C. Pythian-Adams, *Desolation of a City: Coventry and the Urban Crisis of the Late Middle Ages* (Cambridge: Cambridge University Press, 1979).

Orest Ranum, "The Refuges of Intimacy," in *A History of Private Life: Passions of the Renaissance,* edited by Roger Chartier, translated by Arthur Goldhammer (Cambridge, Mass.: Harvard University Press, 1989), pp. 225–230.

Werner Rösener, *Peasants in the Middle Ages,* translated by Alexander Stützer (Urbana: University of Illinois Press, 1992).

## MANNERS

**Need for Manners.** Like clothing, housing, and food, the development of early-modern manners was linked to defining and maintaining social hierarchies. The German sociologist Norbert Elias argued that the early modern era was a period of change and cultural instability. The discovery of the New World unsettled formerly firm notions of geography, the Copernican Revolution obliterated old cosmologies, and the Reformation shattered the unity of Catholicism. Feudalism, as a political and economic system, was giving way to absolutism and capitalism, which, for much of the period, were not fully developed themselves. In a society undergoing such reorganization, recom-posing all its hierarchies, the consolidation of an increasingly complicated system of manners, reinforced through public display and by shaming and ostracizing nonconformists, rendered clear for all the boundaries and limits of social relations. Etiquette thus evolved rapidly between 1500 and 1800 because it was a means for society, in an era of drastic cultural transformation, to redefine order within a newly chaotic world.

**Status Hierarchies.** Meals were designed to remind everyone of each other's status, and table manners were social acts that highlighted these status differentials. Indeed, the word *courtoisie* originally referred to forms of behavior that developed at feudal courts. Seating was established according to the guests' social status. In Tudor England, for instance, the most important guests sat at a higher table placed at the end of the dining hall, and two other tables would be placed at right angles to the main table, forming an open-ended rectangle. If one of the host's servants inadvertently sat one guest further from the main table than his status merited, a feud could develop between the host's family and the offended guest's. For this reason, Tudor etiquette books focused on social hierarchies and who should sit where. Additionally, guests' social status determined the quantity and quality of the plates and bowls placed before them; the most important guests had gilded silver tableware, while others would receive plain silver, pewter, or even pottery. While the cups of important guests were covered, guests of lesser importance had to share open cups. (A sixteenth-century Venetian book that prepared travelers to England, however, interpreted this custom as rooted in the parsimony of the English, who wanted to limit the amount of wine their guests would drink.) Etiquette required that guests who shared cups drink with both hands, as the tables were crowded and there was a lot of reaching, and it was considered rude to spill drink intended for others. Furthermore, guests were served different meals. The highest ranking guests might dine on quail while the lowest ranking guests might receive sausages and gruel. Far from being offensive, this practice was welcomed as a way to delineate the variegated social status of the guests. In Russia, for example, the host might reward a guest of limited status for having provided good service or advice by sending higher quality food from one table to the guest's plate. In Tudor England the status of the host determined, moreover, how much food he could offer his guests. A cardinal was allowed to serve nine dishes, a bishop seven, and the mayor of London six. Such sumptuary laws were not exclusive to the English elite; in Reformation Germany, for instance, Lutheran church officials, seeking to control what they viewed as peasant gluttony and debauchery, limited the number of guests and courses that could be served at baptisms and weddings. At fancy banquets, guests washed their hands before each serving, but this practice, too, was embedded with hierarchical meaning. In Tudor England, a mini-keg fastened on a mini-wagon went around the table, and guests washed their hands, in the order of their rank, with water released from the spigot. The use of communal serving plates also worked to emphasize status hierarchies. Normally four guests ate from one plate, and the order by which they served themselves mirrored their respective status. The Russian book *Domostroi*, written in the mid sixteenth century, counseled its readers not to begin to eat immediately when food is placed before them, but rather to pause to make sure that those more honored serve themselves first. Finally, there was a practical function behind carving the meat at the table in front of the guests. Though at first it seems odd to carve up an animal slowly and deliberately in front of one's guests, it enabled the host to reveal, in front of all, which guests received the most tender parts of the dish, and thereby reinforced social distinctions. Indeed, etiquette books in Tudor England were called "carving books."

**Tableware.** For much of the early modern era, guests brought their own cutlery to a dinner, and almost no one, short of a monarch, owned matching sets of tableware. It is for this reason that privileged infants were given silver spoons at their baptisms, as they would use them throughout their adult lives. (With the exception of Italy, forks were rare throughout Europe for most of the early modern era.)

Guests also brought their own knives to dinner; proper manners dictated that the guests speared the food from communal plates, and then pulled the food off their knives and ate with their fingers. Accepting this custom, Erasmus pointed out in his *On Civility in Boys* (1530) that only three fingers were to be used, not the entire hand. Knives, unlike cups and serving plates, were never shared. Since a knife is also a weapon, an assassination at dinner could have been camouflaged as a simple accident involving the passing of a knife between drunken guests. Knives were gradually phased out as eating utensils, and were replaced by spoons and forks precisely because bringing a weapon to a dinner party (even as an eating utensil) was ultimately seen as incongruous with a system (etiquette) established to consolidate deference.

**Disciplining Process.** In general, the low level of early-modern etiquette would surprise modern readers. A fifteenth-century French etiquette book, *These Are Good Table Manners*, considered it necessary to advise its readers not to be the first to take from a communal dish, not to put back into the communal dish anything that had been in one's mouth, not to blow one's nose into one's hand and then take a piece of meat with it, not to offer the person sitting beside one a piece of food already chewed, not to dip one's food

Hunters enjoying a meal, illumination from the fourteenth-century manuscript *Le Livre de la Chasse* (Bibliothèque Nationale, Paris)

The following is from Antoine de Courtin's *New Treatise on Civility* (1672), an etiquette book that guests at Louis XIV's Versailles probably followed. The relationship between manners and consolidating status hierarchies is quite evident—note the references to "people of higher rank," and "people so delicate." Note also how the disciplining process is evolving, both in terms of relating table manners to feelings of shame, repugnance, and physical pain, but also in terms of sophistication—guests can receive additional spoons and plates from the host if etiquette requires it.

If everyone is eating from the same dish, you should take care not to put your hand into it before those of higher rank have done so, and to take food only from the part of the dish opposite you. Still less should you take the best pieces, even though you might be the last to help yourself. It must also be pointed out that you should always wipe your spoon when, after using it, you want to take something from another dish, there being people so delicate that they would not wish to eat soup into which you had dipped it after putting it into your mouth. And even, if you are at the table of very refined people, it is not enough to wipe your spoon; you should not use it but ask for another. . . . If you have the misfortune to burn your mouth, you should endure it patiently if you can, without showing it; but if the burn is unbearable, as sometimes happens, you should, before the others have noticed, take your plate promptly in one hand and lift it to your mouth, and, while covering your mouth with the other hand, return to the plate what you have in your mouth, and quickly pass it to the footman behind you. Civility requires you to be polite, but it does not expect you to be homicidal toward yourself. It is very impolite to touch anything greasy, a sauce, or syrup, etc., with your fingers, apart from the fact that it obliges you to commit two or three more improper acts. One is to wipe your hand frequently on your serviette and to soil it like a kitchen cloth, so that those who see you wipe your mouth with it feel nauseated. Another is to wipe your fingers on your bread, which again is very improper. The third is to lick them, which is the height of impropriety. . . . As there are many [customs] which have already changed, I do not doubt that several of these will change in the future. Formerly one was permitted . . . to dip one's bread into the sauce, provided that one had only not already bitten it. Nowadays that would be a kind of rusticity. Formerly one was allowed to take from one's mouth what one could not eat and drop it on the floor, provided it was done skillfully. Now that would be very disgusting.

**Source:** Norbert Elias, *The History of Manners*, translated by Edmund Jephcott (New York: Pantheon, 1978), pp. 92–93.

into the saltcellar (salt, like sauces, was served in bowls, and while one could freely dip food into a liquid sauce, dipping food into salt would quickly spoil it), not to sit on a seat upon which a previous guest had urinated, and not to loosen one's clothing and scratch at one's body parts during the meal. Erasmus counseled that because it was unhealthy to retain wind, the dinner guest ought to hide the sound with a loud cough, or reduce the sound by pressing one's buttocks firmly together. Rabelais made fun of the state of contemporary table manners in early sixteenth-century France by listing the offenses committed by Gargantua, and then attributing them to the boy's youthful age. Among Gargantua's indiscretions are wiping his nose with his sleeve at the table, washing his hands in the communal soup, spitting in the dishes, and blowing "a fat fart." In *Galateo* (1558) Giovanni della Casa recommended that his readers not blow their nose in their napkin and then stare at the mucous; and not wipe the sweat off their face, caused, presumably, from eating hot food at a crowded table, with a sullied napkin. The *Domostroi* also tied control of the body to signs of social respect. It advised its readers not to pick their noses, cough, or sneeze while in the presence of a monk. The *Domostroi* further recommends that guests not insult their hosts by publicly denigrating the food "as sour, tasteless, too salty, bitter, moldy, raw, overcooked." Finally, the regulations for dining at the lord's court in Wernigerode (1570) stipulated that no male table guest urinate in front of a lady, and that guests refrain from urinating in doorways or in front of windows. The regulations for dining at the court in Brunswick (1578) stated that guests refrain from urinating or defecating in closets or on staircases. It is important to remember, however, that with such court edicts, those of higher rank were imposing a strict control of impulses and emotions (shame and repugnance) on their social inferiors. Present-day understandings of the health risks involved with dining amid feces, urine, and sputum were not appreciated by early-modern medicine, and so the motivating force behind these etiquette suggestions and court edicts was, ultimately, the desire to discipline one's inferiors and to consolidate social hierarchies.

Sources:
Norbert Elias, *The History of Manners*, translated by Edmund Jephcott (New York: Pantheon, 1978).

Jacques Revel, "The Uses of Civility," in *A History of Private Life: Passions of the Renaissance*, edited by Roger Chartier, translated by Arthur Goldhammer (Cambridge, Mass.: Harvard University Press, 1989), p. 184.

Alison Sim, *Food and Feast in Tudor England* (New York: St. Martin's Press, 1997).

## TOWN AND CITY LIFE

**Fortifications.** Cities at this time were great walled-in islands existing in the midst of fields and pastures. A traveler approaching the early-modern city encountered on either side of the road, cows, sheep, and goats grazing in the pastures lying outside the city's walls. Most cities of Europe were encircled by constantly repaired Roman and Medieval walls, and often by moats filled with flowing water, as well. Gallows and torture wheels (heavy wooden wheels used to crush a convict's bones, and then attached—with the still-living victim twisted among its spokes—to a

Detail from a fifteenth-century painting of Genoa, showing densely packed houses from the town walls to the port (Museo Navalie di Pegli, Genoa)

huge pole) dotted the landscape outside the walls. The rotted corpses of those executed were left deliberately outside the walls to prevent disease and to serve as a warning to newcomers that the city's laws were to be obeyed.

**City Gates.** Due to the almost constant warfare of the era, walls and moats alone were not sufficient to safeguard a city. Defensive towers were therefore inserted periodically within the walls. These were huge battlements usually adjacent to those limited number of gates from which people entered and departed the city during daylight hours. The seriousness attached to the city's defensive structures is revealed in the writings of a Milanese merchant staying in Calais around 1518 (the city was controlled by the English then), who noted that any foreigner seen near the moat or climbing the walls would be put to death. The city's gates would be carved out of the fortified walls at those locations where major highways from neighboring cities intersected the walls; thus, the settlement patterns of neighboring cities dictated where a particular city's gates would be placed. (Though it should be noted that highways linking the major cities of Europe were little better than deeply rutted roads.) Nördlingen, a German city whose late-medieval walls stand intact, represents well what was once fairly typical: a little under two miles of fortified walls surround the entirety of Nördlingen, and along the town walls lie five gates (all of which are so narrow that today's automobiles have trouble squeezing through them) and eleven defensive towers. Florence's wall was five miles in circumference and included seventy-three towers and fifteen gates. The design of these towers was fairly standard: their base was usually square, and was itself about four stories high. Upon the base would stand a circular two- or three-story tower containing a balustrade and firing slits, from which one could shoot at marauders attacking adjacent parts of the wall. Cities with moats had drawbridges inserted at the gates, allowing passage over the flowing water below. Gates were manned, particularly at night, with watchmen and guards. Towers erected at gates also served as the municipal prisons, and the cells—some so small that it would be difficult for a prisoner to lie down in them—often occupied the third or fourth story. As the gate was the first edifice encountered by a newcomer to a city, messages and warnings were often posted on the exterior walls of the gate. For instance, in Dinkelsbühl, visitors can still see, on a building just inside one of the gates, a painting of a cleaver chopping off a hand amid a pool of blood. The message to visitors was clear: stealing was not tolerated.

**City Populations.** Notarial documents, judicial records, hospital registers, tax records, and baptism and death certificates reveal that populations within the larger cities varied considerably, so the following figures are estimates. Around 1500, Paris, Naples, and Venice alone among European cities had populations of at least one hundred thousand, while London, Florence, and Rome each had roughly fifty thousand. Other great cities in 1500 included the Flemish trading centers of Ghent (fifty-five thousand) and Antwerp (forty-five thousand), while Berlin and Madrid were little more than villages at the end of the fifteenth century. The largest cities in German speaking lands—Cologne, Augsburg, Vienna, and Nuremberg—each had populations around twenty thousand. Most striking, however, is the rate of growth these cities experienced. By 1700, Paris and London, for example, each contained about half a million residents, while Amsterdam and Naples had populations of roughly two hundred thousand. Cities were thus full of strangers: merchants in search of new markets, pilgrims, students coming to study at the emerging urban universities, the ever-desired carpenters and masons, and mercenaries. Peasants, seeking to avoid unemployment, hunger, and the dangers of the countryside, would attempt to establish citizenship and obtain work within the city as well. For example, in 1600 about twenty-four thousand people lived in Munich, the capital of the duchy of Bavaria, although fewer than one-half had resided in the city long enough to qualify as actual citizens with full rights, reflecting not only the general increase in population throughout Europe during the sixteenth century but also the dawning of urbanization as well. Indeed, in an era when 30 percent to 40 percent of babies died within their first year, immigration was the only way a city could guarantee a relatively stable population.

**Inside the City.** Within the walls one still found citizens working on vegetable gardens, which nearly every house possessed. In many cities, even the jailer's wife maintained a garden outside the prison, where she grew vegetables to supplement the meager diets of the incarcerated. There was not a sharp distinction between the rural world outside the walls and the urban world inside them: streams flowed everywhere, and the city's landscape was filled with wooden barns, fences, and stables. Animals of all sorts—horses, chickens, pigs, goats, sheep—walked up and down the streets and alleys, which were strewn not only with rubbish heaps, but with feces, both animal and human. People regularly threw their garbage into the street, where pigs or even stray dogs would forage on it. Cities were far from self-sufficient, however, and all depended upon close relationships with the rural communities in their hinterlands. Renaissance Florence established such greatness in part because of the auspicious relations it maintained with sharecroppers in the Tuscan countryside who provided the urban elite with a secure food supply, as well as with grain, oil, and wine, which the Florentine elite in turn sold or traded throughout Europe.

**Building Materials.** Most, if not all, of the typical city's buildings would be made out of wood, though fifteenth-century Paris and seventeenth-century Amsterdam were making the transition to stone. As a safeguard against fire, some exceptionally crowded cities, such as Florence and Bruges (Flanders) had passed ordinances that mandated tiles on all roofs. The risk of fire was especially great because houses were closely packed together, so close in fact that the structures truly held up one another. In early-modern Goslar, Germany, more than 1,500 buildings housed 12,000 people in an area covering just 240 acres.

Mazes of walkways and vaults connected houses to other rows of houses. It is easy to see how fire, once started, could quickly spread. Nearly the entire city of Troyes in France burned to the ground in 1547, Moscow experienced repeated fires throughout the early modern era, and a great fire destroyed 75 percent of London—more than 12,000 homes—in 1666. By the early fourteenth century, Florence had, in addition to mandating tiled roofs, passed laws stipulating that, to prevent fire, all buildings on major streets had to be faced with stone to at least seven feet off the ground. Early-modern urban planning sought to create more open space: in Munich, Duke William V tore down entire neighborhoods and erected in their stead churches, mansions, and monasteries, all with dramatic courtyards, and wider avenues. Those areas untouched retained narrow, interwoven city streets that mingled in a mazelike fashion, seemingly to belie any forethought in their design. Added to the maze of streets in many early-modern cities was an equally elaborate web of canals and smaller, artificially constructed waterways, which were somewhat like aqueducts. These channels provided a water network throughout the city and, in addition to guaranteeing a drinking supply, they also furnished the tanners, dyers, millers, and fullers with the water needed for their operations. Even smaller towns like Goslar had close to thirty mills in the sixteenth century, while larger towns such as Munich had as many as thirty-six wells and eighteen fountains to supply its residents with water. Conversely, fourteenth- and fifteenth-century Pisa lacked an adequate waterworks and consequently saw its population decimated by marsh disease and malaria.

**Darkness and Congestion.** Typically, each story in a house jutted out from the one directly below it. This building style rendered the streets' maximum width at ground level, but meant that little air or light penetrated to ground level, as the distance between buildings facing one another on opposite sides of the street was greatly reduced at the rooftops. In parts of York, England, contemporary visitors can still stroll through serpentine streets, many of which are so narrow that an adult leaning out of a window on the second floor can touch the building on the other side. The oldest part of Florence, near the Piazza della Signoria, possessed streets only about eight feet wide at ground level. As they were lined, however, with relatively tall buildings, light was effectively blocked out on these streets, and the district was infamous for being habitually dark, damp, and fetid. While noteworthy today, these sections of York and Florence would have been all too common in 1500. Signs hung everywhere, protruding from the buildings into the narrow streets, and added to the sensory congestion. Guilds, shops, hotels, taverns, and even private homes were wont to hang a placard or festoon, making the narrow and dark streets all the more congested. By evening, the absence of street lights guaranteed that the city was an eerily dark environment, illuminated only by a burning taper or oil lamp in a house window or by the candles that lighted a neighborhood tavern. Undoubtedly the surest way

for a traveler or new resident, lost in the maze of streets at ground level, to orient oneself within the city would have been to locate the towers of the largest cathedral or church, which almost always lay in the center of the city. Given that the average building in an early-modern city was three or four stories high, the spires of the great cathedrals, such as the Gothic cathedral in Strasbourg, which towered above the city's roofs at a height of over 460 feet, or the summit of the belltower in St. Mark's Cathedral in Venice, which one would have to climb over eight-hundred steps to reach, clearly dominated the skyline.

**Need for Open Spaces.** By all accounts early-modern cities were quite noisy and smelly, and, even by today's standards, the air must have been difficult at times to breathe. Despite their impressive waterworks, only a few wealthy cities, such as Milan, possessed paved (cobblestone) streets, and so, depending on the weather and season, dust or mud could be everywhere, mixing with the garbage and fecal matter on the streets. Due to the narrow and winding nature of the streets, the almost complete lack of circulating air prevented dissipation. The city's slaughterhouses and tanneries, its noxious hospitals, its old, rotting wooden buildings, and its lack of spacious streets created ideal conditions for the spread of smallpox, typhoid, consumption, hydropsy, and pleurisy, as well as workplace injuries. Antonio de Beatis, who recorded his travels through Europe in 1517–1518, noted that the streets of Paris were so muddy and narrow, and that so many carts vied to get through the city's corridors, that simply walking within the city was quite dangerous. In Edmond Rostand's famous play *Cyrano de Bergerac* (1897), the title character is murdered in 1655 Paris by villains who, with no effort, mask the assassination as a simple—and common—street accident. It is not surprising, then, that one of the main goals of nearly every early-modern municipal government was the creation of more open spaces. Fourteenth-century Florence responded to a common problem when it devoted a high percentage of its financial resources to street improvements. The primary reason Florence turned its main streets into rectilinear ones did not stem from abstract aesthetic considerations but rather from the inability of farmers and merchants transporting foodstuffs to reach the city's internal markets.

**Market Squares.** Markets emerged periodically from these mazes of dusty streets. Every city would have a number of markets, each held in a different square: a hay market, coal market, fish market, corn (or vegetable) market, and cloth market. Adding to the din caused by the daily buying, selling, fighting, and bartering (and by all the construction under way in the adjoining streets) was the sound of craftsmen—tanners, leatherworkers, weavers, cobblers, blacksmiths, wheelwrights, swordsmiths—who worked in front of their shops and homes from dawn until the night's darkness prevented further work. In the 1470s Florence had 84 cabinetmakers' shops, 54 stone and marble cutters' shops, 44 goldsmiths' shops, 70 butchershops, and 66 apothecaries and groceries. A century later, Antwerp could

In the following passage Pope Pius II describes Vienna, circa 1458. This portrait of urban life is excerpted from a work titled *The History of Emperor Frederick III*, which was published in 1669. Although Vienna's walls, architecture, churches, and markets impress Pius, aspects of the city's social life trouble him. He also notes how many of Vienna's residents are new to the city, reflecting the general trend toward urbanization. An old proverb, "city air makes one free," referred to the custom which granted liberty and citizenship to former serfs who spent a year and a day within a city's walls. Based on Pius' account, this custom applied to peasants who carried wine into Vienna.

Vienna is surrounded by a wall two thousand paces in circumference, but it has large suburbs with moats encompassing them, and a palisade all around. The city also has a great moat and rising from it a very high rampart. Then there are thick and lofty walls with numerous towers and defenses prepared for war. The houses of the citizens are roomy and richly adorned, yet solid and strong in construction. Everywhere there are arched doorways and broad courts. . . . The stables are full of horses and domestic animals of all kinds. The high façades of the houses make a magnificent sight. Only one thing produces an unpleasant effect; they very often cover the roofs with wooden shingles, and so few are tied. For the rest, the houses are built of stone. . . .

The wine cellars are so deep and so spacious that it is said that Vienna has as many buildings under the earth as above it. The streets are paved only with hard stone, so that the wheels of vehicles are not easily worn out. The churches . . . are both large and splendid, built of dressed stone, full of light, and admirable for their rows of columns. . . .

It is believed that the city numbers fifty thousand communicants. Eighteen men are chosen as magistrates, and there is a judge whose duty it is to interpret the law, and a master of citizens, who has charge of civic affairs. . . .

It is really incredible how much produce is brought into the city day after day. Many wagons come in loaded with eggs and crayfish. Flour, bread, meat, fish, and poultry are brought in tremendous masses; nevertheless, by evening nothing is left to be bought. The wine harvest lasts here for forty days, and every day three hundred carts full of wine are brought in two or three times, and twelve hundred horses are harnessed daily to the horses. In the villages outside Vienna . . . liberty is granted to all who bring wine into the city; it is unbelievable how much wine is brought in. . . .

On the other hand, in so large and noble a city, brawls are fought like military engagements; now the craftsmen against the students, then the citizens against the workers. . . . Hardly a celebration goes by without a man-slaughter; numerous murders are committed. When there is a brawl, there is no one to separate the contending parties; neither magistrates nor the princes try, as they should, to prevent such great evils.

To sell wine in the home is in no way damaging to the reputation. Almost all citizens operate taverns for drinking. . . . The common people worship their bellies and are gluttonous. What a man has earned during the week by the work of his hands, he squanders down to the last penny on Sunday. This is a raggish, boorish lot, and there is a very great number of whores. . . . Old families are rare, and practically all the inhabitants are immigrants or foreigners. . . .

The Viennese live, moreover, without any written law; they say that they live according to ancient customs, which they often distort or interpret as they wish. Justice is wholly venal. Those who have the means sin without punishment; the poor and unprotected are punished with the full rigor of the law.

**Source:** James Bruce Ross and Mary Martin McLaughlin, eds., *The Portable Renaissance Reader* (New York: Penguin, 1958), pp. 208–213.

---

boast of having 594 bootmakers and tailors, 78 butchers, 92 fishmongers, and 110 barbers and surgeons.

**Noise Pollution.** The early-modern city was a symphony of clanging, hammering, chopping, filing, and forging sounds that were periodically supplemented by the pealing of church bells, the yelling of street urchins chasing a cart, the chanting of a choir of monks emanating from the open windows of a monastery, and the crowing of roosters. Vendors roamed urban streets all day long hawking spices, clothes, and sausages; wandering musicians beat their instruments; charismatic preachers attracted crowds with impromptu public sermons that filled city squares; and jugglers, prostitutes, ventriloquists, and mendicant friars sought attention from those congregating in the markets and those gathering at the city's wells. Beggars, some hideously deformed, called out for alms. Begging was a profession in those days and was referred to as "the golden trade." In 1574 Nuremberg, more than seven hundred beggars were officially registered with the municipal authorities, making begging, by far, the largest "occupation" in the city. But there were probably more than one thousand beggars in Nuremberg at that time, most of whom loitered around taverns or in front of the doors of churches and monasteries. Though professional beggars, in this highly charged religious environment, satisfied the elites' need to display publicly their Christian charity, their wailings and importunings surely contributed to the noise in the city. As the Nuremberg city council described the situation in 1588: "The general citizenry here is especially inconvenienced by vagrants, beggars, and tramps, especially by the screaming and bawling of children both day and night in the streets and before the houses. . . ." Because the workday began at 5 A.M., the main meal (dinner) was eaten at noon, and work, for most of the city's residents, ceased around 3 P.M. The night brought relative quiet: people went to bed early by our standards (taverns in most cities were closed by 10 P.M.), and no respectable citizen, save the watchmen patrolling the city walls, alert to fires and would-be thieves, was out much after 9 P.M. Nocturnal crime was relatively rare, partly because crimes committed after dark brought a much harsher penalty than if they had occurred during the day, and partly because cities closed their gates at sunset and imposed curfews that were regarded by the residents as a form of protection, not as an attack on liberty.

**The Wealthy.** Because suburbs did not exist as they are known today (although as city populations expanded, rural settlements and gardens administered by noble families and religious institutions developed outside the city's walls), wealthier families also lived within this crowded jumble, in narrow homes with steep pediments. However, their homes were built along the edges of the major city squares and along the city's widest avenues, thus insuring for themselves dwellings that were airy, dry, and clean. For example, in Erfurt, Germany, most of the patricians resided in beautiful homes—each painted with a unique façade—that form the perimeter of the lovely square known as "Fishmarket," while in another German city, Schwäbisch Hall, the patrician homes stand side by side, facing the large, open square that lies between them and the monumental St. Michael's Church. The Fuggers, as wealthy a family as any in early-modern Europe, including those of kings and emperors, lived in grand style along Augsburg's Maximilian Street, a wide and airy boulevard lined with beautiful mansions and famous, even today, for the elaborately carved bronze fountains which dot its path.

**Availability of Goods.** Just as in contemporary times, the city in the early modern era was a hub of commerce and exchange. A city's status was largely determined by the power and influence of its guilds, by the level of its global economic connections, and by the commodities that could be found within it. Thus, Benedetto Dei, a fifteenth-century Florentine merchant, argued in a famous tract that his city was grander than either Venice or Rome because of its wool and silk trade, counting 270 shops belonging to the wool merchants' guild, and 83 to the silk merchants. Fifteenth-century Venice was famed for its spice trade, as well as for the availability of silks, pearls, precious gems, and rare cloths imported from the Mideast and various Mediterranean ports. Noting Antwerp in 1560, the Florentine

lawyer and diplomat Francesco Guicciardini wrote that the first reason to account for the city's preeminence was its "fairs for merchandise." He praised not only Antwerp's spice and drug trade with India, which brought rare treasures like clove, cinnamon, nutmeg, ginger, and rhubarb to the city, but also celebrated the city for being a place where one could obtain such prized items as Turkish carpets and fustians, armor, delicate glasswork, sugar, silks, wools, velvet cloth, satin, tapestries, and skins of sable, ermine, lynx, and leopard. Although cities were filled with poverty, stench, and disease, they were at the same time exciting places—almost mythical to the rural peasant—where one could hear countless languages spoken, purchase tobacco from the New World or ivory from Africa, and encounter people from all parts of the world.

**Jewish Ghettos.** Although officially expelled from some countries, like Spain and England, Jews built sustainable communities in many European cities, such as Prague, Worms, and Venice. The neighborhoods where Jewish communities lived were known as ghettos and they were, given the congested and mazelike nature of the early-modern city, fairly segregated and recognizable. In Worms, for example, contemporary visitors can still easily find the large block of buildings packed tightly together, forming a little island amid several main thoroughfares, against the city walls by St. Martin's Gate. The boundary of the ghetto in Worms is fixed by a boulevard called *Judengasse* (Jewish Alley); there is hardly a city in Germany today without such a street, and, by locating it, one can find where the ghetto was. Life in the cities was always uncertain for Jews. For example, in 1349, blaming the plague on Jewish intrigue, the citizens of Freiberg burned every adult Jew, except pregnant women, in the city. In 1519 the Jewish community of Regensburg, one of the largest in the Holy Roman Empire at that time, was summarily banished, inspiring similar expulsions in other cities. Even in cities where Jewish communities were allowed to remain, such as Frankfurt am Main, Jews were subjected to great hostility. In early-modern Frankfurt, travelers who entered the city through the Brückenturm Gate gazed upon a large painting of a Christian boy being tortured to death by Jews. Renovated as late as 1678, it was removed only in the 1770s.

**Entertainment.** Like today, cities were worlds filled with all kinds of exciting entertainment. In addition to restaurants and taverns (Munich in 1600 had forty-two wine shops and fourteen alehouses), the early-modern city offered periodic entertainment. Chief among these would be parades, such as the great citywide procession held in Bruges every 3 May, and the processions in London (prior to Henry VIII's break with Rome) that occurred on the feasts of St. John and St. Peter, and for which the streets of the city were covered with flowers. Great fairs were eagerly awaited by city residents. Geneva, for example, held four fairs annually, and though ostensibly commercial, these fairs provided great forms of amusement and distraction for all of Geneva's citizens. Also popular throughout western Europe were dances, horse or pig races through the city streets, outdoor theatrics such as mystery (or miracle) plays staged by religious confraternities (laymen) and religious orders such as the Jesuits (London's Globe Theatre was somewhat unique in its secular status), and minstrel and puppet shows. One famous entertainer, Arnoul Greban, delighted the citizens of the French town of Angers in 1490 with a mystery play about Christ's Passion during which he recited sixty-five thousand verses. Unlike modern cities, there were no museums in the early-modern era. However, royal courts were collecting items of natural history and art that would in later centuries form the basis of the urban museum, and on occasion these would be open to the public.

**Public Executions.** The always popular witch-burning or criminal execution did not always transpire on the gallows hill outside the city's walls and must be considered a form of entertainment. The government of Renaissance Florence viewed highly publicized executions not only as necessary deterrents to crime, but as events that gratified the popular appetite. Thus, a slave girl who had poisoned her master in 1379 was, prior to being burned at the stake, led in a cart through Florence as the executioner periodically tore the flesh from her body with red-hot pincers. In Verona, gallows were built in the Roman amphitheater in the center of the old town.

**Gambling and Prostitution.** For men, there were also games of chance, which were tolerated during the day in squares and markets, and which took place clandestinely at night in back alleys or barns, and prostitution, which was legal and regulated in most of the larger cities. At the start of the sixteenth century, Venice had more than 11,000 registered prostitutes (close to 10 percent of the population!), while Rome, a city just beginning to rebuild after centuries of neglect, listed 6,800. In Valencia, Spain, an entire neighborhood was given over to prostitutes, who were housed in 150 special houses and who illuminated their doorways with three or four candles: hence, the "red-light district." In addition, though London's government attempted to combat syphilis in the early 1500s by confining prostitutes to a single locale at the Bankside in Southwark, soliciting occurred throughout the city, even within St. Paul's Cathedral. City dwellers also enjoyed the use of public baths, and men and women often bathed naked together, eating their meals on a buoy. Late-sixteenth-century Munich had a dozen public bathhouses. Although many maintained that visiting baths was medicinal, many municipalities closed their baths during the sixteenth century in an effort to curb the spread of syphilis. Often the seizure of the bathhouse provoked great anger, as is revealed in the official complaint written to Count Sigmund von Lupfen by the residents of Stühlingen (southwest Germany) in 1525.

Sources:

A. L. Beier and Roger Finlay, "The Significance of the Metropolis," in *London 1500–1700*, edited by Beier and Finlay (London: Longman, 1986), p. 3.

Gene A. Brucker, *Renaissance Florence* (Berkeley: University of California Press, 1969).

Lorenzo Camusso, *Travel Guide to Europe 1492. Ten Itineraries in the Old World* (New York: Holt, 1992).

Ronnie Po-chia Hsia, *The Myth of Ritual Murder* (New Haven: Yale University Press, 1988).

Michael Kunze, *Highroad to the Stake,* translated by William E. Yuill (Chicago: University of Chicago Press, 1987).

Margaret Pelling, "Appearance and Reality: Barber Surgeons, the Body and Disease," in *London 1500–1700,* edited by A. L. Beier and Roger Finlay (London: Longman, 1986), pp. 82-112.

James Bruce Ross and Mary Martin McLaughlin, eds., *The Portable Renaissance Reader* (New York: Penguin, 1958).

Gerald Strauss, ed., *Manifestations of Discontent in Germany on the Eve of the Reformation* (Bloomington: Indiana University Press, 1971).

## VILLAGE LIFE

**Rural Crisis.** By 1300, even after the surge of urbanization that characterized the High Middle Ages, perhaps 90 percent of the European population still lived in the countryside. Throughout Europe at this time, rural society confronted a host of problems, such as uneven levels of population density, inadequate nourishment, overstraining of natural resources, overall economic depression, and surges in population growth that exacerbated all the aforementioned problems. Earlier, between 1100 and 1300, peasant communities throughout central and western Europe had indulged in large-scale clearings, uprooted woodlands, and drained marshes in order to grow more grain and feed a steadily growing population. For certain areas this uninhibited exploitation resulted in unproductive soil under cultivation, upon which some communities were still depending hundreds of years later. In addition, rapid deforestation caused problems of erosion as it lowered the water table and allowed valuable nutrients to wash out of the soil. The gradual reduction of village commons as well as the conversion of woodlands—which in the Middle Ages had been used to graze livestock—into arable farmland caused a notable decrease in the raising of livestock, and as a result the nutrition level of peasants' diets was lowered. The decline of the forests also reduced the supply of mushrooms, nuts, herbs, and berries, further reducing the peasants' diet. Firewood and timber for building became valued commodities, and strict regulations were introduced stipulating when and how much wood a peasant could gather. Moreover, there was no longer enough manure to fertilize adequately all the fields. With the shortage of grazing lands, early-modern lords and village authorities restricted the public use of the commons, which meant villagers became reliant on shepherds to graze their cattle in far-off pastures. Conflicts between shepherds and villagers became a widespread feature of village life. In attempts to meet the increasing demand for grain, many villages in the early modern era were built along rivers on terrain that was too low, and consequently they experienced regular and severe flooding. Petitions that were sent throughout the sixteenth century to the Elector of Saxony from Elster, a village on the Elbe River, exemplify this problem. The villagers pled for reductions in their taxes because severe flooding of the river damaged their harvest every few years. In short, a situation had been created that guaranteed regular famines and bad harvests after 1300.

**Settlement Patterns.** Villages were laid out in a variety of settlement patterns. Some villages were circular in design with all of the houses facing a central common, which would probably be used for pasture. Perhaps the church, if the village had one, or a fish pond might stand in place of a common pasture. Individual farmland would extend behind each house. This design awarded protection to farms and livestock during times of war. Another prevalent pattern involved building the houses along a single road, with the majority of the farmhouses forming a long row. The village settlement was thus arranged in somewhat of a straight line, with strips of farmland extending far back behind each house well into the forests. The advantage of this type of settlement lay in the ease with which one's farmland could be expanded without interfering with one's neighbor. This pattern was preferable if the village lay near a marsh because the peasants could build canals running parallel to the main street that drained the soil nearest to the village. In German lands the most common type of settlement pattern was characterized by a village center reserved for the peasants' homes and individually owned, fenced-in gardens, which would be connected to one another by various paths and lanes. These backyard gardens often meant survival for the great majority of families that lacked the thirty or forty acres of individually owned land necessary for economic independence. The arable land lay in a wide ring surrounding the village, and portions of it were divided among the village's families, some plots permanently and others on a year-to-year basis, according to complicated laws and customs. As there were no paths in the arable land, conflict often ensued because peasants, taking heavy tools and draught animals, had to cross each other's portions to get to their own, and thus were often accused of damaging a neighbor's crop. Finally, surrounding the arable would be an outer ring, this one containing the common pasture and extending into the nearby woodlands. Sometimes referred to as the "common mark," this area was used collectively by all members of the village as a place for grazing livestock, obtaining timber, gathering firewood, picking berries, and finding nuts and honey. In short, the traditional village had a complex topography consisting of individually owned farmhouses and gardens, as well as parcels of meadow and arable, some of which were individually farmed, some of which were communally worked, and some of which changed ownership on a rotating basis. Finally, it should be noted that the famous "three field system" of crop rotation, in which fields alternated between lying fallow and producing either summer or winter crops, did not exist from time immemorial, but rather emerged as the result of complicated mutual restrictions developed by village communities as a response to the crises caused by population growth and land shortage. Its widespread adoption in Western Europe (in grain-producing areas—rarely in wine-growing regions) resulted in the vast

Woodcutters and husbandmen, illumination from a fifteenth-century Flemish codex (from Franco Cardini, *Europe 1492*, 1989)

increase of cereal production that enabled Western Europe to urbanize in the late Medieval and early-modern eras, but it was by no means universally incorporated, and settlement patterns and agricultural practices in Russia, for instance, were quite distinct from West European models.

**Woodlands and Marshes.** In an effort to attract settlers in some wooded and marshy areas, peasants were given better property rights, had minimal ties to the local lord, and had to satisfy fewer feudal obligations. These legal and social improvements compensated those peasants who endured the added hardship of clearing wood, draining swampland, and living in scattered settlement patterns. In areas where villages lacked nucleated centers, manorial institutions were weak or nonexistent, and the predominant mode of agriculture—dairy farming or cattle and pig raising—did not rely on the more cooperative systems of farming typical in open-field villages. In addition, women were given a higher degree of independence, and their labor represented a much higher proportion of the total agricultural labor than it did in villages committed to growing grains. The economic reliance on women in wooded and marsh areas seems to have created a crisis in gender relations by 1600 and might explain both the increase in misogyny and the witch craze of the early seventeenth century.

The following description of a peasant's house in an area near the German city of Frankfurt am Main is written in a tongue-in-cheek style, comparing the home of a peasant to the castle of a king. Despite the author's comic intent, his portrait of a wealthier peasant's home (note the mention of servants) and its furnishings is accurate. The description of the looting of the house by hungry soldiers who, during military campaigns, lived by plundering peasant villages, is less funny, and reveals the frequent and unexpected hardships to which peasants were subjected.

My father . . . owned a palace as good as the next man's. It was so attractive that not a single king could have built one like it with his own two hands; he would rather have put off the construction for all eternity. It was well chinked with adobe, and instead of being covered with barren slate, cold lead, or red copper, it was thatched with straw. . . . He had the wall about his castle not made of fieldstone picked by the wayside, or of indifferently manufactured brick—no, he used oak planking, from a noble and useful tree on which grow pork sausages and juicy hams [peasants relied on the acorns which fell from oaks to feed their pigs which grazed in the forests]. . . . The rooms, halls, and chambers had been tinted black by smoke. . . . The tapestries were of the most delicate texture in the world, for they were made by [spiders]. His windows were dedicated to St. No Glass for no other reason than that he knew windows woven of hemp and flax took more time and trouble than the most precious Venetian glass. . . . Instead of pageboys, lackeys, and stable boys, he had sheep, rams, and pigs, each neatly dressed in its own uniform. They often waited on me in the fields until, tired of their service, I drove them off and home. His armory was sufficiently and neatly furnished with plows, mattocks, axes, picks, shovels, manure forks, and hay rakes. He drilled and exercised these weapons daily; hoeing and weeding was his military discipline . . . hitching up the oxen was his captaincy; taking manure to the fields his science of fortification; plowing, his campaigning; splitting firewood, his troop movements and maneuvers; and cleaning out the stables, his war games and most noble diversion. With these activities he made war on the whole earth . . . and thereby obtained rich harvest every fall.

[Inside the house, robbing soldiers] bundled up big bags of cloth, household goods, and clothes, as if they wanted to hold a rummage sale somewhere. What they did not intend to take along they broke and spoiled. Some ran their swords into the hay and straw, as if there hadn't been hogs enough to stick. Some shook the feathers out of beds and [stole] bacon slabs, hams, and other stuff. . . . Others knocked the hearth and broke the windows. . . . They burned up bedsteads, tables, chairs, and benches, though there were yards and yards of firewood outside the kitchen. Jars and crocks, pots and casseroles all were broken. . . . In the barn, the hired girl was handled so roughly that she was unable to walk away, I am ashamed to report. They stretched the hired man out flat on the ground, stuck a wooden wedge into his mouth to keep it open, and emptied a bucket full of stinking manure drippings down his throat. . . .

Source: Hans Jacob Christoffel von Grimmelshausen, *The Adventures of Simplicius Simplicissimus,* translated by George Schulz-Behrend (Columbia, S.C.: Camden House, 1993), pp. 2–7.

**Government.** While there are exceptions to every rule, the majority of early-modern villages were not preindustrial utopias in which neighbors eagerly helped one another and lived in happy communities. Although the introduction of the common-field system forced village peasants to cooperate with each other, and even though individual farming was increasingly subjected to the stipulations of the village's self-governing institutions, few villages developed a truly communal spirit. For instance, conflicts arose regarding complaints over how fairly the fields in the common had been distributed; accusations that all members of the village had not performed their share of work on the communal fields; disputes involving charges of having damaged another's crop, either by having carelessly trampled over a neighbor's field or by failing to prevent one's livestock from grazing on a neighbor's field; and arguments over where property lines legally existed. As a result each village had its own complex form of government whose members and committees oversaw and strictly regulated every aspect of village life. This system included deciding who would help install a new fence around the village; determining the exact days that villagers would be responsible for sowing their crops, harvesting them, and removing them after the harvest, so that livestock could graze on the stubble fields; allocating how much wood each family could remove from the forest; and coordinating, on an almost day-to-day basis, when different portions of the arable could be farmed, to prevent, given the lack of direct access to most plots, one peasant farmer from interfering with the labor of another. Firewood, the sole fuel supply, was frequently scarce, so the village government would also determine when the communal oven could be lit for baking bread. Most villages possessed a rather large oven housed in a separate structure that was lit at established times and with which multiple households baked their food simultaneously. The use of such an oven also reduced the risk of fire, as it was usually kept apart from the homes and barns.

**Officials.** Villages in German-speaking lands were governed by several officials. The bailiff was in charge of overseeing additional clearings and planning of the settlement. He had high status in the village, generally possessed more land than his neighbors, and mediated between the village community and the secular and ecclesiastical lords who retained feudal rights over the village. The forest ranger regulated how much timber and firewood each household would be allowed. Complaints suggest this official was susceptible to bribes and often committed relatively minor crimes with some degree of impunity. The *Schultheiss*, or chief-administrative official, was a wealthy villager, sometimes appointed for life by the local lord, and sometimes elected by the other wealthy male peasants within the village. He exercised varied political and judicial functions, and usually concerned himself with collecting and channeling the villagers' tax payments to the higher authorities. *Richters* (village officials) were also elected by the wealthier male peasants to sit on a committee that met throughout the year to appoint and hire night watchmen, shepherds, cowherds, and rodent catchers; to deal immediately with any emergency or serious crime; to resolve interpersonal conflicts; and to see that debtors paid their arrears. The superintendent, an official of the church and not officially of the village, monitored the moral life of the village, and made sure that the adults went to church, sent their children and servants to Sunday school, paid their fixed dues to the church, repaired church properties as needed, and received punishment for transgressions such as adultery, abandonment, and the physical abuse of one's elderly parents. Finally, the schoolmaster was involved in certain areas of village politics, notably when a child was involved in a disturbance. For instance, in the village of Leonberg near Stuttgart, in the late seventeenth century, the schoolmaster was forced into the political spotlight when a thirteen-year-old schoolgirl dramatically accused herself of being a witch, of having caused harm to various domestic animals, and of imperiling the eternal souls of her classmates.

**Social Relations.** By the sixteenth century, economic polarization had separated a few relatively well-off peasants from their poorer neighbors. Through luck, hard work, or successful marriage alliances, some peasants had managed to accumulate enough land to be able to sell surplus grain at the regional market. With such funds these peasants built up their herds, produced enough manure to fertilize their fields effectively, and grew even more grain. They then had started lending money to their poorer neighbors, often with the result that they took their neighbors' land as collateral. Eventually they had the wherewithal to hire poorer peasants, some of whose land they now owned, as day laborers. In times of crop failure these poorer peasants had to purchase food from their wealthier neighbors at exorbitant prices, further polarizing the distribution of wealth. This vicious cycle was played out in nearly every village in early-modern Europe, and, not surprisingly, this dynamic created village animosities and conflicts. It is with good cause that more than one historian has identified envy as the paramount emotion of early-modern village life.

**Cottagers.** Beneath the wealthiest peasants (called *Hüfner* in Germany) were those who owned neither draught animals nor farmsteads (a house with a barn and some individual holdings) but possessed only a simple plot with a one-room cottage, usually on the periphery of the village. These peasants were called, appropriately, "cottagers" (*manouvriers* in French and *Kotsassen, Gärtner*, or *Kötter* in German). A high percentage of cottagers were the younger sons who had been denied a partial inheritance of their parents' land. This may seem unfair, but if a family divided its holdings evenly among the sons, all would, within two generations, be reduced to the status of cottager. Other cottagers might originally have possessed their own fields, but, lacking oxen or horses, these peasants were forced to work their fields by hand without access to key technologies such as the wheeled plough and harrow, which were dependent on animal labor. Thus, as regional markets increasingly commercialized agriculture during the fifteenth and sixteenth centuries, those peasants lacking the necessary tools and livestock emerged as the cottagers, for they could not produce enough to sell. Often to make ends meet, cottagers worked as day laborers on the fields of the wealthier peasants or they allowed runaway serfs, escaped convicts, deserters, and itinerant con artists to lodge under their roofs, which vexed their wealthier neighbors. Cottagers also worked as village artisans, performing necessary, though socially embarrassing, jobs such as butcher, tanner, weaver, and gravedigger.

**Day Laborers.** At the lowest level were the day laborers who lived, at best, in tiny houses erected on the land of the wealthy peasant or of the lord, close to the fields on which they would work, and, at worst, in barns and stables. Unlike the cottagers, who at least owned a home, maintained a relatively small backyard garden, and earned money through artisanal enterprise, the day laborers had nothing, and relied upon the charity of their neighbors just to survive. Their wives and children—if they had any—begged in front of the church on Sunday. In times of great inflation (and this covers much of the early-modern period), however, day laborers were probably better off than the cottagers, for the former were generally fed by their employers as part of their labor contract, while the latter would have to spend incredibly high percentages of their household incomes just to keep their families from starving.

**Obligations.** Though the seignorial conditions under which peasants labored varied greatly across Europe—in early modern times French peasants were freer than their counterparts in England, and peasants in Western Germany were much better off than those on lands east of the Elbe, in Eastern Europe and in Russia, where serfdom bordered on slavery—only a small percentage of peasants were able to accumulate land sufficient to achieve economic security. Secular and religious lords, in both Protestant and Catholic lands, siphoned off peasant surpluses through a series of tithe, tax, and rent obligations. The peasant had to endure forced labor for his feudal lord (well after nation-states had clearly emerged, local petty lords still retained privileges over the peasants whose villages stood on their lands), which might amount to several weeks each year. The *courvée* (work tax) included not only farming the lord's fields, fixing his fences, and tending his livestock, but involved gathering timber for his needs, repairing roads, and running errands for him. It was common for peasants to thrash through the woods to scare up the deer or other animals on those days when the lord planned his hunt. Documents from sixteenth-century Germany reveal that church officials punished peasants for missing Sunday services, when, in fact, the peasants had been ordered to help on the hunt; in this instance, peasants were caught between conflicting obligations. In addition, the peasant's wife and daughters would have to spin, weave, and launder for the lord's family. Peasants in some areas of Europe saw their labor obligations converted, roughly between 1100 and 1400, to additional payments of money and farm produce. Such a conversion gave peasants more time to work their own fields, and, even with the added payments, these peasants would be better off at the end of the year. They also enjoyed greater political independence, as the local lord no longer disrupted their lives as frequently. By the sixteenth century, however, population increases caused shortages of land that enabled lords to restore the hated work tax, as few peasants had enough land to satisfy both their family's consumption needs and their payments to the lord. As a result, lords intervened more closely in the daily affairs of the village, causing a great deal of resentment, as most peasants could not appreciate the broad demographic and economic changes transforming Western Europe. They knew only that they were expected to perform duties from which their grandfathers had been exempt. A series of peasant rebellions in Germany, culminating in the Peasants' War of 1524–1525, signify this frustration, and, as the peasant forces were always roundly defeated by the lords' mercenary armies, the peasants' economic and political condition in any given region deteriorated considerably after an uprising, because the lords punished rebellion with further exactions.

**Hardships and Joys.** Life in the peasant village was hardly the rustic idyll celebrated by the Romantics or the pure simple life envisioned by many in modern society. As suggested by close readings of the tales of the Brothers Grimm or those by Mother Goose, the peasant world was filled with danger and hardship. Gangs of drifters and detachments of soldiers frequently descended on the village, pilfering food and supplies, raiding chicken coops, stealing laundry left to dry, and snipping off horses' tails, which they could sell to upholsterers. A village would be lucky if no one was seriously harmed or killed during such raids, or if it was not burned down. Hunting parties made up of dozens of nobles often rode with reckless abandon over peasant fields, destroying in minutes months' worth of work. Wolves and bears attacked domestic animals and ate crops as well as the occasional villager who wandered too far into the woods. Disease came regularly and killed both men and livestock.

**Bees.** Peasants had relatively little free time and worked from sunrise well through sunset. When not involved with toil on his individual strips of land or on the commonly held portions of arable, the peasant, with his family, raised flax for spinning, brewed beer for private consumption, and produced vegetables, cheeses, chickens, and eggs to sell at regional markets. Peasants whittled and spun late into the evening in bees or large gatherings held in a single home to preserve the wood needed for heating and lighting. Such gatherings were important because they provided an opportunity for villagers to talk, sing, and gossip among themselves at the end of a day. Teenagers, segregated during the day by the gendered division of labor, had the chance to flirt with one another at these bees, and their parents negotiated marriages during them. Because of the great amount of gossip and negotiation that went on during these bees, local lords and supraregional authorities tried to prevent them; but, as firewood was truly scarce, the villagers could usually justify the holding of bees with a sound economic argument about the prudence of lighting and heating only one workspace.

**Misconceptions.** Other forms of entertainment included drinking binges and village feasts, which were held to celebrate engagements, weddings, the completion of the harvest, and the major religious holidays of Christmas, Easter, and Pentecost. While these events undoubtedly occurred and provided the peasants with merriment and necessary outlets to relieve the constant stress of living at near-subsistence levels, they probably were not as consistently extravagant and debauched as various sources claim them to be. Surviving sermons, petitions of complaint brought by local lords, essays such as Sebastian Brant's *Ship of Fools* (1490), and the texts of the popular plays that were performed in cities at Shrovetide all attest to the great decadence and carousing that went on during village celebrations. However, when reading these documents, one must remember that they were produced during an age when the secular authorities were obsessed with maintaining the vast differences in rank between the nobility, the city burghers, and the peasants, and when the religious authorities, particularly in Protestant lands, were trying to fashion new forms of piety and sobriety in daily life. The peasants' lifestyle was probably not as extravagant and immodest as either the scolding clerics, or the rapacious tax officials, desirous of increasing the peasants' tax burdens by painting a picture of their ability to feast perpetually, would have had their contemporaries believe. Depictions of peasants feasting and drinking to excess in urban plays should also be seen, partly, as comic stereotyping, in which boorish and gluttonous peasants were in essence stock characters created to delight urban spectators and to confirm for them their sense of cultural superiority. In fact, the so-called luxury regulations, which limited the number of guests who could attend a peasant feast, how much they could be served, and how long the affair could last, existed for the most part to prevent peasants from celebrating in a manner deemed unsuitable for their estate and not to reduce excessively high levels of feasting already intrinsic to village life. Life in the village was quite hard, and few peasants had the wherewithal to celebrate either regularly or regally.

**Changes in the Countryside.** Throughout early-modern Europe, wealthy urban nobles maintained rural estates. These properties enabled the privileged, much like the aristocrats of ancient Rome, to escape the oppressive heat and foul odors that characterized cities in summertime and provided a refuge to which they could turn if plague or political rebellion broke out in their town. Rural estates also gave the urban nobility a place where they could pursue the favored sport of their order—the hunt. A ruling family of Renaissance Florence, the Medici, maintained a fortified rural villa in the Tuscan countryside with its own chapel and gardens, while Henry VIII of England favored Hampton Palace, a residence in London's countryside that he sequestered from Cardinal Thomas Wolsey, for hunting parties, horseback riding, and tennis. However, lesser figures than these copied their betters, and even a relatively obscure fifteenth-century Venetian *condottiere* (a captain of a mercenary army) such as Jacopo Marcello possessed a spectacular castle on the Italian mainland in the Euganean hills south of Padua to which his family retreated whenever plague visited Venice. Likewise, the Westphalian adventurer Heinrich von Staden, who spent part of his adult life in the service of Ivan the Terrible, possessed, even though he was neither Russian nor noble, properties in the countryside to which he turned when political unrest or disease befell Moscow.

**"New Men."** As capitalism developed in the late sixteenth and seventeenth centuries, nonnoble (or recently ennobled) merchants, lawyers, and state bureaucrats accumulated vast sums of wealth. These "new men" invested portions of their fortunes in rural estates, in part to imitate their social betters, and in part because too much wealth had already been invested in the cities. Many of these rural developers (for that is what in essence they became) were able, through their vast economic resources, to seize peasant farms as collateral against unpaid loans, to enclose large areas of the countryside, and to penetrate—and destroy—centuries-old communal institutions. Such dynamics often resulted in violence, such as the infamous "Carnival in Romans" (1580) where street violence during a pre-Lenten holiday feast erupted into a territorial civil war fought by the traditional urban elite of the city of Romans, the long-standing rural elite in the Dauphiné countryside, and the "new men" who were attempting to gain a foothold in both realms.

Sources:

Robert Darnton, *The Great Cat Massacre and Other Episodes in French Cultural History* (New York: Basic Books, 1984).

Margaret L. King, *The Death of the Child Valerio Marcello* (Chicago: University of Chicago Press, 1994).

Michael Kunze, *Highroad to the Stake*, translated by William E. Yuill (Chicago: University of Chicago Press, 1987).

Emmanuel Le Roy Ladurie, *Carnival in Romans*, translated by Mary Feeney (New York: George Braziller, 1979).

Werner Rösener, *Peasants in the Middle Ages*, translated by Alexander Stützer (Urbana: University of Illinois Press, 1992).

David Warren Sabean, *Power in the Blood* (Cambridge: Cambridge University Press, 1984).

David Underdown, "The Taming of the Scold: the Enforcement of Patriarchical Authority in Early Modern England," in *Order and Disorder in Early Modern England*, edited by Anthony Fletcher and John Stevenson (Cambridge: Cambridge University Press, 1985).

# SIGNIFICANT PEOPLE

## PIETRO ARETINO

### 1492-1556
### SATIRIST

**Man of Letters.** Born in 1492 during the Golden Age of Florentine humanism, Pietro Aretino, who died from a stroke in 1556, is most recognized for the more than three thousand letters he published. These letters illuminate all facets of Italian life during the first half of the sixteenth century, from aesthetics to warfare, from sport to complicated religious dogma, from the eating of mushrooms to observations on how drunks stumble after a night spent imbibing. Given his prolific output, the sheer number of his readers, and the diversity of his themes, many intellectual historians regard him as Europe's first "journalist." His writing is often quite licentious, and indeed he indulged his obsession with prostitution both in his writings and in his daily life. Not surprisingly, the Counter-Reformation Church placed his works on the Index of Forbidden Books in 1559. He has remained less famous and less read in our century than either Niccolò Machiavelli or Desiderius Erasmus, two other Renaissance writers whose works were similarly censured, perhaps as a result of the pornographic nature of a good deal of his work.

**Savage Wit.** Aretino's father was a cobbler in the Tuscan countryside. His mother was famous for her beauty, and became, despite her marital status and the fact that she had borne four children, the live-in mistress of a local nobleman, Luigi Bacci. In his youth Aretino lived with his mother in Bacci's household, though he ran away at the age of eighteen to Perugia and became a house servant for the noted humanist Francesco Bontempi. In this capacity the young Aretino was introduced to Perugia's painters and poets, and, primarily as a painter, he began his own lifelong commitment to the humanist cause. After a while in Francesco's service, Aretino moved to Rome, where the wealthy Sienese financier, Agostino Chigi, sponsored him as a humanist in the service of the Chigi family. In Rome, Aretino quickly became noted for his savage wit, intelligence, keen powers of observation, and writing skill. He was invited to meet Rome's leading artists and thinkers, including Raphael, whose later painting of him hangs today in the Louvre in Paris.

**Papal Connections.** In 1521 Giulio de Medici, a candidate for the papacy, hired Aretino to write pro-Medici propaganda pamphlets, as well as pieces that lampooned the other candidates. Unfortunately for Aretino, another candidate, Adrian of Utrecht, whom Aretino's pen had scorched, was selected pope, and the ambitious young humanist was forced to flee Rome. Clearly talented, Aretino secured a position at the court of Federico Gonzaga, the Duke of Mantua. In Federico's service Aretino continued to further his reputation as a skilled writer and satirist. When, in 1523, Giulio de Medici became Pope Clement VII, Aretino was recalled to Rome, and his future seemed bright. Unfortunately, one of Aretino's friends created a scandal by distributing humiliating sketches of Bishop Giberti, a valued adviser to Pope Clement. Aretino angered Giberti by securing the release of his friend from prison, and compounded the bishop's rage by proceeding to write sixteen pornographic pieces, *Sonetti lussuriosi* (Lewd Sonnets, 1524), supposedly chronicling Giberti's favorite sexual maneuvers. Naturally, Clement favored his bishop over his humanist, and Aretino was forced to flee Rome for the second time in two years. He traveled to France, offering his services to the French king, Francis I. Later reconciled with Clement, Aretino returned to Rome. Though a play of his published in 1525, *A Comedy About Court Life,* displays Aretino's great wit, wonderful style, and uninhibited freedom, it also savagely ridiculed the debauchery at the papal court, earning, for Aretino, Clement's displeasure. Had Aretino remained in Clement's good graces, he might have been able to seduce the mistress of a powerful Roman resident, Della Volta, with impunity, but he did not enjoy Clement's favor, and Della Volta avenged his humiliation by trying to have Aretino assassinated. Though he survived the attempt, Aretino's right hand was wounded, preventing him from ever painting again. In 1525, a second flight to Mantua occurred, from where Aretino published satirical sonnets and plays that ridiculed Clement's court and clients. An assassination attempt in 1527 forced Aretino to relocate yet again, and this time he settled in Venice, where he remained for the rest of his life.

**Exile in Venice.** Sixteenth-century Venice was infamous for its tolerance of free speech, its relative religious heterodoxy, and its prostitutes. Wealthy and militarily powerful, Venice safeguarded the entire Italian peninsula from the Ottoman Turks and so could ignore the prohibitions of Counter Reformation Catholicism emanating from Rome. Consequently, Venice attracted scholars and artists seeking freedom, and, like Gentile da Fabriano, Giovanni Bellini, Giorgione, and Titian, Aretino found Venice instantly to his liking. Becoming friendly with Titian gave Aretino instant acceptance in Venice's artistic community and a wide circle of friends. Aretino also befriended Pietro Bembo at this time, a man who had risen to prominence as Pope Leo X's secretary. At the height of his social and political influence, Aretino could concentrate on his literary output, which made him quite wealthy; he could afford to live the lifestyle of a courtier without having to be one. Aretino's satire was so vicious that he, in effect, could "blackmail" Europe's rulers, who voluntarily gave him great sums to avoid being the target of his wit and pen. Artistically free from having to please a patron, and financially free as well, he led what would later be called a "Bohemian" lifestyle in a house in the center of Venice, overlooking the Rialto Bridge on the Grand Canal. In this house he established his own court of sorts, living among his secretaries, collaborators on literary projects, mistresses (both male and female), servants, and various friends. Though he fathered several children, he never married.

**Patron of the Arts.** Aretino championed young writers who bucked convention, and he supported artists who attempted to fashion new artistic styles and social attitudes. William Shakespeare, for example, later claimed Aretino influenced him. Aretino was both loved and hated. He was one of three Venetians chosen by the Senate to meet the Holy Roman Emperor Charles V when the latter traveled to Verona in 1543. He received a papal knighthood and pension in 1550, but his work was placed on the Index in 1559; he earned the favor of King Henry VIII of England by dedicating a book of letters to him in 1542, but England's ambassador to Venice tried to have him assassinated in 1547. His six volumes of published letters, an invaluable source for social historians who concentrate on the Italian Renaissance, contain Aretino's commentaries on food, recipes, types of wine, table manners, household furnishings, clothing styles, and daily life in Venice.

Sources:

James Cleugh, *The Divine Aretino: A Biography* (New York: Stein & Day, 1965).

*Selected Letters of Aretino,* translated by George Bull (Harmondsworth, U.K. and New York: Penguin, 1976).

# MICHEL EYQUEM DE MONTAIGNE

## 1533-1592
### ESSAYIST

**Beginnings.** Michel Eyquem de Montaigne was born near Bordeaux, France, in February 1533. His father was a soldier, lawyer, landowner, merchant, and, later, mayor of Bordeaux. His mother stemmed from a wealthy Spanish-Portuguese Jewish family that had fled to southern France to avoid religious persecution. As a boy, Michel's education was completely overseen by his father, who permitted his son to read and converse only in Latin until the age of six. At that age Michel was enrolled at the Collège de Guyenne in Bordeaux; this school was a leading center of mid-sixteenth-century French humanism. Between the age of sixteen and twenty Montaigne attended the University of Toulouse, one of the foremost hubs of French humanism and an institution noted for championing heterodox religious ideas.

**Noble Savages.** Well-educated as a humanist, Montaigne assumed a legal post in Périgueux in 1554. His father became mayor of Bordeaux that same year, and in 1557 the younger Montaigne took a seat in the Bordeaux *parlement* (a high ranking court, like a regional Supreme Court). He served as a member of the parliament until 1570. While still a member, Montaigne journeyed to Paris on a mission to the king's court in 1561, and he accompanied the king to Rouen in 1562 after the king's troops had captured the city from Huguenot forces during the fighting now known as the French Wars of Religion. In Rouen, Montaigne observed Brazilian natives, an experience that motivated him to write his celebrated philosophical piece "On Cannibals." In this work Montaigne argues that European men are arrogant, foolish, and inclined to evil, and that, for all of Europe's advances in science and technology, the "noble savages" of the New World manage to live a purer, more admirable life, one he believes to be free of pollution, economic inequalities, slums, legal inequalities, prisons, and religiously motivated violence.

**Wealth.** In 1565 Montaigne married an heiress, Françoise de Chassagne, who brought to their marriage a large dowry. This sum, combined with the inheritance from his father's death three years later, made Montaigne an extremely wealthy man. Strangely, Montaigne, a man who wrote so much about himself and his experiences, wrote precious little about his wife or his family life. He had six children, but only one lived more than a few months. He did, however, have a deep attachment to Mademoiselle de Gournay, who had been attracted to him by his writings before ever meeting him, and whom he ultimately adopted as his daughter late in his life.

**Government Service.** During the 1570s Montaigne tried, unsuccessfully, to negotiate a compromise between the Catholics and Henri of Navarre, the Huguenot leader, in an attempt to bring the Wars of Religion to a close. Pestered by gallstones, Montaigne undertook a journey to Germany in 1580 in search of a cure at German and Italian spas. During this trip he also visited parts of Switzerland and was received by the Pope during his stay in Rome. Montaigne published the diaries penned during this trip as *Travel Journey* (1580). In 1581, while still in Italy, Montaigne was elected, as his father once had been, mayor of Bordeaux. He returned to accept the position, one he was to hold for four years. It was a challenging task: the religious wars were still being fought, and Montaigne had to work hard to keep Bordeaux under Catholic control and to pacify the volatile surrounding countryside. He was criticized for abandoning his duty, as he fled the city immediately after concluding a second term as its mayor in order to avoid the plague. However, evidence reveals that Montaigne was no coward; as mayor he always fulfilled his military obligations to guard the city against the Huguenots, and he fought against the raiding parties and minor bands of mercenaries who frequently attacked the city. In the late 1580s Montaigne, who had retired to his estates, ventured once more to Paris, where he served Henri of Navarre during the negotiations that led to the latter's conversion to Catholicism and subsequent coronation as King Henri IV, events that brought the French Wars of Religion to a close. Offered important positions by a grateful Henri in 1590, Montaigne, in declining health, refused them, and died in 1592 at the age of fifty-nine.

**Trials of a Man.** Montaigne is most famous for his *Essais,* a nontraditional autobiographical work compiled in a three-volume series of sketches that he began writing in 1572 and finished in 1588. In fact, it is from this title that the word *essay,* meaning a short, reflective, written work, is derived; but Montaigne meant the title to suggest "trials." His "autobiography," rather than following a linear path relating the events of his life from birth to old age, seeks to depict the true essence of the man (himself) in a timeless setting, by conveying the man's reactions to various events and to disturbing subjects (hence, the trials). The *Essais* explore, to list but a few examples, Montaigne's views on friendship, on the social and medical effects of wearing certain types of clothing, on cruelty, on cripples, on presumption, and on cannibalism.

**Philosophical Skepticism.** This work is also important to the history of Western philosophy, for in it Montaigne developed philosophical skepticism; his famous motto was "Que sais-je?" (What do I know?). Undoubtedly influenced by the intellectual shocks that followed the discovery of the New World, the Copernican Revolution, the Protestant Reformation, and the attack on Aristotelian science by the Paracelsians, Montaigne, through the *Essais,* established a system of thought that stressed how completely relative personal experience was, and how transitory most scientific and moral "truths" actually were. Truth, for him, emerged from one's culture, upbringing, time, and natural preju-

dices. Thus, a child born Catholic believes in the truth of Catholicism; a Muslim child believes in the truth of Islam. Montaigne argued that neither God's existence nor the immortality of the soul could ever be proved, and that the determination of such ultimate questions relied solely on faith. Montaigne has thus been seen as a skeptical nonbeliever, whose questioning of religious truths ushered in the secular-oriented Enlightenment. Indeed, the Vatican put his works on the Index of Forbidden Books in 1676. Others, however, consider Montaigne a champion of the Catholic Counter Reformation, for his writings attacked the ability of reason and rational thought to address religious concerns, and thus, in a real sense, attacked the justification of Martin Luther's arguments. For the social historian, his *Essais* and *Travel Journey* are invaluable sources for glimpses of daily life in sixteenth-century Europe.

Sources:

*The Complete Works of Montaigne,* translated by Donald M. Frame (Stanford, Cal.: Stanford University Press, 1957).

Donald M. Frame, *Montaigne: A Biography* (New York: Harcourt, Brace & World, 1965).

# SILVESTER

## FLOURISHED MID-SIXTEENTH CENTURY

### PRIEST AND SOCIAL DISCIPLINARIAN

**Significance.** There is considerable debate as to how much the priest Silvester influenced Russian Tsar Ivan IV, known as Ivan the Terrible. According to Nikolay Mikhaylovich Karamzin, the great early-nineteenth-century Russian historian, Ivan the Terrible only acted virtuously when he was guided by Silvester, and all that was good in Ivan ought to be attributed to Silvester. Yet, another great nineteenth-century Russian historian, S. F. Platonov, denies Silvester both the credit for Ivan's farsighted policy of strengthening Russia's southern frontier and the opprobrium for Ivan's brutal responses to the social crises that destroyed the Muscovite state by the 1580s. Most twentieth-century experts on Ivan, however, argue that Silvester must assume some blame for Ivan's later violence and debauchery, viewing the Tsar's maniacal behavior as a direct consequence of, and reaction against, Silvester's stern treatment of the youthful Ivan.

**Background.** Little is known about Silvester's early life. As a priest in Novgorod, Silvester was first noticed by Macarius, Archbishop of Novgorod. The latter had set the goal of bringing together "all the reading books that could be found in the Russian land" under one collection, and to this end he created a team of scholars that included Silvester. When Macarius was promoted to the rank of Metropolitan (head of the Orthodox Church in Russia) and relocated to Moscow in 1542, he brought along Silvester. Like other members of Macarius's team, Silvester was famous for his literary knowledge and he espoused nationalistic and political ideas that would have great appeal to Tsar Ivan. Silvester favored the creation of a single, ecumenical Orthodox state under an autocrat who would be "Tsar of Orthodoxy."

In 1547 a great fire consumed Moscow and killed more than 1,700 people. Terrified crowds sought scapegoats to punish for this disaster, which many believed was a form of Divine retribution, and members of the Glinsky clan (a family loyal to Ivan and politically influential) and their servitors were openly murdered, provoking severe retribution by Ivan. At this time, Silvester emerged and rebuked Ivan in God's name and used Holy Scripture to admonish the young Tsar severely. Silvester continued to warn Ivan that God would punish him if he continued to indulge his evil passions. Silvester told Ivan of apparitions and miracles God had sent. A contemporary of Ivan's, Prince Kurbsky, claims in his chronicles that at this point Ivan repented, and became cleansed and docile, though modern historians challenge Kurbsky's assessments. Brought into Ivan's confidence, Silvester worked with a noble, Aleksei Adashev, in urging Ivan to control his violence and to renew himself in goodness. Both Silvester and Adashev ultimately sought a moral improvement in government, but they believed this was unattainable without a moral improvement in Ivan.

**Court Favorite.** Ivan's government was ruled from 1547 until 1557 by a council of men selected by Silvester and Adashev. An all-powerful favorite, Silvester presided over this ruling council. The official chronicle of Ivan's reign records that "this churchman, Silvester, was held in great favor by the Sovereign, who took his advice on spiritual and secular matters. He was, it were, omnipotent, because all heeded him and no one mocked him or opposed him in any way. . . . And he wielded great power over all matters, things both holy and secular alike, as though he were both Tsar and saint . . . although he [was] but a priest." Indeed, Silvester and his council controlled the young Ivan and bent his will with abstruse religious arguments and pleas for the public's welfare. Clearly Silvester was a charismatic man: Prince Kurbsky believed him to be both blessed and a flatterer, while an older Ivan stated that, in his youth, Silvester had been able to oppress him and treat him like a slave. Records left by observers at Ivan's court note that Silvester was able to silence Ivan by reproaching him and accusing him of being childish.

**Guidebook.** Officially Silvester was priest in Moscow's Kremlin Church of the Annunciation, and in that capacity he oversaw the installation of the icons that make this church's interior among the most beautiful in the world. Silvester also oversaw the decoration of Ivan's *Zolotaya Palata* (Golden Palace), personally selecting the subject matter of the frescoes within it and arranging their placement. In fact, the incomparable splendor of these projects enabled his enemies to attack him for heresy and promoting Western influences in Orthodoxy through art, though there was nothing undogmatic in the new style of icons that Silvester favored. Silvester also is credited with authoring the *Domostroi* (circa 1550–1580), a guidebook for moral living.

The dictates of the *Domostroi* reflect Silvester's religious views. Silvester opposed amusement in theory, and he prohibited dancing, singing, and even the playing of chess. He believed laughter was a weapon of the devil; regarded a wife not as a partner, but as the chief servant in a man's house; and argued that a husband should treat a wife as a slave or as a farm animal. Stubborn and stern, even in comparison to other mid-sixteenth-century religious figures like John Calvin, Silvester's *Domostroi* is a manual that links Christianity to the most mundane aspects of daily life, such as how to clean carpet, where to arrange furniture, and how to wash dishes. Its passages aim at total control of daily life, much as its author himself attempted to control Ivan's every action.

**Political Machinations.** In 1553 Ivan became quite ill and was presumed to be dying. Ivan noted that Silvester spent this time trying to consolidate his own position, rather than tending to the needs of his bedridden sovereign. Ivan also discovered that Silvester had been working behind the scenes to champion the Tsar's cousin Vladimir as heir, rather than the heir selected by Ivan himself, his son Dmitry. Ivan became convinced that Silvester's council was working to undermine the policies of his grandfather, Ivan III, who had consolidated central power at the expense of Russia's landowning princes. Silvester believed he was merely improving the moral stature of Russia's government by restoring to influence men whom he considered suitable for state service. From this point on, Ivan viewed Silvester as an opportunist who had cunningly usurped power and who had treasonably appropriated sovereign power unto himself. Though after 1553 Ivan no longer trusted Silvester, he so feared him and the council that he dared not challenge them until 1557.

**Banishment.** Perhaps because of his religious background, Silvester always regarded the Crimean Tatars and the Turks, both Muslim, as Russia's main threats, and he centered his foreign policy recommendations on them. Others at Ivan's court favored Russian intervention in the Baltic, particularly against Livonia and Sweden, and Ivan himself shared this orientation. Ivan used Silvester's and Adashev's opposition to the Livonian War (which, in hindsight, was correct, as the war proved to be a disaster for Russia, despite initial successes) to free himself from their control. Ivan banished Silvester to the distant Kirillov Monastery. Though Silvester had already been cloistered for several years when Ivan's beloved wife, Anastasia, died after a prolonged illness in 1560, Ivan nonetheless blamed Silvester. Ivan believed his wife was the victim of poisoning, assassinated by nobles whose great hatred of her had been stirred up by Silvester and his council during the time when Silvester had opposed her son as heir to the throne. In fact, Ivan vacillated as to whether he should bring Silvester to trial on the charges of witchcraft, believing his former guardian had cast spells on nobles to make them oppose and hate Anastasia. Silvester was ultimately spared this ordeal, though he was transferred to the Solovetsky Monastery, which lies isolated on an island in the White Sea. Here Silvester died, though when and how is unknown. Ivan later took pride in the fact that he spared Silvester's son.

Sources:
Robert Payne and Nikita Romanoff, *Ivan the Terrible* (New York: Crowell, 1975).

S. F. Platonov, *Ivan the Terrible*, edited and translated by Joseph L. Wieczynski (Gulf Breeze, Fla.: Academic International, 1974).

Carolyn Johnston Pouncy, ed. and trans., *The Domostroi: Rules for Russian Households in the Time of Ivan the Terrible* (Ithaca, N.Y.: Cornell University Press, 1994).

# DOCUMENTARY SOURCES

Baldesar Castiglione, *The Book of the Courtier* (1528)—a text on how to dress to succeed at an Italian Renaissance Court. Published in many editions and translated into several languages during the sixteenth century, it also discusses table manners and how to develop skill in various forms of entertainment.

William Caxton, *Book of Courtesies* (circa late fifteenth century)—etiquette book and guide to proper dining popular in late-medieval England.

Antoine de Courtin, *New Treatise on Civility* (1672)—French etiquette book written during the age of King Louis XIV.

Giovanni della Casa, *Galateo* (1558)—Italian etiquette book of the late Renaissance.

Thomas Elyot, *The Castle of Health* (1534)—English book concerned with allowing the reader to identify the constitution of his or her humors (phlegmatic, melancholic, sanguine, or choleric). The text then recommends which foods each of these four physical types should consume to insure health.

Desiderius Erasmus, *The Colloquies* (1518)—a series of playful stories that poke fun at the experiences of daily life and the superstitions that accompany them. It includes interesting pieces on the eating of meat and fish, fasting, and the conditions of certain inns.

Erasmus, *On Manners in Boys* (1530)—a handbook on how to educate young boys in the proper ways of eating specific foods and on how to develop their table manners.

Ludovico Guicciardini, *Descriptions of Everyone in the Low Countries* (1567)—written by a Florentine diplomat and banker who recorded his impressions of city life in what is today Belgium and the Netherlands, focusing on social and economic activity.

Michel Eyquem de Montaigne, *Journey to Germany, Switzerland, and Italy* (1580)—more commonly known as *Travel Journey;* a travel diary of a French philosopher and statesman, rich in descriptions of food, of eating customs, and of the qualities of inns in the countries he visited during his search for a cure for his gallstones in 1580.

François Rabelais, *Gargantua* (1534)—a satirical novel that describes the boyhood life of the prince Gargantua, including passages on how the ideal prince dresses for different occasions, what food his mother ate while pregnant with him, how the interior of princely residences are decorated, and what games he and his friends played.

Silvester, *Domostroi* (circa 1550–1580)—compiled by the chief adviser of Ivan the Terrible, this text provides suggestions for nobles on proper living, including instructions on planning dinner party menus, how to clean clothes, where and how to store eating utensils, and how furniture should be arranged.

Thomas Tusser, *Five Hundred Points of Good Husbandry* (1557)—a lively English tome providing information on everything a householder needs to know, such as how to brew beer and how to trap rats in his house.

Monthly labors depicted in a fourteenth-century manuscript of a manual by Pietro Crescentio (from Franco Cardini, *Europe 1492*, 1989)

# FAMILY AND
# SOCIAL TRENDS

by MERRY WIESNER-HANKS

## CONTENTS

*Sidebars and tables are listed in italics.*

## 1395

- John Rykener, who was going by the name of Eleanor, is arrested in England while wearing women's clothes and offering to perform illegal sexual services, and is brought before court. It is one of the few recorded instances of homosexual and transvestite activity during the Renaissance.

## 1400s*

- There are, on average, 14.4 maternal deaths for every one thousand births in Florence, Italy. The actual figure may be as high as 20 percent.

## 1405

- French poet Christine de Pizan publishes *The Book of the City of Ladies*, which refutes assumptions questioning the ability of women to succeed in public roles.

## 1406

- De Pizan writes an advice book for women titled *The Book of Three Virtues*, which classifies the roles of women.

## 1415

- Florence allows the establishment of public brothels.

## 1419

- Florentine architect Filippo Brunelleschi designs the Foundling Hospital in Florence.

## 1422

- Italian painter Masaccio (Tommaso di Giovanni di Simone Guidi) completes the *Madonna Enthroned with Christ Child* for the central panel of a Pisa altarpiece, which presents Mary as more of an earthly mother, rather than an otherworldly figure, with a human child.

## 1427

- St. Bernardino of Siena delivers forty-five sermons, among which are several on the duties of wives and widows and the relationship between spouses.

## 1435-1444

- Italian humanist, architect, painter, and writer Leon Battista Alberti publishes *On the Family* in the Italian vernacular, rather than in Latin, in order to broaden public access to the work. It is the first in a series of advice books.

*Denotes circa date*

**1480***
- Italian painter Domenico Ghirlandajo, a noted fresco artist of the Florentine school, completes "An Old Man and His Grandson," a portrait of an elderly grandfather, with a disfiguring disease (elephantiasis), tenderly holding his young grandchild.

**1486**
- *Malleus Maleficarum*, the standard handbook for detecting and eradicating witch-craft, which helped inspire a witch-hunting hysteria, is published by Johann Sprenger and Heinrich Kraemer.

**1493***
- Syphilis (*Treponema pallidum*) appears for the first time in Europe, in Barcelona, evidently brought by Christopher Columbus's sailors after his voyage to the West Indies.

**1500s**
- Rise of churching, an after-birthing purification ceremony for infants and mothers.

**1509**
- The well-educated Italian Isabella d'Este becomes the leader of Mantua, and founds a school with a concentration on moral education for young women.

**1513**
- German doctor Eucharius Rösslin publishes *Rosengarten für swangere Frauen und Hebammen* (Rosegarden for Midwives and Pregnant Women), a guide for mid-wives.

**1518**
- German artist Lucas Cranach paints "Reclining River Nymph at the Fountain," one of a series of paintings that portrays the female body in elegant, yet unrealis-tic poses that fit German tastes, which will lead toward more erotic representa-tions in his later work.

**1528**
- Italian diplomat Baldassare Castiglione's *Il cortegiano* (The Book of the Court-ier), which celebrates ideal courtly life, is published.

**1532**
- Abortion is made a capital offense in the Holy Roman Empire.

**1540s***
- Cities in Italy begin enforcing laws restricting the movements and dress of courtesans.

**1558**
- Scottish religious reformer John Knox, a former ordained Catholic priest who converted to Protestantism (Calvinism), publishes *First Blast of the Trumpet Against the Monstrous Regiment of Women,* an attack on the reign of the Catholic Queen Mary that generally assails the competence of women to rule.

**1562**
- The city council of Nuremburg closes its brothels.

**1566**
- German religious reformer Martin Luther's book *On Marriage* is published.
- Flemish painter Pieter Brueghel the Elder completes "The Wedding Dance," one of a series of pieces that reveal the life of ordinary people. Children are often portrayed in his works, such as in "Young Folk at Play" (or "Children's Games," 1560), which reveals nearly eighty different activities, including twenty games.

**1577**
- English writer Hugh Rhodes publishes *Book of Nurture,* detailing what behavior is expected from children and advice on their proper upbringing by adults.

**1584**
- English writer Reginald Scot publishes *Discoverie of Witchcraft,* an attack on the superstition involved in witchcraft.

**1587**
- Start of the Portuguese Inquisition, in which many homosexuals were targeted for discipline and punishment by Catholic authorities.

**1600***
- Luis de León, a Spanish lyric poet and religious writer best known for *De los nombres de Cristo* (1583), writes *La perfecta casada* (The Perfect Wife), which reinforces male-dominated views of the inferiority of women.

# OVERVIEW

**Reciprocal Relationship.** The intellectual and religious changes of the Renaissance and Reformation are often regarded primarily as the shapers of large institutions and structures of society: the churches where people worshipped, the courts where rulers governed, the buildings in which people lived and worked, the schools in which some people were educated. These changes also influenced much smaller structures and institutions as well, including the families in which most Europeans lived, and even people's own bodies, emotions, health, and sense of identity. Conversely, these small and what may seem to be private things—the family and the individual person—also shaped larger developments. Many artists, religious reformers, political leaders, writers, and explorers grew up in a family environment. This fact may seem self-evident, but for many centuries the history of the Renaissance and Reformation has ignored it; ideas were often described as if they were transmitted from brain to brain, with no notice paid to the private life, family surroundings, or even physical existence of their thinkers. Great individuals were discussed as if they never had been children, never married, never become parents, never grew old.

**Seven Ages of Man.** This ignoring of personal development and private life was not shared by people who lived during the period 1350 to 1600, for they thought and wrote often about their own existence and place in society. In a tradition at least as old as the ancient Greeks, people talked about the stages of life, with some scholars arguing that there were four, corresponding to the four seasons, some twelve, corresponding to the months and the signs of the zodiac, and some three, five, six, eight, or ten. The number that was increasingly accepted was seven, corresponding to the seven known planets (the planets out from the Sun to Saturn, plus the moon), and these were often described as the "ages of man": infancy, boyhood, adolescence, young manhood, mature manhood, older manhood, and old age. The seven ages of man began with stages of physical and emotional maturing, and then were differentiated by increasing and decreasing involvement in the world of work and public affairs; only in young manhood was family life usually discussed. The "ages of woman" were harder to differentiate, and many Renaissance discussions of the life-cycle never included women at all. When they did, it was a woman's sexual status and relationship to a man that mattered most, for a woman was thought of as a virgin, wife, or widow, or alternately a daughter, wife, or mother. In the last few decades, however, historians have begun to explore family life and personal development for both men and women, and now have a much better picture of the physical and emotional lives of individuals and families in this era, and the ways these were shaped by intellectual, economic, social, and religious changes.

**Birthing.** Childbirth during the period under consideration took place at home, with the expectant mother assisted by her female relatives and friends. If she lived in a city, a mother might call on the services of a professional midwife, who had been trained by serving an apprenticeship with an experienced midwife. University-trained doctors were largely uninterested in childbirth or other obstetrical issues, and in many parts of Europe the presence of any man in the room where a child was being born, including the child's father, was viewed as unlucky. Midwives and other women assisting in the birth turned to a variety of herbal remedies, nourishing food, prayer, and sometimes magical means to ease the mother's pains and speed the birth along. The risks of dying in childbirth were high compared to today, but not as high as they would be in the nineteenth century when more women gave birth in unsanitary hospitals tended by physicians who did not wash their hands or equipment. Women usually knew someone who had died in childbirth, and they celebrated each successful birth with religious rituals and social gatherings.

**Gender-Specific Tasks.** Most infants were cared for by their own mothers, though wealthier women might use the services of a wet nurse so that they could more quickly resume their economic and social tasks. Infants were sometimes swaddled to keep them warm and safe, and both boys and girls wore long dress-like garments over cloths used for diapers. Parents began to train their children for adult life and work at an early age, so that by four or five children were expected to perform simple tasks around the household or workplace. This training and these tasks were gender-specific, with girls instructed in household skills and boys in work that would assist their fathers. Parents were also expected to provide their children basic religious and moral instruction, telling them stories about individuals regarded as pious and praiseworthy.

**Schooling.** By the age of seven, middle- and upper-class boys in urban areas often began to attend school, either in the language spoken in their area (termed the "vernacular") or in Latin. Wealthier girls might be educated in their homes by tutors, but their opportunities were much narrower than those of their brothers. After the Reformation, more schools that taught basic reading and writing were opened, though never as many as religious reformers hoped, and almost everywhere there were many more schools for boys than girls. School curriculum was also gender-specific, with boys encouraged to study rhetoric and other secular subjects while girls' lessons focused on religion and morals.

**Youth.** Though there was no word for "teenager" in European languages during this era, people did think of "youth" as a distinct phase of life, marked by sexual maturity but not full adult responsibilities. Religious and political authorities often worried about and attempted to control the activities of young men, including drinking, fighting, and other wild behavior. The activities of young women were controlled also by their parents and by cultural norms that sharply distinguished between respectable and unrespectable women, for the sexual double standard was accepted throughout Europe. If a woman did engage in premarital sexual activity and became pregnant, she came before a church or secular court for trial and punishment, which in many places grew increasingly harsh during this period. Thus women who became pregnant out of wedlock often attempted to hide the fact as long as possible or took desperate measures to end the pregnancy, knowing that it might be impossible for them to gain employment or a husband if they became unwed mothers. If they were not able to end the pregnancy, they sometimes left the child at one of the foundling homes opened by cities or churches, though a child's chances of survival in these institutions were slim.

**Prostitution and Homosexuality.** Religious and political authorities also regulated or penalized other types of sexual activity. Before the Reformation, prostitution was widely tolerated, and most cities had official brothels that were taxed and licensed. After the Reformation, brothels in Protestant cities were generally closed and those in Catholic cities regulated more strictly; women who were arrested for prostitution were harshly punished. In many places, authorities attempted to prohibit other activities they saw as immoral, such as dancing or flirting, though such prohibitions were never rigorously enforced. Homosexual activity was also harshly suppressed, and became a crime punishable by death in some parts of Europe. The number of actual executions for homosexuality was small, but the methods of death, such as burning alive, could be grisly. Despite these measures, however, male homosexual subcultures with special behavior, styles of dress, and meeting places began to develop in Europe's largest cities.

**Marriage.** Most people's sexual activities took place inside of marriage rather than outside of it, and opinions about marriage generally became more positive during this period. Learned and popular writers discussed the purposes of marriage, which they generally saw as companionship, children, and the avoidance of sin, and people heard these ideas in wedding sermons and homilies. The ideal marriage was hierarchical, with the husband clearly in charge of his wife and the rest of the household, but not tyrannical; husbands were encouraged to show affection toward their wives and consult them on major decisions. Wives were instructed at great length on the importance of obedience, which was to be cheerful and willing, a reflection of their obedience to God. How many marriages actually conformed to this ideal is difficult to determine, as the marriages likely to show up in court records or other historical sources are those in which there were problems. There is evidence of strong affection and close relations between spouses and between parents and children in many families, but also many references to coldness, authoritarianism, and even violence. It was extremely difficult or impossible to obtain a divorce, however, so spouses simply had to make the best of whatever situation in which they found themselves. Marriage was the goal of most people, for it brought social adulthood and the opportunity to be independent from their own parents, though there was always a significant minority of men and women who did not marry, but supported themselves on their own or joined religious communities.

**Family Unit.** Families in the United States today are primarily residential and emotional units, but during the Renaissance and Reformation families also worked as a unit, raising crops or producing items together. Religious and vocational training occurred within the family, and significant events such as weddings, baptisms, and funerals were often marked by feasts and celebrations. Individuals also socialized with their peers, however, with young men and young women congregating in certain spots, adult men at taverns, and adult women at the neighborhood well or at each others' houses. Perhaps because families spent so much of their work time together, what little leisure time they had was enjoyed apart from the rest of the family.

**The Elderly.** Statistics often give the average life expectancy in premodern Europe as twenty-five or thirty, which might make it seem as if there were no older people around. Such statistics are skewed by the fact that about one-half of those born died before they were five, however, and a large number of people lived into their sixties or seventies. Death did come at a more-variable age, so that the loss of a spouse was not necessarily linked to being older, and there were large numbers of widows and widowers of all ages. Because women often married men who were older than they were, widows outnumbered widowers. Widowhood often brought a decline in a woman's economic status, though it also gave her greater control over her property and circumstances than she had had when her husband was still alive. Widows thus balanced their needs and independence when choosing whether to remarry, and tended to remarry less frequently and more slowly than did widowers. The elderly of both sexes relied generally on their families if they were no longer able to support themselves, though sometimes this support had to be legally guaranteed with a formal contract between an aging parent and adult child. Some people were active in their work or making family decisions well into their eighties, though the stereotype of the elderly in this period was one of physical and mental weakness.

# TOPICS IN FAMILY AND SOCIAL TRENDS

## BIRTH

**Women's Domain.** Throughout the entire period from 1350 to 1600, childbirth was strictly a female affair. The husband was not present unless his wife was dying, and male doctors took little interest in delivery. Male physicians were only called in if the child, mother, or both were dead or dying, so their presence was dreaded. As the time of the birth approached, a woman began to make preparations. She decided which friends and neighbors she would invite to assist her. This determination was a matter taken seriously, for witchcraft accusations occasionally stemmed from the curses and anger of a neighbor who had not been invited. If the expectant mother lived in a rural area, she would generally contact a woman known to be experienced in handling childbirth, along with other friends and relatives. If she lived in a city, however, professional midwives who had undergone a long period of training and apprenticeship might also be available to assist her.

**Labor.** Whether in the countryside or city, once a woman knew she was in labor, the women assisting her transformed a room of the house, or in small houses a bed, into a "lying-in chamber," according to local traditions of what was proper. In many parts of Europe, air was viewed as harmful to the mother, so doors and windows were shut and candles lit. Special objects believed to be helpful in speeding delivery were brought in, such as amulets, relics of saints, or certain herbs. Special prayers were offered, and the women prepared broth or mulled wine (termed "caudle" in England) to nourish the mother through the delivery. They also arranged swaddling clothes for the infant.

**Delivery.** The actual techniques of delivery varied widely, even within the same town. Some midwives and mothers preferred to use a birthing stool, a special padded stool with handles that tipped the mother back slightly; other mothers lay in bed, kneeled, stood, or sat in another woman's lap. The level of intervention also varied from midwife to midwife. Some tried to speed the birth along by making the mother change positions or pulling on the child as it emerged, while others might wait for days during a difficult labor before attempting to interfere. The most-skillful and best-trained midwives took a middle route, intervening only when they thought it necessary. If they were able to read, they might consult a printed midwives' guide, such as the *Rosengarten für swangere Frauen und Hebammen* (Rosegarden for Midwives and Pregnant Women, 1513) written by the German city doctor Eucharius Rösslin.

**Risky Business.** Childbirth was an event with many meanings, at once a source of joy and dread. Most women experienced multiple childbirths successfully, but all knew of or even had watched someone die while giving birth. Using English statistics, it has been estimated that the maternal mortality rate in the sixteenth century was about 1 percent for each birth, which would make a lifetime risk of 5 to 7 percent. Women knew these risks, which is why they attempted to obtain the services of the midwife they regarded as the most skilled. Midwives were responsible for the spiritual as well as the physical well-being of the children they delivered, for they were allowed to perform emergency baptisms on children they thought might die.

**Birth Control.** Mothers recognized that the dangers of childbirth might be intensified when children were born too close together, and attempted to space births through a variety of means. Many nursed their children until they were more than two years old, which acted as a contraceptive, for suckling encourages the release of the hormone prolactin, which promotes the production of milk and inhibits the function of the ovaries. They also sought to abstain from sexual relations during the time of their monthly cycle regarded as most fertile, though this "rhythm method" was based on an incorrect view of the menstrual cycle and was not very effective. Couples regularly attempted to restrict fertility through coitus interruptus, magical charms, and herbal potions, though all of these methods were condemned by religious leaders. Condoms made from animal intestines or bladders were available by the mid sixteenth century to

A wealthy mother and newborn in her lying-in chamber, with her attendants present, as depicted in *The Birth of the Virgin*, by Master of the Life of the Virgin (Alte Pinakothek, Munich)

those who could afford them, but they were originally designed to protect men from venereal disease carried by prostitutes and were only slowly seen as a possible means of birth control for married couples.

**Postpartum Rituals.** The experience of childbirth did not end with actual birth. In most parts of Europe, mothers were advised to undergo a period of "lying-in" after the birth, in which they sharply restricted their activities and contacts with the outside world. Although this seclusion was difficult for many rural and poor women, religious taboos that made a recently delivered mother impure meant that such restrictions were often followed even when this activity brought hardship to the family because the woman was not working. Russia had perhaps the strongest taboos, for Orthodox Christianity taught that everything associated with childbirth, including the midwife, attendants, place, and even the child, was impure. Not until her ritual of purification, which occurred forty days after birth, was anyone supposed to eat in the woman's company; baptism was often delayed until the same day so that the newborn remained impure and could nurse from its impure

mother. Judaism and Catholicism had a similar ritual of purification, though contacts with the mother were not so sharply restricted. Her movements outside the home were, however, which meant a Catholic woman could not attend her own child's baptism; in Italy the midwife who carried the child was the only woman normally present at a baptism. In some parts of Catholic Europe, this purification ceremony was seen as so important that it was performed over the coffin of a woman who had died in childbirth.

**New Rituals.** After the Reformation, Protestants rejected the idea that women needed to be purified after giving birth, but some Protestants retained the ceremony, commonly called churching, terming it instead a service of thanksgiving. In some Lutheran areas, churching was required of all married mothers and forbidden to those who gave birth out of wedlock, which created a distinction between honorable and dishonorable women. Among Protestants in England, unmarried women who had given birth were only to be churched if they named the father and wore a white sheet signifying that they were sorry for their actions during the service.

This selection is from a popular midwives' manual, *Rosengarten für swangere Frauen und Hebammen* (Rosegarden for Midwives and Pregnant Women), written by a German city doctor, Eucharius Rösslin, and published in 1513.

When the pregnant woman nears delivery, she should drink mature wine mixed with water. She should also have a regimen of food and drink, a regimen a month before birth which makes one moist but not too fat, and one should avoid what makes one dry, constipated, weighs down, presses or constricts. When the woman is even nearer to delivery, when she still has twelve or fourteen days and feels some pain and pressure, she should sit in a bath up to her navel every day, sometimes more often, but not too long (so that she doesn't get weak). She should move around with easy work and movements, walking and standing more than she did before. Such things help the fetus come into position.

Another regimen for the time of delivery which the woman should need if she feels pressure, pain and some moistness begins to show and flow out of the vagina. This regimen takes place in two ways. The first is that one brings on a quick descent and delivery. The other way to lessen complications, labor pains, and pain is for her to sit down for an hour and then stand and climb up and down the stairs shouting loudly. The woman should force out and hold her breath (breathe heavily) so that she puts pressure on her intestines and bears down. The woman should also drink those medicines that are written about afterwards for they force the child downward into delivery position. When she feels the uterus dilate and plenty of fluid flow to her genitals (i.e., water breaks), she should lie on her back, but not complete lying down or standing. It should be a middle position between lying and standing. She should tilt her head more towards the back than the front. In southern German and in Italian/French areas, the midwives have special chairs for delivery. They are not high, but hollowed out with an opening in the inside. The chair should be prepared so that the woman can lean on her back. One should fill and cover the back of the same chair with cloth and when it is time, the midwife should lift the cloth and turn them first to the right and then to the left side. The midwife should sit in front of her and pay careful attention to the child's movement in the womb. The midwife should guide and control her arms and legs with her hands which are coated with white-lily or almond oil or the like. And with her hands in the same way, the midwife should also gently grasp the mother, as she well knows. The midwife should also instruct, guide, and teach the mother, and strengthen her with food and drink. She should urge the woman on to work with soft, kind words so that she begins to breathe deeply. One should dry her stomach off gently above the navel and hips. The midwife should comfort the woman by predicting a successful birth of a baby boy. And if the woman is fat, she should not sit, rather lie on her body and lay her forehead on the ground and pull her knees up underneath so that the womb has pressure applied to it. Afterwards, she should anoint her internally with white-lily oil and, if necessary, the mid-wife should open the woman's cervix with her hands and afterwards, the woman will deliver quickly.

Source: Eucharius Rösslin, *Rosengarten für swangere Frauen und Hebammen* (Frankfurt, 1513). Translation by Merry Wiesner-Hanks.

A woman attended her churching in the presence of the women who had been with her during the birth, including the midwife, and often saw churching as the final stage of childbirth; many of the rituals that were part of churching were devised by women themselves, not highly learned theologians. Churching is, in fact, only one of many popular rituals and beliefs surrounding birth that did not die out by 1600. Evidence gathered in the mid twentieth century indicates that people in many parts of Europe continued to regard a woman who had recently given birth as unlucky, and they prohibited her from touching wells or stalls or visiting her neighbors.

Sources:
David Cressy, *Birth, Marriage, and Death: Ritual, Religion, and the Life-Cycle in Tudor and Stuart England* (Oxford & New York: Oxford University Press, 1997).

Jacques Gélis, *History of Childbirth: Fertility, Pregnancy and Birth in Early Modern Europe*, translated by Rosemary Morris (Cambridge: Polity Press, 1991; Boston: Northeastern University Press, 1991).

Jacqueuline Marie Musacchio, *The Art and Ritual of Childbirth in Renaissance Italy* (New Haven: Yale University Press, 1999).

### CHILDHOOD

**Changing View of Children.** Historians used to think that before the eighteenth century, people were harsh or indifferent toward their children and did not regard childhood as a separate stage of life. These views were derived largely from child-raising manuals that advocated strict discipline and warned against coddling or showing too much affection, and portraits of children that showed them dressed as little adults. This bleak view has been altered as people have studied

Children playing a game, from a circa 1475 carved ivory diptych sundial from Nuremburg (Metropolitan Museum of Art, New York, Rogers Fund, 1987)

sources that give information about the way children were actually treated rather than the way they were supposed to be treated; they have discovered that many parents showed great affection for their children and were very disturbed when they died young. Such sentiments can be seen easily in a letter from the wealthy Florentine woman Alessandra Strozzi to her son Filippo Strozzi in 1459. Parents tried to protect their children with religious amulets and pilgrimages to special shrines, made toys for them, and sang them lullabies. Even practices that may seem cruel, such as wrapping children tightly with bands of cloth (termed "swaddling"), were motivated by a concern for the child's safety and health at a time when most households had open fires, domestic animals wandered freely, and mothers and older siblings were doing work that prevented them from continually watching a toddler. Paintings from the period show small children in wheeled walkers that kept them safer until they learned to walk securely, and women's diaries report that they led their toddlers on "leading-strings" attached to their clothing to prevent them from falling or wandering.

**A Boy's World.** In most parts of Europe, boys inherited family land while girls generally did not, and in all parts of Europe men were regarded as superior to women. These practices and attitudes led parents to favor the birth of sons over daughters. Jewish women prayed for sons, and German midwives were often rewarded with a higher payment for assisting in the birth of a boy. English women's letters sometimes apologize for the birth of daughters. Girls significantly outnumbered boys in most orphanages or foundling homes, as poor parents decided their sons would ultimately be more useful; infants had a much poorer chance of survival in orphanages than they did if cared for by their parents. Occasionally parents who could not care for their children killed them outright, but these cases were quite rare and generally involved desperate unwed mothers; one cannot tell from the records whether girls were more likely to be killed than boys, for the court records generally simply refer to "child" or "infant."

**Divergence of Treatment.** It is difficult to know whether boys and girls were treated differently when they were infants. Children were dressed alike in long dresslike garments for the first several years of their lives, rather than put into pink or blue outfits as is often common in contemporary American culture. Until they were about seven, children of both sexes were cared for by women, generally their own mothers if they were poor and servants or nursemaids if they were wealthy. When children began their training for adult life, at the age of four or five, clear distinctions became evident. Girls of all classes were taught skills that they would use in running a household—spinning, sewing, cooking, and the care of domestic animals; peasant girls were also taught some types of agricultural tasks. Boys also began to learn the skills they would use later, assisting their fathers or working in the fields. Many children began to work when they were very young; boys as young as seven might be apprenticed to a man other than their father to learn his trade, and girls might be sent at that age to another household to be a domestic servant. In northern Europe wealthy children might be sent at this age to the homes of even wealthier and more prominent people, with the expectation they would learn good manners as well as make acquaintances and contacts that would later lead to favorable marriages or help them in their careers.

**Early Education.** If parents themselves could read, they might begin teaching their children to read along with learning practical skills. A few medieval authors, such as theologian St. Thomas Aquinas, encouraged both fathers and mothers to take an interest in their young children's education: "For this the activity of the wife alone is not sufficient, but the intervention of the husband is better suited, whose reason is better suited for intellectual instruction and whose strength for the necessary discipline." After the Protestant Reformation, reformers urged both fathers and mothers who could themselves read to pass this knowledge on to their children, or to send their small children to friends or neighbors who could. Older women in many towns and cities

# "I HAVE SUFFERED A GRIEVOUS BLOW"

The following is a letter from a wealthy Florentine woman Alessandra Strozzi to her son Filippo in 1459 describing her feelings about the death of another son.

My dear son. On the 11th of last month, I received your letter of July 29, with the news that my dear son Matteo had become ill, and since you didn't tell me the nature of his malady, I became worried about him. I called Francesco and sent for Matteo di Girgio; and they both told me that he had a tertian fever. I gained some comfort from this, for if some other malady does not develop, one does not become mortally ill from a tertian fever. Then I heard from you that he was improving so that, while I was still concerned, my spirits did improve a little. I then learned that on the 23rd, it pleased Him who gave him to me to take him back. Being sound of mind, he willingly received all of the sacraments as a good and faithful Christian. I am deeply grieved to be deprived of my son; by his death, I have suffered a grievous blow, greater than the loss of filial love, and so have you, my two sons, reduced now to such a small number. . . .

Although I have suffered the greatest pain in my heart that I have ever experienced, I have received comfort from two things. First, he was with you; and I am certain that he was provided with doctors and medicine, and that everything possible was done for his health, and that nothing was spared. Yet, it was all to no avail; such was God's will. I have also been comforted by the knowledge that when he was dying, God granted him the opportunity to confess, to receive communion and extreme unction. He did this with devotion, so I understand; from these signs, we may hope that God

has prepared a good place for him. I realize, too, that everyone has to make this journey; and they cannot foresee the circumstances [of their death], and they cannot be certain that they will die as did my beloved son Matteo (for whoever dies suddenly or is murdered . . . loses both body and soul). So I have been comforted, realizing that God could have done worse to me. And if by his grace and mercy, he conserves both of you, my sons, he will give me no more anguish.

From your letter of the 26th, I know that you have been sorely tried in body and soul as have I, and as I shall continue to be until I receive word from you that you are taking care of yourself . . . I know that you have had sleepless nights, and that you have suffered from this ordeal, so that you are now in a bad state. And I worry so much about this day and night that I cannot rest. . . . I beg you, for love of me, to calm yourself and guard your health, and don't concern yourself so much about the business. It might be a good idea to take a light purgative . . . and then to take some air, if it is at all possible. Do remember that your health is more important than your property. . . .

In burying my son with such ceremony, you have done honor to yourself and to him. Since no services are held here for those in your state [i.e., exiles], it was particularly important to give him a decent funeral there, and I am pleased that you have done so. I and my two daughters, who are disconsolate over the death of their brother, are dressed in mourning . . .

**Source:** Alessandra Strozzi to Filippo Strozzi in Naples, 6 September 1459, *Lettere di una gentildonna fiorentina*, pp. 177–181, translated by Gene Brucker, in *The Society of Renaissance Florence: A Documentary Study* edited by Brucker (New York: Harper & Row, 1971), pp. 47–49.

ran "cranny schools" that combined child care with teaching young children their letters and the recitation of Bible verses or psalms. Jewish women in Italy taught children the Hebrew letters and the correct reading of scripture in Hebrew, though translation and commentary were reserved for male teachers.

**Literacy.** Most parents themselves could not read, however, and practical training in daily tasks was the extent of the education most children received in Renaissance and Reformation Europe; the vast majority of the population was not able to read or write in 1350 nor in 1600. They were not necessarily uneducated, for they may have been highly skilled in a trade and astute about the world around them, but this education came through oral tradition and training, not through books.

Sources:

Hugh Cunningham, *Children and Childhood in Western Society since 1500* (London & New York: Longman, 1995).

Linda A. Pollock, *Forgotten Children: Parent-Child Relations from 1500 to 1900* (Cambridge & New York: Cambridge University Press, 1983).

Richard C. Trexler, *Power and Dependence in Renaissance Florence*, volume 1: *The Children of Renaissance Florence* (Binghamton, N.Y.: Medieval & Renaissance Texts & Studies, 1993).

## EDUCATION

**Schools.** Before the Reformation, other than the informal schools run by older women in their own homes, opportunities for basic schooling came primarily through religious institutions such as convents and monasteries, or schools attached to cathedrals. Convent and monastery schools primarily served boys and girls who were intending

A letter from Florentine humanist Leonardo Bruni to Italian noblewomen Lady Baptista Malatesta in 1405, advising her on the proper subjects for women to study.

Thus there are certain subjects in which, whilst a modest proficiency is on all counts to be desired, a minute knowledge and excessive devotion seem to vain display. For instance, subtleties of Arithmetic and Geometry are not worthy to absorb a cultivated mind, and the same must be said of Astrology. You will be surprised to find me suggesting (though with much more hesitation) that the great and complex art of Rhetoric should be placed in the same category. My chief reason is the obvious one, that I have in view the cultivation most fitting to a woman. To her neither the intricacies of debate nor the oratorical artifices of action and delivery are of the least practical use, if indeed they are not positively unbecoming. Rhetoric in all its forms,—public discussion, forensic argument, logical fence, and the like—lies absolutely outside the province of women.

What Disciplines then are properly open to her? In the first place she has before her, as a subject peculiarly her own, the whole field of religion and morals. The literature of the Church will thus claim her earnest study. Such a writer, for instance, as St. Augustine affords her the fullest scope for reverent yet learned inquiry. . . .

Moreover, the cultivated Christian lady has no need in the study of this weighty subject to confine herself to ecclesiastical writers. Morals, indeed have been treated of by the noblest intellects of Greece and Rome. . . .

But we must not forget that true distinction is to be gained by a wide and varied range of such studies as conduce to the profitable enjoyment of life, in which, however, we must observe due proportion in the attention and time we devote to them.

First amongst such studies I place History: a subject which must not on any account be neglected by one who aspires to true cultivation. For it is our duty to understand the origins of our own history and its development; and the achievements of Peoples and of Kings. . . .

The great Orators of antiquity must by all means be included. Nowhere do we find the virtues more warmly extolled, the vices so fiercely decried. From them we may learn, also, how to express consolation, encouragement, dissuasion or advice. . . .

I come now to Poetry and the Poets—a subject with which every educated lady must shew herself thoroughly familiar. For we cannot point to any great mind of the past for whom the Poets had not a powerful attraction. . . . Hence my view that familiarity with the great poets of antiquity is essential to any claim to true education. For in their writings we find deep speculations upon Nature, and upon the Causes and Origins of things, which must carry weight with us both from their antiquity and from their authorship. Besides these, many important truths upon matters of daily life are suggested or illustrated. All this is expressed with such grace and dignity as demands our admiration. . . .

But I am ready to admit that there are two types of poet: the aristocracy, so to call them, of their craft, and the vulgar, and that the latter may be put aside in ordering a woman's reading. A comic dramatist may season his wit too highly: a satirist describe too bluntly the moral corruption which he scourges: let her pass them by.

Source: William Harrison Woodward, ed. and trans., *Vittorino da Feltre and Other Humanist Educators: Essays and Versions* (London: Cambridge University Press, 1897), pp. 126–129, 132.

to become monks or nuns, but they occasionally also had pupils who were not planning on taking religious vows. Cathedral schools were reserved for boys and young men, often those intending on a church career or further study for a professional vocation in law or medicine at a university. Women were prohibited from studying at universities, which developed in Europe in the twelfth century.

**Elementary Schools.** After the Reformation, first in Protestant areas and then in Catholic, learning to read came to be viewed as a part of religious instruction, and political and religious authorities encouraged the opening of elementary schools to teach boys and girls who could not learn at home. The number of schools that actually opened was always smaller than reformers desired, and more schools were established for boys than for girls; by 1580 in central Germany, for example, 50 percent of the parishes had licensed German-language schools for boys and 10 percent for girls. The education such schools offered was not extensive. Children attended for an hour or so a day, for one to two years, and were to learn, in the words of one school ordinance, "reading and writing, and if both of these can't be mastered, at least some writing, the catechism learned by heart, a little figuring, a few psalms to sing."

A teacher and grammar students, terracotta carving by Luca della Robbia, circa 1431–1438 (Museo dell'Opera del Duomo, Florence)

**Gender Bias.** The schools set up in rural areas often offered an identical curriculum for boys and girls, though the students were usually taught separately, as school authorities thought that having both sexes in one room would be distracting. There were greater gender distinctions in education in cities. In the small German town of Memmingen, for example, boys were engaged in competitions in Latin rhetoric with an eye toward their future university careers, whereas the best student in the girls' school in 1587 was chosen on the basis of her "great diligence and application in learning her catechism, modesty, obedience, and excellent penmanship." Along with reading, writing, and religion, sewing and other domestic skills were frequently part of the curriculum at girls' schools, which worked to the advantage of female teachers, who were hired in preference to male instructors, because they could be paid less; scholarships set up for poor girls read: "To be sent to school, and especially to learn to sew."

**Catholic Schools.** During the sixteenth century, schooling in Catholic areas was even more gender-specific, other than what was offered girls in convents, which were largely limited to the nobility and wealthy. A survey of schools in Venice in 1587–1588 found about 4,600 male pupils, or one-fourth of the school-age boys in the city, and only thirty girls. There were some informal catechism schools in Italy and Spain (those for boys taught by men and for girls by women) where pupils learned to read, but classes only met for about two hours on Sundays and religious holi-days so that the level of literacy achieved was not high. Opportunities for girls increased in the seventeenth century in some parts of Catholic Europe with the spread of the female teaching orders such as the Ursulines, but a survey of school-age children in southern France in the late eighteenth century found about two-thirds of boys receiving some schooling, compared to only one girl in fifty.

**Writing.** Where girls' schools existed, girls attended for a much briefer period than their male counterparts, which often meant they learned to read but not to write because the two were not taught simultaneously. Writing was also more expensive to learn, as pupils had to have some special materials, which parents were often unwilling to provide for their daughters. Parish registers, marriage contracts, and wills throughout the Renaissance and Reformation generally reveal that about twice as many men as women from similar social classes could sign their names, and that the women's signatures are more poorly written than the men's, so that their name might have been the only thing these women ever wrote.

**Notions of Womanhood.** Teaching women to read but not to write was the result not only of an economic decision on the part of parents, but also of contemporary notions about the ideal woman. Learning to read would allow a woman to discover classical and Christian examples of proper female behavior and to absorb the ideas of great (male) authors. Learning to write, on the other hand, would enable her to express her own ideas, an ability that few thinkers regarded as important and some saw as threatening. Many well-educated men also considered certain types of reading materials or subjects as improper for women, as the advice of the Florentine humanist Leonardo Bruni to the noblewoman Lady Baptista Malatesta shows.

Sources:

Paul F. Grendler, *Schooling in Renaissance Italy: Literacy and Learning, 1300–1600* (Baltimore: Johns Hopkins University Press, 1989).

R. A. Houston, *Literacy in Early Modern England: Culture and Education, 1500–1800* (London & New York: Longman, 1988).

George Huppert, *Public Schools in Renaissance France* (Urbana: University of Illinois Press, 1984).

### FACING ADULTHOOD: ADOLESCENCE AND SEXUAL MATURITY

**New Beginnings.** For most boys and girls, any opportunities for school attendance came when they were quite young and ended before they reached adolescence, which brought both sexual maturity and the beginnings of their life as a working person. It was a period when young people, particularly girls, were expected to begin settling down, not a time of "finding themselves" or "exploring their potential."

**Changes.** The onset of menstruation, termed *menarche* in modern English and "the flowers" in the sixteenth century, provided a girl with the clearest signal of bodily changes leading to adulthood. The average age at menarche has declined in the Western world, from about 15.5 in the 1890s to less than 13 at the end of the twentieth century,

*Lovers*, a late-fifteenth-century woodcut, by the Master of the Housebook (Kupferstichkabinett, Staatliche Museen, Berlin)

but it is not clear that the average age in the Renaissance and Reformation period was significantly higher than that in the nineteenth century. In fact, it may even have been lower, because age at menarche is affected by nutrition and other environmental factors, and many girls in the nineteenth century had a poorer diet and performed work that was physically harder than those of earlier times. Somewhere around fourteen years of age was probably about average, with poorer girls starting later than wealthier ones.

**Menstruation.** Because the actual biological function of menstruation had not yet been discovered, it was viewed medically as either a process that purified women's blood or removed excess blood from their bodies. Many authors, such as the unknown medical writer who composed the treatise *On the Secrets of Women* in the early fourteenth century, also thought that menses in women mixed with sperm to create a child. Doctors in this period regarded all bodily fluids as related and viewed illness as caused by an imbalance among fluids in the body; they thus recommended taking blood by cutting a vein or using leeches—termed "bloodletting"—as a treatment for disease in both men and

women. Because of this reasoning, menstruation was not clearly separated from other types of bleeding in people's minds, and was often compared to male nosebleeds, hemorrhoids, or other examples of spontaneous bleeding. Menstrual blood was thought to nourish the fetus during pregnancy, and because the body was regarded as capable of transforming one sort of fluid into another, to become milk during lactation. In the same way, male blood was held to become semen during intercourse. Semen and milk were not viewed as gender-specific fluids, however, for "virile" women who had more bodily heat than normal were seen as capable of producing semen, and effeminate men who lacked normal masculine heat were thought to produce milk.

**Fears.** The cessation of menstruation (amenorrhea) was regarded as extremely dangerous for a woman, either because it left impure blood in her that might harden into an abnormal growth, or because it would allow excess blood to run to her brain, which would become overheated. (The latter idea would be cited as a reason for barring women from higher education in the nineteenth century; education would cause all their blood to remain in their brains, which would halt menstruation and eventually cause the uterus to shrivel away.) Thus, doctors recommended hot baths, medicines, pessaries placed in the vagina, and, for married women, frequent intercourse, to bring on a late menstrual period.

**Taboos.** Menstruation was not simply a medical matter, however, but carried a great many religious and popular taboos, for though all bodily fluids were seen as related, menstrual blood was still generally viewed as somehow different and dangerous. Hebrew Scripture held that menstruation made a woman ritually impure, so that everything she touched was unclean and her presence was to be avoided by all. By the Renaissance, in Jewish communities, this taboo was limited to sexual relations and a few other contacts between wife and husband for the seven days of her period and seven days afterward. At the end of this time, a woman was expected to take a ritual bath (*mikvah*) before beginning sexual relations again. Among the Orthodox Slavs in eastern Europe, menstruating women could not enter churches or take communion. Western Christian churches were a bit milder, but both Catholic and Protestant commentators advised against sexual relations during menstruation. This recommendation was originally based strictly on the religious notion that women were unclean, though during the sixteenth century the idea spread that this activity was medically unwise as it would result in deformed or leprous children. Menstruation was used to symbolize religious practices with which one did not agree; English Protestants, for example, called the soul of the pope a "menstruous rag." According to popular beliefs, menstruating women could by their touch, glance, or mere presence rust iron, turn wine sour, spoil meat, or dull knives. Though these ideas declined among educated Europeans during the seventeenth century, they are recorded well into the twentieth century among many population groups.

This selection is from the medical treatise *On the Secrets of Women*, written in the early fourteenth century by an unknown author but attributed to the famous medieval scientist and philosopher Albertus Magnus.

Now that we have finished our introductory remarks, designed to prepare the reader's mind toward this subject matter, let us turn to the matter of the book, and first let us examine the generation of the embryo. Note therefore that every human being who is naturally conceived is generated from the seed of the father and the menses of the mother, according to all philosophers and medical authorities. And I say "medical authorities" because Aristotle did not believe that the father's seed was part of the substance of the fetus, but rather that the fetus proceeded from the menses alone, and afterwards he states that the seed exudes like vapor from the menses. The doctors, [the Greek physician Galen and his followers] on the other hand, believe that the fetus is made up of male and female seed together.

Having set forth both opinions, we must now see how that seed is received in woman. When a woman is having sexual intercourse with a man she releases her menses at the same time that the man releases sperm, and both seeds enter the *vulva* (vagina) simultaneously and are mixed together, and then the woman conceives. Conception is said to take place, therefore, when the two seeds are received in the womb in a place that nature has chosen. And after these seeds are received, the womb closes up like a purse on every side, so that nothing can fall out of it. After this happens, the woman no longer menstruates. . . .

The menses in woman, just like the sperm in man, is nothing other than superfluous food which has not been transformed into the substance of the body. In woman it is called "menses" because it flows at least once every month when the woman reaches the proper age, that is, 12, 13, or, most frequently, 14. This flow takes place every month in order to purge the body. In some women it begins at the new moon, in some afterwards, and thus all women do not have their pain at the same time. Some have more suffering, some less; some have a shorter flow than others, and this is all determined by the requirement and the complexion of the individual woman.

The third question is why menses, which are superfluous food, flow in women, and sperm does not flow in men, for this is also superfluous food. To this I reply that woman is cold and humid by nature, whereas man is hot and dry. Now humid things naturally flow, as we see in the fourth book of the *Meteorology* [a book by Aristotle] and this is especially true of that humid substance which is in women, for it is watery. In men, on the other hand, the humid substance resembles air, and, further, man has natural heat, and this heat acts upon the humid. Since nature never does anything in vain, as is noted in the first book *On Heaven and Earth*, [another book by Aristotle] and because the heat in women is weaker than that in men, and all their food cannot be converted into flesh, nature takes the best course. She provides for what is necessary, and leaves the excess in the place where the menses are kept. Enough has been said on this subject, for to go into more detail would be to give more than the subject demands. . . .

**Source:** Helen Rodnite Lemay, *Women's Secrets: A Translation of Pseudo-Albertus Magnus' De Secretis Mulierum with Commentaries* (Albany: State University of New York Press, 1992), pp. 63–65.

**Women's Beliefs.** It is difficult to know what women themselves thought about menstruation, for they rarely wrote about it. Women's handwritten personal medical guides, small books in which they recorded recipes for cures and other household hints, include formulas for mixtures to bring on a late menses and to stop overly strong flow. Women turned to midwives and other females for help with a variety of menstrual ailments. Most women seemed to view menstruation not as an illness or a sign of divine displeasure, but as a normal part of life; only in the nineteenth century would menstruation come to be regarded as an illness.

**Masculine Changes.** Sexual maturity in young men was not marked, of course, by one distinct characteristic such as the onset of menstruation, but by several signs of physical maturation such as the growth of facial hair and the deepening of the voice. This transformation seems to have occurred somewhat later than in modern times, but, as is still true, young men varied greatly in the age at which they became physically mature. In many parts of Europe, adolescent boys and young men did not live with their own families, but in the household of an employer or a master-craftsman to whom they were apprenticed. Their master or employer was expected to oversee their work and free time, and keep them from engaging in activities that might bring harm to themselves or others. Many employers and masters—and some parents—complained that the boys and young men under their supervision were difficult to control, and that they frequently engaged in rowdy or disruptive behavior, drinking, fighting, and swearing. According to court records, gangs of young men frequently roamed the streets of many towns in the evening, fighting with one another, threatening young women, and drinking until they passed out. In some places these youth groups were well organized and carried out activities such as throwing rotten fruit at or making noise outside the homes of people whose actions they did not approve of, such as pastors who tried to control them, or older men who had married much younger women. Such actions may in part have been motivated by the fact that the age of marriage in much of Europe was quite late during this period, leaving young men with no legitimate sexual outlet, so they instead proved their masculinity with drinking contests, fighting, and other wild behavior. These activities were frowned upon and the boys were punished if they got out of hand. Still, these activities were also in some ways expected as a normal part of achieving manhood.

Sources:

Patricia Crawford, "Attitudes to Menstruation in Seventeenth-Century England," *Past and Present*, 91 (May 1981): 47–73.

Elizabeth A. Foyster, *Manhood in Early Modern England: Honour, Sex and Marriage* (New York: Longman, 1999).

Michael Mitterauer, *A History of Youth*, translated by Graeme Dunphy (Oxford & Cambridge, Mass.: Blackwell, 1993).

### GRAVE CONCERNS: ATTITUDES TOWARD SEXUALITY

**Maturity.** Opinions about when men and women reached sexual maturity were closely related with attitudes toward sexuality in general, which were also a mixture of medical and religious beliefs. In medical terms, male sexuality was the baseline for any perception of human sexuality, and the female sex organs were viewed as the male turned inside out or simply not pushed out. The great sixteenth-century anatomist Andreas Vesalius depicted the uterus looking exactly like an inverted penis, and his student Baldasar Heseler commented: "The organs of procreation are the same in the male and the female. . . . For if you turn the scrotum, the testicles and the penis inside out you will have all the genital organs of the female." This idea meant that there were no specific names for many female anatomical parts until the eighteenth century, because they were always thought to be the the inverse of some male part, and so were simply called by the same name.

**Bodily Heat.** The fact that the female sex organs were inside the body was viewed as a sign of female inferiority; male organs, it was thought, were pushed out by the greater heat in the male body, which was regarded as a positive and active force. This condition was also used to explain why men go bald more often than women, for heat burned up their hair from the inside. The parallels between male and female organs could lead to alleged unusual sex changes, for many medical doctors throughout Europe solemnly reported cases of young women whose sex organs suddenly emerged during vigorous physical activity, transforming them into men; there are no reports of the opposite, however. Because female sex organs were hidden, they seemed more mysterious to early modern physicians and anatomists, and anatomical guidebooks use illustrations of autopsies on women's

A woman brought up on charges of adultery before a male tribunal, from an undated manuscript for
*Tristan and Isolde* (Munich Library, Cod. Germ. 51)

Andreas Cappelanus's *The Art of Courtly Love* (circa 1185) was a popular treatise during the period of the Renaissance and Reformation. It described how a man can and should fall in love, and how he could get out of a love affair he no longer wanted.

## CHAPTER III: *What the Effect of Love is*

Now it is the effect of love that a true lover cannot be degraded with any avarice. Love causes a rough and uncouth man to be distinguished for his handsomeness; it can endow a man even of the humblest birth with nobility of character; it blesses the proud with humility; and the man in love becomes accustomed to performing many services gracefully for everyone. O what a wonderful thing is love, which makes a man shine with so many virtues and teaches everyone, no matter who he is, so many good traits of character! There is another thing about love that we should not praise in few words: it adorns a man, so to speak, with the virtue of chastity, because he who shines with the light of one love can hardly think of embracing another woman, even a beautiful one. For when he thinks deeply of his beloved the sight of any other woman seems to his mind rough and rude.

## CHAPTER IV: *What Persons Are Fit for Love*

We must now see what persons are fit to bear the arms of love. You should know that everyone of sound mind who is capable of doing the work of Venus may be wounded by one of love's arrows unless prevented by age, or blindness, or excess of passion.

An excess of passion is a bar to love, because there are men who are slaves to such passionate desire that they cannot be held in the bonds of love—men who, after they have thought long about some woman or even enjoyed her, when they see another woman straightway desire her embraces, and they forget about the services they have received from their first love and they feel no gratitude for them. Men of this kind lust after every woman they see; their love is like that of a shameless dog. They should rather, I believe, be compared to asses for they are moved only by that low nature which shows that men are on the level of the other animals rather than by that true nature which sets us apart from all the other animals by the difference of reason.

## CHAPTER VIII: *The Easy Attainment of One's Object*

The readiness to grant requests is, we say, the same thing in women as overvoluptuousness in men—a thing which all agree should be a total stranger in the court of Love. For he who is so tormented by carnal passion he cannot embrace anyone in heartfelt love, but basely lusts after every woman he sees, is not called a lover but a counterfeiter of love and a pretender, and he is lower than a shameless dog. Indeed the man who is so wanton that he cannot confine himself to the love of one woman deserves to be considered an impetuous ass. It will therefore be clear to you that you are bound to avoid an overabundance of passion and that you ought not to seek the love of a woman who you know will grant easily what you seek.

## CHAPTER IX: *The Love of Peasants*

If you should, by some chance, fall in love with a peasant woman, be careful to puff her up with lots of praise and then, when you find a convenient place, do not hesitate to take what you seek and to embrace her by force. For you can hardly soften their outward inflexibility so far that they will grant you their embraces quietly or permit you to have the solaces you desire unless first you use a little compulsion as a convenient cure for their shyness. We do not say these things, however, because we want to persuade you to love such women, but only so that, if through lack of caution you should be driven to love them, you may know, in brief compass, what to do.

Source: Andreas Capellanus, *The Art of Courtly Love*, translated by John Jay Parry, edited by Frederick W. Locke (New York: Ungar, 1957), pp. 4–5, 24.

---

lower bodies as symbols of modern science uncovering the unknown.

**Negative Concepts.** Religious opinion about sexuality was generally more negative than the ideas of scientists and doctors. Orthodox Slavs in eastern Europe had the most negative beliefs, seeing all sexuality as an evil inclination originating with the devil and not part of God's original creation; as in the rest of Europe, women were viewed as more sexual and the cause of men's original fall from grace. Even marital sex was regarded as a sin, with the best marriage one in which there was no sexual intercourse; this concept led to stories about miraculous virgin births among Russian saints, and to the popular idea that Jesus was born out of Mary's ear, not polluting himself with passage through the birth canal.

**Ambivalent Attitudes.** Western Catholic opinion did not go this far, but displayed an ambivalent attitude toward sexuality. Sex was seen as polluting and defiling, with virginity regarded as the most desirable state; members of the clergy and religious orders were expected, at least in theory, to remain chaste. Their chastity and celibacy made them different from, and superior to, lay Christians who married. On the other hand, the body and its sexual urges could not be completely evil, because they were created by God; to claim otherwise was heresy. Writers vacillated between these two opinions or held both at once, and the laws regulating sexual behavior were based on both. In general, early modern Catholic doctrine held that sexual relations were acceptable as long as they were within marriage, not done on Sundays or other church holidays, performed in a way that would allow procreation, and that did not upset the proper sexual order, which meant the man had to be on top.

**Reformed Views.** Protestant reformers clearly broke with Catholicism in their view that marriage was a spiritually preferable state to celibacy. Moreover, Protestants saw the most important function of marital sex not as procreation, but as increasing affection between spouses. Based on his own experience, Martin Luther stressed the power of sexual feelings for both men and women, and thought women in particular needed intercourse in order to stay healthy. Protestants generally agreed with Catholics that sexual relations were permissible as long as they were marital and "natural," though exactly what they meant by natural differed from writer to writer.

**Popular Views.** Opinions about sexuality were expressed in this period not simply by learned scientists and theologians but also by the writers of popular songs and stories. Many of these works celebrate male sexuality—bawdy tales of men who, along with drinking and fighting, slept with other men's wives. Even those works that discussed love along with sex, such as Andreas Cappelanus's *The Art of Courtly Love* (circa 1185), considered force part of male sexuality, at least when lower-class women were concerned. Few of these popular works portray women who engaged in sex outside of marriage in a positive light, and some even praise men who beat women into submission.

Sources:

Joan Cadden, *Meanings of Sex Difference in the Middle Ages: Medicine, Science, and Culture* (Cambridge & New York: Cambridge University Press, 1993).

Thomas Laqueur, *Making Sex: Body and Gender from the Greeks to Freud* (Cambridge, Mass.: Harvard University Press, 1990).

Ian Maclean, *The Renaissance Notion of Woman: A Study in the Fortunes of Scholasticism and Medical Science in European Intellectual Life* (Cambridge & New York: Cambridge University Press, 1980).

### HARD CHOICES: PREGNANCY OUTSIDE OF MARRIAGE

**Social Control.** Cases involving sexual actions and moral behavior were sometimes handled by church courts and sometimes by city or state courts; whatever the venue, because the consequences of sexual misconduct became visible within the bodies of women, they appeared more frequently than men in these courts.

The vast majority of cases involving sexual misconduct were for premarital intercourse, termed fornication. It was often difficult for unmarried women to avoid sexual contacts. Many of them worked as domestic servants, where their employers or employers' sons or male relatives could easily coerce them. They worked in close proximity to men (a large number of cases involved two servants in the same house) and were rarely supervised or chaperoned. Female servants were sent on errands alone or with men, or worked by themselves in fields far from other people; though notions of female honor might keep upper-class women secluded in their homes, in most parts of Europe there was little attempt to protect female servants or day-laborers from the risk of seduction or rape.

**Remedies.** Once an unmarried woman suspected she was pregnant, she had several options. In some parts of Europe, if she was a minor her father could go to court and sue the man involved for "trespass and damages" to his property. The woman herself could go to her local court and attempt to prove there had been a promise of marriage in order to coerce the man to marry her. This might also happen once her employer or acquaintances suspected pregnancy. Marriage was the favored official solution, and was agreed upon in a surprising number of cases, indicating that perhaps there had been an informal agreement, or at least that the man was now willing

The use of pennyroyal as an abortifacient, from a thirteenth-century manuscript (Vienna, Nationalbibliothek, MS lat. 93. fol. 93)

to take responsibility for his actions. In cases where marriage was impossible, such as those involving married men or members of the clergy, the courts might order the man to maintain the child for a set period of years.

**Extreme Measures.** Many women attempted to deny the pregnancy as long as possible. The clothing styles of the period, with full skirts and aprons, allowed most women to go until late in the pregnancy without showing clear visible signs. A woman might attempt to induce an abortion, either by physical means such as tying her waist very tight or carrying heavy objects, or by herbal concoctions that she brewed herself or purchased from a local person reputed to know about such things. Recipes for abortifacients were readily available in popular medical guides, cookbooks, and herbals, generally labeled as medicine that would bring on a late menstrual flow, or "provoke the monthlies." Both doctors and everyday people regarded regular menstruation as essential to maintaining a woman's health, so anything that stopped her periods was considered dangerous. Pregnancy was only one possible reason, and a woman could not be absolutely sure she was pregnant until she quickened, that is, felt the child move within her. This was the point at which the child was regarded as gaining a soul to become fully alive—that is what "quickening" originally meant—so that a woman taking medicine to start her period before quickening was generally not regarded as attempting an abortion. Whether any of these medicines would have been effective is another matter, however. Some of them did contain ingredients that do strengthen uterine contractions, such as ergot, rue, or savin, but these items can also be poisonous in large doses. It was difficult for women to know exactly what dosage they were taking, for the raw ingredients contain widely varying amounts of active ingredients and their strength depends on how one prepares them, so it was likely that a woman would take too little to have any effect or too much and become violently ill or die.

**Punishment.** Penalties for attempting or performing an abortion after the child had quickened grew increasingly harsh during this period. In the Holy Roman Empire, aborting a "living" child was made a capital offense in 1532, with death to be by decapitation for men and by drowning for women. Midwives were ordered "when they come upon a young girl or someone else who is pregnant outside of marriage, they should speak to them of their own accord and warn them with threats of punishment not to harm the fetus in any way or take any bad advice, as such foolish people are very likely to do." Abortion was difficult to detect, however, and most accusations emerged in trials for infanticide, in which a mother's attempts to end her pregnancy before the birth became evidence of her intent.

**Illegitimate Birth.** In most cases women resigned themselves to having the baby even if they could not get

## TAKING RESPONSIBILITY FOR THE BABIES

Church courts heard all cases having to do with marriage and sexuality before the Reformation, and after it in Catholic and some Protestant areas; the following are two cases brought before English Church courts in the town of Lincoln in the early sixteenth century.

[1517] . . . Alice Ridyng, unmarried, the daughter of John Ridyng of Eton in the diocese of Lincoln appeared in person and confessed that she conceived a boy child by one Thomas Denys, then chaplain to Master Geoffrey Wren, and gave birth to him at her father's home at Eton one Sunday last month and immediately after giving birth, that is within four hours of the birth, killed the child by putting her hand in the baby's mouth and so suffocated him. After she had killed the child she buried it in a dung heap in her father's orchard. At the time of the delivery she had no midwife and nobody was ever told as such that she was pregnant, but some women of Windsor and Eton had suspected and said that she was pregnant, but Alice always denied this saying that something else was wrong with her belly. On the Tuesday after the delivery of the child, however, the women and honest wives of Windsor and Eton took her and inspected her belly and her breasts by which they knew for certain that she had given birth. She then confessed everything to them and showed them the place where she had put the dead child. She said further that neither her father nor her mother ever knew that she was pregnant since she always denied it until she was taken by the wives as described. Examined further she said by virtue of the oath she had taken on the gospels that she had never been known carnally by anyone other than the said Thomas and that nobody else urged or agreed to the child's death. She also said that the child had been conceived on the feast of the Purification of the Blessed Virgin Mary last at the time of high mass in the house of Master Geoffrey Wren at Spytell where Master Geoffrey was then ill.

[1519] John Asteley [rector of Shepshed] confessed that he had made Agnes Walles, unmarried, pregnant and that she had given birth to a girl child at Hauxley before Christmas. He had supported the child there from his tithes [taxes paid to the church of which Asteley was rector]. He also confessed that he had made pregnant Margaret Swynerton, unmarried, and had had three children by her. Margaret is now dead. He also had another child by one Joan Chadwyk, now married, then single. Joan lives at Dunstable. John does not know where Agnes lives now. Because he confessed these things . . . the vicar general ordered that from henceforth no other woman should serve in his home and that he should live continently.

Source: P. J. P. Goldberg, ed., *Women in England c. 1275-1525* (Manchester, U.K.: Manchester University Press, 1995).

married, often leaving their normal place of residence to have it with friends or relatives, though it was illegal in many parts of Europe to harbor an unmarried pregnant woman. The consequences of unwed motherhood varied throughout Europe, with rural areas that needed many workers being the most tolerant. In rural Norway, for example, about one-quarter of the unwed mothers married men other than the father of their child one to six years after giving birth. For many unmarried women, however, pregnancy meant disaster, especially when the father was the woman's married employer or was related by blood or marriage. Such a situation was considered adultery or incest rather than simple fornication and could bring great shame on the household. Women in such situations were urged to lie about the father's identity or were simply fired; they received no support from the wife of the father, whose honor and reputation were tightly bound to her husband's. A pregnant woman fired by her employer was often in a desperate situation, as many authorities prohibited people from hiring or taking in unmarried pregnant women, charging them with aiding in a sexual offense.

**Desperate Measures.** Women in such a situation might have decided to hide the birth. They gave birth in outhouses, cow stalls, hay mounds, and dung heaps, hoping that they would be able to avoid public notice, and then they either took the infant to one of the new foundling homes that had opened during the fifteenth or sixteenth centuries in many cities, or they killed it. Before the sixteenth century, church and secular courts heard few cases of infanticide, as jurists recognized that physicians could not make a clear distinction between a stillbirth, a newborn who had died of natural causes, and one who had been murdered. This leniency changed in the sixteenth century, when infanticide became legally equated with murder in most areas of Europe and so carried the death penalty, often specified as death by drowning. These stringent statutes were quite rigorously enforced. More women were executed for infanticide in early modern Europe than any other crime except witchcraft.

**Enforcement.** Midwives were enlisted to help enforce the statutes. They were to report all births and attempt to find out the name of the father by asking the mother "during the pains of birth." If an accused woman denied giving birth, midwives or a group of women from the village examined her to see if she had milk or showed other signs of recent delivery; in the case of foundlings, midwives might be asked to examine the breasts of all unmarried women in a parish for signs of childbirth. Midwives also examined the bodies of infants for signs that they had drawn breath. Courts were intent on gaining confessions, occasionally even bringing in the child's corpse to rattle the accused. Records from a 1549 trial in Nuremburg report: "And then the midwife said, 'Oh, you innocent little child, if one of us here is guilty, give us a sign!' and immediately the body raised its left arm

and pointed at its mother." The unfortunate mother was later executed by drowning.

Sources:

Richard Adair, *Courtship, Illegitimacy, and Marriage in Early Modern England* (Manchester, U.K. & New York: Manchester University Press, 1996).

Peter C. Hoffer and N. E. H. Hull, *Murdering Mothers: Infanticide in England and New England, 1558–1803* (New York: New York University Press, 1981).

Angus McLaren, *A History of Contraception: From Antiquity to the Present Day* (Oxford & Cambridge, Mass.: Blackwell, 1990).

## HOMOSEXUALITY

**Repressing the Aberrant.** Church and state authorities during the Renaissance and Reformation attempted to suppress homosexual as well as premarital and extramarital heterosexual activity. After about 1250 they increasingly defined homosexual actions as "crimes against nature," seeing them as particularly reprehensible because they thought they did not occur anywhere else in creation. Homosexual activity, usually termed "sodomy," became a capital crime in both England and the Holy Roman Empire (Germany) during the 1530s, although the two areas defined it slightly differently: in the empire it included relations between two men, two women, or any person and an animal, while in England relations between two women were not mentioned. Preachers and officials denounced sodomy with strong language, and linked it with other serious crimes such as heresy.

**Sodomy.** Despite harsh language about "sodomites" and "the unmentionable vice" (for example, homosexuality), the number of actual sodomy cases in this period was quite small. The Portuguese Inquisition, for example, compiled two large books with more than 4,400 names of all those accused of or confessing to homosexual acts during the period 1587 to 1794; of these about 400 were actually put on trial and about 30 appear to have been executed. This lack of concern about sodomy in comparison with other types of sexual misconduct resulted in part because homosexual relations did not lead to the birth of a child who might require public support, and in part because most male homosexual relations seem to have occurred between a superior and inferior, such as an older and younger man, or a master and servant. The dominant individual was generally married and heterosexually active, with his homosexual activities not viewed as upsetting the social order. This attitude began to change in a few cities such as Florence—and later London and Amsterdam—and homosexual subcultures began to develop with special styles of dress, behavior, slang terms, and meeting places; these networks brought together men of different social classes and backgrounds and did not necessarily involve a dominant and subordinate partner. Authorities occasionally responded brutally when they discovered homosexual networks and subcultures, though most of these developments occurred well after 1600.

Harsh attacks on homosexual relations, as well as other sexual acts judged sinful such as adultery and premarital sex, were common in the Renaissance and Reformation. This selection is from Franciscan theologian, preacher, and administrator Jean Benedicti's treatise *The Compendium of Sins and the Remedy for Them* (1610).

On Sodomy, the Sin against Nature

This sin is against the natural order because it is committed against the sexual order, a sin that is more grievous than having relations with one's sister, even with one's own mother. Now there is sodomy, and there is the sodomitical act, which are two different things.

I hardly dare speak of this vile and horrible sin, and especially in our France. If I do, however, I will certainly say, that this sin is so enormous that it cannot be mentioned because of its horror. For, in the first place, such sodomites are compared to parricides and murderers. Secondly, they are infamous according to the laws. Thirdly, they should be punished with death and burned. The law of Moses orders that the active one as well as the passive one be put to death. Fourthly, according to ecclesiastical law, if they are lay, they should be excommunicated and expelled from the church, so that there is even a council that forbids giving them communion on the point of death. If they are ecclesiastics, they should, according to the Lateran Council, be confined to a monastery, as to a perpetual prison, to do penance there. But Pope Pius V recently issued an edict by which he deprives all ecclesiastics stained with this sin of every office, benefice, and clerical privilege, ordering that they be demoted and delivered into the hands of justice, to have them put to death according to the disposition of the secular laws. From this extravagant [a type of papal text] one draws a conclusion, that if the clergyman who is accustomed to this sin is irregular [barred from fulfilling his functions because of his faults], he should be removed from his office and deprived of his benefice, which he cannot possess in good conscience. For this reason he should leave and renounce it. What, then, will the confessor do when such a person presents himself to him? He should refer him to the bishop, and, if the penitent is not subject to the bishop, refer him to the Holy Father, the Pope, to have his dispensation. This is understood to apply in the case of someone who has indulged in this sin, which is condemned not only *inforo exteriori* [in the external court], that is to say through public judgment, but also *inforo interiori* [in the internal court], that is to say through the sacrament of confession, just as the same Pope Pius V, by word of mouth, interpreted it afterward. It is understood to be sodomy when it is practiced through sodomitical copulation and not only through the sodomitical act. This sin is so detestable that there are even some demons and wicked spirits who hold it in horror. For even though they sometimes keep carnal company with sorcerers and witches, still there are none who have ever committed the sin against nature. This is the mystical commentary of some Fathers on the passage from the Prophet [Ezekiel] that says, "I will deliver you into the hands of the Spirits of the Philistines," that is to say of the devils, "who, even they, will be ashamed of your wicked life," that is to say of your sins against nature.

Such shameless people fall from this miserable sin into others more terrible, such as apostasy, atheism, heresy, and finally, having reached the height of impiety, die damned. This is why the Apostle [Paul] calls them children of wrath and says that the philosophers were not pushed in the direction of damnation for that reason.

Source: Jeffrey Merrick and Bryant T. Ragan Jr., eds., *Homosexuality in Early Modern France: A Documentary Collection* (New York: Oxford University Press, 2001), pp. 3–4.

**Ultimate Punishment.** Though they were rare, actual executions for sodomy could be grisly, however. Sodomy was punished by burning adult offenders alive, with juvenile offenders—who were not liable for execution—quickly passed through the fire so that, as officials commented, they could get a foretaste of what was to come if they did not change their ways. Those charged with homosexual acts were sometimes tortured to reveal other offenders, so that sodomy accusations often occurred in waves. The executions were generally carried out at public events called autos-da-fé, where bigamists and other individuals regarded as disturbing God's natural order were also either executed or displayed for public ridicule. Punishments were often more severe for the man who took the passive role, because he was perceived as disturbing the natural gender order as well as the sexual order, that is, allowing himself to become feminized.

**Lesbianism.** Women were not immune from sodomy accusations and trials, although there were only a handful in all of Europe during this period. In part, this lack of prosecution was because, in the minds of male authorities, sex always involved penetration, so female homosexuality was seen as a kind of masturbation. The cases that came to trial generally involved women who wore men's clothing, used a dildo or other device to effect penetration, or women who married other women. The horror with which they were regarded sprang more from the fact that they had usurped a man's social role than that they had been attracted to another woman. In all of these cases, the woman who had remained in feminine clothing received a milder punishment, and in none of them is there any discussion of a lesbian subculture, which may seem odd considering the all-female milieus in which many women lived, worked, and slept, and the late age of marriage and high percentage of women who never married in some parts of Europe.

**Cloaked Realities.** It is easier to find clear records of the opinions of those who opposed and prosecuted homosexual activity than those who engaged in it. Other than in pornography, most authors in this period do not discuss sexual relations—either heterosexual or homosexual—explicitly. Some of them do express strong same-sex emotions in sentimental and sensual terms, revealing passionate attachments and close friendships among the characters they create and between themselves and other actual individuals. This move was one period in which educated people were trained in the Platonic

A young man struggling with his sexual interests in the "12th Joy of Marriage," a chapter in French writer Antoine de La Sale's
*The Fyftene Joyes of Maryage* (Folger Shakespeare Library, Washington, D.C.)

ideal of spiritual love and close friendship, however, so that the expression of passionate same-sex emotions might not indicate homosexual relations. Some scholars have thus tried to dismiss all of these writings as simply a literary exercise. However, more-recent scholars agree that the fact that the letters were addressed to someone of the same sex was not accidental. They point out that the notion of a lifelong "sexual identity" as heterosexual or homosexual (bisexual or transgendered) developed long after 1600 in Europe, but it is clear that some people had strong erotic feelings toward members of the same gender, feelings that were sometimes expressed through genital sex even if individuals did not consider themselves to be "lesbian" or "homosexual."

Sources:

John Boswell, *Same-Sex Unions in Premodern Europe* (New York: Vintage, 1994).

Alan Bray, *Homosexuality in Renaissance England,* second edition (New York: Columbia University Press, 1995).

Michael Rocke, *Forbidden Friendships: Homosexuality and Male Culture in Renaissance Florence* (New York: Oxford University Press, 1996).

## INDECENT BEHAVIORS

**Improper Activities.** Along with premarital sexual activity, people engaged in, and were often punished for, a range of other sexual activities and moral offenses during this period. Particularly after the Protestant and Catholic Reformations, religious and political authorities attempted to ban dancing, spinning bees (where young men and women gathered in the evenings to chat while the women worked), and clothing styles that revealed too much of the body or bodily contours. In many southern European cities, women charged with improper behavior such as flirting might be locked up in institutions established by church or city authorities for repentant prostitutes and other "fallen women." Such houses, often dedicated to the biblical figure Mary Magdalene, also began to admit women who were regarded as being in danger of becoming prostitutes, generally poor women with no male relatives; the ordinances stated explicitly that the women admitted had to be pretty or at least acceptable looking, for ugly women did not have to worry about their honor.

"The Bath-house," depicting lax moral activities during the Middle Ages, an illumination by a Bruges master in the *Dresden Prayer Book,* circa 1480 (Universitatsbibliothek, Leipzig)

In the fourteenth century, many cities in Europe supported the opening of houses of prostitution, for reasons similar to those presented below by the municipal council of Florence. In the sixteenth century, city councils, such as the one in Nuremberg, closed the approved brothels, although illicit prostitution continued.

[Florence] Desiring to eliminate a worse evil by means of a lesser one, the lord priors . . . [and their colleges] have decreed that . . . the priors . . . [and their colleges] may authorize the establishment of two public brothels in the city of Florence, in addition to the one which already exists: one in the quarter of S. Spirito and the other in the quarter of S. Croce. [They are to be located] in suitable places or in places where the exercise of such scandalous activity can best be concealed, for the honor of the city and of those who live in the neighborhood in which these prostitutes must stay to hire their bodies for lucre, as other prostitutes stay in the other brothel. For establishing these places . . . in a proper manner and for their construction, furnishing, and improvement, they may spend up to 1,000 florins. . . .

Source: Florentine State Archives, Provissioni 105, fols. 248r–248v, translated by Gene Brucker, in *The Society of Renaissance Florence: A Documentary Study*, edited by Brucker (New York: Harper & Row, 1971), p. 190.

[Nuremberg] [January 5, 1562] The high honorable [city] council asks for learned opinions about whether it should close the city brothel (*Frauenhaus*), or if it were closed, whether other dangers and still more evil would be the result.

[January 19, 1562] The learned counselors, pastors and theologians discussed whether closing the house would lead the journeymen and foreign artisans to turn instead to their masters' and landlords' wives, daughters, and maids. The pastors and theologians urged the city not to break God's word just because

of foreigners, and one argued that the brothel caused journeymen to have impure thoughts about women. If they were never introduced to sex, they would not bother other women. The argument that a man performed a good deed when he married a woman from the brothel, which he could no longer do if the brothel was closed, is to be rejected, as closing the brothel would also pull the women out of the devil's grip. One jurist added his opinion that because there were only ten or twelve women in the brothel, they couldn't possible be taking care of all the journeymen, so closing the house would not make that much difference. The council then asked for an exact report from Augsburg about the numbers of illegitimate children before and after it closed its brothel [in 1532] to see if it had increased or decreased.

[March 18, 1562] On the recommendations written and read by the high honorable theologians and jurists, why the men of the council are authorized and obliged to close the common brothel, it has been decided by the whole council to follow the same recommendation and from this hour on forbid all activity in that house, to post a guard in the house and let no man enter it any more. Also to send for the brothel manager and say to him he is to send all women that he has out of the house in two days and never take them in again. From this time on he is to act so blamelessly and unsuspiciously that the council has no cause to punish him. When this has been completed, the preachers should be told to admonish the young people to guard themselves from such depravity and to keep their children and servants from it and to lead such an irreproachable life that the council has no cause to punish anyone for this vice.

[May 18, 1577] The high honorable city council asks for learned opinions, because adultery, prostitution, immorality and rape have gotten so out of hand here in the city and the countryside.

Source: Nuremberg: Bavarian State Archives, Ratsbücher 31, Fols. 316, 350; 36, Fol. 15. Ratschlagbücher 36, Fols. 150–153. Translation by Merry Wiesner-Hanks.

**Illicit Love.** Prostitution was increasingly regulated during this period, and in some areas prohibited outright. During the Middle Ages most European cities allowed prostitution in licensed brothels; community leaders justified this policy by saying that it protected honorable women and girls from attacks by young men. The women in these brothels were expected to come from outside the city and their customers were supposed to be unmarried men, not married men or priests. During the fifteenth century many city fathers began to feel increasingly uneasy about permitting prostitution and started requiring women to wear distinctive clothing or not appear in public at all. By the sixteenth century, cities in central and northern Europe started closing their houses of prostitution; this movement happened first in Protestant and then in Catholic cities and was supported by religious reformers from all groups. Southern European cities, especially those in Italy, generally licensed prostitutes and restricted their movements but did not prohibit them outright. Forbidding prostitution did not end the activity, however, but it did mean that women—and occasionally men—could now be arrested, fined, and sometimes banished for prostitution. Their customers, however, were rarely charged.

**Rape.** Courts also heard cases of rape, which was a capital crime in many parts of Europe, but the actual sentences handed out were more likely to be fines and brief imprisonments, with the severity dependent on the social status of the victim and perpetrator. The victim had to prove that she had cried out and made attempts to repel the attacker, and had to bring the charge within a short period of time after the attack. Charges of rape were fairly rare, which suggests that it was underreported, but examinations of trial records indicate that rape charges were usually taken seriously because judges and lawyers rarely suggested that the woman herself provoked the attack. Women bringing rape charges were often more interested in getting their own honorable reputations back than in punishing the perpetrator, and for this reason they sometimes requested that the judge force their rapists to marry them. It may be difficult to understand why any victim would do this, but it was often the easiest way for a woman who was no longer a virgin to establish an honorable social identity.

**Unbecoming Conduct.** Certain activities by married people might have also led to their being charged with improper behavior. Religious and political authorities rarely intervened in disputes between spouses unless they created public scandal or disturbed the neighbors, and they usually attempted first to reconcile the spouses. This policy included terrible cases of domestic violence, in which one spouse—almost always the wife—accused the other of beatings with sticks or tools, brutal kicking, stabbing, or choking. Courts generally held that a husband had the right to beat his wife to correct her behavior as long as it was not too extreme; in England "too extreme" meant the stick that he used was narrower than his thumb—the origin of the term "rule of thumb." Accusations of adultery were taken far more seriously than those of domestic violence, because this misbehavior directly challenged the link between marriage and legitimate procreation. Adultery was a capital offense in most of Europe, and in a few cases individuals were actually executed, though usually they were punished with fines, prisons sentences, or banishment. As in rape, the severity of the punishment usually depended on the social status of the accused, and also on the gender of the guilty party; though adultery on the part of married men was theoretically a crime in most of Europe, only infidelity on the part of married women was actually punished.

**Whispered Charges.** Along with courts and other legal authorities, sexual activity of all types was also controlled through less-formal means, such as discussions among neighbors and acquaintances about some-

one's reputation and honor. Such discussions show up in court records when they led to charges of slander. The most serious accusation for a woman was to be termed a "whore," and most sexual slander directed at men—terms such as "cuckold," "whoremaster," or "pimp"—actually involved the sexual activities of the women who were supposed to be under their control.

Sources:

Laura Gowing, *Domestic Dangers: Women, Words, and Sex in Early Modern London* (Oxford: Clarendon Press; Oxford & New York: Oxford University Press, 1996).

Guido Ruggiero, *The Boundaries of Eros: Sex Crime and Sexuality in Renaissance Venice* (New York: Oxford University Press, 1985).

Margaret R. Somerville, *Sex and Subjection: Attitudes to Women in Early-Modern Society* (London & New York: Arnold, 1995).

## OPINIONS ABOUT MARRIAGE

**Expected Roles.** For the majority of people in Renaissance and Reformation Europe, sexual desires and relations did not lead to charges of fornication, infanticide, or homosexuality, but were simply one part of the institution that shaped their lives to a great degree—marriage. Opinions about marriage in this period were varied, but generally became more positive than they had been in the Middle Ages. During the fifteenth century some writers began to argue that God had set up marriage and families as the best way to provide spiritual and moral discipline, and, after the Reformation, Protestants championed marriage with even greater vigor. They wrote many tracts trying to convince men and women to marry or advising spouses (particularly husbands) how best to run their households and families. Johannes Mathesius, for example, a Lutheran pastor, wrote: "A man without a wife is only half a person and has only half a body and is a needy and miserable man who lacks help and assistance." Preachers used the story of Eve being created out of Adam's rib as proof that God wanted women to stand by the side of men as their assistants and not be trampled on or trod underfoot (for then Eve would have been created out of Adam's foot); these directives always mention as well, however, that women should never claim authority over men, for Eve had not been created out of Adam's head.

**Goals of Marriage.** Protestant writers generally cite the same three purposes of marriage, in the same order of importance, that pre-Reformation writers did—the procreation of children, the avoidance of sin, and mutual help and companionship. Some reformers, including Martin Luther, interpreted "mutual help and companionship" to have a romantic and sensual side, so there tended to be less of an antipathy toward sexuality (as long as it was within marriage) among Protestants than Catholics.

**God's Plan.** The ideal of mutuality in marriage was not one of equality, however, and Protestant marriage manuals, household guides, and marriage sermons all stress the importance of husbandly authority and wifely obedience. This obedience, for almost all Protestants,

Martin Luther's opinions about marriage are expressed in many of his writings, including formal theological treatises, letters, and sermons; this piece is from a sermon on marriage preached in 1521.

Those who want to enter into the estate of marriage should learn from this that they should earnestly pray to God for a spouse. For the sage says that parents provide goods and houses for their children, but a wife is given by God alone [Prov. 19:14], everyone according to his need, just as Eve was given to Adam by God alone. And true though it is that because of excessive lust of the flesh lighthearted youth pays scant attention to these matters, marriage is nevertheless a weighty matter in the sight of God. For it was not by accident that Almighty God instituted the estate of matrimony only for man and above all animals, and gave such forethought and consideration to marriage. To the other animals God says quite simply, "Be fruitful and multiply" [Gen. 1: 22]. It is not written that he brings the female to the male. Therefore, there is no such thing as marriage among animals. But in the case of Adam, God creates for him a unique, special kind of wife out of his own flesh. He brings her to him, he gives her to him, and Adam agrees to accept her. Therefore, that is what marriage is.

A woman is created to be a companionable helpmeet to the man in everything, particularly to bear children. And that still holds good, except that since the fall marriage has been adulterated with wicked lust. And now [i.e., after the fall] the desire of the man for the woman, and vice versa, is sought after not only for companionship and children, for which purposes alone marriage was instituted, but also for the pursuance of wicked lust, which is almost as strong a motive.

God makes distinctions between the different kinds of love, and shows that the love of a man and woman is (or should be) the greatest and purest of all loves. For he says, "A man shall leave his father and mother and cleave to his wife" [Gen. 2:24], and the wife does the same, as we see happening around us every day. Now there are three kinds of love: false love, natural love, and married love. False love is that which seeks its own, as a man loves money, possessions, honor, and women taken outside of marriage and against God's command. Natural love is that between father and child, brother and sister, friend and relative, and similar relationships. But over and above all these is married love, that is, a bride's love, which glows like a fire and desires nothing but the husband. She says, "It is you I want, not what is yours: I want neither your silver nor your gold; I want neither. I want only you. I want you in your entirety, or not at all." All other kinds of love seek something other than the loved one: this kind wants only to have the beloved's own self completely. If Adam had not fallen, the love of bride and groom would have been the loveliest thing. Now this love is not pure either, for admittedly a married partner desires to have the other, yet each seeks to satisfy his desire with the other, and it is this desire which corrupts this kind of love. Therefore, the married state is now no longer pure and free from sin. The temptation of the flesh has become so strong and consuming that marriage may be likened to a hospital for incurables which prevents inmates from falling into graver sin. Before Adam fell it was a simple matter to remain virgin and chaste, but now it is hardly possible, and without special grace from God, quite impossible. For this very reason neither Christ nor the apostles sought to make chastity a matter of obligation. It is true that Christ counseled chastity, and he left it up to each one to test himself, so that if he could not be continent he was free to marry, but if by the grace of God he could be continent, then chastity is better.

Thus the doctors [earlier Christian theologians] have found three good and useful things about the married estate, by means of which the sin of lust, which flows beneath the surface, is counteracted and ceases to be a cause of damnation. First, [the doctors say] that it is a sacrament. . . . Second, [the doctors say that] it is a covenant of fidelity. . . . Third [the doctors say] that marriage produces offspring, for that is the end and chief purpose of marriage.

Source: *Luther's Works*, volume 44 (Philadelphia: Fortress, 1956), pp. 8–12.

was to take precedence over women's spiritual equality; a woman's religious convictions were never grounds for leaving or even openly disagreeing with her husband, though she could pray for his conversion. The only exceptions to this view were some of the radical reformers, such as the Anabaptists, who did allow women to leave their unbelieving spouses; but those who did so were expected to remarry quickly and thus come under the control of a male believer. Women were continually advised to be cheerful rather than grudging in their obedience, for in doing so they demonstrated their willingness to follow God's plan. Men were also given specific advice about how to enforce their authority, which often included physical coercion; in both continental and English marriage manuals, the authors use the metaphor of breaking a horse for teaching a wife obedience. Though the opinions of women who read such works were not often recorded, one can tell somewhat from private letters that women knew they were expected to be obedient and silent, for they often excused their

*A Wise Woman*, circa 1525, woodcut by Anton Woensam, depicting the traditional Catholic model for the good wife

actions when they did not conform to the ideal. Such letters also indicate, however, that women's view of the ideal wife was one in which competence and companionship were as important as submissiveness.

**A High Calling.** The Protestant exhortation to marry was directed to both sexes, but particularly to women, for whom marriage and motherhood were a vocation as well as a living arrangement. Marriage was a woman's highest calling, even though it brought physical dangers and restraints on her free-

dom. The words of the Tudor homily on marriage, which the crown required to be read out loud regularly in all English churches, make this clear: "Truth it is, that they [women] must specially feel the griefs and pains of matrimony, in that they relinquish the liberty of their own rule, in the pain of their travailing [for example, labor and delivery], in the bringing up of their own children, in which offices they be in great perils, and be grieved with many afflictions, which they might be without, if they lived out of matrimony." Despite their recognition of the disadvantages of marriage for women, however, most Protestants urged all women to marry, for they thought no woman had the special divine gift of freedom from sexual urges.

**The Pulpit Speaks.** The opinions of Protestant leaders about marriage and women were not contained simply in written works, but were communicated to their congregations through marriage sermons and homilies; because people in many parts of Europe were required to attend church, there was no way they could escape hearing them. Their opinions were also reflected in woodcuts and engravings that illustrated religious pamphlets, an important tool in the spread of Protestant ideas. The ideal woman appears frequently in both sermons and illustrations: she sits with her children, listens to a sermon or reads the Bible, is dressed soberly, and has her hair modestly covered. Negative depictions were also utilized: nuns who blindly follow their superiors; priests' concubines; prostitutes or women dressed extravagantly buying expensive rosaries; and disobedient wives being beaten by their husbands.

**A Differing Doctrine.** The Catholic response to the challenge of the Protestant reformers included a rejoinder to the elevation of marriage. As with so many other issues, Catholic thinkers reaffirmed traditional doctrine and agreed that the most worthy type of Christian life was one both celibate and chaste. There was some disagreement about the relative importance of the three traditional purposes of marriage, with more liberal thinkers stressing the emotional bond between the couple more than procreation or the avoidance of sin, but in general there was a strong sense that all sexuality, including marital, was sinful and disruptive. Catholic authors also realized that despite exhortations to celibacy, most women in Europe would marry, and so they wrote marriage manuals to counteract those offered by Protestants. The ideal wife they described was exactly the same as that proposed by Protestant authors—obedient, silent, pious—and their words give clear indication that they still regarded women as totally inferior. Fray Luis de Leon, for example, in the late-sixteenth-century treatise *La perfecta casada* (The Perfect Wife), comments: "When a woman succeeds in distinguishing herself in something praiseworthy, she wins a victory over any number of men who have given themselves over to the same endeavor. For so insignificant a thing as this which we call woman never undertakes or succeeds in carrying out anything essentially worthwhile unless she be drawn to it, and stimulated, and encouraged by some force of incredible resoluteness which either God, or some singular gift of God, has placed within her soul."

**Jewish Views on Marriage.** In Jewish opinion, like Protestant, all women should marry, and the qualities of the ideal wife had changed little since Old Testament times. According to Isaac ben Eliakim, author of a Yiddish ethical manual written in the early seventeenth century and frequently reprinted, the ideal wife was thrifty, cheerful, obedient, never jealous, and always responsive to her husband's physical and emotional needs. Though this definition differs little from contemporary Christian opinion, the tone of the manual is a

---

## "HE IS NOT TO HIT HER TOO HARD"

Local, territorial, and national law codes all regulated aspects of married life, including financial matters and spousal relations. The following is a section from the Law Code of the territory of Salzburg, Austria, from 1526.

It is to be accepted that both spouses have married themselves together from the time of the consummation of their marriage, body to body and goods to goods. . . .

The husband shall not spend away the dowry or other goods of his wife unnecessarily with gambling or other useless frivolous pastimes, wasting and squandering it. Whoever does this is guilty of sending his wife into poverty. His wife, in order to secure her legacy and other goods she has brought to the marriage, may get an order requiring him to pledge and hold in trust for her some of his property. In the same way he is to act in a suitable manner in other things that pertain to their living together and act appropriately toward her. If there is no cause or she is not guilty of anything, he is not to hit her too hard, push her, throw her or carry out any other abuse. For her part, the wife should obey her husband in modesty and honorable fear, and be true and obedient to him. She should not provoke him with word or deed to disagreement or displeasure, through which he might be moved to strike her or punish her in unseemly ways. Also, without his knowledge and agreement she is not to do business [with any household goods] except those which she has brought to the marriage; if she does it will not be legally binding . . .

The first and foremost heirs are the children who inherit from their parents. If a father and mother leave behind legitimate children out of their bodies, one or more sons or daughters, then these children inherit all paternal and maternal goods, landed property and movables, equally with each other . . .

Women who do not have husbands, whether they are young or old, shall have a guardian and advisor in all matters of consequence and property, such as the selling of or other legal matters regarding landed property. Otherwise these transactions are not binding. In matters which do not involve court actions and in other matters of little account they are not to be burdened with guardians against their will.

Source: Franz V. Spechtler and Rudolf Uminsky, eds., *Die Salzburger Landesordnung von 1526*, Göppinger Arbeite zur Germanistik, Nr. 305 (Göppinngen: Kümmerle, 1981), pp. 119, 154, 197. Translation by Merry Wiesner-Hanks.

---

*The Fiancés*, by Lucas Van Leyden, circa 1519 (Fine Arts Museum, Strasbourg)

bit less dreary, commenting practically, "If you treat him like a king, then he, in turn, will treat you like a queen," rather than dwelling on obedience as a religious duty.

**Sources:**
Eric Josef Carlson, *Marriage and the English Reformation* (Oxford & Cambridge, Mass.: Blackwell, 1994).

Steven Ozment, *When Fathers Ruled: Family Life in Reformation Europe* (Cambridge, Mass.: Harvard University Press, 1983).

Margo Todd, *Christian Humanism and the Puritan Social Order* (Cambridge & New York: Cambridge University Press, 1987).

## PATTERNS OF MARRIAGE

**Foundation of Society.** Marriage was the lived experience of most people during this period. Marital patterns and customs varied widely throughout Europe, but in all places and at all times the vast majority of women and men married at least once, and society was conceived of as a collection of households, with a marital couple, or a person who had once been a spouse, as the core of most households.

**Delayed Matrimony.** Marital patterns varied according to region, social class, and to a lesser degree religious affiliation. The most dramatic difference was between the area of northwestern Europe, including the British Isles, Scandinavia, France, and Germany, and eastern and southern Europe. In northwestern Europe, historians have identified a marriage pattern unique in the world, with couples waiting until their mid- or late twenties to marry, long beyond the age of sexual maturity, and then immediately setting up an independent household. Husbands were likely to be only two or three years older than their wives at first marriage, and though households often contained servants, they rarely included more than one family member who was not a part of the nuclear family. In most of the rest of the world, including southern and eastern Europe, marriage was between teenagers who lived with one set of parents for a long time, or between a man in his late twenties or thirties and a much younger woman, with households again containing several generations. The northwestern European marriage pattern resulted largely from the idea that couples should be economically independent before they married, so that both spouses spent long periods as servants or workers in other households—saving money and learning skills—or waited until their parents had died and the family property was distributed. This period of waiting was so long, and the economic requirements for marriage set so high, that many people did not marry until they were in their thirties, and a significant number never married at all.

**Freedom of Choice.** Did this late age of marriage mean that people had a greater say in who they married? This question has been hotly debated, particularly for England, which provides most of the available research sources in the form of family letters, diaries, and official records regarding marriage. There are many instances, particularly among the upper classes, in which there were complicated marriage strategies to cement family alliances and young people were more or less forced to marry whom their parents wished. Among the lower classes, neighbors and public authorities often helped to determine whether a couple would marry—the neighbors through pressuring courting couples, and officials by simply prohibiting unions between individuals regarded as too poor. Historians who have focused on the middle classes, however, assert that though couples may have received advice or even threats, they were largely free to marry who they wished.

**Good Choices.** In some ways this debate sets up a false dichotomy because both sides tend to focus on cases in which there was clear and recorded conflict between individuals and family or community. In the vast majority of marriages, the aims of the people involved and their parents, kin, and community were the same; the best husband was the one who could provide security, honor, and status, and the best wife was one who was capable of running a household and assisting her husband in his work. Therefore, even people who were the most free to choose their own spouses, such as widows and widowers or individuals whose parents had died, were motivated more by pragmatic concerns than romantic love. This consideration is not to say that their choice was unemotional, but that the need for economic security, the desire for social prestige, and the hope for children were as important as sexual passion. The love and attraction a person felt for a possible spouse could be based on any combination of these concerns.

**Jewish Unions.** The link, rather than conflict, between social and emotional compatibility was recognized explicitly by Jewish authorities. Jewish marriages in most parts of Europe continued to be arranged throughout this period, and the spouses were both young. Authorities expected love to follow, however, and described the ideal marriage as one predestined in heaven. Judaism did allow divorce, which was then sometimes justified on the grounds that the spouses had obviously not been predestined for each other.

**Promoting Marriage.** One of the key ideas of the Protestant Reformation was the denial of the value of celibacy and championing of married life as a spiritually preferable state. One might thus expect religion to have had a major effect on marriage patterns, but this conclusion is difficult to document, in large part because all the areas of Europe that became Protestant lie within northwestern Europe. There were many theoretical differences. Protestant marriage regulations stressed the importance of parental consent more than Catholic ones, allowed the possibility of divorce with remarriage in cases of adultery or impotence

and in some areas also for refusal to have sexual relations, deadly abuse, abandonment, or incurable diseases such as leprosy; Orthodox courts in eastern Europe allowed divorce for adultery or the taking of religious vows. The numbers of people who actually used the courts to escape an unpleasant marriage were small, however, and apparently everywhere smaller than the number of couples who informally divorced by simply moving apart from one another. Women in particular more often used the courts to attempt to form a marriage, such as in breach-of-promise cases, or to renew a marriage in which their spouses had deserted them, than to end one. The impossibility of divorce in Catholic areas was relieved somewhat by the possibility of annulment and by institutions that took in abused or deserted wives; similar institutions were not found in Protestant areas.

**Influences on Marriage.** Social class had a larger impact than religion on marital patterns. Throughout Europe, rural residents married earlier than urbanites and were more likely to live in complex households of several generations or of married brothers and their families living together. They also remarried faster and more often. Women from the upper classes married earlier than those from the lower, and the age difference between spouses was greater among upper-class people. People who had migrated in search of employment married later than those who remained at home, and chose someone closer to their own age.

**Common Trends.** Along with significant differences, there were also similarities in marriage patterns throughout Europe. Somewhere around one-fifth of all unions were remarriages for at least one of the partners, with widowers much more likely to remarry than widows and to do so sooner than their female counterparts. The reasons for this disparity differ according to social class: wealthy or comfortable widows may have seen no advantage in remarrying, for doing so would put them under the legal control of a man again, and poor widows, particularly elderly ones, found it difficult to attract marriage partners. Women of all classes were expected to bring a dowry to their marriage, which might consist of some clothing and household items (usually including the marriage bed and bedding) for poor women, or vast amounts of cash, goods, or property for wealthy brides; in eastern Europe the dowry might even include serfs or slaves. This dowry substituted in most parts of Europe for a daughter's share of the family inheritance, and increasingly did not include any land, which kept property within the patrilineal lineage. Laws regarding a woman's control of her dowry varied throughout Europe, but in general a husband had the use, but not the ownership, of it during his wife's lifetime, though of course if he invested it unwisely this distinction did not make much difference. However, a woman could sue her husband if she thought he was wasting her dowry, and many courts took control of the wife's property from her spouse. The 1526 Law Code from the territory of Salzburg gives one example of how a woman could do this, as well as other provisions

There were many poems and prose works describing ideal wives and husbands or providing advice on domestic relations published in the sixteenth and seventeenth centuries. The following is a typical one.

You that intend the honourable life,
And would with joy live happily in the same,
Must note eight duties do concern a wife,
To which with all endeavour she must frame:
  And so in peace possess her husband's love,
  And all distaste from both their hearts remove.

The first is that she have domestic cares,
Of private business for the house within,
Leaving her husband unto his affairs,
Of things abroad that out of doors have been
  By him performed, as his charge to do,
  Not busy-body like inclined thereto.

Nor intermedling as a number will,
Of foolish gossips such as do neglect,
The things which do concern them, and too ill,
Presume in matters unto no effect:
  Beyond their element when they should look,
  To what is done in kitchen by the cook.

Or unto children's virtuous education,
Or to their maids, that they good housewives be,
And carefully contain a decent fashion,
That nothing pass the limits of degree:
  Knowing her husband's business from her own,
  And diligent do that, let his alone.

The second duty of the wife is this,
(Which she in mind ought very careful bear).
To entertain in house such friends as his
As she doth know have husband's welcome there:
  Not her acquaintance without his consent,
  For that way jealousy breeds discontent.

* * *

Third duty is, that of no proud pretense,
She move her husband to consume his means,
With urging him to needless vain expense,
Which toward the counter or to Ludgate leans,
  For many idle housewives (London knows)
  Have by their pride been husband's overthrows.

A modest woman will in compass keep,
And decently unto her calling go,
Not diving in the frugal purse too deep,
By making to the world a peacock show:
  Though they seem fools, so yield unto their wives,
  Some poor men do it to have quiet lives.

Fourth duty is, to love her own house best,
And be no gadding gossip up and down,
To hear and carry tales amongst the rest,
That are the news reporters of the town:
  A modest woman's home is her delight,
  Of business there, to have the oversight.

At public plays she never will be known,
And to be tavern guest she ever hates,
She scorns to be a street wife (idle one)
Or field wife ranging with her walking mates:
  She knows how wise men censure of such dames,
  And how with blots they blemish their good names.

* * *

Fifth duty of a wife unto her head,
Is her obedience to reform his will,
And never with a self-conceit be led
That her advice proves good, his counsel ill:
  In judgement being singular alone,
  As having all the wit, her husband none.

* * *

When as the husband bargains hath to make,
In things that are depending on his trade,
Let not wife's boldness power unto her take,
As though no match were good but what she made:
  For she that thus hath oar in husband's boat,
  Let her take breech, and give him petticoat.

**Source:** Samuel Rowlands, *The Bride* (London, 1617).

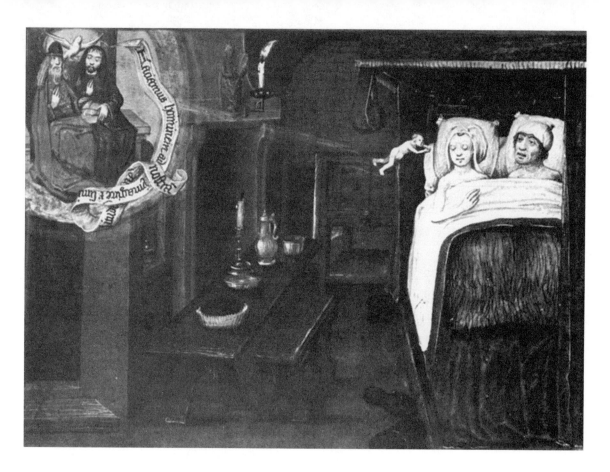

"Lex Epous," depicting the conjugal ideal, an illumination from *Traites Divers de Jean Mansel* (Bibliothèque Nationale, Paris, MS. Arsenal 5206, fol. 174)

regarding property in marriage. This action was clearly something done only as a last resort, as it meant a woman had to admit publicly her husband was a wastrel or spendthrift. During the late medieval period, women appear to have been free to bequeath their dowries to whomever they chose, but in many parts of Europe this right was restricted during the sixteenth century to prevent them from deeding property to persons other than male heirs.

Sources:

Eric Josef Carlson, *Marriage and the English Reformation* (Oxford & Cambridge, Mass.: Blackwell, 1994).

Francis William Kent, *Household and Lineage in Renaissance Florence: The Family Life of the Capponi, Ginori, and Rucellai* (Princeton: Princeton University Press, 1977).

Richard Wall, Jean Robin, and Peter Laslett, eds., *Family Forms in Historic Europe* (Cambridge & New York: Cambridge University Press, 1983).

## PATTERNS OF MARRIED LIFE

**Male Dominance.** The increasing legal emphasis on the male lineage paralleled a rising concern among male religious, literary, and political writers with the authority and role of the male head of household. With few exceptions, Catholics, Protestants, and Jews; English, French, Italians, and Germans; highly educated humanists and illiterate street singers; all agreed that women should be subservient and that husbands should rule over their wives. Indeed, there is no other issue that

men of this period—and apparently most women—agreed upon so completely. This notion was not only an intellectual construct, but shaped legal codes throughout Europe, with married women always under the legal control of their husbands, and adult single women and widows often required to have a male guardian oversee their legal and financial affairs. Husbands were generally given the right to coerce or punish their wives physically, and courts rarely supported a wife's leaving her husband even for serious physical abuse.

**Women's Role.** At the same time, some writers also stressed the wife's authority over children and servants, viewing her as a coruler in the household with her husband. First Protestants and then Catholics stressed that being a wife was the proper vocation for a woman, one worthy of respect from her husband and other household members. The authors of marriage manuals took great care to emphasize the importance of mutual affection between spouses, regarding it as one of the great benefits of marriage.

**Actual Relations.** What about actual marital relations? Did husbands and wives show more or less affection for one another than modern couples? Which idea was followed more in practice, that of husbandly authority or that of mutual respect? Studies that address these questions have been undertaken in various parts of Europe for the last twenty years, but historians have not reached a consensus. Some of them see the Renaissance and Reformation family as patriarchal and authoritative, and relations between spouses, as well as between parents and children, as cold and unfeeling. Others have found that many people suffered serious depression at the loss of a spouse or child; they expected a marriage to include affection and companionship and were distressed when it did not. Examples of abusive spouses and of mutually caring relationships both abound, so it is difficult to make any blanket generalizations.

**Status Earned.** Marriage was the clearest mark of social adulthood for both women and men; for men, marriage often meant that they could now be part of the governing body of their village or town, a role from which unmarried men were excluded. Craft guilds generally required that master-craftsmen be married, because the assistance of a wife was needed to feed and clothe the journeymen and apprentices, purchase supplies, and sell the finished product. Married men were also seen as more stable and less likely to engage in wild behavior.

**A Matriarch's Place.** For women, marriage meant that they would gain authority over dependent members of the household. Middle-class urban women also began, during the early modern period, to redefine what it meant to be a "housewife." After the Protestant Reformation, the wives of Protestant pastors were often the leaders in the creation of this expanded domestic role. Medieval urban "housewives" had had little time for purely domestic labor; cooking was simple, cleaning tasks were few, and many domestic tasks such as baking and laundry were hired out. This workload began to change in the sixteenth century, when foodstuffs were more likely to come into households in a less-finished state and middle-class households contained more consumer goods that needed cleaning and care. Of necessity, the time spent by middle-class women on domestic tasks expanded, particularly as things that had been unavailable or unimportant in the Middle Ages— glass windows, a stone floor instead of a dirt one, and several courses at dinner—became important signs of middle-class status. Now the ideal wife was not simply one who showed religious virtues such as piety and modesty, but also economic ones such as order, industriousness, and thrift; the ideal husband was one who could provide appropriate consumer goods for his household. This division of labor shows up clearly in the poem of advice, titled *The Bride* and published by Samuel Rowlands in London in 1617. The sixteenth century was seen as a time of growing prosperity among the middle classes; the fruits of that prosperity, the "middle-class lifestyle," were determined, and to a large degree created, by middle-class married women, using the disposable income produced by their own labor and that of their husbands and children.

Sources:

Alan Macfarlane, *Marriage and Love in England: Modes of Reproduction, 1300–1840* (Oxford & New York: Blackwell, 1986).

Michael Mitterauer and Reinhard Sieder, *The European Family: Patriarchy and Partnership from the Middle Ages to the Present*, translated

Cistercian nuns in their convent, detail from a thirteenth-century French tombstone at St. Stephan's Shrine

by Karla Oosterveen and Manfred Hörzinger (Chicago: University of Chicago Press, 1982).

Lyndal Roper, *The Holy Household: Women and Morals in Reformation Augsburg* (Oxford: Clarendon Press, 1989; New York: Oxford University Press, 1989).

## UNMARRIED PEOPLE

**Class Strategies.** What about people who could not or chose not to get married? In eastern Europe, with a much earlier average age at first marriage, the number of people who never married was small, and most of them were in convents or monasteries. In southern Europe, most men married, but wealthy or middle-class women who chose not to marry, or whose parents could not raise a dowry large enough to obtain an appropriate husband, ended up in convents, whose standards about strict living were often not very high so that the women lived the same comfortable lifestyle they would have on

The vast majority of people in Renaissance and Reformation Europe married, and there are few comments from those who did not marry about the single life. This poem is one of the few, by Anna Bijns, a writer and poet in Antwerp.

Unyoked Is Best! Happy the Woman Without a Man

How good to be a woman, how much better to be a man!
Maidens and wenches, remember the lesson you're about to hear.
Don't hurtle yourself into marriage far too soon.
The saying goes: "Where's your spouse? Where's your honor?"
But one who earns her board and clothes
Shouldn't scurry to suffer a man's rod.
So much for my advice, because I suspect—
Nay, see it sadly proven day by day—
'T happens all the time!
However rich in goods a girl might be,
Her marriage ring will shackle her for life.
If however she stays single
With purity and spotlessness foremost,
Then she is lord as well as lady. Fantastic, not?
Though wedlock I do not decry:
Unyoked is best! Happy the woman without a man.

Fine girls turning into loathly hags—
'Tis true! Poor sluts! Poor tramps! Cruel marriage!
Which makes me deaf to wedding bells.
Huh! First they marry the guy, luckless dears,
Thinking their love just too hot to cool.
Well, they're sorry and sad within a single year.
Wedlock's burden is far too heavy.
They know best whom it harnessed.
So often is a wife distressed, afraid.
When after troubles hither and thither he goes
In search of dice and liquor, night and day,
She'll curse herself for that initial "yes."
So, beware ere you begin.
Just listen, don't get yourself into it.
Unyoked is best! Happy the woman without a man.

A man oft comes home all drunk and pissed
Just when his wife had worked her fingers to the bone
(So many chores to keep a decent house!),
But if she wants to get in a word or two,
She gets to taste his fist—no more.
And that besotted keg she is supposed to obey?

Why, yelling and scolding is all she gets,
Such are his ways—and hapless his victim.
And if the nymphs of Venus he chooses to frequent,
What hearty welcome will await him home.
Maidens, young ladies: learn from another's doom,
Ere you, too, end up in fetters and chains.
Please don't argue with me on this,
No matter who contradicts, I stick to it:
Unyoked is best! Happy the woman without a man.

A single lady has a single income,
But likewise, isn't bothered by another's whims.
And I think: that freedom is worth a lot.
Who'll scoff at her, regardless what she does,
And though every penny she makes herself,
Just think of how much less she spends!
An independent lady is an extraordinary prize—
All right, of a man's boon she is deprived,
But she's lord and lady of her very own hearth.
To do one's business and no explaining sure is lots of fun!
Go to bed when she list, rise when she list, all as she will,
And no one to comment! Grab tight your independence then.
Freedom is such a blessed thing.
To all girls: though the right Guy might come along:
Unyoked is best! Happy the woman without a man.

Prince,
Regardless of the fortune a woman might bring,
Many men consider her a slave, that's all.
Don't let a honeyed tongue catch you off guard,
Refrain from gulping it all down. Let them rave,
For, I guess, decent men resemble white ravens.
Abandon the airy castles they will build for you.
Once their tongue has limed a bird:
Bye bye love—and love just flies away.
To women marriage comes to mean betrayal
And the condemnation to a very awful fate.
All her own is spent, her lord impossible to bear.
It's *peine forte et dure* instead of fun and games.
Oft it was the money, and not the man
Which goaded so many into their fate.
Unyoked is best! Happy the woman without a man.

**Source:** Kristiaan P. G. Aercke, "Anna Bijns: Germanic Sappho," in Katharina M. Wilson, *Women Writers of the Renaissance and Reformation* (Athens: University of Georgia Press, 1987), pp. 382–383.

the outside. In 1552 in Florence, for example, there were 441 male friars and 2,786 nuns out of a population of 59,000; the difference resulted not from women's great religious fervor, but from a staggering increase in the size of the dowry required for a middle- or upper-class marriage. Families placed their daughters in convents instead of trying to find husbands for them, because convent entrance fees were much lower than dowries.

**Unmarried Poor.** Entrance fees for convents were too high for poor women, however, and special institutions were opened in Italian cities by the Catholic Church and municipal governments for young, attractive unmarried women to allow them to earn a dowry and thus perhaps a husband. Women whose marriage chances were seen as unlikely in any case were also often sent to conventlike religious institutions, where they did not take formal vows and worked at spinning or sewing to support themselves. Unmarried poor women and men also worked as domestic servants for their entire lives, living in the household of their employer and therefore being under his control.

**Few Opportunities.** In the cities of northwestern Europe, the number of unmarried people was more significant; historians estimate that between 10 to 15 percent of the northwestern European population never married during this period, and that in some places this figure may have been as high as 25 percent. Unmarried people, especially women, often moved to cities in search of employment as domestic servants or in cloth production; they frequently found work spinning wool, a situation reflected in the gradual transformation of the word "spinster" from a label of occupation to an epithet for an unmarried woman. The types of employment open to most unmarried people were generally poorly paid; households headed by unmarried people (and widows) were always the poorest in any city; unattached women, in particular, often had to live together in order to survive.

**Controlling the Unwed.** In the late Middle Ages, city governments worried about how to keep unmarried people from needing public welfare, and in the sixteenth century, cities began to view single women living independently as a moral, as well as an economic problem. They were "masterless," that is, not under the authority of a responsible older man. It was during this period that greater stress was being laid on the authority of the husband and father, and unmarried people living alone were perceived as a possible threat to public safety and the proper social order. Unmarried men were regarded as more likely to get drunk and engage in fights than married men, and spinsters risked getting pregnant out of wedlock. Laws were passed forbidding unmarried people to move into cities and ordering them to find a place of residence with a married couple. (Such laws were also passed, and enforced, in colonial New England.) Men who were not married were not allowed to become masters in craft guilds or participate in city government. Both Protestant and Catholic authorities increasingly viewed marriage as "natural"—for everyone in Protestant areas and for all those who were not clergy or members of a religious order in Catholic areas—so that people who did not marry were somehow "unnatural" and therefore suspect.

**Open Opposition.** Some men were proud of their decision to remain unmarried, flaunting their independence to authorities and moving around frequently rather than settling down. It was more difficult for women to move, and some women internalized the stigma attached to never being married. This was particularly true for middle- and upper-class Protestant women, whose letters discuss ways they fulfilled their Christian duties without being a wife or mother, such as taking care of elderly parents or serving the needy. Not all women agreed that marriage was preferable, however, and some celebrated their unmarried state. The most eloquent expression of this situation was a poem by Anna Bijns, a sixteenth-century Antwerp poet.

Sources:

Judith M. Bennett and Amy M. Froide, eds., *Singlewomen in the European Past, 1250–1800* (Philadelphia: University of Pennsylvania Press, 1999).

John Henderson and Richard Wall, eds., *Poor Women and Children in the European Past* (London & New York: Routledge, 1994).

Margaret R. Sommerville, *Sex and Subjection: Attitudes to Women in Early-Modern Society* (London & New York: Arnold, 1995).

## VALUABLE ASSETS: CHILDREN

**Importance of Children.** In all religious traditions, the procreation of children was viewed as one of the most important functions of marriage and childless couples were viewed with pity. Childlessness hit women particularly hard, because it was invariably seen as the woman's fault. This unfortunate condition is one of the reasons that suggestions about how to promote fertility through diet, exercise, potions, and charms were extremely common in midwives' manuals and advice books for women. Childless men could test their fertility outside of marriage with little public condemnation (though not officially condoned, adultery—if one's wife was barren—was rarely punished), but childless wives did not have this opportunity.

**Pregnancy.** Determining whether one was pregnant was not an easy matter, however. The stopping of menstrual periods opened up the possibility, but midwives' manuals and private medical guides cautioned women against regarding this as a clear sign, because it may also have been the result of other medical conditions. Nausea, breast enlargement, and thickening around the middle also pointed toward pregnancy, but only at quickening—that is, when the mother could feel the child move within her body, which usually happens during the fourth or fifth month—and only then was the mother regarded as verifiably pregnant. Until the late eighteenth century on the Continent and the nineteenth century in England, quickening was also viewed as the point at which a child gained a soul, so that charges of abortion could not be brought against a woman who had not yet quickened. This legal definition affected the way women thought about their own pregnancies, for they did not describe a miscarriage

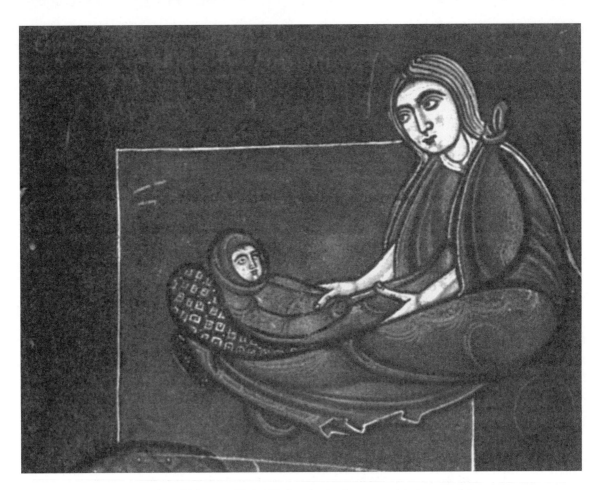

A mother with her swaddled child, illumination from an undated manuscript
(Corpus Christi College, Cambridge, MS 2, f. 147 v)

before quickening as the end of a pregnancy or the death of a child, but as the expulsion of blood curds, leathery stuff, or wrong growths. Pregnancy was not a condition affirmed externally and visually, or with modern home pregnancy tests and ultrasound screening, but internally and tactilely, with only the mother able to confirm that quickening had happened.

**Advice for Pregnancy.** Once a woman suspected or knew she was pregnant, she received a great amount of advice. The first midwives' manuals in most European languages, published in the sixteenth century, contained advice for prenatal care for the mother as well as the handling of deliveries. These manuals were reprinted for centuries, and new ones were published in the seventeenth century, but their advice for expectant mothers changed little. Much of what they recommended was common sense: pregnant women should eat moderately of nourishing foods, including a good amount of proteins, and avoid foods that make them nauseous or that are highly spiced; they should moderate their drinking and avoid strong liquors; they should get regular exercise but avoid strenuous lifting; and they should wear low-heeled shoes and loosen their lacing or corsets. The advisability of sexual intercourse during pregnancy was debated, as was the practice of letting blood from pregnant women. Many of their sugges-

tions have to do with the mental, rather than strictly physical, well-being of the expectant mother and stem from a strong belief in the power of the maternal imagination. Both learned and uneducated people in Europe believed that what a woman saw or experienced during pregnancy could affect the child. The desire to drink red wine or eat strawberries might lead to children with red birthmarks; being frightened by a hare or longing to eat rabbit caused harelip; and sudden frights might cause a miscarriage or deform the fetus in some way. Birth defects were regularly attributed to bad experiences during pregnancy, or to a woman's frequent contact with animals.

**Nursing.** The vast majority of women during this period nursed their own children, often until they were more than two years old and on demand rather than on a set schedule. Women who could not produce their own milk, as well as middle- and upper-class women in many parts of Europe, relied on wet nurses, the very wealthy hiring the nurse to come into their own homes, and the rest sending the child to the home of the wet nurse, often for two or three years. Though by the eighteenth century this practice came to be viewed as a sign of the heartlessness and decadence of wealthy women, it actually stemmed from the fact that nursing was incompatible with many of their familial and social duties. Wealthy women were pressured to produce

Advice books for children and young people were common types of literature in the Renaissance and Reformation. The following selection comes from the advice book of Elizabeth Grymeston, written for her son and published in London about 1600.

To her loving son, Bernie Grymeston

My dearest son, there is nothing so strong as the force of love; there is nothing so forcible as the love of an affectionate mother to her natural child; then no mother can either more affectionately show her nature, or more naturally manifest her affection, than in advising her children out of her own experience to eschew evil and incline them to do that which is good . . . leave thee this portable *veni mecum* for thy counsellor in which thou maist see the true portraiture of thy mother's mind, and find something either to resolve thee in thy doubts, or comfort thee in thy distress; hoping that, being my last speeches, they will be kept in the conservance of thy memories which I desire thou will make a register of heavenly meditations . . .

I have prayed for thee that thou mightest be fortunate in two hours of thy life time: in the hour of thy marriage, and at the hour of thy death. Marry in thine own rank, and seek especially in it thy contentment and preferment: let her neither be so beautiful as that every liking eye shall level at her; nor yet so brown as to bring thee to a loathed bed. Defer not thy marriage till thou comest to be saluted with a *God speed you sir,* as a man going out of the world after forty; neither yet to the time of *God keep you sir* whilst thou art in they best strength after thirty; but marry in the time of you *are welcome sir,* while thou art coming into the world. For seldom shalt thou see a woman out of her own love to pull a rose that is full blown, deeming them always sweetesy at the first opening of the bud . . . Let thy life be formal, that thy death may be fortunate: for he seldom dies well that liveth ill.

To this purpose as thou hast within thee reason as thy counsellor to persuade or dissuade thee, and thy will as an absolute prince with a *fiat vel evetetur;* with a *let it be done or neglected;* yet make thy conscience thy *censor morum [censor of behavior]* and chief commander in thy little world: let it call reason to account whether she have subjected herself against reason to sensual appetites. Let thy will be censured, whether her desires have been chaste or as a harlot she hath lusted after her own delights. Let thy thoughts be examined. If they be good, they are of the spirit (quench not the spirit), if bad, forbid them entrance: for once admitted, they straightways fortify and are expelled with more difficulty than not admitted.

My desire is that thou mightest be seasoned in these precepts in thy youth that the practice of thy age may have a taste of them. And because that is incident to quick spirits to commit rash attempts, as ever the love of a mother may challenge the performance of her demand for a dutiful child, be a bridle to thyself to restrain thee from doing that which indeed thou maist do: that thou maist the better forbear that which in truth thou oughtest not to do; for *he seldom commits deadly sins, that makes a conscience of a venial scandal.* Thou seest my love hath carried me beyond the list I resolved on, and my aching head and trembling hand have rather a will to offer, than ability to afford, further discourse. Wherefore with as many good wishes to thee, as good will can measure, I abruptly end, desiring God to bless thee with sorrow for thy sins, thankfulness for his benefits, fear of his judgment, love of his mercies, mindfulness of his presence: that living in his fear, thou maist die in his favour, rest in his peace, rise in his power, remain in his glory for ever and ever.

Thine assured loving mother, *Elizabeth Grymeston*

Source: Elizabeth Grymeston, *Miscelanea. Meditations. Memoratives* (London: Melch. Bradwood for Felix Norton, 1604).

---

many heirs, and people seem to have been aware of the contraceptive effects of lactation; they were advised that nursing would ruin their physical attractiveness; and they were taught that sexual intercourse would corrupt their milk and that their first duty was to their husbands.

**Wet Nurses.** The decision to hire a wet nurse was often made not by the woman herself but by her husband, who made a contract with the wet nurse's husband for her services. Wet nurses were chosen with great care; those from rural areas who had borne many healthy children were favored. Psychological and moral qualities were also taken into consideration, for it was thought that an infant gained these attributes through the nurse's milk; after the Reformation, for example, parents inquired about the religious affiliation of any prospective nurse, for Catholic parents feared the corruption caused by Protestant milk, and vice versa. The wet nurse and her husband had to agree to refrain from sexual relations during the period of the contract, for it was thought that pregnancy tainted a woman's milk.

**Detrimental Effects.** Along with the children of the wealthy, wet nurses also cared for the children of the poor; communities hired wet nurses to suckle foundlings and orphans. Many of these poor children died, as did many of the more privileged, some no doubt because of neglect or carelessness, but also because the wet nurses themselves were generally impoverished and took on more children than they had enough milk; in many cases these women had sent their own infant to an even poorer woman in order to take on children to nurse in the first place. Wet nurses often became fond of the children they suckled and were reluctant to return them to their parents, sometimes remaining with the children as servants or companions into adulthood. Some historians have speculated that children in Europe also suffered emotional distress because of the wet-nursing system; frequent changes in wet nurses, the absence of their biological mother, and permanent separation from the wet nurse at weaning could prevent small children from forming good relationships with women. Because infant feelings affect later psychological development, wet nursing has been seen as contributing to negative ideas about women, particularly their fickleness and changeability. The irony of these possible consequences is the fact that husbands made the decision about how a child would be nursed.

**Deep Attachments.** Being a parent is, of course, an emotional and intellectual experience as well as a physical one, and, though some historians have argued that parents were cold and uncaring, mothers and fathers generally became deeply attached to their children. The deaths or illnesses of their children often led people into depression or even suicidal despair, and those who showed no attachment to their offspring were viewed as mentally disturbed. Parents' concern over their children became particularly acute during their own illnesses, leading several people to write advice books for their children in case they should die.

Sources:
Valerie A. Fildes, *Breasts, Bottles, and Babies: A History of Infant Feeding* (Edinburgh: Edinburgh University Press, 1986).

Fildes, ed., *Women as Mothers in Pre-industrial England: Essays in Memory of Dorothy McLaren* (London & New York: Routledge, 1990).

Richard C. Trexler, *Power and Dependence in Renaissance Florence,* volume 1: *The Children of Renaissance Florence* (Binghamton, N.Y.: Medieval & Renaissance Texts & Studies, 1993).

## WORK AND LEISURE

**Different Patterns.** In the contemporary world, families in urban areas and in most parts of the developed world rarely work as a unit; economically, families are units of consumption—buying items they use as a group such as cars, houses, and food—rather than units of production. They are also bound together by emotional ties, expected to develop love for one another and to engage in leisure-time activities together. This model is in many ways the reverse of the pattern in Renaissance and Reformation Europe; in that era, most families were units of production, raising crops or making items together. (In this way, they resemble families in less-developed areas in which most people still make their living by farming.) During what little free time they had, family members generally sought out their peers, rather than other family members, for recreational activities.

**Child's Play.** Though work began at an early age for most children, very young children and older children during nonwork hours played with toys and engaged in games that were not that different from modern devices. They had dolls, balls, hoops, tops, sticks, and marbles. Because the houses of the poor were small, children played outside much of the time. Adolescents often congregated together in single-sex groups, the girls most likely in someone's house or yard and the boys in the streets or alleys. Boys were often given toy weapons for both play and practice, and girls were given dolls to train them for their later roles as mothers; even girls who entered convents at a young age, and thus were expected to remain unmarried and childless, played with and owned dolls. From evidence in Florence, girls in convents viewed these dolls as representing the infant Jesus, and saw caring for them as a sign of religious devotion.

**Entertainment.** There were no large-scale public games or professional entertainments in Europe during this period, as there had been during the Roman Empire, but traveling entertainers occasionally sang,

A man warming his feet, from a late-fifteenth-century missal at the abbey of Montierneuf, Poitiers (Bibliothèque Nationale, Paris, Latin 873)

Festivals and celebrations in the Renaissance occasionally got out of hand and led to tragedy. The following is the report of events at a 1393 wedding, recorded by the French royal chronicler Jean Froissart.

There was in the king's household a Norman squire . . . who thought of the following piece of pleasantry to amuse the king and the ladies. . . . For the ball that night, he had six cloth coats made and then had them covered with flax that looked like hair in shape and color. He dressed the king in one, [four young nobles in others], . . . and the sixth one he wore himself. When they were all dressed up by having the coats sewed around them, they appeared to be wild men *(hommes sauvages),* for they were covered with fur from head to foot. This masquerade pleased the king greatly, and he expressed his pleasure to his squire. It was so secretly contrived that no one knew anything about it but the servants who attended on them.

Sir Evan de Foix [one of the masqueraders] . . . said to the king:

"Sire, I advise you to give strict orders that no one come near us with torches, for if but a spark falls on the coats we are disguised in, the flaxen fur will catch fire, and we will burn up before anyone can do anything about it." "In God's name," the king said, "you speak wisely and well, and it shall be done.". . . Then he sent for one of the sergeants at arms who was on duty at the door and told him: "Go to the ballroom and in the king's name command that all the torches be placed on the far side of the room and that none of them come near the six wild men who are about to enter." [It was done, but] soon after this, the duke of Orleans entered, attended by four knights and six torches. He knew nothing of the king's orders or the six wild men who were about to make their appearance. First he watched the dancing and the women, then he began dancing vigorously himself. . . .

At this point the king of France made his appearance with the five others, all dressed like wild men and covered from head to foot with flaxen fur as fine as human hair. No one present could recognize them. Five of them were attached to one another and the king came in first and led the others into the dance. When they entered the hall, everyone was so intent on watching them that the order about torches was forgotten. Fortunately the king left his companions and, impelled by his youth, went to show himself off to the ladies; passing first in front of the queen, he went along next to the duchess of Berry, who was his aunt and younger than he was. For fun the duchess took hold of him and wanted to know who he was, but the king stood there and would not give his name. "You won't ever escape me," the duchess said, "unless I know your name first."

Just then the other five wild men met a great accident caused by the duke of Orleans . . . who was too eager to know who they were. As the five were dancing, he lowered the torch that one of his servants held in front of him, bringing it so close that the flame ignited the flax. And flax, as you know, cannot be put out once it is afire. Moreover, the flames heated the pitch with which the flax was attached to the cloth. The costumes themselves soon burst into flame, for they were covered with pitch and flax, were dry and delicate, and were all yoked together.

Those who wore them were in agony and began to cry out horribly, The situation was so dangerous that no one dared to get near them, although several knights did come up and try to strip the burning costumes off them, but the pitch burned their hands and disabled them for days thereafter. One of the five, Nantouillet, figured that the bar must be nearby, so he broke away and threw himself into a washtub full of water for rinsing out cups and plates. This saved him; otherwise he would have been burned to death like the others, and he still was badly injured.

Source: Jean Froissart, *Chroniques,* translated in Thomas Johnes, *Chronicles of England, France, Spain, and the Adjoining Countries,* volume 2 (London: W. Smith, 1839), pp. 532–533.

danced, and performed plays or puppet shows at markets or fairs. By the sixteenth century in some cities of Europe these traveling players had settled into permanent acting troupes operating out of theaters, such as those made famous by Shakespeare's plays, or in the courts of Europe's monarchs. Attending the theater was not an option for most people, however, whose opportunities to see or hear any professional entertainment were very limited.

**Time for the Soul.** The one leisure-time activity that families often engaged in together was worship. Well-to-do fathers often held morning and evening prayers, or, after the development of the printing press, read out loud to the entire household—servants included—from the Bible or other religious literature. Families attended church services together, the wealthier of them often sitting in special family pews. Religious ceremonies such as weddings, baptisms, and funerals marked major family events, and in Catholic areas the anniversaries of family members' deaths were also the occasion of special ceremonies. Particularly after the Reformation, time spent not working was supposed to be spent in training the soul, whether in the family group, the larger congregation, or, if one were literate, reading and praying on one's own.

**Festivals.** Religious holidays also provided an occasion for community-wide festivals. Most areas celebrated specific saints' days, which were also often linked to important points in the agricultural cycle such as harvest or planting. The whole community would turn out for the festivals, which offered social companionship and a break from the bleakness of work. At festivals and weddings, people of all social classes often engaged in wild public parties and celebrations, wearing costumes and playing games; occasionally these activities led to tragedy. Protestant and Catholic reformers often criticized the drinking, gambling, and dancing that accompanied festivals and weddings, and occasionally succeeded in having festivals prohibited and weddings restricted to solemn ceremonies in a church. In a few instances, such as in Geneva under John Calvin's governance, reformers also banned certain leisure-time activities that occurred outside of festivals, such as gambling, cardplaying, and plays.

**Controlling the Disorderly.** Religious disapproval of raucous recreational activities was accompanied by a growing distaste on the part of upper- and middle-class people for public drinking and brawling. Historians have labeled this view the "reformation of manners" or the "civilizing process," which they also trace through long-term changes in habits of eating, washing, blowing one's nose, spitting, and urinating. These natural functions were increasingly regarded as inappropriate in public by upper- and middle-class Europeans, who began to see polished manners as a sign of their superiority over the common masses. They increasingly carried out their bodily functions and their recreational activities in private, the first in their own homes and the second either in the home or in palaces or other exclusive sites separated from the general public. Events such as those described at the royal wedding of 1393 would have been unusual, almost unthinkable, for a party involving upper-class people in 1600. For members of the elite, family quarrels and concerns also gradually became private matters, to be kept out of the public eye and away from public institutions such as courts whenever possible.

Sources:

Peter Burke, *Popular Culture in Early Modern Europe* (London: Temple Smith, 1978; New York: Harper & Row, 1978).

Norbert Elias, *The Civilizing Process,* translated by Edmund Jephcott (New York: Urizen, 1978).

Ralph A. Houlbrooke, *The English Family, 1450–1700* (London & New York: Longman, 1984).

## YEARS ADVANCED: WIDOWHOOD AND OLD AGE

**A Deep Loss.** The death of a spouse and old age are usually linked in the modern world, but they were not necessarily in Renaissance and Reformation Europe, for people became widowed at all ages and might easily be widowed several times during their lives. The demise of a mate brought a more dramatic change in status for women than it did for men, for women's link to the world of work was often through their husbands, so that his death affected their opportunities for

A diseased grandfather holding his grandson, portrait by Italian painter Domenico Ghirlandaio; circa 1480 (Musée du Louvre, Paris)

making a living while the death of a wife did not. One can see this distinction in the fact that the word for "widower" in most European languages derives from the word for "widow," whereas the more common pattern is for the female designation to derive from the male—princess from prince, actress from actor. "Widower," in fact, does not enter common usage until the eighteenth century, when people began to think about the loss of a spouse more as an emotional than an economic issue.

**Widows.** In many parts of the world women who became widowed returned to their birth families or entered the household of a brother or brother-in-law, but in most areas of Europe, widows became heads of households themselves and were forced to find some way to survive and to support their dependent children. Not surprisingly, widowhood generally brought a decline in a woman's economic status, with the poorest households in towns and villages headed by elderly widows; because the death of his wife did not mean a man had to change occupations, widowers did not become significantly poorer. During times of economic hardship, crime by widows, mostly petty theft, increased, though authorities tended to treat them less harshly than other lawbreakers.

**Some Opportunities.** Whereas widowhood often brought economic adversity for women, it also gave them a wider range of action throughout most of Europe. Widows who had inherited money or property from their husbands or who had

People used wills to divide their goods among family and friends, and, if they were Christian, to make bequests to the church. These wills often give us a glimpse of the values and ideas of people who were not wealthy or powerful and who otherwise left no trace of their lives in the historical record.

**Will of John Jalander, Cranbrook, April 18, 1476**

To the High Altar of Cranbrook for tithes [church taxes] forgotten, 6 pence.

To the construction of the new chapel of the Blessed Mary, 6 shillings/8 pence.

To my godson Nicholas Pend, 6 pence.

To each godchild, 4 pence.

To the repair of the roadway, where most needed, between the crossroads of Hertle and Turneden, 40 pence.

To my wife Alice, my best cow.

To Richard Cryspe, another cow.

To my son Robert, a cow and a calf.

The rest of my goods, to my wife Alice and Richard Cryspe.

Executors: my wife Alice and Richard Cryspe.

To my wife Alice, all my lands and tenements for life.

After her decease, my trustees shall deliver to my son Robert, the said property as a free holding on the con-

dition that the said Robert pay his brother William £ 12 within 6 years after the death of my wife, at the rate of £2 per year.

To be sold to pay my debts and bequests: a garden with a passage to it, called Smythisfield.

Should my son Robert die before age 22 and without lawful issue, then I will that my daughter Alice Cryspe have a croft of land called Loggecroft, as a free holding. And should my daughter Alice die without legitimate heirs of her body, then I will that the said croft be sold and the money be used for charitable works.

And if, as just said, my son Robert should die before 22 without lawful issue, all my lands and tenements (except the croft bequethed to Alice) shall be sold. The money therefrom shall be distributed as follows:

to my son William, 26 shillings/8 pence

to a suitable priest to celebrate in the church of Cranbrook for a year, for my soul and the souls of the faithful departed, £ 10.

the remainder of the money shall be used to buy a chalice for the church of Cranbrook.

Robert shall pay Margaret, the daughter of my daughter Alice, 26 shillings/8 pence towards her marriage.

My wife shall have her quarters in my house, and a fire in the hall, and her easement there, and the use of the bakehouse, for 8 years.

Source: Jules de Launay, *Abstracts of Cranbrook Wills Proved in the Diocesan Courts of Canterbury* (Canterbury, U.K.: English Records Collection, 1984), p. 28.

---

received their dowry back at his death were usually quite free to invest or spend it as they wished. Aristocratic widows were often active managing their families' business affairs, and identified the rights and privileges attached to their position as *theirs,* and not simply belonging to them in trust for their sons. Widowhood could also place a woman in a position of great power over her children, deciding the amount of dowry for her daughters and assisting her sons in gaining positions of political influence.

**Challenging Convention.** This social and economic independence was disturbing to many commentators, who viewed men being in charge as the norm, and they recommended that widows remarry. Remarriage was also troubling, however, for

it lessened a woman's allegiance to the family of her first husband and could have serious economic consequences for the children of her first marriage. It might also give a wealthy widow what was seen as an inappropriate amount of power over her spouse. Laws regarding widows often reflect this ambivalence. In many parts of Europe laws made remarriage more attractive by requiring a widow to have a male guardian cosign all financial transactions, even religious donations, and giving him power over her own children. The same law code might also make it less attractive by stipulating that a widow could lose all rights over her children, including the right to see them. Not wishing to contemplate either the independence or remarriage of their wives, lawmakers were thus attempting somehow to keep a widow dependent on the family of her first husband.

**Reality.** In actual practice, whether a widow remarried or not was determined more by her economic and personal situation than by laws or theoretical concerns. Younger widows remarried much more readily than older ones, and widows with few children more readily than those with many. The opposite is true in the case of widowers; those with many children were most likely to remarry, and to do so quickly. In general, widowers were far more likely to remarry than widows; French statistics indicate that 50 percent of widowers remarried, as opposed to 20 percent of widows.

**The Elderly.** Widowhood was a clear legal status, but "old age" in the early modern period is harder to define. For women, the best marker might be menopause, which usually occurred somewhere in a woman's forties; the mean age at which women in northwestern Europe bore their last child was forty. Because life expectancy was less than in modern times, however, even if people stopped having children before forty they still had offspring in their households for most of their later years of life. Older men and women whose children had all left home generally continued to live on their own as long as possible. Evidence from England indicates that middle-class children were more likely to assist their elderly parents by providing them with servants so that they could stay in their own households rather than taking them in; the elderly lived with their married children only among the poor. Though earlier periods are often romanticized as a time when the elderly were cherished for their wisdom and experience, this concept was not necessarily so. In many parts of Europe, parents made formal contracts with their children to assure themselves of a certain level of material support, or included clauses in their wills. In her advice book for women written in 1407, the French author Christine de Pizan reminds young women that "you owe honor to the elderly, so it follows that at all costs you must avoid mocking them and doing or saying injurious, derisive, or outrageous things, or bad things of whatever kind. Do not displease or find fault with them, as some wicked young people do who are very much to be reproached for it, who call them 'old boys' or 'old biddies'."

**Support of the Elderly.** Older women were generally more in need of public support than older men, in part because their spouses were less likely or able to care for them than were the wives of older men, who were generally younger or had no way to leave an ailing spouse. Younger relatives were also more willing to take in elderly men than women; older women often formed joint households with other elderly female relatives or simply acquaintances to pool their resources and expenses, a practice almost unknown among men. The higher percentage of elderly female welfare recipients may have also been partly the result of the fact that there were simply more older women than men around. Despite the dangers of childbirth, female life expectancy seems to have been gradually growing longer than that for men throughout this period; by the eighteenth century in France, female life expectancy at birth was about thirty-four and male about thirty-one.

**New Challenges.** Aging brought physical as well as economic changes, and there is evidence that these were viewed as more of a problem for women than men already in the sixteenth century. Postmenopausal women were widely believed to experience increased sex drive, which might even lead them to seek demonic lovers in order to satisfy themselves. They were believed to emit vapors from their mouths that could cause nursing women's milk to dry up or animals and children to sicken. They were thought to be especially concerned with the lessening of their physical attractiveness, for a Spanish physician's remedies to combat wrinkles were all directed to women. At the very end of life, both men and women were viewed as physically and mentally infirm; many illustrations of the ages of man show the man in the seventh (and last) stage as bent over and supported by a cane, and in William Shakespeare's play *As You Like It,* the character Jacques describes this stage as "second childishness and mere oblivion."

Sources:

Sandra Cavallo and Lyndan Warner, eds., *Widowhood in Medieval and Early Modern Europe* (New York: Longman, 1999).

Joan Larsen Klein, ed., *Daughters, Wives and Widows: Writings by Men about Women and Marriage in England, 1500–1640* (Urbana: University of Illinois Press, 1992).

Joel T. Rosenthal, *Old Age in Late Medieval England* (Philadelphia: University of Pennsylvania Press, 1996).

# SIGNIFICANT PEOPLE

## LEON BATTISTA ALBERTI

### 1404-1472

### MATHEMATICIAN, WRITER, ARCHITECT

**Rough Beginnings.** Leon Battista Alberti was an Italian scholar, architect, and author, one of those people who might easily be called a "Renaissance Man." Born 14 February 1404, he was the illegitimate son of a Florentine banker, but, like many young men in Renaissance Italy whose fathers were wealthy, the circumstances of his birth did not keep him from gaining an excellent education. He studied Latin as a young boy, began studying literature from a private teacher at the age of eleven, and at fourteen or fifteen went to the University of Bologna to study law. Shortly afterward his father died, and he was apparently cheated out of his inheritance by his cousins, though this situation also did little to affect his rise in status. He began writing Latin plays and dialogues and met many prominent humanists and writers, who were impressed by his talents.

**Literary Roots.** When he was about twenty-four, Alberti completed his legal studies and took a position as the secretary to one of the pope's assistants. Along with his work as a papal official and secretary, Alberti spent much of his time writing works on decidedly non-religious topics. He wrote two works in Italian on love, which were very popular; they were printed and translated into other languages during his lifetime. (The first printing presses were introduced into Italy in the 1450s.) He wrote a long dialogue, divided into four parts, on the family, which would be copied and plagiarized by many people for years to come.

**On the Role of the Patriarch.** In this dialogue *Della famiglia* (On the Family), Alberti has various men of his clan discuss such matters as education, marriage, and household management. The book begins with a long discussion of the duties of the father, in which one of the characters quotes his own father's advice to male family members:

> The duty of a father is not only, as they say, to stock the cupboard and the cradle. He ought, far more, to watch over and guard the family from all sides, to check over and consider the whole company, to examine all the practices of every member, inside and outside the house, and to correct and improve every bad habit. He ought preferably to use reasonable rather than indignant words, authority rather than power. He should appear to give wise counsel where this would help more than commands, and should be severe, rigorous, and harsh only where the situation really calls for it. He ought in every thought always to put first the good, the peace, and the tranquillity of his entire family. This should be a kind of goal toward which he, using his intelligence and experience, guides the whole family with virtue and honor. He knows how to steer according to the wind's favor, the waves of popular opinion, and the grace given him by his fellow citizens, toward the harbor of honor, prestige, and authority.

**A Mother's Role.** Considerations of the duties of a mother are much more brief, but they do appear in the second part of the book:

> For the procreation of children, no one can deny that man requires woman. Since a child comes into the world as a tender and delicate creature, he needs someone to whose care and devotion he comes as a cherished trust. This person must also nourish him with diligence and love and must defend him from harm. Too much cold or too much sun, rain, and the wild blowing of a storm are harmful to children. Woman, therefore, did first find a roof under which to nourish and protect herself and her offspring. There she remained, busy in the shadow nourishing and caring for her children. And since woman was busy guarding and taking care of the heir, she was not in a position to go out and find what she and her children required for the maintenance of their life. Man, however, was by nature more energetic and industrious, and he went out to find things and bring what seemed to him necessary. Sometimes the man remained away from home and did not return as soon as his family expected. Because of this, when he came back laden, the woman learned to save things in order to make sure that if in the future her husband stayed away for a long time, neither she nor her children would suffer. In this way it seems

clear to me that nature and human reason taught mankind the necessity of having a spouse, both to increase and continue generations and to nourish and preserve those already born.

**Speaking to the People.** It may seem unusual to us that a man who was officially a priest and employee of the pope wrote on subjects such as love and the family, but Alberti, like all Renaissance authors, based his writings not on personal experience but on classical Greek and Roman writings that provided both the form and content. The dialogue form, particularly one in which a group of men sit around and discuss a particular topic, had been a common literary device since the time of Plato, and many Renaissance writers found it appealing. Alberti broke with other authors in that he wrote his major works in Italian so that they could be read by people who were not literate in Latin. He revised his treatise on the family to make it even more readable, and he later composed the first grammar of the Italian language to assist people as they learned to read.

**Varied Contributions.** Alberti continued to compose a variety of types of works in both Italian and Latin, and in the 1430s he became interested in artistic issues as well, first writing about and then trying his hand at architecture. He composed a treatise on painting in 1435, in which he discussed issues of linear perspective, and he received a commission to design an arch that would support an equestrian statue of Nicolo III d'Este, a member of a powerful Italian noble family and the ruler of the city-state of Ferrara. His work in architecture continued throughout the rest of his life; his architectural writings expanded into a ten-volume work, *De re aedificatoria*, which covered every aspect of the subject—proportion, symmetry, decoration, proper restoration of existing buildings, and urban planning. He designed new buildings, such as the Palazzo Rucellai in Florence, a huge mansion for the Rucellai family, and he planned the restorations and renovations of several churches in Florence, Rome, and Mantua. In some ways his architectural work was similar to his writings on love and the family, in that it was based on theoretical principles and not on day-to-day experiences. Just as he wrote about the family from afar—never marrying or having children himself—he did not supervise the building of his architectural designs but left that to others.

**Codes.** Toward the end of his life Alberti became interested in a new subject, cryptology, and wrote a treatise on how to devise codes, probably to assist a friend, Leonardo Dati, who was in charge of encoding papal correspondence so that it could not be read if it came into the wrong hands. Historians of codes, in fact, often regard Alberti as the father of Western cryptology, as he was the first to invent a code with multiple letter substitutions. As in his writings on other subjects, he drew on many different traditions and yet developed his own ideas. This blend of classical and modern elements marks all of Alberti's work, both written and architectural, and is what has led contemporary historians to view him as a model Renaissance man.

Sources:

Leon Battista Alberti, *The Family in Renaissance Florence,* translated by Rene Neu Watkins (Columbia: University of South Carolina Press, 1969).

Franco Borsi, *Leon Battista Alberti,* translated by Rudolf G. Carpanini (Oxford: Phaidon, 1977).

Joan Kelly, *Leon Battista Alberti: Universal Man of the Early Renaissance* (Chicago: University of Chicago Press, 1969).

# GIOVANNI DI SER LODOVICO DELLA CASA

## 1420-1480

### AND

# LUSANNA DI GIROLAMO

## c. 1420-?
## ROMANTIC LITIGANTS

**Examined Lives.** The easiest thing for historians to research is the public life of famous people. The private lives of such individuals are also often open to view; because they were important, private documents such as letters and diaries were saved, and other people often commented about their private lives. Thus, much more is known about the marriages and child-rearing practices of the elite—monarchs and their heirs—than about anyone else. Because of their standing, however, the personal and family life of wealthy and powerful individuals cannot be considered typical, and one cannot make generalizations based only on their experiences.

**Legal Disputes.** The private lives of ordinary people from the Renaissance and Reformation period are largely lost to us, as they rarely leave a trace in the records. One of the times that they do become visible, however, is when events led to a legal dispute. The situation involving Giovanni di Ser Lodovico della Casa and Lusanna di Girolamo is one of those cases. In the summer of 1455, Lusanna, the daughter of an artisan and the widow of a cloth maker, brought a case to the Archbishop's court in Florence, requesting the marriage of Giovanni to another woman be ruled invalid because he was already married to her. (The case was actually brought to court by a male legal representative, called a procurator, because women did not usually argue their own cases; Lusanna was the plaintiff, however.) She asserted that she had married Giovanni after the death of her first husband and wanted the marriage recognized. The case was extremely complex, involving the testimony of twenty-nine people and eventually leaving three hundred pages of records handwritten by a notary. Though it is also not typical—most people's marriages did not lead to long legal disputes—the parties in this case were very ordinary, and through their words and those of the witnesses, one can get a better glimpse of commonly held Renaissance ideas about love and marriage than from sources that concern elite people. The exploration of a single individual or situation is termed "micro-history," and it has become a popular type of historical study.

**The Case.** According to the testimony of witnesses in the case, Lusanna was an extremely beautiful woman; Giovanni was infatuated with her even before her first husband died, and immediately after the death began following her and showing up at her house. Her father would only allow the relationship to continue if the couple were married, but Giovanni would not agree to a public marriage as his family was much wealthier and more prominent than Lusanna's and his father would disinherit him if he learned of it. The witnesses for Lusanna testified that there had been a secret ceremony, in which the couple had formally agreed to marry in front of a friar and several other people, and an exchange of rings. If this ritual indeed had happened, it was a legal marriage according to Christian law, which simply required consent of the spouses and witnesses for a marriage to be binding. The witnesses for Giovanni testified in response that there had been a sexual relationship between the two, but that it had begun before Lusanna's first husband died and had never involved marriage. They swore that Lusanna was promiscuous, with other lovers besides Giovanni, and that she and her family were inventing the story of the wedding to get Giovanni's money; they hinted that she might even have poisoned her first husband. Both sides charged the other with bribing witnesses, and attacked the honor and credibility of opposing witnesses. The case dragged on for several months, with many affidavits and petitions. Finally the archbishop, who was well versed in church law, ruled that the wedding had indeed taken place, that Giovanni's second marriage was annulled, and that he should acknowledge Lusanna publicly as his wife and treat her as one should treat a wife. The case did not end there, however. Giovanni's family was linked by connections of business and friendship to the powerful Medici family of Florence, and they used their influence with the pope to get the archbishop's decision reversed. The marriage of Giovanni and Lusanna was declared null and void; Giovanni stayed with his other wife, had several children by her, and continued to carry out business activities for his family business all over Europe. Lusanna disappeared from the records; she may have entered a convent or married a man from outside of Florence.

**Lessons.** What can this case teach us about love and marriage in the Renaissance? It is clear that despite the church's prohibition of adultery, love affairs involving married individuals were quite common. Giovanni's side, not Lusanna's, brought up his having an affair with her before her husband died. For young men who were members of the upper classes, such affairs were common. Well-to-do men usually did not marry until they were in their thirties, and frequently had liaisons with servants, prostitutes, or lower-class women; censuses from Florence list hundreds of illegitimate children living in the households of their fathers or in the foundling homes. (In addition to the illegitimate son of his father, Giovanni himself had two illegitimate sons who lived with him, whose mothers are not listed but were neither Lusanna's nor his wife's.) Women involved in sexual relationships outside of marriage were criticized more than men, and some of the witnesses called Lusanna a "bad woman" (*mala femina*), but they did not refuse to associate with her; other men sought her hand in marriage after the death of her first husband. What was unusual in this case was the fact that she held out for Giovanni rather than accepting any of these other men and ultimately brought her case to court. The witnesses on her side attribute this action to her love for Giovanni (and describe his public displays of affection for her as well), and those on his side attribute this stubbornness to her desire for wealth and higher social standing. From their words, it is clear that both love and money made sense as motives for marriage in the Renaissance.

Sources:

Gene Brucker, *Giovanni and Lusanna: Love and Marriage in Renaissance Florence* (Berkeley: University of California Press, 1986).

David Herlihy and Christiane Klapisch-Zuber, *Tuscans and their Families: A Study of the Florentine Catasto of 1427* (New Haven: Yale University Press, 1985).

# ELISABETH OF BRAUNSCHWEIG

## 1510-1558
### REGENT AND EVANGELIST

**Early Marriage.** The life of Elisabeth of Braunschweig, author of four books and many hymns, as well as the ruler of a small German state, demonstrates the ways in which religious, political, and family concerns could all intersect. She was born in 1510 as the third child of Archduke Joachim I of Brandenburg and his wife Elisabeth. When she was fifteen her father arranged for her to be married to the widowed Duke Erich I of Braunschweig-Calenberg, who was forty years her senior. Despite the age difference, the spouses appear to have gotten along, and Elisabeth bore four children—three daughters and a son—over the next fifteen years. In 1540 Erich died, naming Elisabeth as the regent for his young son, also named Erich.

**A Volatile Situation.** Relations among the rulers of the many states of the Holy Roman Empire were often competitive and unfriendly, with all seeking to advance their own interests and expand their own territories, making and breaking alliances with great frequency as the fortunes of allies and enemies rose and fell; one of Elisabeth's key aims was keeping Braunschweig-Calenberg strong for her son. Beginning in the 1520s, religious differences made the situation even more volatile, as rulers within the Holy Roman Empire opted to side with Martin Luther or remain loyal to the pope. In some cases their choices were the results of real religious convictions, in others of practical assessments of the political situation, and in still others—and probably most commonly—a mixture of the two.

**A Mother's Trials.** Elisabeth of Braunschweig was right in the middle of this upheaval, both because of her family connections and her own religious convictions. In 1527 her mother became Lutheran when her husband was away; he was furious when he returned, and contemplated executing or divorcing her or imprisoning her for life. Her mother decided to flee, and spent the next eighteen years wandering, sometimes in great poverty, from one sympathetic Lutheran court or household to another, refusing to come back to Brandenburg until her husband assured her she could worship in the manner she chose. Even his death in 1535 did not convince her to return, as her sons had remained Catholic; only their subsequent turn to Lutheranism and personal promises of financial support convinced her to come back.

**Conversion.** Elisabeth of Braunschweig's own religious conversion occurred about a decade after her mother's, apparently in 1538 after a visit by her mother. As was common for rulers interested in the new Lutheran teachings, she invited a well-known Lutheran pastor, Antonius Corvinus, to the court to instruct her further. Her husband's reaction was far different from that of her father toward her mother, and he let her follow her own beliefs. Elisabeth got the opportunity to make her religious convictions a public rather than a private matter two years later when Erich died and she became the regent for her twelve-year-old son. With the assistance of Corvinus, she introduced Lutheran services and beliefs, instructing her subjects to behave morally and obey her as they would their own mothers.

**A Literary Bent.** Elisabeth was not only a mother toward her subjects, but also to her own children, and she wrote personal books of instruction for her son and daughters. They were not designed to be published, but Elisabeth expected them to be passed around to other family members and handed down to subsequent generations. She included advice about marriage, and was actively engaged in arranging the marriages of her children. She linked her oldest daughter Elisabeth and her son Erich to Protestant noble families through marriage, and in 1546 she remarried, to Duke Poppo of Henneberg, the younger brother of her daughter's husband. The most brilliant marriage—in terms of the hierarchy of nobility—was the marriage between her second daughter Anna Maria and Albrecht of Prussia, which took place in 1550. Like her mother, Anna Maria married a widower four decades her senior, and Elisabeth apparently hoped this marriage would prove to be as satisfactory as hers had.

**Shifting Alliances.** Despite her mother's hopes and advice, Anna Maria's marriage was not happy, but Elisabeth had more serious problems. The year after he took over rule, Erich II reconverted to Catholicism, banished most of the Lutheran ministers, imprisoned Corvinus in solitary confinement, and went off to fight for the emperor in Spain. Erich's officials were ordered to maintain strict Catholicism, and he paid no attention to his mother's impassioned letters begging him to

release Corvinus and warning of God's wrath if he persisted in disobeying her and treating the Protestant clergy harshly. Though he paid her no heed, Erich II was influenced by political circumstances and shifting levels of power, and on returning from Spain he decided to become a Protestant again and ally himself with various Protestant princes. Elisabeth appears to have been pleased by this decision, but she also wanted to assure Erich's hold on his territory and so pledged all of her money, jewels, and property to finance a war against her main opponent, the Catholic Heinrich of Braunschweig-Wolfenbüttel. Heinrich and his allies won, and he confiscated all of Elisabeth's property. She moved with her youngest daughter Katharina to Hanover, and was forced to borrow money from its citizens in order to have food and shelter. Her bitter letters to her son, sons-in-law, and brothers during this period complain of little food, wood, or clothing, and a series of illnesses; following the advice of his relatives, her husband stayed on his own lands and did not help her.

**Frustrated Plans.** In 1555 the emperor was finally persuaded by various nobles to allow Elisabeth to leave Hanover, and she alternated living with her husband and on one of her own estates. Her lack of control over her own circumstances was made dramatically clear several years later, when Erich dealt his mother a final blow by arranging a marriage between her beloved daughter Katharina and a Catholic nobleman from Bohemia. Elisabeth did not approve of the marriage—nor did Katharina—but she decided to attend anyway. Erich misled her about when the wedding was to take place, and, as she was on her way, Elisabeth learned it had already occurred and that Katharina had left for Bohemia with her husband. Elisabeth returned to her property and died several months later.

**Assessment.** It would be easy to assess Elisabeth of Braunschweig's life as a failure and a good example of the inability of women, including those of the highest social class, to shape their own situations. She was married by her father to a man more than three times her own age, and the fact that she and her husband grew to care for one another was a fortunate accident. Her son rejected what she clearly regarded as her major accomplishment—the introduction of the Protestant Reformation into Braunschweig—and spent his life following the emperor on military campaigns, thus rejecting her advice about how to be a good ruler. Anna Maria, for whom she had provided such careful advice became alienated from her husband and died young. Elisabeth's second husband followed the wishes of his family rather than defending her, and the child she felt closest to was whisked away without her being able to say goodbye. If one takes a somewhat longer view, however, Elisabeth's legacy becomes more positive. All of Braunschweig eventually became Lutheran and has remained so. Elisabeth was one of the many female rulers in Renaissance and Reformation Europe, such as Isabella in Castile, Mary and Elizabeth Tudor in England, Mary Stuart in Scotland, Catherine de' Medici in Italy, and Anne of Austria in France, who were influential in creating a new and more active role for matriarchs.

Sources:
Roland H. Bainton, *Women of the Reformation in Germany and Italy* (Minneapolis: Augsburg Publishing House, 1971).

Margaret L. King, *Women of the Renaissance* (Chicago: University of Chicago Press, 1991).

# VERONICA FRANCO

## 1546-1591
### COURTESAN AND POET

**Early Life.** Veronica Franco's life suggests both the possibilities and limitations for an educated woman in Renaissance Italy and also highlights the ways in which intellectual connections and literary or artistic talents occasionally worked to offset a life that otherwise went against convention. Franco was the daughter of Francesco Franco, a Venetian merchant, and Paola Fracassa, a woman not his wife who made her living arranging sexual partners and companions for leading Venetian men. Franco's father did not deny that she was his daughter, but officially recognized her, which meant that, like her father, she was considered a citizen of Venice and had an official coat-of-arms. Her father arranged for her to be educated by private tutors along with her brothers, and from a young age she showed great skill in writing.

**Multiple Relationships.** As was to be expected for a young woman in Italy at this time whose father was quite well-off, she was married when she was less than twenty to another Venetian citizen, but she separated from him soon afterward and apparently never had any children by him. At that point she began a series of relationships with leading intellectuals and writers in Venice, providing them with intellectual and emotional companionship; she had six children by several different fathers, although, as was common in this period, only half of her children survived infancy.

**The Honest Courtesan.** Franco never denied her activities, and she became known as an "honest courtesan," one of a handful of women in the large cities of France or Italy during this period who achieved prominence and near-respectability through their sexual connections with nobles, intellectuals, and officials. Such courtesans were often glamorized in plays and poetry as they dressed and lived lavishly and seemed to flaunt the normal expectations for sexual morality in women. This

assessment was true to some degree, but the chances for such a life were slim, possible only to those with beauty, talent, and usually family connections. Courtesans often came from well-to-do urban families or the lesser nobility, and were often born out of wedlock; they and their families realized that they had greater opportunities for gaining wealth and stature through informal relations with prominent men than through marriage. Compared with the lives of most women, the life of a courtesan seemed elegant and independent, but their status was still set primarily by the men to whom they were attached, just as a married woman's status was set by her husband.

**An Unusual Independence.** Franco was able to be more independent than many courtesans because of her own abilities. Her literary talents brought her to the attention of Domenico Venier, an acclaimed poet and the head of the most important literary academy in Venice, where writers and other learned individuals came together to read their work and discuss other cultural topics. Venier became her patron, inviting her to the meetings of the academy and other gatherings and encouraging her literary pursuits. Franco began her publishing career with a type of work viewed as especially appropriate for a woman: she requested poems from male writers and gathered them into an anthology honoring prominent Venetian men.

**Literary Boldness.** In 1575 Franco published a book of her own poetry, *Terze rime*, in which she was frank about her own life, including its sexual aspects. This boldness was unusual in a female writer, for most women of the Renaissance and Reformation periods who wrote chose religious topics, and those who did write about secular topics rarely discussed sexual issues. She was attacked by some of her male acquaintances for this boldness, perhaps because it went against what they expected women to be both in real life and in poetry. In real life, women were expected to be chaste and obedient; in poetry, they were expected to be reserved, beautiful, and unattainable—the inspiration for men's poetry about love and longing, not women who felt love or sexual passion themselves.

**Letters.** Along with her poetry, in 1580 Franco also published a volume of fifty letters addressed to various prominent individuals. Such volumes were common for Renaissance humanists, who saw the letter as an opportunity to show off their literary skills as well as a means to convey information. Most people who wrote letters during this period did not expect them to be private, and they took great care in crafting their prose. Letters were often handed around at literary gatherings or read aloud, with readers or listeners commenting on their style and skill. The letters in Franco's collection were, in fact, never sent to their addressees, but, as was the case with similar collections published by other writers, simply published as a collection, allowing their author to describe her life and provide advice to the well-to-do men to whom they are addressed.

**A Troubling Accusation.** In the same year that her book of letters was published to great acclaim, Franco was accused by her son's tutor of performing magical incantations and was brought to trial by the Venetian Inquisition. The trial was a sensation and it damaged Franco's reputation, even though she was eventually cleared of all charges through her own efforts and those of her supporter Venier. She died in poverty at the age of forty-five, having outlived her patrons and no longer able to attract the attention of new ones. Some of her loss of wealth was the result of the plague in Venice, but it was also a common situation for women who had made their reputations as courtesans. Franco is unusual in that her literary works have survived her and have lasting importance as significant and beautiful examples of Renaissance love poetry.

Sources:

Veronica Franco, *Poems and Selected Letters,* edited and translated by Ann Rosalind Jones and Margaret F. Rosenthal (Chicago: University of Chicago Press, 1998).

Rosenthal, *The Honest Courtesan: Veronica Franco, Citizen and Writer in Sixteenth-Century Venice* (Chicago: University of Chicago Press, 1992).

# CARITAS PIRCKHEIMER

## 1466-1532
### ABBESS AND HUMANIST

### AND

# WILLIBALD PIRCKHEIMER

## 1470-1530
### LAWYER AND HUMANIST

**Elite Roots.** Caritas and Willibald Pirckheimer were a sister and brother, members of a prominent family from Nuremberg in southern Germany, renowned for their education and concern for religion. Their lives point out the ways in which gender shaped the opportunities for learning open to men and women, but also demonstrate the ways in which family background and personal characteristics could work to lessen gender differences. Caritas and Willibald were born into a family that prized education and cultural achievements. Their great-grandfather and grandfather both studied law in Italy, where they became acquainted with the new style of learning, termed humanism, that prized reading and study of texts in their original languages rather than depending on the opinions of more recent commenta-

tors. Their grandfather was a member of the city council of Nuremberg, and also wrote philosophical treatises and studied the works of Italian humanists. He encouraged his son Johannes (circa 1440–1501), the father of Caritas and Willibald, to study further and to buy books; eventually Johannes came to own one of the largest private libraries in all of Germany, which he passed on to his son, and that has survived largely intact until today, now part of a public library in Germany.

**Opportunities for Learning.** Caritas and Willibald thus grew up in a household centered on education and literary pursuits. Their father was employed as a lawyer for the bishop of a city near Nuremberg and made a good income; he gathered other people who were interested in learning into an informal discussion group that met in his own house—termed a sodality—and the children were often welcome at these meetings. Along with Caritas and Willibald, seven of Johannes's other daughters survived infancy.

**Divergent Paths.** During adolescence the paths of Caritas and Willibald diverged in terms of their living situations, though not in terms of their values and ideas. Like his ancestors, Willibald studied law and Greek philosophy in Italy and returned to Nuremberg to become a member of the city council, a position he held for more than twenty-five years. He married in 1495, and his wife quickly had several children; she died in childbirth in 1504, leaving him a widower with five small daughters. In contrast to the usual pattern for widowers, Willibald did not remarry but found another solution to the problem of raising his daughters: he placed three of them when they were quite young in one of the local convents, already the home of several of his sisters.

**Studies Pursued.** Willibald continued his humanistic studies throughout his life, teaching himself Greek to a level at which he could skillfully translate it into Latin. He also became friends with many cultural and intellectual leaders of Germany, including the painter Albrecht Dürer (who was also from Nuremberg), and the Dutch humanist scholar Desiderius Erasmus; they corresponded with him and joined the Pirckheimer sodality when they were in Nuremberg. Willibald's letters to them survive and provide much information about the personal and intellectual connections among Germany's leading thinkers.

**Chosen Path.** In the late 1510s, discussion among educated people in Nuremberg as elsewhere in Germany began to revolve around the ideas of Martin Luther and other reformers. Willibald acquired many of Luther's writings for his library, and he became personally acquainted with Luther in 1518 when the reformer stopped in Nuremberg. When in 1525 the city of Nuremberg decided to break with the Catholic church and become Protestant, however, Willibald was not convinced that this path was the correct one; he hoped to reform the Catholic Church from within rather than split it apart. His desires for reconciliation and peace among different religious factions made him seem old-fashioned, and at the end of his life he resigned from the city council and sought comfort in his classical studies.

**Convent Studies.** Caritas was also caught in the middle of the Reformation, and this movement has made her better known than her brother. Along with six of her seven sisters, she entered a convent in Nuremberg when she was still a girl; four of the Pirckheimer sisters later became abbesses, as did two of their nieces (Willibald's daughters). For many decades Caritas's life in the convent was much like that in her father's house, filled with study, writing, translations of classical works, and correspondence with other learned people throughout Europe. Though the convent cut her off from the world to some extent, it also gave her the opportunity and time to continue her studies, and she gained a reputation as one of the most-learned women in Europe.

**Disrupted Life.** Convent walls could not protect her and the other nuns from the disruptions of the Reformation, however. In 1524, as various families in Nuremberg were rejecting Catholicism and becoming Protestant, they also rejected Catholic teaching about the value of convent life and decided to remove their daughters from the Saint Klara convent where Caritas was abbess. These girls had been in the convent since they were young and did not wish to leave. Caritas attempted to prevent their removal, but the families had the backing of the city council. The girls were dragged out forcibly, with Protestant residents of the city looking on and shouting their encouragement. Caritas describes the scene in her memoirs—titled the *Denkwürdigkeiten:*

> All three children fell around me howling and screaming and begging me not to abandon them, but unfortunately I could not help them . . . The mothers told the children that it was their duty according to God's commandment to obey them, that they wanted them to come out to save their souls from hell . . . The children cried that they did not want to leave the pious, holy convent, that they were absolutely not in hell, [and that] although they were their mothers, they certainly were not obliged to obey them in matters that went against their souls. . . . Each of them was pulled by four people—two in front pulling, two behind pushing . . . the wretched children called out in loud voices to the people and complained to them that they had suffered violence and injustice, that they had been pulled out of the cloister forcibly.

Though these girls were not allowed to return to the convent, the violence of these events disturbed many people; Caritas's learned friends supported her desire to let convent residents decide for themselves, and this stance, combined with Caritas's bravery, convinced the city council not to allow any more forcible removals or to shut down the entire convent. Convent residents were not allowed to hear Catholic services, however, and the convent was not permitted to take in new novices. Caritas's memoirs became a testimony to freedom of religious choice, and have now been translated into several languages, while her humanist works and those of her brother are of interest only to scholars.

**Sources:**

Paula S. Datsko Barker, "Caritas Pirckheimer: A Female Humanist Confronts the Reformation," *Sixteenth Century Journal of Early Modern Studies,* 26 (Summer 1995): 259–272.

James H. Overfield, *Humanism and Scholasticism in Late Medieval Germany* (Princeton: Princeton University Press, 1984).

Lewis William Spitz, *The Religious Renaissance of the German Humanists* (Cambridge, Mass.: Harvard University Press, 1963).

# CHRISTINE DE PIZAN

## 1364–CIRCA 1430
### POET AND AUTHOR

**Privileged Upbringing.** Christine de Pizan was born in Italy, the daughter of a highly-educated man who was appointed medical and astrological adviser to the French king Charles V. Christine thus grew up at the French court, where her father made sure she received an excellent education, arranging for her to be tutored along with her brothers. She married at fifteen to a young man, Étienne du Castel, who looked as if he would also have a brilliant career at court, and the couple quickly had three children. Étienne died in an epidemic in 1390, however, leaving Christine widowed at twenty-six with young children and an elderly mother to support, as her father had also died. Women in this situation would normally rely on their family members for support and go to live in the house of a brother or sister. This option was not one that Christine liked, and she decided to support her family through writing, an unusual choice for anyone in this era before the printing press and unheard of for a woman.

**Patronage.** Christine began to write prose works and poetry, sending them to wealthy individuals in hopes of receiving their support. (In this era before the invention of the printing press, the few authors who supported themselves by writing did so by gaining the patronage of rulers, nobles, or other wealthy people, who either paid them to write specific works or rewarded the authors financially for works that were dedicated to them.) She initially used literary forms that were popular, such as ballads and allegories, though later she employed a wider range of styles. She was successful in her efforts, gaining commissions to write specific works, including biographies, histories, and books of military tactics. Among these was a biography of Charles V, the French king who had supported her father, written in 1404, and *The Book of Deeds of Arms and of Chivalry* (1410), a work describing the duties of a military leader. This latter title was so useful, it was one of the earliest books (in English translation) published by the first printer working in England, William Caxton. Christine recognized that her wide education allowed her to succeed, and she made sure her own children received similarly broad training.

**Antiwar Activist.** During Christine's entire life, England and France were involved in the Hundred Years' War, a conflict fought completely in France in which certain French nobles often sided with the English. Christine recognized that the war was devastating France, and wrote several works calling for its end, such as *Lament on the Evils of Civil War, Lamentations on the Woes of France,* and *The*

*Book of Peace* (1413). The disruption and danger caused by the war eventually led Christine to enter the Abbey of Poissy, where her daughter was already a nun. She never took religious vows but continued to write until the end of her life. Her last surviving work is a poem in praise of Joan of Arc. While residing in the Abbey, Christine learned of Joan's brave acts, which inspired the French troops and future French king at the siege of Orléans. The poem was composed in 1429, right after the siege, and before Joan had been captured; it is not known exactly when Christine died, or whether she knew that in the end Joan had been burned at the stake.

**Character of Women.** Christine's political writings were extremely important in her day, but she has become better known for a group of writings that addressed the situation of women. During the late Middle Ages, many writers of romances about noble knights and ladies also wrote cynical satires mocking chivalry and bitterly criticizing women as devious, domineering, and demanding. Toward the end of the fourteenth century, several writers in Europe decided to answer misogynist attacks on women directly, beginning a debate about women's character and nature that would last for centuries, usually called the "debate about women." Christine was the first female author to enter this debate. She was not content simply to list famous and good women as earlier pro-women writers had, but she also explored the reasons behind women's secondary status. She wrote a series of works in defense of women, the most important of which was *The Book of the City of Ladies* (1405), in which she ponders the question about why misogynist ideas are so widely held. She attacks these ideas in a sophisticated way, noting that the authorities usually cited in criticism on women were usually all men; that they disagree among themselves, and with reason and logic; that the language of the attacks is open to inter-pretation, and that they are often based on men's projection of their own fears and weaknesses. Instead of using extraordinary female counterexamples to argue against women's inferiority, she admits that women are inferior in many things, but this condition comes from their lack of education, economic dependence, and subordinate status.

**Feminist?** Because she explicitly discusses the historical misrepresentation of women and recognizes the social and economic bases of women's weakness, Christine is sometimes termed the "first feminist." Others have seen this label as misleading because Christine does not use her analysis to call for social change, as later feminist thinkers would. Keeping in mind the time in which she wrote, however, her conclusion that women's oppression and suffering made them better able than men to live virtuous lives in imitation of Christ is not simply a resigned acceptance of the realities of male power but also a positive affirmation of women's spiritual superiority. Along with theoretical discussions of women's status, she also wrote a book of practical advice for women, *The Book of Three Virtues* (1406), in which she instructs women of all social classes how to act and survive in the world; much of her advice, particularly that for widows, was based on her own experience. Neither of these works was printed in France during the early modern period, though an English translation of *City of Ladies* appeared in 1521. Both of them have become popular more recently, however, and *City of Ladies* has joined Niccolò Machiavelli's *The Prince* (1513) as a standard text in courses on the Renaissance.

Sources:

Renate Blumenfeld-Kosinski, ed., *The Selected Writings of Christine de Pizan: New Translations, Criticism,* translated by Blumenfeld-Kosinski and Kevin Brownlee (New York: Norton, 1997).

Enid McLeod, *The Order of the Rose: The Life and Ideas of Christine de Pizan* (London: Chatto & Windus, 1976).

Charity Cannon Willard, *Christine de Pizan: Her Life and Works* (New York: Persea, 1984).

# DOCUMENTARY SOURCES

**Note:** The vast majority of people during the period 1350–1600 could not read. Most individuals received their ideas about the family and the proper roles of men and women, as with everything else, from listening to other people, attending sermons or formal presentations, or looking at stained-glass windows, statues, or other images. If they were literate, most of what they read was religious material. Thus the most influential work on family life, sexuality, personal development, and gender roles was the Bible.

Leon Battista Alberti, *On the Family* (1435–1444)—An advice book by an Italian humanist. Alberti wrote the text in the vernacular (as opposed to Latin) in order to make it more accessible to the general population.

Giovanni Boccaccio, *Decameron* (1348–1353)—Also known as *Ten Days' Work.* Ten fictitious people, fleeing from plague-stricken Florence, tell stories of adventure, deception, and love. Boccaccio declares that true happiness is found in accepting one's fate without bitterness as well as the consequences of one's own actions.

Baldassare Castiglione, *Il cortegiano* (The Courtier, 1513–1518)—A classic of Italian literature, *Il cortegiano* examines in the form of dialogue the qualities of the ideal courtier or royal court attendant. Among these qualities are graceful behavior, *sprezzatura* (the impression of effortlessness), humor, proper speech, discreet modesty, and honorable love. Castiglione's book went through many editions (at least one a year for the century after its initial publication) and was translated into Spanish (1534), French (1537), Latin (1561), English (1561), German (1565), and Polish (1566).

John Knox, *First Blast of the Trumpet Against the Monstrous Regiment of Women* (1558)—A vehement expression of the common belief that the exercise of power by women is both unnatural and irreligious. The pamphlet was aimed specifically at England, Scotland, and France where females held the reins of government.

Luis de León, *La perfecta casada* (The Perfect Married Woman, 1583)—Written by a Spanish monk, this text provides a picturesque glimpse of feminine customs of the day.

Martin Luther, *On Marriage* (1566)—Luther's major statement on the religious and social responsibilities of matrimony and family.

Christine de Pizan, *Le Livre de la cité des dames* (The Book of the City of Ladies, 1405)—A volume on contemporary women known for their heroic and virtuous behavior.

Pizan, *Le livre des trois vertus* (The Book of Three Virtues, 1406)—A sequel to *The Book of the City of Ladies* which classifies women's roles in medieval society and provides moral instruction for women in various social settings.

Juan Luis Vives, *Instruction of a Christian Woman* (1540)—A guide to women's proper religious and moral education by the Spanish humanist who was tutor to Princess Mary Tudor of England.

The Laurentian Library in Florence, designed in the Proto-Baroque style by Michelangelo, in 1523

# RELIGION AND PHILOSOPHY

by FREDERIC J. BAUMGARTNER

## CONTENTS

*Sidebars and tables are listed in italics.*

**1350**

- Approximately one million pilgrims flock to Rome for the celebration of the Holy Year, a religious festival proclaimed by Pope Clement VI.

**1365**

- The University of Vienna is founded by the Duke of Austria.

**1370**

- Gert Groote enters the monastery but leaves three years later. He begins to preach in the Netherlands and his brand of piety, called the Modern Devotion, spreads quickly. Groote's followers continue to accept Catholic doctrine and practices while insisting upon more emotion and feeling in religion.

**1377**

- The papal residence officially returns to Rome following a seventy-three-year stay in Avignon, France.

**1378**

- The Great, or Western, Schism begins after the death of Pope Gregory XI in Rome. Amid demands for an Italian pontiff, the Sacred College of Cardinals elects the archbishop of Bari as Pope Urban VI. He soon proves to be so inflexible that a group of cardinals pronounce his election invalid and they appoint one of their own, Robert, Cardinal of Geneva, as Pope Clement VII. Urban VI promptly excommunicates the rebel cardinals and their Pope. Meanwhile, Clement VII returns to Avignon with a majority of the old cardinalate. For the next thirty-nine years, the followers of these two Popes are divided chiefly along national lines, resulting in a great deal of confusion and loss of prestige for the papacy.

**1400**

- A new approach to learning known as civic humanism appears in Florence, Italy; it emphasizes the study of Latin classics as the best way to learn rhetoric, poetry, and history.

**1409**

- The Great Schism intensifies with the election of a third Pope by the Council of Pisa. Twenty-four cardinals from both sides convene the council in an attempt to resolve the conflict. Denouncing both Gregory XII (Rome) and Benedict XIII (Avignon), they elect the archbishop of Milan as Pope Alexander V. Neither Gregory XII nor Benedict XIII accept this ruling. A year later Alexander V dies and is succeeded by Pope John XXIII.

*Denotes circa date*

**1414**

- The Council of Constance begins. Under pressure from the newly elected Holy Roman Emperor, Sigismund, king of Hungary, Pope John XXIII convenes the council, which promptly deposes him, accepts the resignation of Gregory XII, and dismisses the claims of Benedict XIII.

**1415**

- The Czech theologian and priest John Hus is executed for heresy after leading a religious rebellion in Bohemia. His followers, the Hussites, soon devolve into factions. The more-conservative element, the Utraquists (from *sub utraque specie,* meaning "both the cup and the bread"), support religious liberty and anticlericalism. The more-radical Taborites, composed of the lower classes, reject any liturgy and doctrine not specifically found in the Bible. Intermittent Hussite wars plague the Church and Holy Roman Empire for the next fifty years.

**1417**

- The Council of Constance finally deposes Benedict XIII and elects a new Pope, Martin V; the Great Schism officially ends.

**1430**

- The Council of Basel convenes in order to address the question of papal supremacy and the Hussite heresy; it ends in 1449.

**1434**

- The Utraquists defeat the outnumbered Taborites in battle. Two years later the Hussites are recognized as members of the Catholic Church.

**1438**

- A council of French clerics issues the Pragmatic Sanction of Bourges, which reasserts the practice of the cathedral clergy electing bishops and terminates the right of the papacy to collect revenues from the French clergy.

**1439**

- Byzantine Emperor John VII agrees to recognize the Pope as the head of the Greek Orthodox Church in exchange for military assistance against the Turks.

**1458**

- After the election of the first humanist Pope, Pius II, the papacy begins to take an active role in Renaissance culture.

| | |
|---|---|
| **1460** | • Pope Pius II declares conciliarism, the belief that the general council of the Catholic Church is superior to the pontiff, a heresy. |
| **1462** | • The Platonic Academy is founded in Florence by Cosimo de Medici. |
| **1471** | • Thomas à Kempis finishes writing *Imitation of Christ*, in which he states that he would rather feel sorrow for his sins than be able to define what sorrow is. |
| **1474** | • *The Platonic Theology* by Marsilio Ficino is published. It proposes that Plato believed in the immortality of the soul and that his philosophy of love prefigures the Gospel. |
| **1478** | • Queen Isabella of Spain requests that the Pope establish the Inquisition, an official tribunal for the discovery and punishment of heresy. |
| **1480** | • The Spanish Inquisition begins when six *Conversos* (Spanish Jews converted to Christianity) are executed for practicing Judaism. Several thousand others are executed over the next one hundred years. |
| **1492** | • Spain begins to expel all Jews who refuse to convert to Christianity. |
| **1494** | • The German legal scholar Sebastian Brant finishes writing *Ship of Fools*, a satire of European society that makes especial fun of clergymen. |
| **1500\*** | • Spanish missionaries arrive in the West Indies and start to convert Native Americans.<br>• Printed copies of humanist and classical texts begin to appear in Northern Europe. |

**1502**

- King Ferdinand and Queen Isabella decree the expulsion of unconverted Muslims from Spain.

**1506**

- The German humanist Johannes Reuchlin writes a Hebrew grammar book and dictionary.

**1509**

- Desiderius Erasmus's *The Praise of Folly*, a satire on European society and the hypocrisy of high churchmen, is published.
- The French theologian and reformer Jacques Lefevre d'Etaples publishes an edition of the Psalms.
- The University of Alcala is founded in Spain by Cardinal Ximenez de Ciscneros.

**1514**

- A Polyglot version of the New Testament, written in the original languages of Hebrew, Aramaic, and Greek, is published. A Polyglot edition of the complete Bible appears in 1522.

**1516**

- The Concordat of Bologna replaces the Pragmatic Sanction of Bourges by allowing the French king authority to appoint bishops in his realm, although papal approval of the appointment is still needed. The concordat also restores the pope's right to receive revenues from France.
- Pietro Pomponazzo finishes writing *On the Immortality of the Soul*. He opposes the notion of an afterlife where the soul would be punished or rewarded, and instead argues that doing good is its own reward, while evil is its own punishment.
- *Utopia* by Sir Thomas More is published. It describes an ideal society free of sloth, greed, pride, ambition, and other vices.

**1517**

31 Oct.
- The Protestant Reformation begins when the German priest and professor Martin Luther posts his Ninety-five Theses on the door of the church at the University of Wittenberg. The theses question primarily the value of indulgences and condemn the means used in selling them.

**1518**

- The First Reformed Church is founded in Zurich, Switzerland.

**1519**

- In *History of Florence,* Niccolò Machiavelli argues that the Italian city-states should follow the ancient Roman model for creating a society.

- The Leipzig Debate begins and lasts for three weeks. The prominent Ingoldstadt theologian Johann Eck and Luther argue various issues, including the authority of the pope and the councils. Eck's identification of Luther as a Hussite is the first time Luther is openly accused of heresy.

**1520**

- Luther publishes three major essays on the state of the Catholic Church: *Address to the Christian Nobility of the German Nation, Babylonian Captivity of the Church,* and *On the Freedom of the Christian.* As a result, Pope Leo X issues a papal bull demanding a retraction of his statements. Luther reacts by burning the bull in a ceremonial fire at Wittenberg.

**1521**

- Leo X excommunicates Luther. Meanwhile, the Diet of Worms is held to determine various administrative issues of the Holy Roman Empire. Luther is summoned to the diet to answer the charges of heresy and treason. An edict is passed condemning the German theologian's doctrines, along with all those who aid, condone, publish, or read his views.

- *Defense of the Seven Sacraments* is written for King Henry VIII of England. An attack on Luther's doctrines, it is not published until 1687.

**1523**

- Huldrych Zwingli persuades the city council to declare Zurich a Protestant city.

**1524**

- Zwingli writes *A Commentary on True and False Religion* in which he declares that the only true sacraments are the Eucharist and baptism.

**1528**

- The Capuchins, a branch of the Franciscans, are approved by the papacy as a religious order specializing in preaching to the urban poor.

**1529**

- Henry VIII replaces More with Thomas Cromwell as chancellor because of More's refusal to assist the king in his attempts to gain an annulment from the Pope. (The queen, Catherine, had failed to produce a male heir.)

**1530**

- The College of Three Languages, dedicated to the study of ancient Latin, Greek, and Hebrew, is established in France.

**1531**

- The Schmalkaldic League is created by Lutheran princes to counter papal authority.

**1533**

- Henry VIII issues a degree forbidding appeals to the papal court. He also secretly weds Anne Boleyn after having his marriage to Catherine declared invalid.

**1534**

- Luther completes a German translation of the Bible.
- In an attempt to create a new Jerusalem, Anabaptists seize control of the German city of Münster.
- St. Ignatius of Loyola founds a religious order known as the Society of Jesus (Jesuits).
- Because of his ongoing conflict with papal authority, Henry VIII obtains from Parliament the Act of Supremacy, which establishes a national church separate from the Roman Catholic Church and appoints the king protector and sole supreme head of the church in England.

**1535**

- The Company of St. Ursula is founded. An order of nuns, it is dedicated to the teaching of young girls.

**1536**

- John Calvin's *Institute of Christian Religion* is printed. Calvin spends his life revising the work, and the last edition appears in 1561. *Institute* is a major theological statement on church law, faith, sermons, and the sacraments.
- Henry VIII begins closing monasteries in England and confiscating their funds.

**1539**

- *Six Articles*, written by Henry VIII, confirms most Catholic doctrine.

**1540**
- Pope Paul III officially recognizes the Society of Jesus.

**1541**
- John Calvin's system of church governance, the "Ecclesiastical Ordinances," is accepted by the city of Geneva.
- The Jesuit St. Francis Xavier arrives in India to begin missionary work.

**1542**
- Pope Paul III institutes the Inquisition in Rome.

**1545**
- The Council of Trent opens to examine ways in which to reform the Church and to contest Protestantism.

**1549**
- Thomas Cranmer, the Archbishop of Canterbury, writes the *Book of Common Prayer*.

**1559**
- Pope Paul IV orders the publication of the *Index Librorum Prohibitorum* (Index of Forbidden Books), a list of "dangerous and unholy" tomes written by heretical authors such as Luther, Zwingli, and Calvin.

**1560**
- Presbyterianism, a form of Calvinism, begins to spread throughout Scotland.

**1564**
- Pope Pius IV publishes the Council of Trent decrees, which reaffirm Catholic doctrine, including papal supremacy.

**1594**
- In *The Three Truths* Pierre Charron states that the Protestant insistence upon individual reading of the Bible causes too much discord.

**1595**

- According to Montaigne in *Essais,* individual behavior is determined by experience and not some ultimate truth.

**1600**

- The Italian philosopher Giordino Bruno is burned at the stake for heresy because he advances the theory that the universe is infinite.

Johannes Tezelius Dominicaner Münch/mit seinen Römischen Ablaßkram/welchen er im Jahr Christi 1517. in Deutschenlanden zu marckt gebracht/wie er in der Kirchen zu Pirn in seinem Vaterland abgemahlet ist.

O ihr deutschen merckel mich recht/
    Des heiligen Vaters Papstes Knecht/
Bin ich/vnd br in euch jst allein/
    Zehn tausent vnd neun hundert carein/
Gnad vnd Ablaß von einer Sünd/
    Vor euch/ewer Elter n/Weib vnd Kind/
Sol ein jeder gewehret sein
    So viel ihr leg e ins Kästelein/
So bald der Gülden im Becken klingt/
    Im huy die Seel im Himel springt/

A woodcut, circa 1517, of Johann Tetzel, one of the first antagonists of Martin Luther, selling indulgences from the back of a donkey

# OVERVIEW

---

**Crises.** In 1350 the Catholic Church faced two major crises. One was the Black Death (1347–1351), which led to a preoccupation with death and the appearance of a highly mechanical form of religiosity that depended upon the performance of many pious acts and religious devotions to lessen God's wrath. The other was the residence of the pope in Avignon, France, for the past four decades, away from Rome, where his position as bishop provided the basis for his authority over the Church. Pressure on the pope to go back to Rome secured a return in 1377. When Pope Gregory XI died in 1378, the process of selecting a new pontiff resulted in threats of violence that led to the election of an Italian Pope (Urban VI) who remained in Rome and a rival Pope (Clement VII) who returned to Avignon. This Great, or Western, Schism created an even greater scandal and led to the theory of conciliarism, which declared that the general council of the Church was superior to the pontiff. In 1409, the Council of Pisa attempted to solve the problem by electing its own Pope (Alexander V), but that merely resulted in three pontiffs claiming legitimacy. In 1415, the Council of Constance ended the schism by persuading two of the popes to resign and deposing the third before proceeding to the election in 1417 of Pope Martin V, who was accepted by all Catholics. Conciliarism did not disappear; it continued to exercise influence until the Reformation, especially in its call for the reform of Catholic clergy.

**Heresy.** The Church also wrestled with the problem of heresy in the late Middle Ages. Groups such as the Brethren of the Free Spirit denounced the authority of the clergy. John Wycliffe, an English theologian, rejected the authority of the pope as well as the Catholic definitions of several key doctrines. His beliefs influenced a religious rebellion in Bohemia led by John Hus, who was executed for heresy in 1415 at the Council of Constance. Followers of Hus, the Hussites, formed an independent church called the Utraquist Church from their practice of making the Eucharist available in both the bread and wine. A radical wing of the Hussites, convinced that the Second Coming was at hand, used violence to cleanse the world of sinners before Christ's return. The violence ultimately led to a civil war between the moderate and radical Hussites factions. The moderates eventually won and reached an agreement with Rome.

**Turks and Jews.** The other major division of Christianity, the Orthodox Church, faced the threat of the Ottoman Turkish invasion of the Byzantine Empire. Hoping to get aid from the Westerners, Orthodox leaders agreed to negotiate a reunion between the Orthodox and Catholic Churches, but their efforts floundered on the Catholic insistence on papal supremacy. In 1453 the Muslim Turks conquered Constantinople (present-day Istanbul) and effectively ended the Byzantine Empire. The Turks tolerated the presence of Christians and also accepted Jews in their lands to a greater extent than in Catholic Europe. The Catholic record toward the Jews in the Middle Ages was a mix of toleration and persecution; Poland and Italy were unusually tolerant places, whereas Spain became the most-intolerant land in the late fifteenth century. Heavy pressure was put on both Jews and Muslims there to convert to Christianity. Those who did convert were not treated well, but those who refused to be baptized were expelled from Spain—the Jews in 1492 and the Muslims in 1502.

**Nominalism.** The system of scholastic theology that dominated the late Middle Ages was founded by William of Ockham. It is called nominalism, from the Latin for name, because it argued that human minds are capable of recognizing the similarities among things of the same kind and coming up with a name for them. There are no universals that exist in the mind of God, as previous theologians maintained. Ockham also promoted the concept of the absolute and the ordained powers of God. In his absolute power, God could have created any kind of universe, but he has chosen to create the one that exists. Nominalists used the idea to speculate what kind of universe God might have created, for example, one in which the Earth orbits the Sun. In theology Ockham emphasized that God has established a system of salvation by which he has chosen to accept as worthy of grace the good deeds of humans, although they are not in themselves of any real merit. Nominalism coincided with the post–Black Death era's emphasis on pious acts and provided a theological justification for such activities, although many theologians in the ever-growing number of universities denounced it as heresy. These debates over fine points of theology and the emphasis on quantity, not quality, in performing religious acts led to a more personal mystical relationship with God. Some women, such as St. Catherine of

Siena, became famous for their writings on how to achieve mystical union with God. The movement known as the Modern Devotion, arising in the Netherlands, combined a desire for emotion and feelings in religion with an active life teaching and nursing. Communities of the Brothers and the Sisters of the Common Life sprang up across northwestern Europe in the fifteenth century. The Brothers' schools provided a quality grammar school education to boys.

**Civic Humanism.** In Italy a new approach to learning appeared in the mid fourteenth century. Called humanism, it emphasized the study of the Latin classical works as the best way to learn rhetoric, poetry, and history. Humanists believed this approach would be the best way to prepare a middle-class boy for an active life in the business and politics of his city-state. Petrarch and other early humanists traveled extensively uncovering the manuscripts for the Latin classics to make them available to a wider reading public. Once two or more manuscripts of a Latin classic were found, scholars realized that errors had crept in during the centuries of recopying. The second phase of humanism involved text edition, establishing the original text of the work. In Florence humanists used "civic humanism" to rally the defense of the city against its enemies. By the late fifteenth century, the Italian political situation, in which humanism appeared, had greatly changed, and humanists emphasized the idea that knowing classical Latin was a good in itself, without any practical benefit. The fall of Constantinople brought many Greek scholars to Italy, and knowledge of classical Greek literature became part of humanism. Study of Aristotle and Plato in their original language revealed the mistakes in the scholastic theologians' interpretations of the two great philosophers, leading to increasing antagonism between humanists and scholastics.

**Christian Humanism.** In northern Europe the hostility between the two sets of scholars became serious. Humanism appeared in the North only after 1450 and was influential first in Germany, where it was taught in the schools of the Brothers of Common Life. There, Northern humanism took on its interest in studying the sources of Christianity in their original languages and reforming the Church, for which it is known as Christian humanism. Many humanists, especially Desiderius Erasmus, wrote biting satires against the clergy that highlighted their vices and abuses. These humanists also attacked the mechanical formalism of late medieval worship. Erasmus traveled widely and had contacts with humanists in nearly every European land. He was a friend of the English humanist, Sir Thomas More, the author of *Utopia* (1516). Erasmus's crowning work was his text edition of the Greek New Testament, which pointed out errors in the official Bible used by the Church. Christian humanists have been seen as a prelude to the Reformation because the first Protestants used their work extensively.

**Luther.** Martin Luther drew some ideas from Christian humanism, but his role in the Reformation (the sixteenth century religious movement that resulted in the establishment of the Protestant Church) grew out of a bitter struggle with himself over his eternal salvation. Convinced that he was a depraved sinner, Luther became a monk, priest, and professor of theology at the University of Wittenberg. All failed to give him any sense that he was worthy of Heaven, until he found in the Epistle to the Romans a passage that revealed to him the concept of "salvation by faith alone." Luther now saw grace to believe in Christ as redeemer as an unmerited gift from God to some souls and not to others. When indulgence peddlers appeared in the region attempting to sell the St. Peter's indulgence in 1517, Luther was enraged and wrote up his Ninety-five Theses as a call to debate the issue. The Ninety-five Theses were spread across Germany, making Luther enormously popular. A public debate in 1519 further spread his ideas and enhanced his popularity. He wrote three books in 1520 that made clear his break with the Catholic Church on papal authority and key points of doctrine. He was called before a meeting of the Imperial Diet in 1521 to answer charges of heresy but refused to yield. He was declared an outlaw and hid for a year at a remote castle, where he began the German translation of the Bible. Putting the Bible in the hands of the laity, and in their own languages, became a hallmark of Protestantism. Radical unrest in Wittenberg brought Luther back home, which is where he was when the German Peasants' Revolt broke out in 1524. Luther soon condemned the peasants for their use of violence, which cost him much of his popular support. It also caused him to emphasize the need for obedience to established authority. Luther became involved in controversies with Erasmus and Huldrych Zwingli, which prevented a unified reform movement. Lutheranism became a largely Germanic movement, with success in much of Germany and the Scandinavian countries.

**Anabaptists.** Luther's example was important to other early Reformers, even if they did not accept his specific points of doctrine. Zwingli led the reform of Zurich in Switzerland, where he succeeded in persuading the city council to adopt his vision of true Christianity in 1523. He differed from Luther in his understanding of the Eucharist, which led to their inability to forge a common bond when they met in 1529. Zwingli was the founder of the Reformed Churches, but he also influenced the early Anabaptists, who required adult baptism as a sign of adult commitment to the Church. Some Anabaptists organized communes where the saints would live in isolation from the sinners of the outside world; the most successful were the Moravian Brethren. Others believed that the end of the world was at hand, and they had to cleanse the world of sinners. The most notorious episode occurred in a German city, Münster, where in 1534 radical Anabaptists seized control and held it for a year while trying to turn it into the new Jerusalem. Anabaptism was saved from such excesses by committed pacifists like Mennos Simons, founder of the Mennonites. Simons and other reformers after the 1534–1535 Münster siege were careful to avoid militant radicalism.

**Calvin.** John Calvin, a reformer after the Münster incident, was careful in his early writing to convince readers that he was not a dangerous radical. A Frenchman, he came to

Geneva in 1536, where he emerged as the leading theologian of Reformed Christianity, although he was extensively influenced by Zwingli. Calvin is noted for his doctrine of predestination, in which God is seen as choosing both the saved and damned from all eternity, and his form of church governance that provided a role for the laity through the consistory. His theology had special appeal to the middle classes, which used it to justify their active involvement in business and worldly pursuits. Calvinism became the predominant religion in several European lands. One of these lands was Scotland, where the political chaos resulting from the succession of Mary Stuart as an infant to the throne created an opportunity for Protestants, led by the ardent Calvinist John Knox, to establish a version of Calvinism called Presbyterianism as the official religion of the realm in 1560.

**Henry VIII.** In England the Reformation depended heavily on the monarch. When the Pope refused to grant Henry VIII an annulment from his marriage to Catherine of Aragon, he broke the ties between Rome and the Church of England in 1531. Henry was conservative in religion, but he closed the monasteries and introduced the English language into worship services, which until that time were primarily in Latin. His son Edward VI made the Church doctrinally more Protestant; his elder daughter Mary I returned it to union with Rome; his younger daughter Elizabeth I largely reestablished her father's Church. The Elizabethan settlement established a vague statement of doctrine while keeping much of traditional practice.

**Catholic Response.** The Catholic Church had both internal currents of reform (Catholic Reformation) and responses to Protestantism (Counter-Reformation). Catholic reform included establishing new religious orders. In 1534 St. Ignatius of Loyola had not organized the Society of

Jesus (or Jesuits) to purposely combat the Protestants, but it soon emerged as the "cutting edge of the Counter-Reformation." The Council of Trent in 1545 was intended both to reform the Church by setting higher standards for the clergy and to contest Protestantism by defining Catholic doctrine as distinctly as possible from the Protestant.

**End of Humanism.** The vehement doctrinal disputes largely ended humanism. Those few humanists who tried to carry on their work after 1530 usually found themselves harassed by church authorities from one side or the other. Peter Ramus, an anti-Aristotelian humanist, was a victim of the St. Bartholomew's Massacre (1572) during which thousands of Huguenots (French Protestants) were murdered. Some thinkers used the dialogue as a literary device to discuss dangerous ideas without being accused of accepting them. Michel de Montaigne used skepticism as a way to promote toleration of religion and other controversial ideas by arguing that the human mind was incapable of knowing the truth. His French Catholic followers would use skepticism as a tool against the Protestants. In addition, Giordano Bruno demonstrated the dangers of ideas such as heliocentrism (the belief that the Sun is the center of the universe) by discussing the possibility of an infinite number of worlds with human beings, leading to his execution in 1600 for heresy.

**Conclusion.** The Black Death, the Great Schism, the rise of Italian civic humanism and its northern counterpart Christian humanism, and the emergence of Protestantism all contributed to the tumultuous changes of the period from 1350 to 1600. Ultimately, by the beginning of the seventeenth century a new world had emerged, a world of religious separation and intolerance.

# TOPICS IN RELIGION AND PHILOSOPHY

## CATHOLIC REFORMATION, COUNTER-REFORMATION

**Future Opportunities.** In 1517, the future of the Catholic Church seemed brighter than it had been for some time. Christian humanists were working to reform the Church without badly disrupting it. The *reconquista* of the Iberian peninsula from the Muslims had recently been completed. The Medici Pope, Leo X, was a brilliant diplomat and patron of art and humanism who was successfully

defusing the long-standing political issues between the papacy and the monarchies. Most significantly, the voyages of exploration by European sailors had opened new opportunities for bringing Christianity to millions of unbelieving souls and offered the promise of outflanking Islam, the great nemesis of medieval Christendom. Christopher Columbus was motivated by ambition and greed but also by orders from Ferdinand and Isabella to Christianize the

The Council of Trent was a series of religious councils held from 1545 until 1563 that sought not to condemn Protestantism but rather to consolidate the power and prestige of the Catholic Church, centralize and strengthen its organization, eliminate obvious church abuses, define ambiguous doctrine, and restate its position on challenged doctrines. The following are excerpts from the Thirteenth and Twenty-second sessions that address the seven sacraments.

Examples of the Decrees of the Council of Trent, 1545-1563.

Thirteenth Session, Chapter IV: Since Christ our Redeemer declared that it was truly His body which He offered up in the form [sub specie] of bread, and since the church has moreover always accepted this belief, this holy council declares once more that by the consecration of the bread and the wine the whole substance of the bread is converted into the substance of the body of Christ our Lord, and the whole substance of the wine into the substance of his blood, which change is aptly and properly termed trans-substantiation by the Catholic church.

Thirteenth Session, Canon I: If any one shall deny that the body and blood of our Lord Jesus Christ together with his spirit and divinity, to-wit, Christ all in all, are not truly, really and materially contained in the holy sacrament of the Eucharist, and shall assert that the Eucharist is but a symbol or figure, let him be anathema.

Thirteenth Session, Canon VI: If any one shall say that Christ, the only-begotten son of God, is not to be worshipped with the highest form of adoration (Latrioe) including external worship, in the holy sacrament of the Eucharist, or that the Eucharist should not be celebrated by a special festival, nor borne solemnly about in procession according to the praiseworthy and universal rite and custom of the holy church, nor held up publicly for the veneration of the people and those who adore it are idolaters, let him be anathema.

Twenty-second Session, Canon I: If any one shall say that a real and fitting sacrifice is not offered to God in the mass, or that nothing is offered except that Christ is given us to eat, let him be anathema.

Twenty-second Session: Canon II: If any one shall say that the words, "This do in remembrance of me," Christ did not institute the apostles as priests, or did not ordain that they themselves and their successors should offer up His body and blood, let him be anathema.

Twenty-second Session, Canon III: If any one shall say that the sacrifice of the mass is only a praiseworthy deed or act of edification, or that it is simply in commemoration of the sacrifice on the cross and is not in the nature of a propitiation; or that it can benefit only him who receives it and ought not to be offered for the living and the dead, for sins, punishment, atonement, and other necessary things, let him be anathema.

Sources: Edward McNall Burns and Louis Snyder, eds., *The Counter Reformation* (Princeton: Van Nostrand, 1964), pp. 136–137.

*Translations and Reprints,* Volume II (Philadelphia: University of Pennsylvania, 1897), pp. 28–29.

---

nonbelievers he might find in the "Indies," and the same was true of the Portuguese captains in their voyages to the Indian Ocean. When Pope Alexander VI issued his decree of 1493 dividing the unknown lands between Spain and Portugal, he mandated the bringing of the Gospel to the pagans as their first responsibility. The realization that the Europeans had encountered an entirely unknown people in the Americas raised a serious problem: Medieval theologians had denied the possibility of humans living outside of the known world. Were the American natives human and capable of becoming Christian? Some clergymen defended the medieval tradition, but most were eager for an affirmative answer so that the vast populations being found could become part of the Church.

**Las Casas.** Missionaries arrived in the West Indies before 1500 and had immediate success in gaining converts. They found that the demands of the other Spaniards for labor from the natives were disrupting the work of conversion. They also quickly recognized how rapidly the American Indian populations were declining from European diseases, disruption of their societies, and over exploitation for labor. In 1511 a Dominican preached a sermon denouncing the treatment of the natives. One of those who heard the sermon was a priest, Batholeme Las Casas, who was deeply affected. He spent the rest of his long life defending the rights of the American Indians, and he had many allies among the Spanish missionaries. Las Casas and his allies had little long-term influence in reducing the burden of Spanish colonization on the Native Americans, but the process of Christianizing them proceeded rapidly. By 1600, with few exceptions, the natives had become Christian wherever the Spanish had conquered.

**Xavier and Ricci.** The Portuguese missionaries faced a different situation in Asia. There they found sophisticated religions such as Hinduism and Buddhism, whose members were not likely to be impressed by European military power, and Islam, whose members were familiar with Christianity and hostile to it. The rate of conversion to Christianity was far less there than in the Americas, yet enough converts had been won by 1534 that the Pope erected a bishopric at Goa in India. Portuguese missionary activity, however, is always associated with the Jesuit St. Francis Xavier. He arrived in India in 1541, where he baptized thousands mostly from the lowest castes. He moved on to the Malay Peninsula and Japan before dying on an island off the coast of China in 1552. The goal of Christianizing China was taken up by the Italian Jesuit, Matteo Ricci. Ricci learned an enormous amount about Chinese culture and society, and his own accomplishments in European science and mathematics made him one of the most respected Europeans in China ever. His synthesis of Chinese culture with Christianity won him great success among the Chinese, but he also set the stage for a bitter controversy over the use of Chinese traditions by Chinese Catholics in the next century.

**Slow Response.** Catholic success overseas helped to balance the losses Catholicism suffered in Europe following the rise of Protestantism. The failure of Pope Leo X and the cardinals to grasp the nature of the issues raised by Martin Luther prevented any effective response for two decades, by which time Protestantism was too well established to be rooted out. One reason for the slow response was that for many in the upper levels of the Church, Luther's beliefs seemed little different from the reform advocated by Christian humanism. The presence of a Catholic reform predating Luther is the principal reason why many historians prefer the term *Catholic Reformation* over *Counter-Reformation,* which has the connotation that whatever reform the Church undertook in the sixteenth century was done only in response to Protestantism. The best-known movement was the Oratory of Divine Love, a number of local institutions across Italy that arose largely from the life and charitable work of St. Catherine of Genoa. She inspired priests and laymen in Genoa to form the group in 1497. Similar organizations appeared across Italy, but the most significant was organized in Rome by 1517, and its main activity was hospital visitations. Its members included future cardinals Gasparo Contarini and Gaetano da Thiene, as well as Gian Pietro Caraffa, who later became Pope Paul IV.

**Other Orders.** New religious orders arose in the early sixteenth century. The Capuchins were a strict branch of the Franciscans, whose name came from the four-cornered hood that became their identifying feature. Their rule, approved by the papacy in 1528, stated that they were to live in small groups with an emphasis on preaching to the urban poor. They also staked out roles as chaplains to soldiers and sailors. Another new order that had its roots in Italy was the Company of St. Ursula, founded in 1535 when Angela Merici heard the pledges of perpetual virginity from twenty-eight young women. They dedicated themselves to an active life of teaching girls while living at home and wearing ordinary clothing. They made a sharp break with the traditional cloistered orders of nuns, but their success in attracting women raised fears in the higher clergy of unsupervised single women. By 1600 the Ursulines were forced to return to a more traditional type of convent, housing schools for upper-class girls within their walls. The Capuchins, early Ursulines, and several smaller orders that were organized in the same era reflected the attitudes of the Brethren of the Common Life and the Christian humanists against the restrictions of traditional monastic life and in favor of an active life in the world.

**Jesuits.** By far the most successful in breaking the mold of traditional religious orders was the Society of Jesus, founded in 1534 by St. Ignatius Loyola. He drew up a rule for the order that was highly innovative for its time. The name he chose, the Society of Jesus, was controversial because no previous order had presumed to include Christ's name in its title. Also controversial was Loyola's idea that the members not be required to assemble regularly during the day for common prayer, as was true for all monks previously, but be permitted to say those prayers alone. This innovation had the effect of allowing the Jesuits to be active in the world, for they did not have to return to their houses several times a day. The refusal to wear a monk's habit had a similar effect of permitting the Jesuit priest to be an active participant in the world's business. Despite opposition from such influential prelates as Cardinal Caraffa, Pope Paul III gave his approval to the Society of Jesus in 1540. At a time when the Protestants' major challenge to Catholicism was their denunciation of the authority of the papacy, Loyola emphasized that obedience to the pope was necessary to be a good Christian. His declaration that Jesuits ought to be ready "to believe what seems to us to be white is black, if the Church so defines it" refuted the Protestant rejection of the authority of the Catholic Church.

**Dedicated Members.** These innovations and attitudes would not have had much impact if Loyola had not found an approach to religious life that had strong appeal to the young Catholic men of his era and ever since. The Society had demanding admission requirements. New members were carefully screened for intelligence, good health, and social skills before being accepted for a lengthy probationary period. Only after nine years of proving that they were committed to accepting the Society's discipline and living up to its goals were they permitted to become full members by taking a fourth vow of obedience to the papacy along with the traditional three vows of a monk. The number of Jesuits increased at an astounding rate throughout the sixteenth century. Loyola had devised a system of training that yoked together intelligence, discipline, and the freedom to take personal initiative when appropriate to the goal of doing "All for the Greater Glory of God." Nearly all of what Loyola devised for the Jesuits was intended to enhance the goal of being active in the service of God among His people. This active service may have been the principal source of its great appeal, for the Jesuit could see the results of his labors, whether as preacher, teacher, or missionary, unlike the monk whose task of praying for the salvation of souls rarely produced obvious successes. Yet, the Jesuit remained a part of a committed group who provided encouragement, constructive criticism, companionship, and a sense of belonging largely absent from the life of the parish priests. The result was to form a group of men who were the elite of Catholic Europe, whose highly successful labors for the Church deemed them the cutting edge of the Counter-Reformation.

Detail from *The Ship of Church*, by an anonymous sixteenth-century Spanish artist (Descalzas Reales, Madrid)

**Clement VII.** For all of Loyola's brilliance in designing his new order, it might not have had much success if the church it served had remained less than worthy of such commitment and service. The election of a reforming Pope, Adrian VI, in 1522 as successor to Leo X was quickly undone by his death a year later. His successor, Clement VII, was, like Leo, a member of the Medici family. Not as great a patron of artists as Leo, Clement was just as obtuse when it came to understanding the issues involved in creating the Reformation. His vacillation in decision making was made worse by being caught between French king Francis I and Emperor Charles V in their wars to control Italy. It was in the context of those wars that the major event of Clement's reign, the sack of Rome by imperial troops, took place in 1527. Under Charles's thumb for

most of the rest of his reign, he refused Henry VIII's request for an annulment from Catherine of Aragon. While Clement was ready at the Emperor's urging to grant some concessions to the Lutherans, such as clerical marriage, he adamantly refused Luther's demand that a general council of the Church meet in Germany as the only way of healing the division in the Church. The popes refused to consider a council unless it remained under their control. The Lutherans refused to accept a papal-dominated council as legitimate. Despite calls for a council from Catholics as well, Clement and his successor Paul III did not yield to the entreaties until Paul felt secure that he could control any council convened.

**Council of Trent.** Paul III, elected in 1534, was little different from his predecessors. He was trained a humanist, had four illegitimate children before becoming a priest, and actively promoted his relatives as any other pope. He was, however, more willing to act to reform the Church. One decision was approving the Society of Jesus in 1540, although he could not have foreseen the large role the Society would have in the Counter-Reformation. In 1542 he instituted the Inquisition in Rome, which never became as notorious as its Spanish counterpart. He named prominent reformers as cardinals, including Contarini and Caraffa. Paul III appointed Contarini to head a commission to investigate the papal court and recommend reforms. Its report detailed the problems all too thoroughly and laid them at the foot of the papacy, to Protestant delight and Paul's chagrin. Paul shelved it without action. Contarini served as papal delegate to a meeting at Regensburg in Germany in 1541 to try to reach a compromise with the Lutherans, whose spokesman was Philip Melanchthon. Agreement was reached on several key issues, but the meeting collapsed over the definition of the Eucharist. At last secure that he would control it, Paul III agreed to summon a general council. The place chosen was Trent, which was in lands ruled by Emperor Charles V yet Italian-speaking and on the south side of the Alps, thus satisfying both emperor and Pope. When the Council of Trent opened in December 1545, only four archbishops and thirty-one bishops, mostly Italians, were present. Attendance increased slowly during this first set of sessions that lasted until March 1547 and never exceeded one hundred bishops. France's king refused to send any French bishops on the grounds that the French Church did not need reforming, and if it did, he and his bishops would do it without outside interference. The Lutherans were invited to send observers, but it was made clear that they could not address the council nor take part in the discussions or voting. Some Lutherans did go to Trent but left when they realized they had no voice. In March 1547 the outbreak of war between Charles V and the Lutherans forced the suspension of the council, which Pope Julius III reconvened in 1551. The second set of sessions lasted just over a year when renewed fighting in Germany again halted it.

**Assertion of Power.** Pope Paul IV, elected in 1555, strongly opposed the council. He believed the Pope had the authority to reform the Church without it. Already seventy-nine years old when elected, he had a hot temper and an overwhelming sense of papal power. He hated Protestants and Spaniards with about equal passion, the latter because of their abusive rule in southern Italy, his homeland. He provoked a war with Spain in which he used the French and German Lutherans in an effort to drive the Spanish out of Italy. Despite using Protestant mercenaries, he made draconian demands for Catholic rulers to eradicate heresy, pushing Mary of England into rash acts of repression. Paul IV established the *Index of Forbidden Books* to make it clear to Catholics what works they could not read. The *Index* listed individual books as suspect in doctrine, such as Niccolò Machiavelli's *The Prince* (1513), and those authors whose entire body of works were banned.

Luther and Calvin were listed, but also Erasmus. Paul attempted to cleanse the city of Rome as Calvin had Geneva, prohibiting gambling, dancing, and prostitution. He also placed severe restrictions on the Jews in the Papal States, imposing heavier taxes on them, segregating them more completely from Christians and placing numerous Judaic works on the *Index*.

**Successor.** Paul IV became the model Counter-Reformation Pope, although no other was as harsh as he. His successor Pius IV, was determined to maintain traditional Catholicism. Pius IV believed that the council was the best way to strengthen the Church in combat with the Protestants. In 1561 the largest number of bishops, 270 in all, including finally a French delegation, arrived at Trent to resume the council. Although the earlier sessions had done some defining of doctrine, the third set of sessions, which lasted until December 1563, was the most productive. The key consideration was defining Catholic doctrine as distinct as possible from Protestant positions. Every Catholic doctrine and practice that had come under challenge was affirmed in the most conservative interpretation found in scholasticism, which usually came from St. Thomas of Aquinas. Thomist theology gained victory over Christian humanism. Papal supremacy was also affirmed, and the popes emerged from the council with more control over the bishops and the national churches than it had before. Trent also made important strides in reforming the Church. The role of the bishop as pastor of his diocese was emphasized, and his authority over the clergy in it, including over monasteries, which often had independence from episcopal oversight, was enhanced. The bishops were required to build seminaries in their dioceses for educating their priests, which by the early seventeenth century largely eliminated the complaints about the ignorance of the common priest. Bishops were also required to be in residence in their dioceses for six months of the year and to undertake visitations of all their parishes every two years. The obligation of clerical celibacy was reaffirmed, and the bishops were required to enforce it strictly on their priests. As the Tridentine decrees began to take effect across Catholic Europe, the quality of the clergy improved dramatically, and the complaints against it that had fueled the Reformation became a thing of the past.

**Increased Tension.** The Council of Trent exacerbated the differences between Catholic and Protestant, not reduced them, as many had hoped for when it began. No one could argue, as some did before 1545, that they did not know what the official Catholic positions on the contested doctrines were. Compromise was impossible once Pius IV published the council's decrees in early 1564. Philip II ordered them accepted in his realms immediately, although he included reservations on points that threatened to reduce royal authority over the Church. In the next several years the other Catholic rulers and authorities accepted them. The one exception was France, where Trent's decrees were denounced as undermining the liberties of the Gallican Church, and the French never did accept them before the French Revolution. Nonetheless, the implementation of Trent's decrees in northern Italy, Spain, and the Spanish Netherlands surrounded France with lands where they were transforming the Church. It created something of a moral imperative for the French bishops to adopt them in practice as well.

**Implications.** Trent clearly identified the enemy for both sides of the confessional divide. Any hope lingering among the Protestants that the entire Church might accept their doctrines was unsustainable after 1563, while any possibility that the Catholic Church might offer a compromise to the Protestants to bring them back to unity with Rome was also gone. Religious war had already reared its ugly head two decades earlier, but there now was a new militancy on both sides that would lead to nearly a century of bloody religious warfare across Europe.

Sources:

Henry Outram Evennett, *The Spirit of the Counter-Reformation* (Cambridge & London: Cambridge University Press, 1968).

Hubert Jedin, *A History of the Council of Trent*, 2 volumes (London: Thomas Nelson, 1957–1961).

John O'Malley, *The First Jesuits* (Cambridge, Mass.: Harvard University Press, 1993).

John Olin, *Catholic Reform: From Cardinal Ximenes to the Council of Trent, 1495–1563* (New York: Fordham University Press, 1990).

## CHRISTIAN HUMANISM

**Printing Press.** Italian humanists were slow to take their understanding of the liberal arts beyond the Alps. An occasional northerner could be found in Italy studying humanism in the early fifteenth century, and an occasional Italian steeped in humanism traveled northward. Only after 1450 were enough of both groups present in the rest of Europe to speak about the Northern Renaissance. After 1450 there were several developments that helped form Northern humanism. One was the printing press, traditionally attributed to Johannes Gutenberg of Mainz and invented around 1450, although several printers helped perfect movable type. By 1470 printing had reached Italy. When Aldus Manutius founded his press in 1490, Venice became an important center of printing. Manutius developed the style of typeface that became known as italics and specialized in printing humanist and classical literature. His humanist books were compact and cheap but well made. The printing press was a major factor in making the Renaissance permanent since it was impossible to again lose copies of classical works. It also helped to spread humanism across the Alps, since booksellers carried copies northward where they found a good market. Northern printers also began printing humanist texts, often pirating them from Italian publishers. By 1500, printed copies of humanist and classical texts had made their way across northern Europe, and books replaced teaching as the key to the spread of humanism.

**Court Trophies.** When popes became patrons of humanists, monarchs and great nobles also began to hire Italian humanists as ornaments for their courts. King Matthias Corvinus gained the throne of Hungary in 1458 and used his ties to Venice to become the first northern king to create a "renaissance court." Italian artists and humanists flourished there, but the most outstanding aspect of his patronage was the Corvinian Library with its 2,500 volumes mostly of classical literature. Unfortunately, nothing of this outpost of humanism in Eastern Europe survived the catastrophic Ottoman invasion of 1526. To the north in Poland, an early center for humanism appeared in Cracow, at both the university and the royal court of King Casimir IV. The courts of Western Europe were slower to become humanist centers. War distracted the Spanish and English monarchs from humanism until about 1500. In France, the powerful hold that the theology faculty of the University of Paris had on French intellectual life delayed the flourishing of Renaissance culture until after Charles VIII returned in 1495 from the First French Invasion of Italy.

**Brothers of Common Life.** A third source for Northern humanism was the schools of the Brothers of the Common Life. Few Brothers were humanists, but they were sympathetic to the idea of educating young men with the best texts available. Humanists began to appear as teachers in their schools in Germany and the Netherlands. Germany had many autonomous cities, called Free Imperial Cities, that were similar in government to the Italian city-states, in which humanistic studies flourished. The first important German humanist was known as Agricola. He went to Italy in 1469 and studied there for ten years. His classical Latin was so good that he was asked to give lectures in the language at the University of Pavia, a rare honor for a northerner in Italy at that time. When Agricola returned to Germany, he concentrated on teaching classical Latin. Conrad Celtis, a son of peasants, learned classical Latin from Agricola, but his program went beyond appreciating classical Latin for its own sake. He was a German patriot and saw to the printing of the Roman historian Tacitus's *Germania* (98 C.E.). Celtis disliked Italy and spent only a short time there. He criticized the Germans for being dominated by the Italians.

**Reuchlin.** Johannes Reuchlin became the most-famous German humanist because of his dispute with Johannes Pfefferkorn. Reuchlin was a true Renaissance man. He earned a law degree, served as a diplomat in Italy, wrote poetry and comedies and was fluent in classical Latin, Greek, and Hebrew. His interest in Hebrew sparked the "Reuchlin Controversy." In 1506 he wrote a Hebrew grammar and dictionary, the first done by a Christian. Four years later he came under attack for his interest in Hebrew and Judaism from Pfefferkorn, a Jewish convert to Christianity, who was eager to erase all memory of his former religion. Reuchlin defended the right of Christians to study Hebrew texts, and the controversy spread. It was taken to the University of Paris in 1514, where the theologians rejected Reuchlin's position, deeply angering the humanists, who had taken up his cause. Among the humanist works supporting Reuchlin was the notorious *Letters of Obscure Men* (1515–1517), written by Ulrich von Hutten

Ulrich von Hutten, a German knight and humanist, was one of the most articulate spokesmen for a kind of German cultural nationalism. He resented Rome's claims of cultural and political superiority and championed ecclesiastical reform. In this 1520 letter to Elector Frederick of Saxony, Hutten accuses the Roman Curia of corruption and calls for reform.

We see that there is no gold and almost no silver in our German land. What little may perhaps be left is drawn away daily by the new schemes invented by the council of the most holy members of the Roman Curia. What is thus squeezed out of us is put to the most shameful uses. Would you know, dear Germans, what employment I myself have seen that they make at Rome of our money? It does not lie idle! Leo X gives a part to nephews and relatives (these are so numerous that there is a proverb at Rome, "As thick as Leo's relation."). A portion is consumed by so many most reverend cardinals (of which the holy father created no less than one and thirty in a single day), as well as to support innumerable referendaries, auditors, prothonotaries, abbreviators, apostolic secretaries, chamberlains and a variety of officials forming the elite of the great head Church. These in turn draw after them at untold expense, copyists, beadles, messengers, servants, scullions, mule drivers, grooms, and an innumerable army of prostitutes and the most degraded followers. They maintain dogs, horses, monkeys, long-tailed apes and many more such creatures for their pleasure. They construct houses all of marble. They have precious stones, are clothed in purple and fine linen and dine sumptuously, frivolously indulging themselves in every species of luxury. In short, a vast number of the worst of men are supported in Rome in idle indulgence by means of our money. . . . Does not your Grace perceive how many bold robbers, how many cunning hypocrites commit repeatedly the greatest crimes under the monk's cowl, and how many crafty hawks feign the simplicity of doves, and how many ravening wolves simulate the innocence of lambs? And although there be a few truly pious among them, even they cling to superstition and pervert the law of life which Christ laid down for us.

Now, if all these who devastate Germany and continue to devour everything might once be driven out, and an end made of their unbridled plundering, swindling and deception, with which the Romans has overwhelmed us, we should again have gold and silver in sufficient quantities and should be able to keep it.

Source: Merrick Whitcomb, *A Literary Sourcebook of the German Renaissance*, volume 2 (Philadelphia: University of Pennsylvania, 1899), pp. 6, 19–20.

**Desire for Reform.** The Reuchlin affair brought out several key elements that made Northern humanism a distinctive school of thought from the Italian. Reuchlin's interest in Hebrew was part of the movement of returning to the original sources of Christianity. Church reform was another essential element of Northern humanism. The Northern humanists applied the techniques of text criticism developed by the Italians for the study of the largely pagan Latin and Greek classics to what they called the Christian classics—the earliest manuscripts of the Bible and the works of the Church fathers. The goal of this work was to clear out the accumulated weight of the centuries of misinterpretation of Christian doctrine by the medieval theologians. For Christian humanists "returning to the sources" meant returning to the pure doctrine of the earliest Church. They felt themselves qualified to discuss theology because they often knew Greek and in some cases Hebrew, while both languages were almost unheard of among scholastic theologians. The theologians began to conclude that humanism was not merely an inappropriate emphasis on ancient languages but also a threat to their fiercely defended monopoly on the right to interpret doctrine. They reacted by denouncing the most outspoken humanists as heretics. The humanists responded with biting satire and parody against the theologians and the Catholic clergy in general. The abuse of office rampant in the clergy distressed many humanists, some of whom were clerics themselves. Church reform was important to them, and since the humanists were first of all experts in the use of rhetoric, they used their talents as writers to push their program. Beyond reforming a corrupt clergy of its abuses, Christian humanists also were interested in eliminating the mechanical formalism found in Catholic worship. The humanist interest in the classics joined with the currents of mysticism found in the North and the attitude of the Brothers of the Common Life to seek to develop a more personal approach to religious life. Despite the seriousness of the goal, satire was often the means the humanists used to gain attention for the need for reform. The first major satire came from the pen of Sebastian Brant, a talented Latinist and legal scholar who was the secretary for the city of Strasbourg. He wrote *The Ship of Fools* in 1494 as a sweeping satire on all of European society. It took the form of a description of a boat, filled with insane people, floating down the Rhine River. The Rhineland cities allegedly had rid themselves of their insane by putting them on such boats. Brant satirized everyone, but the clergy were the special targets of his wit.

**Erasmus.** The same characterization was true of Erasmus who had the sharpest wit of the Northern humanists and the best sense of how to use it effectively. He used it against what he regarded as the unchristian papacy under Julius II, the Warrior Pope, who had personally commanded the papal army in its successful assault of Bologna, which had revolted against papal rule. Erasmus always denied writing *Julius Excluded from Heaven* (1513), but the evidence for his authorship of this biting satire against Julius is strong. In *Praise of Folly* (1509) Erasmus's satire

and Crotus Rubeanus. The work was a biting satire against the clergy and scholastic theologians. Eventually the issue went to Pope Leo X, who decided against Reuchlin in 1520. By then, the Lutheran movement had overshadowed the Reuchlin controversy, and it quietly disappeared.

The mythical Utopia, woodcut from Basel's 1518 edition of English humanist Sir Thomas More's *Utopia* (British Library)

was gentler but more broadly aimed. He depicts Folly as a cheerful goddess who praises her followers in European society. No part of society escapes his scathing wit, but the sharpest barbs are aimed at the churchmen: popes and prelates whose concerns are war, politics, and aggrandizement; monks and nuns who believe that they can compensate for a life of sensuality by empty prayers; priests who try to make up for their violations of their vow of chastity by saying an endless number of masses; theologians who are vainly proud of the trivia they call knowledge.

**Travels.** Erasmus spent his life traveling across Western Europe except for Spain and Portugal. To a large extent he traced out the course of Northern humanism, although it should not be concluded that he was responsible for its development in the North. Alexander Hegius, Erasmus' tutor in Latin at a school of the Brothers of the Common Life in the Netherlands, learned classical Latin from Agri-

cola. Hegius also introduced Erasmus to Greek. Erasmus went to Paris to study theology but soon abandoned it to take part in the growing circle of humanists in Paris. Robert Gaguin, who helped Erasmus improve his classical Latin, was the first noteworthy French humanist. He made several visits to Italy before publishing his first humanist work in 1495, a history of France that incorporated the humanist approach to writing history. Erasmus wrote the dedicatory poem for it. He published his first humanist work, the *Adages,* in Paris in 1500 and then left France, leaving Jacques Lefèvre d'Étaples as the outstanding humanist in the realm.

**Lefèvre.** After becoming a master of arts at Paris, Lefèvre visited Italy, where he was inspired to translate several of Aristotle's works directly into Latin from Greek. Upon his return to France, LeFèvre turned to the Christian classics. He bypassed the scholastic commentaries and went directly to the sources in order to understand the true meaning of the texts. In 1509 he published an edition of the Psalms in which he placed four early Latin translations in columns alongside his own critical text. Three years later he edited St. Paul's epistles by placing the Latin text from the Vulgate (official version of the Bible approved by the Catholic Church) side by side with his own translation from the Greek, pointing out where he regarded St. Jerome's text was in error. His commentary on St. Paul owed nothing to scholastic theology; it was a simple exposition of the literal meaning of the apostle's words. By 1525 Lefèvre was on the edge of involvement in early French Protestantism, only to draw back because of pressure from the monarchy.

**Budé.** The other leading French humanist, Guillaume Budé, had mostly secular interests. He was the best Greek scholar in France in the early sixteenth century as well as the best legal scholar. Sharply attacking the way law was taught in the universities, Budé published critical editions of codes of Roman law and demanded that law students study them directly instead of reading medieval commentaries. His reputation as a humanist was established by *On Coins and Measurements* (1515), a study of the Roman system of weights and measurements and coinage. King Francis I, whom the humanists called "the Father of Letters," appointed Budé royal librarian in 1522. Francis and Budé shared responsibility for founding the College of the Three Languages in 1530, which received royal funds to support the teaching of ancient Latin, Greek, and Hebrew.

**Colet.** Erasmus had left France for England in 1500. Among the humanists he met there were John Colet and Sir Thomas More. Colet was in key respects not a humanist. He knew little classical Latin and had less interest in humanist scholarship, but he was committed to the Modern Devotion. He believed that the epistles of Paul had to be read as rhetoric. Colet's influence was extensive: he became dean of St. Paul's Cathedral in London in 1504 and founded St. Paul's School five years later. Erasmus met him soon after he arrived in England, and Colet persuaded him to become learned in Greek so he could use the original text of the New Testament instead of having to rely on a Latin translation. Erasmus went to Italy in 1506 to improve his Greek but found that there was little the Italian humanists could teach him. He spent a year in Venice with Aldus Manutius publishing a expanded edition of his *Adages*. This edition had more than three thousand proverbs collected from the Greek and Latin classics with a commentary that allowed Erasmus to criticize those aspects of the Church and society that he felt violated the spirit of Christ.

**More.** By 1509 Erasmus was back in England, where he lived in Sir Thomas More's house. More was both a talented humanist and a busy civil servant. He knew classical Latin and a little Greek, and he was a successful lawyer who became a high official for Henry VIII. His place in humanism was established through his *Utopia*, published in 1516. The plot of the book is simple. More is introduced to a sailor named Raphael Hythloday, who has returned after

## MIRANDOLA

Giovanni Pico della Mirandola is best known for his *De hominis dignitate oratio* (Oration on the Dignity of Man, 1486). This short work is an excellent summary of neo-Platonic thought during the mid-Renaissance. Mirandola believed that humans have the capacity to determine their own fate. God created everything and gave all a determined place in the cosmos, and then he created humans and gave them the freewill to be godlike or to behave like beasts. The notion that humans are capable of perfecting their existence on earth evolved into a moral obligation to improve oneself and one's society.

At the time of man's birth the Father plants every kind of seed and the germs of every kind of existence; and the ones which each man cultivates are the ones which will grow, and they will bear their fruit in him. If they are vegetative, he will be a plant; if animal, he will be a brute; if they are rational, he will become a celestial creature; if intellectual, he will be an angel and the son of God. But if, not content with the lot of any kind of creature, he draws into the center of his own unity, his spirit will become one with God. . . .

Let a sacred ambition enter into our souls so that we do not satisfy ourselves with mediocre things, and strive with all our strength to reach them. From the moment that we wish it, we can. Let us despise earthly objects, let us disdain celestial ones, and leaving aside whatever is worldly, let us soar to that supramundane court which is close to the high dignity. There, according to the sacred mysteries, the Seraphim, Cherubim, and Thrones have the primacy. Unable to give up, and impatient of second place, let us emulate their dignity and glory and, if we desire it, we shall be in no way inferior to them.

Source: Eugen J. Weber, *The Western Tradition* (Lexington, Mass.: D. C. Heath, 1972), pp. 297–300.

five years on an island called Utopia. Hythloday explains life on Utopia, and he and More engage in a dialogue in which they compare life there with life in Europe. The ideal society that More describes for Utopia is one where there is no sloth, greed, pride, or ambition. Utopia is free of those vices, responsible for most of the evils More sees around him in Europe, because it has a society based on a community of property and goods instead of private property and a money economy. Gold is used only for children's toys and other ignoble things. Everyone works six hours a day regardless of job and receives compensation adequate to their needs. Just laws and fair institutions ensure that all receive what they need to live well without envying what others have. *Utopia* has been interpreted in many different ways. Some have proclaimed More as the first socialist, while others have seen him as a reactionary man unable to accept the changes in English society that were leading to the development of capitalism.

**Gentle Satire.** The second view has some merit, since More objected to the hardships on the peasants that capitalistic activities such as enclosing land to use for sheep raising were causing, but the key to understanding the work is the fact that the Utopians are not Christians. Although they are virtuous, moral, and just, they are so without the benefit of the teachings of Christ. The Europeans have the Bible to guide them and should therefore be better than the Utopians, yet they are not better. *Utopia* is gentle satire, playing up the irony that the pagan Utopians are so superior in virtue to the Christians. *Utopia* is also noteworthy as the first European work that takes account of the European discovery of the New World. By the time *Utopia* was published, More had turned to his political career, one that would eventually take him to the highest office of chancellor. In office, More showed little toleration of dissenting religious views, which was Erasmus's hallmark. Heresy was a crime for which More could give no leniency, and he sought the execution of English heretics, only to fall under the ax himself in 1535 for refusing to accept the king's supremacy in the Church of England.

**Simple Christian Truth.** The crowning work of Erasmus's six years in England was his Greek edition of the New Testament. Not until 1510 did Erasmus feel secure enough in his Greek to begin working on a critical edition of the Greek text. He used four early manuscripts for establishing what he considered the definitive Greek text. Modern scholars have found some errors in Erasmus's work, but they agree that he did an excellent job. Next to his Greek text Erasmus placed his translation into Latin. He pointed out places where the Church's official Vulgate version did not agree with the Greek text, and his commentary showed how he believed the scholastic theologians had misused the Vulgate's Latin to define doctrine erroneously. His work challenged the reliability of the official biblical text at a time when others were calling into question aspects of late medieval doctrine and practice that conservative Catholics relied on the Vulgate to support. Christian humanists and early Reformers argued that the Church needed to reject what they saw as medieval errors and return to the simplicity and purity of the early Church. In the preface to the Greek edition, Erasmus called on the pious Christian laity to read and discuss the Bible in the vernacular languages. One purpose of his work was to provide the proper basis for accurate translations into the vernaculars so that everyone could read. He proclaimed that even women and Muslims should read the Gospels. He believed theology should not be reserved to the university theologians who lacked the proper training in the ancient languages and who were overly trained in logic to understand the Bible correctly. Scholastic theology, said Erasmus, was best ignored. He wanted it replaced by the philosophy of Christ, the simple Christian truth found in the New Testament.

**Polyglot Bible.** A similar Spanish project was the Polyglot Bible, which was the first attempt to produce the text of the Bible in all of its original languages of Hebrew, Aramaic, and Greek. Jewish scholars participated despite the royal policy of intolerance. The New Testament was published in 1514, and the entire Bible in 1522. The texts of the three languages plus the Latin Vulgate were placed side by side, so that scholars could compare them, but the editors of the Polyglot Bible made no effort at pointing out possible errors in translation, as Erasmus did. It was the great achievement of the Spanish humanism centered in the University of Alcala, founded in 1509 by Cardinal Ximenez de Cisneros, Queen Isabella's principal adviser. He believed that knowledge of ancient languages made better Christians of those who knew them. He founded Alcala as a place where innovative teaching of the ancient languages could take place unencumbered by the tradition surrounding the older universities.

**Prelude to the Reformation.** After leaving England in 1516, Erasmus lived mostly in the Swiss city of Basel. It was a center of humanism with several major presses that printed his works. Swiss humanists were congenial to Erasmus because many of them were pacifists. He denounced rulers for ignoring the desire for peace from their peoples and engaging in war for dynastic ambitions, greed, and vengeance. The Swiss had been involved as mercenaries in Italian wars since 1494. Pope Julius II's use of Swiss mercenaries left a sour taste for many Swiss humanists, helping to give rise to the Swiss Reformation. By 1525 Erasmus had fallen out of the limelight, despite continuing to write major works of scholarship until his death. The coming of the Reformation cost the "Prince of the Humanists" enormously. For Protestants, who expected he would step to the forefront and use his enormous prestige as the leader of the Reformation, his desire to reform the traditional Church without breaking with papal authority led to his reputation as the lost leader of the Reformation. For Catholics he was a traitor who paved the way for the Reformation with his inflammatory satires and criticisms of the clergy and scholastic theologians. For both sides, the saying "Luther hatched the egg that Erasmus laid!" was true. The history of Northern humanism is usually seen as a prelude to the Reformation, not as a noteworthy intellectual movement in its own right.

Sources:

Anthony Goodman and Angus McKay, *The Impact of Humanism on Western Europe* (London & New York: Longman, 1990).

De Lamar Jensen, *Reformation Europe: Age of Reform and Revolution* (Lexington, Mass.: D. C. Heath, 1981).

Lewis Spitz, *The Religious Renaissance of the German Humanists* (Cambridge, Mass.: Harvard University Press, 1963).

**John Hus.** The Council of Constance (1413–1415) dealt with a major issue concerning a charge of heresy against John Hus, a theologian from Bohemia. Heresy can be defined as holding a doctrine condemned as erroneous by a proper church authority. The Church had asserted its right to hand over heretics to the secular arm—the state—for execution based on a law enacted by the Roman emperor Constantine. As of 1350 there was little in the way of organized heretical groups across Europe, but shadowy groups appeared and disappeared often in a haze of blood. The most notorious were the Brethren of the Free Spirit, although what is known about them comes almost entirely from their opponents and is therefore most certainly biased. As recorded in their heresy trials, the Free Spirits believed that they could attain union with God directly without the agency of the Church. They allegedly said that they could achieve perfection and become sinless, which permitted them to do anything; breaking laws and commandments provided evidence to them that they had become perfect. The surest fact about the Free Spirits was that they rejected the authority of the clergy. Their sense that they were perfect made it impossible for them to obey the clergy, whom they regarded as hopelessly corrupt.

Other groups, even some Flagellants, were strongly anti-clerical. The wealth and corruption of the Catholic clergy in the late Middle Ages made anticlericalism a common response, especially among the poor. More often it was anticlericalism and not any specific doctrinal deviation that led to condemnation for heresy.

**John Wycliffe.** Heresy was also found among elites, such as the Englishman John Wycliffe. A distinguished theologian at Oxford University, Wycliffe developed a fierce hostility to the papacy because of the Great Schism. In the last years before his death, he wrote several works in which he attacked virtually everything about the medieval Church, including the Catholic doctrine of the sacrament of the Eucharist. Defining the Lord's Supper was the most difficult task for medieval theologians. It was second in difficulty only to the Trinity, which had been carefully defined in the early Church. The doctrine of the Eucharist was established only in 1215 at the Fourth Lateran Council, which accepted transubstantiation: during Mass the bread and wine of the Sacrament are transformed completely into the body and blood of Christ, although the appearances of the bread and wine remain. The doctrine depended heavily on Aristotle's ideas of substance and accidents, and thinkers like Wycliffe who were not Aristotelians were inclined

The burning of John Hus at the Council of Constance on 6 July 1415, woodcut from Ulrich Richenthal's *Das Concilium*, printed in 1483 (Beinecke Rare Book and Manuscript Library, Yale University)

The following is an excerpt from a 1428–1431 heresy trial in the Diocese of Norwich. The defendant was forced to confess a range of heretical beliefs regarding the necessity of certain holy sacraments.

In the name of God, before you, the worshipful father in Christ, William, by the grace of God bishop of Norwich I, John Reve, a glover from Beccles in your diocese, your subject, feeling and understanding that I have held, believed, and affirmed errors and heresies which be counted in this confession, that is to say:

That I have held, believed, and affirmed that the sacrament of baptism done in water in the form customary to the church is of no avail and not to be demanded if the father and mother of the child are christened and of Christian beliefs.

Also that the sacrament of confirmation done by a bishop is not profitable or necessary to man's salvation.

Also that confession ought not to be made to any priest, but only to God, for no priest has the power to forgive a man of sin.

Also that I have held, believed, and affirmed that no priest has the power to make God's body in the sacrament of the altar, and that after the sacramental words said by a priest at mass nothing remains except a loaf of the material bread.

Also that only consent of love in Jesus Christ between a man and woman of Christian beliefs is sufficient for the sacrament of matrimony, without any contract of words or solemnizing in church.

Also that I have held, believed, and affirmed that only God has power to make the sacraments, and no other creature.

Also that I have held, believed, and affirmed that no creature of Christian belief is required to fast in Lent, on the Umber Days, Fridays, vigils of saints nor any other times which the Church commands should be fasted, but it is lawful for people of Christian beliefs to eat meat at all such times and days. And in affirming this opinion I have eaten meat on Fridays and the other aforementioned days.

Also I have held, believed, and affirmed that it is lawful for all Christ's people to do all bodily work on Sundays and all other days which the Church has commanded to be held holy, if people keep themselves from other sins at such days and times.

Also I have held, believed, and affirmed that every man may lawfully and without sin hold and withdraw his tithes and offerings from churches and curates, if it is done prudently.

Also I have held, believed and affirmed that it is lawful for God's people to act contrary to the precepts of the Church.

Sources: Norman P. Tanner, ed., *Heresy Trials in the Diocese of Norwich, 1428-1431,* volume 20 (London: Royal Historical Society, 1977), pp. 111–113.

---

to reject it. For Wycliffe, the Eucharist was not Christ's body and blood but a special sign of them concealed in the bread and wine. His views of the Church and clergy were even more radical. Popes, bishops, and priests were not necessarily among the saved; and if they were not, they had no right of authority in the Church. This position led to Wycliffe's doctrine of "dominion of grace." He believed God granted the right to property; only those without sin were rightful property holders. In Wycliffe's opinion this excluded most of the clergy from holding property. It also led to the idea that those who were true Christians had the right to seize property from sinners, that is, everyone else. This doctrine became part of the view of many cults that proclaimed that they were the only true Christians; some used violence to seize what they believed was rightfully theirs through the dominion of grace.

**Lollards.** In England, Wycliffe's views helped to stimulate the formation of a group known as the Lollards, who came mostly from humble origins. The Lollards denounced clerical ownership of property, clerical celibacy, transubstantiation, and papal authority while demanding a pure clergy who used the Bible in the language of the people. The Lollards, composed of only a few thousand persons, persisted despite active repression by the English government. Some historians argue that the Lollards maintained an active underground movement up to the time of the English Reformation. Wycliffe's impact was greater in Bohemia, where some Czech theologians taught his theology when they returned home after being educated at Oxford. Hus, who did not study in England, emerged to lead the Czech theologians who adopted Wycliffe's theology. By 1400 Bohemia was ready for a religious rebellion. The mostly German prelates controlled much of the property of the realm, and papal revenue demands on the Bohemian Church were high. Ethnic tensions between Germans and Czechs in the University of Prague created a volatile situation in which the former opposed the call for church reform while the latter supported it. The antipapal, nationalistic aspects of the Czech theologians' call for church reform resonated among the Czech people. Hus taught Wycliffe's theology in the university and preached it as the chief preacher of a major Prague church. He was called before the

Council of Constance in 1415 to answer charges of heresy. Emperor Sigismund, who had jurisdiction because Bohemia was part of the Holy Roman Empire, gave Hus a safe conduct, ensuring his safety at the council. The council first condemned Wycliffe for heresy and then found Hus guilty of the same errors. Hus and a second Czech theologian were executed despite the safe conduct, violated on the grounds that one must not keep faith with a heretic.

**Rebellion.** The Czech population in Bohemia responded to Hus's execution with rebellion against the Catholic Church and the German emperor. Emerging as the central focus of the rebellion was the Eucharist. The Hussites demanded that the sacrament be made available to the laity in both the bread and the wine. Giving the cup to the laity had disappeared in the twelfth century, largely out of fears of spilling Christ's blood. "Utraquist," from the Latin word for "both," was the name given to the church the Hussites organized in Bohemia. With the support of most Czech nobles, the Hussites established a national church free of the pope and rid of the German prelates. Meanwhile, Emperor Sigismund gathered an army and invaded Bohemia. Led by John Zizka, the Hussites defeated Sigismumd's Germans in a series of battles between 1416 and 1420. Many Hussites, whose anxieties had been raised to a fever pitch by the war, became convinced that Christ's Second Coming would occur immediately. Following Jesus' admonition to flee to the mountains, the Hussites assembled on hilltops. One site south of Prague was identified as Mount Tabor, which tradition had designated as the place where Christ's return would occur. The Taborites believed that they had to prepare the world for Christ's Second Coming. They differed from most of the many previous groups who believed the Second Coming was at hand in that they used violence against the nonbelievers. Taborites were admonished to cleanse the earth of sinners because Christ would not return until it was purified. Violence against the moderate Hussites, who refused to join the Taborites, led to civil war in Bohemia. In 1434 the moderate Hussites defeated the Taborites and largely destroyed their movement. The moderates then reached an accommodation with the Pope that permitted Utraquism in the Bohemian Church while it returned to union with Rome. This situation prevailed in Bohemia until the Reformation began in the next century.

**Primacy of the Pope.** It is possible that the Orthodox Churches, which never stopped giving the cup to the laity, influenced the Utraquists, since Zizka and other Czech soldiers had served as mercenaries in the Orthodox lands to the east and south of Bohemia. The question of the cup was less important as a point of contention between the Eastern and Western Churches than was the primacy of the pope. Catholics insisted that the Orthodox accept the pope as superior to the patriarch of Constantinople; the Orthodox refused. Several attempts at forging reunion had floundered on that issue before 1350. The rise of the Ottoman Turks, who crossed from Asia Minor into the Balkans in 1361, persuaded leaders in the Byzantine

Empire to seek aid from the Westerners. In 1439 Byzantine emperor John VIII and Patriarch Michael III arrived in Florence to discuss reunion. They capitulated to the Catholics on most points, agreeing to recognize the pope as the head of the Greek Orthodox Church; in exchange the Pope called for a crusade against the Turks. The Turks defeated a small crusader army in Bulgaria in 1444, while most Orthodox rejected the union with Rome. One of the most outspoken of those denouncing reunion was the duke of Moscow, who deposed the bishop of Moscow for accepting papal supremacy.

**Turks.** In 1453 Sultan Mehemmed II arrived before Constantinople's walls with an enormous force. Anti-Western feelings were so strong among the Greeks that the saying in the city was "Better Turk than Pope." The Greeks believed that the sultan would allow them to keep their religion while the Westerners would demand acceptance of Catholic liturgy and papal supremacy. On 29 May 1453, Turkish troops poured over the city's walls. Three days later, the sultan announced his policy of toleration of Christianity and designated the patriarch as the spokesman for the Christians in his empire. Mehemmed chose an outspoken foe of reunion as patriarch to replace Patriarch Michael, who had fled to Rome. One result of the Turkish conquest was the enhancement of the patriarch's authority in the Greek Church, since he no longer had to submit to the Byzantine emperor in matters of doctrine and discipline, but overall the Orthodox people suffered. They were now a conquered people who, as non-Muslims, had to pay a burdensome tax to the sultan. They also had to provide a levy of young boys to be raised as soldiers (known as Janissaries) in the Ottoman army. There was tremendous pressure on Christians in the Ottoman Empire to convert to Islam. However, Islamic tradition taught not to seek conversion, and this creed was retained after the conquest. Across the Balkans, communities of Muslims appeared alongside their Christian neighbors. The Orthodox ossified under Ottoman rule. Largely sealed off from contact with the West and currents of change, they clung to the past, insisting on maintaining every point of traditional doctrine and ritual. The Orthodox churches in the Ottoman Empire did not have problems with schism, heresy, and anticlericalism as did the Western Church. Since Orthodox priests could be married (although bishops could not), the scandal of clergy violating their vows of celibacy that outraged so many Western Christians did not exist in the Orthodox Church. In addition, the Orthodox clergy did not control the same amount of property as did their Western counterparts, thereby eliminating another source of antagonism toward clergy.

**Russia.** One Orthodox land that maintained its independence from the Turks was Russia. The Russians proclaimed that Moscow was the "Third Rome," since the second Rome, Constantinople, had fallen just as the first Rome had earlier. They declared that they were protectors of all Christians under Ottoman rule. The Russian Church severed ties with the Greek patriarchate, but it allowed

Patriarch Jeremias II to travel to Moscow in 1589 to establish a new patriarchate there. The patriarch of Moscow henceforth was a rival to the patriarch of Constantinople for leadership of Orthodox Christians.

**Judaism.** A third officially tolerated religion in the Ottoman Empire was Judaism. Although the Jews were a small minority in the Empire, in at least one city, Salonica in Greece, they may have constituted a majority of the residents in 1500. Judaism was also in theory tolerated in Catholic Europe during the Middle Ages, but practice was often quite different. The Church had decreed that Jews, as witnesses to the faith of Moses and the prophets, had a legitimate place in European society, unlike pagans and Muslims, who were eradicated from Christian lands. In 1120 the Pope declared the papacy the special protector of the Jews, who had to pay heavily for that protection. The popes also mandated that Jews identify themselves by wearing a special yellow hat or a Star of David and living in a designated part of the cities, which in Italian was called the *ghetto.* Early in the Middle Ages rulers also defended the Jews, since they provided useful banking and business services. Church law, drawing on Mosaic law, which prohibited the ancient Hebrews from taking interest from fellow Hebrews, had defined any interest-taking between Christians as usury. Jews were permitted to provide the services of bankers and pawnbrokers to Christians, including popes and kings. The common resentment toward those who performed such services was combined in respect to the Jews with the charge that they were "Christ killers," often inciting Christians to inflict violence against Jews, especially in times of tension and stress. Ordinary Christians, indoctrinated in the view that the only source of truth was their faith, found it hard to understand why nonbelievers of any sort should be tolerated in a Christian society, especially when popular rumor accused the Jews of having accumulated great sums of ill-gotten wealth. They were quick to blame the Jews for disasters such as the Black Death (1347–1351), and during this time hundreds of Jews were killed on charges that they had poisoned the wells. The hostility to Jews among medieval Christians was based on religion, not race; a Jew who converted to Christianity was assured of the safety of life, limb, and property.

**Jewish Havens.** The kings of England and France in the late fourteenth century believed the rumors of Jewish wealth and sought it by expelling the Jews and confiscating their properties. With the rise of Italian bankers, rulers were less dependent on Jewish bankers. Jews from those kingdoms migrated into the Holy Roman Empire only to be expelled from all but a few Free Imperial cities in the fifteenth century. They continued to move eastward into Poland-Lithuania, where they finally found a refuge. The Jagellonian dynasty of Poland-Lithuania issued privileges to the Jews that allowed them to be represented in a separate estate in the Polish Diet and provided them with freedom of worship, self-government in the towns, equal rights to justice, and protection of property. By 1500 Poland-Lithuania had Europe's largest Jewish population. In Italy,

Jews also found a measure of toleration. The late-medieval popes, with a few exceptions, continued as protectors of the Jewish people, and the city of Rome was an important center of Jewish culture. In the commercially active city-states of northern Italy, Jewish success in business created less resentment, and in cities such as Venice large Jewish communities were active in economic and cultural life.

**Spanish Inquisition.** Although Jews found success in Poland-Lithuania and Italy, their worst catastrophe occurred in Spain. Added to their liabilities there was their close association with the Muslims. Once the *reconquista* (reconquest) returned control of most of the peninsula to Christian rulers, the presence of Jews and Muslims was regarded as threatening to the Christian rule and faith. Beginning in the late fourteenth century pressure was placed on Jews and Muslims to convert to Christianity. Those who did become Christian were called *Conversos.* Although there were fewer Jews, they made up a larger proportion of the *Conversos,* because the Muslims found it easy to immigrate to North Africa and join their coreligionists, an option unavailable to the Jews. *Conversos* with Jewish backgrounds had wide success in business, finance, and government offices. Descendants of *Conversos* even filled some high church offices. However, resentment by the "Old Christians" grew rapidly. Hostility to the *Conversos* took on racial overtones, as many Old Christians began to proclaim that "purity of blood" was necessary for royal and church office. Being baptized was no longer adequate to save *Conversos* from persecution and prejudice. The issue of *Conversos* who continued to practice their former religions in secret led Queen Isabella of Castile in 1478 to ask the Pope to establish the Inquisition, which had authority only over baptized persons. The Spanish Inquisition was under the control of the Spanish monarchy, not the Pope. In 1480 six *Conversos* were executed for practicing Judaism, the first of several thousand victims over the next century. As the Inquisition expanded its reach, many *Conversos* took refuge with unconverted Jews. This prompted the royal decision of 1492 to expel all unbaptized Jews from Spain. About three-fourths of the Jewish population chose to leave rather than accept baptism. Most migrated to the Ottoman Empire, although some fled to southern French cities that had not been under royal control at the time of the expulsion decree.

**Muslim Expulsion.** The Spanish Muslims were largely unaffected by the campaign against Jewish *Conversos,* but in 1502 Ferdinand and Isabella suddenly decreed the expulsion of unconverted Muslims. The issue at hand was largely one of military security created by the rise of Ottoman power in the Mediterranean Sea. Nothing terrified the Spanish as much as the prospect of a Turkish attack coordinated with a Muslim revolt. Any Muslim who remained in Spain was assumed to have accepted baptism and was therefore subject to the Inquisition. Many Muslims neither emigrated nor accepted baptism, and the Spanish continued to face the problem of a large Muslim population throughout the sixteenth century. Portugal followed Spain's lead in these matters, but the Portuguese never were as insistent about racial purity as their neighbors were. Spain emerged from the *reconquista* with a powerful belief in the need for religious conformity and unity as well as a conviction of the identity between being Spanish and Catholic. When Protestantism appeared, the Spanish government had the Inquisition in place to deal with the heretics quickly and ruthlessly. When the wars of religion erupted in the sixteenth century, few Spanish doubted their role as the defenders of Catholicism against infidel and heretic.

Sources:

Christopher Dawson, *The Dividing of Christendom* (New York: Sheed & Ward, 1965).

Gordon Leff, *Heresy in the Later Middle Ages: The Relation of Heterodoxy to Dissent, c. 1250–c. 1450,* 2 volumes (Manchester, U.K.: Manchester University Press, 1967).

George H. Williams, *The Radical Reformation* (Philadelphia: Westminster, 1962).

## HUMANISM

**Origins.** While scholasticism dominated northern Europe in the fourteenth century, humanism came to the fore among Italian intellectuals. Humanism is the term used for the literary side of the Renaissance. The word came from *studia humanitatis,* the Latin phrase for the liberal arts. The liberal arts the Italians emphasized were rhetoric, poetry, and history, not logic and metaphysics. These were subjects that placed mankind at the center of attention. The humanists were by no means irreligious, but theology had little place among their interests. Humanism developed out of the attitudes and prejudices of the Italian bourgeoisie, who looked to Rome as the ideal city-state. Italian humanists hoped the glory of Rome could be reestablished in the Italian city-states. Thus, they believed that Roman literature had a great deal to say on politics, the economy, and society to the secular, urbane merchants who governed the city-states.

**Center of Activity.** Italy was the home of humanism for several reasons. One was the presence, largely in the north, of various independent city-states. These areas were run by prosperous merchants who believed that their sons needed a different education for success in business and politics than could be found in the northern universities, where students were being prepared primarily for careers as churchmen. Naturally, merchants preferred rhetoric over logic; the best rhetoricians were ancient Romans, especially Cicero. A second reason humanism flourished in Italy was that the universities of Italy concentrated on the teaching of Roman law, which sparked interest in Roman culture and history. Third, throughout the Middle Ages many secular schools were founded in northern Italy where boys learned elementary subjects without any thought of becoming clerics. Most early humanists were educated in such schools and received an introduction to the *studia humanitatis* in them. Fourth, there were many physical reminders of the grandeur of Rome found throughout Italy. Fifth, the wealth of the larger city-states, in particular Florence, pro-

## THE LATIN LANGUAGE

Florentine Humanist Lorenzo Valla extols the importance of the Latin language in the development of civilized society.

As our ancestors, winning high praises, surpassed other men in military affairs, so by the extension of their language they indeed surpassed themselves, as if, abandoning their dominion on earth, they had attained to the fellowship of the gods in Paradise. If Ceres, Liber, and Minerva, who are considered the discoverers of grain, wine, oil, and many others have been placed among the gods for some benefaction of this kind, is it less beneficial to have spread among the nations the Latin language, the noblest and the truly divine fruit, food not of the body but of the soul? For this language introduced those nations and all peoples to all the arts which are called liberal; it taught the best laws, prepared the way for all wisdom; and finally, made it possible for them no longer to be called barbarians.

Why would anyone who is a fair judge of things not prefer those who were distinguished for their cultivation of the sacred mysteries of literature to those who were celebrated for waging terrible wars? For you may most justly call those men royal, indeed divine, who not only founded the republic and the majesty of the Roman people, insofar as this might be done by men, but, as if they were gods, established also the welfare of the whole world. Their achievement was the more amazing because those who submitted to our rule knew that they had given up their own government, and what is more bitter, had been deprived of liberty, though not perhaps by violence. They recognized, however, that the Latin language had both strengthened and adorned their own. . . . First, that our ancestors perfected themselves to an incredible degree in all kinds of studies, so that no one seems to have been pre-eminent in military affairs unless he was distinguished also in letters, which was not inconsiderable stimulus to the emulation of others; then, that they wisely offered honourable rewards to the teachers of literature; finally, that they encouraged all provincials to become accustomed to speak, both in Rome and at home, in the Roman fashion.

Source: Lorenzo Valla, *The Glory of the Latin Language,* in *The Portable Renaissance Reader,* edited by James Bruce Ross and Mary Martin McLaughlin (New York: Viking, 1968), pp. 131–132.

vided patronage for specialists in the subjects that interested the merchants. The Church had been the only patron of learning in the Middle Ages, and few prelates were interested in the subjects that enthralled the humanists, although late in the Renaissance popes and cardinals would become patrons of humanists.

**Classical Literature.** The core of humanism was studying the literature of classical antiquity. While interest in the contents of the classical works was never absent from the Middle Ages, the monks were more pleased to possess the manuscripts in their libraries than to read them. Early monks had done so fine a job of copying the Latin classics

1420 most of the Latin classics known today were circulating among the educated elite of Italy.

**Boccaccio.** Unlike later humanists, who wrote in classical Latin, Petrarch and Boccaccio wrote extensively in their vernacular, Tuscan Italian, helping to establish it as the literary language of modern Italy. Boccaccio's most famous work, the *Decameron* (1353), was a set of one hundred tales told by ten young Florentines who had fled their city to escape the Black Death (1347–1351). The tales are about contemporary Italian life, especially romance and love, often depicting nuns and priests involved in illicit sexual affairs. The *Decameron* is noteworthy both for being unusually risqué for its era, and for its keen understanding of human nature. For all of their talent in writing in Italian, Petrarch and Boccaccio had much to do with the decline in writing in the vernacular among humanists who followed them. Both men were unabashed admirers of classical Latin as the only proper way to express themselves. They consciously imitated classical forms in their literary works in Latin. They agreed that the style of Latin in use by the Church and the scholastics was corrupt and barbarian. Medieval Latin was seen as proof of how far from the heights of civilization Europe had fallen since the Roman Empire had collapsed. The term *Middle Age* was coined by a humanist well after Petrarch, but the basic division of history into classical, medieval, and modern was present in his thought. For them the classical world was a golden age to which they sought to return their era by overcoming the corruption and barbarism of the centuries since. They established the basic principle of humanism: Anything the Romans had done was superior to their own time. Only by returning to the ancient models could Italy and Christendom recover its past greatness.

**Errors in the Text.** By 1400 the large number of manuscript copies of the Latin classics the humanists had uncovered was creating a new problem. It soon became clear that two copies of the same work were rarely identical. As the monks of past centuries had copied them, errors had crept in. Words, lines, and even whole paragraphs had been skipped, copied twice, or misread. The task of determining what is the original text of a work is called textual criticism, and humanists of the early fifteenth century were the first critical scholars. Textual criticism required excellent knowledge of not only classical Latin, but also knowledge of the culture and history in which the Roman author had lived. The humanists met these challenges amazingly well, so well that modern scholars often find little to improve on when producing critical editions of the classics. The most-famous figure in the second phase of humanism was Lorenzo Valla, a native of Rome who spent much of his life as secretary to the king of Naples. Valla established his reputation by producing critical editions of Latin classics, especially those written by Cicero. He had much to do with establishing the late Republican period in which Cicero had lived as the true golden age for the Latin language. Late in life, Valla turned his attention to early Christian works. He criticized the style and accuracy of the Vulgate,

A mid-fourteenth-century miniature of Francesco Petrarch in his study (Biblioteca Trivulziano, Milan)

that early humanists were convinced they were reading copies done by the Romans themselves and adopted the style of handwriting from them. The copies had in fact been made during the Carolingian Period (seventh century to tenth century C.E.), and thus the Carolingian minuscule became the modern style of handwriting. What might be called the first phase of humanism—the search for manuscripts of the Latin classics—was under way by 1350, when Francesco Petrarch and Giovanni Boccaccio, two Florentines, met for the first time. They and other humanists began a systematic search for the classical manuscripts across Europe and improved on the rather haphazard search that Petrarch had been pursuing for twenty years. Boccaccio, for example, is credited with finding Tacitus's *Histories* (circa 100–110 C.E.), a major work by a Roman historian. Patrons supported the effort by buying the manuscripts or having them copied for their libraries. By the official Catholic translation of the Bible done by St. Jerome. Valla's most notorious act was demonstrating that the document called the *Donation of Constantine* (circa 775) was a forgery. It was supposedly a grant of power over the Western Roman Empire that Emperor Constantine had given to the Pope when Constantine had departed Rome for Constantinople. The papacy and its lawyers had used it frequently to argue for papal control over the rulers of Catholic lands. Valla proved, through his analysis of its words and style, that it could not have been written before feudalism had become established in the ninth century. This revelation did not hurt Valla's career, and he died as a papal secretary.

**Civic Humanism.** While humanists like Valla pursued scholarly careers in the classics, others made greater use of the ancients for political purposes. What has been called civic humanism appeared in Florence around 1400 at a time when Florence was under attack by the duke of Milan. Several men who were major figures in Florentine government were important humanists. Most prominent among them were Coluccio Salutati and Leonardo Bruni. They applied the principles that they learned from classical literature to Florentine politics. The ideal for them was the Roman Republic, which was the most successful city-state in history, and Cicero, the outspoken supporter of the republic, was their favorite classical author. History, a major concern of humanism, was the central focus of the civic humanists. They studied the great Roman historians such as Livy and Tacitus and wrote histories of the postclassical era that imitated them. Bruni's *History of the Florentine People* (1610) used Roman sources to prove that Florence had been founded during the Roman Republic and shared in the same republican virtues. Both Petrarch and Boccaccio had retired late in their lives from their scholarship and turned to religion. For the civic humanists, being active in the world and especially in their city-state served as the highest form of human activity; the possibility of retreating into religious life was foreign to them. It was not that they were irreligious, but they could not conceive of entering a monastery and being shut off from the world. They argued that one could attain salvation as a busy merchant or politician as easily as a monk could. This view began to sanctify daily life, a notion absent from the medieval worldview. It also resulted in the humanists' ever increasing criticism of monks and nuns as parasites, who were denounced for living unproductive lives. Civic humanists took a deep interest in education, since they understood the need to prepare boys from the governing classes for an active life as businessmen and politicians through the right curriculum. Their concept of education involved a broader development of the person, including physical education, than was true of most medieval schools. The development of moral character and virtue was important to the humanists, and their choice of models came from classical literature. Pietro Paulo Vergerio made the case well in his *On the Manners of a Gentleman and on Liberal Studies* (1393). Skill in reading and writing classical Latin would necessarily lead to an appreciation of the values and virtues found in the classics and make the student a worthy citizen as well as a good Christian. Humanists saw nothing incompatible between the two.

**Limited Tenure.** The length of time in which civic humanists held power in Florence and other city-states was brief. After 1450 the political situation in northern Italy shifted greatly from what it had been a century earlier. Most of the small cities had been absorbed into the larger ones, which had no intention of allowing local republican institutions of self-government to exist in their subjects. The remaining city-states were being taken over by tyrants, a term that indicated someone who had illegally seized power and thereby violated the civic humanists' concept of good politics. In Florence, the Medici family dominated politics while keeping the trappings of republicanism. The result was a shift from practical elements in humanism, especially the sense that it was preparation for an active life in politics. A shift in patronage for the humanists also took place in the mid fifteenth century. With the election in 1458 of a humanist as pope, Pius II, the papacy began to take an active role in Renaissance culture, something it had largely ignored up to then, due to its preoccupation with the Great Schism and conciliarism. The popes began to employ humanists as secretaries, whose eloquence in classical Latin was regarded as appropriate ornamentation for the papal court. Also, after the Councils of Constance (1413–1415) and Basel (1430–1449) met north of the Alps, Italian humanists began leaving Italy for the royal courts of northern realms.

**Measure of All Things.** In the third phase of humanism there occurred the cultivation of classical learning as a good in itself without any practical value. Humanists began to argue that anything worth saying had to be said in classical Latin. Literary style became more important than the content of the classical works. For instance, Cicero's eloquence and flair for public speaking became more valued than his political commentary. A second feature of later humanism was the study of Greek and Greek literature. The interest in Greek began with the arrival of the Greeks in 1439 for the Council of Florence, but the key development was the fall of Constantinople in 1453. Its fall brought many Greek scholars to Italy, often with their manuscripts of ancient Greek works. As humanists came to appreciate the learning found in the ancient sources, learning Greek became a badge of honor for them. Unlike classical Latin, which was easily mastered by an audience educated in the despised medieval form, classical Greek was difficult to learn and thus limited to a small number of humanists. Those humanists turned to manuscripts of the Greek philosophers Plato and Aristotle. The scholastics had known the works of Plato and Aristotle largely through Latin translations from Arabic, not the original Greek. Critical editions of the original Greek texts and translations in Latin directly from the Greek demonstrated that there was much in their thought that the scholastics had misunderstood. Humanist study of philosophy received a boost with the founding of the Platonic Academy in Florence, when Cosimo de Medici in 1462 gave a villa to Marsilio Ficino as a center for the study of Plato. Plato appealed to humanists because of his eloquence and compatibility with Christian beliefs. Ficino was convinced that a great spiritual revival could be brought about through the study of Plato. He wrote *The Platonic Theology* in 1474 to propose that Plato had believed in the immortality of the individual soul, unlike Aristotle who had denied it, and that Plato's philosophy of love prefigured the Gospel. Ficino and the Platonists also found in Plato support for the humanist principle: "Man is the measure of all things."

**Pomponazzi.** The humanists found Aristotle less appealing, but the critical editions of his works pointed out how the scholastics had misread him, which was a useful stick with which the humanists could beat their rivals, as the antagonism between them and the scholastics heated up after 1500. Providing accurate texts of Aristotle's scientific works revealed how mistaken his medieval commentators had been in their understanding of his scientific thought, which helped lay the foundation of the Scientific Revolution. The center of Renaissance Aristotelian studies was the University of Padua in Italy, where scholars were eager to claim the true Aristotle for humanism. The most prominent Aristotelian among the humanists was Pietro Pomponazzi. In his major work, *On the Immortality of the Soul* (1516), Pomponazzi dealt with the fact that Aristotle had not believed in an immortal soul. He affirmed that as a philosopher he found Aristotle was correct in denying it, but as a Christian he believed it by faith. Pomponazzi opposed the idea that moral behavior required belief in an afterlife where the soul would be punished or rewarded. He argued that doing good is its own reward, while evil is its own punishment. This was a step on the way to a natural code of morality not dependent on religious belief.

**Machiavelli.** Pomponazzi's contemporary, Niccolò Machiavelli, is far more notorious for proposing that political activity also was not dependent on religion. Machiavelli served in the Florentine government during the years 1494 to 1512, when he lost his office. He then turned to writing, and in his first work, *The Prince* (1513), he bemoaned his misfortune under the guise of discussing the nature of politics and history. Unlike St. Augustine's view of history, which provided the basic framework for medieval history, Machiavelli did not see the hand of God in the unfolding of historical events. In his *History of Florence* (1519) he argued that studying Roman history provided the best foundation for a life in politics. He believed that since human nature was unchanging, patterns in history would repeat themselves, including the decline of states, the situation into which he saw Florence and all of Italy slipping. By imitating the Romans of the Republic, Italians could reestablish the golden age of Rome and drive the foreign armies from Italy. Francesco Guicciardini, another historian who served Florence after 1512, was less confident that Rome's golden age could be restored. He was also aware that people had changed since the time of Rome. Thus, he

was more realistic in his major work, *The History of Italy* (1534). Guicciardini understood how individuals could influence history by their vices and virtues. While greed and love of power, the principal motives involved in politics, were largely the same everywhere, their interplay with a given situation would be different from one time to another, so that there were no general patterns that repeated themselves. Guicciardini believed each historical era was unique, even if it had similarities to earlier ones.

**Castiglione.** By 1512 the political situation in Italy had changed vastly from what it had been two centuries earlier. Most of the once independent city-states had lost their autonomy, and the large territorial states that now existed were being ruled by princes, as happened in Florence where the Medici had taken the title of duke for themselves. The Spanish king ruled Milan and Naples. The changing political scene in Italy was well reflected in Baldassare Castiglione's *The Courtier* (1528). Although he received an excellent training in classical Latin and Greek, he wrote the book in Italian. Castiglione describes at great length the qualities of the ideal gentleman. He should be skilled in the use of the sword but slow to use it, be good at gambling but not addicted to it, know Greek and Latin and their literatures, write and speak well, know music, paint with some skill, and in general be a "Renaissance man." Castiglione also described the ideal Renaissance lady. She had her own distinctive qualities that were to complement those of the males. Castiglione insists that a lady ought to be equally well educated in liberal arts, for a well-educated mind is as valuable to a woman as to a man. It no longer was the hurly-burly of city politics that was the central focus of the proper life, but service at the court of a powerful duke or king.

Sources:
De Lamar Jensen, *Renaissance Europe: Age of Recovery and Reconciliation* (Lexington, Mass.: D. C. Heath, 1981).

Donald Kelly, *Renaissance Humanism* (Boston: Twayne, 1991).

Paul Kristeller, *Renaissance Thought: The Classic, Scholastic, and Humanistic Strains* (New York: Harper, 1961).

## THE LATE MEDIEVAL CHURCH

**Beseeching the Lord.** In 1350 a spectacular religious event took place in Rome. As many as one million pilgrims crowded into the city for the celebration of the Holy Year proclaimed by the Pope. The assembling of so many people, from every region west of Russia to distant Iceland, demonstrated the unity of western Christianity under the papacy. While there were a few dissenters and non-Christians, the vast majority of western Christendom accepted the unchallenged authority of the Catholic Church as divinely ordained. Although there was greater variation in Catholic ritual and belief from region to region than there would be in 1600, one could travel from Iceland to Sicily and from Portugal to Latvia and find the same religion. The presence of pilgrims in Rome from across Europe demonstrated Catholic unity, but the purpose behind their pilgrimages was far less positive. They came to beg God to end the catastrophic epidemic that had been sweeping

Europe for the previous three years. Lacking any understanding of a natural cause for the Black Death, the common explanation was that God was punishing humanity for its sins. In the Middle Ages making a pilgrimage was regarded as one of the most effective means to seek atonement for sin and lessen God's wrath. Men took to the road as Flagellants, publicly whipping themselves as penance in the hope that this would persuade God to end this time of trial. One consequence of the Black Death was that God came to be seen as more of an avenger of sin and evil than He had in earlier times.

**Preoccupation.** The plague also led to a preoccupation with death, which was never far from the mind throughout the Middle Ages, but now it was preeminent. Artists and writers depicted scenes of death, rotting corpses and skeletons, dances of the dead, and the final judgment. The doctrine of Purgatory as a place of cleansing the soul from the stain of sin before it went to heaven was not new, but it became more important in Catholic practice. Clerics used vivid descriptions of the plight of the souls in Purgatory to admonish the faithful to live sinless lives. Indulgences, by which one could shorten time in Purgatory by pious acts,

prayers, and donations to the Church, became far more common. Counting indulgences became almost a mania for the next 150 years. Charity was extended to the dead, whose time in Purgatory could be reduced by applying indulgences to them. The wealthy prepared for their own deaths and cared for their relatives in Purgatory by leaving money in their wills for hundreds of masses; Henry VII of England was reported to have provided for the saying of ten thousand masses for his soul. Artisan confraternities existed largely to provide for masses for dead members. The poor did the same with votive candles.

**Piety.** A vast increase in popular piety also occurred in the late Middle Ages. One result of the new piety was a greater emphasis on quantity, such as conducting masses, pilgrimages, and prayers, as well as collecting relics to allay God's wrath. The tendency was toward placing more and more emphasis on the act itself rather than the state of mind or the condition of the soul of the priest and members of the congregation. If the mass was performed correctly or the formula of the sacrament was recited exactly, then it was effective in helping to bring Catholics to salvation, even if the priest had just come from the arms of his

The Palace of the Popes at Avignon, France, which served the papacy from 1309 to 1377 and the Avignonese popes from 1378 to 1417

concubine. This mechanical formalism, which emphasized external acts rather than internal feelings, was stifling to the spiritual life of many late medieval Catholics.

**Avignon Captivity.** One person not present in Rome in 1350 was Pope Clement VI, the Pope responsible for proclaiming it a Holy Year. Since 1307, the popes had resided in Avignon in southeastern France. The papacy had purchased the city, so it was not in the kingdom of France; but the French king's influence over the popes, all French during their residence in Avignon, was extensive. The other Catholic rulers resented this Francophile papacy, and it became a serious problem when the Hundred Years' War broke out in 1337. The English king reduced papal authority in his lands by denying the right of appeal from an English church court to the papal court and by limiting the pope's ability to raise revenues from England. Papal finances became a burden during "the Avignon Captivity of the papacy." The loss of revenues from the Papal States in Italy, resulting from the pope's absence from Rome, and the creation of a luxurious papal court at Avignon created a severe financial crisis. The popes responded to their need for more income by creating a large bureaucracy and devising new ways to collect more from the Catholic lands. Papal exactions, which technically were placed only on the clergy but in effect had an impact on an entire realm, continued to increase through the remainder of the Middle Ages and led to ever more resentment toward the papacy.

**Great Schism.** The long absence of the popes from Rome created a major scandal because a pope's claims to authority over the Church arose from his position as bishop of Rome. As the decades passed, the pressure on the popes to return increased, and by 1370 two strong-willed female mystics, St. Bridget of Sweden and St. Catherine of Siena, added their formidable voices. In 1377 Gregory XI moved back to Rome, but the city was in terrible condition. Papal absence had devastated its economy and allowed it to sink into lawlessness. A year later Gregory was planning to return to Avignon when he died. As the cardinals met to elect a successor, a Roman mob surrounded their palace and demanded a Roman pope. The cardinals chose an Italian, Urban VI, who quickly alienated them by reducing their privileges. The mostly French cardinals, once they had gotten away from Rome, denounced the election as void because of coercion and proceeded to elect a French cardinal as Pope Clement VII. He returned to Avignon, and the result was the Great, or Western, Schism, in which both Popes had claims to legitimacy.

**Choosing Sides.** Obedience to either the Pope at Rome or the one at Avignon largely was determined by the political alliances of the time: England, Portugal, Aragon, Italy, and Germany supported Urban at Rome; France, Castile, and Scotland accepted Clement at Avignon. Both pontiffs created their own colleges of cardinals, and when they died, successors were chosen who continued the schism. Previous situations of this sort in the papacy had been resolved quickly, but the Great Schism lasted for more than forty years, largely because of the Hundred Years' War (1337–

1453). The scandal of having two popes led to deep spiritual anxiety, as ordinary Catholics worried that they would be doomed if their ruler made the wrong choice about which pontiff to support. Both popes continued to maintain large courts and bureaucracies on reduced revenues, which led to increased efforts to raise money from the lands under their obedience. One result was that the national churches looked to their rulers for protection from rapacious demands of the papal fiscal officers. It was an important boost to the idea that the national churches were quasi-independent with governance over them shared between king and pope.

**Council of Pisa.** Of the ways proposed to solve the Great Schism, the one that had the most support was a general council of the Church. A major issue was whether only the pope could call a council and preside over it. Theologians from the University of Paris made a convincing case that one could be convened independently of the pope. Accordingly, prelates and representatives from Catholic rulers assembled in 1409 at Pisa in Italy. The council found both popes guilty of destroying the unity of the Church and liable to being deposed. When neither resigned, the council declared them antipopes and elected a new, third, pontiff. This attempted solution simply expanded the Great Schism. While the Pisan Pope had the most support, the other two kept a following. The situation was intolerable, and in 1413 a new council met at Constance in Germany. The council prevailed on the Pisan and Roman popes to resign and deposed the one at Avignon when he refused. It then elected Pope Martin V and put an end to the schism. The Great Schism damaged the prestige of the papacy and increased the power of the rulers over the national churches, to the detriment of papal authority. It led to a period of more than a century in which the popes, now back in Rome, were nearly all Italians who concentrated largely on Italian affairs. It ended the more international focus of the papacy of the previous three centuries, and still remains the longest period of time in which popes were non-Italians.

**Conciliarism.** The Council of Constance affirmed conciliarism (the belief that the general council of the Church was superior to the pontiff) by ending the Great Schism. Theologians at the University of Paris were its strongest advocates. They proclaimed that the general council, which the Council of Constance decreed was to meet every five years, was the supreme authority in the Church, including the right to reform the Church. In 1430 another council met at Basel in Switzerland. It had an activist agenda for reforming the papacy, which led to serious confrontations with Martin V and his successors. The council lasted until 1449 because a small group of die-hard conciliarists insisted on remaining in session. Conciliarism received a deadly blow when Pope Pius II decreed in 1460 that it was heresy to hold that the council was superior to the pope.

**Pragmatic Sanction.** Conciliarism did not disappear, however. It lived on largely in France, where it became part of Gallicanism. After a century of having friendly popes who usually accommodated the French king and clergy, the French found that the election of Italian pontiffs drastically reduced the favors they had been receiving. Gallicanists argued that the French Church was free of papal control over its offices and finances while conceding the popes authority over doctrine and discipline. In the fifteenth century, Gallicanists could not agree whether the French king or the clergy, acting as a body, had the power to administer the French Church. In 1438 the clergy gained the upper hand when a national council of clergy issued the Pragmatic Sanction of Bourges, which King Charles VIII accepted. The Pragmatic Sanction reestablished in France the ancient practice of the cathedral clergy electing bishops and ended the papacy's right to collect revenues from the French clergy. The popes protested, and the kings found that the system of local bishop election led to bitter factionalism and often two rival bishops. Thus, in 1516 Pope Leo X accepted King Francis I's invitation to renegotiate the Pragmatic Sanction. The result was the Concordat of Bologna, which gave the king authority to appoint French bishops but also required papal approval of the appointment and restored the pope's right to receive revenues from France. The Concordat of Bologna gave the French ruler a degree of control over the national Church that other rulers, such as England's Henry VIII, would seek during the Reformation. It remained the document by which the French Church was governed until the onset of the French Revolution in 1789.

**Reform Movement.** In addition to believing that the council had superiority over the pope, most conciliarists also promoted church reform. The meaning of this reform varied considerably in the fifteenth century, but the point on which most could agree was the need for a better clergy. Rarely in the Middle Ages had the Catholic Church faced any challenge to its domination over the spiritual life of the laity. This situation made it difficult for the clergy to pay attention to its spiritual duties. One major source of distraction was the enormous amount of property the Church controlled. Despite making up less than 5 percent of the population, the clergy collected about one-third of the income of the lands in Catholic Europe. In church law, the revenues of the clergy were exempt from secular taxation. The papacy collected mandatory fees from the clergy, but the ordinary lay person resented the idea that the wealthy clergy was exempt from paying taxes to the secular authorities. Many in the clergy, and outside of it, denounced the idea of the Church holding property. They saw property as the principal cause of the ills that affected the Church and demanded that the clergy give it up and live in "apostolic poverty" as Christ and his apostles had done.

**Priests.** The quality of the priesthood in the late Middle Ages was poor. There were no seminaries for training priests, many of whom had only a rudimentary education and could barely read Latin. Since they usually came from the same class of people they served, they frequented the same taverns and participated in activities such as the carni-

vals with their parishioners. Drunkenness was a frequent problem, but sexual misbehavior was the most common vice of the clergy. The twelfth-century mandate for clerical celibacy did not create a celibate clergy. Perhaps a majority of priests had concubines, women with whom they had long relationships but whom they legally could not marry. The problem of priests' children vexed the Church. Most parish priests were poverty stricken despite the wealth of the Church, and they were often forced to resort to manual labor or even brigandage. Many ordinary priests revealed their alienation from the Church by participating in movements that challenged it.

**Contrast.** The poverty of the common clergyman contrasted sharply with the opulent lifestyle of the prelates. Cardinals, bishops, and abbots were elites, with wealth and prestige matching the great nobles. They often came from the great noble families, and their outlooks usually coincided with their relatives. Kings regarded the high clergy as a pool of talented, well-born men who could be put to work for the monarchy without being paid, since they could draw on their church revenues. Royal service was one reason for the rampant absenteeism among the prelates. In any given year, before the Council of Trent (1545–1563), a majority of bishops had probably never set foot in their dioceses. Another problem that created absenteeism was pluralism—the practice of allowing high churchmen to hold several church offices. It was common for cardinals to be the bishop for several dioceses simultaneously while spending most of their time in Rome. The high clergymen displayed the same vices that appeared among the lower clergy. The popes themselves were too often guilty of those vices, as proven by Alexander VI's three children. The Council of Constance called for the reform of the Church in leaders and members, but those in authority resisted the conciliarists' pleas until the onslaught of the Reformation forced them to reconsider.

Sources:
Christopher Allmand, *The New Cambridge Medieval History*, volume 7, c. 1415–c. 1500 (Cambridge & New York: Cambridge University Press, 1998).

Francis Oakley, *The Western Church in the Later Middle Ages* (Ithaca, N.Y.: Cornell University Press, 1979).

Steven E. Ozment, *The Age of Reform (1250-1550): An Intellectual and Religious History of Late Medieval and Reformation Europe* (New Haven: Yale University Press, 1980).

## LATE MEDIEVAL THOUGHT

**William of Ockham.** In 1350 the dominant intellectual system in Europe was still scholasticism. The scholastic theologians at the major universities remained the most influential thinkers of the time. Popes and kings frequently called on them to render judgments on issues that were often far from being theological matters. The last of the great scholastics, William of Ockham, died in 1347. The history of scholasticism over the next century involved working out the impact of Ockham's ideas. Before Ockham, the dominant scholastic view in philosophy was Thomism, named after the great scholastic thinker St. Thomas Aquinas. The debate between two systems involved the issue of how the mind knows things. Thomism accepted realism, which proposed that the mind understands what the five senses present to it because it recognizes them from their universals. The universals were concepts that existed on a higher metaphysical plane from things on earth, which reflected the reality of those universals. Christian realists placed the universals in the mind of God, which provided certainty that most people correctly understand the nature of things because God does not deceive. In contrast, Ockham argued that the universals in which the realists believed did not exist. Human minds are capable of recognizing the similarities among things of the same kind and come up with a name for them; therefore, Ockham's position was called nominalism.

**God's Absolute Power.** In theology Ockham promoted the concept of the ordained power of God. He possesses absolute power and accordingly is capable of doing anything, but he has chosen to establish a specific system in which humans gain salvation. God has committed himself to that ordained system, which he will never violate. For nominalists, the concept of God's absolute power opened up an opportunity to speculate about what might be true in a different universe that he could have created. If Church authorities challenged the nominalists for their outrageous ideas, nominalists would answer that they were merely speculating about what God might have done in his absolute power; but they knew that the existing universe was the best of all possible worlds because God had chosen to create it. Few nominalists actually went so far as to discuss anything outrageous, but they took advantage of the concept of God's two powers to investigate the possible options that God could have chosen in designing the universe. Nominalists at the University of Paris, for example, discussed the possibility of the Earth moving around the Sun, contrary to the established belief in the geocentric universe, and they provided extensive arguments in favor of that theory. Yet, they conceded that God had chosen to create a geocentric universe.

**Gift of Grace.** In nominalism, the system for human salvation in God's ordained power was largely the same as that defended by Aquinas. The Catholic doctrine of salvation proclaimed that grace, the undeserved gift from God to humans that makes them worthy of salvation, was imparted by the sacrament of baptism into the soul that otherwise was damned because of original sin. Grace could be lost through sin, a decision to do evil freely made by a soul, but it could be regained or strengthened through the other six sacraments—the Eucharist, penance, confirmation, marriage, ordination as a priest, and the final anointing. However, the issue of how a soul first came to receive baptism and the other sacraments was controversial. This issue had been debated in the early Church between St. Augustine and Pelagius. Augustine had argued that Adam's fall marked souls from birth with original sin, thereby making it impossible for humans to gain salvation by their own efforts. Nothing the individual could do was good enough to break the hold of sin on the soul. Only

---

## THE MODERN DEVOTION

Thomas à Kempis, the author of *The Imitation of Christ*, offers the following description of Geert Groote and followers of the Modern Devotion. It conveys the emotions of the followers and the basic feeling of communal togetherness among the believers.

Such was the inclination amongst the people to hear the Word of God that the Church could scarcely contain the crowd that came together. Many left their food, and, being drawn by a hunger after righteousness, postponed their urgent business and ran together to hear his discourses: he often delivered two sermons in one day, and sometimes continued preaching for three hours or more when fervency of spirit took hold upon him. . . . Blessed be God, who sending His Holy Spirit from Above kindled the hearts of His faithful people, and mightily increased them, so that from the seed of a few converts there grew many companies of devout brethren and sisters who served God in chastity; and to them several monasteries of monks and holy nuns owed the origin of their godly life.

It is the great glory of Master Gerard [Groote] that by his preaching so great a tree was planted and watered, a tree which after his death, though but newly set in the ground, ceased not to flourish in the field of the Lord. Although this religious order and these communities of devout persons were first planted in the nearer parts of Holland, Gelders and Brabant, they afterwards spread rapidly to the more remote regions of Flanders, Frisia, Westphalia, and Saxony, for God prospered them, and the sweet savour of their good reputation reached even to the Apostolic See.

Now the venerable Master Gerard, being filled with the Holy Ghost, and perceiving that by little and little the number of his disciples was increasing and that they were burning with zeal for heavenly warfare, took due care and forethought that the devout might come together from time to time into one house for mutual exhortation, and that they might deal faithfully with one another of the things pertaining to God and to the keeping of the law of Charity: and he ordained that if any should wish to abide continually together, they should earn their own living by the labor of their own hands, and, as far as might be, live in common under the discipline of the church.

**Source:** Thomas à Kempis, *True Christian Piety: The Brethren of Common Life*, in *The Portable Renaissance Reader*, edited by James Bruce Ross and Mary McLaughlin (New York: Viking, 1968), p. 712.

---

God could do so by imparting grace, which he freely gave to some and not to others. It was entirely God's decision, uninfluenced by any foreseen good done by those to whom grace was given. This doctrine is called predestination. In contrast, Pelagius argued that the soul has within itself the ability to do good; Adam's sin reduced that ability but did not destroy it entirely. God would reward those who do good with salvation. After decades of vigorous debate, the Church decided largely in favor of Augustine's position and condemned Pelegianism as a heresy. However, by de-emphasizing Augustine's strong support for predestination, the Church left unanswered the question of how God decided to grant grace to one soul and not to another. Ockham made a key change in the doctrine of salvation that earned him the charge of being Pelagian, which meant that a theologian was giving too much power to humans to shape their own eternal destiny. Ockham maintained that God has chosen to accept the good that humans do as meriting salvation. Certainly it was true that the good deeds of sinful humans are not worthy of influencing the will of the all-powerful God, but he has chosen to allow them to do so. God has established a covenant with humanity that he accepts good deeds as worthy of salvation as if they are of far greater value than they truly are. As expressed by a fifteenth-century nominalist, "God does not deny grace to those who do what is within them." The nominalist emphasis on "Do what is in you" coincided with the post–Black Death era's emphasis on pious acts, prayers, almsgiving to the poor, and donations to the Church. Nominalism provided a theological justification for such activities and thus enhanced the role of pious acts in the late medieval church.

**Universities.** The issues of grace and predestination are good examples of the sort of bitter debates that late medieval theologians carried on in the universities across northern Europe. The number of universities increased greatly between 1350 and 1500. One reason for the increase was the rivalry among rulers, who considered the presence of a university in their lands a source of pride. The duke of Austria founded the University of Vienna in 1365 to counter the one at Prague established by his rival, the Holy Roman Emperor, and the two branches of the ducal house of Saxony each founded a university, one being the University of Wittenberg. The kings of Scotland founded three universities as rivals to Oxford and Cambridge, which bucked the trend by remaining the only ones in England. During the Hundred Years' War the English and French kings both established new universities in the regions of France they controlled. Another reason for founding new universities was the dramatic increase in the study of Roman law. This was most obvious in France, where Paris was prohibited from teaching Roman law because the papacy feared it would lure students away from theology. Three French universities were founded expressly to teach Roman law; the one at Bourges emerged as the best. The Italian universities also proliferated, as the rivalries among the city-states led to the foundation of new schools. The focus of the Italian schools remained law, not theology, and the University of Salerno retained its place as the best medical school. The Church controlled the Italian universities far less than the northern schools. Italians wanted to educate young men for secular careers, not as clerics. They also had greater freedom to teach controversial subjects. The University of Padua in northeastern Italy became the most noted for that after it passed under Venetian control in 1405, as the Venetians protected the faculty members against efforts by

Thirteenth-century seal of the University of Paris, depicting the relationship between religion and learning (Cabinet des Medailes, Bibliothèque Nationale, Paris)

the Church to censure them. After 1400 it was the major center for the study of mathematics, astronomy, and anatomy. It alone provided its medical students with routine dissections of the human body, a practice that the Church had outlawed.

**Mysticism.** For many Europeans in the era after the Black Death, debates among theologians and lawyers were sterile and meaningless and distracted people from the true path to God. Often the same people also felt that the system of salvation promoted by the Church, with its piling up of pious act after pious act with no consideration of what was in the heart of the believer, was equally sterile and meaningless. The yearning for a direct, mystical relationship with God was nothing new to Christianity, but previously those who felt that way usually acted on it by becoming monks and nuns or going off into the wilderness as hermits. Mysticism came out of the monastery after 1350 and spread among the laity who remained active in the world. It was largely free of clerical control. In the Rhine Valley the greatest outpouring of this late medieval mysticism occurred. Because it emphasized feeling over practice and the use of vernacular languages over Latin, it had an unusually strong appeal to women, who rarely had the opportunity to learn Latin. It was probably the most strongly female of all the medieval movements. The two women, St. Bridget of Sweden and St. Catherine of Siena, who had significant roles in persuading the Pope to return from Avignon to Rome, were both famous for their mystical visions and their writings that gave instructions on how to achieve mystical union with God. In England, the illiterate Margery Kempe dictated accounts of her visions to local priests. *The Book of Margery Kempe* (written circa 1432–1436) became a major work of mysticism. Her chastisement of the local archbishop for abusing his office is an example of how mystics posed a threat to the established system. Kempe also demonstrated the appeal of pilgrimage to the people of her time. Although she was married to a merchant of modest means and had fourteen children, she went on pilgrimages to Compostela in Spain, Rome, and the Holy Land before her death in 1439.

**Modern Devotion.** In addition to mysticism, women were attracted in large numbers to another major religious movement of the late Middle Ages, the Modern Devotion. Its founder was Geert Groote, from a Dutch artisan family who became a master of arts at Paris. He seemed on his way to a high position in the Church when he entered a monastery about 1370. After three years he left it and spent his last decade preaching in Dutch towns. Groote turned over his house to a community of women who took no vows and had no habit but lived a communal life of service to God among the urban population. They were called the Sisters of the Common Life. Soon the Brothers of the Common Life appeared. By 1400 more than a hundred of their houses were sprinkled across Germany and the Netherlands. Groote was sympathetic to those who entered a monastery and then found themselves trapped in monastic life. He refused to require vows from his followers and allowed them to come and go from his houses as they pleased. This situation was one reason why church authorities were suspicious of the Common Life, but its members remained loyal to the Church despite harassment from the local bishops. Groote had a distinct type of piety that its practitioners called the Modern Devotion, indicating that they believed it was a new approach to religious life. Its best expression is found in the *Imitation of Christ* by Groote's disciple, Thomas à Kempis, who finished it before 1471. It is the best known of the many devotional works written by adherents to the Modern Devotion. They emphasized the need for emotion and feeling in religion over the scholastics' urge to define doctrine. As Kempis states, he would rather feel sorrow for his sins than be able to define what sorrow is. There was nothing heretical about the Modern Devotion, however. Its followers continued to accept Catholic doctrine and practices but insisted that the liturgy and pious acts be done in a spirit of internal devotion. They sharply attacked the formalism of their era. Groote refused to accept donations to support his communities. The Sisters made their living largely by nursing and childcare, and the Brothers made their way as teachers of boys. They insisted on a quality education for their students, including a solid foundation in Latin. The Brothers believed in reading the original sources of Christianity, and for that reason they found Italian humanism compatible to their views as it made its way into northern Europe in the mid fifteenth century. Their schools provided basic education to several prominent thinkers, most notable among them Desiderius Erasmus and Martin Luther.

Sources:

Heiko Oberman, *The Harvest of Medieval Theology: Gabriel Biel and Late Medieval Nominalism* (Cambridge, Mass.: Harvard University Press, 1963).

Steven Ozment, *The Age of Reform 1250–1550: An Intellectual and Religious History of Late Medieval and Reformation Europe* (New Haven: Yale University Press, 1980).

## LATE-SIXTEENTH-CENTURY THOUGHT

**Sarpi.** By 1560 Catholics and Protestants alike had rejected the nondogmatic, tolerant approach to religious belief exemplified by Desiderius Erasmus. His thought continued to influence the few thinkers who sought to remain apart from the religious debates and violence, but the religious issues were so pervasive that it was almost impossible to remain above the fray. The late sixteenth century was not a productive era for secular thought. In Italy, Pope Julius III was the last active papal patron of humanists; most of his successors were openly hostile to humanism. In Venice, however, there was a late flowering of humanism made possible in large part because of the city's determination to remain free of papal domination. The greatest name among the Venetian intellectuals of the late sixteenth century was Pietro Paulo Sarpi. He was a priest and a theologian who also mastered mathematics and astronomy. He has been called "the loftiest intellect that Venice ever produced." His greatest work is his *History of the Council of Trent* (1619) in which he argued that the papacy had used the council to accentuate the religious divide instead of working to heal it. His attitude toward the religious doctrines that created the division was largely the same as Erasmus's, deploring the rigid dogmatism that led to religious war. The Venetians rebuffed papal demands that Sarpi be censored and punished.

*Magdeburg Centuries.* In Germany the religious controversies largely eliminated humanism as an intellectual activity. The one significant contribution to come out of Germany was decidedly a partisan religious polemic. In 1552 the city council of Magdeburg commissioned a work of church history known as the *Magdeburg Centuries,* a collection of historical documents intended to show that Lutheranism was on solid ground in its claim that it was returning the Church to its early roots. The editor, Matthias Flacius, was a Croatian Lutheran theologian who organized the materials he and his coworkers collected according to divisions of a hundred years. This was the first use of the term *century* as a way of dividing time. While the work was badly skewed toward the Protestant position, it was an important step in the development of the idea that history ought to be written from sources coming from the era under study.

**Ramus.** In Spain and England the impact of the religious divide was equally strong in largely eliminating humanism. The one country where a modicum of secular thought continued to be produced was France. Petrus Ramus was so committed to Calvinism that he was mur-

*The Cuisine of Opinions,* a late-sixteenth-century engraving urging different sects to work together (Societe de l'Historie du Protestantisme Francais, Paris)

dered during the St. Bartholomew's Massacre in 1572, but he had received an excellent humanist training in classical Latin and rhetoric. In 1536 he chose as his thesis for his master of arts degree at the University of Paris the proposition: "Everything said by Aristotle is false." Seven years later Ramus published two works that openly challenged the way Aristotle was taught in the university and attacked the Aristotelians who dominated it. His attack was centered on the proposal that Aristotelian logic, the heart of the arts curriculum, should be replaced by rhetoric. The arts faculty responded by persuading the king to form a commission to settle the matter and arranged for a debate between Ramus and his fiercest opponents. The commission decided against him, and he was prohibited from teaching logic and philosophy. Since he remained a member of the arts faculty, he turned to mathematics, in which he was self-taught. Ramus's curiosity extended to being one of the few Frenchmen of the sixteenth century who was acquainted with the heliocentric theory (the Sun is the center of the universe).

**Dialogue.** One humanist literary device that remained popular after 1550 was the dialogue. By presenting the differing opinions of the participants and allowing the author to serve as the moderator who has the final word, the dialogue permitted the discussion of dangerous ideas that, if presented in a different context, would have exposed the author to censorship and perhaps prosecution. A skillful practitioner of the dialogue form was Pontus de Tyard, a French bishop and a noted poet. In his *L'univers,* for example, one of his speakers presents heliocentrism in a positive

way, while a second speaks strongly against it. Tyard, as the final speaker and moderator, concludes that the human mind finds it difficult to know the truth in matters such as that, where the human senses seem to present evidence in support of both positions. Tyard was the closest France came to a competent astronomer. The marginal notes found in his copy of Copernicus's *De revolutionibus* (1543) indicate a good understanding of the book. Tyard's attitude toward heliocentrism was typical for some Frenchmen of that era: Astronomy was one of many areas concerning nature in which the human mind was incapable of reaching certainty. Hypotheses about the physical world could be neither proved nor disproved.

**Philosophical Skepticism.** Michel de Montaigne became even more identified with the skeptical approach to knowledge. He was born near Bordeaux into a family of wealthy merchants; his mother's family included converted Iberian Jews who had settled in France. His father was a committed humanist who gave his son a tutor who could not speak French, thereby forcing Michel to speak to him in Latin exclusively from early childhood. Montaigne became exceptionally fluent in classical Latin. He was deeply pained by the religious strife he saw about him and the inability of the legal system to end the violence and injustice. He first tried Stoicism, staying indoors with his books and remaining aloof from the world's problems. By 1575 he had moved toward philosophical skepticism— questioning the ability of human reason to reach the truth. In a famous statement he asked: "When I play with my cat, how do I know that she is not playing with me more than I

In this excerpt from *In the Defense of Raymond Sebond*, famed French essayist Michel de Montaigne questions the arbitrary, transient, and region-specific nature of law and religion.

Moreover, if it is from ourselves that we draw the government of our loves, what confusion we are casting ourselves into! For the most acceptable advice our reason can offer us is in general for each to obey the laws of his own country. This is the opinion of Socrates, inspired, he declares, by divine counsel. And what does our reason mean by this declaration except that the only principle governing duty is a fortuitous one? The truth must be always and universally one. If man knew any virtue and justice which had a real form and essence, he would not make them dependent upon the set of customs of this country or that; it would not be from the peculiar notions of Persia or India that virtue would derive its form. There is nothing subject to more continual dispute than laws. . . .

How could that god of antiquity more clearly mark in human knowledge our total ignorance concerning the divine being, and inform men that religion was only a product of their imagination, useful as a unifying bond to their society, than by declaring, as he did to those who inquired about it before his tripod, that the true worship for each man was the one that he found observed by the custom of the place where he was? O God! What obligation do we not have to the goodness of our sovereign creator for having rid our belief of those stupid, vagabond, and arbitrary forms of worship, and for having established it upon the eternal foundation of his holy word!

What, then, will philosophy tell us in this need of ours? That we should follow the laws of our country, that is to say that billowing sea of opinions of a people or of a prince, which will paint justice for me with as many colors and will recast it into as many aspects as there will be changes of passion among them? I cannot have so flexible a judgment. What virtue is it which I saw yesterday esteemed, and which tomorrow will be so no more, and which becomes a crime as soon as one crosses a river?

What kind of truth is it for which these mountains mark the limit, and which is falsehood for those people who dwell on the other side?

**Source:** Michel de Montaigne, *In Defense of Raymond Sebond,* translated by Arthur H. Beattie (New York: Ungar, 1965).

am with her?" Philosophical skepticism led him to two positions that were not inherently contradictory but seemed so in the context of his era. One was that the human mind was incapable of knowing the truth on its own; hence, one should rely on the collective wisdom of vast numbers of people over centuries of time. This view led him to remain a Catholic, but not a zealous one. The other was a strong belief in religious toleration. It is, he believed, putting a high price on one's own beliefs to burn someone else for them, since no one can be certain of the truth of those beliefs.

**New World.** Montaigne was keenly interested in the peoples of the New World, whom he accepted as fully human. He used their lifestyles, often so strange to Europeans, as further support for skepticism about the possibility of certainty in human knowledge. Montaigne expressed his ideas in short pieces he called *Essais* from the French word "to test" or "try out." In his *Essais* he tried out ideas and presented them to others for response. He published his first two books in 1580, and the public response was enormous. Although his writing was interrupted by two terms as mayor of Bordeaux from 1581 to 1585, he published a third book in 1588. Montaigne died in 1592 while attending mass. His adopted daughter, Marie de Gournay, did most of the work of putting his scraps of writing, marginal notes, and the published *Essais* into a coherent edition in 1595. Few literary works have had the profound long-term impact as Montaigne's essays, which still serve as exemplars of good French style. Montaigne stands as a prime example of the "Renaissance man." He was at home in an enormous range of topics but especially in classical literature, eager to achieve the golden mean in every respect, including religion, and fiercely individualistic. The *Essais* are modern in their psychological understanding of human nature and sense of the relativism of experience. It is experience, Montaigne argued, that determines an individual's behavior, not some sort of ultimate truth.

**Charron.** In the first decades after the publication of the *Essais,* skeptical philosophy had a great impact. Pierre Charron, a churchman from Bordeaux and a friend of Montaigne, made skepticism a key part of the French Counter-Reformation. In *The Three Truths* (1594) he argued that Protestantism necessarily sowed confusion because of its insistence on the ability of the individual to read and understand the Bible. The inability of the human mind to be certain of the truth meant that the sixteen centuries of the collective experience and tradition of Catholicism had to be relied upon, and not the ever-erring minds of Protestant leaders. In 1601 Charron published a second skeptical text, *Wisdom,* which again made the case that only the Catholic Church's understanding of divine revelation leads to the truth, but he added that there is a natural code of ethics that can be discerned from the study of human societies. Christian morality is superior to this natural code because it is based on divine revelation, but Charron was one of the first in Europe to propose that a code of ethics could exist separate from religion. Charron's use of skepticism became a mainstay of Catholic controversialists after

1594. The Jesuits were skilled in using it to confound the Huguenots, and their college at La Flèche was the stronghold of skepticism for the next several decades, when René Descartes was educated there. He left the college a skeptic, against which he later would react. Montaigne's skeptical toleration, on the other hand, was not much in evidence during the century after his death.

**Astronomy.** Skepticism also played a role in creating interest in the new astronomical ideas proposed by Nicholas Copernicus. Montaigne argued that the only conclusion to be drawn from the Polish astronomer's skill in arguing for heliocentrism was that one should be unconcerned over which of the systems of cosmology was true. The human mind was incapable of reaching correct knowledge on such matters; therefore, discussion of them was not dangerous to the faith but was simply hypothesizing. Such a position hardly seems productive of scientific advances, but it did have a positive aspect. It allowed French thinkers to discuss Copernicanism in the midst of the religious wars, when zealous Catholics declared that heliocentrism was another Satan-induced error of the times. The skeptical position continued to serve French Catholic thinkers after 1616 when Rome condemned heliocentrism.

**Palace Academy.** Skepticism appeared in the Palace Academy that King Henry III of France established in 1576. Jacques Davy Du Perron, a Calvinist who later converted to Catholicism and became a cardinal, annoyed the king when, after arguing in favor of heliocentrism, he told him that he could argue equally well against it. The Palace Academy involved prominent thinkers who were invited to discuss their ideas before the king and his courtiers. It included two noblewomen who took an active part in the discussions on moral and natural philosophy. The Academy emphasized rhetoric and philosophy, but its sessions always ended with a musical selection. The Palace Academy may have held its last meeting when the notorious Italian thinker Giordano Bruno lectured before the king in 1581 under the auspices of the academy. Bruno came from near Naples and became a Dominican. He earned a degree in scholastic theology but soon was caught up in more dangerous philosophical interests. He left Italy under suspicion of heresy and traveled widely through northern Europe from 1576 to 1592. Bruno's notoriety came mainly from his belief in the infinity of the universe, which came from his acceptance of heliocentrism. He was not an astronomer and did nothing to provide verification of the theory, but he drew intriguing conclusions from it. He proposed that there is an infinity of stars in an infinite universe; each star has planets circling it. In such a universe there is no center, nor was it necessarily true that earth is the only planet with human beings or life. His discussion of other planets with intelligent life was the point that created the most trouble for him, since it raised the question of whether humans on other planets had sinned and had to be redeemed, and if Christ died once for our sins, how was salvation achieved elsewhere? When Bruno returned to Italy in 1592, he went to Venice with its reputation for toleration. Even the Venetians found his ideas too much to accept, and they handed

him over to the Roman Inquisition. Bruno languished in prison for seven years until he was burned at the stake in 1600. He was not, as often claimed, a martyr for science but rather for his radical cosmology. Far more than Nostradamus, his better-known contemporary who never was accused of heresy, Bruno's leaps of imagination about the nature of the universe and time came much closer to being correct as scientists understand them today.

Sources:

William Bouwsma, *Venice and the Defense of Republican Liberty: Renaissance Values in the Age of the Counter Reformation* (Berkeley: University of California Press, 1968).

De Lamar Jensen, *Reformation Europe: Age of Reform and Revolution* (Lexington, Mass.: D. C. Heath, 1981).

Richard Popkin, *The History of Scepticism from Erasmus to Spinoza* (Berkeley: University of California Press, 1979).

## MARTIN LUTHER AND THE REFORMATION

**Primary Motivation.** Christian humanists were eager for church reform, but they were surprised by the direction it took when the German cleric Martin Luther emerged as its leader. He accepted much of the humanist program, but he found infuriating its indifference to the importance of precise definitions of doctrine and sense that human imperfection made finding truth impossible. Luther emerged from his youthful confusion and doubt over how he or anyone could be saved with a profound conviction that he had found the correct answer. This confidence that they had found the truth of the gospels marked all the major Protestant leaders and suggests that the primary motivation behind the Reformation was the reform of doctrine, not the reform of clerical abuses, as much as the first Protestants complained about them.

**Importance of Faith.** Young Luther engaged in a ferocious struggle with himself over the issue of his salvation. How could one as sinful as he be saved? Becoming a monk, a priest, and a theologian, confessing his sins, and performing the many pious acts that Catholicism declared would bring the human soul to salvation failed to assure him that he could be saved. His appointment as professor of biblical theology at the University of Wittenberg led him to read the Bible far more carefully than before. Not even Catholic priests then read the Bible extensively. Luther's friend, Andreas von Karlstedt, said that despite being a priest, he had never actually seen a Bible until he joined Luther at Wittenberg. Most scholastic theologians used the Bible little, depending on the commentaries written by their precursors. Luther was unusual in his era in the extent to which he read the Scriptures. He made the Scriptures the keystone of the Reformation because he found in them the answer he was desperately seeking to the question of how he could attain salvation. In Paul's Epistle to the Romans (1, 17) Luther found the words that created Protestantism: "The just shall live by faith." This opened up to him the concept of justification by faith alone or solafideism, from Latin *sola fide* for "faith alone." Luther took solace in the idea that it is faith in Christ alone that brings salvation. The grace to have faith in Christ is entirely a gift from a

The following is an excerpt from *Twelve Articles*, a list of twelve demands of the Swabian peasants in 1524. The 1524–1525 Peasants' War was the first peasant revolt after the Reformation to employ the doctrines of Martin Luther to justify political and social causes. The Swabian peasants believed that their ideas were consistent with Lutheran beliefs so they sent a copy to Luther and solicited his response. Luther rejected the peasants' advocacy of violence in *Admonition to Peace, A Reply to the Twelve Articles of the Peasants in Swabia*. After the peasants openly rebelled he wrote a second treatise in 1525 entitled *Against the Robbing and Murdering Hordes of Peasants*.

To the Christian Reader Peace and the Grace of God through Christ.

There are many Antichrists who on account of the assembling of the peasants, cast scorn upon the gospel, and say: Is this the fruit of the new teaching, that no one obeys but all everywhere rise in revolt, and band together to reform, extinguish, indeed kill the temporal and spiritual authorities. The following articles will answer these godless and blaspheming fault-finders. They will first of all remove the reproach from the word of God and secondly give a Christian excuse for the disobedience or even the revolt of the entire peasantry. . . . Therefore, Christian reader, read the following articles with care, and then judge. Here follow the articles:

The First Article. First, it is our humble petition and desire, indeed our will and resolution, that in the future we shall have power and authority so that the entire community should choose and appoint a minister, and that we should have the right to depose him should he conduct himself improperly. The minister thus chosen should teach us the holy gospel pure and simple, without any human addition, doctrine, or ordinance. . . .

The Second Article. Since the right tithe is established in the Old Testament and fulfilled in the New, we are ready and willing to pay the fair tithe of grain. Nonetheless, it should be done properly. The word of God plainly provides that it should be given to God and passed on to His own. If it is to be given to a minister, we will in the future collect the tithe through our church elders, appointed by the congregation and distribute from it, to the sufficient livelihood of the minister and his family elected by the entire congregation. The remainder shall be given to the poor of the place, as the circumstances and the general opinion demand. . . .

The Third Article. It has been the custom hitherto for men to hold us as their own property, which is pitiable enough considering that Christ has redeemed and purchased us without exception, but the shedding of His precious blood, the lowly as well as the great. Accordingly, it is consistent with Scripture that we should be free and we wish to be so. . . .

The Fourth Article. In the fourth place, it has been the custom heretofore that no poor man was allowed to catch venison or wild fowl, or fish in flowing water, which seems to us quite unseemly and unbrotherly, as well as selfish and not according to the word of God. . . .

The Fifth article. In the fifth place we are aggrieved in the matter of woodcutting, for our noble folk have appropriated all the woods to themselves alone . . . It should be free to every member of the community to help himself to such firewood as he needs in his home. Also, if a man requires wood for carpenter's purposes he should have it free, but with the approval of a person appointed by the community for that purpose. . . .

Sources: Hans J. Hillerbrand, ed., *The Protestant Reformation* (New York: Walker, 1968), pp. 64–65.

Hillerbrand, ed., *The Reformation. A Narrative History Related by Contemporary Observers and Participants* (New York: Harper & Row, 1964), pp. 389–391.

merciful and gracious God, and the human soul is not capable of rejecting it. However, not all souls receive the grace of faith. Good works or pious acts cannot influence God's decision about who will receive grace. There is no spark of goodness in the soul that divine grace can kindle, as the nominalist theologians maintained. It follows that God has chosen from eternity who will be saved, but who they are is hidden in the mind of God. Luther accepted the doctrine of predestination, but he did not wish to emphasize it because he concentrated on the importance of faith.

**Sale of Indulgences.** When Luther had this transforming experience of faith has never been precisely determined. Most biographers of Luther believe it did occur before the posting of the Ninety-five Theses in 1517, as their content suggests that he had already begun to reject elements of Catholicism. The Indulgence Controversy, which sparked the writing of the theses, encompassed two major aspects of Catholic doctrine and practice that the Protestants could not accept because they found them lacking a basis in Scripture. The concept of the indulgence, that one could shorten the time in Purgatory by prayer, a pious act, or a donation, had come to include the possibility that it could be applied to the souls of those already dead, not just to one's own soul. When Julius II decided to raze old St. Peter's basilica and build a new church, he proclaimed a special indulgence for donations for building it. Most Catholic rulers prevented the collection of the St. Peter's indulgence, but the Holy Roman Emperor's weakness in Germany made it impossible for him to do the same. Indulgence preachers fanned out across Germany along with bankers' agents to handle the money. An indulgence preacher, Johann Tetzel, arrived in the region near Wittenberg in mid 1517. He recited a ditty encouraging peasants to give the small sum for a St. Peter's indulgence: "Whenever a coin in this box rings, a soul from purgatory springs." When Luther learned of Tetzel's activity, he was enraged. The sale of indulgences offended him in at least three ways. Even worse than the theologians suggesting that good works could earn salvation, it proposed that salvation could be bought. The idea that the living could reduce the punishment for the dead challenged his new understanding that forgiveness and salvation was a personal matter between God and the individual soul, not a collective matter for the Christian community. Luther believed that the peasants were being defrauded, since they were getting nothing for their money.

Ninety-five Theses. In October 1517, Luther wrote, in Latin, ninety-five points of theology that he wanted the Wittenberg faculty to debate. According to tradition, he posted them on the door of the university church on 31 October. While many of the Ninety-five Theses dealt with indulgences, others touched broadly on salvation and forgiveness. A century earlier the matter would have resulted in a debate at Wittenberg and some other universities; in 1517 the presence of the printing press led to a far different outcome. Luther's text was translated into German and printed in thousands of copies that rapidly spread across Germany, reducing greatly the income from the indulgence and making Luther a household name throughout Germany. Although Pope Leo X first dismissed the dispute as a "drunken monks' quarrel," he changed his mind when the income from the indulgence dropped and Luther's popularity became known. Pressure was applied to silence Luther, but it only succeeded in angering a man who had a strong stubborn streak.

True Culprit. The key event in the path to Luther's open break with Rome was the Leipzig debate of mid 1519. In time-honored academic fashion, Johann Eck, a scholastic theologian, challenged Luther to debate publicly the issues raised. Eck was a talented theologian, and he succeeded in pushing Luther into making public statements that revealed how deeply the doctrine of solafideism undercut many traditional practices of the Catholic Church. The key issue of the debate was the nature of the pope's authority, whether it came from God as Eck declared or it was merely human, as Luther argued. Eck charged Luther with being a Hussite, the first time that Luther was openly charged with heresy. It forced Luther to read Hus's works carefully, and he found that he agreed with much of what the Czech theologian had argued a century earlier. The debate persuaded Luther that the corruption of doctrine in the Church was not simply a matter of recent generations of clergymen but extended far into the past. The record of the three-week-long debate was printed up and spread across Germany, raising Luther's popularity still higher. After the Leipzig debate Luther concluded that it was the papacy itself that was corrupting the Church, and a true Christian could not accept papal authority.

Clarifying Statements. In 1520 Luther published three major treatises that put forward in a more-systematic way all his insights about the errors in doctrine, ritual, and church governance that he saw present in the Catholic Church. The first was *Address to the Christian Nobility of the German Nation,* in which he urged the German princes to overthrow the unjust domination of the pope over the German Church. He denounced papal claims of authority over secular rulers, the sole right to call church councils, and the unique power to interpret the Bible. Luther also revealed that he had rejected clerical celibacy and monasticism. He called on the German ruling class to take the lead in reforming the Church. Luther's second treatise, written in Latin for theologians, was the *Babylonian Captivity of the Church.* It set out the implications of Luther's beliefs for the Catholic sacramental system. He found only two sacraments—baptism and the Eucharist—with a basis in the New Testament. In respect to baptism he had little disagreement with the Catholic practice, but his doctrine of the Eucharist was different in two key ways. Luther agreed with Hus that the sacrament would be complete only if the cup was shared with the laity, but his doctrine of Christ's presence in the sacrament was consubstantiation, not transubstantiation. Luther believed Christ's body and blood were truly present along with the bread and wine of the sacrament. Luther's third work of 1520 was *On the Freedom of the Christian.* His use of the word freedom referred to the believer as being free from sin and the devil. He also defined his doctrine of the priesthood of the believers. There can be no difference among Christians between clergy and laity; all stand equal before God in faith and grace. All the baptized are priests because they share in the spiritual estate. Luther did agree that there is an office of minister, who preached the Gospel and presided over the sacraments. Being a minister, however, conferred no special privileges on earth. Every occupation had equal merit as an opportunity to serve God in the world. This view led to the Protestant definition of "vocation" as referring to a career in the secular world, not a calling to the life in the clergy.

Outlaw. In December 1520 a papal bull (document sealed with a lead bulla) was sent to Luther threatening excommunication if he did not retreat from his views. He responded by burning it along with a book of church law. This made it clear that he did not accept the authority of the Pope to judge him. Leo X demanded that Emperor Charles V arrest Luther for heresy. Charles summoned Luther before a meeting of the Imperial Diet at the city of Worms in June 1521. The emperor provided him with a safe conduct to ensure his safety there. Luther's friends in the Diet defended him, but the decision to condemn him was a foregone conclusion. He was called upon to retract his errors but instead made one of the great addresses of history, which concluded: "I am bound by the Scriptures I have cited and my conscience is captive to the Word of God. I cannot and will not recant anything, for it is neither safe nor right to go against conscience. God help me.

Amen!" Despite Luther's address he was condemned as an outlaw, which removed him from the protection of the law, and meant that anyone could legally strike him dead. Honoring the safe conduct, the emperor allowed Luther to leave Worms, and his friends whisked him away to Wartburg Castle.

**Exile.** At the castle Luther set to work translating the Bible into German, using Erasmus's Greek New Testament for that part of the Scriptures. He finished the German New Testament in eleven weeks, but did not complete his translation of the entire Bible until 1534. The vernacular translation of the Scriptures became one of the key characteristics of Protestantism. The laity, who were not likely to know Latin, were encouraged to read the Bible, because the Word of God does not require theologians and priests in order to be understood. Luther felt that the truth of the Bible was open to anyone who read or heard it with an open mind and a pure heart. He was convinced that everyone should reach the same conclusions as he and was highly intolerant of those who did not. Luther quickly faced the problem arising from making the Bible available to all. Not all who read it agreed with his interpretation, and they demanded the freedom to reach their own, often different conclusions. Luther objected that this would lead to chaos and denounced it as the work of the devil to undermine the truth. While he never proposed that he had the sole authority to establish the correct interpretation of Scripture, he often acted as if he did. When word came to him at Wartburg in 1522 that preachers in and around Wittenberg, including his friend Andreas Karlstadt, were promoting more-radical changes in the Church than he thought right, he returned home to retake control.

**Peasants' War.** Karlstadt and Thomas Müntzer were the leading radical preachers at Wittenberg of what has become called the Radical Reformation. As befitting for those who believed that everyone had the right to interpret Scripture, they disagreed with each other as much as with Luther or the Catholic Church. Müntzer went well beyond Karlstadt in proposing a radical transformation of society. Müntzer believed that the age of revelation had not ended with the death of the last apostle and God could give new revelation to some men, such as himself. He proclaimed that God had revealed to him that the harvest time of the world was at hand and he would be God's scythe for his harvest. Violence against the ungodly was necessary to prepare the world for Christ's second coming. Luther's return enabled him to wrestle control of the Reformation in Wittenberg back from the radicals, but expelling them from the city simply moved them into different locales to preach their ideas. By early 1523 Müntzer's gospel of violence was finding an audience among German peasants. Economic and social changes were having a severe impact on the peasants, who looked to Luther, the man who challenged the authority of pope and emperor, for leadership against the established powers. The peasants misinterpreted such Lutheran terms as the freedom of the Christian and the priesthood of the believers as referring to the material

Nineteenth-century bronze doors, inscribed with a Latin version of Martin Luther's Ninety-five Theses, at Castle Church in Wittenberg, Germany. The original wooden doors on which Luther nailed his list were destroyed by fire in 1760.

world. Since they as Christians were free, they should be free from serfdom, and as priests they had the right to the clergy's property. Müntzer himself led the peasants into battle against the nobles in May 1525. He promised his followers that God would protect them from their enemies by empowering him to catch the cannonballs in his sleeves. It proved untrue, and they were slaughtered. As this and other violent episodes of the German Peasants' War unfolded, the peasants found that Luther was not as sympathetic to their cause as they thought. Early in the rebellion he had urged the nobles to satisfy the just demands of the peasants, but as the violence and chaos escalated, he turned against them. He called on the nobles and princes to use whatever violence was necessary to put down the rebellion. The authorities did not need his encouragement to do it, but his angry attack on the peasants was damaging to his popularity among the lower classes. Catholics meanwhile were making the case to the nobles that rebellion and chaos were exactly what would happen if heretics were allowed to go free. Consequently, large numbers in both the upper and lower classes returned to Catholicism, blunting what had been the Reformation's triumphant advance until then. The Peasants' War proved to be a significant factor in the subsequent religious division of Germany.

**Political Authority.** Luther responded to the chaos of the Peasants' War by defining more precisely his concept of political authority. Since Scripture requires obedience to authority "which is from God" (Romans 13:1), the Christian has the obligation to obey properly constituted rulers. Christians who rebel against legitimate rulers dare to put themselves above God. Should the ruler order the subjects to do something evil, such as denouncing true religion, Christians have the obligation of passive resistance, disobeying but accepting what punishment the ruler might impose for rebellion. Luther needed the support of German princes for his reform of religion to go forward. He had hoped at first that the German bishops would provide the leadership for the reformed Church. Few did, however, and Luther turned to the princes. He had not intended to turn over control of the Church to them, but what was intended as a temporary arrangement in which the princes would administer the church's resources and see that true religion was taught to the people became permanent. From the princes' perspective, Luther's views were an opportunity to enhance their authority, and many eagerly accepted it.

**Controversy with Erasmus.** The Peasants' War had barely ended when Luther found himself in a heated dispute with Erasmus. The humanist had hoped to keep out of the emerging Reformation, since his agenda did not include any break with Rome. Although he defended Luther's right to be heard, he objected to his position on Scripture, which, he declared, allowed even cobblers to decide matters of theology. The issue that pushed Erasmus into the fray was the issue of free will. Did the soul have freedom to accept or reject divine grace? Luther maintained that the soul was incapable of rejecting grace. In 1525 Erasmus stated his case that souls have free will, but beyond that he did not want to dispute theology with Luther. That same year Luther responded with *On the Bondage of the Will*. It presented the fullest case for his position that grace is an entirely free gift from God that the soul can not resist. Erasmus had tried to be conciliatory, since he had always sought to avoid this sort of theological debate; Luther's response was harsh and personal. Many humanists were dismayed at its tone, feeling that the Prince of Humanists deserved more respect, and they concluded that Luther's cause was not necessarily theirs. Younger humanists largely supported Luther. Philip Melanchthon, the best Greek scholar among the Lutherans, remained loyal to Luther, although he had tried in vain to persuade Luther to tone down his language toward Erasmus. Humanism's time, however, had largely passed.

**Zwingli.** Luther became involved in another theological controversy three years later. As Lutheranism gained success in the south German cities, it ran into competition with a different approach to reform led by Huldrych Zwingli of Zurich. With Emperor Charles V declaring his intentions of enforcing the imperial ban against Luther and his followers, the two Protestant leaders hoped to unite against the Catholic forces. The key issue of difference between them was in the definition of the Eucharist. Zwingli denied the real presence of Christ in the bread and wine of the Sacrament and proclaimed only a symbolic presence. An exchange of pamphlets on the issue had already marked out their disagreement when Luther and Zwingli met at Marburg Castle in October 1529. Although they agreed on a wide range of issues, the definition of the Eucharist remained a stumbling block. For Luther, the word *is* in the words of the Sacrament "For this is my body" truly meant "is." For Zwingli, it meant "symbolizes." Luther stomped out of the meeting in anger, and the two branches of Protestantism went their separate ways.

Martin Luther defending his beliefs at the 1521 meeting of the Diet of Worms, relief from Luther Monument in Worms

**Protestants.** Emperor Charles V had called a meeting of the Imperial Diet for 1529 to deal with the Lutherans. Although the meeting was cut short by war with France and the Turkish attack on Vienna, it is noteworthy because the German princes and cities signed a petition they intended to present to Charles asking for religious freedom. They signed it as "the protesting estates," which gave rise to the term *Protestant*. The following year a meeting of the diet did take place. An effort led by Melanchthon to forge a compromise failed to gain acceptance. The diet then decreed that the Lutherans would have one year to return to Catholicism and give back the church lands they had seized or face the emperor's full military might. Before the year was up, war resumed with France and the Ottoman Empire, the same problems that had prevented Charles from dealing forcefully with the Lutherans ever since 1521, and he had to call on the Lutheran princes for help. They organized the Schmalkaldic League in 1531 to create a united front. It succeeded in winning temporary toleration of their religion while Charles had to deal with his major foes outside of Germany. By the time he gained a long enough respite from war with the French and the Turks in 1547 to deal militarily with the Lutherans, they had become too well entrenched to be rooted out. Eight years of off-and-on war resulted in defeat for Charles, who was forced to accept the Peace of Augsburg in 1555. It recognized the right of the German princes to choose between Catholicism and Lutheranism as the religion of their states and established legal existence for Lutheran churches in those principalities that chose Lutheranism. Germany became permanently divided between Catholic and Lutheran.

**Germanic Movement.** Luther was largely concerned about the German Church; he took little interest in other parts of Europe. Perhaps for that reason Lutheranism remained a Germanic movement. It had success where there was a strong Germanic element—the Scandinavian countries, where the kings of Denmark and Sweden imposed Lutheranism on their churches in 1537 and 1540 respectively, and Prussia, where in 1525 the grandmaster of the Teutonic Knights proclaimed himself Duke Albert and turned his new duchy Lutheran. Elsewhere there were few who were fully committed to Lutheran theology, even if they were called Lutherans by their Catholic opponents. Aspects of Luther's theology influenced other Protestants, and, more importantly, his example and courage inspired them. The Evangelical Church, the term the Lutherans preferred, was more conservative than the other forms of Protestantism—the Reformed Churches and the Anabaptists.

Sources:

Eric Gritsch, *Lutheranism: The Theological Movement and Its Confessional Writings* (Philadelphia: Fortress Press, 1964).

Bernhard Lohse, *Martin Luther: An Introduction to His Life and Work* (Philadelphia: Fortress Press, 1986).

Heiko A. Oberman, *Luther: Man Between God and the Devil* (New Haven: Yale University Press, 1989).

Gerald Strauss, *Luther's House of Learning: The Indoctrination of the Young in the German Reformation* (Baltimore: Johns Hopkins University Press, 1978).

## THE SPREAD OF THE REFORMATION

**Zwingli.** The first Reformed church was founded in Zurich, Switzerland. Huldrych Zwingli convinced city officials to accept his vision of true religion shortly after he arrived as chief preacher in 1518. Zwingli, the son of Swiss peasants, received an excellent education at Basel and Vienna and became attracted to Erasmus's Christian humanism. When he was ordained a priest in 1506, he showed none of the sense of being a sinner that had plagued Luther, and he cheerfully admitted having had an affair. Zwingli's work as a parish priest involved serving as chaplain to Swiss mercenaries fighting in Italy for Julius II, and the heavy casualties they suffered turned him against the papacy. When he began his preaching in Zurich, Zwingli was a radical Erasmian. He always bristled when it was suggested to him that he owed his theology to Luther and insisted that he had arrived at it independently. Yet, clearly he owed much to Luther although he disagreed with him on several key issues.

**Public Debate.** In his first sermon in Zurich, Zwingli preached "the pure gospel of Christ" and revealed that he rejected many Catholic practices. As he stepped up his criticism and many in Zurich took up his message, pressure was placed on the city council to deal with the problem. In early 1523 the council arranged for a public debate between Zwingli and some Catholics. The use of a public debate between Catholics and Protestants before the local city council was a common device through which most of the German and Swiss cities formally adopted the Reformation. The Zurich council decided that Zwingli had won the debate, as well as a second one later that year, and began to implement his changes. Clerical celibacy was no longer required, and Zwingli married. Monasteries and convents were closed, and the city took over the relief for the poor they had been providing. In 1525 a third debate before the council secured for Zwingli the abolition of the mass and the institution of his Communion service as proper worship. By rejecting both transubstantiation and consubstantiation, Zwingli removed the special role of the priest/minister in worship. No special power or privilege was needed for the pastor to assemble God's people to commemorate the Lord's Supper and affirm Christ's symbolic presence in his people.

**Eucharist and Baptism.** In 1524 Zwingli wrote *A Commentary on True and False Religion*, which was the fullest presentation of his theology. Besides the Eucharist he accepted only baptism as a sacrament. He favored infant baptism, in contrast with some of his early followers, who required adult baptism. The baptized become members of the Christian community, but membership in it does not ensure that they are among the saved. Only God knows who is saved and who is damned. The saved, however, are likely to demonstrate their faith through good works, a

Ulrich Zwingli, the people's priest in the Swiss city of Zurich, believed that the Word of God was the purest authority and he increasingly worked for reform in the church. On 29 January 1523, he invited six hundred friends and foes to the Zurich town hall for a discussion. The basis for this discussion was sixty-seven articles that Zwingli had prepared, ranging from the nature of the Gospel to the practice of selling indulgences. Some of the more interesting ones appear below.

1. All who say that the gospel is invalid without the confirmation of the Church err and slander God.

2. The sum and substance of the gospel is that our Lord Jesus Christ, the true Son of God, has made known to us the will of His heavenly Father, and has with His innocence released us from death and reconciled God.

3. Hence Christ is the only way to salvation for all who ever were, are, and shall be.

5. Hence all who consider other teachings equal to or higher than the gospel err and do not know what the gospel is.

14. Therefore all Christian people shall use their best diligence that the gospel of Christ be preached alike everywhere.

15. For in the faith rests our salvation, and in unbelief our damnation; for all truth is clear in Him.

16. In the gospel one learns that human doctrines and decrees do not aid in salvation.

17. That Christ is the only eternal high priest, wherefrom it follows that those who have called themselves high priests have opposed the honor and power of Christ, yea, cast it out.

18. That Christ, having sacrificed Himself once, is to eternity a certain and valid sacrifice for the sins of all faithful, wherefrom it follows that the mass is not a sacrifice, but is a remembrance of the sacrifice and assurance of the salvation which God has given us.

22. That Christ is our justice, from which [it] follows that our works insofar as they are good, so far they are of Christ, but insofar that they are ours, they are neither right nor good.

23. That all which God has allowed or not forbidden is righteous, hence marriage is permitted to all human beings.

24. That all who are called clericals sin when they do not protect themselves by marriage after they have become conscious that God has not enabled them to remain chaste.

**Sources:** Samuel Macauley Jackson, ed., *Selected Works of Huldreich Zwingli (1484–1531)* (Philadelphia: University of Pennsylvania, 1901), pp. 40, 47–54, 111–117.

Lewis W. Spitz, ed., *The Protestant Reformation* (Englewood Cliffs, N.J.: Prentice-Hall, 1966), pp. 82–85.

highly moral life, and love of God and neighbor. Zwingli promoted broader change in ritual than Luther did. His worship service differed more from the mass. Music and images in church were banned, and images in the existing churches were either broken or whitewashed over. Marriage became a civil contract, and divorce was accepted. Concerning church governance, Zwingli looked to the magistrates in the city council, not to the princes, for leadership in the church. He saw no real distinction between the church and the city; preachers and magistrates alike had the task of establishing God's rule. His political views have been described as theocratic, meaning civil and religious laws are derived from divine sources and thus ecclesiastical authorities have an important role in civil government. As Zurich and other Swiss cities, persuaded by Zwingli's disciples, became Reformed, the ever-present tension with the mountain cantons, which remained Catholic, increased. By 1529 Zwingli was sufficiently worried about civil war that he met with Luther at Marburg to forge a united front. After the meeting's failure, war erupted between Protestant and Catholic Swiss. Zwingli was killed leading the troops from Zurich into battle in 1531. Zwingli, the forgotten man of the Reformation, had a strong influence on two branches of Protestantism—Anabaptism and Calvinism.

**Anabaptists.** The idea that baptism must be administered to an adult, who thereby makes a public commitment to a Christian life, was present in the early church and appeared in heretical movements throughout the Middle Ages. It reappeared soon after Zwingli began preaching in Zurich. Rebaptism rose out of the concept of the gathered church as a community of true believers who make an adult decision to join. Conrad Grebel was the most prominent of the Zurichers who rejected the idea accepted by Catholics and most Protestants that a child at birth was automatically a member of a church coextensive with the state. Several major consequences followed from requiring adult baptism. First, the church consisted only of the elect, who were few; the traditional view that it included saints and sinners whom Christ would separate at the end of time was rejected. The saints must keep apart from the children of darkness. Second, it requires the separation of church and state. If the church consists of only a few true believers, then it is not synonymous with the state but distinct from it. It follows that true believers were not obliged to pay taxes, swear oaths, and perform military service. Third, Emperor Constantine had condemned rebaptizing as a heretical practice and mandated death for it. The radicals insisted that they did not rebaptize because infant baptism was not valid; they usually called themselves simply the Brethren. Catholic and Protestant authorities called them "Anabaptists" to bring them under legal liability to administer to them a "third baptism": death by drowning.

**Hutter.** Grebel provided a coherent theology for the gathered church of the saints. The model for a community of true believers was the Apostolic Church, and the Anabaptists sought to emulate it. Their practices included common ownership of goods, a greater role for women, shunning nonbelievers, a rigid moral code, and nonresistance to persecution. Refusal to use violence was common to most early Anabaptists. Grebel died a natural death, but Swiss authorities imposed the death penalty on the most outspoken of the Anabaptists. Other Anabaptists scattered across Europe, carrying their ideas to a wide audience, although many radical groups sprang up without Swiss influence. Most Anabaptists insisted on a rigorous moral code, but some proclaimed that faith permitted anything. Since they were the saints of God living in the new age, human laws no longer bound them. Such lawlessness helped to discredit Anabaptism in the eyes of most people, but Jakob Hutter came close to establishing Anabaptism as a viable way of life. Influenced by the Swiss Brethren, Hutter became an Anabaptist in Austria. Persecution forced him to flee to Moravia in 1533 where he became head of a commune of Moravian Brethren. His concept of the apostolic community required that both production and consumption of goods be done in common. Hard work, discipline, and dedication among the Moravian Brethren allowed their communities to flourish. The passing of centuries failed to dampen the enthusiasm of most Brethren, and their communities survived, despite frequent persecution, through migration to the Ukraine and then America.

**Münster.** Little is known about Melchior Hoffman before he arrived in Strasbourg in 1529. As the prophet of the end times, he declared it would become the New Jerusalem in 1533. Hoffman had success in gaining followers among the urban poor of the German and Dutch cities, where economic recession and bad harvests had created enormous stress. In such troubled times the promise of being among those who would receive eternal reward while the nobles, merchants, and prelates would be vanquished, was too powerful to give up, even when the year 1533 ended without Christ's return. Hoffman did not visit Münster, a German city that would always be associated with his doctrines. Before a public debate between Lutheran and Catholic theologians in August 1533, Anabaptist preachers were invited to the city to bolster the Protestant cause. The result was a stalemated city council that refused to take action against the Anabaptists, and the city quickly became a refuge for radicals. They included Jan Bokelson and Jan Matthys, whose forceful personalities gave them a major role in the Anabaptist takeover of Münster in early 1534. They sent a letter to cities and villages of the region announcing that Münster was the New Jerusalem and inviting the true believers to go there and avoid the vengeance of the Lord. About 2,500 people accepted the invitation. The expulsion of both Lutherans and Catholics persuaded local Lutheran nobles to join the Catholics and lay siege to Münster in March 1534. As the siege tightened, Matthys declared he had received a command from God to drive the enemy away. On Easter, the appointed day for Christ's return, he led a sortie, promising his troops that God would protect them. Matthys was killed and his body hacked to pieces. Bokelson now took control of Münster. He revealed that God demanded establishment of a government based on ancient Israel, and he drew up rules for the city based entirely on the Bible. Polygamy as practiced by the Hebrew patriarchs was mandated, since there was a serious imbalance of women in the city. Bokelson declared himself king of the entire world with Münster as the New Jerusalem. By early 1535 an effective siege was in place, reducing the people to starvation. A reign of terror kept the starving people from overthrowing their king. Finally two men escaped and revealed weak points in the defenses to the besiegers, who in June broke through the walls, massacred the defenders, and captured Bokelson. They put him in a cage and exhibited him around Germany until early 1536, when he was returned to Münster and executed. The cage with his corpse was hung in the cathedral tower, where it remained for centuries.

**Simons.** The events in Münster seemed to justify harsh persecution of Anabaptists. Anabaptism was saved from possible extinction by the work of several theologians who returned to its earlier pacifism. The most important was Menno Simons, a priest who became a radical through Hoffman's influence. Simons condemned all violence despite persecution. He believed that only a few saints, who had to suffer persecution until Christ's return, made up the true church. Then they would be lifted up to the New Kingdom while the wicked would suffer unending torments. By convincing Anabaptists that suffering persecution from the wicked was a sign of their election as saints, Simons turned them away from violent resistance to the authorities. Simons emphasized that only God knows the day and the hour of Christ's return; the saints must wait patiently until it happens. Modern followers of his doctrines are the Mennonites and Amish.

**Calvin.** The first days of John Calvin as a Protestant coincided with events at Münster. This situation helps to explain his desire to persuade authorities that his political and social views were not radical. Like Zwingli, Calvin came to Protestantism through humanism. His first publication was a humanist commentary on the Roman author Seneca the Younger's *On Mercy* (55–56 C.E.). Seneca's Stoicism appealed to Calvin with its emphasis on self discipline and belief in natural law; even the most depraved persons understand what is good and moral, although they fail to do it. By 1534 Calvin had become Protestant, although he seems not to have had a dramatic conversion experience of the kind that Luther did. Calvin traveled widely for the next two years, staying for a time in Basel, where Zwinglians had led the Reform. The influence of Zwingli and Luther can be seen in Calvin's first work on

Meeting in the Calvinist Temple at Lyon, 1564 (Bibliotheque Publique et Universitaire, Geneva)

religion, *Institutes of the Christian Religion*, which was printed in early 1536. It was his major theological work, although he revised it extensively for the rest of his life, with the final edition appearing in 1561. Yet, the first edition is a surprisingly mature work for someone who only three years earlier was not sure of his beliefs. In July 1536, on his way to Strasbourg to become pastor of the French Protestant community there, he passed through Geneva, which had already accepted Protestantism. The local Protestant leaders, Zwinglians in theology, persuaded him to stay. The publication of his *Institutes* earlier in 1536 marked him as a major Protestant theologian and Calvin quickly became the dominant figure in Geneva. In his haste to make it a truly reformed city, however, he made enemies who secured his ouster in 1538. He went to Strasbourg, where he worked closely with Martin Bucer, whose Lutheran beliefs had been heavily influenced by Zwingli. In 1541 supporters regained control of Geneva and invited Calvin to return, which he did only reluctantly.

**Governing the Church.** Upon his return Calvin drew up his "Ecclesiastical Ordinances" to establish a system of church governance. The city council accepted them in 1541 as his condition for staying. Calvin based his form of church governance on the Acts of the Apostles, where he found four divine offices—pastors, whose duties involved preaching and ministering the two sacraments of baptism and holy communion; teachers, who instructed the faithful; elders, who oversaw the conduct of the congregation; and deacons, who directed the administering of relief to the poor. The key body was the consistory, made up of all nine pastors in Geneva in 1541 and twelve elders who were chosen from the members of the city council. The dozen elders were laymen, so in theory the laity controlled the consistory, although Calvin's views almost always dominated. The consistory had the task of overseeing and correcting the doctrine of the pastors and the conduct of lay people who refused to accept correction from the elders. Excommunication, expulsion, and in some cases, execution, were imposed on those who refused to submit to the consistory. The consistory imposed Calvin's strict moral code on the people, which in the hands of his later followers in England became known as Puritanism.

**Predestination.** Calvin gave a major place to the doctrine of predestination. The doctrine was not new to him; many earlier Christian theologians, especially St. Augustine, had accepted it. Most of its previous defenders had maintained that God had chosen the elect for salvation, but the damned were responsible for their fate because of their sins. Calvin argued that there was nothing that a human could do, whether good or evil, to influence God's will. He did not shrink from what he called the doctrine's "awful consequences": God has predestined both the saved and the damned from all eternity. Calvin was eager, however, to keep his followers from lapsing into fatalism—the belief that it makes no difference what people do in life, since their fate has already been determined—which some Anabaptists were preaching. He proclaimed that those who lived a good Christian life should have reasonable confidence that they were among the elect. This confidence, taken more as a guarantee by his followers, gave the Calvinists the courage to confront the evildoers and correct them, especially the princes who were harming the true religion.

**Protestant Work Ethic.** Predestination was a stumbling block for many who otherwise were attracted to Calvin's vision of Christianity, but it gave to those who did accept it a powerful courage of their convictions to change the world. It made them a revolutionary force in western Christendom in the century to come. As interpreted by later Calvinists, the doctrine also had the consequence of seeing success in the world, especially in business, as a sign of election, since God would favor his saints. Along with Calvin's denunciation of monasticism and his emphasis on doing one's best in day-to-day life, it helped to create what has been called the Protestant work ethic.

Sacraments. What Calvin meant by a good Christian life included receiving the two sacraments of baptism and the Eucharist. Baptism is the sign of joining the fellowship of the Church and being counted among the children of God. In one sense Calvin literally meant children, for he accepted infant baptism as an authentic practice of the early Church, taking the place of circumcision as the sign of initiation for Jewish infants. Calvin believed in Christ's real but spiritual presence in the bread and wine of the Eucharist. It served well as a compromise between Luther's consubstantial real presence and Zwingli's symbolic presence. Calvin did not agree with Zwingli that the Lord's Supper should be celebrated only four times a year, but the Zwinglians who reformed the city before he arrived had established the practice, and it remained so in the Calvinist liturgy. Consequently, the center of ordinary Sunday worship became Scripture readings and the sermon. Calvin followed Luther in proclaiming that biblical truth was open to anyone with an open mind and a pure heart, but he was not so convinced that most people could understand it correctly. He had seen how the practice of reading the Bible "alone, for oneself" had led to what he regarded as the excesses of the Anabaptists. The pastors and teachers had the great responsibility of guiding the people though the Bible, which was done first of all by Sunday preaching. Attending Sunday services was another necessary sign of leading a good Christian life. "Keep thou holy the Lord's day!" received greater emphasis in Calvinism than in other mainstream branches of Christianity. While accepting Zwingli's ban on images in church, Calvin promoted the singing of Psalms, and the singing of Psalms in vernacular translation became one of the marks of Calvinists.

**Eagerness to Reform.** Calvin's experiences were entirely within the context of urban bourgeois life. His religious beliefs and practices reflected it, as, for example, in abandoning the prohibition on interest. The pastors in concert with the prosperous merchants and artisans governed the Church of Geneva. Calvinism appealed largely to the bourgeoisie across Europe, who put an emphasis on certain points in it that supported the development of capitalism. The theory that Protestantism and in particular Calvinism gave rise to capitalism is overstated, but there is some connection between the two. Calvin was clearer in separating the Church from the city council than Zwingli had been in Zurich. Both church and state have the tasks of bringing sinners to praise God, but they do it in distinct ways. The church can flourish under any type of government, provided it is not a tyranny, and the Christian is obliged to obey secular authority. Yet, if the state orders what is against the law of God, then the Christian must resist, although Calvin seems to rule out violent resistance. He accepted monarchy as a legitimate form of government, but he felt that a single person holding authority was more likely to require his subjects to violate God's law, while he could not trust the rule of the mob, democracy, to avoid anarchy, the other great evil besides tyranny. Thus, he felt that rule by the few, oligarchy, was the best government, as it existed in Geneva. When Calvinists found themselves confronting the Catholic monarchs in the various religious wars after 1560, they found it easy to interpret Calvin's thoughts on these matters to justify armed resistance to monarchy. Unlike Luther, Calvin was eager to reform all Christendom and founded the Geneva Academy in 1559 for training pastors to send across Europe. By the time he died in 1564, strong Calvinist movements had been established in France, England, the Netherlands, and Scotland; in the latter two countries it became the dominant religion.

**Presbyterians.** Scotland remains today the most Calvinist land except perhaps for Geneva itself. Before 1540, isolated Scotland had seen little in the way of heresy. A greater impact on Scotland's religious future was England's break with Rome. A pro-English party long had been active in Scots politics, and now it took on a pro-Protestant position, especially in contrast with the monarchy's pro-French policy, eager to maintain the "Auld Alliance" with France. James V had married Mary of Guise, from a strongly Catholic French noble family, as part of that policy. When he died in 1542, his only child was his week-old daughter, Mary, who became Mary Queen of Scots despite her age. Chaos followed in Scotland, which became worse when Mary was taken at age six to be raised at the French court with her Guise relatives. The pro-English party gained support, as opposition to the role of Mary of Guise in governing Scotland became extensive. In 1546 a group of Scots, including a young priest, John

Knox, murdered the pro-French archbishop of St. Andrews and seized his castle until French troops drove them out. Knox served a term as a slave on French galleys. After being freed he went to Geneva and became an ardent Calvinist. His opportunity to strike against French influence and Catholicism came in 1559, when he returned to Scotland. Mary of Guise died in 1560 while her daughter was still in France, and Knox and the Protestant party persuaded the Scottish Parliament to abolish the authority of the papacy in Scotland and adopt the Scottish Confession of Faith, which was largely Calvinist. Special emphasis was placed on the role of the presbyters (elders) hence the name Presbyterian Church.

**House of Stuart.** Queen Mary returned to Scotland in 1561. She was a Catholic in what was now a Protestant realm, but she might have kept power if it had not been for her marital problems. When her second husband Lord Darnley was murdered in 1567, she married one of those believed responsible. The outrage of the Scots forced her to flee to England for protection, and her infant son by Darnley was crowned King James VI of Scotland (ruled 1567–1625). He later ruled England as James I (1603–1625), the first Stuart king of England. He was put under the control of Protestant regents who saw to it that he was raised Calvinist. Scotland became solidly Protestant.

**English Response.** Despite a tradition of antipapal attitudes and a native heretical group, the Lollards, England responded slowly to Protestantism. Henry VIII (ruled 1509–1547) had a *Defense of the Seven Sacraments* (first published in 1687) ghostwritten for him attacking Luther's doctrine, but his chancellor, Cardinal Thomas Wolsey, angered the English people and clergy with his demands for money and his use of church and political offices to advance his ambition to become pope. What might have happened in England had it not been for the "King's Great Matter" is impossible to say. Henry had married his older brother's widow, Catherine of Aragon, to maintain a Spanish alliance. By church law, such a relationship was incest, and Henry had received a dispensation from Julius II to marry her. By 1527, when Catherine was past the age of childbearing, the marriage had resulted in only one surviving child, Princess Mary. Since a female's right to rule in England was unclear, Henry was worried about the future of his dynasty. By then he had also fallen in love with Anne Boleyn, Catherine's lady-in-waiting. Henry's sense that he was being punished for violating divine law against incest and his passion for Anne led him to ask the Pope for an annulment of his marriage. Unfortunately for him, Catherine's nephew, Emperor Charles V, controlled Rome. When Henry's petition reached Pope Clement VII, Charles refused to allow his aunt to be humiliated and his cousin cut out of a chance of ruling England. The Pope's response was to delay, hoping the problem would solve itself by someone's death or change in the political situation.

**Finding a Solution.** Henry, exasperated by the delays, replaced Wolsey as chancellor with the humanist Sir Thomas More in 1529. More refused to participate in the quest for the annulment, so the office soon went to Thomas Cromwell, who was sympathetic to moderate Protestantism and persuaded Henry to pressure Clement by reducing ties to Rome beginning in 1531. The Pope did not concede, so in 1533, with Anne Boleyn now pregnant, Henry issued a decree forbidding appeals to the papal court, the last step in the break with Rome. The Parliament was asked to approve of it in order to gain popular support. The archbishop of Canterbury could now hear the annulment request, and the archbishop, Thomas Cranmer, granted it. Henry had already married Anne, who gave birth to the future Queen Elizabeth I. A 1534 decree defined any denial of the king's authority over the Church as treason, and several persons, most notably Sir Thomas More and Bishop John Fisher, were executed for denying Henry's supremacy in religion. Henry was conservative in religion despite being "the supreme head of the Church of England on earth," but he made some changes beyond rejecting papal authority. He replaced Latin with English in the church services. Cromwell received authority to investigate monasteries and convents for corruption, and in 1536 he ordered that the smaller ones be closed and their properties given to the king. Three years later all remaining religious houses were closed. Monastic properties were either given to the king's favorites or sold at good prices, which committed many influential people to support the break with Rome. Yet, Henry reconfirmed most Catholic doctrines including transubstantiation and clerical celibacy in his Six Articles of 1539. Many persons who rejected traditional doctrine were executed as heretics.

**Multiple Wives.** Henry's marital problems continued after his marriage to Anne. After she had several miscarriages, Henry accused her of adultery, which was treason, and she was executed. He then married Jane Seymour, who in 1537 gave birth to Edward and died twelve days later. He had three more wives; the last survived him upon his death. His will called for his children to succeed him in the order of Edward, Mary, and Elizabeth. As a minor Edward VI needed a regent, his uncle Edward Seymour. The latter was favorable to Protestantism, and as a result Zwinglian and Calvinist preachers arrived from the Continent. In 1549 Cranmer wrote the *Book of Common Prayer* to provide a moderate Protestant text for church services, while clerical marriages were permitted. When Seymour fell from power in 1551, the duke of Northumberland took power and moved further toward Reformed Protestantism. A new *Book of Common Prayer* appeared in 1552 with a largely Zwinglian definition of the Eucharist.

**Puritan Movement.** The next year Edward was dead, and his Catholic sister Mary took the throne. She immediately set to work to undo what her father and brother had done. Under the influence of moderates, Mary's first two years involved gradual restoration of traditional Catholicism, but when vehemently anti-Protestant Pope Paul IV was elected in 1555, he put strong pressure on her to cleanse her realm of heretics. Some three hundred persons were executed (including Thomas Cranmer) for which she became known as "Bloody Mary." About eight hundred English Protestants fled to Geneva and other Reformed cities. After Mary died childless in 1558 and her Protestant sister Elizabeth became queen, most "Marian exiles" returned home, full of zeal for Calvinism. They helped create the Puritan movement, so called because they wanted to purify the Church of England of the Catholic practices and beliefs that they still saw in it.

**Elizabethan Religious Settlement.** Elizabeth I (ruled 1558–1603) never revealed her religious beliefs, but as soon as she took the throne she proclaimed that she would return the Church of England to what it had been under her father's rule. In fact she accepted many of the Protestant changes made under Edward. A revised edition of Cranmer's *Common Book of Prayer* took out some of the most openly Reformed statements while vaguely phrasing definitions of controversial doctrines in hope that Protestant and Catholic alike could find them acceptable. What is called the Elizabethan Religious Settlement was intended to satisfy both sides as much as possible. In Elizabeth's international policy, however, she clearly came down on the side of the Protestant states; politically England was a Protestant land, even if doctrinally the Church was not clearly so. Some Catholics and Puritans found that they could not accept the middle of the road in religion. Eliza-

beth handled the Puritan demands for further reform deftly without giving in and deflected any political threat they might have posed. The Catholics were seen as a greater threat because of the religious wars going on across Europe. Catholic refusal to take the oath recognizing her as "supreme governor in spiritual affairs" was deemed treasonous, and by 1570, when the Pope excommunicated Elizabeth, executions of Catholics for treason began. Some two hundred Catholics accepted death rather than swear the oath. Called Recusants for refusing the oath, a small number of the English people remained Catholic.

Sources:

A. G. Dickens, *The English Reformation* (London: B. T. Batesford, 1964).

Dickens and John M. Tonkin, *The Reformation in Historical Thought* (Cambridge, Mass.: Harvard University Press, 1985).

Gordon Donaldson, *The Scottish Reformation* (Cambridge: Cambridge University Press, 1960).

Robert M. Kingdon, ed., *Transition and Revolution: Problems and Issues of European Renaissance and Reformation History* (Minneapolis: Burgess, 1974).

Menna Prestwich, ed., *International Calvinism 1541-1715* (Oxford: Clarendon Press, 1985; New York: Oxford University Press, 1985).

# SIGNIFICANT PEOPLE

## JOHN CALVIN

### 1509-1564
### THEOLOGIAN AND REFORMER

**Studies.** Born at Noyon in northern France, John Calvin was the son of the notary to the local bishop, which made him part of the bourgeoisie. Eager for a high-church career for John, his father sent him to the University of Paris for training as a theologian. Calvin also began to study with several prominent humanists. After his father had a falling out with the clergy, he sent his son to Orléans for a law degree, which Calvin received in 1532. He returned to Paris, where he continued his study of classical literature. In that year he published a commentary on the Roman author Seneca the Younger's *On Mercy* (55–56 C.E.) It was a typical piece of humanist scholarship and shows no sign of Protestantism. By 1534 he had become Protestant,

for in the aftermath of the posting of anti-Catholic placards by Zwinglians in Paris, he fled from France, although he seems not to have had any role in the episode.

**Geneva.** Calvin traveled widely for the next two years, going to Ferrara in Italy and Basel in Switzerland. In July 1536, on his way to Strasbourg to become pastor of the French Protestant community there, he passed through Geneva, which had already accepted Protestantism. The local Protestant leaders persuaded him to stay. The publication of his *Institutions of the Christian Religion* earlier in 1536 had already marked him as a major Protestant theologian. Calvin quickly became the dominant figure in the city. In his haste to make it a truly Reformed city, he made enemies who secured his ouster in 1538. Calvin went to Strasbourg, where he married in 1540. His wife Idelette died eight years later. In 1541 supporters regained control of Geneva and invited Calvin to return, which he did reluctantly. He spent the rest of his life there.

**Model Christian City.** Upon his return Calvin set about to make Geneva into the model Christian city. He drew up his "Ecclesiastical Ordinances" to establish the system of church governance for its church. The city council accepted them in 1541 as his condition for returning from Strasbourg. Calvin based his form of church governance on the Acts of the Apostles, where he found four divine offices of pastors, teachers, elders, and deacons. The key institution was the consistory, made up of all nine pastors in Geneva in 1541 and twelve elders who were chosen from the members of the city council. It had the task of correcting the doctrine of the pastors and the conduct of laypeople who refused to accept correction from the elders. The consistory imposed Calvin's strict moral code on the people, which in the hands of his later followers in England became known as Puritanism. John Knox, the Scots reformer, would call Geneva "the most perfect city of Christ."

**Predestination.** Calvin's place in the history of theology arises from the major role he gave to the doctrine of predestination, the belief that God has determined a soul's fate from all eternity. The doctrine was not new to Calvin; various earlier Christian theologians had argued for it. What was different for Calvin was that he could not accept what most previous defenders of the doctrine maintained: God chose the elect for salvation, but the damned were responsible for their fate because of their sins. Calvin, because of his emphasis on God's absolute power, argued that there was nothing that a human could do, whether good or evil, to influence God's will. Calvin did not shrink from what he called the doctrine's "awful consequences": that God has predestined both the saved and the damned from all eternity. Calvin was eager, however, to stop his followers from lapsing into fatalism: the belief that it makes no difference what they do in life, since their fate has already been determined. He proclaimed that those who lived a good Christian life should have reasonable confidence that they were among the elect. This confidence, taken more as a guarantee by his followers, gave the Calvinists the courage to confront the evildoers and correct them, especially the princes who were harming the true religion, and go to their deaths with Psalms on their lips. Predestination was a stumbling block for many who otherwise were attracted to Calvin's vision of Christianity, but it gave to those who did accept it a powerful courage of their convictions to change the world. It made them a revolutionary force in western Christendom in the century to come. As interpreted by later generations of Calvinists, the doctrine also had the consequence of seeing success in the world, especially in business, as a sign of election, since God would surely favor his saints. Along with Calvin's denunciation of monasticism and his emphasis on doing one's best in day-to-day life, it helped to create what has been called the Protestant work ethic.

**Enemies.** Although Calvin dominated Geneva after 1541, he faced opposition from many who did not accept his beliefs or moral code. Some were condemned to death for heresy or sedition. The most notorious case involved an outsider, Michael Servetus, a Spaniard who denied the doctrine of the Trinity. Eager to debate Calvin, Servetus arrived in Geneva in 1553 and was quickly arrested and convicted of heresy. His execution by burning demonstrated that Calvin was not a supporter of religious toleration.

**Academy.** Calvin was eager to reform the entire Christian Church and founded the Geneva Academy in 1559, later known as the University of Geneva, for training pastors to send across Europe. By the time he died in 1564, vibrant Calvinist churches had been established in France, Hungary, England, the Netherlands, and Scotland. Theodore Beza, an exiled French nobleman, who had been his associate for twenty years, took his place as the leader of Reformed Christianity.

Sources:
William Bouwsma, *John Calvin: A Sixteenth-Century Portrait* (New York: Oxford University Press, 1988).

Alister McGrath, *A Life of John Calvin: A Study of the Shaping of Western Culture* (Cambridge, Mass.: Blackwell, 1990).

John T. McNeill, *The History and Character of Calvinism* (New York: Oxford University Press, 1954).

# ST. CATHERINE OF SIENA

## 1347-1380
### CATHOLIC NUN

**Special Destiny.** Born Katerina di Benincasa at Siena in western Italy, she was the second youngest child in a family of twenty-four children. She was a twin, whose sister was given to a wet nurse because her mother did not have enough milk for two babies. Catherine lived while her twin sister died in a few months. This tragedy gave Catherine a sense of having a special destiny. Her father was a dyer, who, as a member of the class of tradesmen and artisans, was active in the politics of Siena. His faction held power from 1355 to 1368. This situation probably was the root of Catherine's strong interest in politics and her good sense of how to achieve political goals.

**Divine Vision.** Catherine was barely a year old when the Black Death swept through Siena, taking several of her siblings and many relatives. Her entire life was darkened by recurring outbreaks of the plague, and it may explain her interest in caring for the sick. As a child Catherine was fascinated by the Dominican friars who preached in her hometown, and at age seven she had a vision of Christ smiling at her, which led her to decide to become a nun. She remained committed to that goal despite her family's wishes that she marry, and her resolve was made all the stronger when an older sister died in childbirth. In her early teens Catherine began to practice a life of severe self-denial that included whipping herself and extended periods of fasting. Throughout her life she ate so little that those around her often believed that she went without food. She was extremely thin yet active for most of her life. Her fasting may also explain her many visions.

**Sisters of Penance.** By the time Catherine reached her sixteenth year, her family accepted her commitment to becoming a nun and allowed her to join the Sisters of Penance. That order did not have any convents, and she lived isolated in a small room in her parents' house with almost no contact with other people. After three years filled with constant prayer and visions, she underwent a mystical experience in 1366 in which Christ promised to be her heavenly spouse, and she emerged from her room in order to care for the sick and the poor. In 1370 Catherine fell into a long trance, in which she received a divine command to leave her home and enter the public life of the world. In short order, despite her inexperience in politics, she became deeply involved in the issues of her time. The major issue was the absence of the Pope from Rome. Since 1307 the popes had been residing at Avignon in southern France, which created a problem since the Pope's authority rested on the claim to be the successor of St. Peter as bishop of Rome. It was a major blow to Italian pride as well as the Roman economy. Catherine began to exhort Pope Gregory XI to return to Rome while also actively supporting his call for a crusade against the Muslims. The crusade never took place, but she impressed the Pope with the zeal and effort she put into advocating it.

**Raymond of Capua.** In 1374 Catherine was summoned to an assembly of church leaders in Florence to investigate whether this woman who wrote to popes, cared for the sick and poor, and fasted constantly was authentic. She convinced them of her divine mission, although they assigned Raymond of Capua as her confessor and companion to ensure that she did not starve herself to death. He became her principal confidant and biographer. Catherine also impressed the leaders of Florence, who asked her to mediate for them with the Pope over the war that had broken out between the city and the papacy over land in the Papal States. She went to Avignon in 1376 as the city's representative, which also gave her the opportunity to admonish Pope Gregory to return to Rome. She failed to secure a peace between Florence and the papacy but did influence Gregory's decision to leave Avignon for Rome in late 1376. This event is the one for which she is best known.

**Death.** Catherine also returned to Italy, where her reputation had grown so high that other governments asked her to mediate their disputes. At Florence in 1378 she found herself in the midst of the popular uprising known as the "Ciompi." When an attempt was made on her life, she was bitterly disappointed in surviving it, believing that she had been denied martyrdom. Nonetheless, she played a role in settling the uprising and then returned to Siena, where she wrote (literally for the first time—she apparently was illiterate until this point in her life) the *Dialogue of Divine Providence.* It was a dialogue between the Heavenly Father and a human soul in which she set out her theology of love and service. Her wish to retire from the political scene received a severe setback when a major crisis erupted in the papacy. After Gregory XI's death in 1378, factionalism among the cardinals resulted in the election of two popes, one residing in Rome and the other in Avignon. The Roman Pope Urban VI called her to Rome to support his cause. Catherine wrote vehement letters seeking to resolve the Great Schism. Believing that she was at fault for her sinfulness, she reduced even further the tiny amount of food she consumed, and in early 1380 she died in Rome. She is a prime example of what historian Rudolph Bell has called "holy anorexia."

**Biography.** Fifteen years later, Raymond of Capua wrote Catherine's biography, which had a large role in securing her canonization as a saint in 1461. Besides the *Dialogue,* her major literary work is the enormous collection of her letters. While many are eloquent exhortations to their recipients to love Christ and serve humanity, most are to popes, cardinals, and kings, often amazingly blunt in their language, on solving problems and correcting abuses in the Church. Her commitment to the unity and authority of the Catholic Church was the principal reason why Pope Paul VI in 1970 declared Catherine a Doctor of the Church, which means that her works are recommended for study by Catholics.

Sources:

Rudolph Bell, *Holy Anorexia* (Chicago: University of Chicago Press, 1985).

Sigrid Undset, *Catherine of Siena;* translated by Kate Austin (New York: Sheed & Ward, 1954).

# DESIDERIUS ERASMUS

## 1466-1536
### HUMANIST

**Dissatisfaction.** The illegitimate son of a man who at some point became a priest and his housekeeper, Desiderius Erasmus was born in Rotterdam, Holland. He received a good foundation in classical literature both from his father, who knew some classical Latin, and the Brothers of the Common Life. At age twenty-one he entered a monastery and five years later was ordained a priest. Dissatisfied with life in the monastery, he received permission to leave. He went to the University of Paris to study scholastic theology but soon found that distasteful as well, later making a crack that the University was a place "where the eggs were stale and the theology was staler." Having experienced life as a monk and a theologian and having developed a deep aversion to both lifestyles, Erasmus made monks and theologians the special targets of his biting wit.

**Ancient Wisdom.** Despite his complaints about the lack of learning in his monastery, Erasmus had continued his classical studies there, and while in Paris he earned a living teaching classical literature to wealthy young men. One of them, an English nobleman, took him to England in 1499. There he met the English humanist, John Colet, and became fast friends with Sir Thomas More. Colet persuaded him to improve his Greek, which allowed Erasmus to make his first mark as a humanist in 1500 by publishing *Adagia (Adages),* a collection of Greek proverbs. Erasmus greatly expanded it through six subsequent editions. Besides demonstrating his command of classical Greek, Erasmus intended the work to serve the cause of the reform of education. Like all humanists, he believed that ancient wisdom provided a surer guide to moral instruction and a productive life in the world than could be found in the contemporary schools. Other major works on this theme included *The Handbook for the Christian Knight* (1503) and *Instructions for a Christian Prince,* written in 1516 for the future emperor, Charles V. An important aspect of his political views was a belief in pacifism.

**Folly.** Erasmus traveled across Europe over the next nine years but returned to England in 1509, living for six years with More. There he wrote the best known of his literary works, *The Praise of Folly* (1509), which in Latin is a pun on More's name, *moria* being both folly and the Latinized spelling of More. Erasmus depicts Folly as a cheerful goddess who praises her followers in all elements of European society, but no groups are satirized as sharply as monks and theologians. Perhaps the sharpest piece of satire, which Erasmus always denied writing but common consensus has attributed to him, is the poem *Julius Excluded.* It depicts the notorious warrior Pope Julius II as having died and arriving at the gates of Heaven only to have St. Peter deny him entrance because he does not recognize him as Pope with his armor and weapons. Erasmus's purpose in his satires, directed largely against the clergy, was church reform. He believed that the Church needed to return to the purity of the early Church, from which the Church of his era had strayed in its emphasis on formal ritual and scholastic theology. His remedy for the ills of the Church was *Philosophia Christi,* by which he meant that ancient wisdom should be integrated into Christian belief. The tools of humanism must be put to work for the benefit of religion. Thus, Erasmus produced many critical editions of Greek classical authors. He believed that humanistic learning should be employed for the restoration of the earliest texts of the Bible and the Christian classics by the church fathers. He accordingly provided critical editions of the works of a dozen church fathers, including St. Jerome and St. Augustine.

**Greek New Testament.** The crowning work among Erasmus's editions was his critical edition of the Greek New Testament. In 1511 he was appointed to the faculty at the University of Cambridge, where he began work on it. Erasmus included his own Latin translation of his Greek text and pointed out places where he felt the official Latin version used by the Catholic Church, Jerome's Vulgate, was in error. In his annotations to the text, he expressed his disagreement with the scholastic theologians' interpretation of biblical texts. Although it was in itself a major accomplishment of biblical scholarship, Erasmus's Greek New Testament is best known as the source for Martin Luther's German translation of the Bible and, through a French translation of it, the King James Version. The Greek New Testament's publication in 1516, by which time Erasmus had left England, established his reputation as "Prince of Humanists." He was lionized across Europe, and his program for both church and education reform seemed within reach.

**Religious Toleration.** Luther's bursting forth on the scene in late 1517 proved a disaster for him, even if Luther proclaimed at first that he was simply following Erasmus's lead. There is no question that Erasmus, with his calls for Church reform, biting satire against the clergy, and critical editions of major texts of the early Church, played a role in the first stage of the Reformation. Erasmus, however, could not accept the radical break with the Catholic Church that Luther soon was leading. Both sides in the emerging religious split castigated him: Catholics, for providing so much ammunition to the Protestants; and Protestants, as the "failed first reformer" who lacked courage to lead the Reformation. In 1525 he and Luther became involved in a bitter debate over the question of human free will, in which Erasmus defended the ability of humans to make moral judgments on their own. His disdain for debating theology led him to advocate religious toleration, one of few who did so in the sixteenth century. He remained a Catholic until his death in Basel, although the papacy later placed his books on the *Index of Forbidden Books.*

**Significance.** Perhaps no other intellectual sums up in himself the essence of a period of thought the way Erasmus does for Northern humanism. He touched on every theme found in it; he knew or corresponded with nearly every other Christian humanist; and he spent time in nearly all the centers of Northern humanism. His own path from the most respected and lionized man in Europe in 1517 to becoming almost an afterthought in the wake of the coming of the Reformation traces the destiny of Christian humanism as well.

Sources:
De Lamar Jensen, *Renaissance Europe: Age of Recovery and Reconciliation* (Lexington, Mass.: D. C. Heath, 1981).

Margaret Phillips, *Erasmus and the Northern Renaissance* (London: Hodder & Stoughton, 1949).

Albert Rabil, *Erasmus and the New Testament: The Mind of a Christian Humanist* (San Antonio, Tex.: Trinity University Press, 1972).

# MARSILIO FICINO

## 1433-1499
### PHILOSOPHER AND TRANSLATOR

**Platonic Academy.** As the son of the physician of Cosimo de Medici, Marsilio Ficino was also intended for a medical career, and he received an excellent education at Florence and Bologna. He was distracted from medicine by developing a strong interest in Plato, and in 1456, Cosimo provided him support to learn Greek. Previously the city of Florence had hosted a meeting of leaders of the Catholic and Orthodox Churches in hopes of bringing about church reunion, and it stimulated Greek studies in the city. After the fall of Constantinople (1453) many Greek scholars fled to Florence, and Cosimo was eager to enhance his city's reputation as the center of Greek learning in Italy. By 1462 Ficino had become fluent enough in Greek that Cosimo commissioned him to translate all of Plato's works into Latin, working from a complete manuscript of the ancient scholar's writings that Cosimo had received from the Byzantine emperor in 1439. Cosimo also gave him a villa in which to do his work. A group of like-minded scholars began to meet at Ficino's villa, and it became known as the Platonic Academy of Florence. Ficino served as its leader and carried on an enormous correspondence across all of Europe that helped spark interest in Plato and other Greek philosophers.

**Ancient Mysteries.** Ficino had barely started translating Plato's dialogues, when Cosimo asked him to turn to translating a Greek manuscript that one of his agents had acquired in Greece. It supposedly was written by Hermes Trismegistus, who was believed to be Moses' contemporary and credited with being the source of eloquence and reason and the inventor of language and writing. (Two centuries later the text was shown to have been written about 400 C.E.). The *Corpus Hermeticum,* as the work became known, was seen as the link between the Bible and the learning of the ancient world. It appeared to show that Greek philosophy and Christianity had a common source, and for Ficino it explained why Plato seemed so often to have foreseen Christian doctrine. Much of the *Corpus Hermeticum* was devoted to examining the forces of the universe and unveiling the secrets of controlling those forces, that is, magic. It gave a powerful boost to the occult sciences such as alchemy, and although Ficino believed in these disciplines, he was not a practicing astrologer or alchemist.

**Major Works.** Ficino finished translating the *Corpus Hermeticum* in 1464 and returned to Plato's works, completing them in 1470 although they were not printed until 1484. By then Ficino had been ordained a priest (1473) and received a position in the cathedral of Florence. While he continued to translate other Greek philosophers into Latin, he also turned his attention to writing his own works. In 1474 he finished his major work, the *Theologica Platonica* (Platonic Theology), which was printed in 1482. Its purpose was to provide a synthesis of Platonic philosophy and Christian theology. He called it the *prisca theologia,* which predated the coming of Christ. Also in 1474 after a serious illness, Ficino published a smaller but similar book, *Liber de Christiana religione* (The Christian Religion), to show the relationship between Plato's philosophy, Christianity, and the other religions of the world. Ficino of course believed that Christianity was the best religion, but he found ideas of value in the others. A major concern for Ficino was the immortality of the individual human soul, which Aristotle had denied and on which not all the scholastic theologians had agreed. It was only at the Fifth Lateran Council (1512–1517) that the Catholic Church proclaimed it an official doctrine, in part because of Ficino's influence. His commentary on Plato's *On Love* can be seen as almost an original work since it went well beyond simply commenting on Plato's work. It became one of the best-known works on the theme of love and is largely responsible for the concept of Platonic love.

**Synthesis.** Ficino's last significant work was *De vita libri tres* (On Life, 1489). It was intended to bring together all the themes that had appeared in his earlier writings and the works that he had translated. It shows his interest in astronomy and mathematics, largely for their value for astrology and natural magic. The forces of nature for which they provide knowledge are benevolent, not evil. His vision of humanity was that of the great chain of being in which humans stand halfway between the physical world and the spiritual, capable of understanding and being influenced by both.

**Fall from Grace.** Ficino led a busy life outside of his scholarship. He served as tutor to Cosimo's grandson Lorenzo, who continued to give him patronage when he became head of the Medici family. When there was an outbreak of plague in Florence in 1478, Ficino wrote a guide to its treatment. Written in Italian to be of use to his fellow citizens, the treatise remained a standard medical work for several centuries. When the Medici fell from power in Florence in 1494, Ficino also lost his posts. At the time of his death, he was working on a commentary to St Paul's Epistle to the Romans.

**Significance.** Ficino was one of the first scholars to have his works printed on the newly developed printing press, and large numbers of printed copies of his books were distributed across Europe, helping to spread his ideas and his reputation. He can be described as the first intellectual with European-wide readership, despite having never traveled outside of Italy. The influence of his translations, works, and correspondence permeated the sixteenth century.

Sources:

Michael Allen, *The Platonism of Marsilio Ficino* (Berkeley: University of California Press, 1984).

James Hankins, *Plato in the Italian Renaissance,* 2 volumes (Leiden, Netherlands & New York: E. J. Brill, 1990).

Paul Oskar Kristeller, *The Philosophy of Marsilio Ficino,* translated by Virginia Conant (New York: Columbia University Press, 1943).

# ST. IGNATIUS OF LOYOLA

## 1491-1556

### SCHOLAR AND MISSIONARY

**Military Background.** The founder of the Society of Jesus (Jesuits) was born into a noble Basque family in northern Spain. Raised in the typical manner of his class, trained for war with little formal education, St. Ignatius of Loyola volunteered for service during a conflict against the French for control of Navarre. In 1521 he suffered a crushed leg from a cannon ball and lay in bed at his family castle for nearly a year while his leg was twice rebroken in hopes of straightening it, but he always walked with a limp.

**Time to Reflect.** He spent his time reading religious books; his favorite was Thomas à Kempis's *Imitation of Christ.* When he was sufficiently healed, he spent another year as a hermit meditating about his purpose in life. Loyola's experiences during that year laid the foundation for his major work on religious life, the *Spiritual Exercises.* He then went on a pilgrimage to Jerusalem, where his hopes to stay on and convert the Muslims were dashed when the city authorities refused to allow him to remain. When he returned to Spain in 1524, he decided to become a priest. He had to return to grammar school in Barcelona with boys less than half his age to become proficient in Latin. He entered the University of Acala, where his unusual lifestyle caught the attention of the Spanish Inquisition; but there were no consequences. In 1528 Loyola went to the University of Paris and received a master of arts degree five years later. He then began the study of theology but never finished a degree.

**Papal Approval.** While at Paris, Loyola gathered around him six young men, mostly Spaniards, whom he directed in his *Spiritual Exercises.* In 1534 they took a vow to go to Palestine as missionaries to the Muslims. On their way to the Middle East in 1537, they had to remain in Italy because of war in the Mediterranean. Loyola and his followers decided to organize a new religious order, which they called the Society of Jesus, and its members became known as Jesuits. They asked Pope Paul III to give it official recognition, but they ran into resistance from those who felt that the name was highly presumptuous and who objected to the new order's innovative rules. In particular, there was opposition to Loyola's proposal that the members not be required to assemble regularly during the day for common prayer as was true for all monks up to his day but be allowed to say those prayers by themselves. This innovation had the effect of allowing the Jesuits to be active in the world, for they did not have to return to their houses several times a day. The refusal to adopt a habit, unlike other religious orders, had a similar effect. Paul III, persuaded probably by Loyola's promise to place his group completely under the obedience to the pope, gave his approval to the Society of Jesus in September 1540.

**Obedience and Hierarchy.** Loyola was immediately elected superior general of the new order and took up permanent residence in Rome. In 1547 he produced the Society's Constitutions, which was the first significantly new rule for a religious order since the Rule of St. Benedict from the sixth century. Although the general body of the Society did not formally accept the Constitutions until 1558, two years after Loyola's death, they were followed from the Society's beginning. Authority within the Society was concentrated in the hands of the superior general, who was elected for life by all of the full members. Regarded as essential was obedience to the superior general and to the men to whom he delegated authority in the Jesuit provinces. The society's emphasis on obedience and its tightly hierarchical organization has been often described as based on the military, although Loyola's actual time in the army was brief.

**Preaching.** Loyola was determined to create an order of Catholic elite through rigorous rules for admitting new members. Prospective members were carefully screened for intelligence, good health, and social skills before being accepted for a lengthy probationary period of testing. New Jesuits were expected to receive a college education, often becoming masters of theology, and undergo Loyola's *Spiritual Exercises.* Only after nine years of proving that they were committed to accepting the Society's discipline and living up to its goals were they permitted to become full members by taking a fourth vow of obedience to the papacy along with the traditional three vows of a monk. While Loyola himself was not a good preacher, his new order attracted many excellent ones, and the earliest mark that the Society made was through preaching, especially in areas where there was a growing Protestant presence. Loyola did not intend for the Society to become "the cutting edge of the Counter-Reformation," as it has been described, but the talented men it attracted could not help but be drawn into the religious controversies of the era. Nor did he expect that the Jesuits would become prominent as confessors to the Catholic rulers of Europe, which gave them great influence in politics but also created deep resentment against them.

**Education.** Loyola did intend from the beginning that the Jesuits would be involved in education. Jesuit colleges, promoting a balanced education in religion and humanism, acquired immediately a reputation for the quality of the education they provided mostly to the sons of the Catholic elite. Loyola never lost sight of his original goal of missionary work, but it was not to the Muslims but to the inhabitants of the lands the Europeans were then exploring that Jesuit missionaries were dispatched. The first, St. Francis Xavier, "the Apostle of the Indies," was on his way to Asia even before the Pope had recognized the Society in 1540.

**Last Years.** As the Jesuits increased rapidly in number, reaching perhaps one thousand by 1556, Loyola had to deal with an enormous range of problems, and his surviving correspondence is the most extensive from any sixteenth-century figure. His last years were made difficult by a rebellion against his authority in the Portuguese province and the election in 1555 of volatile anti-Spanish Pope Paul IV, who had opposed approving the society. Loyola died while at prayer. The Catholic Church canonized him a saint in 1622.

Sources:

Jean Delumeau, *Catholicism Between Luther and Voltaire: A New View of the Counter Reformation* (London: Burns & Oates; Philadelphia: Westminster, 1977).

William Meissner, *Ignatius of Loyola: The Psychology of a Saint* (New Haven: Yale University Press, 1992).

John O'Malley, *The First Jesuits* (Cambridge, Mass.: Harvard University Press, 1993).

# BARTOLOMÉ DE LAS CASAS

## 1484-1566
### MISSIONARY AND HISTORIAN

**Journey to the New World.** The son of a merchant who would accompany Christopher Columbus on his second voyage and a woman who owned a bakery, Bartolomé de Las Casas was born in Seville, Spain, probably in 1484. He was there in March 1493, when Columbus returned triumphantly from his first voyage. Las Casas prepared for a career in the church, studying theology and law. In 1502, because of his family connections, he accompanied the first governor of the island of Hispaniola to the New World. Shortly before he left, he received the tonsure, making him a member of the clergy, but he was not yet a priest.

**Native American Treatment.** Upon landing in Hispaniola, Las Casas took part in a military expedition against natives who had rebelled against the Spanish demands for labor. His reward was an *encomienda*, a grant of land and native labor, and he immediately observed the harsh treatment of the Indians. In 1510 the first Dominican friars arrived in Hispaniola and immediately began protesting the treatment of the natives. They deeply influenced Las Casas, who was ordained a priest in 1512, the first man to receive ordination in America. He served as a chaplain to the Spanish force that conquered Cuba with much bloodshed in 1513. Stunned by the violence he saw and meditating on the Book of Ecclesiastes, he renounced his *encomienda* in 1514 and began to denounce the system as slavery. The other settlers opposed him vehemently, and he decided to return to Spain to press his case to King Ferdinand of Aragon.

**Royal Audience.** In 1515 he and several Dominicans sought an audience with the king, in which they hoped to present a wide-ranging proposal for changing the relationship between the Spanish and the Indians in the New World. They were eager to Christianize the natives but objected to the use of war and forced conversion. Las Casas also proposed using Africans as slave laborers to replace the Native Americans, but he soon repented of that idea as well and denounced all forms of slavery. When the king died in 1516 without granting an audience, Las Casas turned to the powerful chief minister of Castile, Cardinal Ximenez de Cisneros, who was highly sympathetic. Cisneros approved of much of what Las Casas proposed in respect to ending the *encomienda,* founding free native communities, and encouraging the migration of Spanish peasants to America, but stubborn resistance from the colonists prevented their implementation. Las Casas persuaded the new king Charles I (Emperor Charles V of the Holy Roman Empire) to allow him to found a religious colony on the coast of Venezuela. In 1521 twenty-one missionaries sailed from Spain but only five reached the colony, and continued slaving raids provoked a native uprising that doomed the plan. By late 1522 Las Casas was back in Spain.

**Personal Crusade.** Disappointed by this failure, Las Casas decided to withdraw from the world and joined the Dominican Order, taking his vows in 1524. For six years he lived in a Dominican house in Hispaniola, devoting his time largely to writing the *History of the Indies,* one of the most valuable sources on the early voyages of discovery and the conquest. The continued mistreatment of the Native Americans persuaded him to return to the fray. In 1535 the king gave him a commission to investigate the Spanish conquest of Peru, but he was shipwrecked on the coast of Nicaragua, where he spent two years working to convert the natives and watching them be enslaved by colonists. Returning to Europe he went to Rome and persuaded Pope Paul III to declare in 1537 that the Indians were rational humans and equally worthy to any other people of receiving Christian instruction. The pope strongly condemned forced conversion. Las Casas began to write the many works in which he expounded those ideas. His work paid off with the publication of the New Laws in 1542, in which Charles I abolished the *encomienda* system and prohibited the enslavement of Native Americans. Two years later Las Casas was named bishop of Chiapas in southern Mexico. He soon found that neither the New Laws nor his new position ended the exploitation and misery of the Indians. The colonial authorities for the most part refused to implement the laws and honor his status as bishop. Badly frustrated in Chiapas, Las Casas returned to Spain for good in 1547.

**Debate.** Las Casas had not given up the struggle for native rights. He soon found himself in the most famous episode of his life: the debate with a noted scholar. Juan de Sepulveda defended Aristotle's thesis that some men were natural slaves and their betters had a right to enslave them, which he applied to the natives of the Americas and the Spanish colonists. In August 1550 at Valladolid the two faced off before a panel of theologians and lawyers, who were to report to the king. Sepulveda spoke for only three hours, while Las Casas went on for five days. His orations were published as *In Defense of the Indians.* The panel made no formal recommendation to Charles I, but the consensus of the time and since has been that Las Casas got the better of the debate. He was given oversight over the selection of missionaries sent to the Americas. In the New World, however, his work had little impact, as the colonists largely ignored the royal commands on improving the natives' treatment, threatening revolt if the king enforced his orders.

**Legacy.** After 1552, Las Casas spent most of his time in Valladolid, writing and editing his extensive body of works but going often to the royal court despite his age to argue on behalf of the American Indian cause. He died in Madrid while on one such mission. His dying words were an admonition to those around his deathbed to continue to work for the protection of the Native Americans. His vast writings, which probably did exaggerate Spanish cruelty in the Americas, were a major source of the "Black Legend" in which Spain was unfairly denounced for its atrocities, especially in England through its emotionally charged English translation. Although he was not a pacifist, he denounced waging war against the Indians as unjust, and he ardently affirmed that the only proper means of conversion was through persuasion and example, not by war. Especially since his labors were on behalf of a people to whom he did not belong, Las Casas serves as the model defender of human rights in history.

Sources:

Juan Friede and Benjamin Keen, eds., *Bartolomé de Las Casas in History: Toward an Understanding of the Man and His Work* (DeKalb: Northern Illinois University Press, 1971).

Lewis Hanke, *All Mankind Is One; A Study of the Disputation between Bartolomé de Las Casas and Juan Gines de Sepulveda in 1550 on the Intellectual and Religious Capacity of the American Indians* (DeKalb: Northern Illinois University Press, 1974).

# MARTIN LUTHER

## 1483-1546

### RELIGIOUS REFORMER

**Promise to God.** Born into a prosperous peasant family in Saxony, Germany, Martin Luther received his early education in a school of the Brothers of the Common Life. His father wanted him to become a lawyer to continue the family's rise in status, and Luther earned a masters of arts degree from the University of Erfurt in 1505. During the summer before he began his law studies, he was caught outdoors during a violent thunderstorm. Terrified when lightning knocked him down, he vowed to become a monk if his life was spared. Despite his father's outrage, he entered a monastery and was ordained a priest in 1507. In 1512 he finished his master's degree in theology and was appointed professor of biblical theology at the University of Wittenberg in Saxony, where he stayed until his death.

**Faith.** Despite being a pious and obedient monk, Luther was convinced that he deserved damnation for his sinfulness, although there is no reason to believe that he was especially sinful. The answer the Catholic Church provided to the question "How can I be saved?"—receiving the sacraments and doing good works—did not give him any consolation. He plagued Johann von Staupitz, the superior of his monastery, with his scruples and doubts. Staupitz arranged for him to get his faculty position at Wittenberg in hope that it would distract him. While preparing a theology lesson on the Epistle to the Romans, Luther was struck by the passage "The Just shall live by faith." When Luther had this transforming experience of faith has never been determined with precision. It may have occurred as early as 1514, shortly after he began his lectures on the Bible at Wittenberg, or as late as 1519, as he suggested in his reminiscences from 1545. Regardless, it opened up for him the idea that faith in Jesus as Redeemer is the sole source of salvation. He began to act on this insight in 1517 when he drew up his Ninety-five Theses objecting to the sale of indulgences. The debate over whether he actually posted them on a church door on 31 October 1517 does not detract from their significance, as they were quickly translated from Latin into German and spread across Germany.

**Spreading the Word.** What Luther had intended to be a scholarly debate among theologians rapidly became a major popular cause across Germany. In 1519 he publicly debated the issues he had raised with a Catholic theologian, Johann Eck, at Leipzig. Eck, a skillful debater, drew Luther into making statements based on his new beliefs that denied the authority of priests and the pope. The record of the debate was distributed widely, raising Luther's popularity further. Pope Leo X condemned several of Luther's positions, and Luther burned the papal document in June 1520, making clear his rejection of papal authority. In the same year Luther published three major books on theology and church reform, which were printed in thousands of inexpensive copies and spread across Germany. The use by Luther and other reformers of the printing press, then less than a century old, to spread their ideas was a major factor in the success of the Reformation.

**Motto of Protestantism.** In June 1521, pressured by the Pope, Emperor Charles V summoned Luther to a meeting of the Imperial Diet at Worms, where he was ordered to recant his beliefs. The best source for his response does not include the stirring "Here I stand. I can do no other." It may have been added several years later. Nonetheless, it became the motto of Protestantism. Declared an outlaw, Luther hid out for ten months, when he began translating the Bible into German. Making the Bible available in the vernacular, so that lay people could read it in their own languages, while the Catholic Church continued to insist on the use of Latin, was one of the great strengths of Protestantism. It also gave rise, however, to a multitude of differing interpretations of Scripture, especially since Protestants rejected any central authority like the papacy to settle doctrinal disputes. That problem arose in Wittenberg while Luther was at the Wartburg. Several preachers began to push a more-radical reform of religion and society. When word came to him of the outburst of radicalism in Wittenberg, Luther returned home to regain control of the Reformation. The radicals helped touch off the German Peasants' Revolt in 1524. Luther was at first sympathetic to the peasants, but his inherent conservatism in politics led him to condemn their excesses in the most vehement language in his notorious *Against the Murdering and Plundering Peasants* (1525). This book cost him much of his popular support. It also led him to emphasize the need for obedience to established authority.

**Attempts at Consolidation.** Protected by the duke of Saxony against the imperial ban, Luther felt secure enough to marry Katherine von Bora in 1525. She was a former nun with whom he had a large family. By marrying, Luther demonstrated his belief that a minister of God did not have to be celibate in order to serve the Church. Katherine served as a model for a new office in European society, the minister's wife. Also in 1525 Luther became involved in a bitter debate with Desiderius Erasmus over the question of free will. His early hopes that Erasmus might join with him and even take over the leadership of the Reformation had been dashed by then. As Protestantism spread, disputes over interpretation of doctrine, especially with the Zurich reformer Ulrich Zwingli, threatened to undercut the movement in the face of the opposition of Charles V. In 1529 he met with Zwingli at Marburg in an unsuccessful attempt to form a united Protestant Church. Luther had a bad temper, and it betrayed him at Marburg, as it had during the Peasants' Revolt, when he stomped out of the meeting in anger.

**Reminiscences.** As Luther aged, he remained active in the movement he had founded, teaching theology at Wittenberg and settling disputes among Lutherans. Many students boarded in his house, and at the dinner table he talked at great length about his family and the early days of the Reformation, which they wrote down. This "table talk" provides historians with far greater knowledge about his life than is true for any other figure of his era. In 1546 he went to settle a dispute between

two Lutheran princes, took ill, and died upon his return to Wittenberg.

Sources:

Roland Bainton, *Here I Stand: A Life of Martin Luther* (New York: Abingdon-Cokesbury, 1950).

Richard Marius, *Martin Luther: The Christian between God and Death* (Cambridge, Mass.: Belknap Press of Harvard University Press, 1999).

Heiko A. Oberman, *Luther: Man Between God and the Devil* (New Haven: Yale University Press, 1989).

# FRANCESCO PETRARCH

## 1304-1374
### POET AND SCHOLAR

**Beginnings.** Born in Arezzo, Italy, to a family in exile from its native city of Florence, Francesco Petrarch was raised in Avignon, France, where his father, a lawyer, gained a position at the papal court in 1312. He studied law at the University of Bologna until the death of his father in 1326, and then he returned to Avignon. There at church on Good Friday in 1327, he first saw Laura, a married Frenchwoman whose name he immortalized in his poems and who inspired him with a passion that has become proverbial for its constancy and purity. Despite his love for her, or perhaps because of it, he entered the clergy but was never ordained a priest. He received an income from his church position, although he lived as a layman. As a young man he traveled widely in the Low Countries and Germany as well as Italy and France. His travels helped convince him that Italy was the cultural heir of the Roman Empire, which persuaded him to abandon law and develop his interest in the study of classical Latin literature. He embarked on a career as a writer and scholar.

**Love for Laura.** Petrarch first gained recognition as a poet in Tuscan Italian, thereby helping, along with his Florentine predecessor Dante, to make that dialect the literary language of Italy. His early love poems to Laura were collected in *Il Canzoniere* (The Songbook), which are regarded as the first examples of the sonnet. He was influenced both by the French chivalric romance and Dante's poems to Beatrice, but Petrarch's poetry is about a real woman, albeit one with whom he never became as intimate as he wished, rather than the idealized lady of French feudalism or Dante's personification of divine truth. His poems differ also because they are as much about his own reflections on his frustrated love for Laura as about the lady herself. When she died during the Black Death in 1348, Petrarch wrote another set of poems about her, collected in *I Trionfi*. They are more similar to Dante's poems to Beatrice in that Laura becomes an allegorical figure of love and truth. Largely because of his early Italian poems, the Senate of Rome named him poet laureate in 1341.

**Classical Latin.** Petrarch also tried his hand at writing poetry in classical Latin. He regarded as his masterpiece the epic poem *Africa*, finished in 1342, about the Roman commander Scipio who defeated Hannibal. Literary critics agree that his genius was in lyrical rather than epic poetry and do not have a high opinion of *Africa*. He wrote extensively in classical Latin, both poetry and prose. Among his notable works in that language were a set of biographies of illustrious men of the ancient world and a dialogue titled the *Secretum* (1343) between himself and St. Augustine, in which Petrarch has the great theologian chastise him for his love of fame and pleasure. Among the things in which Petrarch took great pleasure was classical Latin itself. He believed that the language as used by the ancients was the purest and most beautiful form of expression and contrasted it with the corrupted Latin in use in the Middle Ages, which was a term he had a significant role in creating.

**Proper Education.** Petrarch, however, did not ignore the content of the classical works, especially those written before the end of the Roman republic. He possessed the attitudes and prejudices of the Italian bourgeoisie, even if he spent much of his life in France; so he looked to Rome as the ideal city-state, which he hoped could be reestablished in the Italian city-states. Thus, he believed that Roman literature had a great deal to say to the wealthy, secular, and urbane merchants who governed the Italian city-states about how to run a successful city-state in respect to politics, the economy, and society. According to Petrarch and other humanists, the proper form of education and culture for the successful businessman/politician of a city-state was *studia humanitas*, the study of the classics.

**Italian Humanism.** The man called the "Father of Humanism" contributed greatly to the creation of Italian humanism both by his praise of ancient learning and his search for the manuscripts of the classics. What he and his fellow humanists of the first generation did was to ferret out the manuscripts of the classics, which were found mostly in monastery libraries, and make copies available to a larger and more eager reading public. It was not that the monks failed to recognize the value of their manuscripts, but they were making little use of them. The search for the classical manuscripts received a large boost when in 1350 Petrarch met the poet Giovanni Boccaccio at Florence, with whom he had been corresponding. The two humanists, enlisting the help of several like-minded men, embarked on a more systematic hunt throughout Italy and across Europe, which succeeded in putting most of the extant Latin classics into the hands of humanists by 1400.

**Last Years.** Petrarch lived in Italy the last twenty years of his life, first in Milan and then on a small farm near Padua, where he died in 1374. During his last years an illegitimate daughter and her family lived with him. The last production of an enormously busy literary life was a collection of his letters to other humanists, the *Familiares*. They provide clear evidence of both his love of the Latin language and classical literature and his largely unrealized goal of fusing classical ethics with Christian morality.

**Sources:**

John Whitfield, *Petrarch and the Renascence* (New York: Russell & Russell, 1965).

Ernest Wilkins, *Life of Petrarch* (Chicago: University of Chicago Press, 1961).

# ST. TERESA OF AVILA

## 1515-1582
### CATHOLIC NUN

**Beginnings.** Teresa Sanchez Cepeda Davila y Ahumada was the daughter of a wealthy merchant of Avila west of Madrid, who was descended from converts from Judaism, and his second wife, a woman from an Old Christian family. Teresa was one of ten children in the family. Her mother died when she was thirteen, and without maternal supervision she engaged in less-than-saintly behavior for three years until her father, worried about her reputation (and his), sent her to a convent school. After reading the letters of St. Jerome, Teresa decided to enter religious life. In 1536 at age twenty-one, against her father's wishes, she joined a convent of Carmelite nuns in her hometown, taking the name of Teresa of Jesus. The convent was quite lax in its discipline, allowing the nuns plenty of opportunity to entertain guests and acquire luxuries. Teresa at first indulged in such behavior while yet yearning for a more devout spiritual life. She turned sharply against the lax lifestyle in 1555 after a serious illness in which she experienced a period of temporary paralysis in her legs. She also began to hear voices and have visions, including one of her place in hell should she fail to repent. Convinced of the need for stricter discipline for nuns, she founded her own convent at Avila in 1562 with a group of like-minded nuns from her original convent, who adopted the original strict rule of the Carmelites. As a symbol of their commitment to a more severe lifestyle, its nuns gave up their shoes for rough sandals, hence the name of Discalced (shoeless) Carmelites. One of her primary concerns was the conversion of Protestants through constant prayer.

**Official Recognition.** Teresa quickly encountered serious opposition from a variety of sources, including the people of Avila who were not eager to support another religious house in their city at a time when perhaps 20 percent of the Spanish population were priests, monks, or nuns. Many church authorities doubted that she had any divine or church sanction to organize a new convent. She eventually won the confidence of King Philip II, whose control over the Spanish Church stifled the opposition. Over the next twenty years Teresa built seventeen additional convents, whose nuns acquired a reputation for sanctity and seclusion from the world. In 1567 she met a fellow mystic, the Spanish Carmelite St. John of the Cross, whom she persuaded to found two monasteries for men similar to her convents. In 1580 Pope Gregory XIII gave her Discalced Carmelites official recognition as a religious order within the Catholic Church. He was also the Pope who imposed the Gregorian Calendar on Catholic countries, which dropped ten days in October 1582; so when Teresa died on 4 October of that year, the next day was 15 October.

**Importance.** Teresa's place in history has come largely from her religious writings in which she describes her mystical visions. She believed that she had achieved a mystical union with God and described how others could also achieve it. The account of her spiritual life, found in the *Book of Her Life* (first written in 1562 but constantly revised until her death), *The Way of Perfection*

(1566), and *The Interior Castle* (1582), forms one of the most remarkable accounts of a spiritual biography. Only St. Augustine's *Confessions* compares with it. Her mystical writings and independent ways brought her to the attention of the Spanish Inquisition, which investigated her at least six times but never found sufficient reason to put her on trial. Despite such suspicions about her Catholic orthodoxy, she was declared a saint in 1622, and in 1970 Pope Paul VI declared her a Doctor of the Church, making her, along with St. Catherine of Siena, one of two Catholic women so recognized. Along with her friend St. John of the Cross, she is regarded as the most beloved religious writer of early modern Catholicism. Her vivid description of her heart being pierced by an arrow of divine love, which happened to her in a vision of 1559, is the subject of *The Ecstasy of St. Teresa*, Gian Lorenzo Bernini's Baroque sculpture masterpiece finished in 1645.

Sources:

Stephen Clissold, *St. Teresa of Avila* (New York: Seabury, 1979).

Alison Weber, *Teresa of Avila and the Rhetoric of Femininity* (Princeton: Princeton University Press, 1990).

# DOCUMENTARY SOURCES

John Calvin, *Christianae religionis Institutio* (Institutes of the Christian Religion, 1536)—Calvin's major work of theology emphasizing worship, morals, and church administration. Its preface is addressed to the King Francis I of France, imploring him to reject the superstitions of Catholicism and to listen to "righteous teaching." The first edition has six chapters: Law and Decalogue; Faith; The Sermon; True Sacraments; False Sacraments; and Christian Liberty.

Baldassare Castiglione, *Il cortegiano* (The Courtier, 1513–1518)—First published in Venice in 1528. A dialogue on ideal courtly life, *Il cortegiano* is one of the most- celebrated works of the late humanist period.

St. Catherine of Siena, *Dialogue of Divine Providence* (circa 1378)—The principal work on medieval mysticism.

Desiderius Erasmus, *Adagia* (Adages, 1500)—A collection of sayings from ancient Greek authors that established Erasmus's reputation as a humanist.

Erasmus, *The Praise of Folly* (1509)—The author's best known work; a satire on European society with a special emphasis on the clergy.

St. Ignatius of Loyola, *Spiritual Exercises* (circa 1521)—An important text on Christian spirituality used extensively for the training of new members of the Society of Jesus (Jesuits).

Bartolomé de Las Casas, *In Defense of the Indians* (1550)— The author's arguments in the famous debate with the scholar Juan de Sepulveda. Las Casas rejected the notion that Native Americans were mere natural slaves to be exploited by Spanish colonists.

Martin Luther, *On the Bondage of the Will* (1525)—In a response to an attack made by Erasmus, Luther denies the existence of human free will.

Luther, *On the Freedom of the Christian* (1520)—The most influential of the three pamphlets written by Luther in 1520 (the other two are *Address to the Christian Nobility of the German Nation* and *Babylonian Captivity of the Church.*) In *On the Freedom of the Christian*, Luther defines what it means to be free of sin and describes his doctrine of the priesthood.

Michel Eyquem de Montaigne, *Essais* (Essays, 1572–1580, 1588)—Innovative literary work that advocates religious toleration, philosophical skepticism, and the study of the classics.

Sir Thomas More, *Utopia* (1516)—A major humanist work that describes an imaginary society where there is communal ownership of land, education for all men and women, and religious toleration.

St. Teresa of Avila, *The Interior Castle* (1582)—A masterpiece of Christian spirituality and mysticism.

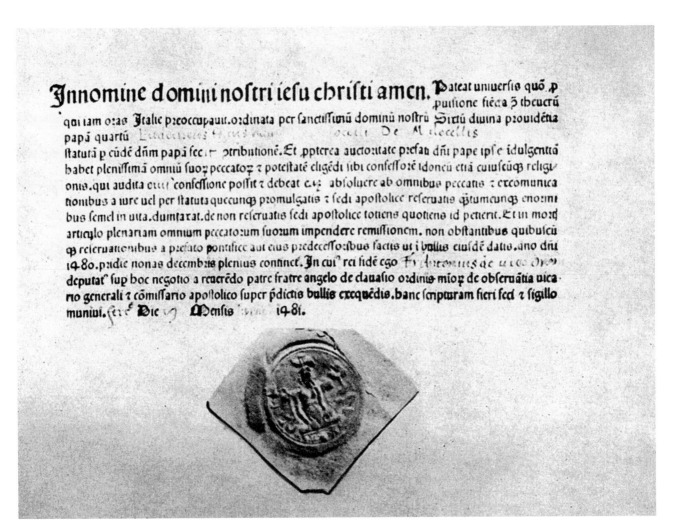

An indulgence blank, a prepared form with spaces for name and date, used by Johann Tetzel from Brandenburg

# SCIENCE, TECHNOLOGY, AND HEALTH

by JOLE SHACKELFORD

## CONTENTS

*Sidebars and tables are listed in italics.*

**1351**
- The Black Death, a form of bubonic and pneumonic plague from Asia, ends after four years of devastating Europe. It is the first major pandemic in the region in about eight hundred years.

**1364**
- The University of Cracow is founded in Poland. Over the span of the next two and one-half decades, universities are also established at Heidelberg, Germany, and Cologne, France.

**1397**
- Manuel Chrysoloras begins teaching Greek to Italian humanists, inaugurating a Renaissance passion for Greek literature.

**1410**
- *Geography*, a second-century C.E. tome by the Greek astronomer, mathematician, and geographer Ptolemy, is rediscovered. Ptolemy estimates the size of Earth, describes its surface, and lists places located by a system of latitude and longitude.

**1415**
- Prince Henry of Portugal establishes a school of navigation at Sagres.

**1450**
- The Vatican Library is founded by Pope Nicholas V and soon contains a massive collection of ancient Greek and Roman manuscripts, as well as medieval poetry and literature.

**1454**
- Georg Puerbach writes *Nova theorica planetarum*, a treatise on the Aristotelian (homocentric spheres) and Ptolemaic (Earth is the center of the cosmos) models of astronomy; it is not published until 1472.

**1455**
- A forty-two-line (per page) Bible is the first surviving book printed on Johannes Gutenberg's press. This new technology quickly revolutionizes learned culture. By 1501 more than one thousand printing offices in Europe have produced approximately 35,000 books with approximately 10 million copies.

**1457**

- The University of Freiberg is founded in eastern Germany.

**1463**

- Marsilio Ficino translates the *Corpus Hermeticum*, a group of texts ostensibly written before Plato and conveying ancient religious and cosmological wisdom. Hermetic philosophy, as it came to be known, supports the neoplatonist worldview favored by Renaissance alchemists and chemical philosophers.

**1464**

- An academy is founded in Florence as a center of studying and discussing Platonic thought. Marsilio Ficino is appointed the principal instructor.

**1477**

- The University of Uppsala is founded in Sweden and the University of Tübingen is established in Germany.

**1485**

- The English Sweat, a rapidly developing and quickly fatal disease, first appears. Four more epidemics strike England, and then the disease mysteriously vanishes in the sixteenth century.

**1489**

- A fast-spreading and frequently fatal illness begins to appear among Spanish troops besieging the Moorish stronghold of Granada. Characterized by a high fever, rash, headache, and delirium, it is later diagnosed as typhus.

- Marsilio Ficino's *De vita libri tres* (Three Books on Life) is published and becomes a model for natural philosophers and magi (sage magicians) who wish to wield cosmic power through the use of talismans, incantations, proper choices of food, medicines, and clothing, and other ritual aspects. In this same year, Giovanni Pico Della Mirandola finishes *Heptaplus*, a treatise that applies Jewish Kabbala to interpret *Genesis*, helping to create the Renaissance tradition of Christian Cabala. The idea of Cabala, that knowledge and power is encoded into the Book of Scripture, is extended to apply to the Book of Nature in the sixteenth century, and alchemists begin to try to work out the divine chemical coding for natural processes.

**1492**

- Christopher Columbus reaches the islands of the Caribbean Sea. Knowledge of the plants, animals, minerals, lands, diseases, and people of the New World streams back to Europe in the sixteenth century, challenging science and medicine.

**1494**

- The first reported case of venereal syphilis occurs among French troops in southern Italy. An epidemic of this disease shocks European medicine and social life.

**1508**

- The University of Alcalá is founded in Spain.

**1509**

- *De arte distillandi simplicia et composita* is published. This book by Hieronymus Brunschwig gives detailed instructions for making furnaces used in the production of chemical drugs.

- Throughout Europe a concerted effort begins on the part of town officials to limit the right of practicing medicine to licensed and qualified doctors.

**1514**

- The Polish astronomer Nicholas Copernicus refutes the geocentric beliefs of Ptolemy and advances the heliocentric theory in which the Earth and other planets revolve around the Sun.

**1521**

- *Commentary on the Anatomy of Mondino* is published. In this volume Berengario da Carpi urges his readers to study the ancient Greek texts of Galen in conjunction with performing actual dissections.

**1527**

- The German alchemist and physician Paracelsus throws an expensive volume of Avicenna's *Canon of Medicine* on a midsummer's bonfire in Basel, Switzerland, symbolizing his rejection of classical medical theory.

**1530**

- The German physician and botanist Otto Brunfles begins to write *Herbarum vivae eicones* (Portraits of Living Plants), a study of the minute characteristics of individual flora.

**1531**

- Publication of a Latin translation of the rediscovered text by Galen, *On anatomical procedures*, acquaints European anatomists with Galen's techniques for vivisecting animals.

**1537**

- In *Nova Scientia* (A New Science), Niccolo Tartaglia examines the kinematics of falling bodies and projectiles.

**1538**

- Girolamo Fracastoro finishes writing *Homocentrica sive de stellis* (Homocentrics, or On the Stars), an attempt to defend Eudoxian astronomy (the cosmos is a complex system of concentric spheres, each moved by the prime mover).

**1542**

- *Summa perfectionis magisterij,* a thirteenth-century text on alchemy, and *De historia stirpium commentarii insignes* (History of Plants) are published.

**1543**

- Copernicus's heliocentric hypothesis is published (*On the Revolutions of the Celestial Orbs*), as is Vesalius's anatomical treatise with lavish, detailed illustrations (*On the Architecture of the Human Body*).

**1545**

- Botanical gardens are created at Italian universities, which signals a new interest in botany, herbal drugs, and acclimatizing foreign plants.

**1546**

- In *De contagione et contagiosis morbis et curatione* (On Contagion, Contagious Diseases, and Their Cure), Girolamo Fracastoro introduces the theory that illnesses are spread by "seeds" or material agents.

**1551**

- *Prutenic Tables,* a collection of astronomical charts based on Copernicus's theorems, is compiled by Erasmus Reinhold.

**1556**

- *De re metallica* (On the Nature of Metals) by Georg Agricola is the first detailed study on mining, metallurgy, and glassmaking.

**1559**

- *De re anatomica* (On Anatomy), a text on vascular systems written by Realdo Columbo, is published.

**1564**

- In *Dix livres de la chirurgie* (Ten Books on Surgery), the French surgeon Ambrose Pare discusses proper wound dressings and surgical procedures.

**1566**

- A decree by the French Parlement in Paris forbids the internal use of antimony-based chemical drugs, making official the rift between Paraclelsian and Galenist physicians and touching off a period called the "Antimony Wars," during which Paracelsian rememdies are discouraged by the Paris medical faculty but encouraged by physicians employed by the crown and aristocracy. The conflict lasts through most of the seventeenth century.

**1570**

- *Theatrum orbis terrarum* (Theater of the World), an atlas by Abraham Ortelius, is published.
- Christoph Clavius, a Jesuit priest, defends Ptolemaic astronomy in *In sphaeram Joannis de Sacro Bosco commentarius* (Commentary on the Sphere of Johannes Sacrobosco).

**1571**

- Petrus Severinus, a follower of Paracelsus, advances the theory that diseases are chemical in nature and caused by specific "entities."

**1572**

- The Danish astronomer Tycho Brahe observes a supernova. The next year he compiles his findings in the acclaimed *De nova stella* (The New Star).
- Thomas Erastus launches a four-volume attack on Paracelsian medicine, linking it to magic and religious heresy.

**1574**

- Nicolas Monardes writes a treatise on the medicinal plants of the New World. In 1596 John Frampton produces an English translation titled *Joyful News Out of the New-Found World.*

**1576**

- Brahe begins to build an observatory on the island of Hven for his patron Frederick II of Denmark.

| | |
|---|---|
| **1583** | • In *De Plantis* (Plants), the botanist Andrea Cesalpino describes more than 1,500 plants. |
| **1584** | • Giordano Bruno publishes four books that contain his main ideas on the infinity of the cosmos, a reformation of knowledge, and the nature of God. Bruno's views on the last subject lead to his arrest in Venice and public execution in Rome in 1600 by being burned alive at the stake. |
| **1588** | • Brahe announces a new cosmological model that affirms Copernican astronomy, while still maintaining that Earth is the center of the cosmos. |
| **1597** | • Andreas Libavius published *Alchymia*, in which he champions chemical methods as useful additions to medicine and natural philosophy. Libavius subsequently engages in a long and vigorous campaign against Paracelsian chemistry as founded on bad philosphical, religious, and pedagogical principles. |
| **1598** | • Brahe publishes *Mechanica astronomiæ instauratæ* (The Mechanics of a Restored Astronomy), in which he describes his laboratory and observatories Uraniborg and Stjæneborg, giving specifications for the intruments he uses for measuring the stars and planets. |
| **1600** | • Dutch opticians invent the telescope. |
| | • William Gilbert's *De magnete* (On the Magnet) combines traditional lore about the occult properties of magnets with careful experimentation on the nature of magnets and magnetic effects. Such experimentalism becomes a hallmark of the foundation of modern science in the seventeenth century. |

# OVERVIEW

**Dark Ages.** Greek culture produced great advances in natural philosophy (science) and medicine in classical antiquity. These developments were written in Greek, even after the Roman empire expanded and incorporated regions previously ruled by Greek kings. Educated Romans of the empire studied these subjects in Greek and some, such as Emperor Marcus Aurelius, even wrote in Greek. When the economy of the Western Empire began to collapse in the fifth and sixth centuries C.E., the best works of Greek scientific and medical literature had not yet been translated into Latin and, as a result, largely disappeared in the West as knowledge of the Greek language faded. Roman authority crumbled, and ensuing centuries of rule by various Germanic tribes contributed to a general decline of education. This period, from the sixth to the ninth century, has been called the Dark Ages because scholarship sank to a low ebb.

**Intellectual Appetite.** Gradually, during the ninth, tenth, and eleventh centuries, the Christian religion obtained better control on the European population, literacy began to gain ground, and cathedral schools were established. Western scholars' renewed appetites for ancient knowledge had to be satisfied by traveling abroad to locate manuscripts, many of which were written in Arabic or Greek and required translation. By the early thirteenth century European learned culture was heavily engaged in evaluating and adapting a rich heritage of scientific and medical knowledge from Greco-Roman antiquity, but the process would not be adequately completed until the sixteenth century. Only at that time did scholars of scientific subjects begin to go beyond their predecessors, exploring nature more directly than their forebears had and venturing radically new theories. The Middle Ages had been a time of great technological innovation, also, but the widespread application of medieval techniques and tools took place in the Renaissance, transforming the production of raw materials, goods, and even scientific research itself. The Renaissance, which for historians of science and medicine is generally regarded as extending through the sixteenth century, was therefore a period in which the intellectual, technological, and economic changes that had begun to sprout in the Middle Ages flourished and embraced a greater geographic area as well as a larger sector of society.

**Agent of Change.** One great event distinguishing the fourteenth century—a watershed event that can be used to mark the end of the Middle Ages and the beginning of the Renaissance—was the Black Death (1347–1351), a great epidemic of plague that caught Europeans by surprise and inaugurated an extended period of recurring epidemics. Historians argue about the relative importance of the Black Death itself in altering European culture, but that it was an important agent of change and a salient feature of the century is not disputed. Clearly, tremendous changes in the intellectual and material culture of Europe after the Black Death helped to lay the foundation for the development of new approaches to the study of nature in the seventeenth century, a process commonly referred to by historians as the Scientific Revolution. Therefore, the application of the term Renaissance for the period 1350–1600 is warranted, because the intellectual, economic, and technological rebirth of Europe was a necessary preparation for what followed. In many respects, this era was a rebirth of classical humanistic values, which occurred against a background of late-medieval academic institutions and cultural pluralism.

**New World.** By 1350 the universities were flourishing and proliferating across Europe, and the first wave of the recovery of classical knowledge in the twelfth and thirteenth centuries had passed. European intellectuals with a command of Latin now possessed a sense of the richness and sophistication of Greco-Roman antiquity, but the West had just suffered the worst demographic disaster to befall the European area since the last days of Imperial Rome. The Black Death proved to be a harbinger of a cycle of plagues and pandemics that visited and revisited Europe well into the early modern period. The persistence of epidemic disease slowed population recovery and radically altered the outlook of all classes of people, thus presenting challenges to religious and political authority and to medical scholarship, both of which underwent a period of reevaluation. Demographic crises provided a stimulus to technological innovation, too, as agricultural production and markets responded to labor shortages. Meanwhile, the discovery of the New World and further exploration of Africa and the East spurred the development of navigation and mapmaking and resulted in a wealth of information about distant climates and their natural products, which in turn fired the imagination of natural philosophers and forced a revision of old ideas about the world and its inhabitants. From the New World came not only new crops and new medicines but also new diseases. By 1600 European nations began to dominate the sea lanes of the Atlantic Ocean and colonize remote lands, bringing Western ways, religion, and people to distant coasts.

**Cosmology and Natural History.** At the same time, the European intellectual world was undergoing a tremendous transformation. In the wake of Nicholas Copernicus's hypothesis that Earth was not the center of everything but revolved around the Sun, astronomers began to examine the heavens more thoroughly, searching for answers to how the cosmos was put together. Cosmologists ventured speculations about the extent and nature of the universe that greatly departed from the comfortable, closed world of medieval Aristotelian theory. By 1600 Giordano Bruno had suggested that Earth was but one planet circling one sun among countless suns in an endless universe, and William Gilbert was sowing the seeds of gravitation theory with his idea that Earth was a huge magnet. At the same time, reports and specimens of the abundant and exotic plant and animal life of distant habitats were returning from voyages of exploration and trade. This new information led to a revision of natural history, which began in the sixteenth century and ultimately led to the taxonomy of Carolus Linnaeus in the eighteenth century and Charles Darwin's theory of evolution by natural selection in the nineteenth century.

**Other Sciences.** Scholars' vision turned inward as well. The institutionalization of human anatomy in the university curriculum in the fourteenth century encouraged the reexamination of received lore about the structure of the body and facilitated comparative anatomy, which in later periods spurred research into physiology and established both botany and zoology as autonomous sciences. By 1600 key developments in the coming scientific revolution of the seventeenth century, which would create the basis for modern science, were already in place. New technologies not only permitted European nations to reach out and exploit the rest of the world but also hastened the end of the old feudal order and shaped the nature of nations as political states. In many ways the creation of a new science and a new world order, which Francis Bacon was to call the "Great Instauration" in the beginning of the seventeenth century, was already in the offing by 1600.

# TOPICS IN SCIENCE, TECHNOLOGY, AND HEALTH

## ALCHEMY AND METALLURGY

**Economic and Military Resource.** The term *alchemy* originated in medieval Islam as an Arabization of the Greek word *chemia*, which referred to working with melted metals. Metallurgy and alchemy remained intimately connected through the Renaissance, although by 1600 the metallurgical arts had attained a degree of professional distinction and were producing their own descriptive and theoretical literature. Indeed, the mining, smelting, and refining of metals constituted an important industry in central Europe during the sixteenth century, and the princes who ruled emerging nation-states sought to encourage its development everywhere as an economic and military resource.

**Coinage.** Metals were the basis of coinage, too, and control of money was crucial to maintaining political authority and stability. For this reason the production and debasement of precious metals, whether by smelters or alchemists, was a sensitive matter and conferred on alchemy the dual status of desirable secret technology and feared violation of the economic order. For the latter reason in 1317 Pope John XXII prescribed severe punishment for alchemists.

**Transmutation.** Educated people believed that things of the world were materially distinct because of differing qualities and that there was a single underlying matter that took varying forms. Gold differed from lead not because of any fixed elemental nature but because it possessed different qualities—it was yellower, more ductile, and resisted corrosion better than lead. Therefore, few doubted that the transmutation of one metal into another was possible, since in theory one could add or subtract qualities to vary the form of the material object. However, many writers were skeptical of any particular individual's claims to have mastered the art and become an adept, or expert, at transmutation. As a result, the deceiving false-alchemist who demands advanced payments for the secret to making gold from cheaper metals, only to escape before the fraud is detected, and the deluded alchemist who wastes his family's wealth in search of the "elixir" or "philosophers' stone" that will enable transmutation, became familiar figures in literature from Geoffrey Chaucer's *Canon's Yeoman's Tale* (circa 1386–1400) to Ben Jonson's *The Alchemist* (1612) and Ludvig Holberg's *The Arabian Powder* (1722–1727). By the late sixteenth century, alchemy was much more than the dream of making gold (*chrysopoeia*) and the object of the poet's derision; it was also a means to make new medicines that held out the promise of treatment of "incurable" diseases, longevity, and inexpensive drugs for the poor. No wonder the Rosicrucians and other sectarian reformers of the late sixteenth and early seventeenth centuries were interested in alchemy as a means to create a better society.

**Translated Texts.** Alchemy as a science, with a complicated theoretical structure, practical procedures, and professional vocabulary, came to the Latin West from the Islamic world in the twelfth and thirteenth centuries, when manuscripts attributed to Abū Mūsā Jābir ibn Hayyān and other Arabic alchemists were rendered into Latin. These texts taught that metals comprised varying blends of philosophical principles called sulfur, which conveyed color, odor, and inflammability, and mercury, which gave metal its weight and fluidity (fusibility). The sulfur-mercury theory embodied the Aristotelian idea that metals and minerals were produced in the earth by various kinds of terrestrial vapors, or exhalations, which yielded metals, if they were moist and cold, or friable minerals, if they were dry and hot. Therefore, the sulfur-mercury theory was readily assimilated to Aristotelian matter theory in the thirteenth century by such renowned scholars as Roger Bacon and Albertus Magnus.

**Exoteric versus Esoteric.** An indigenous European Latin alchemical scholarship, drawing heavily on Arabic theory, took root in the thirteenth century, of which the most influential text was the *Compendium of Perfection*, written by Paul of Taranto under the pseudonym Geber (Jābir). This treatise, which was widely copied and eventually printed, proved to be one of the most important sources of basic theory and laboratory procedures for exoteric alchemy. Exoteric alchemy is distinguished from esoteric alchemy by a general disregard for spiritual metaphysics and religious mysticism, concerns that came to characterize much alchemical writing of the sixteenth and subsequent centuries. Exoteric alchemical tracts often admonished practitioners to be morally pure and regard knowledge of the philosopher's stone as the ultimate gift of God, achievable through hard study and divine illumination. Writers of this tradition often cloaked alchemical procedures in elaborate religious or mythological allegory. Nevertheless, exoteric alchemy was not in itself a religious practice. The esoteric tradition, however, fed on late antique Stoic and Platonic ideas attributed to sages such as

Hermes Trismegistus and Plato, and later on the Renaissance Neoplatonism of Marsilio Ficino and his followers. This approach incorporated a more-spiritual, less-materialist metaphysics that appealed to Reformation intellectuals such as Paracelsus and Jacob Boehme. By the early seventeenth century, alchemy as a species of matter theory that emphasized the chemical nature of all being and all change—from the original divine creation of the world described in Genesis (Gen. 1) to the body's internal processes of digestion, disease, and healing—was a salient feature of religious, philosophical, and medical discussion. There is, in fact, no historical justification for distinguishing between alchemy and chemistry in this period, since the terms were used without consistent distinction.

**Medicinal Purposes.** The use of alchemical methods to prepare medicines is found already in treatises attributed to Arnald of Villanova and John of Rupescissa (fourteenth century), who were concerned with extracting the essences of herbs, minerals, and animal products by distillation. The idea that the alchemist could prepare a tincture or elixir that could complete imperfect metals and make them into gold, the fully perfected metal, naturally extended to the belief that elixirs could perfect humans, too, healing their infirmities and conveying longevity. By the late sixteenth century, some alchemists were caught up in the quest for specific chemical preparations to treat particularly intractable diseases, such as epilepsy and syphilis, as well as general, cure-all elixirs called panaceas. Most such medical chemists, or chemical physicians, considered themselves to be followers of Paracelsus or were labeled Paracelsians by their critics, who found mystical alchemy to be impious and regarded alchemical drugs as dangerous poisons.

**Causal Connections.** Paracelsus and his followers radically altered alchemy and medical chemistry by elaborating a spiritual matter theory that added a salt principle to the sulfur-mercury theory and by making explicit and metaphorical connections between spiritualist theology, alchemy, and astrology. In general, the Paracelsians have been criticized for failing to distinguish adequately between identity and analogy. This problem is clearly evident in the Paracelsian theory that the human body reflects the greater world, or macrocosm, and that tremors of the body are phenomenally the same as earthquakes, having the same remote causes.

**Iatrochemistry.** As alchemists accumulated experience in constructing, fueling, and regulating furnaces and condensers to cool and recover the distilled vapors, they were able to prepare purer and stronger mineral acids to use as reagents, enabling them to separate mineral ores and recombine their constituents in new ways. Some of the metal compounds that they produced were highly poisonous and produced strong symptoms in humans, which the Paracelsians took to be indications of their great healing virtues, too. These products could be safely administered as medicines if the specific toxicities could be removed chemically. By 1600 iatrochemistry (medical chemistry) was emerging as a distinct part of medicine; chemically pre-

Large alchemical alembics used for distillation

pared drugs were beginning to find their way into traditional medical practice and would claim increasingly large portions of the official pharmacopoeias (books describing drugs, chemicals, and medicinal preparations) in the new century.

**Great Promise.** Knowledge of how to use acids, distillations, and metallic agents such as antimony to separate mineral ores into their components was useful in nonmedical applications as well, particularly in assaying and refining silver and gold. As mining and refining became more commercially and strategically important in the sixteenth century, treatises on assaying, distillation, and metallurgy began to appear, reflecting a growing specialization in these professions. Princes often supported alchemists not only in the hopes that they might command the secrets of gold-making, but also to staff court laboratories for testing the purity of metals and ores, preparing iatrochemical medicines and various cosmetics and confections for domestic use. Laboratories, such as those found in the palace of Landgraf Wilhelm of Hesse-Kassel and the basement of Tycho Brahe's villa, gradually moved into the public domain in the seventeenth century. Alchemists were also called on to prepare inks for printing, dyes for textiles and glass production, and other industrial chemicals. Alchemy held great promise for late-Reformation idealists, who sought the improvement of society through new methods of producing cheaper and more-effective drugs and other material goods.

Sources:

Allen G. Debus, *The Chemical Philosophy: Paracelsian Science and Medicine in the Sixteenth and Seventeenth Centuries,* 2 volumes (New York: Science History Publications, 1977).

Charles Nicholl, *The Chemical Theatre* (London & Boston: Routledge & Kegan Paul, 1980).

Piyo Rattansi and Antonio Clericuzio, eds., *Alchemy and Chemistry in the 16th and 17th Centuries* (Dordrecht, Holland & Boston: Kluwer Academic Publishers, 1994).

## ASTROLOGY AND MEDICINE

**Astrological Power.** Paracelsus's emphasis on the essentially astral character of humans and the active powers that dwell within nature can be readily understood in the context of Renaissance Neoplatonic theories that were elaborated in the late fifteenth century by Marsilio Ficino and spread north with Italian humanism. Ficino and his followers believed that the properly trained scholar-practitioner, the *magus* (magician-sage), could rearrange his physical surroundings and mental state in order to channel the cosmic forces that constantly rained down on him and interconnected every part of the world, forming an organic entity. Through proper choice of foods and clothing, the preparation of elaborate talismans from herbs and minerals selected for their astrological virtues, and the singing of ancient hymns and poems, the wise man could wield cosmic power to achieve health and longevity and otherwise alter the natural flow of the stellar influences. In short, he could manip-

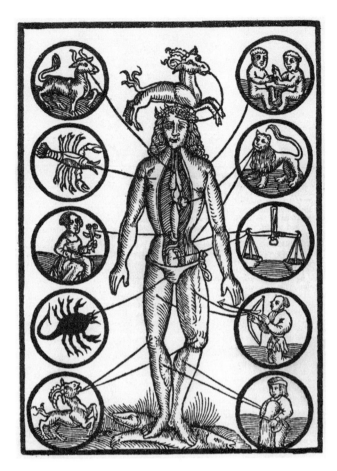

Woodcut of the signs of the zodiac showing the parts of the body with which they are allegedly associated

Explanations for epidemic diseases at that time focused on regional explanations rather than on the individual's state of health. These beliefs resulted in medical theories based on the supposed effects of comets and conjunctions of harmful planets (chiefly Saturn and Mars, but influenced by Jupiter and Mercury) in unfavorable constellations.

**Moon.** During the late Middle Ages consideration of the phase of the Moon and the positions of the major planets within a horoscope cast for the patient by an astrologer-physician became an entrenched part of treatment. The constellation in which the Moon was to be found at the onset of an individual's illness determined what part of the body was afflicted, and the physician estimated the nature, severity, and likely outcome of the disease on the basis of favorable or unfavorable planetary aspects. These considerations were important, but treatment was also based on other factors, such as the patient's age, sex, occupation, and general treatment.

**Accurate Calculations.** The medical need for astrology was a powerful stimulus to the recovery and perfection of ancient astronomical methods. Accurate astronomical calculations were required to create and modify the reference tables of planetary positions (*ephemerides*) that were then used to calculate their specific positions at a particular time and geographic location. Beyond the requirements of the Christian church for an accurate liturgical calendar, which would ensure the proper timing and coordination of Easter, feast days, and other holy rituals, no motive for astronomical reform loomed larger than the demands of medicine.

**Tycho Brahe.** Owing to the complexity of astrological theory and the mathematical competency required to construct and interpret an accurate medical horoscope, sophisticated astrology was practiced mainly by university-educated physicians and astronomers, although, as with other aspects of elite practice, a certain amount of astrological lore filtered down to lay practitioners who would use the astronomical data in almanacs or calendars for basic astrological practices. Like other natural sciences, astrology came under intense scrutiny in the sixteenth century, when attempts were made to integrate it with physical theory, subject it to more rigorous mathematical requirements, and verify its principles through systematic observation. Tycho Brahe, who set out to reform all of astronomy by means of careful, systematic measurement and mathematical analysis of the motions of the planets, also kept a detailed astrological and meteorological diary, in which planetary positions were recorded in the context of weather and notable events. Although Brahe was not a physician, he had studied the basics of medicine informally and was committed to a Neoplatonic and Paracelsian world view, in which the heavens above (the macrocosm) were connected to the herbs and minerals of the earth and to the major organs of the body (the microcosm). This correspondence between the macrocosm and microcosm unified the dual aspects of Brahe's research program—what he called "celestial astronomy" (astronomy as we know it) and "terrestrial astronomy" (alchemy). Clearly he viewed astronomy and astrology as essential parts of a general study of nature.

ulate astrological power. Such a fanciful view of a world ruled by magical forces was not the outgrowth of medieval tales of King Arthur's court and folk mythology, but a renewal and reinterpretation of ancient scientific astrology which, along with other aspects of Greek natural philosophy, became the object of intense investigation by medieval and Renaissance European scholars. Humanist interest in recovering ancient astrological knowledge is evident in the printing of Philipp Melanchthon's edition of the Greek text of Ptolemy's *Tetrabiblos* (second century C.E.), the source of much of Western astrological theory. Melanchthon, perhaps Martin Luther's most scholarly student, was a great reformer of education at Wittenberg, where he fostered an academic environment that encouraged the study of Copernicus's ideas about cosmology, among other recent developments in natural philosophy. He was also committed to the validity of astrology as a science.

**Comets and Planets.** The ancient Greek astronomer and mathematician Ptolemy of Alexandria had rationalized and codified astrology in the second century C.E., and this work, along with the mathematical astronomy necessary to make astrological predictions, was eagerly translated from Arabic and Greek sources by European medical scholars from the twelfth century onward. Viewed as helping the physician to establish the remote causes of diseases, astrology became an established part of medical theory and practice during the course of the fourteenth century.

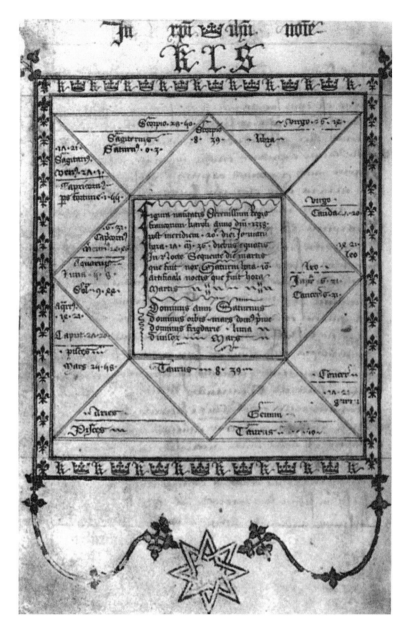

The horoscope of Charles V of France, circa 1377, including the exact hour and day of his birth and the constellation under which it took place (St John's College, Oxford)

**Sources:**

Roger French, "Astrology in Medical Practice," in *Practical Medicine from Salerno to the Black Death*, edited by Luis Garcia-Ballester et al. (Cambridge & New York: Cambridge University Press, 1994), pp. 30–59.

Robert S. Westman and J. E. McGuire, *Hermeticism and the Scientific Revolution: Papers Read at a Clark Library Seminar, March 9, 1974* (Los Angeles: William Andrews Clark Memorial Library, University of California, 1977).

Frances Amelia Yates, *Giordano Bruno and the Hermetic Tradition* (Chicago: University of Chicago Press, 1964).

## THE BLACK DEATH

**Terrifying Illness.** When violent and relatively abrupt sickness and death struck seemingly healthy individuals without warning and began to sweep across Europe in 1347–1348, these occurrences shocked and baffled members of every class of society. Medical lore had preserved distant memories of plague in Athens in 430–427 B.C.E., and scattered historical chronicles noted plagues that had eroded the economy and military might of late Imperial Rome in the sixth century C.E. By the late Middle Ages these events were, for the most part, forgotten. No one in medieval Europe had experienced anything like the epidemic death that arrived in Italy on board ships from the East, ravaged almost all of Europe, and recurred every ten to twenty years, terrifying people and hindering population recovery, until it disappeared without explanation in the early eighteenth century.

**Case Fatality.** Symptoms of the Black Death, as it was eventually named, were striking and exceedingly painful. Guy de Chauliac, physician and surgeon to the Pope, described the onset of the epidemic as a quickly spreading disease that caused high fever, expectoration of blood from the lungs, and death within three days. Soon another clini-

The following selection is an extract from the report of the University of Paris medical faculty on the causes of the Black Death, October 1348.

We say that the distant and first cause of this pestilence was and is the configuration of the heavens. In 1345, at one hour after noon on 20 March, there was a major conjunction of three planets in Aquarius. This conjunction, along with earlier conjunctions and eclipses, by causing a deadly corruption of the air around us, signifies mortality and famine. . . . Albertus Magnus in his book *Concerning the causes of the properties of the elements* (treatise 2, chapter 1) says that the conjunction of Mars and Jupiter causes a great pestilence in the air, especially when they come together in a hot, wet sign, as was the case in 1345. For Jupiter, being wet and hot, draws up evil vapours from the earth, and Mars, because it is immoderately hot and dry, then ignites the vapours, and as a result there were lightnings, sparks, noxious vapours and fires throughout the air.

These effects were intensified because Mars—a malevolent planet, breeding anger and wars—was in the sign of Leo from 6 October 1347 until the end of May this year. . . . Mars was also looking upon Jupiter with a hostile aspect, that is to say quartile, and that caused an evil disposition or quality in the air, harmful and hateful to our nature. . . . And this is enough about the distant or universal cause for the moment.

Although major pestilential illnesses can be caused by the corruption of water or food, as happens at times of famine and infertility, yet we still regard illnesses proceeding from the corruption of the air as much more dangerous. This is because bad air is more noxious than food or drink in that it can penetrate quickly to the heart and lungs to do its damage. We believe that the present epidemic or plague has arisen from air corrupt in its substance. . . and this corrupted air, when breathed in, necessarily pene-

trates to the heart and corrupts the substance of the spirit there and rots the surrounding moisture, and the heat thus caused destroys the life force, and this is the immediate cause of the present epidemic.

And moreover these winds, which have become so common here, have carried among us. . . bad, rotten, and poisonous vapours from elsewhere: from swamps, lakes, and chasms, for instance, and also (which is even more dangerous) from unburied or unburnt corpses—which might well have been a cause of the epidemic. Another possible cause of corruption, which needs to be borne in mind, is the escape of the rottenness trapped in the centre of the earth as a result of earthquakes—something which has indeed recently occurred. But the conjunctions could have been the universal and distant cause of all these harmful things, by which the air and water have been corrupted.

The bodies most likely to take the stamp of this pestilence are those which are hot and moist, for they are the most susceptible to putrefaction. The following are also more at risk: bodies bunged up with evil humours, because the unconsumed waste matter is not being expelled as it should; those following a bad life style, with too much exercise, sex, and bathing; the thin and weak, and persistent worriers; babies, women, and young people; and corpulent people with a ruddy complexion. However, those with dry bodies, purged of waste matter, who adopt a sensible and suitable regimen, will succumb to the pestilence more slowly.

We must not overlook the fact that any pestilence proceeds from the divine will, and our advice can therefore only be to return humbly to God. But this does not mean forsaking doctors. For the Most High created earthly medicine, and although God alone cures the sick, he does so through the medicine which in his generosity he provided.

**Source:** Rosemary Horrox, ed., *The Black Death*, translated by Horrox (Manchester & New York: Manchester University Press, 1994), p. 56.

cally distinct form became evident: its victims also experienced high fever, but not bleeding from the respiratory tract. In many cases, rashes and carbuncles on the skin followed, as did headaches, chills, and other symptoms. The most obvious and characteristic signs, or "tokens," of this longer infection were swollen lymph nodes in the armpits and groin, which were sufficiently distressing to demand opening and draining, even though it seemed that death soon followed anyway, usually about five to seven days after the first signs appeared. Not everyone who developed the disease died, but case fatality was high. Bodies quickly piled up in villages and cities, leading authorities to create sepa-

rate plague cemeteries. At the peak of the Black Death, rotting corpses were lined up in trenches and buried en masse, layer upon layer.

**Assumed Causes.** Contemporaries cited multiple explanations for plague. The most widespread belief was that it was a divine punishment for a misbehaving populace, but scientific, social, and political explanations also abounded. Astrologers explained that a rare conjunction of Mars, Jupiter, and Saturn occurred in a particularly unfavorable aspect in 1345. Some scholars drew on Arabic medical treatises and blamed the plague on a poisonous atmosphere. The ancient medicine of Hippocrates and Galen had correlated disease with air fouled by poisonous vapors and evil smells (miasmas) and with physical substances that afflicted individuals through direct contact (contagion). These local, or proximate, causes were regarded as triggered by remote causes, such as comets, unfavorable planetary aspects, and earthquakes, as well as by accidental or unintentional infection through contact with diseased animals, clothing, and persons.

**Prayer, Medicine, and Flight.** The Black Death severely traumatized those who survived it, but records indicate that people resumed the business of living only to meet the next wave of plague, and then the next, striking one part of Europe or another every year for three centuries. Estimates of mortality for the initial wave of Black Death range from an astounding 30 percent to 50 percent, but individual locations could be passed over entirely (for instance, Iceland, Finland, and some parts of Bohemia were not affected) or suffer 100 percent depopulation through death and subsequent abandonment (as in some valleys of Norway). The violence of subsequent outbreaks varied considerably by location and demography. The second plague, for example, is referred to as the children's plague, because it was perceived to claim mainly young victims who were born after the initial wave. Popular and learned perceptions of the plague throughout the period emphasized its sudden viciousness and the hope that one might avoid it through prayer, medicines, or flight to healthy regions.

**Affixing Blame.** These last factors led to some of the public health measures that were applied in times of plague: the killing of cats, dogs, and other carriers of contagion; the placing of cities and ships under quarantine, to hinder movement of people and goods that might harbor contagion; the isolation of infected households; the burning of clothing and other suspected items that were found in the homes of plague victims; the burning of sulfur or incense to purify bad air; and the destruction of Jews or other people suspected of maliciously tampering with urban water supplies. Jews had already been implicated in the spread of leprosy earlier in the fourteenth century, so the onslaught of plague merely provided a new excuse for an established social practice. When plague threatened Strasbourg early in 1349, for example, the pleading of enlightened city authorities did not stop the crowds from rounding up two thousand Jews and killing them. One chronicler reported that it took six days to burn them. Such was the terror inspired by plague.

*The Triumph of Death,* by an anonymous Sicilian artist, circa 1445 (Galleria Nazionale da Sicilia, Palermo)

**The Culprit.** Scholars today still debate the scientific explanations of the Black Death and subsequent plague epidemics. Most agree that it was caused by the bacillus *yersinia pestis,* which normally afflicts rats and other rodents and is spread among them by fleas. For unknown reasons, *yersinia pestis* periodically becomes epidemic, killing most or all of an extended family of rats, causing their infected fleas to seek neighboring rat packs or other warm-bodied hosts. When this situation happened, humans, who lived in relatively close proximity to household rats (black rats) in medieval and early modern Europe, were also infected, leading to a form of the disease now called bubonic plague (after the swellings, or buboes, in the armpits and groin). Infected fleas can live for months and travel easily in clothing and grain shipments, and presumably they were carried by human commerce to other communities of people and rats. This situation explains why plague seems to have traveled quickly by well-established commercial land and sea routes, reaching even the remote, sparsely populated upland valleys of Norway and Sweden. These areas needed to import grain and therefore imported rats and their fleas as stowaways in grain shipments. However, the observations of de Chauliac and others also imply that plague was on some occasions spread directly from human to human, probably carried by water droplets coughed up by victims of bubonic plague and then inhaled by their neighbors. This form of the disease is called pneumonic plague and spreads rapidly among humans living in densely populated circumstances.

**Impact.** Once brought to Europe, bubonic plague remained a constant part of the disease picture until the late seventeenth century. It would smolder in one place or another for a period and erupt into a regional epidemic every ten or twenty years. Such repeated outbreaks combined with other epidemic diseases, such as typhus, influenza, tuberculosis, and smallpox, to reduce the population and encourage a slower rate of reproduction as couples delayed marriages. The overall result was that Europe's population continued to decline until about 1450 and did not recover its early thirteenth-century levels until the 1500s. The vestiges of abandoned medieval village lots, their roads, and their long field strips remain to this day as evidence of communities that never recovered from the plague.

Sources:

Ole Jørgen Benedictow, *Plague in the Late Medieval Nordic Countries: Epidemiological Studies* (Oslo: Middelalderforlaget, 1992).

Rosemary Horrox, ed., *The Black Death* (Manchester & New York: Manchester University Press, 1994).

Colin Platt, *King Death: The Black Death and Its Aftermath in Late-Medieval England* (Toronto & Buffalo: University of Toronto Press, 1997).

## COSMOLOGY

**The Cosmos.** Despite the persistent myth that scholars in Christopher Columbus's day feared he would sail off the edge of a flat earth, there is ample evidence in texts from the early Middle Ages suggesting a basic understanding of Earth's sphericity, its location at the center of the spherical cosmos, and its immobility. These ideas survived the economic collapse of the Western Roman Empire. The seven liberal arts that well-born Roman citizens studied included the study of astronomy. This curricular model became the foundation for the revival of education in the Carolingian period and was a presumed basis for advanced study in the high medieval university; hence, rudimentary knowledge of cosmology never wholly disappeared from learned culture. However, a working knowledge of astronomy, sufficient to cast a medical horoscope, was a rarity in the Latin West before Arabic treatises were sought out and translated during the first great wave of the recovery of classical knowledge in the eleventh and twelfth centuries. At that time Europeans learned to use the astrolabe, a sighting instrument perfected in the Moslem East for calculating celestial coordinates. Also in the twelfth century the treatises of Aristotle were translated. By the thirteenth century these texts became the basis for all branches of philosophy taught at the university. Aristotle had disregarded observational astronomy, which he considered as a subdiscipline of mathematics, and instead elaborated a model of the physical structure of the cosmos, the study of which is called cosmology.

**Two Distinct Realms.** Aristotelian cosmology taught that the terrestrial world comprises four concentric elemental spheres, into which the four basic material elements—earth, water, air, and fire—generally settle. Earth, being the heaviest, seeks the center of the cosmos, which is why earth is central. Water settles in around earth, then air, then fire. The outer reaches of the sphere of fire extended almost to the invisible sphere that allegedly carried the Moon around Earth. The four elements were in constant motion, mixing with one another and penetrating each other's native region, which explains moisture in the air, fire within wood, and so on. In stark contrast, the large region that began with the sphere of the Moon and extended out to the celestial sphere, which was the physical limit of the cosmos and held all of the visible stars, was regarded as eternal and unchanging and composed of a fifth element, quintessence. All motions in this region, which encompassed the orbs of Mercury, Venus, the Sun, Mars, Jupiter, and Saturn, were obliged to be circular and of constant rotational speed, because only uniform spherical (circular) motion was at once moving and unchanged, inasmuch as all parts of a sphere remain at a constant distance from its center and cyclically and regularly return to the same locations. The divinely inspired motive power for the cosmos originated in the outermost sphere and propagated inward toward the center, turning each planet and eventually stirring up the terrestrial elements. Thus, Aristotle divided the cosmos into two distinct realms—terrestrial and celestial—each with its own intrinsic laws and nature. In the celestial world nothing changed and all beings naturally moved in circles, and there was perfect order. In the terrestrial world, birth, growth, death, and decay, which entailed the combination and recombinations of the elements, ensured a constant state of change and disorder.

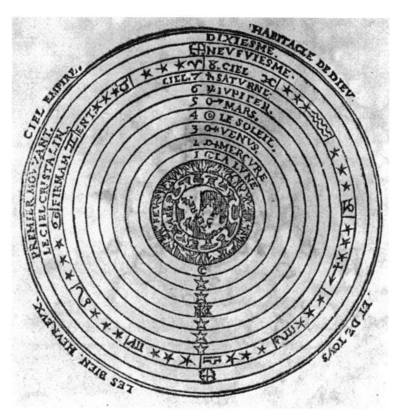

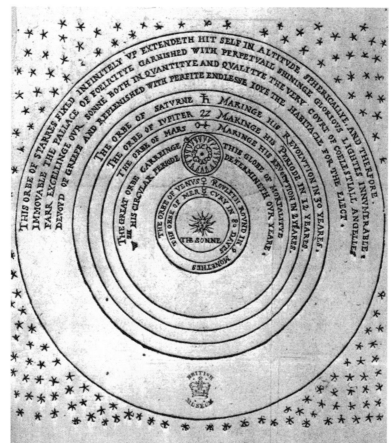

The geocentric (Aristotelian) universe (top), as depicted in Peter Apian's *Cosmographia* (1524) and the heliocentric (Copernican) universe (bottom), as depicted in a 1576 edition of Leonard and Thomas Digges's *Prognostication Everlastinge* (1555)

In this passage from book one of his "On the Revolutions of the Heavenly Spheres" (1543), Nicholas Copernicus describes the physical makeup of the cosmos as he sees it, with the Earth having been replaced by the Sun as the center. Chief among the reasons he expresses here such a radical shift in cosmology are spacial symmetry, mathematical ordering, and a feeling that the Sun, which is a visible emblem of life-giving divinity, should hold a central place in the system. It is crucial to Copernicus's argument that he convince readers that all the apparent movements of the stars and planets can be accounted for by the relative motions of the earth and planets and by the great distance between the Sun and the stars.

The first and highest of all is the sphere of the fixed stars, which contains itself and all things, and is therefore motionless. It is the location of the universe, to which the motion and position of all the remaining stars is referred. For though some consider that it also changes in some respect, we shall assign another cause for its appearing to do so in our deduction of the Earth's motion. There follows Saturn, the first of the wandering stars, which completes its circuit in thirty years. After it comes Jupiter which moves in a twelve-year long revolution. Next is Mars, which goes round biennially. An annual revolution holds the fourth place, in which as we have said is contained the Earth along with the lunar sphere which is like an epicycle. In fifth place Venus returns every nine months. Lastly, Mercury holds the sixth place, making a circuit in the space of eighty days. In the middle of all is the seat of the Sun. For who in this most beautiful of temples would put this lamp in any other or better place than the one from which it can illuminate everything at the same time? Aptly indeed is he named by some the lantern of the universe, by others the mind, by others the ruler. Trismegistus called him the visible God, Sophocles' Electra, the watcher over all things. Thus indeed the Sun as if seated on a royal throne governs his household of Stars as they circle round him. Earth also is by no means cheated of the Moon's attendance, but as Aristotle says in his book *On Animals* the Moon has the closest affinity with the Earth. Meanwhile the Earth conceives from the Sun, and is made pregnant with annual offspring. We find, then, in this arrangement the marvellous symmetry of the universe, and a sure linking together in harmony of the motion and size of the spheres, such as could be perceived in no other way. For here one may understand, by attentive observation, why Jupiter appears to have a larger progression and retrogression than Saturn, and smaller than Mars, and again why Venus has larger ones than Mercury; why such a doubling back appears more frequently in Saturn than in Jupiter, and still more rarely in Mars and Venus than in Mercury; and furthermore, why Saturn, Jupiter and Mars are nearer to the Earth when in opposition than in the region of their occultation by the Sun and re-appearance. Indeed Mars in particular at the time when it is visible throughout the night seems to equal Jupiter in size, though marked out by its reddish colour; yet it is scarcely distinguishable among stars of the second magnitude, though recognised by those who track it with careful attention. All these phenomena proceed from the same cause, which lies in the motion of the Earth. But the fact that none of these phenomena appears in the fixed stars shows their immense elevation, which makes even the circle of their annual motion, or apparent motion, vanish from our eyes. For every visible object has some limit of distance, beyond which it is no longer seen, as is shown in the *Optics*. That there is still a very great distance from Saturn, the highest of the wandering stars, to the sphere of the fixed stars is shown by the scintillation of their lights. It is by this mark that the planets are particularly distinguished, for there had to be a particular point of difference between the moving and unmoved stars. Such truly is the size of this structure of the Almighty's.

Source: Nicholas Copernicus, *Copernicus: On the Revolutions of the Heavenly Spheres*, translated by A. M. Duncan (Newton Abbot, U.K.: David & Charles, 1976; New York: Barnes & Noble, 1976), pp. 49–51.

**Accepted Theory.** This cosmos was the one Dante described in *The Divine Comedy* (circa 1308–1321) and was, with a few modifications, warmly embraced by Christian theologians, philosophers, and the learned laity. The order of Aristotle's cosmos reflected the wisdom, order, and benevolence of the Creator, who placed his special creature, man, in the center. This view made perfect sense, since Earth seems at rest, heavy objects seem to fall and light ones rise, and the heavens seem to go through their cycles of conjunctions with unchanging regularity, shaping the seasons and their effects. The gradient of perfection, beginning with the most perfect, outermost heaven, where the souls of the departed joined Christ and awaited resurrection, passed inward through the celestial orbs, where the angelic intelligences dwelled, and then through the changeable fiery, aerial, and watery spheres, ending up in the interior elemental earth, where base matter seethed and spontaneously generated snakes, insects, and other "infernal," or lower, creatures.

**Mirror of Society.** Dante's Aristotelian image of the physical world mirrored the social and political structure of medieval Europe, where the unquestioned perfection and authority of the kings and popes trickled down through the feudal and ecclesiastical hierarchies to touch the basest bondsmen, whose world also was characterized by constant change, imperfection, birth, corruption, and death. To paraphrase the *Tabula smaragdina* (Emerald Tablet of Hermes)—a compilation of ancient alchemical, occultic, and theological works reputedly by the Hellinistic author Hermes Trismegistos—what is below reflects and is governed by that which is above; every being in the cosmos owes its livelihood to its superiors, and its condition mirrors their wisdom and benevolence. By the late Middle Ages, Aristotelian cosmology was well integrated into the political, religious, and moral order of Europe, which is why its eventual demise has been considered by historians as a "scientific revolution" concurrent with the painful social, religious, and economic revolutions that marked the transition from medieval feudalism to the modern nation-state.

**The Almagest.** Ironically, the effort to perfect the Aristotelian cosmology is what eventually destroyed it and laid the basis for a more modern view of the universe as a huge, largely empty space, in which the Sun is but one of many and Earth just another planet. The need for a more accurate calendar and a refined astrology, along with a general humanist zeal to recover and understand the wisdom of the ancient Greeks, Egyptians, Hebrews, and Chaldeans, encouraged scholars to seek out Greek astronomical and mathematical manuscripts and improve on their science. In the fifteenth century Georg Puerbach and Johannes Regiomontanus searched out new manuscripts of Ptolemy's *Almagest* (second century C.E.), the greatest ancient treatment of astronomy, and set about adapting his methods to the three-dimensional, physical cosmology of the medieval Aristotelians. Regiomontanus wrote an epitome, or digested form, of the *Almagest,* which helped explain the details of Ptolemy's mathematical approach, and a humanist Greek edition of the text was printed in the sixteenth century. However, by then astronomers were beginning to realize that refinement in Ptolemy's methods was not enough to correct the errors that kept throwing off the calendar and would also, logically, reduce the accuracy of astrological prediction.

**Copernicus.** In the next generation, a young Pole from the Baltic north named Nicholas Copernicus determined that a true restoration of ancient astronomy required rejection of the geocentric model that formed the basis of Ptolemy's astronomy and Aristotle's cosmology. Instead, he went back to the earlier astronomy of Aristarchus of Samos, who was reported to have taught that the Sun is the center of the cosmos and Earth revolves about it, as a planet. Copernicus had studied both astronomy and cosmology at the University of Cracow in Poland before heading to Italy to study law and medicine. After his return to his homeland, he set down his ideas in a short manuscript called the *Commentariolus,* or "Little Commentary" (1514), which was copied and circulated among astronomers.

**Wandering Earth** Copernicus's hypothesis was that Earth rotated on its axis, rather than lying stationary, while the huge celestial sphere turned round once every twenty-four hours, giving the illusion that the planets and the stars rise in the east, stretch across the vault of the sky, and set to the west. He also thought that the Sun, as symbol of God and source of life-giving warmth, was the true center of the cosmos, and that the Earth revolved about it, traveling at a considerable speed. In short, he argued that Earth was a planet or "wanderer" (*planetoi*), like Mars or any other. The idea was generally greeted as idle speculation, contrary to both common sense and intellectual tradition, but it eventually sparked the curiosity of a Lutheran philosopher at Wittenberg named Georg Joachim Rheticus, who traveled to Poland to learn more from Copernicus and persuade him to publish the details of his new astronomy. The result was the *Narratio prima* (First Narration), which Rheticus published in 1540, followed by Copernicus's fully articulated mathematical astronomy, *De revolutionibus orbium coelestium* (On the Revolutions of the Celestial Orbs) in 1543.

**Heliocentrism.** From the beginning, the religious implications of the Sun-centered cosmology (heliocentrism) were of concern, since the Bible taught that Earth was stationary and central and that the Sun rose and set, moving about it. However, the absurdity of a moving Earth, both from the standpoint of Aristotelian cosmology and the common-sense view that the Earth did not seem to be moving and that stones fell "downward" toward the center, prevented the new system from being seriously considered as reality before the arguments of Galileo and the mathematical refinements of Kepler began to win converts to heliocentrism in the seventeenth century. In the intervening half century or more, astronomers who taught the Copernican system and used it to calculate planetary movements did so because it was mathematically convenient, not because they regarded it as a step toward grasping the cosmological truth. It was in fact not astronomers who first defended the Copernican model as a plausible physical system, but rather natural philosophers, who rejected elements of Aristotelian philosophy for other reasons and were drawn to heliocentrism as an alternative. The most flamboyant of these was the renegade Dominican monk and philosopher, Giordano Bruno.

**Dissenter.** Bruno ran afoul of his Dominican brothers in southern Italy for holding religious and cosmological views that were at variance with Catholicism. He abandoned his monastery and headed north. After a brief stay in Paris, he traveled to England, where he espoused his doctrine of the infinity of the universe, in which Earth was not central. His argument was more theologically than scientifically motivated, since he reasoned that the cosmos must reflect God and be infinitely large, with no particular center—or rather that its center was present everywhere, just as God was fully present everywhere. Nevertheless, Bruno's vision of a radically new world order attracted the attention of his contemporaries, who were just beginning to undo the Aristotelian cosmology. In the hindsight of nineteenth-century historians, Bruno became something of an emblem of the struggle of scientific truth against the

A 1326 astrolabe, used to determine the position of the Sun or stars for navigation (British Museum)

intransigence of tradition and the totalitarian authority of the Church, which ordered Bruno to be burned alive at the stake in Rome in 1600. His crime, however, was not Copernicanism, but espousing heretical ideas about Christ. The Catholic Church did not yet have an official, legal policy about the Copernican hypothesis.

**Ellipses.** Bruno was not alone in questioning traditional cosmology in the late sixteenth century. The English mathematician Thomas Digges believed that there was no celestial sphere, but that the stars filled an extended (perhaps boundless) space, and this notion supported Copernicus's claim that the cosmos was larger than the ancients had supposed. However, he was not ready to put Earth in motion. His countryman, William Gilbert, likewise could

not abandon the idea of a central Earth, but did argue that it rotated on its axis every day. Medieval scholars had entertained this notion in the early fourteenth century, arguing that it would be more economical for the Earth to rotate once every twenty-four hours than to have the entire mass of the cosmos—all the stars, planets, Sun, Moon, and their various spheres—revolve about the fixed Earth. However, where the fourteenth-century scholastic philosophers considered this idea as a logical possibility and dismissed it for want of philosophical merit, Gilbert attributed Earth's motion to its intrinsic magnetic soul, the existence of which he demonstrated through careful experimentation and reported in his *De magnete* (On the Magnet, 1600). Gilbert's proposal planted the seed of an idea in the head of

Johannes Kepler, who argued that all the celestial bodies have intrinsic moving souls, which account for the motions of the Moon about Earth and Earth and other planets about the Sun. Kepler argued that a magnetic soul, such as the kind postulated by Gilbert for Earth, accounted for why the planets did not orbit in perfect circles but were alternately attracted and then repelled, bending the circles into ellipses.

**Royal Favorite.** The extent to which Renaissance theorists resisted discarding the belief that Earth was at rest in the center of the cosmos is well illustrated by the work of its greatest astronomer, Tycho Brahe, whose publications were authoritative at the close of the sixteenth century. Brahe's astronomy was shaped by his conviction that the real problem with the science in his day, which was obviously not capable of accurate predictions, was not a failure of theory but an absence of dependable observational facts. His determination to systematically scrutinize and measure the heavens and reform astronomy was stimulated by his 1572 observation of a *nova stella* (new star) in the constellation Cassiopeia. Brahe's observation was but one of many in Europe, but it was more detailed and accurate than others and was published at a time when it attracted the attention of the king of Denmark, who was anxious to reward Brahe and also foster natural philosophy in his kingdom. The result was that Brahe, already a wealthy member of Denmark's high nobility, was granted state funding to build Europe's first scientific research institution on the island of Hven. There he built an observatory and alchemical laboratory, both of which surpassed their contemporaries.

**Alternative.** The key to the significance of the "new star," which appeared out of nowhere, went through a sequence of color changes, and then vanished, was that it occurred in the perfect and unchanging celestial region and was therefore in violation of Aristotelian theory. Subsequent observations by Brahe and his assistants revealed that comets also were celestial but passed through the supposed celestial orbs that moved the planets, descending toward Earth and then ascending again to the stars. This view, too, ran counter to Aristotelian cosmology, according to which comets were meteorological phenomena and occurred in the terrestrial atmosphere, but Brahe's measurements proved decisively that comets were extraterrestrial. Despite his readiness to break down the terrestrial-celestial distinction in medieval cosmology, Brahe was unwilling to abandon the stationary central Earth. None of his observations supported Copernicus's claim that Earth revolved about the Sun, and Brahe found no reason to oppose the religious consensus that God, speaking through the Bible, taught that the Earth was at rest. Instead, he devised a compromise model, in which the Sun and the Moon revolve about the Earth, while the planets revolve around the Sun. This model was mathematically equivalent to the Copernican, heliocentric system, but did not require Earth to be in motion. It was sufficiently successful to be adopted by Catholic educators in the seventeenth century. Since the church rejected Galileo's Copernican model on the grounds that it violated Scriptural authority, which required a central Earth, Brahe's system was a logical alternative to the ancient Aristotelian/Ptolemaic model of the cosmos, which Galileo's telescopic observations of the phases of Venus had disproved.

**Staying Power.** As the sixteenth century closed, the classical cosmology was in serious disrepair but still the dominant view. It would eventually fall during the course of the seventeenth century, partly put to rest by the successful mathematical astronomy of Isaac Newton, which brought the observations and arguments of Galileo, Kepler, Brahe, and others into a coherent explanation of celestial motions that was based solely on matter, inertial motion, and gravitational attraction. In 1600, however, little of this development was in evidence. Indeed, arguments about cosmology then seemed to occupy not only a philosophical but also a theological space. Bruno's imaginative universe was postulated on his view of the creative and sustaining divinity that powered it. His philosophical writings assume a divine, Platonic world soul that unifies everything. Brahe's assistant, Kort Aslakssøn, argued that the processes at work in the heavens were also those that work on Earth and in the alchemical laboratory, and that these were essentially spiritual. Quite likely his views reflected those of his mentor, and he carried them with him into a theological career at the University of Copenhagen. Even Kepler's early arguments about the structure and functioning of the planetary system were founded on ideas of divinity, soul, and a kind of intelligence that was part of created matter, accounting for how remote objects could influence one another—how the things above could affect those below, as the Emerald Tablet of Hermes taught. Modernity had not arrived.

Sources:

Marie Boas, *The Scientific Renaissance 1450-1630* (New York: Harper, 1962).

James M. Lattis, *Between Copernicus and Galileo: Christoph Clavius and the Collapse of Ptolemaic Cosmology* (Chicago: University of Chicago Press, 1994).

C. S. Lewis, *The Discarded Image: An Introduction to Medieval and Renaissance Literature* (Cambridge: Cambridge University Press, 1964).

## EPIDEMIC DISEASE AND MEDICINE

**Syphilis.** Approximately two years after Columbus reached the New World, an unknown disease appeared among the ranks of a French army that was laying siege to the southern Italian city of Naples. Characterized by terrible pain, swelling, and open sores on the penis and scrotum, the disease was recognized by the surgeons and physicians who treated it as a new kind of venereal disease. Unlike gonorrhea, this new disease led to secondary skin lesions on almost any part of the body, along with skeletal pains that made sleep difficult. The French army blamed it on the locals, calling it the Neapolitan Disease. Much of the rest of Europe associated it with the invading French, whose army disbanded in 1495, further spreading it, and called it the French Disease, or simply the pox. It became known as syphilis, a name first used by the Italian poet, physician, and natural philosopher Girolamo Fracastoro, who described the travails of a shepherd boy he called "Syphilis" in a poem describing the new disease.

**Mercury Cure.** Historians continue to debate whether syphilis was brought to Europe from the West Indies with returning Spanish ships or if it was caused by a sudden mutation of a milder, nonvenereal form of *treponemosis* that was already present in Europe and Africa. Whatever its origin, European observers, many of them victims, reacted to the disease as if it were new to the Continent and quickly associated it with prostitution and the loose morality of the Renaissance. Associated with adultery, it was foisted on unsuspecting spouses and transmitted congenitally to innocent children. Owing to the open sores and skin lesions, physicians and surgeons treated syphilis as a disease of the blood that provoked rashes and sores as a result of the body's effort to expel corrupted matter. Skin diseases were sometimes treated with salves containing mercury and other toxic metals, and mercurial salves soon became the standard treatment for syphilis, because in large doses, mercury provoked both sweating and salivating, another means of ridding the body of "morbific" (disease-causing) matter. Physicians who believed that chemically prepared metallic drugs were useful as orally administered medicines against the pox and other diseases distilled various mercury salts to dose patients. The apparent success of these "chemical physicians," as they were called, upset the established medical profession and led to vigorous debate that shook the foundations of medical theory and education. Patients treated with mercury achieved some degree of cure, although if treatments were not long enough or not repeated, the disease sometimes went into dormancy only to reemerge years later as tertiary syphilis. This disease, which is characterized by lesions of the cranium, nasal bones, shin bones, and occasionally other parts of the skeleton, resulted in horrible disfigurement and death.

**English Sweat and Typhus.** Syphilis was not the only new disease in the late fifteenth and sixteenth centuries, merely the most physically and morally horrifying. A more mysterious disease struck England in 1485, first appearing among mercenary troops. Called simply the English Sweat, it reoccurred four more times, the last in 1551, and often killed within hours of the appearance of symptoms. Even in a society faced with the constant presence of fatal disease, such a sudden death was astonishing. Typhus was another apparent newcomer, appearing among Spanish troops who were attempting to expel the Muslim Moors from the city of Granada in southern Spain in 1489–1490. Characterized by high fever, rash, headache, delirium, and high fatality, typhus became a constant companion of European armies into the twentieth century, often accounting for more casualties than did armed conflict.

**Smallpox.** Another major illness that erupted in the sixteenth century was smallpox. Possibly long extant in Europe in a mild form and not distinguished from other "fevers," smallpox became a major killer when introduced to natives of the Western Hemisphere. Never exposed to this disease, nor typhus, measles, and influenza, Native Americans had no immunities or experience to help them respond to epidemics. Both factors enabled diseases to spread rapidly, wiping out large populations and discouraging survivors from resisting the Europeans. Under these circumstances, smallpox apparently mutated into a more virulent form and became a serious, disfiguring disease when it was reintroduced to Europe in the seventeenth century.

**Guaiacum Wood.** The appearance of new diseases stimulated the medical community to find new treatments and new theories to account for disease. For a time, guaiacum wood was imported from South America and powdered for use as an infusion against syphilis, partly on the reasoning that divine providence would have placed a cure near the source of the disease, which was widely regarded as the New World. Moreover, guaiacum also provoked sweating, which medical theory at the time regarded as curative.

**Contagion Theory.** In the sixteenth century, syphilis began to be viewed as being spread by contagion, or contact, rather than arising as an imbalance in the body's basic fluids (known as humors). This latter theory had dominated medicine since the time of Hippocrates, and even plague was thought to arise possibly from a miasma in the air that people inhaled, causing an imbalance in their blood. During the course of the 1500s, however, medical theorists began to give new attention to an ancient contagion theory that was described by the Roman poet Lucretius in the first century B.C.E. Fracastoro's study of syphilis, which he published in 1530, had suggested that the disease was caused by invisible but material "seeds"—a term Lucretius had used to describe atoms—that were physically transmitted from one person to another. This idea appealed to physicians and public health authorities, who thought plague was spread by impurities in hair and woolen goods as well as by miasmas in the air. The seed theory also implied that some diseases had a specific material origin, which challenged the traditional conception of disease as a physiological condition.

**Organic Pathology.** Roughly contemporary with Fracastoro, a Swiss-German physician named Paracelsus came to a similar conclusion that diseases were caused by specific entities, but he regarded them as infective spirits rather than material seeds and thought that they could be countered with spiritually active chemical drugs. This spiritual-seed theory was further developed by one of Paracelsus's followers, Petrus Severinus, into a general theory of organic pathology that influenced seventeenth-century ideas about the specificity of diseases. The idea that disease was a specific entity, regardless of whom it affected, rather than an imbalance or physiological malfunction that was unique to each victim, revolutionized the medical marketplace. Once diseases were identified as particular entities, or types, specific drugs could be prescribed against them or bought without the need for expensive medical consultation. (Why pay the doctor, when one can get the cure from the druggist?) The seed theories of Fracastoro and Severinus also provided justification for the practices of quarantine, isolation, and the destruction of infected clothing and furs, as

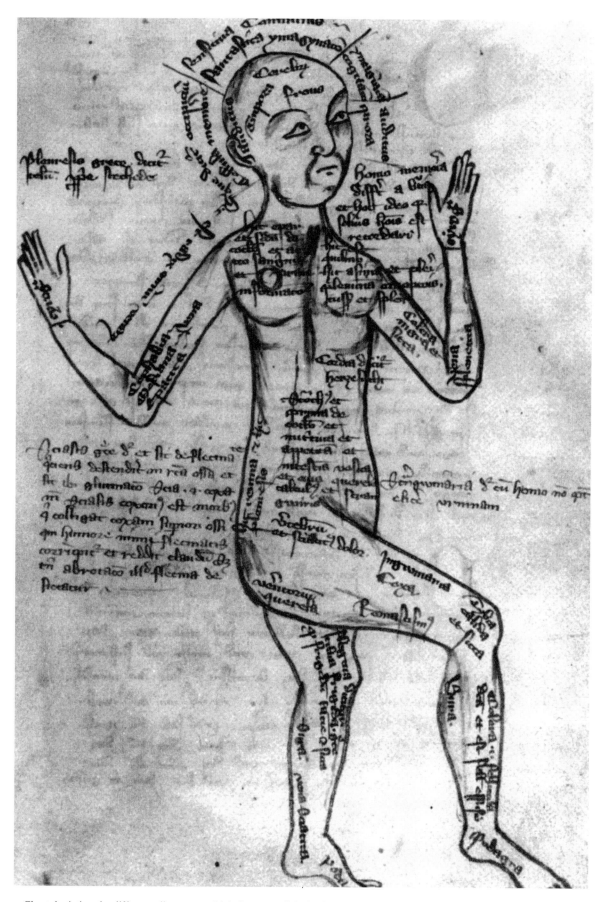

Chart depicting the different ailments to which the parts of the body are liable, from a fifteenth-century German manuscript (British Library, Arundel MS 252, f. 37)

well as cats and dogs, which public health authorities had already recommended during times of plague. Enforcement of such measures became stricter and more universal in the seventeenth century and may have contributed to the disappearance of bubonic plague from Europe. In any case, the amount of money spent on control of epidemic plague and the economic losses that were suffered because of quarantine are witnesses to contemporaries' belief that such measures were warranted.

Sources:

Robert S. Gottfried, *The Black Death: Natural and Human Disaster in Medieval Europe* (New York: Free Press, 1893; London: Collier Macmillan, 1983).

Vivian Nutton, "The Seeds of Disease: An Explanation of Contagion and Infection from the Greeks to the Renaissance," *Medical History*, 27 (1983): 1–34.

Claude Quétel, *History of Syphilis*, translated by Judith Braddock and Brian Pike (Baltimore: Johns Hopkins University Press, 1990).

## MEDICAL MARKETPLACE

**Home Remedies.** Most people in the modern world experience medicine either in a physician's or dentist's office, a local clinic, or a hospital. However, in Renaissance Europe educated physicians were few, clinics as such did not exist, and hospitals served mainly as shelters for the poor and provided only limited medical care. University-trained physicians and surgeons in the late Middle Ages numbered no more than ten to fifteen per ten thousand inhabitants and were concentrated in larger towns and cities, where their expensive services were utilized chiefly by the elite. The bulk of healing was done at home, not by medical doctors making house calls but by family members, by men and women of the community who were experienced in folk ways and had empirical knowledge of herbs, or by a whole range of professional healers who made up what historians call "the medical marketplace." These healers included apothecaries, bonesetters, oculists who removed cataracts, lithotomists who removed bladder stones, midwives, barber-surgeons, and other specialists. Medical treatment was not a sustaining profession for many healers, so they often combined it with other activities. The early apothecaries, for example, were often put into the same guilds as grocers and spice traders.

**Organization.** Medieval guilds, which incorporated to protect craftsmen and merchants from the uncertainties brought by an unregulated free market, served as models for providers of surgical and medical care as well. The Doctor of Medicine degree (M.D.), like other advanced university degrees, was an educational credential, conferring upon the holder the right to teach. In order to elevate medical practice to a high professional standard, M.D.s in urban areas formed colleges of medicine, which functioned like craft guilds. Surgeons and barber-surgeons, whose services were generally limited to bloodletting and simple surgical procedures, also organized into colleges or companies. They sought to control licensing and limit the number of practitioners, thereby defining both the quality and the cost of medical care.

An apothecary shop, illumination from a fourteenth-century French manuscript (British Library, Sloane MS 1977, f. 49 verso)

**Measures of Control.** In the largest cities, such as London and Paris, the various colleges of surgeons, physicians, barber-surgeons, and apothecaries constantly strove to defend their privileges while seeking to encroach on competing professionals. In seventeenth-century London, for example, the College of Physicians frequently engaged in lawsuits against unlicensed physicians, as well as barbers and apothecaries who persisted in diagnosing illnesses and prescribing remedies, which was legally the province of the trained physician. In other places, particularly Mediterranean cities such as Venice, the colleges of medicine had a vertical organization similar to the textile guilds, and included physicians and surgeons. In Venice, the guilds were also supervised by the republic's government, which resulted in a better-regulated, if less open, system of health care.

**Physicians and Surgeons.** The higher orders of medical care—surgeons and physicians—had not always been so distinct. When medicine began to emerge as a learned craft in Salerno, Italy, during the ninth to the eleventh centuries, surgery was a prominent part of the curriculum. The inclusion of medicine in the university curriculum in the thir-

The same year that Andreas Vesalius published his epoch-making *On the Architecture of the Human Body* (1543), he produced a more concise version (or *Epitome*), intended for the student dissector. His approach in that text is similar to his fuller treatment, but more direct, less detailed, and lacking the many expensive woodcuts that made the *Architecture* so costly. The following section from the preface to *Epitome* explains why Vesalius thought that such a book was needed.

It is a charge to be laid most gravely at the door of the mob of physicians that they perform their duty so carelessly in distinguishing the parts of the human body that not even enumeration is made use of in learning them. For when, beyond the function and use of each part, its location, form, size, color, the nature of its substance, the principle of its connection with the other parts, and many things of this sort in the medical examination of the parts may never be sufficiently perceived, how many can be found who know even the number of the bones, cartilages, ligaments, muscles, and veins, arteries, and nerves running in a numerous succession throughout the entire body and of the viscera which are found in the cavities of the body? I pass over in silence those pestilent doctors who encompass the destruction of the common life of mankind, who never even stood by at a dissection: whereas in the knowledge of the body no one could produce anything of value who did not perform dissections with his own hands as the kings of Egypt were wont to do and in like manner busied himself frequently and sedulously with dissections and with simple medicines. Whence also those most prudent members of the household of Asclepius [that is, physicians] will never be sufficiently praised, who, as children in the home learn reading and writing, so they exercised the dissection of cadavers and, learning in this wise, under the happy auspices of the Muses, they bent to their studies. . . . Indeed, those who are now dedicated to the ancient study of medicine, almost restored to its pristine splendor in many schools, are beginning to learn to their satisfaction how little and how feebly men have labored in the field of Anatomy to this day from the times of Galen, who, although easily chief of the masters, nevertheless did not dissect the human body; and the fact is now evident that he described (not to say imposed upon us) the fabric of the ape's body, although the latter differs from the former in many ways."

Source: Andreas Vesalius, *The Epitome of Andreas Vesalius,* translated by L. R. Lind (New York: Macmillan, 1949), pp. xxxiv–xxxv.

---

teenth century combined with teachings from the newly recovered writings of Galen of Pergamon and Aristotle—ancient Greece's most prominent medical and philosophical writers—helped physicians define medicine not only as the craft of healing, but also as a philosophical subject. Galen had emphasized that the physician should be well grounded in Aristotelian philosophy, and university medicine became oriented more toward theoretical training as physicians increasingly viewed surgical procedures as a lower-order, nonintellectual pursuit. Although medical and surgical training were not completely divorced in the southern universities, such as Bologna (Italy), even there professional distinctions developed, with surgery occupying a subordinate position in the social and educational hierarchy. In the North the gulf between physicians and surgeons was much more radical and complete. In fifteenth-century Paris, for example, surgery was not taught at the university. M.D.s were expected to command medical philosophy and offer diagnosis and therapeutic advice to the patient and leave the cutting, salving, bandaging, and bloodletting to the surgeons and barber-surgeons. For their part, surgeons sought to lift their own educational status, sometimes requiring students to learn Latin and, increasingly in the fifteenth century, demanding that students attain firsthand anatomical knowledge by attending annual dissections.

**Clinical Experience.** During the sixteenth century, efforts by humanist physicians to reunite surgery, drug-

making, and medicine according to the ancient Greek ideal met with limited success, although they produced some noteworthy advances in anatomical knowledge. Andreas Vesalius, perhaps the foremost anatomist of the century, instructed surgeons by anatomical demonstration at Bologna, while a physician lectured on theory. However, the separation between physician and surgeon did not discourage Vesalius from confronting his students with observational facts that ran counter to Galen's teachings. Vesalius published *On the Architecture of the Human Body* (1543) and brought active anatomical research to a new level. Of greater benefit to the surgeon, however, was the increased frequency of military campaigns. These excursions provided both employment and opportunity to experiment with new procedures, and led to the gradual transformation of the large general hospitals, such as the Hotel Dieu in Paris, from hostels into treatment facilities for the poor. As Europe's population increased and as the poor migrated to the cities, these institutions offered physicians and surgeons alike the chance to gain clinical experience that was unrivaled in the private sector.

**Improved Hospitals.** Medieval hospitals in the West were originally Christian charitable hospices that provided basic food and shelter for the poor and for travelers, though sometimes rudimentary medical care was also provided. Hospitals as institutions that focused primarily on treatment emerged earlier in the Byzantine and Islamic worlds than in the Latin

West, owing to the greater continuity of classical traditions and, in Byzantium, to the maintenance of centralized imperial order. The Pantokrator Hospital, founded in Constantinople in the twelfth century, was arguably the first well-staffed hospital in Christendom, with separate wards for men and women, wards for patients with different kinds of ailments, and a professional medical, administrative, and operational staff. Hospitals that served a dual medical and instructional function were also a part of medieval Islam and may have served as examples for the Latin West. Knowledge of both Byzantine and Islamic health care filtered into the West, as crusaders returned from the Holy Land or from Constantinople.

**Specialized Facilities.** The first true hospitals of Latin Europe evolved from hospices in the city states of northern Italy in the fourteenth century. This type of institution gradually spread north in the fifteenth century. Specialized facilities for isolating lepers (*lazarettos*) were prevalent earlier but were not mainly treatment oriented. Leprosy declined in most parts of Europe during the fourteenth century, and the larger lazarettos were adapted to house and treat victims of plague during the centuries that followed. These were temporary public health measures that were utilized when epidemics of bubonic plague were declared, and not continuous, permanently staffed health care centers. However, beginning in northern Italian cities such as Florence, Milan, and Venice, specialized institutions were maintained for other designated segments of the population: the old and infirm, abandoned and victimized women, unwed mothers, and orphans. Such hospitals did not exclusively serve medical purposes, nor were they intended for those who could afford treatment at home.

**Training Centers.** By the fifteenth century, large general hospitals, such as Florence's Santa Maria Nuova, began to provide regular medical care for those who could not afford it at home. In France the Hotels Dieu that were established in Paris and in major provincial cities shifted toward caring for the sick poor. One hospital was even founded in colonial Quebec to provide for the natives and the immigrant poor. In England, hospitals continued to have an ecclesiastical foundation, such as London's St. Bartholomew's Hospital, but there, too, they served an increasingly clinical function, more so in the seventeenth and eighteenth centuries. Not until the late Enlightenment (1750–1800) did northern municipal hospitals begin to serve as routine training grounds for clinicians, and then medicine and surgery were again brought together in the service of both healing and medical research. In both these areas, Italy and Spain were ahead of their northern neighbors, but by then Bologna and Padua (Italy) were surpassed by Leiden (Holland), Paris, and Vienna as Europe's most prestigious centers of medical training.

Sources:

Ole Peter Grell and Andrew Cunningham, eds., *Health Care and Poor Relief in Protestant Europe, 1500–1700* (London & New York: Routledge, 1997).

Margaret Pelling and Charles Webster, "Medical Practitioners," in *Health, Medicine and Mortality in the Sixteenth Century*, edited by Webster (Cambridge & New York: Cambridge University Press, 1979), pp. 165–235.

Guenter Risse, *Mending Bodies, Saving Souls: A History of Hospitals* (New York: Oxford University Press, 1999).

## MEDICAL THEORY AND PRACTICE

**Galen.** At the top of the pyramid of medical care providers that characterized the medical marketplace was a small group of elite physicians who were extensively trained in the liberal arts and academic medicine at one of Europe's universities. Medicine for this group was defined by an intimate knowledge of classical Greek theories about health and disease that was conveyed principally in the works of antiquity's greatest medical writer, Galen (second century C.E.). Galen's medicine came to the Latin West first by way of Arabic versions of his writings or commentaries on them, which were rendered into Latin in the eleventh to the thirteenth centuries, and later in translations made directly from Greek manuscripts imported from Byzantium or discovered in remote monastic libraries. Recovery of these texts was uneven, with the therapeutic and general-theory treatises reaching Western readers before the research-oriented anatomical and physiological works, owing in part to Islamic emphasis on therapy and disinterest in anatomical knowledge for its own sake, beyond what was required for surgery.

**Physician and Physiology.** Galen had insisted that a proper physician be well versed in philosophy, particularly that of Aristotle, and this approach suited medieval readers, who wished to develop medicine from the mere craft of healing, handed down by apprenticeship, into a learned profession. Aristotle's philosophy was introduced into the curriculum of medieval universities early in the thirteenth century and came to dominate the curriculum by midcentury. By the time of the Black Death, medicine had joined law and theology as one of the three graduate departments that a well-endowed university featured, and achieving a medical degree presupposed a solid preparation in Aristotelian philosophy, especially natural philosophy. So close was the connection between theoretical medicine and natural philosophy that the Greek terms for nature (*physis*) and natural philosopher (*physiologos*) caused the term *physicus* to replace *medicus* for the educated physician, resulting in the modern usage of the terms *physician* and *physiology* in a predominantly medical sense.

**Emergence of Modern Science.** This connection is crucial for understanding the nature of elite medicine in the Renaissance and Reformation as well as the importance medicine as a field had for the development of natural philosophy and thus the emergence of early modern science. Even in 1600 there were few professional opportunities for those engaged in scientific research or teaching, other than in philosophy and medical departments at the universities or the practice of medicine. Consequently, many of the innovators in science and technology were, like Nicholas Copernicus and Georg Agricola, trained in medicine, the concerns of which bore directly on fields such as astronomy, alchemy, and physics, as well as on the early development of zoology and botany.

**Conservatism.** The practice of elite medicine was intrinsically conservative and did not change much from the time of Galen until the nineteenth century, nor was it

At age 45, after a years of wandering from court to court, job to job, the Swiss-born physician Paracelsus settle down for a couple of years in Carinthia (Austria), where he composed three treatises that are known collectively as his Carinthian Trilogy. The first of these is a vigorous defense of his novel medical ideas, which were ridiculed by contemporary court physicians, titled *The Reply to Certain Calumniations of His Enemies* or *Seven Defences*. The following is an excerpt from the fourth defense, "Concerning my journeyings." In it one sees Paracelsus' praise for the Spartan life of the wandering student of nature, who sacrifices personal comfort and monetary gain for sake of true knowledge of nature. His demand that one must travel to learn must have been old already, but appealed to his sixteenth-century followers, who took up his cry to abandon books and seek the knowledge of medicine from alchemy and other experiential sciences; by talking to artisans and peasants, rather than reading the books of Galen and Aristotle. The Book of Nature (*codex naturae*) that he mentions at the conclusion of this passage refers to the idea that God's revelation is written in both the Book of Scripture and in the Book of Nature, and therefore personal study of nature is a religious process analogous to formal theology.

A physician should first of all be an *Astronomus*. Now necessity demands that his eyes should give him evidence, in order that he may be such: without this evidence he is only an astronomical gossip. It demands too that he should be a *Cosmographus:* not to describe how the countries wear their trousers, but to attack more bravely what diseases they have. Although it be thine intention and desire to be able to make the costumes of this land from what thou hast learned here, and thou excusest thyself thus from gaining knowledge of strange lands, what concern is it of the physicians's that thou art a tailor. Wherefore, as the things now mentioned must be experienced, they belong to us *Parabolanis* [doctors who attended patients in their homes] and are bound up with medicine and not to be separated from it. Thus it is necessary that the physicians should be a *Philosophus* and that his eyes inform him in order that he may be such: if he desires to be one, he must gather together from all quarters what is

there. . . . For the arts have no feet . . . English *humores* are not Hungarian, nor the Neapolitan Prussian, wherefore must thou go where they are; and the more thou seekest them out and the more thou learnest of them, the greater is thine understanding in thy native land. Thus it is also necessary that the physician be an alchemist: if now he desire to be one, he must see the mother from whom grow the *Mineralia.* Now the mountains go not after him, rather must he go after them. Now where the *Mineralia* lie, there are the artists: if a man wish to seek out artists in the analysis and preparation of nature, he must seek them in the place where the *Mineralia* are. How then can a man find out the preparation of nature, if he does not seek it out where it is? Should I then be blamed because I have wandered among my *Mineralia* and learned the temper and heart, and grasped in my hands the art of those who teach me to separate the pure from the dross, by which I anticipated much evil? Nonetheless I must also repeat the philosophic saying, that wisdom is despised only by the ignorant; thus, too, art by those who do not profess it. . . . Wisdom is a gift of God. Where he gives it, there should one seek it out. Thus too where he has placed art, there should it be sought. It shows great perception in man that man is reasonable enough to seek the gifts of God where they lie, and understands that we are obliged to go after them. If then there is an obligation here, how can one despise or spit upon a man who carries it out? It is true, those who do not thus, have more than those who do: those who sit in the chimney-corner eat partridges and those who pursue the arts eat a milk-soup. The corner-trumpeters wear chains and silk: the wanderers can scarcely pay for ticking [straw for a mattress]. Those within the walls have it cold and warm according to their wishes; those in the arts, were it not for a tree, would have no shade. Now he who would serve the belly, he follows me not; he follows those who go in soft raiment, although these are unfit for wandering. . . . I think it praiseworthy and no shame to have thus far journeyed cheaply. For this I would prove through nature: He who would explore her, must tread her books with his feet. Scripture is explored through its letters; but nature from land to land. Every land is a leaf. Such is the *Codex Naturae;* thus must her leaves be turned.

Source: Paracelsus, *Four Treatises of Theophrastus von Hohenheim, called Paracelsus,* translated by C. Lilian Temkin and others, edited by Henry E. Sigerist (Baltimore: Johns Hopkins University Press, 1941), pp. 26–29.

ever particularly successful from the modern point of view. However, while it is true that therapeutic methods as a whole remained much the same over this period, inasmuch as bloodletting was still a preferred treatment for "fevers" in the eighteenth-century Enlightenment, there were, nevertheless, several innovations, such as the use of chemically prepared, mineral-based drugs. Also, the use of even traditional therapeutic methods varied by practitioner and was often subject to changes in theory and debates over proper procedures. Moreover, the historical actors themselves—patients and physicians—clearly believed that they could achieve some measure of relief, if not always a cure. In a world characterized by frequent mortality at any age in life, and lacking adequate record keeping, medical care and longevity could not easily be correlated.

**Balance of Fluids.** Galen's medicine was based on theories of health and disease that were handed down from the earliest medical writers, the Hippocratic physicians, but supplemented by the extensive anatomical and physiological researches carried out at the Museum of Alexandria during the Hellenistic period (the third and second centuries B.C.E.). Galen regarded health as a state of balance, where the body's four basic fluids—blood, phlegm, yellow bile (choler), and black bile (melancholia)—are mixed in a proportion that is suitable to the individual's natural state. Each of these four fluids was associated with a pair of the four basic qualities that Aristotle had defined as fundamental to material substances—hot, cold, wet, and dry. Blood was wet and hot, phlegm was wet and cold, yellow bile was hot and dry, and black bile was cold and dry. According to this system, an old man, for example, would naturally be drier and colder than a young man, who would have a warmer and moister temperament, or natural constitution. One would expect an elderly patient to have a balance characterized by more black bile, which was by nature dry and cold, and less blood, which was warm and moist. Older people were, therefore, by nature more melancholic, since they had more black bile, and younger ones more sanguine (from *sanguis*, the Latin word for blood). Women were naturally colder and moister than men and therefore had more phlegm (were phlegmatic) in a state of health, although old women were as a rule drier than young women. The system was extraordinarily complex, taking into consideration many factors that were idiosyncratic, such as one's profession (students and scholars tend to be naturally melancholic, that is, rich in black bile), the positions of the planets at one's birth, the time of the year one became ill, which part of the body was affected, and so on. The first job of the physician was to know the patient's normal constitution and evaluate the various factors that may have affected it in order to determine if he or she were imbalanced and in what way. Such an imbalance was not regarded as a symptom of disease, but rather as the disease itself.

**Therapeutic Approaches.** Treatment for a fluidic imbalance, a state of disease, took one of three forms, according to classical medicine. The physician first sought to rebalance the patient's fluids by adjusting his or her diet and lifestyle (regimen), in an attempt either to diminish those fluids that were in excess or to supplement those that were deficient. If this approach failed, or if the disease was acute and demanded more-radical therapy, drugs would be administered in order to alter specific qualities in the body or to force the expulsion of the excess fluids by vomiting, excreting, secreting, and sweating. Medieval and Renaissance pharmacies were filled with diverse natural drugs that were harvested from various parts of plants, derived from animals and their excrements, and mined from the earth as mineral salts. These drugs were used alone as "simples" or were compounded together according to recipes, and used either to alter the body's qualitative balance directly or else to promote vomiting (emetics), excretions (purgatives), sweating (sudorifics), and various other real or imagined means of evacuating excess fluids and restoring balance. As a guide to adjusting the patient's temperament, according to the principle of contraries (that is, use a hot, dry drug to cure a cold, wet disease), Galen associated qualities with drugs and rated these on a scale of one to four degrees. A drug might be hot in the third degree and dry in the first, for example. Such a mathematical system pleased those who sought certainty in medicine, but stymied physicians who thought that the specific characteristics of diseases and drugs could not be reduced to a calculus of the four qualities.

**Bloodletting.** In cases where blood was in excess, as evident by fevers, inflammation, and skin lesions, which were thought to indicate the body's natural attempt to get rid of excess and corrupt blood, balance was restored by the removal of blood by one of several methods, the most drastic of which was venesection, the cutting of a vein to let out some blood. This process was regarded as a surgical procedure, the third form of chemical therapy, and was routinely practiced by surgeons or barbers in the Renaissance. The professional symbol of the barber, the red and white striped barber's pole, is thought to have represented the blood and bandages that were associated with this trade when such emblems were needed to advertise to an illiterate public. Elaborate theories dictated the part of the body from which the blood was to be removed and how much. Bloodletting was so common that it was even used as a preventative, along with diet, and patients would ask to be bled in the spring, in anticipation of an outbreak of plague, and at other times they deemed healthful. Bleeding patients with acute fevers seems particularly misguided from a modern standpoint, but the loss of an appreciable amount of blood would have cooled and calmed the medieval and early modern patient, giving relief from the symptoms, if not actually curative. Moreover, having blood let was probably less stressful than another surgical treatment, the use of caustic chemicals or hot iron rods to cauterize the skin and thus heat and dry the body.

**Other Options.** Surgery also comprised other sorts of invasive surgical procedures, such as lithotomies (cutting to remove bladder stones), repairing hernias, excising cancers, and lancing infected glands. However, throughout the Renaissance and Reformation, treatment involved a mix of the three forms of therapy, and physicians and surgeons attempted to heal wounds by administering oral drugs as well as through surgery. The application of drugs to the outside of the body as oils, salves, and poultices, for example, was commonly regarded as the province of the surgeon, even if they were being used to heal such diseases as leprosy, syphilis, and plague, and although internal medicine was in theory left to the physician, in reality practices overlapped. One must keep in mind that there were few physicians per capita and that the prescribed methods of treatment were often known and practiced by surgeons, elders in the community, or members of the family. This situation was especially true in rural areas and provincial towns where M.D.s were rare.

**Chemical Malfunctions.** Galenic medicine underwent several significant changes in the period from 1350 to 1600. On the one hand, university medicine moved closer to Galen's ideal, as new texts from Galen's formidable medical scholarship were discovered and better translations were printed and absorbed into the curriculum. The medical faculty at the University of Paris, to take the most extreme example, became more radically Galenist during the course of the sixteenth century, to the legal exclusion of competing theories and therapies. On the other hand, a novel blend of alchemical theory and use of mineral drugs that was associated with the Swiss-German physician, religious radical, and iconoclast Paracelsus challenged Galenism and won many adherents, particularly among surgeons and physicians trained in several German universities, as well as Basel, Switzerland, and Montpellier, France. The Paracelsians, or chemical physicians, viewed diseases as the result of specific chemical processes or malfunctions of natural, healthy chemical processes that took place at specific locations in the body, rather than as imbalances, and they sought to correct them by administering chemical drugs to restore the body's normal, healthy chemistry. This approach was a very different way of conceptualizing diseases and conflicted with Galen's theory.

**Spiritual Elements.** Where the Galenists reduced disease to a fluid imbalance resulting in a qualitative state—too hot, cold, moist, or dry (or an appropriate combination of these)—the Paracelsians characterized diseases as being caused by "inflamed sulfur," "copper salts," "nitre," or other chemical substances. They thought that all such substances were reducible to combinations of the three spiritual elements: salt, sulfur, and mercury. Therefore, where the Galenist might prescribe a bleeding or a complex compound mixture of herbal drugs that was designed to provide just the right amount of heat and moisture to counteract a cold and dry disease condition, the Paracelsian might administer a somewhat toxic chemical elixir with the aim of expelling the harmful products of the disease process and helping the body's native healing tendency restore its proper chemical operations.

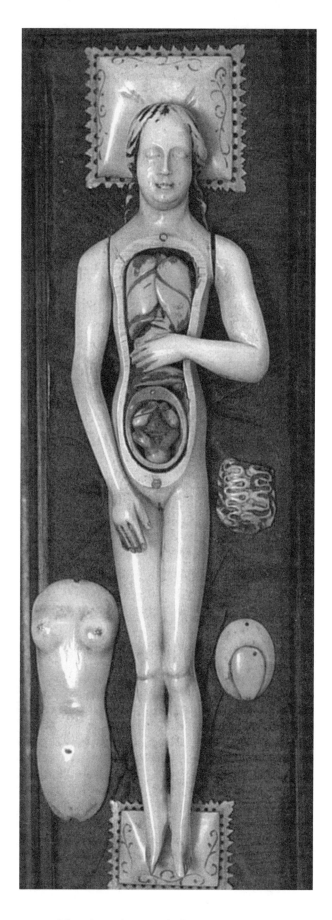

A late-sixteenth-century Italian ivory anatomical figure (Wellcome Historical Medical Museum & Library, London)

**Professional Differences.** The differences between the Galenist and chemical approaches to medicine were striking on many levels of theory and therapy and were even reflected in the religious consequences of their philosophies. Controversies arose between the two kinds of medicine. Medical disagreements sometimes divided along political, confessional (religious), professional, and social lines. In late-sixteenth-century Paris, for example, chemical physicians were banned by the university, which controlled medical practice in the city, but were supported by the French crown and found employment at royal institutions and in aristocratic households. Chemical medicine was consequently shunned by Paris-educated physicians, while often adopted by those with degrees from the University of Montpellier, in southern France, and by apothecaries and surgeons. In addition, while French Galenists tended to be Catholic, chemical physicians were often Protestant Huguenots, although such distinctions were not so simple elsewhere in Europe. The ensuing controversy raged within the medical community during the latter part of the sixteenth century and through the seventeenth century, with the result that chemically prepared medicines came into wide use against diseases that were recognized as particular kinds (generic) rather than as imbalances limited to individual constitutions. As time went by, chemical drugs were slowly adopted by Galenist physicians, too, although their application was given new explanations that were consistent with Galenic theory.

**Dissections.** Another major change that medicine underwent in the Renaissance and Reformation was the increasing investigation of the human body and the teaching of anatomy to both physicians and surgeons. Before the rise of university medicine, surgeons and physicians dissected animals to study anatomy, if they bothered at all. Such training had apparently disappeared in the West during the early Middle Ages, and when medicine was again taught at Salerno, in the ninth to eleventh centuries, scholars depended on translations of Arabic medical treatises for guidance. Islamic medicine did not view knowledge of the anatomy of cadavers as useful to healing the living, and Galen's anatomical research was not incorporated into their teaching, beyond what applied directly to surgery. Galen had been an avid student of human anatomy and physiology, and beginning in the fourteenth century, as his teachings gained influence, surgical and medical professors sought to emulate his example. By 1400 Europe's best medical schools required its students to attend at least one annual public dissection of a human body. Sometimes these mandatory dissections included male and female cadavers for comparison. Cadavers were provided by the municipal or royal governments, which arranged to have condemned criminals executed at an appropriate time so their bodies would be fresh for the scheduled dissections. These events would be accompanied by dissections of various kinds of animals—a sheep, pig, or pregnant dog, for example—to enable greater understanding of human anatomy through comparison of similar parts.

English anatomist John Banister lecturing in London, 1581 (Wellcome Historical Medical Museum & Library, London)

**Spread of the Practice.** At the same time, particularly at southern European universities and municipalities, autopsies were made on the bodies of those who died destitute and without family, or in instances when the cause of death needed to be determined. These procedures were conducted by noted surgeons and physicians in front of an audience of their clinical students. The regular practice of dissection gradually spread to northern Europe in the course of the fifteenth and sixteenth centuries, and by the mid seventeenth century the foremost human anatomists were to be found in Copenhagen, Leiden, Amsterdam, Stockholm, London, Paris, Oxford, and several of the universities in Germany, as well as in the traditional medical strongholds of northern Italy.

**Vesalius.** Anatomists and their students at first relied on a dissection manual composed in the early fourteenth century by Mondino da Luzzi or on a commentary or other text based on it. Galen's anatomical treatises were translated during the fourteenth to sixteenth centuries, but his level of knowledge and technical proficiency were not matched until the sixteenth century, when the Paris humanists began to consciously pattern their research after his. The most famous of these men were Jacques Dubois (Sylvius) and Johannes Guinter of Andernach, whose student Andreas Vesalius is credited with surpassing Galen and drawing attention to the fact that there was still much to be discovered through dissection. Vesalius insisted that people should dissect diligently and look for themselves rather than rely on written authorities alone. During Vesalius's lifetime, the Italian universities of Bologna and Padua, where he taught in the late 1530s and early 1540s, became the premier schools of anatomy and drew students from all over Europe. They, in turn, took his techniques and insistence on verifying written texts through personal observation to other schools, thereby laying the foundation for many new discoveries about the organs, their functions, and the various systems of the body, all of which revolutionized human physiology in the seventeenth century.

**Influence of Hippocrates.** While some humanists were reviving Galen's methods of anatomical and physiological research, others were seeking to emulate Hippocratic medicine, with its attentiveness to the individual patient's clinical manifestations. Again, the northern Italian universities were leaders, making clinical (bedside) experience a part of a student's education already in the thirteenth and fourteenth centuries, but the Paris humanists self-consciously promoted the clinical approach, in terms of writing down exemplary case histories, in emulation of the Hippocratic *Epidemics* (circa 420–350 B.C.E.). Although true clinical teaching in the modern sense was not developed until the early nineteenth century, the ideals and rhetoric of patient-oriented medicine were being touted by renowned physicians such as Jean Fernel in the mid sixteenth century and provided a needed corrective to what had become an overly elaborate, theory-dominated medicine of the university-educated Galenists.

**Conclusions.** In summary, four medical contributions emerged from the sixteenth century to fertilize medical discussion during the scientific revolution of the seventeenth and eighteenth centuries. First, the high level of ancient Greek medicine was recovered with Galen's theoretical and therapeutic system. Second, his anatomical expertise was surpassed, providing the means to wholly revise understanding of the body and its operations. Third, physicians were again promoting the collection and recording of symptoms and results at their patients' bedsides, which encouraged a reexamination of the nature of diseases and what seemed to avail against them. Finally, chemical medicine, which owed little to classical Greek medicine, emerged as a new way of looking at the human body, its diseases, and the workings of the world in general. These multiple streams of medical thinking flowed together to reshape medical theory in early modern Europe.

Sources:
Vivian Nutton, ed., *Medicine at the Courts of Europe, 1500–1837* (London & New York: Routledge, 1990).

Katherine Park, *Doctors and Medicine in Early Renaissance Florence* (Princeton: Princeton University Press, 1985).

Andrew Wear, Roger French, and Iain Lonie, eds., *The Medical Renaissance of the Sixteenth Century* (Cambridge & New York: Cambridge University Press, 1985).

## PRINTING AND ILLUSTRATION

**Printing Press.** Few technological innovations have had as profound an impact on intellectual culture as did the introduction of mechanical printing with movable type—the printing press. The medieval university had created an immense appetite for books, which grew along with literacy in the late Middle Ages. However, prior to the press, these tomes were copied out by hand, either by the individual student or by professional scribes and stationers hired for the task. Early manuscripts were written on parchment, or vellum, made by carefully removing the hair from the skin of a sheep, goat, or calf and scraping, drying, and trimming it to produce a medium that excels even modern papers in strength and durability.

**Papermaking.** Both parchment and hand copying were labor intensive and therefore expensive, and this fact limited book production and consumption to ecclesiastical and state institutions and wealthy individuals. When the technology for making paper from cotton fibers reached western Europe from the Islamic world in the twelfth century, paper quickly became the medium of choice for textbooks, enabling ordinary students to make their own copies of important texts, helping to accelerate the dissemination of scholasticism, and contributing to the rapid growth of the Latin university system throughout Europe.

**Impact.** Manuscript books had drawbacks. Besides being costly, hand copying permitted errors to creep into texts and virtually limited illustrations to certain luxuriously crafted, hand-colored treatises, where they served to decorate, not inform. These factors were ameliorated by the

SECVNDA MVSCVLO. RVM TA BVLA

The human musculature, woodcut from Flemish anatomist Andreas Vesalius's *De humani corporis fabrica* (On the Architecture of the Human Body, 1543)

which was used to squeeze grapes. By 1400 such presses were used to print illustrations from blocks of wood that were cut out in such a way as to leave raised lines that could be inked (bas-relief). The real revolution came with the development of easily replicated, movable type, from which entire pages of text could be set and printed as a block. A type designer styled and cut a set of master dyes for each font, and these sets were used to punch the type itself, which was made of an alloy of lead, tin, and antimony.

**Gutenberg.** Various people were beginning to experiment with mechanical printing in the 1440s, but the man credited with successfully merging these technologies is Johannes Gutenberg, whose Bible is the earliest surviving European printed book (circa 1455). Gutenberg set up shop in Mainz, Germany, and printing spread from there to other towns on the Rhine River and its tributaries and then to France, reaching northern Italy by the 1460s. The early German printers created fonts that resembled the German manuscript minuscule and are generally called black-letter Gothic, variations of which were still in use in the early twentieth century. However, when presses were set up in Italy, Roman type fonts were created to mimic the lighter, humanist hands of Renaissance Italy, and these quickly dominated Latin scientific printing and were the forerunners of modern styles.

**Standard Editions.** Printing and humanism went hand in hand. Authors worked closely with printers to see that pages were free of typesetting errors, and print houses employed scholars with expertise in Greek and oriental languages (Hebrew, Syriac, and occasionally Arabic) to produce the many humanist editions of classical treatises and commentaries that began to issue forth. With mechanical printing it was possible to replicate thousands of similar pages without introducing scribal errors, enabling humanists to produce standard editions by scrutinizing manuscript copies and restoring what they judged to be the original text. Sometimes university-educated men, such as the German astronomer Johannes Regiomontanus, set up their own presses to facilitate scientific publication. Scholars were authors and editors of early books and were also a major market for printed editions, especially academic treatises, so it is hardly surprising that they would work closely with presses and with the network of trade fairs that sprang up at regional centers such as Frankfurt, Lyon, and Venice to provide a means for widely marketing books.

**Improved Artistic Quality.** The marriage of printed text and printed illustration revolutionized scientific writing in particular, especially natural histories and medical and biological treatises. The ability to replicate an illustration meant that it was worthwhile to invest time and expertise in it. The artistic quality of illustrations quickly improved, as artist-illustrators, some of whom were trained by the masters of Renaissance painting, were contracted to make realistic woodcuts of specific flowers, animals, and parts of the body. By 1500 woodcuts were widely used in scientific books and for reproducing maps. Roughly contemporary with the spread of early presses, illustrators began to exper-

press. Once type was set, a thousand identical sheets of paper, containing several pages of text each, could be printed in a single day. Prices fell, bringing pamphlets and even books within easy reach of the growing urban middle class and fueling an information revolution. Printing presented new challenges to political authority and social stability. Arguably, the Protestant Reformation would not have succeeded had it not been for the press, which permitted religious and political ideas to be inexpensively and widely circulated in vernacular languages. This development, in turn, fostered vernacular literacy, a hallmark of the Renaissance. The Catholic authorities also realized the potential of the press, and it became a powerful tool for the Counter Reformation in the hands of the Jesuits in the second half of the sixteenth century.

**Illustrations and Type.** Printing brought together several extant technologies, which were adapted to give the press the basic form it had in early modern Europe. The screw press itself was a modification of the wine press, iment with metal-plate engraving, which produced an even higher quality print but required greater control over metal fabrication techniques and the use of a new kind of press, the roller press.

**Pedagogical Tools.** Dependable, artistic illustrations completely changed the way pictures were used. Once serving as decorations for expensive manuscripts that were elaborated to delight the eyes of wealthy patrons, illustrations began to serve as pedagogical tools, since they could be reproduced accurately. An outstanding example of the synergy between printed word and scientific illustration is Andreas Vesalius's *De humani corporis fabrica* (On the Architecture of the Human Body, 1543), in which various anatomical illustrations are beautifully depicted by an artist trained in the workshop of the Renaissance painter Titian and keyed to the text by letters, much as in present-day books. This technique permitted text and illustration to work together and brought the artistic talents of painters to bear on naturalistic portrayals of plants, minerals, and animals. This development in turn focused scholars' attention on precise description and eventually on classification of natural forms. The result was an explosion of information of unprecedented accuracy and quality at the time that global exploration was bringing home specimens of previously unknown species to be introduced to Europeans.

Sources:

Elizabeth Eisenstein, *The Printing Press as an Agent of Change: Communications and Cultural Transformations in Early Modern Europe* (Cambridge & New York: Cambridge University Press, 1979).

James Moran, *Printing Presses: History and Development from the Fifteenth Century to Modern Times* (London: Faber & Faber, 1973).

John W. Shirley and F. David Hoeniger, eds., *Science and the Arts in the Renaissance* (Washington, D.C.: Folger Shakespeare Library / London: Associated University Presses, 1985).

## TECHNOLOGY AND INVENTION

**Mastering the Technology.** In many respects, the European Middle Ages was a period of technological change and mastery, inasmuch as many of the techniques for improving agriculture, large-scale textile manufacturing and shipping, controlling water flow in order to flood moats, and fortifying towns were developed well before the Renaissance. The medieval world was a world of specialists, whose tools and techniques were brought to a high level of accomplishment and guarded by guilds and secrecy. However, in many cases, medieval innovations were not fully deployed until the Renaissance, when they were stimulated by the expansion of European markets, discovery of New World crops, nascent capitalism, and new methods for extracting, refining, and working metals and industrial chemicals.

**Military Innovations.** The Renaissance deployment of medieval innovations is evident in military technology. Gunpowder was introduced to Europe in the Middle Ages, and the cannon and arquebus eventually displaced the trebuchet and crossbow. Early cannon were large siege weapons and were cumbersome to transport and of little tactical value. Firearms were still a novelty on the battlefield at the beginning of the fourteenth century, but by 1500 they were decisive in winning the field. Smaller and more portable artillery pieces came into use during the sixteenth century and were used collectively to break down the walls of medieval strongholds, which had played a significant part in determining the geography of feudal society and the defense of towns. In response, military forces became more mobile and relied on mercenaries and on innovations in fortification design, both of which favored larger national political units that could more readily raise greater funding through taxation. Carefully designed and mathematically engineered, star-shaped fortresses, with polygon-shaped bastions to deflect cannon balls and provide overlapping fields of defensive fire, along with elaborate earthworks to soften the impact of artillery, were pioneered in Italy in the sixteenth century and quickly spread northward. One can still see a seventeenth-century star fort on the island of Vardø, guarding the Arctic Sea passage to the White Sea via Norway's north cape.

**Naval Power.** Cannon were also mounted on naval vessels, requiring larger, more powerful ships that were capable of blockading ports and bombarding towns from the water. In the sixteenth and seventeenth centuries, maritime nations such as England, Holland, Denmark, and Sweden rose in prominence as control of the seas became more strategic to commercial development. At stake was not only trade and colonization of New World and Old World colonies, but also domination of trade with Russia, Poland, and Scandinavia, which supplied much of the grain and herring to Europe.

**Farming.** Agriculture offers further examples of the Renaissance implementation of medieval innovations. Medieval economic historians have long argued that decisive agricultural changes occurred in the early and high Middle Ages, when oxen were abandoned in favor of horses as a source of draft power and when annual crop rotations changed from a two-stage to a three-stage rotation. These medieval technologies enabled faster plowing and the cultivation of heavier soils and a reduction in the time that fields were left fallow between cropping, resulting in higher annual yields of grain. However, historians are coming to realize that this process was slow and may not have extended throughout Europe until the early sixteenth century, by which time new innovations were being put into practice.

**Forage Crops.** Probably the most significant change in agriculture during the Renaissance and early modern period was the introduction of forage crops. This situation permitted a changeover from depletive grain farming to a sustainable agriculture based on manuring and increased animal husbandry. Production of forage crops required relatively flat, well-plowed fields, a sufficient supply of water, and suitable crop varieties, such as clover and alfalfa. Field preparation was enhanced by the enclosure of the rotational strips of medieval open-field grain farming, which was fostered by economic changes in the wake of the Black Death, but the introduction of cross-plowing and irrigation were also important factors.

A late-fourteenth-century castle, built by Sir Edward Dalyngrigge, at Bodiam, East Sussex, England

Plowing a second time across the ridges produced by the first plowing yielded a flatter field, which was suitable for broadcast seeding and mowing. Irrigation by damming and diverting rivers spread in Italy, southern France, and Spain in the sixteenth century, and in England and northern Europe the practice of seasonally flooding forage fields was introduced. Irrigation in the Mediterranean regions also allowed the cultivation of rice and mulberry trees for the production of silkworms, which reduced Europe's dependency on Asian imports.

**Agricultural Base.** Alfalfa, one of the important modern forage crops, was cultivated in the Roman Empire and described in classic agricultural treatises, but knowledge of its use disappeared during the Middle Ages. It was reintroduced to Spain by the Moors, but it was not cultivated in Italy and France until renewed attention to agricultural methods and the fifteenth-century printing of humanist editions of Roman agricultural treatises by Varro and Cato encouraged innovation. Books produced in the sixteenth century combined descriptions of Roman practices with Islamic methods of controlling water. Also in the sixteenth century, botanical gardens were established in northern Italy and later at all major universities. These gardens facilitated the testing of seeds and the acclimation of new crops. New World crops such as maize, which was widely cultivated in Spain within a decade of Columbus's discovery of Hispaniola, and sweet potatoes began to alter the traditional agricultural base, although the large-scale production of the white potato did not appear until the seventeenth century.

**Dutch.** The invention and application of the wind-driven water pump in Holland in the early fifteenth century, coupled with large-scale dyking and pouldering, enabled the Dutch to reclaim large tracts of fertile land from lakes, swamps, and the North Sea and carefully manage their irrigation. The resulting increase in agricultural production enabled the Low Countries to rise to international prominence and extend their mercantile, industrial, and military might around the globe in the early modern period.

**Metalworking.** The mining and working of metals enjoyed a boom that began in the second half of the fifteenth century. This boom was brought about both by the increasing demand for advanced military weaponry and armament and by the transformation of the European economy from the manorial accumulation of goods in kind to a cash economy, which required quantities of precious metals. Depletion of mines and the infusion of New World bullion into the European market created inflation and effectively ended this boom in the middle of the sixteenth century, but improvements in chemical extraction of metals and assaying techniques indicated the continued importance of mining into the seventeenth century, particularly in northern Europe.

**Mining Operations.** The growth of the mining industry in the boom period (1450–1550) involved both an extensification, as new areas were opened up, and an intensification, as mines were sunk deeper into the earth and production and processing were mechanized.

Well-illustrated books on mining and metallurgy, the best known of which are Vannoccio Biringuccio's *Pirotechnia* (1540), Georg Agricola's *De re metallica* (1556), and Agostino Ramelli's *Le diverse et artificiose machine* (1588), reveal the elaborate water, human, and horse-powered devices that were contrived to pump and ventilate deep shafts, break up and sieve ore, and fan the fires of roasters and smelters that were used to refine the ore into ductile metal. The availability of capital and the need to capitalize nonagricultural forms of production were incited by the sudden and persistent rent depression and labor inflation in the wake of the Black Death, as landholders sought new ways to generate new wealth, and these factors hastened the large scale mechanization of the industry. The technology of these machines was not radically different from medieval designs, but during the Renaissance it was systematized and made more central to commercial metal production.

**Glass Production.** Biringuccio and Agricola also described the technology for glass production, which like metal extraction required complex furnaces and handling methods, including blowing and casting in molds. Glass had been produced in the Mediterranean basin during the Roman Empire and persisted in the Byzantine Levant and Egypt after the collapse of the Western empire. When revived in Italy during the Middle Ages, glassmaking produced mainly utilitarian products and was concentrated in towns with access to Egyptian natron, which was a necessary raw material. As Venice grew to dominate Mediterranean trade, it also developed a practical monopoly on certain kinds of glass production, which the government fostered and regulated on the island of Murano in the Venetian lagoon.

**Venetian Influence.** Glassmaking declined in the fourteenth century in both Islam and the West, possibly because of the economic disruptions caused by warfare and the Black Death. When it was revived in the fifteenth century, Venice emerged as the center of a new focus on fine wine glasses and other luxury products that were coming into vogue in Europe's courts and wealthy houses. By the mid sixteenth century northern European demand for Venetian glass encouraged a transfer of technology, and furnaces were set and manned by expatriate Venetians, particularly in England, Germany, Spain, and the Netherlands. By the late seventeenth century these nations began to surpass Venice in quality and quantity of glassware.

**Earthenware.** Ceramics was another important Renaissance industrial product, sharing some common technology and raw materials with glassmaking, but using clay rather than vitrified silica sand as a base. The well-known majolica (Italian) and faience (French) types of ceramic required an earthenware object to be fired with a tin glaze, which yielded an opaque white background on which intricate patterns could be painted, and then a second glazing, or lustering. This technology was brought to Christian Spain from Muslim Grenada in the fifteenth century and spread to Italy in the sixteenth, where newly discovered classical Roman murals encouraged the creation of elaborate Renaissance patterns of decoration.

**Clocks.** Improvements in precision instrumentation went hand in hand with the growth of science and technology generally. The increasing sophistication of clockworks is a case in point. Large, weight-driven clocks began to appear in thirteenth-century Europe, rapidly becoming sources of civic pride and emblems of orderly government. Springs began to replace weights in the fifteenth century, enabling clocks to be made smaller, which allowed their use in navigation and as scientific instruments. Such clocks were used by Tycho Brahe in the last quarter of the sixteenth century for making accurate measurements of the stars and planets as they passed through the meridian (due north or south), which needed to be meticulously timed. Brahe himself was a technological innovator and serves to illustrate the productive interaction between craftsmen and theorists in the period. His earliest instruments for measuring the angular separations of celestial bodies were fabricated entirely of wood and ordered from instrument makers in Germany. These instruments were easy for skilled craftsmen to produce using traditional, medieval tools and techniques, but were not stable with respect to changes in humidity and temperature, and therefore not entirely suitable to Brahe's needs. Therefore, he brought craftsmen to him and established workshops near his observatories. Working with them, he experimented with various new instrument designs, using combinations of wood, brass, iron, and steel to maximize strength and stability. Brahe also built a water-powered paper mill, a printing house, and a glass factory on his island research facility, bringing technology and science into close cooperation.

**Market Demands.** Although there were specific technological innovations during the Renaissance and into the sixteenth century, as illustrated by the instruments developed and used by Brahe, the period is better characterized as a time when medieval technologies were put into practice on a large scale in response to changing market demands that accompanied economic and military expansion in the Renaissance and the age of discovery. Advances in design and construction enabled higher temperature furnaces and greater precision in instrumentation, for example, but the actual mechanization of industrial processes owed more to the increased cost of human labor and the greater demand for industrial products than to breakthroughs in basic design.

Sources:

Jean Gimpel, *The Medieval Machine: The Industrial Revolution of the Middle Ages,* second edition (Aldershot, U.K.: Wildwood House, 1988).

W. Patrick McCray, *Glassmaking in Renaissance Venice: The Fragile Craft* (Aldershot, U.K. & Brookfield, Vt.: Ashgate, 1999).

Charles Singer, ed., *A History of Technology* (Oxford: Clarendon Press, 1954–1958).

# SIGNIFICANT PEOPLE

## GEORG BAUER (GEORGIUS AGRICOLA)

### 1494-1555

PHYSICIAN, MINERALOGIST, AND SCHOLAR

**Humanism.** Georg Bauer, better known as Georgius Agricola, was born in Saxony, Germany, attended the University of Leipzig from 1514 to 1518, and then taught Greek and Latin, first at the municipal school in Zwickau and then as a lecturer at Leipzig. His early training in grammar and classical literature suggests that he followed the humanist program, as does his adoption of a Latin form of his name, Agricola (meaning, like Bauer, "farmer"). Humanism, which was a scholarly movement to recapture the elegance of classical rhetoric and the civic-mindedness of Athens and Rome at their greatest moments, was flourishing in the universities of Italy, France, and Germany in the early sixteenth century at the time that the seeds of the Lutheran Reformation were being sown. Although Agricola was critical of the papacy in his early years, like his humanist friend Erasmus of Rotterdam, he remained formally a Catholic.

**Medical Training.** In 1524 Agricola left Germany and traveled to Italy, where he studied medicine at the University of Bologna. After receiving a degree he moved to Venice, where he worked for the humanist printer Aldus Manutius, preparing a new Greek edition of treatises written by antiquity's greatest physician and medical author, Galen of Pergamon. In 1526 Agricola returned to Germany, and the following year was appointed municipal physician in Joachimsthal, Bohemia, which was a new and growing mining town located in what was sixteenth-century central Europe's largest mining district. In this setting he realized that classical scholars had never studied mining and metallurgy in depth and set about preparing *Bermannus sive de re metallica* (Bermannus, or On Metals), which was published in 1530. The secondary title of the book was reminiscent of Cicero's *De re publica* (On the Republic), the quintessential humanist text from the height of the classical Roman civilization. Similar titles in the sixteenth century, such as Realdo Colombo's treatise *De re anatomica* (On Anatomy) mark their authors as humanists.

**International Audience.** Written as a dialogue (again, a humanist style) between a fictional miner, scholar, and poet named Bermannus and two friends, who were educated physicians, the book was the first on this subject written in Latin and aimed at an international, scholarly audience. In 1530 he left his position at Joachimsthal and traveled widely in the area, studying mining and beginning work on *De re metallica* (On Metals), a more extensive, folio edition on the subject with almost three hundred woodcut illustrations, which was not published until 1556. This book comprehensively treated all aspects of metal production from mining and assaying ore to refining and working the finished products, with detailed descriptions and illustrations of the elaborate machines employed in the industry. It was widely circulated in the sixteenth century and soon translated into German and Italian. A modern English translation was made by mining engineer and later U.S. president Herbert Clark Hoover and his wife, Lou Henry Hoover, and published in *The Mining Magazine* in 1912. In 1533 Agricola took a position as municipal physician in the Saxon town of Chemnitz, where he married, served on the town council, was appointed mayor for four terms, and finally died in 1555.

**Model Approach.** Agricola's approach to the subject of mining and metallurgy served as a model of open discourse and access to scientific and technological information and stood in direct contrast to the work of his contemporary, Paracelsus, whose treatises were written in obscure language and intended for a select audience of practitioners. Critics of the secrecy that pervaded alchemy and other occult sciences, such as Andreas Libavius at the end of the sixteenth century, lauded the approach of authors such as Agricola and accused the Paracelsians of disregard for the public good, the promotion of which was a central tenet of civic humanism.

Sources:

Georgius Agricola, *De re metallica,* translated by Herbert Clark Hoover and Lou Henry Hoover (New York: Dover, 1950).

Marco Beretta, "Humanism and Chemistry: The Spread of Georgius Agricola's Metallurgical Writings," *Nuncius,* 12 (1997): 17–47.

R. F. Tylecote, *A History of Metallurgy* (London: Metals Society, 1976).

# TYCHO BRAHE

## 1546-1601
## ASTRONOMER

**Beginnings.** Born into Denmark's high nobility, Tycho Brahe opted to become a prince of scientific researchers instead of pursuing a military or diplomatic career, as befit his aristocratic heritage. Like many of his noble peers, he was tutored in Latin at home and traveled widely in his youth, visiting various European universities—enrolling at Copenhagen, Leipzig, and Rostock—and making the acquaintance of natural philosophers and noblemen wherever he went. Astronomy captured his interest early, and he bought books and instruments for private study of the subject. When he realized that his observations in Leipzig of the conjunction of Jupiter and Saturn did not agree with the date predicted by the astronomical tables then in use, he determined to reform astronomy and bring it up to date with new observations. Such tables were of great importance in Renaissance Europe because the accuracy of astrological prediction depended on them, and such predictions affected medical diagnostics and therapy as well as providing the widely popular horoscopes that guided kings and commoners alike. The needs of state, in particular, made astrology a suitable science for an aristocrat to dabble in, as was alchemy, which Brahe also studied in Germany. When his father's death forced him to return to Denmark and settle his inheritance, Brahe sold his share of the family estate to his brother and moved into the former Herrevad Abbey, which was in the possession of his aunt and uncle. There he built a laboratory and set about what would become his lifelong pursuit of both alchemy and astronomy.

**Birth of a Star.** In fact, Brahe viewed alchemy and astrology as two aspects of a single science. He believed that there was a sympathetic correspondence between the stars and planets, metals, minerals, stones, and plants, and also the organs of the human body. The operations of the cosmos could therefore be studied in the observatory, by means of what he called "celestial astronomy," or in the laboratory, by "terrestrial astronomy," which referred to alchemy. Brahe recalled that he was returning to the main house from his laboratory at Herrevad in 1572 when he first noticed a new star in the sky, a phenomenon that is still called a *nova* (new). Such a thing was unknown to Europeans and was presumed not to be possible in the celestial realm, since the region of the stars and planets was generally thought to be perfect and incapable of any novelty or decay. Accordingly, astronomers throughout Europe were eager to observe the new star and publish their interpretations of what it might be and what its appearance portended. Brahe carefully observed the new star and determined it to be a long distance from the Earth, and therefore not simply an atmospheric phenomenon of some sort, as Aristotle had taught.

**Uraniborg.** Brahe published his findings and interpretations in *De nova stella* (The New Star) in 1573. The small volume demonstrated that he was a competent and well-educated astronomer, bringing him to the attention of Europe's scholars and encouraging the king of Denmark to offer him a feudal endowment if he would build a research facility on royal land and reside in Denmark as an aristocrat in service to the crown. This position was the kind that suited a member of one of Denmark's most powerful families. The result was Uraniborg, a Renaissance villa that Brahe erected on the island of Hven, within sight of Copenhagen and the royal fortresses of Kronborg and Landskrona, between which every ship entering the Baltic Sea from the Atlantic must pass. The location was in many respects ideal: it was central to the kingdom, within easy reach of the capital and the court, and yet isolated by water, providing a measure of privacy and undisturbed study. The island rises abruptly out of the Danish sound that today separates Sweden from Denmark, and often enjoys clear weather when the nearby shores are clouded over, making it a suitable location for an observatory.

**Laboratory.** Uraniborg was not expansive by Danish aristocratic standards, but expensive to build and maintain. It featured the latest Dutch and Italianate architectural styles, statuary, Dutch paintings, and a stone-faced earthen perimeter wall with gate houses, surrounded by an elaborate garden with gazebos and walkways. Uraniborg was more than an aristocrat's house, though. Its clever design also accommodated a library, where the research staff could gather, sleeping rooms for his assistants, and observation decks with removable roof sections on the north and south ends of the second story. On these decks Brahe placed various devices for measuring the angles between stars and planets, which enabled him to record their positions. In the basement he built a well-equipped alchemical laboratory, which in complexity rivaled those owned by kings and princes elsewhere in Europe. Although he claimed to have spent an equal amount of time and money on alchemical research, no records of his work in that area have survived, except for a couple of recipes for medical elixirs. Nevertheless, reports from visitors to the island support Brahe's description of an elaborate facility with many kinds of furnaces and condensers.

**Accurate Data.** As his need for greater astronomical precision developed, he constructed another observatory nearby, one that was dug into the ground in order to provide a protected place to mount even larger instruments out of the wind, which vibrated them and introduced errors. Several large observation pits, with stable stone foundations on which to set various enormous quadrants and armillary astrolabes, had removable covers to shield them from the rain and permit sighting of the major celestial phenomena. With the best of these instruments, Brahe was able to double the accuracy of previous astronomical data.

He commemorated the irony of observing the heavens from underground in a Latin poem, one of many that revealed his training as a Renaissance scholar.

**Quest for Perfection.** Construction of Uraniborg commenced in 1576 and was largely completed by 1580, but Brahe was an incessant builder and tireless researcher, always trying to improve his research methods and tinkering with the design of his villa and his instruments. Besides the underground observatory, which he intended to connect to Uraniborg by tunnel, he built a printing house and a paper mill, so that he could publish his work on location. The mill was water powered, but since there was no sufficient stream of water on Hven, Brahe created a system of fish ponds that acted as reservoirs to collect rainwater to drive the water wheel. He also built a workshop and a glassworks to supply his instruments, alchemical glassware, and household needs.

**Published Work.** Brahe accumulated an immense amount of observational data while resident on Hven, which was eventually published as the Rudolphine astronomical tables in the next century. Besides positional data, from which he hoped to construct a new theory of planetary motion, he made an important observation on a comet in 1577, which proved that it was a celestial and not an atmospheric phenomenon, as the Aristotelians believed. Tycho's realization that comets crossed through the orbs that were supposed to carry the Sun, Moon, and planets around Earth suggested to him that the celestial spheres were not substantial enough to hinder penetration. On this basis, he created his own planetary model, in which the Sun and Moon revolved around Earth, as was the case in ancient astronomy, but the other planets revolved around the Sun, as in the Copernican system. Brahe published the details of this new model in 1588 and it became quite influential in the seventeenth century.

**Rudolf II.** That same year King Frederik of Denmark, Brahe's patron and friend, died and was succeeded by his son Christian IV. For various reasons, he fell out of favor with the new king and his advisers, who began to revoke his royal endowments. The result was that Brahe abandoned Uraniborg in 1597 and eventually secured an appointment at the court of Rudolf II, the Holy Roman Emperor, where he hoped to reproduce the research facilities he had developed in Denmark. To that end, he moved his household into Benatky Castle outside Prague, the imperial capital, shipped his instruments from Denmark, build a new observatory and laboratory, and continued his work. To help him with the tedious mathematical work of correlating observations with theory, Brahe recruited a German mathematician named Johannes Kepler. When Brahe died in 1601, Kepler took possession of the tomes of data that Brahe and his students had produced over the course of three decades and used them to establish a brand new theory: that all planets—including the Earth—traversed elliptical orbital paths around the Sun.

**Legacy.** Brahe's many-sided research effort reflected a complex Renaissance view of the cosmos and a commitment to understanding it through systematic study. Besides astronomy and alchemy, he also kept a meteorological record, with which he hoped to grasp the relationship between astrology and weather conditions, he wrote Latin poetry, and began to make accurate maps of Hven and its surroundings. All of these activities were woven together into life at Uraniborg, which is regarded as Europe's first dedicated research institute. Uraniborg itself fell into ruin in the decades after Brahe left it, cannibalized for building material for local projects. Brahe's program, however, lived on in Copenhagen, where the king established a royal observatory where his student Christian Sørensen (Longomontanus) was installed as royal astronomer, and a royal laboratory, where a Paracelsian physician was hired to distill elixirs and make other chemical medicines.

Sources:

John Robert Christianson, *On Tycho's Island: Tycho Brahe and His Assistants, 1570-1601* (Cambridge & New York: Cambridge University Press, 2000).

Christine Jones Schofield, *Tychonic and Semi-Tychonic World Systems* (New York: Arno, 1981).

Victor Thoren, *The Lord of Uraniborg: A Biography of Tycho Brahe* (Cambridge & New York: Cambridge University Press, 1990).

# GUY DE CHAULIAC

## CIRCA 1290-CIRCA 1370
### SURGEON

**Wealthy Patrons.** Guy de Chauliac was born into the peasant class in southern France, but with the help of aristocratic benefactors, he was able to learn Latin, attend the universities of Montpellier and Bologna, and reach the highest level of professional medicine. Although mainly interested in surgery, de Chauliac studied the liberal arts and advocated a broad philosophical training for surgeons. There was already a tradition of Latin surgical treatises by de Chauliac's day, dating back to Roger of Salerno's *Practica chirugiæ* (The Practice of Surgery, late twelfth century), but de Chauliac recognized the importance of scrutinizing the available translations of both ancient Greek medical authorities and the Arabic digests and commentaries on them by such authors as Rhazes, Avicenna, and Albucasis. Prominent medical and surgical teachers and students of Montpellier before him, foremost among them Arnald of Villanova and Henri of Mondeville, had recognized the importance of making surgery a learned profession that incorporated the classical philosophical medical theories of Hippocrates, Galen, and Aristotle, while retaining the emphasis on the practical art of healing that Galen's Arabic followers emphasized in their medical texts. By basing surgery on natural philosophy and deductive logic, Arnald and Henri had supported the inclusion of surgery among the academic professions taught by the universities and commanded the respect of a wealthy clientele. De Chauliac followed their lead, writing in Latin and grounding his opinions in the authority of past medical writers.

**Anatomical Instruction.** In the early fourteenth century, when he was a medical student, anatomical instruction was just being introduced into the medical curriculum. Mondino da Luzzi was a pioneer in teaching human anatomy at the University of Bologna, where de Chauliac studied surgery. By the end of the fourteenth century, attendance at an annual anatomical demonstration was required of medical students at Europe's best medical schools. Such instruction was intended to provide physicians with a basic understanding of the place and normal condition of the organs of the body, but it also served to acquaint surgical students with the interior of the body and where it was safe to make an incision. It also provided employment for surgeon-anatomists in the universities and encouraged the practice of anatomy. Mondino's textbook, *Anathomia* (1316), became the basis for anatomical instruction in European medical schools for the next two centuries, and commentaries on it were still in use when Andreas Vesalius published his anatomical masterpiece in 1543.

**Papal Favorite.** Historians of medicine have criticized de Chauliac's bookish approach to surgery, even arguing that while he professed the surgical procedures of his predecessors and criticized his contemporaries for erroneous methods, he avoided cutting whenever possible. Nevertheless, de Chauliac received a first-rate education, spent much of his adult life in service as surgeon to the Roman Catholic popes, and was one of the first to incorporate anatomical knowledge drawn from Galen's second century C.E. treatise *De usu partium* (On the Use of the Parts), which had only recently been translated into Latin and proved too long and complicated to find use in the medieval curriculum.

**Astute Observation.** De Chauliac survived the Black Death in 1348 and also witnessed the second European epidemic in 1360. He observed that some victims coughed up blood and invariably died within a couple of days of the appearance of the first symptoms, while others developed painful swellings in the armpits, neck, and groin and then either died within several days or survived. This report and others that corroborate it have led scholars to suspect that the Black Death was a disease caused by the pathogen responsible for modern bubonic plague, but spread by two different means. If transmitted from person to person via airborne water droplets that are coughed out—a common way of spreading infection—the pathogen would settle in the lungs first and lead to bleeding and rapid death. On the other hand, the pathogen can be transmitted by fleas and cause a swelling in the main lymph nodes (buboes) draining the area where the fleas have bitten and infected the person, commonly in the armpits, groin, or neck. Fatality in this mode of plague, called bubonic plague, is lower. The actual cause and epidemiological mechanisms behind the Black Death and subsequent epidemics are still debated, but de Chauliac's observations, coming as they do from a knowledgeable and trained medical observer, cannot easily be discounted.

**Surgical Text.** Toward the end of his life, de Chauliac wrote a textbook on surgery, *Inventorium sive collectorium in parte chirurgiciale medicine* (Inventory or Collection on the Surgical Part of Medicine, 1363), commonly called the *Chirugia magna* (Great Surgery), which was the first such book on the subject to include a chapter specifically on anatomy. Otherwise, de Chauliac drew much of his material from the chief Arabic treatises and has been criticized for being less original and personally engaged in surgical practice than his predecessors William of Saliceto, John of Arderne, and even Henri of Mondeville. Nevertheless, de Chauliac's *Great Surgery* proved to be popular as a surgical textbook, perhaps because of his authority as a papal surgeon, and was translated into several vernacular languages, including Middle English. These translations enabled it to be of use outside the university, reaching the majority of surgical trainees, who never learned Latin. When one considers the relative rarity of M.D.s in rural areas, where the majority of Europe's population lived, the importance of such translations to surgeons and other healers who relied on vernacular treatises for instruction becomes evident.

Sources:
Ira M. Rutkow, *Surgery: An Illustrated History* (St. Louis: Mosby-Year Book, 1993).

Nancy Siraisi, *Medieval and Early Renaissance Medicine: An Introduction to Knowledge and Practice* (Chicago: University of Chicago Press, 1990).

# NICHOLAS COPERNICUS

## 1473-1543
### ASTRONOMER

**University of Cracow.** Nicholas Copernicus was born in Torun in the far north of Poland in 1473. With the support of his uncle, a prominent member of the Catholic Church, Copernicus was able to attend the University of Cracow, Poland, from 1491 to 1496, where he became interested in astronomy. Cracow was among the leading north European universities, and Copernicus would have been exposed to the latest methods and controversies within astronomy and natural philosophy there. By the late fifteenth century, astronomy was suffering from a lack of precision—the mathematical models and techniques for predicting planetary alignments were out of date—as well as a fundamental disagreement about the proper foundations and purposes of the field. The mathematical astronomy developed in the second century C.E. by Ptolemy was technically sophisticated and worked reasonably well when used with high-quality, recent observations but violated some of the basic principles of Aristotle's philosophy, which demanded that the Moon, Sun, and five planets

(Mercury, Venus, Mars, Jupiter, and Saturn) be carried around the stationary Earth on orbs, or spheres.

**Entering the Fray.** Aristotle's treatises taught that the celestial world was perfect, where nothing changed or decayed. The only kind of physical motion appropriate to this region was one that did not change. The only such motion is produced by a sphere's rotating in place at a constant speed—ever moving, but endlessly and changelessly repeating the same movement. According to this view, the cosmos was constructed of a complex system of concentric spheres, each moved by a kind of intelligence that sought to emulate the motion of the outermost sphere, which was moved by the prime mover. Cosmologists from Eudoxus (fourth century B.C.E.) down through the ages retained this ideal of an astronomy based on homocentric spheres, but no mathematical model was constructed on this basis that could make acceptable predictions. By the late Renaissance, two distinct approaches existed: that of Ptolemy, whose mathematical approach was workable, if not philosophically acceptable, and that of Averroes, an Arabic commentator on Aristotle's philosophy and an ardent opponent of Ptolemy's approach. During this time Copernicus began to study astronomy.

**Bologna.** While Copernicus was at Cracow, his uncle was appointed bishop of Warmia (northern Poland), and Nicholas was made a canon of the cathedral of Frauenburg. A canon was a salaried member of the church and usually expected to function as an administrator and serve as a juror in the church court. To prepare Copernicus for this career, the church permitted him to use his salary to further his education in canon law (church law), and he left Cracow for northern Italy, where he enrolled at the University of Bologna in 1496. At Bologna, Copernicus neglected his legal studies and continued to study astronomy while also becoming interested in medicine. The two sciences were connected by astrology, which was necessary to determine the kind, and timing, of treatment appropriate to a particular patient. At Bologna, Copernicus would have found himself in the thick of controversy over Averroes's interpretations of Aristotle, which opposed not only mathematical astronomy, but also the Christian teaching on the immortality of the soul. Thus, theology, astronomy, and physical cosmology intersected in arguments about the nature of the soul, the celestial intelligences that moved the planets, and how they so moved them.

**Padua.** Copernicus left Bologna without a degree in 1501, and after briefly returning to Poland, studied medicine at Padua (Italy), one of the foremost centers of Aristotelian philosophy in the sixteenth century and the scene of arguments between the Averroists and the Thomists (adherents to St. Thomas Aquinas's version of Aristotelian theory) over the mortality of the soul. The Averroists interpreted Aristotle strictly where he taught that the human soul was a material form and therefore dissolved when the body decayed, an idea that was condemned by the Catholic Church in 1512.

Copernicus stayed at Padua for two years, only to take his doctorate in law at the University of Ferrara, another northern Italian school.

**Startling Theory.** Having completed his education, Copernicus returned to Frauenburg, where he served as a secretary to his uncle, the bishop, and practiced medicine, astronomy, and engineering. In 1513 he built an observation tower, where he set up instruments for observing the relative positions of the celestial bodies. The following year he circulated a six-page manuscript treatise that first detailed his novel theory that the Sun was the real center of the cosmos, with the Earth just another planet revolving about it in an orb.

**Realist Tradition.** Despite a later interpretation that Copernicus intended his new, heliocentric model merely as a mathematical device to enable greater precision to correct the Christian calendar, it is now clear that Copernicus was working within a realist tradition, as were all other parties to the Averroist-Ptolemaist controversy during the late fifteenth and sixteenth centuries. Realists are concerned to put forth hypotheses about the world that reflect physical reality rather than merely convenient instruments for discovery and calculation. This situation explains not only Copernicus's later reasoning for why objects would not fall off a moving Earth and other answers to critics of heliocentrism, but also his low profile—he did not sign his name to the 1514 treatise and he only reluctantly committed his ideas to print more than a quarter of a century later.

**Historical Impact.** In 1539 a German Lutheran student who had come to Frauenburg to learn more about Copernicus's ideas drafted the *Narratio prima* (First Report) of Copernican astronomy, which was printed and circulated the following year. Copernicus completed the full version of this theory, *De revolutionibus orbium coelestium* (On the Revolutions of the Celestial Orbs), which was a chapter-by-chapter answer to Ptolemy's *Almagest*, including the mathematical means of calculating planetary positions, and published it in 1543, the year that he died. However, Andreas Osiander, who was overseeing the printing, surreptitiously added an anonymous statement on the back side of the title page indicating that the hypotheses discussed in the book were not to be construed as statements about the reality of the cosmos. No doubt Osiander was aware that heliocentrism would be controversial, inasmuch as it ran counter to literal interpretations of the Bible, and sought to cushion its reception by the subterfuge. People familiar with Copernicus and his work were not fooled by the preface, but it did serve to confuse historians of science in the nineteenth and early twentieth centuries, who misunderstood its historical impact.

Sources:

Thomas Kuhn, *The Copernican Revolution: Planetary Astronomy in the Development of Western Thought* (Cambridge, Mass.: Harvard University Press, 1957).

Edward Rosen, *Copernicus and His Successors* (London & Rio Grande: Hambledon Press, 1995).

Robert Westman, ed., *The Copernican Achievement* (Berkeley: University of California Press, 1975).

# GIROLAMO FRACASTORO

## CIRCA 1478-1553

## ASTRONOMER, PHYSICIAN, AND POET

**French Disease.** Girolamo Fracastoro was a "Renaissance man" both in the banal sense of his historical context and in the broader meaning of an active intellect with a broad range of cultural interests and achievements. His reputation as a scholar has faded since the sixteenth century, when his contributions to mathematical astronomy and poetry were noted, and if he is remembered at all by historians, it is for his poem called *Syphilis sive morbus gallicus* (Syphilis, or the French Disease, 1530), which gave a new name to a disease that was new to late-Renaissance observers.

**Stargazing.** Fracastoro was a younger son of a wealthy family of the northern Italian town of Verona and was schooled at home in Latin literature and philosophy by his father before being sent to the University of Padua. As an undergraduate, Fracastoro studied literature, mathematics, and astronomy as well as Aristotelian philosophy, which was taught by Pietro Pomponazzi. The latter acquired a European-wide reputation as a champion of an extreme version of Aristotelian natural philosophy, which challenged some of the accepted interpretations of medieval theory. It is perhaps not surprising, then, that Fracastoro would later write a treatise attempting to revive the Aristotelian model of the universe as a series of homocentric (concentric) spheres that bore the stars and planets about the central earth. This theory was rather complicated mathematically and suffered from a serious drawback—if planets are fixed to a sphere with Earth at the center, why do they seem to vary in brightness, as if they approach and recede from Earth? For both reasons, the homocentric model was superceded by the epicycle-deferent models of Ptolemy (second century C.E.), which explained that planets moved as if affixed to small circles (epicycles), which were themselves moved around Earth by larger circles or spheres (deferents). Ptolemy's model was mathematically simpler and more accurately accounted for the observed movements of the Sun, Moon, and planets, and was therefore suitable for making predictions and casting horoscopes, and was used in one form or another by all mathematical astronomers in medieval Islam and Christendom. The Aristotelian homocentric model persisted through the Middle Ages as an explanation of how the world might be physically structured (cosmology), but no attempt to revive it as a plausible mathematical model was made before the late fifteenth century, when Georg Puerbach tried to reconcile Aristotle's spheres with Ptolemy's epicycles. Fracastoro's work, which he published as *Homocentrica sive de stellis* (Homocentrics, or On the Stars, 1538), should accordingly be seen as an attempt to restore Aristotle's

place in natural philosophy in the face of a growing body of evidence that the old theories were inadequate. In this effort Fracastoro was less a revolutionary than a humanist scholar, seeking to understand what the ancients thought rather than overturning it.

**Medical Studies.** Fracastoro also studied medicine while at Padua, and upon receiving his degree in 1502 he was appointed as an instructor in logic and adjunct in anatomy. At this time he made the acquaintance of Nicholas Copernicus, who had enrolled at Padua to study medicine the previous year. When war threatened between the Venetian Republic and the Holy Roman Empire, whose lands pressed on the northeastern border of the republic, the university closed, and Fracastoro went to serve on the frontier before returning to his native Verona. Established in town and owning a villa in the mountains, Fracastoro settled down to a life of intellectual pursuit as a landed gentleman and active physician. He was a regular member of the local college of physicians and hosted philosophical meetings at his country estate. Through his expanding reputation and personal contacts within the Church he was appointed physician to the Council of Trent in 1545 and given a benefice (a salaried position in the Church). He remained active as a philosophical and medical scholar until a stroke killed him in 1553.

**Clavius.** Fracastoro's *Homocentrics,* like other sixteenth-century attempts to force Aristotle's cosmology to agree with observation, was not successful, but was important enough in contemporary astronomical and philosophical discussions to be considered a threat to the prevailing Ptolemaic cosmology by Christoph Clavius. The latter was the leading teacher of astronomy at the *Collegio Romano* in Rome, which was the academic center of Catholicism of the new Jesuit order, which was interested in using science education as a tool for winning converts to the Catholic religion. Clavius's assessment and refutation of Fracastoro's ideas points out that Copernicus's heliocentric hypothesis was not the only challenge to the Ptolemaic system, which Clavius defended in his book *Commentary on Sacrobosco's Sphere* (1570) even after Galileo's discoveries seemed to deny its validity.

**Cause and Effect.** Of greater significance to sixteenth and seventeenth century philosophical discussion was Fracastoro's *De sympathia et antipathia rerum* (On Sympathy and Antipathy, 1546), which addressed a persistent problem in medieval, Renaissance, and early modern natural philosophy, namely how one thing could affect another at a distance—without physically touching it. Such causation was obviously fundamental to the action of celestial bodies on terrestrial objects, including people, but also governed the observed behavior of magnets, the attraction of dry bits of straw to a piece of amber that was rubbed with a cloth, and even magical and medical phenomena, such as why amulets seemed to "work like a charm," why people could inflict harm on each other by giving "the evil eye," and why menstruating women would cause a mirror to become discolored merely by looking at it. Obviously such cases, attributed to sympathy or antipathy between the forms or souls inherent in people and objects, were of wide significance, from physical theory to medical practice and even the prosecution of witches.

**Contagion.** Fracastoro did not deny the existence of a spiritual order in the material world that was responsible for the evident sympathies and antipathies between remote objects, but he did explain such actions with material mechanisms in the specific case of contagious diseases. He discussed this situation in *De contagione et contagiosis morbis et curatione* (On Contagion, Contagious Diseases, and Their Cure, 1546), which was appended to his treatise *On Sympathy and Antipathy.* Contagion, related to the root word for "contact," was by the Renaissance a well-established popular explanation for how epidemic diseases could spread from person to person or object to person, accounting for some of the public health measures that were enforced in response to plague. However, Fracastoro elaborated the theory in terms of the atomic hypothesis that had been promoted by Cicero's contemporary Lucretius, which had been considered and discarded as atheistic in the Middle Ages. Lucretius's lengthy poetic treatise *De rerum natura* (On the Nature of Things, written in the first century B.C.E.) was printed and again was a topic for discussion in late-fifteenth- and early-sixteenth-century Italy. Fracastoro used Lucretius's idea that the material world was composed of small bits of atomic matter, which he called "seeds," to explain how disease could spread by remote contact, carried by the air or lodged in clothing, from one person to another, or from a dog or cat or a garment to a person. Fracastoro's theory helped legitimize unpopular public health measures, which called for the destruction of cats and dogs and expensive cleaning and fumigating (or burning) of infected belongings during outbreaks of plague. However, his idea of disease as caused by a physical agent, a seed or particle of disease, also contributed to the perception that epidemic diseases and all other natural actions must occur through contact—a point made in 1569 by Fracastoro's contemporary Francisco Valles. This idea was to become a founding principle of the much-touted mechanical philosophy that is associated with René Descartes and the scientific revolution of the seventeenth century.

Sources:

Girolamo Fracastoro, *Fracastoro's Syphilis,* edited and translated by Geoffrey Eatough (Liverpool, U.K.: Cairns, 1984).

James M. Lattis, *Between Copernicus and Galileo: Christoph Clavius and the Collapse of Ptolemaic Cosmology* (Chicago: University of Chicago Press, 1994).

Vivian Nutton, "The Reception of Fracastoro's Theory of Contagion: The Seed That Fell Among Thorns?" *Osiris,* 6 (1990): 196–234.

# PARACELSUS

## 1493-1541
### ALCHEMIST AND PHYSICIAN

**Early Years.** Philippus Aureolus Theophrastus Bombast von Hohenheim, later known by the simpler cognomen Paracelsus, was born in the Swiss village of Einsiedeln, where his father practiced medicine. Paracelsus's mother died while he was still a child, and the family moved to Villach, a mining town in Austria, where he grew up observing his father treat the particular diseases that afflicted miners. Paracelsus also absorbed the chemistry and lore surrounding mining and metallurgy. He was schooled by local clerics, from whom he received a wide-ranging exposure to both orthodox and mystical religion and philosophy, which were feeding the discussions and social unrest in the early sixteenth century that gave rise to the Reformation. It is no wonder, then, that Paracelsus's extensive writing, popular preaching, and teaching as an adult revealed a syncretistic combination of chemical theory, medicine, and heterodox religious ideas, which he gave vague philosophical expression in terms of medieval mysticism and Renaissance Platonism.

**Medical Approach.** Paracelsus claimed to be a doctor of both medicine and surgery, and historians have speculated that he may have attended the University of Vienna and perhaps received the M.D. from the University of Ferrara, where Copernicus completed his graduate study a decade earlier. His writings show a familiarity with concepts found in academic natural philosophy and medicine, but his poor knowledge of Latin, cloudy explanations of theory, and open hostility to the chief tenets of Galenic medicine and Aristotelian philosophy suggest that his knowledge was gleaned from a variety of oral and vernacular written sources and not through the contemporary university medical curriculum. His rejection of any medical use for human anatomy, for example, is not without precedent, inasmuch as medieval Islamic physicians regarded knowledge of anatomy gained from dead bodies to be of little use in healing the living, beyond what might help a surgeon to mend a bone or remove an arrow. Even in Galen's day, there were physicians identified as Empiricists, who denied the therapeutic value of anatomical knowledge and elaborate theories. Members of this medical sect taught that healing was a matter of careful observation of the patient, who should be treated according to the physician's experience with like cases. However, Paracelsus probably was neither an Empiricist nor an Arabist, given his deprecation of Islamic and pagan Greek medicine (except that of Hippocrates) and his readiness to apply magical lore and alchemical theory to describe the hidden workings of the body and its diseases. More likely, he rejected traditional medical theory as part of a Reformation-era antirationalism, combined with a commitment to alchemical theory, Neoplatonist ideas about the relationship between the learned magus and the divinity present in nature, and the German mystics' view of the divinity of the inner man.

**Unpopular Stance.** Paracelsus was violently opposed to the prevailing medical doctrine that health and disease were governed by the state or temperament of the four cardinal qualities (hot, cold, wet, dry), which were determined by the patient's particular mixture of the four basic fluids (blood, yellow bile, phlegm, and black bile). This concept was central to the diagnostic and therapeutic parts of Galen's medicine, and by rejecting it Paracelsus was denying the validity of university medical education. Paracelsus's utter disdain for traditional medicine is symbolized in the story that while employed as a town physician in Basel, Switzerland, in 1527, he threw a copy of Avicenna's *Canon of Medicine*, an expensive book that had been one of the mainstays of medieval medical education, onto the St. John's Eve bonfire. Not surprisingly, he was not popular with professional physicians and apothecaries (druggists), whose livelihood depended on their knowledge of Galenic medicine, not to mention the professors themselves, who viewed Paracelsus as a crackpot and a serious threat to health care and medical education.

**Inner Alchemical Agents.** Instead of the four basic fluids and qualities, Paracelsus regarded all physiological processes as chemical in nature, whether occurring in the body of the greater world (the macrocosm) or in the human body (the microcosm). He described human digestion, excretion, and metabolism as a series of chemical "digestions" or separations that were governed by a kind of innate intelligence. He likened these processes of separating pure nutrients from impurities to the operations of a metallurgist or alchemist, who separated the pure metal or chemical from the dross or dregs. He imagined these processes to be distributed around the body, governed by inner alchemical agents that he called *archei* (singular *archeus*). When operating properly, the archei that were present at various places, most obviously the stomach, perfectly separated pure nutrients from the dregs and excreted the latter. However, when affected by an external influence, caused by a stronger chemical archeus or perhaps a malign ray from a planet or star, the inner alchemist could malfunction and permit a buildup of toxic salts in the body. Inflammations, for example, were regarded as caused by inflamed sulfurous or nitrosulfurous salts.

**Divine Calling.** In keeping with his alchemical view of physiology, Paracelsus recommended drugs on the basis of their chemical properties, which could combat bad inner chemistry, expel toxic excrements, and help the body's natural tendency to restore health. Like Hippocrates, whom he admired, Paracelsus viewed the physician as nature's assistant or minister and demanded that the physician be morally upright. Unlike the Greeks, though, he saw the physician as having a particularly divine calling, since Christ himself was the prototype healer, able to cure the incurable and even raise the dead to life.

**Life of Wandering.** Paracelsus's career was troubled. Owing to his medical iconoclasm, which offended the medical establishment, and his irregular religious preachings, which offended both Catholic and Lutheran religious authorities, he was seldom resident in any one town for long before being chased out, sometimes fleeing in great haste and leaving unfinished treatises behind him, to be puzzled over and reconstructed a generation later by his followers. His reputation for successfully treating diseases that academically trained physicians deemed incurable led to his being repeatedly summoned to heal aristocrats and other prominent people, such as the humanist printer and friend of Erasmus, Frobenius. However, the forces of medical and theological order gave him little respite to work or publish before making him resume his life of wandering. Few of his treatises were printed during his lifetime, which came to an end in Salzburg in 1541, where he died without fanfare.

**Lasting Impact.** Paracelsus's reputation both as a healer and as an author of an alternative medical system grew rapidly after the publication of his main medical ideas during the 1560s. In the last quarter of the century, a new generation of medical students began to embrace these ideas, giving them a more rigorous theoretical explanation and incorporating them into an eclectic medical practice. Petrus Severinus, for example, composed an influential biological philosophy that explained human physiology, generation, and pathology according to Paracelsian principles, which he showed to be compatible with ancient ideas of Hippocrates, Pliny, and other authors. After publishing this book, *Idea medicinæ philosophicæ* (An Ideal for Philosophical Medicine, 1571), Severinus was appointed royal physician to the king of Denmark and took part in the intellectual circle around the famous astronomer Tycho Brahe—who was also a Paracelsian alchemist. Severinus's career typifies the reception of Paracelsian ideas in the late sixteenth century: many students were fascinated by Paracelsus's ideas, but the universities generally opposed them. As a result, Paracelsus's followers often relied on the patronage of kings, queens, and other nobility, who were open to alternative philosophies and treatments.

Sources:

Allen G. Debus, *The Chemical Philosophy: Paracelsian Science and Medicine in the Sixteenth and Seventeenth Centuries*, 2 volumes (New York: Science History Publications, 1977).

Walter Pagel, *Paracelsus: An Introduction to Philosophical Medicine in the Era of the Renaissance* (Basel, Switzerland & New York: S. Karger, 1958).

Andrew Weeks, *Paracelsus: Speculative Theory and the Crisis of the Early Reformation* (Albany: State University of New York Press, 1997).

# ANDREAS VESALIUS

## 1514-1564
### ANATOMIST

**Influence.** Andreas Vesalius is best known today as the founder of modern medical anatomy, on account of his technique, his challenge to receive ideas about the structure of the human body, and his innovative design for an anatomical textbook. His volume initiated a revolution in how anatomy was taught in the late-Renaissance and early-modern curriculum. Yet, if one can place him among the pioneers of modern anatomy, he is perhaps better regarded as the last and best of the ancient anatomists and taken as a measure of the success of medical humanism in sixteenth-century Europe.

**Education.** Vesalius was born in Brussels, Belgium, which was then a part of the Holy Roman Empire. His father was an apothecary in service to the emperor, Charles V. Vesalius mastered Latin in Brussels and then enrolled at the University of Louvain in 1530, where he must have made the acquaintance of Gerardus Mercator, who was also beginning his studies at that time. Vesalius studied philosophy and liberal arts in the arts faculty, as did all beginning students, but soon turned his attention to medicine. At that time medical education was not as advanced in the north European universities as at Paris, Montpellier, and the schools of Spain and northern Italy, and Vesalius traveled to Paris. In Paris he studied under Jacobus Sylvius and Johannes Guinter of Andernach, two prominent humanist medical scholars, physicians, and teachers.

**Dissections.** The humanist movement began in art and literature in Italy in the late fourteenth century, as scholars turned their attention away from the scholastic method and medieval sensibilities and instead emphasized participation in human affairs, the study of history, and the recovery of ancient artistic, architectural, and intellectual forms. The method applied to the latter involved the search for and careful assessment of manuscripts written in the ancient languages. Initially, humanists were enthusiastic about the poetry, prose, dramaturgy, and design of ancient Greece and Rome, but by the early sixteenth century, humanism had become a widespread intellectual movement and embraced other subjects as well, including medicine. New attention was brought to bear on the medical writings of Galen and Cornelius Celsus, whose Ciceronian-era Latin prose provided a model for Renaissance medical treatises. Some of Galen's treatises, such as *On the Use of the Parts*, were known and translated already in the thirteenth and fourteenth centuries, but were long and complicated and therefore were only slowly incorporated into learned medicine. This treatise and other tracts in which Galen discussed human anatomy aroused the interest of surgery students and anatomists in the fourteenth century and contributed to the dissection manuals that guided students of anatomy through the annual human and animal dissections that the better medical schools required students to attend. Galen had been an avid dissector of animals and his descriptions of human anatomy and physiology led medieval readers to suppose that he had dissected humans as well—which he surely would have, had not the mores of the Imperial Greco-Roman culture discouraged him. Princes and city councils of medieval Europe, eager to facilitate surgical training, authorized the annual anatomical demonstrations and provided some bodies of executed criminals for this purpose. Before Vesalius, such demon-

strations served to illustrate what was described in the texts rather than to encourage research and verification of traditional knowledge, and often the actual dissection would be undertaken by a surgeon or other paid *sector*, who would dissect the body as the professor of anatomy read the appropriate section of a surgical text. This process was how anatomy was taught when Vesalius was a student, but he soon discovered the virtue of firsthand experience, practice, repetition, and close attention to anatomical detail.

**Surgical Lectures.** During the fifteenth century, *On anatomical procedures*, Galen's primary presentation of how dissection should be performed, was translated and published and served to invigorate interest among humanist physicians in anatomical method. Vesalius's teacher, Johannes Guinter of Andernach, used it as a basis for his own *Institutiones anatomicæ* (Anatomical Institutions, 1536) and sought to replicate Galen's methods. Vesalius must have been an avid student, since Guinter spoke well of him in this treatise. Vesalius was forced to leave Paris in 1536 on account of war between France and the Holy Roman Empire, and he returned to Louvain, where he received a bachelor's degree in medicine in 1537. That same year he headed for Padua in northern Italy, where he enrolled, took his examination, and was awarded the M.D. in one semester. Such was his expertise that he was immediately appointed to a surgical lectureship and began giving the annual dissections, which he performed himself as he lectured—breaking with the usual tradition. To facilitate his teaching, Vesalius produced six anatomical charts in 1538. These proved immediately popular, and he quickly published them to forestall plagiarism and secure his reputation. Vesalius also edited and published an augmented version of Guinter's *Anatomical Institutions*, in which he first pointed out in print several of the shortcomings of Galen's observations.

**Popular Teacher.** Vesalius was popular as a teacher and was reappointed in 1539 with an increase in salary. The following year he accepted an invitation from the students at the University of Bologna to hold a series of lectures and demonstrations there in tandem with lectures on Galenic anatomy given by Professor Curtius. During the course of these lectures Vesalius realized that anatomical knowledge must be based on firsthand observation rather than dependence on Galen's writings, which contained many errors that reflected his reliance on animal specimens.

**God's Handiwork.** When Vesalius returned to his lectureship at Padua, he began to compose *De humani corporis fabrica* (On the Architecture of the Human Body), which he published in Basel, Switzerland, in 1543. The title of the book is often rendered literally, *On the Fabric of the Human Body*, but the Latin word *fabrica* clearly refers to a design that is fabricated by a maker or craftsman (a *faber*), and therefore ought to be conceived in the sixteenth-century Christian context, where Creation immediately implied Creator. Thus, *fabrica* is better translated here as architecture to reflect Vesalius's opinion that study of human anatomy was a form of appreciation of the Creator's handiwork. In this way he followed Galen, who, though not at all a Christian, viewed anatomy as a kind of appreciation and worship of the divinity and intelligence that he considered to be manifest in all nature and foremost in the human body.

**Classic Text.** Vesalius went to considerable expense and effort, hiring artisans from the foremost shops in Venice to supply the ample illustrations in his book, which set a new standard both for the quality of anatomical illustration and for medical pedagogy. Vesalius keyed the parts of the body in these illustrations to their descriptions in the text, carefully linking prose explanation to pictorial representation. The result was an enormously sought-after and widely emulated book that is among the most valuable in medical history collections today.

**Royal Service.** Following the publication of his book, Vesalius took a position as Imperial Physician to Emperor Charles V, who had previously employed his father. In this job he also worked as a military surgeon and learned techniques being practiced on the battlefield—always a source of surgical innovation. After Charles abdicated the throne to his brother Ferdinand, Vesalius entered the service of Charles's son, the future emperor Philip II, and moved to the new imperial court in Spain. He remained there until 1564, when he embarked on a trip to the Holy Land. The return voyage was troubled by storms, and Vesalius was put ashore on a Greek island, where he died.

**Medical Humanist.** In retrospect, Vesalius must be seen as a medical humanist, whose mission was to restore the art and science of anatomy to the level of expertise evident in Galen's works. His approach to anatomy was wholly within the Galenic tradition, as was his understanding of human biology and medicine. However, in the process of reviving Galen's methods, which included a forgotten technique that enabled the chest of a live pig or other animal to be opened without collapsing the lungs and killing it, he observed and noted several instances in which Galen had erred. As a result of his direct anatomical experiences, and perhaps in keeping with the methodological teachings of Aristotle, which specified that knowledge of general structures was acquired through repeated observations of individual examples, Vesalius stressed that anatomy must be experienced firsthand. Both of these traditions led William Harvey, who studied at Padua at the end of the century, to break with Galen's understanding of human physiology and discover the true operation of the heart and the circulation of the blood through the body.

Sources:

Baldasar Heseler, *Andreas Vesalius' First Public Anatomy at Bologna, 1540: An Eyewitness Report,* translated by Ruben Eriksson (Uppsala, Sweden: Almquist & Wiksel, 1959).

G. A. Lindeboom, *Andreas Vesalius and His Opus Magnum: A Biographical Sketch and an Introduction to the Fabrica* (Nieuwendijk: De Forel, 1975).

Charles Donald O'Malley, *Andreas Vesalius of Brussels 1514–1564* (Berkeley: University of California Press, 1964).

# DOCUMENTARY SOURCES

Georgius Agricola, *De re metallica* (On Metals), 1556—Agricola's final treatment of the technology and theory of mining, metallurgy, glassmaking, and related arts. His work was the first scholarly treatment of these subjects.

Tycho Brahe, *De mundi ætheri recentioribus phænomena* (On the Very Recent Phenomena of the Celestial World), 1588—The treatise in which Tycho published his new cosmological model, the geoheliocentric, or Tychonic system, which retained the best features of Copernican astronomy, while permitting the Earth to remain at the center of the cosmos.

Brahe, *De nova stella* (The New Star), 1573—This publication was Tycho's first and won him an international reputation as a serious astronomer. As the best account of the supernova of 1572, it was widely read in Europe.

Otto Brunfels, *Herbarum vivæ eicones* (Portraits of Living Plants), 1530–1540—The author was a pioneer in using real specimens of plants as models for illustrations, showing individual characteristics naturalistically rather than being composite ideal types, according to the Aristotelian tradition.

Hieronymus Brunschwig, *De arte distillandi simplicia et composita* (On the Art of Distilling Simples and Compounds), 1509—An early and influential book on the art of making furnaces for distilling, which was a fundamental technical skill for the production of chemical drugs in the sixteenth century.

Berengario da Carpi, *Commentaria super Anatomia Mundini* (Commentary on the Anatomy of Mondino), 1521—Commentary on the standard late medieval anatomical guide by Mondino introduced woodcut illustrations and the idea that anatomical knowledge must be based on study of Galen's authoritative texts plus direct personal examination of bodies, ideas that Vesalius expanded on in his more-detailed book twenty-two years later.

Andrea Cesalpino, *De Plantis* (On Plants), 1583—Regarded as a pioneering treatment of botany in which the author introduces a binomial classification system, and classifies more than 1,500 plants. Cesalpino's binomial classification system was superceded by Linnæus's system in the eighteenth century.

Christoph Clavius, *In sphaeram Joannis de Sacro Bosco commentarius* (Commentary on the Sphere of Johannes Sacrobosco), 1570—One of many editions of Clavius's defense of Ptolemaic astronomy against attempts to reintroduce homocentric cosmology by Fracastoro and the heliocentric innovation of Copernicus. As a learned and respected Jesuit astronomer, Clavius influenced church opinion about the Copernican hypothesis.

Realdo Colombo, *De re anatomica* (On Anatomy), 1559—The author demonstrated that the valves of the heart required blood to be moved from the right side of the organ to the left side by way of the lungs, which William Harvey would later use in arguing for a new view of how the heart, lungs, and vascular system function.

Nicholas Copernicus, *De revolutionibus orbium coelestium* (On the Revolutions of the Celestial Orbs), 1543—A painstaking revision of Ptolemaic astronomy that replaces his geocentric system with one in which the Sun, not Earth, is central. Although Copernicus took the radical step of putting Earth in motion about the Sun, which he though better reflected reality, most astronomers in the next generation after Copernicus did not accept this important innovation, they nevertheless used his mathematical methods.

Girolamo Fracastoro, *De contagione et contagiosis morbis et curatione* (On Contagion, Contagious Diseases, and Their Cure), 1546—An exposition that diseases are not always qualitative imbalances, as traditional medicine taught, but could be spread by material agents or seeds of diseases.

Fracastoro, *Homocentrica sive de stellis* (Homocentrics, or On the Stars), 1538—Fracastoro's attempt to restore the credibility of Eudoxian astronomy, which was compatible with Aristotle's cosmology. Astronomers and physicists before the seventeenth century were plagued by the failure of a single model to satisfy the requirements of both physical cosmology and mathematical astronomy; Fracastoro attempted to heal the rift by going back to older systems.

Leonhard Fuchs, *De historia stirpium commentarii insignes* (History of Plants), 1542—A landmark humanist botanical study, Fuchs's work was subject to much copying.

Geber (Abū Mūsā Jābir ibn Hayyān), *Summa perfectionis magisterij*, 1542—A printed edition of a treatise from the thirteenth century, which was fundamental to alchemical education. Presented basic alchemical matter theory as well as practical instruction in the art.

William Gilbert, *De magnete* (On the Magnet), 1600—An interesting combination of Renaissance speculation about the World Soul and compilation of observational and experimental evidence for the physics of the lodestone and magnetic nature of Earth.

Nicolas Monardes, *Ioyfull newes out of the new-found vvorlde*, 1596—An English translation by John Frampton of Monardes's *Primera y segunda y tercera partes de la historia medicinal de las cosas que se traen de nuestras Indias Occidentales que sirven en medicina* (1574), which was one of the early books to describe the medicinal plants from the New World.

Abraham Ortelius, *Theatrum orbis terrarum* (Theater of the World), 1570—The first atlas in the modern sense of a collection of maps intended to describe the world. Map making in early modern Europe was one of the means that political authorities had of staking and maintaining territorial claims and was therefore an important part of the European expansion and hegemony process.

Theophrastus Paracelsus, *Chirurgischer Bücher unnd Schrifften* (Surgical Works), 1591—Several of Paracelsus's books were published in the last quarter of the sixteenth century, but this edition by Johan Huser was the first collection. Paracelsus was known as a successful healer and his surgical writings were consulted for practical hints on wound treatment. His unconventional philosophical theories are scattered throughout his writings.

Ambrose Pare, *Dix livres de la chirurgie* (Ten Books on Surgery), 1564—Pare was sixteenth-century France's greatest surgeon. He adapted and published Italian wound-dressing techniques, which called for mild salves in field dressings for gunshot wounds rather than cautery with hot oil, as was commonly practiced in France previously.

Georg Puerbach, *Nova theorica planetarum* (A New Theory of the Planets), 1472—An attempt to reconcile the Aristotelian homocentric sphere model with the Ptolemaic epicycle model in astronomy. It shows that late-fifteenth-century astronomers were pursuing a realist agenda and were not content with Ptolemaic instrumentalism.

Puerbach and Johannes Regiomontanus, *Epitome of Ptolemy's Almagest*, 1493—When Puerbach died before finished his translation of the *Almagest*, his student Regiomontanus completed the job of digesting the classical astronomical text to make it more readable for Renaissance scholars. This treatise helped rekindle interest in mathematical astronomy and precision, which led to basic revisions of cosmology.

Erasmus Reinhold, *Prutenic Tables,* 1551—Astronomical tables based on Copernicus's mathematical astronomy. It is tangible evidence that Copernicus's work was being read and used, even if those who were using it remained unconvinced of the reality of the heliocentric hypothesis.

Petrus Severinus, *Idea medicinæ philosophicæ* (The Ideal of Philosophical Medicine), 1571—One of the first generation of medical writers to interpret the ideas of Paracelsus, Severinus explained Paracelsian theory in terms of traditional philosophy and promoted the idea that diseases were of a chemical nature and caused by disease entities.

Niccolo Tartaglia, *Nova Scientia* (A New Science), 1537—This treatise on ballistics was an important forerunner of studies by Galileo that established the kinematics of falling bodies and projectiles. With the importance of artillery increasing in the Renaissance, ballistics was becoming a crucial strategic science.

Andreas Vesalius, *De humani corporis fabrica* (On the Architecture of the Human Body), 1543—A pioneering textbook in human anatomy for its use of extensive, carefully drawn figures to illustrate various human systems and structures as well as for its insistence that the anatomist perform his own demonstrations. Vesalius realized that Galen had introduced error into anatomy by using animals in place of humans as subjects of research.

A detail from sixteenth-century Flemish painter Jan van der Straet's (Giovanni Stradano) *Distillation,* showing workers in an alchemist's laboratory (Palazzo Vecchio, Florence)

The room in Frauenberg, Poland, in which Nicholas Copernicus carried out most of his astronomical research

# GLOSSARY

**Aide:** A French sales tax.

**Alchemy:** A medieval science and philosophy that attempted to achieve the transmutation of base metals into gold, discover a universal cure for disease, and establish a means to prolong life indefinitely.

**Anabaptist:** A Protestant sect founded by Conrad Grebel in the early sixteenth century, which required adult baptism as a sign of commitment to the Church.

*Archei* (singular *archeus*): Inner alchemical agents that regulated human digestion, excretion, and metabolism.

*Armeggerie:* Competitive equestrian races held during Italian city festivals to honor the wealthy noble families and city governments.

**Arquebus:** A matchlock firearm invented in the fifteenth century. A portable but heavy weapon, it was usually fired from some type of support.

*Audiencia:* Royal courts in the Spanish colonies.

**Auto de fe:** "Act of Faith." Public events where the church sentenced heretics, homosexuals, bigamists, and other individuals who were believed to disturb "God's natural order." After sentencing, the convicted were turned over to the government for punishments that included public burning. The term is commonly used for the public sentencing by the church as well as the public punishment by the government.

**Barbicans:** A set of towers defending a fortress gate.

**Bastion:** A projecting section of a fort usually located at each of the four corners.

**Bill of Exchange:** A written agreement between bankers and their clients in two different locations that allowed for the balancing of money holdings in both places.

**Black Death:** The term used for the pandemic of plague, probably both bubonic and pneumonic, that swept Europe from 1347 to 1351, killing one-quarter of the population (approximately 25 million people). There were recurrences in 1361–1363, 1369–1371, 1374–1375, 1390, and 1400. It was named after the dark buboes or swellings that developed in a victim's groin and armpits.

**Bloodletting:** The medical procedure of removing blood from the body, through cuts or the use of leeches.

**Bombard:** An early short-barreled artillery piece that had a wide muzzle.

**Breviary:** A book containing religious psalms, prayers, and readings for canonical hours.

**Bubonic Plague:** An illness caused by the bacterium *Yersinia pestis,* which was carried by fleas on household (black) rats. See **Black Death.**

**Bull:** From the word *bulla,* meaning "a round lead seal." A papal edict or decree sealed with a bulla or with a red-ink imprint of the device on the bulla.

**Canon Law:** Ecclesiastical or church law codes.

**Caravel:** A type of ship first developed by the Portuguese in the fifteenth century. It was capable of trans-oceanic voyages and had a large cargo hold. A caravel usually had three or four masts but only one deck.

**Case Law:** A series of statutes based upon previous court cases.

**Casemate:** An enclosure in a fort from which cannons, crossbows, and other weapons are fired through embrasures.

**Catholic Reformation:** An internal reform movement of the Catholic Church in the sixteenth and seventeenth centuries.

**Caudle:** Mulled wine used in England to nourish a mother during delivery.

**Chivalry:** A model for social behavior that stressed valor, loyalty, and attention to personal honor as the key signs of high social status.

*Chrysopoeia:* The process by which alchemists attempted to make gold.

**Code Law:** Written statutes based on ancient Roman law.

**Codex:** A manuscript book usually comprised of scriptural illustrations.

**Codpiece:** An ornamental bag or cover attached to the front of the tightly worn breeches of urban men, so that their genitals would not be seen. Codpieces were often quite excessive, to suggest that their wearers had a great deal to cover.

**Cog:** A cargo ship used by the Baltic nations; it had a straight keel and a single square sail.

**Commission:** A contractual agreement between an artist and patron for a work of art. The commission may be generated by an individual, a guild, confraternity, or religious organization.

**Commons:** The fields of a village that were shared by all, maintained either as common pasture, upon which everyone could graze their animals, or as arable land. In the latter case, specific areas within the commons would be allocated to every family, with annual reallocations, so that, through this rotation of land, maximum fairness would develop over time.

**Condottieri:** Leaders of mercenary forces in Italy.

**Confraternity:** An urban organization, usually formed by educated and wealthy laymen, who would meet regularly to pray, to sponsor city feasts and celebrations, to fund charitable activities, and to provide for the care and well-being of the widows and children of deceased members.

**Conquistador:** A leader of the Spanish conquests in the Americas in the sixteenth century.

**Consistory:** A group of nine pastors and twelve elders who were chosen from the members of the Geneva city council in 1541. Established by John Calvin, it supervised pastors and the conduct of laypeople who refused to accept correction from the elders. The consistory could impose sentences of excommunication, expulsion, and even execution on those who did not submit.

*Conversos:* Jews in Spain who converted to Christianity.

*Cortes:* The representative body in Spain.

*Cosmographia:* World maps designed in the sixteenth century.

**Conciliarism:** A theory advanced during the **Great Schism** which declared that the general council of the Church was superior to the pontiff.

**Counter-Reformation:** Efforts on the part of the Catholic Church in the sixteenth and seventeenth centuries against the Protestant Reformation.

**Counterscarp:** The defended side of a ditch along a city wall.

**Courtly Civility:** A term used to describe the spread of polite manners, decorous behavior, and other mechanisms that promoted social control among aristocratic elites in Renaissance Europe. The proliferation of etiquette manuals in the sixteenth and seventeenth centuries made courtly manners accessible in the rising middle class.

**Cranny Schools:** Small nursery-type schools that taught young children literacy as well as Bible verses or psalms.

**Culverin:** A bronze muzzle-loading cannon of the late fifteenth century. By the 1540s cheaper culverins were being made of iron.

**Curtain Wall:** The main structure of the defenses of a city.

**Danegeld:** An annual tax in England originally believed to have been imposed to bribe Danish raiders or to maintain armed forces against them. By 1350 the danegeld had become a land tax.

**Decretal:** A papal decree giving a decision on some point of canon law.

**Demi-Lunes:** Small bastions placed in front of larger ones.

**Doge:** The elected head (duke) of some Italian city-states such as the Republic of Venice.

**Drum Tower:** A broad-based edifice, used in fortifications, that was the same height as the city walls.

**English Sweat.** A disease of unknown origin that first appeared among English mercenary troops in 1485. The victim usually died a few hours after the symptoms appeared. There were four recurrences during the period, with the last happening in 1551.

**Engraving:** A process in which lines are cut in a metal plate with a tool called a burin. A dampened piece of paper is placed over the ink-filled lines and run through a press. The printed design produced is reversed.

**Ephemerides:** Planetary positions calculated in astronomical reference tables.

**Estates:** See Orders.

**Estates General:** The representative body in France consisting of churchmen (First Estate), nobles (Second Estate), and commoners (Third Estate).

*Fluyt:* Flyboat. A Dutch ship with a long hull and a flat bottom. The *fluyt* was the precursor of the heavy commercial freighter.

**Free Imperial Cities:** Autonomous cities in the Holy Roman Empire similar to Italian city-states.

**Gabelle:** A French tax on salt.

**Gabion:** A basket filled with soil and rocks and used for building earthworks.

**Galleass:** A type of large, rowed ship capable of carrying heavy cannons.

**Galleon:** A three-masted ship developed by the Italians. Capable of open ocean travel, it had limited cargo space. The galleon was the prototype of the frigate and ship-of-the-line in the seventeenth and eighteen centuries.

**Galley:** A vessel found primarily in the Mediterranean Sea and propelled by oars.

**The Gaze:** The concept that viewing a person is a socially charged act related to gender, social class, desire, and power. The artist's authoritative gaze is an example of the relationship established in portraiture.

**Glacis:** A slope that runs downward from a fortification and which softens the impact of cannon balls.

**Grand Vizier:** The chief administrative officer in the Ottoman Empire.

**Great Schism:** Also known as the Western Schism. The period from 1378 to 1417 in the Roman Catholic Church when there were rival popes, each with his own following, Sacred College of Cardinals, and administrative offices.

**Guaiacum:** Evergreen trees and shrubs indigenous to South America and used in a powdered form as a remedy for syphilis. It caused the patient to sweat, which was viewed as a sign that the disease was leaving the body.

**Guild:** An association of merchants and artisans that regulated a specific craft or industry in a city.

**Halberd:** A battle-ax mounted on a long pole.

**Handcannon:** An early gunpowder firearm.

**Hanseatic League:** A commercial confederacy founded by northern European towns in the thirteenth century. Lübeck became the administrative center in 1358, and members included Bremen, Cologne, Danzig (present-day Gdansk), Hamburg, Lüneburg, Magdeburg, Reval, Riga, and Rostock. The League reached the peak of its power in the late 1300s; its last general assembly was held in 1669.

**Hedgehog:** A Swiss military formation in which pikemen form a defensive circle against a stronger enemy force.

**Heresy:** The belief in a doctrine condemned as erroneous by the proper church authorities.

**Holy Roman Empire:** Latin *Sacrum Romanum Imperium.* The political entity encompassing various lands in western and central Europe ruled over first by Frankish and then German kings from 800 to 1806. Because the empire was established by the papacy, many popes viewed it as the secular arm of the Catholic Church.

**Huguenots:** French Protestants in the sixteenth and seventeenth centuries who were persecuted for their faith. The term might have been derived from the name Besançon Hugues, a leader of the faction who died in 1532, and the word *aignos,* meaning "confederates bound together by oath."

**Humanism:** A term derived from the Latin phrase *studia humanitatis* (or study of the humanities), which refers to educational reforms that emphasized a philological and historical approach to the study of ancient texts in Latin, Greek, and Hebrew. The study of ancient texts, especially those from the Greco-Roman period encouraged fifteenth-century scholars to question the fundamental values of medieval society and embrace the virtues of political engagement, wealth, and marriage.

**Iconoclasm:** A term that means "the breaking of images," which refers to the objections raised by sixteenth-century Protestant reformers to various devotional practices that had developed around visual and plastic representations of the Crucifixion, the Virgin Mary, and the saints.

**Illuminated Manuscript:** A handwritten book illustrated with border decorations and paintings created by teams of artists.

**Incunabula:** Books printed before 1501.

**Indulgence:** A written remission of the temporal punishment imposed for sins that had been confessed to, and absolved by, a priest.

**Inns of Court:** Four institutions in London (Inner Temple, Middle Temple, Lincoln's Inn, and Gray's Inn) dedicated to the study of the law. Since the Inns of Court are voluntary societies without charters, their early history is obscure, although they appear to have arisen during the Middle Ages.

**Inquisition:** An institution, often highly ritualized, by which Roman Catholics attacked heresy and other acts considered detrimental to the church. Beginning in the mid thirteenth century, torture was included as a means of obtaining confessions from the accused. Although employed in France and Italy during the Medieval era, the most famous manifestation of the Inquisition occurred in Spain after 1478, when Pope Sixtus IV allowed the Spanish royal house to target Muslims and Jews. The institution spread to other European countries controlled by Spain, as well as to the Americas, and lingered in Europe into the early nineteenth century.

**Italian Trace:** A system of fortifications capable of withstanding prolonged artillery fire. It uses lower walls, ditches, and bastions with clear fields of fire.

**Janissaries:** An elite corps of Turkish troops organized in the fourteenth century.

**Jerkin:** A short, fairly tight waistcoat worn by men, usually made of leather, and similar to a tight leather jacket worn today. Religious authorities condemned peasants who wore it, as its close-fitting nature, and its ability to be opened up the front, made it a sexually charged item of clothing.

**Junker:** A feudal aristocratic landowner in German-speaking lands who wore distinctive clothing and hairstyles. Martin Luther adorned himself as a Junker to disguise himself after the Diet of Worms in 1521.

*Landsknechts:* German infantrymen armed with pikes and halberds.

*Lanteen* **Sails:** Three-sided sails.

**Lazarettos:** Specialized facilities geared toward isolating but not treating lepers.

**Loxodromes:** Lines of constant magnetic heading drawn on maps as arcs.

**Machicolation:** A projection off a stone wall with holes in its floor allowing defenders to throw spears and other objects at enemy soldiers below.

**Magus:** Magician-sage.

*Mappae Mundi:* World maps.

**Marginal Lands:** Acres that were least likely to generate large harvests.

**Marian Devotion:** The veneration of the Virgin Mary that was an integral feature of medieval religious practice and which inspired the proliferation of statues, images, and relics of the Virgin across western Europe.

**Marian Statutes:** A series of English laws passed in 1554–1555 during the reign of Mary Tudor. They are the basis of the modern English system of justice in which a justice of the peace examines defendants and witnesses as well as keeps a written record of all testimony.

**Mercator Projection Map:** Devised by Gerardus Mercator in 1569, this type of map allows for the globe's surface to be projected onto a flat surface. The parallels of latitude are drawn as straight lines whose distance from each other increases with their distance from the equator.

**Miasma:** The poisonous, usually sticky, atoms believed to rise from putrid matter that attached themselves to passers-by and caused the plague and other illnesses.

*Mikvah:* A ritual bath performed by Jewish women after their menstrual period and before beginning sexual relations again.

*Nao:* A square-rigged cargo ship larger than a caravel.

**Ninety-five Theses:** Martin Luther's list of major theological points that he wanted the University of Wittenberg faculty to debate, and which, according to tradition, he posted on the door of the university church on 31 October 1517. They dealt with such topics as indulgences, salvation, and forgiveness.

**Nominalism:** A school of late scholastic thought that emphasized particulars instead of universals. Some nominalist theologians embraced a theological system of salvation by which God chooses to accept as worthy of grace the good deeds of men and women.

**Ordeal:** A physical test administered by medieval authorities to see whether or not somebody was telling the truth. If the person could endure the test, which usually involved hot water or hot irons applied to parts of the body, then the individual passed.

**Orders:** The "estates" in the hierarchically organized society of Europe. The clergy was the First Estate; the nobility was the Second Estate; and the general populace was the Third Estate.

**Patriciate:** A small group of families that had the largest fortunes and controlled most of the political offices of a town.

**Pleurisy:** A disease, caused by poor sanitary conditions, that was common in the cities. An inflammation of the membrane in the lungs, its symptoms include fever, severe pain in the chest, difficulty in breathing, and the exuding of mucuslike fluids from the mouth.

**Pluralism:** The practice of allowing a person to hold several church offices simultaneously.

**Pneumonic Plague:** A form of the **bubonic plague** transmitted by water droplets. *See* **Black Death.**

**Polyphony:** A term applied to the ornamented, contrapuntal, or counterpoint music of the Renaissance, which juxtaposed independent voices and/or melodies beside each other.

**Portolan Chart:** A navigational aid that was marked with straight lines that intersected. This type of chart was used by mariners to do "plain sailing" in the Mediterranean where the distances covered by ships was not great.

*Portolani:* Notebooks used by mariners to record mathematical formulas used in navigation, sailing distances, and so forth.

**Privilege:** A quasi-legal term designating the entitlements of a specific social group. For example, only nobles could receive tax exemption status and carry swords at all times.

**Quattrocento:** The fifteenth century, especially in regard to Italian literature and art.

**Quickening:** The point at which a pregnant woman could feel her child within her body; considered the point at which the fetus received its soul.

**Ravelin:** A detached triangular bastion located in front of a curtain wall.

*Reconquista:* The Christian reconquest of the Iberian peninsula from Muslim armies in the late fifteenth century.

**Reformation:** The religious revolution that occurred in the Catholic Church in the sixteenth century and which led to the founding of Protestantism, one of the three major branches of Christianity. Among the leaders of the Reformation were Martin Luther and John Calvin.

*Reichskamergericht:* Imperial Chamber Court; the supreme court of the Holy Roman Empire.

**Reliquary:** A container, often gilded or covered in precious stones, for sacred relics, such as pieces of bone or fragments of cloth of the saints.

**Renaissance:** Literally "rebirth." A revival throughout Europe in classical learning and wisdom following the cultural decline and stagnation of the Middle Ages. Beginning in the fourteenth century, it was marked by the discovery and exploration of the New World, advances in scientific theory, the decline of feudal institutions, and the expansion of commerce.

**St. Bartholomew's Day Massacre:** The killing of approximately three thousand French Huguenots (Protestants) in Paris on 24–25 August 1572. Plotted by Catherine de' Medici, the massacre was carried out by Roman Catholic nobles, artisans, and shopkeepers. The violence quickly spread to the provinces and was not fully extinguished until October.

**Scabies:** Contagious human skin diseases caused by mites.

**The Scrutiny:** A process started in Florence by which the eligibility of guild members to hold public office is assessed.

**Scurf:** A skin disease, characterized by extreme scaling all over the body and the subsequent shedding of this scaly matter, similar to extreme body dandruff.

**Scutage:** An English tax imposed on a vassal or knight in lieu of military service.

*Sejm:* The representative body in Poland-Lithuania.

*Signoria:* An eight-man executive council in Florence.

**Sodality:** An organized brotherhood or fellowship.

*Solafideism:* Martin Luther's concept of justification by faith alone, taken from the Latin *sola fide* for "faith alone."

**Spanish Square:** A military formation developed in the late fifteenth century that consisted of infantrymen armed with pikes and arquebuses.

**Spelt:** A species of wheat that is grown in the winter or spring.

**Spinning Bees:** Gatherings held at night in villages, usually in someone's home, where women would work together to spin cloth. Ostensibly done at night so that the women could work in the fields during the day, these gatherings provided occasion for women to gossip, settle feuds between their husbands, teach their daughters herbal lore, and arrange marriages.

**Strappado:** A pulley system used by the Inquisition to torture heretics and other criminals. The person's hands are tied behind his or her back and then the victim is lifted off the ground, resulting in extreme pain.

*Studiolo:* A humanist's room containing books, works of art, and other objects collected for private use and enjoyment.

**Sumptuary Laws:** Statutes that prohibited people of a certain class from wearing clothing or jewelry that was reserved for people of higher status.

**Swaddling:** Wrapping newborn children tightly in cloth.

**Syphilis:** A venereal disease that first appeared among French troops besieging Naples in 1494. It received its name from Girolamo Fracastoro's poem about "Syphilis," a young shepherd. Also called the French Disease, Neapolitan Disease, and the pox.

**T–O Map:** Designed by Isidore of Seville in the late sixth century–early seventh century. This Spanish prelate and scholar envisioned the habitable world as being divided into three continents: Asia, Africa, and Europe. He drew the ocean as a vast "O" that encircled the continents and the Mediterranean Sea and various river networks as a large "T" that divided the land masses.

**Taille:** Originally a war tax collected from French commoners.

**Thomism:** A type of scholasticism named after St. Thomas Aquinas and which is based upon realism, the notion that the mind understands what the five senses present to it because it recognizes them from their universal concepts.

**Three-course Crop Rotation:** The practice of allowing one field out of three to remain fallow every year in order to replenish lost nutrients.

**Tonsure:** The shaven hairstyle often worn by monks during the Renaissance.

**Usufruct:** The "use-right" of land accorded to farmers. In return for this right, they had to recognize the overlordship of the landowner by paying rents and acknowledging various other prerogatives of lordship.

**Vulgate:** A Latin version of the Bible authorized and used by the Roman Catholic Church.

*Wagenburg:* A cluster of wagons upon which were placed infantrymen to ward off enemy cavalry.

**War Wagons:** Military vehicles carrying soldiers armed with edged weapons as well as handcannons. First used in 1415 by Jan Žižka's forces in the Hussite war in Bohemia.

**Wergeld:** Literally "the price of a man." An ancient English custom by which a killer pays his victim's family a certain sum in order to avoid a blood feud.

**Western Schism:** *See* **Great Schism.**

**Wet Nurse:** A woman, other than the mother, used to breast-feed a newborn child.

**Woodcut:** A print produced by carving an image in reverse on a woodblock. The raised surfaces are inked, then the block is covered with a damp piece of paper and run through a press.

**Workshop:** The place where an artist has his studio. The term may also refer to the members of his studio, such as assistants and apprentices.

# GENERAL REFERENCES

## GENERAL

John Bossy, *Christianity in the West, 1400–1700* (Oxford & New York: Oxford University Press, 1985).

Thomas A. Brady Jr., Heiko A. Oberman, and James D. Tracy, eds., *Handbook of European History during the Late Middle Ages, Renaissance, and Reformation, 1400–1600,* 2 volumes (Leiden & New York: Brill, 1994; Grand Rapids, Mich.: Eerdmans, 1996).

Peter Burke, *The European Renaissance: Centres and Peripheries* (Oxford & Malden, Mass.: Blackwell, 1998).

Euan Cameron, ed., *Early Modern Europe: An Oxford History* (Oxford & New York: Oxford University Press, 1999).

Carlo M. Cipolla, *Before the Industrial Revolution: European Society and Economy, 1000–1700,* third edition (New York: Norton, 1993).

G. R. Elton, *Reformation Europe, 1517–1559,* second edition (Malden, Mass.: Blackwell, 1999).

Christopher R. Friedrichs, *The Early Modern City, 1450–1750* (London & New York: Longman, 1995).

Paul F. Grendler, ed., *Encyclopedia of the Renaissance* (New York: Scribner, 1999).

John R. Hale, *The Civilization of Europe in the Renaissance* (New York: Atheneum, 1994).

Hans J. Hillerbrand, ed., *Oxford Encyclopedia of the Reformation,* 4 volumes (New York: Oxford University Press, 1995).

Lisa Jardine, *Worldly Goods: A New History of the Renaissance* (London: Macmillan, 1996; New York: Talese, 1996).

De Lemar Jensen, *Reformation Europe: An Age of Reform and Revolution,* second edition (Lexington, Mass.: Heath, 1992).

Jensen, *Renaissance Europe: An Age of Recovery and Reconciliation,* second edition (Lexington, Mass.: Heath, 1992).

Carter Lindberg, *The European Reformations* (Oxford, U.K. & Cambridge, Mass.: Blackwell, 1996).

Charles G. Nauert Jr., *Humanism and the Culture of Renaissance Europe* (Cambridge & New York: Cambridge University Press, 1995).

Steven E. Ozment, *The Age of Reform (1250–1550): An Intellectual and Religious History of Late Medieval and Reformation Europe* (New Haven: Yale University Press, 1980).

Eugene F. Rice Jr. and Anthony Grafton, *The Foundations of Early Modern Europe, 1460–1559,* second edition (New York: Norton, 1994).

Bob Scribner, Roy Perter, and Mikulás Teich, eds., *The Reformation in National Context* (Cambridge & New York: Cambridge University Press, 1994).

James D. Tracy, *Europe's Reformations, 1450–1650* (Lanham, Md.: Rowman & Littlefield, 1999).

Donald J. Wilcox, *In Search of God and Self: Renaissance and Reformation Thought* (Boston: Houghton Mifflin, 1975).

Jonathan W. Zophy, *A Short History of Renaissance and Reformation Europe: Dances over Fire and Water* (Upper Saddle River, N.J.: Prentice Hall, 1996).

## GEOGRAPHY

Fernand Braudel, *The Mediterranean and the Mediterranean World in the Age of Philip II,* 2 volumes, translated by Siân Reynolds (New York: Harper & Row, 1972–1973; London: Collins, 1972–1973).

R. A. Butlin and R. A. Dodgshon, eds., *An Historical Geography of Europe* (Oxford: Clarendon Press, 1998; New York: Oxford University Press, 1998).

W. Gordon East, *The Geography Behind History,* revised edition (London: Nelson, 1965).

Edward Augustus Freeman, *The Historical Geography of Europe,* edited by J. B. Bury (Chicago: Aves Press, 1920).

Susan W. Friedman, *Marc Bloch, Sociology and Geography: Encountering Changing Disciplines* (Cambridge & New York: Cambridge University Press, 1996).

Emanuel Le Roy Ladurie, *Times of Feast, Times of Famine: A History of Climate Since the Year 1000,* translated by Barbara Bray (Garden City, N.Y.: Doubleday, 1971).

N. J. G. Pounds, *An Historical Geography of Europe,* 3 volumes (Cambridge & New York: Cambridge University Press, 1973–1985).

## THE ARTS

Christiane Andersson and Charles Talbot, eds., *From a Mighty Fortress: Prints, Drawings, and Books in the Age of Luther, 1483–1546* (Detroit: Detroit Institute of Arts, 1983).

Michael Baxandall, *The Limewood Sculptors of Renaissance Germany* (New Haven: Yale University Press, 1980).

Baxandall, *Painting and Experience in Fifteenth Century Italy: A Primer in the Social History of Pictorial Style* (Oxford: Clarendon Press, 1972).

Peter Burke, *The Historical Anthropology of Early Modern Italy: Essays on Perception and Communication* (Cambridge & New York: Cambridge University Press, 1987).

Michael Camille, *The Gothic Idol: Ideology and Image-Making in Medieval Art* (Cambridge & New York: Cambridge University Press, 1989).

Roger Chartier, *The Cultural Uses of Print in Early Modern France* (Princeton: Princeton University Press, 1987).

Chartier, *Passions of the Renaissance,* volume 3 of *A History of Private Life,* edited by Philippe Aries and Georges Duby (Cambridge, Mass.: Belknap Press of Harvard University Press, 1989).

Natalie Zemon Davis, *Society and Culture in Early Modern France: Eight Essays* (Stanford, Cal.: Stanford University Press, 1975).

Marilyn Desmond, ed., *Christine de Pizan and the Categories of Difference* (Minneapolis: University of Minnesota Press, 1998).

Eamon Duffy, *The Stripping of the Altars: Traditional Religion in England, c.1400–c.1580* (New Haven: Yale University Press, 1992).

David Freedberg, *The Power of Images: Studies in the History and Theory of Response* (Chicago: University of Chicago Press, 1989).

Richard A. Goldthwaite, *Wealth and the Demand for Art in Italy, 1300–1600* (Baltimore: Johns Hopkins University Press, 1993).

Stephen Greenblatt, *Renaissance Self-Fashioning: From More to Shakespeare* (Chicago: University of Chicago Press, 1980).

Aron Gurevich, *Medieval Popular Culture: Problems of Belief and Perception,* translated by János M. Bak and Paul A. Hollingsworth (Cambridge & New York: Cambridge University Press, 1988; Paris: Maison des sciences de l'homme, 1988).

Barbara A. Hanawalt and Kathryn L. Reyerson, eds., *City and Spectacle in Medieval Europe* (Minneapolis: University of Minnesota Press, 1994).

Francis Haskell and Nicholas Penny, *Taste and the Antique: The Lure of Classical Sculpture, 1500–1900* (New Haven: Yale University Press, 1981).

Mary Hollingsworth, *Patronage in Renaissance Italy: From 1400 to the Early Sixteenth Century* (Baltimore: Johns Hopkins University Press, 1994).

David Landau and Peter Parshall, *The Renaissance Print, 1470–1550* (New Haven: Yale University Press, 1994).

Cynthia Lawrence, ed., *Women and Art in Early Modern Europe: Patrons, Collectors, and Connoisseurs* (University Park: Pennsylvania State University Press, 1997).

Ruth Mellinkoff, *Outcasts: Signs of Otherness in Northern European Art of the Late Middle Ages* (Berkeley: University of California Press, 1993).

Keith Moxey, *Peasants, Warriors, and Wives: Popular Imagery in the Reformation* (Chicago: University of Chicago Press, 1989).

Edward Muir, *Ritual in Early Modern Europe* (Cambridge & New York: Cambridge University Press, 1997).

Henk van Os, *The Art of Devotion in the Late Middle Ages in Europe, 1300–1500,* translated by Michael Hoyle (Princeton: Princeton University Press, 1994).

R. W. Scribner, *For the Sake of Simple Folk: Popular Propaganda for the German Reformation* (Cambridge & New York: Cambridge University Press, 1981).

Philip M. Soergel, *Wondrous in His Saints: Counter-Reformation Propaganda in Bavaria* (Berkeley: University of California Press, 1993).

Randolph Starn and Loren Partridge, *Arts of Power: Three Halls of State in Italy, 1300–1600* (Berkeley: University of California Press, 1992).

Paola Tinagli, *Women in Italian Renaissance Art, Gender, Representation, Identity* (Manchester & New York: Manchester University Press, 1997).

Richard C. Trexler, *Public Life in Renaissance Florence* (Ithaca, N.Y.: Cornell University Press, 1980).

Lee Palmer Wandel, *Voracious Idols and Violent Hands: Iconoclasm in Reformation Zurich, Strasbourg, and Basel* (Cambridge & New York: Cambridge University Press, 1995).

Barbara Wisch and Susan Scott Munshower, eds., *Art and Pageantry in the Renaissance and Baroque* (University Park: Pennsylvania State University Press, 1990).

## COMMUNICATION, TRANSPORTATION, AND EXPLORATION

Luce Boulnois, *The Silk Road,* translated by Dennis Chamberlin (New York: Dutton, 1966).

C. R. Boxer, *Four Centuries of Portuguese Expansion, 1415–1825: A Succinct Survey* (Johannesburg: Witwatersrand University Press, 1961).

Fernand Braudel, *The Mediterranean and the Mediterranean World in the Age of Philip II*, 2 volumes, translated by Siân Reynolds (New York: Harper & Row, 1972–1973; London: Collins, 1972–1973).

Jerry Brotton, *Trading Territories: Mapping the Early Modern World* (Ithaca, N.Y.: Cornell University Press, 1998).

Palmira Brummett, *Ottoman Seapower and Levantine Diplomacy in the Age of Discovery* (Albany: State University of New York Press, 1994).

Peter Burke, *The Italian Renaissance: Culture and Society in Renaissance Italy,* revised edition (Princeton: Princeton University Press, 1987).

Carlo M. Cipolla, *Guns and Sails in the Early Phase of European Expansion* (London: Collins, 1965); reprinted as *Guns, Sails and Empires: Technological Innovation and the Early Phase of European Expansion, 1400–1700* (New York: Pantheon, 1966).

Alfred W. Crosby, *Ecological Imperialism: The Biological Expansion of Europe, 900–1900* (Cambridge & New York: Cambridge University Press, 1993).

Crosby, *The Measure of Reality: Quantification and Western Society, 1250–1600* (Cambridge & New York: Cambridge University Press, 1997).

Allen G. Debus, *Man and Nature in the Renaissance* (Cambridge & New York: Cambridge University Press, 1978).

Elizabeth L. Eisenstein, *The Printing Press as an Agent of Change: Communications and Cultural Transformations in Early Modern Europe*, 2 volumes (Cambridge & New York: Cambridge University Press, 1979).

Lucien Febvre and Henri-Jean Martin, *The Coming of the Book: The Impact of Printing, 1450–1800,* translated by David Gerard, edited by Geoffrey Nowell-Smith and David Wootton (London: N.L.B., 1976).

J. B. Harley and David Woodward, eds., *The History of Cartography* (Chicago: University of Chicago Press, 1987–1994).

Halil Inalçik and Donald Quataert, eds., *An Economic and Social History of the Ottoman Empire, 1300–1914* (Cambridge & New York: Cambridge University Press, 1984).

Lisa Jardine, *Worldly Goods: A New History of the Renaissance* (New York: Doubleday, 1996).

Garrett Mattingly, *The Armada* (Boston: Houghton Mifflin, 1959).

William H. McNeill, *Plagues and Peoples* (N.Y.: Anchor/Doubleday, 1976).

Anthony Pagden, *European Encounters with the New World: From Renaissance to Romanticism* (New Haven: Yale University Press, 1993).

Pagden, *Lords of All the World: Ideologies of Empire in Spain, Britain and France c.1500–c.1800* (New Haven: Yale University Press, 1995).

J. H. Parry, *The Age of Reconnaissance: Discovery, Exploration and Settlement, 1450–1650* (Berkeley: University of California Press, 1981).

J. R. S. Phillips, *The Medieval Expansion of Europe,* second edition (Oxford & New York: Clarendon Press, 1998).

William D. Phillips Jr. and Carla Rhan Phillips, *The Worlds of Christopher Columbus* (Cambridge & New York: Cambridge University Press, 1992).

G. V. Scammell, *The First Imperial Age: European Overseas Expansion, c.1400–1715* (London & Boston: Unwin Hyman, 1989).

Stuart B. Schwartz, ed., *Implicit Understandings: Observing, Reporting, and Reflecting on the Encounters between Europeans and Other Peoples in the Early Modern Era* (Cambridge & New York: Cambridge University Press, 1994).

John Thornton, *Africa and Africans in the Making of the Atlantic World, 1400–1800* (Cambridge & New York: Cambridge University Press, 1992).

James D. Tracy, ed., *The Political Economy of Merchant Empires* (Cambridge & New York: Cambridge University Press, 1991).

Tracy, ed., *The Rise of Merchant Empires: Long Distance Trade in the Early Modern World, 1350–1750* (Cambridge & New York: Cambridge University Press, 1990).

Richard W. Unger, *The Ship in the Medieval Economy, 600–1600* (London: Croom Helm, 1980).

Donald Weinstein and Rudolph M. Bell, *Saints & Society: The Two Worlds of Western Christendom, 1000–1700* (Chicago: University of Chicago Press, 1982).

## SOCIAL CLASS SYSTEM AND THE ECONOMY

Fernand Braudel, *Civilization and Capitalism 15th–18th Century*, 3 volumes, translated by Siân Reynolds (New York: Harper & Row, 1982–1984).

Carlo M. Cipolla, *Before the Industrial Revolution: European Society and Economy, 1000–1700,* third edition (New York: Norton, 1993).

Alexander Cowan, *Urban Europe, 1500–1700* (London & New York: Arnold, 1998).

Alfred W. Crosby Jr., *The Columbian Exchange: Biological and Cultural Consequences of 1492* (Westport, Conn.: Greenwood Press, 1972).

Jonathan Dewald, *The European Nobility, 1400–1800* (New York: Cambridge University Press, 1996).

Christopher R. Friedrichs, *The Early Modern City, 1450–1750* (London & New York: Longman, 1995).

Martha Howell, *Women, Production, and Patriarchy in Late Medieval Cities* (Chicago: University of Chicago Press, 1986).

George Huppert, *After the Black Death: A Social History of Early Modern Europe* (Bloomington: Indiana University Press, 1986).

Huppert, *Les Bourgeois Gentilshommes: An Essay on the Definition of Elites in Early Renaissance France* (Chicago: University of Chicago Press, 1977).

Robert Jütte, *Poverty and Deviance in Early Modern Europe* (Cambridge & New York: Cambridge University Press, 1994).

Peter Kriedte, *Peasants, Landlords, and Merchant Capitalists: Europe and the World Economy, 1500–1800* (Cambridge & New York: Cambridge University Press, 1983).

Richard Mackenney, *Tradesmen and Traders: The World of the Guilds in Venice and Europe, c.1250–c.1650* (Totowa, N.J.: Barnes & Noble, 1987; London: Croom Helm, 1987).

Harry A. Miskimin, *The Economy of Early Renaissance Europe, 1300–1460* (Englewood Cliffs, N.J.: Prentice-Hall, 1969).

Douglass C. North and Robert Paul Thomas, *The Rise of the Western World: A New Economic History* (Cambridge: Cambridge University Press, 1973).

Immanuel Wallerstein, *The Modern World-System*, volume 1: *Capitalist Agriculture and the Origins of the European World-Economy in the Sixteenth Century* (New York: Academic Press, 1974).

Merry E. Wiesner, *Working Women in Renaissance Germany* (New Brunswick, N.J.: Rutgers University Press, 1986).

## POLITICS, LAW, AND THE MILITARY

Larry H. Addington, *The Patterns of War through the Eighteenth Century* (Bloomington & Indianapolis: Indiana University Press, 1990).

Manuel Fernández Alvarez, *Charles V: Elected Emperor and Hereditary Ruler*, translated by J. A. Lalaguna (London: Thames & Hudson, 1975).

M. S. Anderson, *The Origins of the Modern European State System, 1494–1618* (London & New York: Longman, 1998).

John Bennett Black, *The Reign of Elizabeth, 1558–1603* (Oxford & New York: Oxford University Press, 1994).

Gisela Bock, Quentin Skinner, Maurizio Viroli, eds., *Machiavelli and Republicanism* (Cambridge & New York: Cambridge University Press, 1990).

Richard Bonney, *The European Dynastic States, 1494–1660* (Oxford & New York: Oxford University Press, 1991).

J. H. Burns, *Lordship, Kingship, and Empire: The Idea of Monarchy, 1400–1525* (Oxford: Clarendon Press, 1992; New York: Oxford University Press, 1992).

Christopher Coleman and David Starkey, eds., *Revolution Reassessed: Revisions in the History of Tudor Government and Administration* (Oxford: Clarendon; New York: Oxford University Press, 1986).

Hans Delbrück, *History of the Art of War Within the Framework of Political History*, translated by Walter J. Renfroe Jr., volume 4, *The Modern Era* (Westport, Conn.: Greenwood Press, 1985).

Christopher Duffy, *Siege Warfare: The Fortress in the Early Modern World 1494–1660* (London: Routledge & Keegan Paul, 1979).

David Eltis, *The Military Revolution in Sixteenth Century Europe* (London & New York: I. B. Tauris, 1995).

Julian H. Franklin, *Jean Bodin and the Rise of Absolutist Theory* (Cambridge: Cambridge University Press, 1973).

Thomas A. Fudge, *The Magnificent Ride: The First Reformation in Hussite Bohemia* (Aldershot, Hants & Brookfield, Vt.: Ashgate, 1998).

Christopher Haigh, ed., *The Reign of Elizabeth I* (Athens: University of Georgia Press, 1985).

Bert S. Hall, *Weapons and Warfare in Renaissance Europe: Gunpowder, Technology, and Tactics* (Baltimore: Johns Hopkins University Press, 1997).

Marco van der Hoeven, ed., *Exercise of Arms: Warfare in the Netherlands, 1568–1648* (New York: Brill, 1997).

De Lamar Jensen, *Reformation Europe: Age of Reform and Revolution* (Lexington, Mass. & Toronto: D. C. Heath, 1981).

Jensen, *Renaissance Europe: Age of Recovery and Reconciliation* (Lexington, Mass. & Toronto: D. C. Heath, 1981).

Henry Kamen, *The Spanish Inquisition: A Historical Revision* (New Haven: Yale University Press, 1998).

John Keegan, *The Face of Battle* (New York: Viking, 1976).

John H. Langbein, *Prosecuting Crime in the Renaissance: England, Germany, France* (Cambridge: Harvard University Press, 1974).

Jaroslav Lugs, *Firearms Past and Present: A Complete Review of Firearm Systems and Their Histories*, 2 volumes (London: Grenville, 1973).

Garrett Mattingly, *Renaissance Diplomacy* (Boston: Houghton Mifflin, 1971).

David Nicholas, *The Transformation of Europe 1300–1600* (New York: Oxford University Press, 1999).

Geoffrey Parker, *The Military Revolution: Military Innovation and the Rise of the West, 1500–1800* (Cambridge & New York: Cambridge University Press, 1988).

Simon Pepper, *Firearms and Fortifications: Military Architecture and Siege Warfare in Sixteenth-Century Siena* (Chicago: University of Chicago Press, 1986).

Richard A. Preston, and others, *Men in Arms: A History of Warfare and Its Interrelationships with Western Society* (Fort Worth, Tex.: Holt, Rinehart & Winston, 1991).

Eugene F. Rice Jr. and Anthony Grafton, *The Foundations of Early Modern Europe, 1460–1559* (New York: Norton, 1994).

Steven W. Rowan, *Law and Jurisprudence in the Sixteenth Century: An Introductory Bibliography* (St. Louis: Center for Reformation Research, 1986).

J. H. M. Salmon, *Society in Crisis: France in the Sixteenth Century* (New York: St. Martin's Press, 1975).

J. H. Shennan, *The Origins of the Modern European State, 1450–1725* (London: Hutchinson, 1974).

Quentin Skinner, *The Foundations of Modern Political Thought,* two volumes (Cambridge & New York: Cambridge University Press, 1978).

Pieter Spierenburg, *The Prison Experience: Disciplinary Institutions and Their Inmates in Early Modern Europe* (New Brunswick, N.J.: Rutgers University Press, 1991).

Spierenburg, *The Spectacle of Suffering: Executions and the Evolution of Repression: From a Preindustrial Metropolis to the European Experience* (Cambridge & New York: Cambridge University Press, 1984).

Laura Ikins Stern, *The Criminal Law System of Medieval and Renaissance Florence* (Baltimore: Johns Hopkins University Press, 1994).

Gerald R. Strauss, *Law, Resistance and the State: The Opposition to Roman Law in Reformation Germany* (Princeton: Princeton University Press, 1986).

F. L. Taylor, *The Art of War in Italy, 1494–1529* (Cambridge: Cambridge University Press, 1921; reprint, Westport, Conn.: Greenwood Press, 1973).

## LEISURE, RECREATION, AND DAILY LIFE

A. L. Beier and Roger Finlay, eds., *London 1500–1700: The Making of the Metropolis* (London & New York: Longman, 1986).

Philip Benedict, ed., *Cities and Social Change in Early Modern France* (London & New York: Unwin Hyman, 1989).

Fernand Braudel, *Civilization and Capitalism 15th-18th Century,* volume 1: *The Structures of Everyday Life: The Limits of the Possible,* translated by Siân Reynolds (New York: Harper & Row, 1982).

Gene A. Brucker, *Renaissance Florence* (New York: Wiley, 1969).

Lorenzo Camusso, *Travel Guide to Europe, 1492: Ten Itineraries in the Old World* (New York: Holt, 1992).

Roger Chartier, *Passions of the Renaissance,* translated by Arthur Goldhammer, volume 3 of *A History of Private Life,* edited by Philippe Aries and Georges Duby (Cambridge, Mass.: Belknap Press of Harvard University Press, 1989).

Natalie Zemon Davis, *The Return of Martin Guerre* (Cambridge, Mass.: Harvard University Press, 1983).

Davis, *Society and Culture in Early Modern France: Eight Essays* (Stanford, Cal.: Stanford University Press, 1975).

Carlo Ginzburg, *The Cheese and the Worms: The Cosmos of a Sixteenth-Century Miller,* translated by John and Anne Tedeschi (Baltimore: Johns Hopkins University Press, 1980).

R. Po-chia Hsia, *The Myth of Ritual Murder: Jews and Magic in Reformation Germany* (New Haven: Yale University Press, 1988).

Emmanuel Le Roy Ladurie, *Carnival in Romans,* translated by Mary Feeney (New York: Braziller, 1979).

Ladurie, *The Peasants of Languedoc,* translated by John Day (Urbana: University of Illinois Press, 1974).

Steven Ozment, *Flesh and Spirit: Private Life in Early Modern Germany* (New York: Viking, 1999).

Ozment, ed., *Three Behaim Boys: Growing Up in Early Modern Germany: A Chronicle of Their Lives* (New Haven: Yale University Press, 1990).

Magdalena Balthasar Paumgartner, *Magdalena and Balthasar: An Intimate Portrait of Life in 16th-Century Europe Revealed in the Letters of a Nuremberg Husband and Wife,* compiled by Ozment (New Haven: Yale University Press, 1989).

Carolyn Johnston Pouncy, ed., *The "Domostroi": Rules for Russian Households in the Time of Ivan the Terrible,* translated by Pouncy (Ithaca, N.Y.: Cornell University Press, 1994).

Werner Rösener, *Peasants in the Middle Ages,* translated by Alexander Stützer (Urbana: University of Illinois Press, 1992).

James Bruce Ross and Mary Martin McLaughlin, eds., *The Portable Renaissance Reader* (New York: Viking, 1953).

Guido Ruggiero, *Binding Passions: Tales of Magic, Marriage, and Power at the End of the Renaissance* (New York: Oxford University Press, 1993).

David Warren Sabean, *Power in the Blood: Popular Culture and Village Discourse in Early Modern Germany* (Cambridge & New York: Cambridge University Press, 1984).

Alison Sim, *Food and Feast in Tudor England* (New York: St. Martin's Press, 1997).

## THE FAMILY AND SOCIAL TRENDS

Eric Josef Carlson, *Marriage and the English Reformation* (Oxford, U.K. & Cambridge, Mass.: Blackwell, 1994).

David Cressy, *Birth, Marriage, and Death: Ritual, Religion, and the Life-Cycle in Tudor and Stuart England* (Oxford & New York: Oxford University Press, 1997).

Rudolf M. Dekker and C. van de Pol Lotte, *The Tradition of Female Transvestism in Early Modern Europe* (New York: St. Martin's Press, 1989).

Audrey Eccles, *Obstetrics and Gynaecology in Tudor and Stuart England* (London: Croom Helm, 1982; Kent, Ohio: Kent State University Press, 1982).

Catalina de Erauso, *Lieutenant Nun: Memoir of a Basque Transvestite in the New World*, translated by Michele and Gabriel Stepto (Boston: Beacon, 1996).

James R. Farr, *Authority and Sexuality in Early Modern Burgundy* (New York: Oxford University Press, 1995).

Elizabeth A. Foyster, *Manhood in Early Modern England: Honour, Sex and Marriage* (New York: Longman, 1999).

Paul F. Grendler, *Schooling in Renaissance Italy: Literacy and Learning, 1300–1600* (Baltimore: Johns Hopkins University Press, 1989).

Joel F. Harrington, *Reordering Marriage and Society in Reformation Germany* (Cambridge & New York: Cambridge University Press, 1995).

Ralph A. Houlbrooke, *The English Family, 1450–1700* (London & New York: Longman, 1984).

Martin Ingram, *Church Courts, Sex, and Marriage in England, 1570–1640* (Cambridge & New York: Cambridge University Press, 1987).

Susan Karant-Nunn, *The Reformation of Ritual: An Interpretation of Early Modern Germany* (London & New York: Routledge, 1997).

David I. Kertzer and Richard P. Saller, eds., *The Family in Italy from Antiquity to the Present* (New Haven: Yale University Press, 1991).

Margaret L. King, *Women of the Renaissance* (Chicago: University of Chicago Press, 1991).

Robert Kingdon, *Adultery and Divorce in Calvin's Geneva* (Cambridge, Mass.: Harvard University Press, 1995).

Christiane Klapisch-Zuber, *Women, Family, and Ritual in Renaissance Italy*, translated by Lydia Cochrane (Chicago: University of Chicago Press, 1985).

Joan Larsen Klein, ed., *Daughters, Wives and Widows: Writings by Men about Women and Marriage in England, 1500–1640* (Urbana: University of Illinois Press, 1992).

Peter Laslett, *Family Life and Illicit Love in Earlier Generations: Essays in Historical Sociology* (Cambridge & New York: Cambridge University Press, 1977).

Eve Levin, *Sex and Society in the World of the Orthodox Slavs, 900–1700* (Ithaca, N.Y.: Cornell University Press, 1989).

Ian Maclean, *The Renaissance Notion of Woman: A Study in the Fortunes of Scholasticism and Medical Science in Euro-*pean *Intellectual Life* (Cambridge & New York: Cambridge University Press, 1980).

Hilary Marland, ed, *The Art of Midwifery: Early Modern Midwives in Europe* (London & New York: Routledge, 1993).

Angus McLaren, *A History of Contraception: From Antiquity to the Present Day* (Oxford, U.K. & Cambridge, Mass.: Blackwell, 1990).

McLaren, *Reproductive Rituals: The Perception of Fertility in England from the Sixteenth to the Nineteenth Century* (London & New York: Methuen, 1984).

Sara Mendelson and Patricia Crawford, *Women in Early Modern England, 1550–1720* (Oxford & New York: Clarendon Press, 1998).

Rosemary O'Day, *Education and Society, 1500–1800: The Social Foundations of Education in Early Modern Britain* (London & New York: Longman, 1982).

Orest Ranum and Patricia Ranum, eds., *Popular Attitudes toward Birth Control in Pre-industrial England and France* (New York: Harper & Row, 1972).

Lyndal Roper, *The Holy Household: Women and Morals in Reformation Augsburg* (Oxford: Clarendon Press, 1989; New York: Oxford University Press, 1989).

Guido Ruggiero, *Binding Passions: Tales of Magic, Marriage, and Power at the End of the Renaissance* (New York: Oxford University Press, 1993).

Margaret R. Somerville, *Sex and Subjection: Attitudes to Women in Early-Modern Society* (London & New York: Arnold, 1995).

Richard C. Trexler, *Power and Dependence in Renaissance Florence*, volume 1: *The Children of Renaissance Florence* (Binghamton, N.Y.: Medieval and Renaissance Texts and Studies, 1993).

Merry E. Wiesner, *Christianity and the Regulation of Sexuality in the Early Modern World: Regulating Desire, Reforming Practice* (London & New York: Routledge, 2000).

Wiesner, *Women and Gender in Early Modern Europe*, second edition (New York: Cambridge University Press, 2000).

## RELIGION AND PHILOSOPHY

Christopher Allmand, *The New Cambridge Medieval History*, volume 7: *c.1415–c.1500* (Cambridge & New York: Cambridge University Press, 1998).

Frederic J. Baumgartner, *France in the Sixteenth Century* (New York: St. Martin's Press, 1995).

Brenda Bolton, *The Medieval Reformation* (Baltimore: Johns Hopkins University Press, 1983).

William J. Bouwsma, *Venice and the Defense of Republican Liberty; Renaissance Values in the Age of the Counter Reformation* (Berkeley: University of California Press, 1968).

Euan Cameron, *The European Reformation* (Oxford: Clarendon Press; Oxford & New York: Oxford University Press, 1991).

Richard DeMolen, ed., *The Meaning of the Renaissance and Reformation* (Boston: Houghton Mifflin, 1973).

A. G. Dickens, *The English Reformation* (London: Batesford, 1964).

Anthony Goodman and Angus McKay, *The Impact of Humanism on Western Europe* (London & New York: Longman, 1990).

Paul F. Grendler, ed., *Encyclopedia of the Renaissance* (New York: Scribner, 1999).

Eric W. Gritsch and Robert W. Jensen, *Lutheranism: The Theological Movement and Its Confessional Writings* (Philadelphia: Fortress Press, 1976).

Hans J. Hillerbrand, ed., *Oxford Encyclopedia of the Reformation*, 4 volumes (New York: Oxford University Press, 1996).

Hubert Jedin, *A History of the Council of Trent*, 2 volumes, translated by Ernest Graf (London & New York: Nelson, 1949–1961).

De Lamar Jensen, *Reformation Europe: Age of Reform and Revolution*, second edition (Lexington, Mass.: Heath, 1992).

Jensen, *Renaissance Europe: Age of Recovery and Reconciliation*, second edition (Lexington, Mass.: Heath, 1992).

Paul Kristeller, *Renaissance Thought: The Classic, Scholastic, and Humanistic Strains*, revised edition (New York: Harper, 1961).

Gordon Leff, *Heresy in the Later Middle Ages: The Relation of Heterodoxy to Dissent, c.1250–c.1450*, 2 volumes (Manchester, U.K.: Manchester University Press, 1967; New York: Barnes & Noble, 1967).

Franklin Hamlin Littell, *The Anabaptist View of the Church: A Study in Origins of Sectarian Protestantism*, revised edition (Boston: Starr King, 1958).

Bernhard Lohse, *Martin Luther: An Introduction to His Life and Work*, translated by Robert C. Schultz (Philadelphia: Fortress, 1986).

Alister E. McGrath, *Reformation Thought: An Introduction*, third edition (Oxford, U.K. & Malden, Mass.: Blackwell, 2000).

Francis Oakley, *The Western Church in the Later Middle Ages* (Ithaca, N.Y.: Cornell University Press, 1979).

Heiko Augustinus Oberman, *The Harvest of Medieval Theology: Gabriel Biel and Late Medieval Nominalism* (Cambridge, Mass.: Harvard University Press, 1963).

John Olin, *Catholic Reform: From Cardinal Ximenes to the Council of Trent, 1495–1563: An Essay with Illustrative Documents and a Brief Study of St. Ignatius Loyola* (New York: Fordham University Press, 1990).

Steven Ozment, *The Age of Reform (1250–1550): An Intellectual and Religious History of Late Medieval and Reformation Europe* (New Haven: Yale University Press, 1980).

Richard H. Popkin, *The History of Scepticism from Erasmus to Spinoza*, revised edition (Berkeley: University of California Press, 1979).

Menna Prestwich, ed., *International Calvinism, 1541–1715* (Oxford: Clarendon Press, 1985; New York: Oxford University Press, 1985).

Lewis William Spitz, *The Religious Renaissance of the German Humanists* (Cambridge, Mass.: Harvard University Press, 1963).

Larissa Taylor, *Soldiers of Christ: Preaching in Late Medieval and Reformation France* (New York: Oxford University Press, 1992).

Charles Trinkaus, *The Scope of Renaissance Humanism* (Ann Arbor: University of Michigan Press, 1983).

Donald J. Wilcox, *In Search of God and Self: Renaissance and Reformation Thought* (Boston: Houghton Mifflin, 1975).

George Huntston Williams, *The Radical Reformation*, third edition (Kirksville, Mo.: Sixteenth Century Journal Publishers, 1992).

## SCIENCE, TECHNOLOGY, AND HEALTH

James Ackerman, "The Involvement of Artists in Renaissance Science," *Science and the Arts in the Renaissance*, edited by John W. Shirley and F. David Hoeniger (Washington, D.C.: Folger Shakespeare Library, 1985; London: Associated University Presses, 1985), pp. 94–129.

Georg Agricola, *De re metallica*, translated by Herbert Clark Hoover and Lou Henry Hoover (London: *The Mining Magazine*, 1912; New York: Dover, 1950).

Ole Jørgen Benedictow, *Plague in the Late Medieval Nordic Countries: Epidemiological Studies* (Oslo: Middelalderforlaget, 1992).

Marco Beretta, "Humanism and Chemistry: The Spread of Georgius Agricola's Metallurgical Writings," *Nuncius*, 12 (1997): 17–47.

John Robert Christianson, *On Tycho's Island: Tycho Brahe and His Assistants, 1570–1601* (Cambridge & New York: Cambridge University Press, 2000).

Allen G. Debus, *The Chemical Philosophy: Paracelsian Science and Medicine in the Sixteenth and Seventeenth Centuries*, 2 volumes (New York: Science History Publications, 1977).

Elizabeth L. Eisenstein, *The Printing Press as an Agent of Change: Communications and Cultural Transformations in Early Modern Europe*, 2 volumes (Cambridge & New York: Cambridge University Press, 1979).

Roger French, "Astrology in Medical Practice," in *Practical Medicine from Salerno to the Black Death*, edited by Luis Garcia-Ballester and others (Cambridge & New York: Cambridge University Press, 1994), pp. 30–59.

Marie Boas Hall, *The Scientific Renaissance, 1450–1630* (New York: Harper, 1962).

J. B. Harley and David Woodward, eds., *The History of Cartography* (Chicago: University of Chicago Press, 1987–1994).

Baldasar Heseler, *Andreas Vesalius' First Public Anatomy at Bologna, 1540: An Eyewitness Report,* translated by Ruben Eriksson (Uppsala, Sweden: Almquist & Wiksel, 1959).

Rosemary Horrox, ed., *The Black Death* (Manchester & New York: Manchester University Press, 1994).

Thomas Kuhn, *The Copernican Revolution: Planetary Astronomy in the Development of Western Thought* (Cambridge, Mass.: Harvard University Press, 1957).

James M. Lattis, *Between Copernicus and Galileo: Christoph Clavius and the Collapse of Ptolemaic Cosmology* (Chicago: University of Chicago Press, 1994).

C. S. Lewis, *The Discarded Image: An Introduction to Medieval and Renaissance Literature* (Cambridge: Cambridge University Press, 1964).

Pamela O. Long, "Power, Patronage, and the Authorship of *Ars:* From Mechanical Know-how to Mechanical Knowledge in the Last Scribal Age," *Isis,* 88 (March 1997): 1–41.

W. Patrick McCray, *Glassmaking in Renaissance Venice: The Fragile Craft* (Aldershot, U.K. & Brookfield, Vt.: Ashgate, 1999).

Charles Nicholl, *The Chemical Theatre* (London & Boston: Routledge & Kegan Paul, 1980).

Vivian Nutton, "The Reception of Fracastoro's Theory of Contagion: The Seed That Fell Among Thorns?" *Osiris,* second series, 6 (1990): 196–234.

Nutton, "The Seeds of Disease: An Explanation of Contagion and Infection from the Greeks to the Renaissance," *Medical History,* 27 (January 1983): 1–34.

Charles Donald O'Malley, *Andreas Vesalius of Brussels, 1514–1564* (Berkeley: University of California Press, 1964).

Walter Pagel, *Paracelsus. An Introduction to Philosophical Medicine in the Era of the Renaissance* (Basel & New York: Karger, 1958).

Katherine Park, *Doctors and Medicine in Early Renaissance Florence* (Princeton: Princeton University Press, 1985).

Margaret Pelling, "Medical Practitioners," *Health, Medicine, and Mortality in the Sixteenth Century,* edited by Charles Webster (Cambridge & New York: Cambridge University Press, 1979), pp. 165–235.

Colin Platt, *King Death: The Black Death and Its Aftermath in Late-Medieval England* (Toronto & Buffalo: University of Toronto Press, 1996).

Claude Quétel, *History of Syphilis,* translated by Judith Braddock and Brian Pike (Baltimore: Johns Hopkins University Press, 1990).

Guenter B. Risse, *Mending Bodies, Saving Souls: A History of Hospitals* (New York: Oxford University Press, 1999).

Ira M. Rutkow, *Surgery: An Illustrated History* (St. Louis: Mosby, 1993).

John W. Shirley and F. David Hoeniger, eds., *Science and the Arts in the Renaissance* (Washington, D.C.: Folger Shakespeare Library, 1985; London: Associated University Presses, 1985).

Charles Singer and others, eds., *A History of Technology,* eight volumes (Oxford: Clarendon Press, 1954–1984).

Nancy Siraisi, *Medieval & Early Renaissance Medicine: An Introduction to Knowledge and Practice* (Chicago: University of Chicago Press, 1990).

Victor E. Thoren, *The Lord of Uraniborg: A Biography of Tycho Brahe* (Cambridge & New York: Cambridge University Press, 1990).

A. Wear, R. K. French, and I. M. Lonie, eds., *The Medical Renaissance of the Sixteenth Century* (Cambridge & New York: Cambridge University Press, 1985).

Charles Webster, ed., *Health, Medicine, and Mortality in the Sixteenth Century* (Cambridge & New York: Cambridge University Press, 1979).

Andrew Weeks, *Paracelsus: Speculative Theory and the Crisis of the Early Reformation* (Albany: State University of New York Press, 1997).

Robert S. Westman, ed., *The Copernican Achievement* (Berkeley: University of California Press, 1975).

Frances Amelia Yates, *Giordano Bruno and the Hermetic Tradition* (Chicago: University of Chicago Press, 1964).

# CONTRIBUTORS

Frederic J. Baumgartner received his Ph.D. from the University of Wisconsin-Madison in 1972 and has taught at Georgia College and Virginia Polytechnic Institute and State University, where he is currently Professor of History. His books include *Radical Reactionaries: The Political Thought of the French Catholic League* (1976); *Change and Continuity in the French Episcopate: The Bishops and the Wars of Religion, 1547–1610* (1986); *Henry II, King of France 1547–1559* (1988); *Louis XII* (1994); *France in the Sixteenth Century* (1995); and *Longing for the End: A History of Millennialism in Western Civilization* (1999).

Melanie Casey graduated from Methodist College in Fayetteville, North Carolina, in December 2000 with degrees in History and English. She was a member of the Methodist College Honors Program and was chosen to present her paper, "Shakespearean Comedy: License for Licentiousness," at the 1999 Methodist College Lyceum. She currently serves as a Program Coordinator for a child-abuse prevention program and works as a writing tutor at Methodist College.

Amanda Eurich is an Associate Professor of History at Western Washington University in Bellingham, Washington. She is the author of *The Economics of Power: The Private Finances of the House of Foix-Navarre-Albret during the Religious Wars* (1994), and many articles on confessional identity, culture, and conflict in early modern France.

Jay Goodale is Assistant Professor of History and Chair of the Department of European Studies at Beloit College (Wisconsin). He received his Ph.D. from UCLA in 1995. He taught at UCLA and Bucknell University before assuming his present position in 1997. He worked as a research fellow in residence at the Max Planck Institute for History in Göttingen (Germany) during 1998 and in 1999 was appointed the Visiting Chair in Historical Anthropology at the University of Erfurt (Germany). Professor Goodale is completing a book on how social conflict within rural parishes affected the process of the Reformation in sixteenth-century Germany.

Carol Janson is an Associate Professor in Art History at Western Washington University in Bellingham, Washington. She was the book-review editor for *Studies in Iconography* (1993–1999). Her recent papers and publications include studies of classical myths in Northern Renaissance paintings and prints, the stained-glass cycles of Reformation churches in Holland, and the animal fable in Northern print culture.

Jole Shackelford completed his Ph.D. in the History of Science and Medicine at the University of Wisconsin-Madison in 1989. He is currently a temporary Assistant Professor in History of Medicine (Department of Surgery) at the University of Minnesota Medical School. He is completing a scholarly monograph on the Danish Paracelsian physician Petrus Severinus and a book on the English anatomist William Harvey for the secondary market. His recent publications include "Documenting the Factual and the Artifactual: Ole Worm and Public Knowledge," *Endeavour*, 23 (1999); "Seeds with a Mechanical Purpose: Severinus's *Semina* and Seventeenth-Century Matter Theory," in *Reading the Book of Nature: The Other Side of the Scientific Revolution*, Sixteenth Century Essays and Studies, volume 41, edited by Allen G. Debus and Michael T. Walton (1998); and "Rosicrucianism, Lutheran Orthodoxy, and the Rejection of Paracelsianism in Early Seventeenth-Century Denmark," *Bulletin of the History of Medicine*, 70 (1996).

John Theibault received his Ph.D. in history from Johns Hopkins University in Baltimore, Maryland, in 1986. He has taught early modern European history and German history at the University of Oregon, Princeton University, and Loyola College of Maryland. He is the author of *German Villages in Crisis: Rural Life in Hesse-Kassel and the Thirty Years' War, 1580–1720* (1995) and co-author of *A Short History of Early Modern Europe, 1600–1815: Contests for a Reasonable World* (2000).

**Merry E. Wiesner-Hanks** is Professor and Chair of the Department of History at the University of Wisconsin-Milwaukee. She is one of the editors of the *Sixteenth Century Journal* and the author of *Working Women in Renaissance Germany* (1986), *Women and Gender in Early Modern Europe* (1993, 2000); *Gender, Church, and State in Early Modern Germany: Essays* (1998); *Christianity and Sexuality in the Early Modern World: Regulating Desire, Reforming Practice* (2000); and more than forty articles and publications on various aspects of women's lives and gender structures in early modern Europe, especially in Germany. She is also one of the authors of two books of sources and methodology for introductory history courses, *Discovering the Western Past: A Look at the Evidence* (1989, fourth edition 2000) and *Discovering the Global Past: A Look at the Evidence* (1997).

**Norman J. Wilson** is Assistant Professor of History and Coordinator of International Studies at Methodist College in Fayetteville, North Carolina. He received his Ph.D. from UCLA in 1994. He is the author of *History in Crisis?: Recent Directions in Historiography* (1999). His recent papers and publications focus on Free Imperial Cities in the Early Modern Period.

# INDEX OF PHOTOGRAPHS

# INDEX

*Page numbers in boldface refer to a topic upon which an essay is based.*
*Page numbers in italics refer to illustrations, figures and tables.*

Gonzaga, Francesco il, Marchese of Mantua, 92
Goslar, Germany, 295, 296
Gournay, Marie de, 306, 399
Government, **219–231**
    administration, 225–231
    architecture, 61
    bankers and banking, 160, 178
    building materials, 287
    Calvin, 409, 412
    clothing, 274
    drink, 277
    government officials, 216–217, 225–231
    homosexuality, 330
    human body representation, 65
    humanism, 69, 258, 259
    Cosimo de Medici, 177
    monarchies, 216
    Montaigne, 307
    nobility, 162
    open space, 296
    patriciates, 149
    public function, 153
    rituals, 80
    towns, 174
    trade, 176
    unmarried people, 345
    villages, 301–302
    Zwingli, 406
Gozzoli, Benozzo di Lese, 71, 177
Grace, 395–396, 400–401, 404
Grammar, 112
Grammar schools, 111
Granada, 223, 243, 258, 444
*Grand Testament* (Villon), 114
Grand vizier, 229–230
Granville, Cardinal, Archibishop of Mechelen, 90
Gratian of Bologna, 218, 246
    *Concordance of Discordant Canons*, 218, 246
    *Decretum*, 218, 246
Great Council, 226
Great European Plain, 37, 40, 41, 42, 123
Great Mongol Empire, 118
Great Schism
    canon law, 248
    Catherine of Siena, 413
    conciliarism, 372
    humanism, 390
    papal authority, 59, 74, 107, 393
    Wycliffe, 384
Great seal, 227
*Great Triumphal Chariot*, 81–82
Greban, Arnoul, 299
Grebel, Conrad, 406, 407
Greece, 40, 58
Greek language
    Dark Ages, 430
    Erasmus, 414
    Ficino, 415
    humanism, 74, 380, 381, 382, 383, 390
    Indo-European languages, 39
    Manutius, 137, 138
    Petrarch, 112
    print culture, 454
Greek literature
    Alberti, 354
    astrology, 434
    astronomy, 441
    Dark Ages, 430

    humanism, 373, 380, 390, 466
    Manutius, 137, 138
    medicine, 447, 448, 453
    Petrarch, 112
Greek mountains, 41
Greek Orthodox Church, 228, 386
Greek-cross plan, 63
Greenland, 114, 115, 139
Gregorian calendar, 109–110
Gregory I (the Great), 64
Gregory IX, 238, 246
Gregory X, 110
Gregory XI, 372, 393, 413
Gregory XIII, 107, 110, 139, 140, 257, 421
Groote, Geert, 395, 397
Grymeston, Elizabeth, 347
Guaiacum wood, 444
Guarini, Battista, 137
Guarino, Giovanni Battista, 92
Gui, Bernard, 238
Guicciardini, Francesco, 298, 391
    *The History of Italy*, 391
Guicciardini, Ludovico, *Descriptions of Everyone in the Low Countries*, 309
Guilds
    architecture, 70
    artisans, 149, 164–167
    artistic training, 66
    arts, 57, 58
    church festivals, 80
    churches, 84
    cities, 174, 296
    city-states, 216
    colleges of medicine, 446
    depiction of, *164*
    economics, 148–149
    marriage, 343, 345
    theater, 86–87
    women, 67
Guinea, 126, 127, 135
Guinter, Johannes, 453, 466
    *Instutiones anatomicae*, 466
Gulf of Guinea, 127
Gunpowder
    fortifications, 218, 241, 242
    innovations, 217, 234
    naval warfare, 217, 253
    weaponry, 250
Gustavus I (king of Sweden), 222
Gutenberg, Johannes
    humanism, 379
    print culture, 74, 88, 107, 120, 454
    printing workshop reconstruction, *121*
Guy de Chauliac, 435, 438, **460–461**
    *Chirugia magna*, or *Inventorium sive collectorium in parte chirurgiciale medicine*, 461

# H

Habsburgs, 220, 221, 228, 255–256
Hakluyt, Richard, 43
Halberd, 217, 232–234, 250
Hamburg, 224
Hampton Palace, 304
*The Handbook for the Christian Knight* (Erasmus), 414

Handcannons, 234, 250, 252
Handguns, 217, 250, 252, 258, 261
Hannibal, 420
Hanseatic League, 39, 40, 123, 157, 216, 224
Harrison, William, 155, 281
Harvey, William, 467
Havana, 245
Hawthorne, Nathaniel, 276
    *The Scarlet Letter*, 276
Health care
    children, 320
    food, 280
    medical marketplace, 446–448
    women's work, 167, 170, 315, 397
    *See also* Medicine
Hebrew, 379, 380, 382, 383, 454
Hegius, Alexander, 381
Heinrich of Braunschweig-Wolfenbüttel, 356
Heliocentrism
    Brahe, 443
    Bruno, 374
    Copernicus, 441, 443, 462
    cosmology, 431
    depiction of, *439*
    Kepler, 460
    nominalism, 395
    Ramus, 398
    skepticism, 400
Hellenic languages, 39
Hellenic mountains, 41
Hellenistic period, 450
Heller, Jacob, 59, 92
Henri III (king of France), 222, 223, 254, 400
Henri IV (king of France), 223, 254, 271, 307
Henri of Mondeville, 460, 461
Henry II (king of England), 116–117
Henry (king of Portugal), 223
Henry (prince of Portugal), 125–126, 127, 128, **135–136**, 157
Henry V (king of England), 231
*Henry V* (Shakespeare), 276
Henry VII (king of England), 125, 392
Henry VIII (king of England)
    Aretino, 306
    Catholic Church, 237
    Charles V, 221, 410
    Church of England, 374, 410
    Clement VII, 377, 410
    *Defense of the Seven Sacraments*, 410
    Elizabeth I, 256
    food, 283
    fortifications, 243
    Francis I, 256
    Hampton Palace, 304
    Luther, 410
    More, 382, 410
    Parliament, 228
    Protestant Reformation, 394, 410
    weaponry, 244
*Heptaméron* (Margaret of Navarre), 276
*Herbarum vivae eicones* (Portraits of Living Plants) (Brunfels), 467
Heresbach, Conrad, 181
    *Four Books on Husbandry*, 181
Heresy
    baptism, 406
    Bruno, 374, 400, 442
    Council of Nicea, 246
    conciliarism, 393

Columbus, 129–130
Cortés, 131, 133
Las Casas, 375, 417, 418
smallpox, 444
Indies, 39, *115*, 129, 255
*See also* West Indies
Indo-European languages, 39
Indulgences, 59, 373, 392, 401–402, 406, 418,
*422*
Industrial Revolution, 150
Infanticide, 329, 330, 335
Infants, 315, 320, 405, 409
Inflation, 162, 254, 270, 456
Influenza, 438, 444
Innocent VIII, 240
Innovation
arts, 60
cartographers, 128
exploration, 126–127
military, 455
population, 430
print culture, 120, 453
shipbuilding, 124, 128
weaponry, 217, 231, 234, 236, 250–251, 260
woodcuts, 89
Inns, 287, **290–291**, 296
Inns of Court, 245
*Inns* (Erasmus), 287
Inquisition
crime, 236
law, 218, 219, 247–248
Portuguese Inquisition, 330
Roman Inquisition, 378, 400
Spanish Inquisition, 129, 238, 256, 378,
387, 416, 421
Venetian Inquisition, 358
Inquisitorial justice, 236, 237–238
*Institutes of the Christian Religion* (Calvin), 408,
411, 421
*Instruction of a Christian Woman* (Vives), 361
*Instructions*, 238
*Instructions for a Christian Prince* (Erasmus), 414
*Instutiones anatomicae* (Anatomical Institutions)
(Guinter), 466
Intaglio, 89
*The Interior Castle* (Teresa of Avila), 421, 422
Interiors, **283–286**
International Gothic style, 72
International Style, 58, 95
*Inventorium sive collectorium in parte chirurgicale
medicine* (Inventory or Collection on the
Surgical Part of Medicine) (Guy de Chauliac),
461
Ireland, 42, 218, 236, 245, 280
Irrigation, 455–456
Isabella I (queen of Aragon and Castile)
Columbus, 130, 132, 134
Fernández de Córdoba, 257
humanism, 383
influence of, 357
Islam, 387
Joan the Mad, 222, 255
joint monarchy, 216, 222
religion, 374
Spanish Inquisition, 387
warfare, 243
Isidore of Seville, 33
Islam and Islamic culture
agriculture, 456

alchemy, 432
anatomy, 448, 464
Asia, 375
astrolabes, 127
astronomy, 463
Bodin, 254
Ceuta, 125
eradication, 387
glassmaking, 457
Henry (prince of Portugal), 135
medicine, 447, 448, 452
Ottoman Empire, 221, 228, 386
papermaking, 453
Spain, 129, 372, 387–388
tolerance of, 114
trade, 126, 156
travel literature, 117
warfare, 157, 217, 234
Islands
Africa, 127, 135
Columbus, 135
food, 283
geography, 40
Isthmuses, 40
Italian language, 39, 111, 354, 389, 391, 419
Italian Peninsula, 40, 123, 157
Italian trace, 218, 243, 244, 245
Italy
agriculture, 456
architecture, 61–62
arts, 58, 60, 68, 92
baptism, 318
Black Death, 57, 172, 435
calendar reform, 110
ceramics, 457
Charles V, 255
Charles VIII, 223
cities, 175, 270, 390
city-states, 223
Clement VII, 377
clocks, 109
clothing, 273–274
Council of Trent, 379
education, 111, 321, 323
Fernández de Córdoba, 258
food, 280, 281
fortifications, 242, 243, 244, 245, 455
French invasions, 223, 234, 243, 244, 252,
258, 379
glass, 457
government administration, 225, 226
Great Schism, 393
Holy Roman Empire, 219
hospitals, 448
house interiors, 283
houses, 287, 290
humanism, 373, 379, 382, 388, 397, 458,
466
Jews, 372, 387
law, 245
luxury products, 156
Machiavelli, 259
medicine, 453, 466
merchant exchanges, 162
money, 159
navigation, 127
poverty, 170
princely courts, 71
print culture, 121, 454

prostitution, 334
rice, 282
sculpture, 85
shipbuilding, 124
tableware, 292
theater, 87–88
trade, 39, 123
universities, 396
unmarried people, 345
warfare, 218
wine, 277, 278
witchcraft trials, 240
Ivan III (tsar of Russia), 308
Ivan IV (tsar of Russia), 304, 307–309

# J

Jābir Ibn Hayyān, Abū Mūsā, 432
Jadwiga (queen of Poland), 221
Jafuda of Aragon, 119
Jagiello, duke of Lithuania, 221, 228
James of Bourbon, 232
James I (king of England), 223, 257, 410
James V (king of Scotland), 409
James VI (king of Scotland), 223, 257, 410
Janissaries, 229, 230, 234, 386
Japan, 128, 134, 376
Jean de France, Duc de Berry, 58, 70, 94, 95
Jeremias II (patriarch of Constantinople), 387
Jerome, Saint, 121, 390, 414, 420
Jesuits. *See* Society of Jesus (Jesuits)
Jesus Christ
human body representation, 63, 95
sculpture, 85
suffering body, 63–64
Jews and Judaism
banking, 159
Black Death, 437
Bodin, 254
Catholic Church, 372
children, 320
circumcision, 409
cities, 298
clothing, 276
education, 321
marriage, 338–339, 340
menstruation, 324
Ottoman Empire, 217, 292, 372, 387
Paul IV, 378
Poland-Lithuania, 228
Polyglot Bible, 383
postpartum rituals, 318
Reuchlin, 379
Jiménez de Cisneros, Francisco, 71, 383, 417
Joachim I of Brandenburg, 355
Joan of Arc, 217, 231, 237, 238, *247*, 360
Joan the Mad, 222, 255
John of Arderne, 461
John of the Cross, Saint, 421
John of Gaunt, 125
John of Genoa, 59
John I (king of Portugal), 125, 135, 157
John II (king of France), 231, 323
John II (king of Portugal), 125, 127, 129
John of Nassau, 260
John of Rupescissa, 432
John VIII (Byzantine emperor), 386

Tenochtitlán, *129*, 131, 133
Terence, 87
Teresa of Avila, Saint, **420–421**, 422
   *Book of Her Life*, 421
   *The Interior Castle*, 421, 422
   *The Way of Perfection*, 421
*Terze rime* (Franco), 357
*Tetrabiblos* (Ptolemy), 434
Tetzel, Johann, *371*, 401–402, *422*
Textiles, 455
Thames River, 40
Theater, **86–88**
   Aretino, 306
   church festivals, 80
   Commedia dell'Arte, 87–88
   devotional theater, 95
   disguise, 276
   entertainment, 299, 349
   peasants, 303
   religion, 299
   *tableaux vivant*, 81
*Theatrum orbis terrarum* (Theater of the World)
   (Ortelius), 43, 45, 141, 468
*Theologica Platonica* (Platonic Theology)
   (Ficino), 71, 391, 415
Theology
   Anabaptists, 373, 406–407
   Calvin, 373–374, 408–409, 411
   Catholic Church, 375, 376–379, 383,
     391–394
   Copernicus, 462
   dissenters, 384–388
   education, 448
   Erasmus, 383
   God's absolute power, 372, 395, 412
   humanism, 379, 380–383
   late medieval thought, 394–397
   late-sixteenth-century thought, 397–400
   Latin, 74
   Luther, 78, 373, 400–411, 418–419
   print culture, 78, 121
   scholasticism, 372–373, 380, 383, 394–396,
     401
   Zwingli, 404, 405–406
*There is no Greater Treasure Here on Earth than an*
   *Obedient Wife* (Schön), 76
*These Are Good Table Manners*, 292–293
Thiene, Gaetano da, 376
Third Estate, 148, 149, 150, 153, 154, 155, 228
Thirty Years' War (1618-1648), 252, 258
Thomas Aquinas, Saint, 82, 320, 378, 394–395,
   462
Thomas à Kempis, 395, 397, 416
   *The Imitation of Christ*, 395, 397, 416
Thomism, 394–395
*The Three Musketeers* (Dumas), 274
*The Three Truths* (Charron), 399
Tithe, 282, 303
Titian, 93, *100*, 306, 455
Tobacco, 283, 298
Toledo, 277
Topography, 32, 41, 61
Tornabuoni, Giovanni, 84
Torresani, Andrea, 137
Torture
   Bodin, 254
   cities, 293, 295
   confessions, 237
   forms of, 219, 238–239

homosexuality, 331
   ordeals, 236
Toscanelli dal Pozzo, Paolo, 43, 128
Tower of London, 242
Town halls, 61
Towns, **173–174, 293–299**
   agriculture, 151–152
   court city, 175
   cultural geography, 38
   economics, 148–149, 150
   fortifications, 218, 241, 242, 244
   guilds, 167, 174
   poverty, 169
   Third Estate, 155
Trade, **155–159**
   Black Death, 57
   Bodin, 254
   Columbus, 129
   cultural geography, 39
   economics, 149
   exploration, 126
   geography, 33
   Henry (prince of Portugal), 136
   luxury products, 149, 155–156, 157
   maps, *38*
   New World, 133
   physical geography, 40, 41
   shipbuilding, 124–125
   shipping, 123
   slave trade, 127
   towns, 173
*Traites Divers de Jean Mansel*, *342*
Transportation, **123–125**
   agriculture, 150
   geography, 33
   overland transportation, 123–124
   technology, 107
   wine, 277–278
Transylvanian Alps, 41
*Travel Journey* (Montaigne), 45, 307
Travel literature, **116–120**
   cities, 296
   communications, 108
   geography, 33, 36
   inns, 291
   Islamic, 117
   Montaigne, 45, 309
   Polo, 108, 118–119
*Travels* (Odoric of Pordenone), 119
*The Travels of Sir John Mandeville*, 36, 108, 119,
   121, 141
*Treasures of the City of Ladies* (Pisan), 112
*Treatise on the Orders and Dignities* (Loyseau),
   181
Treaty of Combrai, 255
Treaty of Passau, 256
Treaty of Tordesillas, 108, 127, 132, 133, 136
*Treponemosis*, 444
*Très Riches Heures* (Limbourg brothers), 94, 95,
   *141*, *268*
Triangulation, 116, 139
Tridentine decrees, 378
Trissino, Giangiorgio, 93
   *Ritratti*, 93
*Tristan and Isolde*, *326*
Tristão, 125
*The Triumph of Death* (anonymous), 437
*The Triumph of Death* (Bruegel the Elder), 90
*The Triumphal Arch* (Dürer), 92

Triumphal entries, 81
*The Triumphal Procession* (Dürer), 92
Tropic of Capricorn, 42
Troyes, 270, 296
Tsar of Orthodoxy, 308
Tuberculosis, 438
Turkey, food, 280
Turkish language, 39–40
Turks. *See* Ottoman Empire
Tuscany, duchy of, 227
Tusser, Thomas, 181, 309
   *Five Hundred Points of Good Husbandry*,
     181, 309
*Twelve Articles*, 401
Twelve Year Truce (1609), 260
Tyard, Pontus de, 398
   *L'univers*, 398
Typhoid, 296
Typhus, 438, 444
Tyranny, 409

# U

Uffizi, 97
Ugric languages, 39
Ukraine, 41, 407
Ukrainian language, 39
Underwear, 274
Unfortunate Islands, 137
Union of Kalmar (1397), 216, 222
*L'univers* (Tyard), 398
University of Alcala, 383
University of Bologna, 461, 462
University of Cracow, 441
University of Montpellier, 452, 466
University of Padua, 391, 396, 453, 462
University of Paris, 379, 393, 395, 398, 436, 451,
   466
University of Prague, 385, 396
University of Salerno, 396
University of Vienna, 396
University of Wittenberg, 396, 400
Unmarried people, **343–345**
Ural Mountains, 32, 37, 40, 41, 42
Uraniborg, 459–460
Urban IV, 80
Urban planning, 62–63, 68
Urban VI, 372, 393, 413
Ursulines, 323, 376
Usury, 159, 387
*Utopia* (More), 152, 181, 245, 262, 276, 281, 373,
   *381*, 382–383, 422
Utraquist Church, 261, 372, 386

# V

Valdés, Fernando, 238
Valencia, Spain, 299
Valla, Lorenzo, 118, 388, 389–390
Valladolid, 238
Valles, Francisco, 464
Van der Straet, Jan, *469*
Van Eyck, Jan, 58, 81
Van Leyden, Lucas, *339*
Van Mander, Karl, 90